Lecture Notes in Computer Science 8368

Commenced Publication in 1973
Founding and Former Series Editors:
Gerhard Goos, Juris Hartmanis, and Jan van Leeuwen

For further volumes:
http://www.springer.com/series/7408

Steve Counsell · Manuel Núñez (Eds.)

Software Engineering and Formal Methods

SEFM 2013 Collocated Workshops:
BEAT2, WS-FMDS, FM-RAIL-Bok,
MoKMaSD, and OpenCert
Madrid, Spain, September 23–24, 2013
Revised Selected Papers

 Springer

Editors
Steve Counsell
Brunel University
Uxbridge, Middlesex
UK

Manuel Núñez
Universidad Complutense de Madrid
Madrid
Spain

ISSN 0302-9743   ISSN 1611-3349 (electronic)
ISBN 978-3-319-05031-7   ISBN 978-3-319-05032-4 (eBook)
DOI 10.1007/978-3-319-05032-4
Springer Cham Heidelberg New York Dordrecht London

Library of Congress Control Number: 2014932689

LNCS Sublibrary: SL2 – Programming and Software Engineering

Printed on acid-free paper

Springer is part of Springer Science+Business Media (www.springer.com)

Preface

This volume contains selected papers of the workshops collocated with the 11th International Conference on Software Engineering and Formal Methods, SEFM 2013. These workshops were held in Madrid, Spain, during September 24–25, 2013. Each of the workshops had a different slant on the topic of formal methods in software engineering, but each made a significant contribution toward advancement of the respective areas. The depth and range of papers illustrate this.

The aim of the *Second International Workshop on Behavioral Types Workshop* (BEAT 2) was to pursue research topics in the use of behavioral type theory as the basis for new foundations, programming languages, and software development methods for communication-intensive distributed systems.

The aim of the *Third Workshop on Formal Methods in the Development of Software* (WS-FMDS) was to bring together scientists and practitioners active in the area of formal methods and interested in exchanging their experiences in the industrial usage of these methods.

In many engineering-based application areas such as in the railway domain, formal methods have reached a level of maturity that already enables the compilation of a so-called body of knowledge. The purpose of the *Workshop on a Formal Methods Body of Knowledge for Railway Control and Safety Systems* (FM-RAIL-BOK) was to bring together practitioners and researchers in this area and to that end.

The *Second International Symposium on Modelling and Knowledge Management for Sustainable Development* (MoKMaSD) brought together researchers and practitioner from academia, industry, government, and non-government organizations to present research results and exchange experience, ideas, and solutions for modelling and analyzing complex systems. In particular in areas including economy, governance, health, biology, ecology, climate, and poverty reduction.

The aim of the *7th International Workshop on Foundations and Techniques for Open Source Software Certification* (OpenCert) was to bring together researchers from academia and industry interested in the quality assessment of OSS projects, as well as the metrics, procedures, and tools used in OSS communities and for the measurement and assessment of OSS quality.

For each of the workshops at SEFM 2013, we thank the organizers for developing a vibrant and interesting set of papers and resulting talks. We also thank the paper contributors to these workshops and those who attended them.

January 2014

Steve Counsell
Manuel Núñez

Beat 2 Organizers' Message

BEAT 2 (full title: Second International Workshop on Behavioural Types), affiliated to SEFM, followed on from the BEAT 2013 workshop, which was affiliated to POPL 2013, and an invitational meeting that took place in Lisbon in April 2011.

Behavioral type systems go beyond data type systems in order to specify, characterize, and reason about dynamic aspects of program execution. Behavioral types encompass: session types; contracts (for example, in service oriented systems); typestate; types for analysis of termination, deadlock-freedom, liveness, race-freedom and related properties; intersection types applied to behavioral properties; and other topics. Behavioral types can form a basis for both static analysis and dynamic monitoring. Recent years have seen a rapid increase in research on behavioral types, driven partly by the need to formalize and codify communication structures as computing moves from the dataprocessing era to the communication era, and partly by the realization that type-theoretic techniques can provide insight into the fine structure of computation.

The aim of BEAT 2 was to bring together researchers in all aspects of behavioral type theory and its applications, in order to share results, consolidate the community, and discover opportunities for new collaborations and future directions. The workshop was organized under the auspices of COST Action IC1201: Behavioural Types for Reliable Large-Scale Software Systems (BETTY), and the Program Committee for the workshop was formed by taking a representative from each country participating in BETTY.

Papers were submitted in two categories: original research papers, and presentations of papers already published elsewhere. There was also an invited lecture from Dr. Achim Brucker of SAP, whose participation was funded by COST Action IC1201 and by the workshop registration fees. The workshop program was completed by several talks offered by members of BETTY and by participants in the workshop. The list of talks that do not have a corresponding paper in this proceedings volume is as follows:

- Globally Governed Session Semantics
  Dimitrios Kouzapas and Nobuko Yoshida
- Types for Resources in Psi-Calculi
  Hans Hüttel
- Static Deadlock Resolution in the Pi Calculus
  Marco Giunti and António Ravara
- Multiparty Compatibility in Communicating Automata: Characterisation and Synthesis of Global Session Types
  Pierre-Malo Deniélou and Nobuko Yoshida
- Typing Actors Using Behavioural Types
  Adrian Francalanza and Joseph Masini
- Linear Types in Programming Languages: Progress and Prospects
  Simon Gay

- Behaviour Inference for Deadlock Checking
  Violet Ka I Pun, Martin Steffen and Volker Stoltz
- Specification and Verification of Protocols for MPI Programs
  *Eduardo R. B. Marques, Francisco Martins, Vasco T. Vasconcelos, Nicholas Ng,
  Nuno Dias Martins, César Santos and Nobuko Yoshida*
- Distributed Governance with Scribble: Tutorial and Demonstration
  Raymond Hu, Rumyana Neykova, Nicholas Ng and Nobuko Yoshida

Finally, I would like to thank the Program Committee members for their hard work, and the SEFM workshop chair and local organizers for their help.

Simon Gay

Program Committee

Karthikeyan Bhargavan	Inria Paris-Rocquencourt, France
Gabriel Ciobanu	Romanian Academy, ICS, Iaşi, Romania
Ricardo Colomo Palacios	Universidad Carlos III de Madrid, Spain
Ugo de'Liguoro	University of Turin, Italy
Adrian Francalanza	University of Malta, Malta
Tihana Galinac Grbac	University of Rijeka, Croatia
Simon Gay	University of Glasgow, UK
Vaidas Giedrimas	Šiauliai University, Lithuania
Thomas Hildebrandt	IT University of Copenhagen, Denmark
Einar Broch Johnsen	University of Oslo, Norway
Georgia Kapitsaki	University of Cyprus, Cyprus
Vasileios Koutavas	Trinity College Dublin, Ireland
Aleksandra Mileva	Goce Delčev University of Štip, Macedonia
Samir Omanović	University of Sarajevo, Bosnia and Herzegovina
Jovanka Pantović	University of Novi Sad, Serbia
Nikolaos Sismanis	Aristotle University of Thessaloniki, Greece
Peter Thiemann	University of Freiburg, Germany
Vasco Vasconcelos	University of Lisbon, Portugal
Björn Victor	Uppsala University, Sweden
Paweł T. Wojciechowski	Poznań University of Technology, Poland
Peter Wong	SDL Fredhopper, The Netherlands

WS-FMDS Organizers' Message

The Third International Workshop on Formal Methods in the Development of Software, WS-FMDS 2013, was held in Madrid, Spain, on September 24, 2013. The purpose of WS-FMDS is to bring together scientists and practitioners who are active in the area of formal methods and interested in exchanging their experiences in the industrial usage of these methods. This workshop also strives to promote research and development for the improvement of theoretical aspects of formal methods and tools focused on practical usability for industrial applications.

After a careful reviewing process in which every paper was reviewed by at least three WS-FMDS PC members and additional reviewers, the Program Committee accepted five regular papers. The program of WS-FMDS 2013 was enriched by the keynote of Alexey Gotman, on "Abstraction for Weakly Consistent Systems".

Several people contributed to the success of WS-FMDS 2013. We are grateful to the general chair of the 11th International Conference on Software Engineering and Formal Methods SEFM 2013, Professor Manuel Núñez, for his support and help. We also would like to thank the Program Committee members as well as the additional reviewers for their work on selecting the papers. The process of reviewing and selecting papers was significantly simplified through using Easy-Chair.

We would like to thank the attendants of the workshop and hope that they found the program useful, interesting, and challenging.

Carlos Gregorio-Rodríguez
Fernando L. Pelayo

Program Committee

Rui Abreu	University of Porto, Portugal
Mario Bravetti	University of Bologna, Italy
Haitao Dan	Brunel University, UK
Carlos Gregorio-Rodríguez	Universidad Complutense de Madrid, Spain
Raluca Lefticaru	University of Bucharest, Romania
Luis Llana	Universidad Complutense de Madrid, Spain
Jasen Markovski	Eindhoven University of Technology, The Netherlands
Fernando L. Pelayo	Universidad de Castilla - La Mancha, Spain
Pascal Poizat	University of Evry Val d'Essonne, France
Franz Wotawa	Graz University of Technology, Austria
Fatiha Zadi	University of Paris-Sud, France

FM-RAIL-BOK Organizers' Message

Formal methods in software science and software engineering have existed at least as long as the term "software engineering" (NATO Science Conference, Garmisch, 1968) itself. Its various methods and techniques include algebraic specification, process-algebraic modelling and verification, Petri nets, fuzzy logics, etc. Especially in railway control and safety systems, formal methods have reached a considerable level of maturity. For example, the B-method has been used successfully to verify the most relevant parts of a model of the Paris Metro underground railway system. Thus, it appears timely to begin the compilation of a so-called body of knowledge (BoK) dedicated to this specific area.

The FM-RAIL-BOK WORKSHOP 2013 (Towards a Formal Methods Body of Knowledge for Railway Control and Safety Systems), held on September 23, 2013 in Madrid, http://ssfmgroup.wordpress.com, was a first successful step toward this aim. This international workshop was affiliated to SEFM 2013, the 11th International Conference on Software Engineering and Formal Methods, Madrid. Workshop proceedings, which include all papers presented at the FM-RAIL-BOK WORKSHOP, are available online at the workshop site.

Here, we compile selected, revised papers of this workshop. Not necessarily presenting new scientific results, these papers compile case-based "best practice" knowledge in the spirit of classic engineering handbooks. All workshop authors were invited to submit extended versions of their original papers. This gave them the opportunity to react to feedback and discussions at the workshop. In total, we received eight contributed papers, out of which six were selected for inclusion in this volume, based on a thorough reviewing process.

In addition, we include an extended abstract by Tom Maibaum, who reflects upon the topic of "BoKs and Engineering Knowledge." Alessandro Fantechi extended his keynote "Twenty-Five Years of Formal Methods and Railways: What Next?" to a contributed, fully reviewed paper.

As FM-RAIL-BOK co-chairs we would like to thank all authors who submitted their papers to this compilation, the workshop participants, our reviewers, Manuel Núñez and Steve Counsell for the smooth cooperation with SEFM 2013, and Erwin R. Catesbeiana (Jr.) for help with workshop organization on the fly.

Stefan Gruner
Anne E. Haxthausen
Tom Maibaum
Markus Roggenbach

Program Committee

Martin Brennan	British Rail Safety Standards Board, UK
Simon Chadwick	Invensys Rail, UK
Meena Dasigi	Network Rail, UK
Lars-Henrik Eriksson	Uppsala University, Sweden
Alessandro Fantechi	University of Florence, Italy
Stefan Gruner	University of Pretoria, South Africa
Anne E. Haxthausen	Technical University of Denmark, Denmark
Michaela Huhn	Technical University of Clausthal, Germany
Tom Maibaum	McMaster University, Canada
Kirsten Mark-Hansen	Cowi A/S, Denmark
Hoang Nga Nguyen	University of Swansea, UK
Jan Peleska	University of Bremen, Germany
Markus Roggenbach	Swansea University, Wales, UK
Holger Schlingloff	Humboldt University of Berlin, Germany
Eckehard Schnieder	Technical University of Braunschweig, Germany
Kenji Taguchi	AIST, Japan
Helen Treharne	University of Surrey, UK
Laurent Voisin	Systerel, France
Kirsten Winter	University of Queensland, Australia

MoKMaSD Organizers' Message

The Second International Symposium on Modelling and Knowledge Management for Sustainable Development, MoKMaSD 2013, was held in Madrid, Spain, on September 24, 2013. The aim of the symposium was to bring together practitioners and researchers from academia, industry, government, and non-government organizations to present research results and exchange experience, ideas, and solutions for modelling and analyzing complex systems and using knowledge management strategies, technology, and systems in various domain areas, including economy, governance, health, biology, ecology, climate and poverty reduction, that address problems of sustainable development.

Papers submitted to MoKMaSD 2013 were carefully reviewed by the members of the Program Committee, with the help of a few external experts. The program consisted of seven presentations and an open discussion. Paloma Cáceres García de Marina kindly accepted to open the program with a presentation on "A Transport Sharing Platform to Improve the Sustainability." Then, we had a presentation by Joris Hulstijn on XBRL-driven business process improvement, followed by a presentation by Alain Perez on sustainability idea management. Subsequently, we had four presentations on modelling languages and tools for population dynamics and ecological systems by Suryana Setiawan, Pasquale Bove, Mauricio Toro, and Pierluigi Penna.

Several people contributed to the success of MoKMaSD 2013. We are grateful to Antonio Cerone, who invited us to chair this edition of the symposium and assisted us in some organizational aspects of the event. We would like to thank the organizers of SEFM 2013, and in particular General Chair Manuel Núñez and Workshops Chair Steve Counsell. We would also like to thank the Program Committee and the additional reviewers for their work on reviewing the papers. The process of reviewing and selecting papers was significantly simplified through using EasyChair.

Paolo Milazzo
Adegboyega Ojo

Program Committee

Giulio Caravagna	DISCo, University of Milano-Bicocca, Italy
Antonio Cerone	UNU-IIST, United Nations University, UN/Macau SAR China
Luis M. Camarinha-Matos	Universidade Nova de Lisboa, Portugal
Ed Curry	DERI, National University of Ireland, Ireland
Simone D'Alessandro	University of Pisa, Italy
Rocco De Nicola	IMT - Institutions Markets Technologies, Italy
Alexeis Garcia-Perez	Coventry University, UK
Marijn Janssen	Delft University of Technology, The Netherlands
Erik Johnston	Arizona State University, USA

Hong-Gee Kim	Seoul National University, Korea
Siu-Wai Leung	University of Macau, Macau, SAR China
Paolo Milazzo	University of Pisa, Italy
Alessandra Mileo	DERI, National University of Ireland, Ireland
Gianluca Misuraca	European Commission, JRC-IPTS, Spain
Giovanni Pardini	University of Pisa, Italy
Adegboyega Ojo	DERI, National University of Ireland, Ireland
Matteo Pedercini	Millennium Institute, USA
Barbara Re	University of Camerino, Italy
Pallab Saha	National University of Singapore, Singapore
Marco Scotti	COSBI, Italy
Siraj A. Shaikh	Coventry University, UK
Carron Shankland	University of Stirling, UK
Michael Sonnenschein	University of Oldenburg, Germany
Efthimios Tambouris	University of Macedonia, Greece
Massimo Tavoni	FEEM - Fondazione Eni Enrico Mattei, Italy
Luca Tesei	University of Camerino, Italy
Shaofa Yang	Chinese Academy of Sciences, IOS, China

Additional Reviewers

Muhammad Intizar Ali, Harsha Kalutarage, Simone Tini.

OpenCert Organizers' Message

Over the past decade, the open source software (OSS) phenomenon has had a global impact on the way software systems and software-based services are developed, distributed, and deployed. Widely acknowledged benefits of OSS include reliability, low development and maintenance costs, as well as rapid code turnover.

However, state-of-the-art OSS, by the very nature of its open, unconventional, distributed development model, makes software quality assessment, let alone full certification, particularly hard to achieve and raises important challenges both from the technical/methodological and the managerial points of view. This makes the use of OSS, and, in particular, its integration within complex industrial-strength applications, with stringent security requirements, a risk but also an opportunity and a challenge for rigorous methods in software analysis and engineering.

Moreover, OSS communities are, at heart, learning communities formed by people that share the same values, passion, and interest for software development. From this perspective, OSS is the product of a highly diverse, highly distributed collaboration effort. Looking through the glass, the multifaceted aspects of these dynamically evolving, loosely structured OSS communities require an expansion of the typical certification process, beyond traditional frameworks and toward a multidisciplinary approach that would take into account not only technical, but also social, psychological, and educational aspects at individual and community level. Such a certification process could potentially increase participation and enhance visibility.

In such a context, following the success of the six previous editions (collocated with ETAPS 2007, in Braga, OSS 2008, at IFIP WCC, in Milan, ETAPS 2009 in York, SEFM 2010 in Pisa, SEFM 2011 in Montevideo, and SEFM 2012 in Thessaloniki), the *7th International Workshop on Foundations and Techniques for Open Source Software Certification (OpenCert2013)* was held in Madrid, Spain, on September 23, 2013, and collocated with SEFM 2013. The aim of the workshop was to bring together researchers from academia and industry who are broadly interested in (a) the quality assessment of OSS projects and in (b) metrics, procedures, and tools that could be useful in assessing and qualifying individual participation and collaboration patterns in OSS communities.

This report includes a total of four regular papers, each of them reviewed by at least two Program Committee members. It also features the abstract of the keynote given by Jesus M. Gonzalez-Barahona from Universidad Rey Juan Carlos, Spain, on "Using Software Analytics to Characterize FLOSS Projects and Communities."

Several people contributed to the success of OpenCert 2013. We would like to express our gratitude to all members of the Program Committee for their efforts and support. We also thank the OpenCert Steering Committee: Bernhard Aichernig, Antonio Cerone, Martin Michlmayr, David von Oheimb, and José Nuno Oliveira as well as the Organizing Committee formed by Luis Barbosa and Antonio Cerone. They constantly provided their feedback for the sake of the workshop's success.

We would also like to thank members of the SEFM 2013 Organizing Committee, in particular Manuel Núñez (conference chair) and Steve Counsell (workshop chair), who were really helpful on all occasions.

We thank all attendants to the workshop and hope that they found the program compelling and relevant to their interests.

Pantelis M. Papadopoulos
Bruno Rossi

Steering Committee

Bernhard Aichernig	Technical University of Graz, Austria
Antonio Cerone	UNU-IIST, United Nations University, Macau SAR China
Martin Michlmayr	University of Cambridge, UK
David von Oheimb	Siemens Corporate Technology, Germany
José Nuno Oliveira	Universidade do Minho, Portugal

Organizing Committee

Luis Barbosa	University of Minho, Portugal
Antonio Cerone	UNU-IIST, Macau SAR China

Program Committee

Bernhard Aichernig	Technical University of Graz, Austria
Luis Barbosa	University of Minho, Portugal
Jaap Boender	Middlesex University London, UK
Peter Breuer	Brunel University, UK
Andrea Capiluppi	Imperial College London, UK
Antonio Cerone	UNU-IIST, Macau SAR China
Stavros Demetriadis	Aristotle University of Thessaloniki, Greece
Roberto Di Cosmo	Université Paris Diderot / Inria, France
Yannis Dimitriadis	University of Valladolid, Spain
Gabriella Dodero	Free University of Bozen-Bolzano, Italy
George Eleftherakis	CITY College, Greece
José Emilio Labra Gayo	University of Oviedo, Spain
Fabrizio Fabbrini	ISTI-CNR, Italy
João F. Ferreira	Teesside University, UK
Jesus Arias Fisteus	Carlos III University of Madrid, Spain
Imed Hammouda	Tampere University of Technology, Finland
Maria João Frade	University of Minho, Portugal
Andreas Karatsolis	Carnegie Mellon University in Qatar, Qatar
Paddy Krishnan	Oracle Labs, Australia
Thomas Lagkas	CITY College, Greece

Martin Michlmayr	University of Cambridge, UK
Paolo Milazzo	University of Pisa, Italy
José Miranda	MULTICERT S.A., Portugal
John Noll	Lero - the Irish Software Engineering Research Centre, Ireland
David von Oheimb	Siemens AG, Germany
José Nuno Oliveira	University of Minho, Portugal
Pantelis M. Papadopoulos	UNU-IIST, Macau SAR China
Alexander K. Petrenko	ISP RAS, Russia
Simon Pickin	Universidad Complutense de Madrid, Spain
Dirk Riehle	University of Erlangen-Nürnberg, Germany
Bruno Rossi	Free University of Bozen-Bolzano, Italy
Gregorio Robles	King Juan Carlos University, Spain
Alejandro Sanchez	Universidad Nacional de San Luis, Argentina
Siraj Shaikh	Coventry University, UK
Ioannis Stamelos	Aristotle University of Thessaloniki, Greece
Ralf Treinen	Paris Diderot University, France
Tanja Vos	Polytechnic University of Valencia, Spain
Tony Wasserman	Carnegie Mellon Silicon Valley, USA

Service Compositions: Curse or Blessing for Security?

Achim Brucker

Product Security Research Team, SAP AG, Germany

Keynote Speaker of BEAT 2

Building large systems by composing reusable services is not a new idea, it is at least 25 years old. Still, only recently the scenario of dynamic interchangeable services that are consumed via public networks is becoming reality. Following the Software as a Service (SaaS) paradigm, an increasing number of complex applications is offered as a service that themselves can be used composed for building even larger and more complex applications. This will lead to situations in which users are likely to unknowingly consume services in a dynamic and ad hoc manner.

Leaving the rather static (and mostly on-premise) service composition scenarios of the past 25 years behind us, dynamic service compositions have not only the potential to transform the software industry from a business perspective, they also requires new approaches for addressing the security and trustworthiness needs of users.

The EU FP7 project Aniketos develops new technology, methods, tools and security services that support the design-time creation and run-time dynamic behaviour of dynamic service compositions, addressing service developers, service providers and service end users.

In this talk, we will motivate several security and trustworthiness requirements that occur in dynamic service compositions and discuss the solutions developed within the project Aniketos. Based on our experiences, we will discuss open research challenges and potential opportunities for applying type systems.

Abstraction for Weakly Consistent Systems

Alexey Gotsman

Institute for Advanced Studies in Software Development Technologies
(IMDEA Software), Madrid, Spain

Keynote Speaker of WS-FMDS 2013

When constructing complex concurrent and distributed systems, abstraction is vital: programmers should be able to reason about system components in terms of abstract specifications that hide the implementation details. Nowadays such components often provide only weak consistency guarantees about the data they manage: in shared-memory systems because of the effects of relaxed memory models, and in distributed systems because of the effects of replication. This makes existing notions of component abstraction inapplicable.

In this talk I will describe our ongoing effort to specify consistency guarantees provided by modern shared-memory and distributed systems in a uniform framework and to propose notions of abstraction for components of such systems. I will illustrate our results using the examples of the C/C++ memory model and eventually consistent distributed systems. This is joint work with Mark Batty (University of Cambridge), Sebastian Burckhardt (Microsoft Research), Mike Dodds (University of York), Hongseok Yang (University of Oxford) and Marek Zawirski (UPMC).

Using Software Analytics to Characterize FLOSS Projects and Communities

Jesus M. Gonzalez-Barahona

Universidad Rey Juan Carlos, Spain

Keynote Speaker of OpenCert 2013

FLOSS (free, libre, open source) software projects, and the development communities that are built around them, may become really large, complex, and difficult to understand. At the same time, the IT strategy of many organizations is increasingly dependent on FLOSS components, and therefore in the corresponding projects and development communities. Therefore, the analysis of those projects to inform strategic and tactic decisions of those organizations is a matter of first necessity for them. Fortunately, FLOSS projects provide plenty of details about their development processes and actors, in the form of traces in their development repositories (source code management systems, issue tracking systems, mailing lists, forums, etc.). Those traces can be retrieved, analyzed and visualized to gain deep knowledge about how the project is performing. Key parameters and indicators can be produced based on those analysis that allow for the tracking of the evolution of the project, and its main trends. The talk will discuss which kind of information is available in such repositories, which kind of indicators can be obtained from it, and will show some real examples of how it is being used to build development dashboards for real FLOSS projects.

Contents

FM-RAIL-BOK 2013

MoKMaSD 2013

OpenCert 2013

BEAT 2

Towards Global and Local Types for Adaptation

Mario Bravetti[1]([✉]), Marco Carbone[2], Thomas Hildebrandt[2], Ivan Lanese[1],
Jacopo Mauro[1], Jorge A. Pérez[3], and Gianluigi Zavattaro[1]

[1] Lab. Focus, University of Bologna/INRIA, Bologna, Italy
{bravetti,jmauro}@cs.unibo.it
[2] IT University of Copenhagen, Copenhagen, Denmark
[3] CITI and Departamento de Informática, FCT - Universidade Nova de Lisboa,
Lisboa, Portugal

Abstract. Choreographies allow designers to specify the protocols followed by participants of a distributed interaction. In this context, adaptation may be necessary to respond to external requests or to better suit a changing environment (a self-update). Adapting the behavior of a participant requires to update in a coordinated way possibly all the participants interacting with him. We propose a language able to describe a choreography together with its adaptation strategies, and we discuss the main issues that have to be solved to enable adaptation on a participant code dealing with many interleaved protocols.

1 Introduction

Modern complex distributed software systems face the great challenge of adapting to varying contextual conditions, user requirements or execution environments. Service-oriented Computing (SOC), and service-oriented architectures in general, have been designed to support a specific form of adaptation: services can be dynamically discovered and properly combined in order to achieve an overall service composition that satisfies some specific desiderata that could be known only at service composition time. Rather sophisticated theories have been defined for checking and guaranteeing the correctness of these service assemblies (see, e.g., the rich literature on choreography/orchestration languages [2,14], behavioral contracts [6,7], and session types [4,5,12]). In this paper, we consider a more fine-grained form of adaptation that can occur when the services have been already combined but have not yet completed their task. This form of adaptation may arise, for instance, when the desiderata dynamically change or when some unexpected external event occurs. In particular in the context of computer-supported case management, e.g. for health-care or financial services, changes are the norm rather than the exception. This has lead to an increasing interest both from academia and industry in the development of technologies supporting dynamic changes in choreographies and processes, collectively referred to as *adaptive case management* (ACM) [17,19] and being addressed in the recent proposal for a Case Management Model and Notation (CMMN) from OMG [18]. For such technologies, it is crucial

S. Counsell and M. Núñez (Eds.): SEFM 2013 Collocated Workshops, LNCS 8368, pp. 3–14, 2014.
DOI: 10.1007/978-3-319-05032-4_1, © Springer International Publishing Switzerland 2014

that modifications occur in a consistent and coordinated manner in order to avoid breaking the correctness of the overall service composition.

In this paper, we initiate the investigation of new models and theories for service composition that properly take into account this form of adaptation. First of all, we extend a previous language for the description of service choreographies [2] with two operators: the first one allows for the specification of *adaptable scopes* that can be dynamically modified, while the second may dynamically update code in one of such scopes. This language is designed for the *global description* of dynamically adaptable multi-party interaction protocols. As a second step in the development of our theory, we define a service behavioral contract language for the *local description* of the input-output communications. In order to support adaptation, also in this case we enhance an existing service contract language [2] with two new operators for adaptable scope declaration and code update, respectively. The most challenging aspect to be taken into account is the fact that, at the local level, peers should synchronize their local adaptations in order to guarantee a consistent adaptation of their behavior. As mentioned above, these two languages are expected to be used to describe multi-party protocols from global and local perspectives, respectively. The relationship between the two languages is formalized in terms of a *projection* function which allows us to obtain endpoint specifications from a given choreography.

The complete theory that we plan to develop will also consider a concrete language for programming services; such a language will include update mechanisms like those provided by, for instance, the Jorba service orchestration language [13]. The ultimate aim of our research is to define appropriate behavioral typing techniques able to check whether the concretely programmed services correctly implement the specified multi-party adaptable protocols. This will be achieved by considering the global specification of the protocol, by projecting such specification on the considered peer, and then by checking whether the actual service correctly implements the projected behavior. In order to clarify our objective, we discuss an example inspired by a health-care scenario [16]. Two adaptable protocols are described by using the proposed choreography languages: the first protocol describes the interaction between the *doctor* and the *laboratory* agents, while the second involves a *doctor*, a *nurse*, and a *patient*. In case of emergency, the doctor may speed up the used protocols by interrupting running tests and avoiding the possibility that the nurse refuses to use a medicine she does not trust —this possibility is normally allowed by the protocol. Then, using a π-calculus-like language, we present the actual behavior of the doctor and discuss the kinds of problems that we will have to address in order to define appropriate behavioral type checking techniques.

Structure of the Paper. The next section introduces choreography and endpoint languages with adaptation constructs, and the projection function that relates global and local specifications. Then, in Sect. 3 we outline a concrete specification language and discuss the health-care scenario. In Sect. 4 we present some concluding remarks and briefly review related works.

Disclaimer. This paper discusses ongoing work supported by the "Behavioural Types for Reliable Large-Scale Software Systems" (BETTY) Cost Action. Our main aim is to report about the current state of this research activity.

2   Choreography and Endpoint Languages for Adaptation

In the paper, we use the following sets: *channels*, ranged over by $a, a', \ldots$; *scope names*, ranged over by $X, X', \ldots$; and *roles/participants*, ranged over by $r, r_1, r_2, \ldots$. Also, we use $T, T', \ldots$ to denote sets of roles.

2.1   Choreography Language

Syntax. We describe here the syntax of our choreography language. To this end, we first define a set of so-called *choreography terms*. Then, by requiring some well-formedness conditions on such terms, we obtain actual *choreographies*.

The syntax of choreography terms is as follows:

$$
\begin{array}{llll}
C ::= a_{r_1 \to r_2} & \text{(interaction)} & \mid C \; ; \; C & \text{(sequence)} \\
\quad\mid \; C \mid C & \text{(parallel)} & \mid C + C & \text{(choice)} \\
\quad\mid \; C^* & \text{(star)} & \mid 1 & \text{(one)} \\
\quad\mid \; \mathbf{0} & \text{(nil)} & & \\
\quad\mid \; X : T[C] & \text{(scope)} & \mid X_r\{C\} & \text{(update)}
\end{array}
$$

The basic element of a choreography term C is an interaction $a_{r_1 \to r_2}$, with the intended meaning that participant r_1 sends a message to participant r_2 over channel a. Two terms C_1 and C_2 can be composed in sequence ($C_1 \; ; \; C_2$), in parallel ($C_1 \mid C_2$), and using nondeterministic choice ($C_1 + C_2$). Also, a choreography term may be iterated zero or more times using the Kleene star *. The empty choreography term, which just successfully terminates, is denoted by 1. The deadlocked choreography term $\mathbf{0}$ is needed for the definition of the semantics: we will assume that it is never used when writing a choreography (see Definition 1).

The two last operators deal with adaptation. Adaptation is specified by defining a *scope* that delimits a choreography term that, at runtime, may be replaced by a new choreography term, coming from either inside or outside the system. Adaptations coming from outside may be decided by the user through some adaptation interface, by some manager module, or by the environment. In contrast, adaptations coming from inside represent self-updates, decided by a part of the system towards itself or towards another part of the system, usually as a result of some interaction producing unexpected values. Adaptations from outside and from inside are indeed quite similar, e.g., an update decided by a manager module may be from inside if the manager behavior is part of the choreography term, from outside if it is not. Construct $X : T[C]$ defines a scope named X currently executing choreography term C — the name is needed to designate it as a target for a particular adaptation. Type T is the set of roles (possibly) occurring in the scope. This is needed since a given update can be applied to a scope only if it specifies how all the involved roles are adapted. Operator $X_r\{C\}$ defines *internal updates*, i.e., updates offered by a participant of the choreography term. Here r denotes the participant offering the update, X is the name of the target scope, and C is the new choreography term.

Not all choreography terms generated by the syntax above are useful choreographies. To formally define the choreography terms which actually represent choreographies, we rely on some auxiliary definitions. The set of roles inside a choreography term C, denoted $roles(C)$, is defined inductively as follows:

$$roles(a_{r_1 \to r_2}) = \{r_1, r_2\} \qquad roles(X_r\{C\}) = \{r\}$$
$$roles(X : T[C]) = T \cup roles(C) \qquad roles(C^*) = roles(C)$$
$$roles(C_1 \,;\, C_2) = roles(C_1 \mid C_2) = roles(C_1 + C_2) = roles(C_1) \cup roles(C_2)$$
$$roles(\mathbf{1}) = roles(\mathbf{0}) = \emptyset$$

Notice that for $X_r\{C\}$ we consider role r but not the roles in C. This is because $X_r\{C\}$ may correspond to an external update on some different choreography term. We are now ready to define choreographies.

Definition 1. (Choreography). *A choreography term C is a choreography if:*

1. *C does not contain occurrences of $\mathbf{0}$;*
2. *all names of scopes in C are pairwise distinct;*
3. *C is well-typed, i.e. for every scope $X : T[C']$ occurring in C:*
   - *$roles(C') \subseteq T$ and*
   - *every update prefix $X_r\{C''\}$ occurring in C is such that $roles(C'') \subseteq T$.*

We use $type(X)$ to denote the type T associated to the unique scope $X : T[C']$.

Semantics. We now define the semantics of choreography terms via a labeled transition system. As in the syntax, the most interesting part of the semantics concerns update constructs. Recall that T is a set of roles. In the definition below, we use $C[C'/X]$ to denote the substitution that replaces all scopes $X : T[C'']$ with name X occurring in C (not inside update prefixes) with $X : T[C']$. As usual, transition $C \xrightarrow{\alpha} C'$ intuitively says that choreography term C may evolve to C' by performing an action represented by a label α. Our set of labels includes $\sqrt{}$ (termination), $a_{r_1 \to r_2}$ (interaction), and $X_r\{C\}$ (update).

Definition 2. *The semantics of choreography terms is the smallest labeled transition system closed under the rules in Table 1.*

We briefly comment on the rules in Table 1. Rules in the first four rows of the table are standard (cf. [2]). Rule (ONE) defines termination for the empty choreography term. Rule (COMM) executes an interaction, making it visible in the label. While rule (SEQ) allows the first component of a sequential composition to compute, rule (SEQTICK) allows it to terminate, starting the execution of the second component. Rule (PAR) allows parallel components to interleave their executions. Rule (PARTICK) allows parallel components to synchronize their termination. Rule (CHO) selects a branch in a nondeterministic choice. Rule (STAR)

Table 1. Semantics of Choreography Terms

$$(\text{One}) \; \frac{}{1 \xrightarrow{\checkmark} 0} \qquad (\text{Comm}) \; \frac{}{a_{r_1 \to r_2} \xrightarrow{a_{r_1 \to r_2}} 1} \qquad (\text{Seq}) \; \frac{C_1 \xrightarrow{a_{r_1 \to r_2}} C_1'}{C_1; \, C_2 \xrightarrow{a_{r_1 \to r_2}} C_1'; C_2}$$

$$(\text{SeqTick}) \; \frac{C_1 \xrightarrow{\checkmark} C_1' \quad C_2 \xrightarrow{\alpha} C_2'}{C_1; \, C_2 \xrightarrow{\alpha} C_2'} \qquad (\text{Par}) \; \frac{C_1 \xrightarrow{a_{r_1 \to r_2}} C_1'}{C_1 \mid C_2 \xrightarrow{a_{r_1 \to r_2}} C_1' \mid C_2}$$

$$(\text{ParTick}) \; \frac{C_1 \xrightarrow{\checkmark} C_1' \quad C_2 \xrightarrow{\checkmark} C_2'}{C_1 \mid C_2 \xrightarrow{\checkmark} C_1' \mid C_2'} \qquad (\text{Cho}) \; \frac{C_1 \xrightarrow{\alpha} C_1'}{C_1 + C_2 \xrightarrow{\alpha} C_1'}$$

$$(\text{Star}) \; \frac{C \xrightarrow{a_{r_1 \to r_2}} C'}{C^* \xrightarrow{a_{r_1 \to r_2}} C'; \, C^*} \qquad (\text{StarTick}) \; \frac{}{C^* \xrightarrow{\checkmark} 0}$$

$$(\text{CommUpd}) \; \frac{}{X_r\{C\} \xrightarrow{X_r\{C\}} 1} \qquad (\text{SeqUpd}) \; \frac{C_1 \xrightarrow{X_r\{C\}} C_1'}{C_1; \, C_2 \xrightarrow{X_r\{C\}} C_1'; (C_2[C/X])}$$

$$(\text{ParUpd}) \; \frac{C_1 \xrightarrow{X_r\{C\}} C_1'}{C_1 \mid C_2 \xrightarrow{X_r\{C\}} C_1' \mid (C_2[C/X])} \qquad (\text{StarUpd}) \; \frac{C_1 \xrightarrow{X_r\{C\}} C_1'}{C_1^* \xrightarrow{X_r\{C\}} C_1'; (C_1[C/X])^*}$$

$$(\text{ScopeUpd}) \; \frac{C_1 \xrightarrow{X_r\{C\}} C_1'}{X : T[C_1] \xrightarrow{X_r\{C\}} X : T[C]}$$

$$(\text{Scope}) \; \frac{C_1 \xrightarrow{\alpha} C_1' \quad \alpha \neq X_r\{C\} \text{ for any } r, C}{X : T[C_1] \xrightarrow{\alpha} X : T[C_1']}$$

unfolds the Kleene star. Note that the unfolding may break uniqueness of scopes with a given name—we will come back to this point later on. Rule (STARTICK) defines termination of a Kleene star.

The remaining rules in Table 1 deal with adaptation. Rule (COMMUPD) makes an internal adaptation available, moving the information to the label. Adaptations propagate through sequence, parallel composition, and Kleene star using rules (SEQUPD), (PARUPD), and (STARUPD), respectively. Note that, while propagating, the update is applied to the continuation of the sequential composition, to parallel terms, and to the body of Kleene star. Notably, the update is applied to both enabled and non enabled occurrences of the desired scope. Rule (SCOPEUPD) allows a scope to update itself (provided that the names coincide), while propagating the update to the rest of the choreography term.Rule (SCOPE) allows a scope to compute.

We can now define the notion of *closed* traces that correspond to computations of stand-alone choreography terms.

Definition 3. (Traces). *Given a choreography term C_0 a trace is a (possibly infinite) sequence $C_0 \xrightarrow{\alpha_1} C_1 \xrightarrow{\alpha_2} C_2 \xrightarrow{\alpha_3} \cdots$.*

In order to model choreography terms that can be externally updated we need to introduce the notion of *open* transitions.

Definition 4. (Open transitions). *The choreography term C has an open transition of the form $C \xrightarrow{X\{C''\}} C[C''/X]$ if:*

– there is a choreography C_0 with a trace $C_0 \xrightarrow{\alpha} \cdots \xrightarrow{\alpha'} C_0' | C$;
– $C_0' \xrightarrow{X_r \{C''\}} C_0''$ where $r \notin roles(C)$ and X is the name of a scope in C.

We can now define the notion of *open traces* corresponding to computations including also open transitions.

Definition 5. (Open Traces). *Given a choreography term C_0 an open trace is a (possibly infinite) sequence $C_0 \xrightarrow{\alpha_1} C_1 \xrightarrow{\alpha_2} C_2 \xrightarrow{\alpha_3} \cdots$ where every $C_i \xrightarrow{\alpha_{i+1}} C_{i+1}$ is either a transition of the semantics in Table 1 or an open transition.*

As we have said, in a choreography we assume scope names to be unique. However, uniqueness is not preserved by transitions. Nevertheless a slightly weaker property (arising from the fact that we consider Kleene star as the only form of recursion) is indeed preserved, and it simplifies the implementation of the adaptation mechanisms at the level of endpoints.

Proposition 1. *Let C be a choreography and let C' be a choreography term reachable from C via zero or more transitions (possibly open). For every X, C' contains at most one occurrence of a scope named X which is enabled (i.e., which can compute).*

An Example. Below we give an example of an adaptable choreography to illustrate the features introduced above. The example is based on a health-care workflow inspired by field study [16] carried out in previous work. The field study was also considered as inspiration for recent work on session types for health-care processes [11] and adaptable declarative case management processes [17], but the combination of session types and adaptability has not been treated previously.

In the considered scenario, doctors, nurses and patients employ a distributed, electronic health-care record system where each actor (including the patient) uses a tablet pc/smartphone to coordinate the treatment. Below, iteration C^+ stands for $C; C^*$.

$$X : \{D, N\}[((prescribe_{D \to N})^+;$$
$$(sign_{D \to N} + X_D\{sign_{D \to N}\}; up_{D \to N}); trust_{N \to D})^+];$$
$$medicine_{N \to P}$$

where D, N, P denote participant doctors, nurses, and patients, respectively.

The doctor first records one or more prescriptions, which are sent to the nurse's tablet $(prescribe_{D \to N})^+$. When receiving a signature, $sign_{D \to N}$, the nurse informs the doctor if the prescription is trusted. If not trusted then the doctor must prescribe a new medicine. If trusted, the nurse proceeds and gives the medicine to the patient, which is recorded at the patient's smartphone, $medicine_{N \to P}$. However, instead of signing and waiting for the nurse to trust the medicine, in emergency cases the doctor may update the protocol so that the possibility of not trusting the prescription is removed: the nurse would have to give the medicine to the patient right after receiving the signature. In the example, this is done by a self-update

$(X_D\{sign_{D\to N}\})$ of the running scope. In other scenarios, this could have been done by an entity not represented in the choreography, such as the hospital director, thus resulting in an external update. The doctor notifies the protocol update to the nurse using the $up_{D\to N}$ interaction.

Now consider the further complication that the doctor may run a test protocol with a laboratory, after prescribing a medicine and before signing:

$$X'\{D, L\} : [orderTest_{D\to L} \; ; \; (results_{L\to D} + X'_D\{\mathbf{1}\})]$$

We allow the test protocol also to be adaptable, since the doctor may decide that there is an emergency while waiting for the results, and thus also having to interrupt the test protocol. If the two protocols are performed in interleaving by the same code, then the updates of the two protocols should be coordinated. We illustrate this in Sect. 3 below.

2.2   Endpoint Language

Since choreographies are at the very high level of abstraction, defining a description of the same system nearer to an actual implementation is of interest. In particular, for each participant in a choreography (also called *endpoint*) we would like to describe the actions it has to take in order to follow the choreography. The syntax of endpoint processes is as follows:

$$
\begin{array}{lllll}
P ::= \bar{a}_r & \text{(output)} & | \; a_r & \text{(input)} \\
\quad | \quad P \; ; \; P & \text{(sequence)} & | \; P \mid P & \text{(parallel)} \\
\quad | \quad P + P & \text{(choice)} & | \; P^* & \text{(star)} \\
\quad | \quad \mathbf{1} & \text{(one)} & | \; \mathbf{0} & \text{(zero)} \\
\quad | \quad X[P]^F & \text{(scope)} & | \; X_{(r_1,\dots,r_n)}\{P_1,\dots,P_n\} & \text{(update)}
\end{array}
$$

where F is either A, denoting an active (running) scope, or ε, denoting a scope still to be started (ε is omitted in the following).

As for choreographies, endpoint processes contain some standard operators and some operators dealing with adaptation. Communication is performed by $\bar{a}_r$, denoting an output on channel a towards participant r. Dually, a_r denotes an input from participant r on channel a. Intuitively, an output $\bar{a}_r$ in role s and an input a_s in role r should synchronize. Two endpoint processes P_1 and P_2 can be composed in sequence ($P_1 \; ; \; P_2$), in parallel ($P_1 \mid P_2$), and using nondeterministic choice ($P_1 + P_2$). Endpoint processes can be iterated using a Kleene star $*$. The empty endpoint process is denoted by $\mathbf{1}$ and the deadlocked endpoint process is denoted by $\mathbf{0}$.

Adaptation is applied to scopes. $X[P]^F$ denotes a scope named X executing process P. F is a flag distinguishing scopes whose execution has already begun (A) from scopes which have not started yet (ε). The update operator $X_{(r_1,\dots,r_n)}\{P_1,\dots,P_n\}$ provides an update for scope named X, involving roles $r_1,\dots,r_n$. The new process for role r_i is P_i.

Endpoints are of the form $[\![P]\!]_r$, where r is the name of the endpoint and P its process. Systems, denoted S, are obtained by composition of parallel endpoints:

$$S ::= [\![P]\!]_r \qquad \text{(endpoint)} \quad | \ S \| S \qquad \text{(parallel system)}$$

As for choreographies, not all systems are endpoint specifications. By a slight abuse of notation we extend $type(X)$ to endpoints associating a set of roles to each scope name X. Endpoint specifications are defined as follows.

Definition 6. *A system S is an endpoint specification if the following conditions hold:*

(i) *no active scopes are present*
(ii) *endpoint names are unique*
(iii) *all roles r occurring in terms of the form $\overline{a}_r$, a_r, or such that $r \in type(X)$ for some scope X are endpoints of S*
(iv) *a scope with name X con occur (outside updates) only in endpoints $r \in type(X)$*
(v) *every update has the form $X_{type(X)}\{P_1, \ldots, P_n\}$*
(vi) *outputs $\overline{a}_r$ and inputs a_r included in $X_{type(X)}\{P_1, \ldots, P_n\}$ are such that $r \in type(X)$.*

In this presentation, we do not formally define a semantics for endpoints: we just point out that it should include labels corresponding to all the labels of the semantics of choreography terms, plus some additional labels corresponding to partial activities, such as an input. We also highlight the fact that all scopes which correspond to the same choreography scope evolve together: their scope start transitions (transforming a scope from inactive to active) are synchronized, as well as their scope end transitions (removing it). The fact that choreographies feature at most one scope with a given name is instrumental in ensuring this property.

2.3 Projection

Since choreographies provide system descriptions at the high level of abstraction and endpoint specifications provide more low level descriptions, a main issue is to derive from a given choreography an endpoint specification executing it. This is done using the notion of *projection*.

Definition 7. (Projection). *The projection of a choreography C on a role r, denoted by $C\!\restriction_r$, is defined by the clauses below*

$$a_{r_1 \to r_2}\!\restriction_r = \begin{cases} \overline{a}_{r_2} & if\, r = r_1 \\ a_{r_1} & if\, r = r_2 \\ 1 & otherwise \end{cases}$$

$$X_{r'}\{C\}\!\restriction_r = \begin{cases} X_{(r_1,\ldots,r_n)}\{C\!\restriction_{r_1}, \ldots, C\!\restriction_{r_n}\} with \{r_1, \ldots, r_n\} = type(X) \ if\, r = r' \\ 1 \hspace{8cm} otherwise \end{cases}$$

$$X : T[C]\!\restriction_r = \begin{cases} X[C\!\restriction_r] & if\, r \in type(X) \\ 1 & otherwise \end{cases}$$

and is an homomorphism on the other operators. The endpoint specification resulting from a choreography C is obtained by composing in parallel roles $[C \lceil_r]_r$, where $r \in roles(C)$.

As an example, the endpoint projection obtained from the prescribe choreography introduced in Sect. 2.1 is $[P_N]_N \| [P_D]_D \| [P_P]_P$ where processes P_N, P_D, and P_P are as follows (we omit unnecessary 1 processes):

$$P_N = X[((prescribe_D)^+ ; (sign_D + up_D); \overline{trust}_D)^+] ; \overline{medicine}_P$$
$$P_D = X[((\overline{prescribe}_N)^+ ; (\overline{sign}_N + X_{D,N}\{\overline{sign}_N, sign_D\} ; \overline{up}_N); trust_N)^+]$$
$$P_P = medicine_N$$

One can see that the system S obtained by projecting a choreography is an endpoint specification. Ideally, traces of the projected system should correspond to the traces of the original choreography. Actually, we conjecture that this occurs only for choreographies satisfying suitable connectedness conditions that we plan to formalize extending those in [14]. This is not an actual restriction, since choreographies that do not respect the conditions can be transformed into choreographies that respect them [15].

Conjecture 1. Traces of projection of connected choreographies correspond to traces of the original choreography.

We point out two main aspects of the correspondence. First, labels $X_r\{C\}$ of transitions of the choreography should be mapped to labels $[X(r_1, \ldots, r_n) \{P_1, \ldots, P_n\}]_r$ of the transitions of the endpoint specification, where $type(X) = \{r_1, \ldots, r_n\}$ and $P_1 = C \lceil_{r_1}, \ldots, P_n = C \lceil_{r_n}$ are obtained by projection from C. Second, endpoint traces should not consider unmatched input and output labels.

3   Typing a Concrete Language

As demonstrated by our examples, choreography and endpoint terms provide a useful language for expressing protocols with adaptation. In this section, we investigate the idea of using such protocols as specifications for a programming language with adaptation. We plan to follow the approach taken in multiparty session types [12], where choreographies (and endpoints) are interpreted as behavioral types for typing sessions in a language modeled as a variant of the π-calculus. In the sequel, we investigate the core points of such a language by giving an implementation that uses the protocols specified in the examples of the previous sections. In particular, we discuss what are the relevant aspects for developing a type system for such a language, whose types are the choreographies introduced in Sect. 2.1.

In both prescribe and test protocols, the doctor plays a key role since (s)he initiates the workflow with prescriptions, decides when tests have to be requested, and decides when the protocols have to be interrupted due to an emergency. A possible implementation of the doctor could be given by the following program:

```
1. P_D  = pr̄(k);  X[ repeat {repeat {
2.                  k : prescribe̅_N⟨e_pr⟩;  test̅(k');
3.                  X'[k' : orderTest̅_L⟨e_o⟩;
4.                  (k' : results_L(x)+
5.                      X'_(D,L){X_(D,N){k : sign̅_N⟨e_s⟩, k : sign_D(z)}, 1})]
6.                  } until ok(x);
7.              (k : sign̅_N⟨e_s⟩ + X_(D,N){k : sign̅_N⟨e_s⟩, k : sign_D(z)} ;  k : u̅p̅_N⟨⟩);
8.              k : trust_N(t)} until trusted(t) ]
```

In the code there are two kinds of communication operations, namely protocol initiation operations, where a new protocol (or session) is initiated, and in-session operations where protocol internal operations are implemented. The communication $\overline{pr}(k)$ is for initiating a protocol called pr and its semantics is to create a fresh protocol identifier k that corresponds to a particular instance of protocol pr. In-session communications are standard.

The novelty in the process above is in the scope $X[\ldots]$ and update $X_{\ldots}\{\ldots\}$, which state respectively that the program can be adapted at any time in that particular point, and that an adaptation is available. Interestingly enough, the way the program P_D uses the protocols needs care. If the doctor wants to adapt to emergency while waiting for tests, both the test protocol and the prescription protocol need to be adapted as shown in line 5. If the doctor adapts to emergency after having received tests that are ok, then only the prescription protocol needs to be adapted. One can see that session pr can be typed using the prescribe endpoint specification and session $test$ using the test endpoint specification. The update of X in line 4 does not appear in the protocol test since it acts as an external update for a different protocol.

4   Concluding Remarks and Related Work

Adaptation is a pressing issue in the design of service-oriented systems, which are typically open and execute in highly dynamic environments. There is a rather delicate tension between adaptation and the correctness requirements defined at service composition time: we would like to adapt the system's behavior whenever necessary/possible, but we would also like adaptation actions to preserve overall correctness.

In this paper, we have reported ongoing work on adaptation mechanisms for service-oriented systems specified in terms of choreographies. By enhancing an existing language for choreographies with constructs defining adaptation scopes and dynamic code update, we obtained a simple, global model for distributed, adaptable systems. We also defined an endpoint language for local descriptions, and a projection mechanism for obtaining (low-level) endpoint specifications from (high-level) choreographies.

We now briefly comment on related works. The work in [9] is closely related, and indeed was a source of inspiration for the current work. It develops a framework for rule-based adaptation in a choreographic setting. Both choreographies and endpoints are defined; their relation is formally defined via projection. The main difference w.r.t. the work described here is our choice of expressing adaptation in terms of scopes and code update constructs, rather than using rules. Also, we consider choreographies as types and we allow multiple protocols to interleave inside code. These problems are not considered in [9].

Our work is also related to the recent work [8], which considers self-adaptive systems monitored by different global descriptions. The description specifies also when the used monitor should change, and the new monitor to be used is determined by an adaptation function. A main difference is that in their approach the code does not change because processes should be able to implement all the global descriptions since the very beginning.

Our approach bears some similarities with works on multiparty sessions [4, 12], and in particular with works dealing with exceptions in multiparty sessions [3]. Our focus so far has been on formally relating global and local descriptions of choreographies via projection and trace correspondence; investigating correctness properties (e.g., communication safety) via typing in our setting is part of ongoing work. We also note that exceptions and adaptation are similar but conceptually different phenomena: while the former are typically related to foreseen unexpected behaviors in (low-level) programs, adaptation appears as a more general issue, for it should account for (unforeseen) interactions between the system and its (varying) environment.

We have borrowed inspiration also from [17], in which adaptive case management is investigated via Dynamic Condition Response (DCR) Graphs, a declarative process model.

Finally, the adaptation constructs we have considered for choreographies and endpoints draw inspiration from the *adaptable processes* defined in [1]. The application of adaptable processes in session-typed models of structured communications (focusing on the case of binary sessions) has been studied in [10].

An immediate topic for future work is the full formalization of the concrete language and its typing disciplines. Other avenues for future research include the investigation of refinement theories with a testing-like approach, enabled by having both systems and adaptation strategies modeled in the same language, and the development of prototype implementations.

Acknowledgments. This work was partially supported by COST Action IC1201: Behavioural Types for Reliable Large-Scale Software Systems (BETTY). Jorge A. Pérez was partially supported by grants SFRH/BPD/84067/2012 and CITI of the Portuguese Foundation for Science and Technology (FCT).

References

1. Bravetti, M., Di Giusto, C., Pérez, J.A., Zavattaro, G.: Adaptable processes. Logical Methods Comput. Sci. **8**(4), 1–71 (2012)
2. Bravetti, M., Zavattaro, G.: Towards a unifying theory for choreography conformance and contract compliance. In: Lumpe, M., Vanderperren, W. (eds.) SC 2007. LNCS, vol. 4829, pp. 34–50. Springer, Heidelberg (2007)
3. Capecchi, S., Giachino, E., Yoshida, N.: Global escape in multiparty sessions. In: FSTTCS. LIPIcs, vol. 8, pp. 338–351. Schloss Dagstuhl - Leibniz-Zentrum fuer Informatik (2010)
4. Carbone, M., Honda, K., Yoshida, N.: Structured communication-centered programming for web services. ACM Trans. Program. Lang. Syst. **34**(2), 8 (2012)
5. Carbone, M., Montesi, F.: Deadlock-freedom-by-design: multiparty asynchronous global programming. In: POPL, pp. 263–274. ACM (2013)
6. Carpineti, S., Laneve, C.: A basic contract language for web services. In: Sestoft, P. (ed.) ESOP 2006. LNCS, vol. 3924, pp. 197–213. Springer, Heidelberg (2006)
7. Castagna, G., Gesbert, N., Padovani, L.: A theory of contracts for web services. In: POPL, pp. 261–272. ACM, New York (2008)
8. Coppo, M., Dezani-Ciancaglini, M., Venneri, B.: Self-adaptive monitors for multiparty sessions. In: PDP (2014) (to appear)
9. Dalla Preda, M., Lanese, I., Mauro, J., Gabbrielli, M., Giallorenzo, S.: Safe runtime adaptation of distributed applications, 2013. Submitted. Available at http://www.cs.unibo.it/lanese/publications/fulltext/adaptchor2.pdf.gz
10. Di Giusto, C., Pérez, J.A.: Disciplined structured communications with consistent runtime adaptation. In: SAC, pp. 1913–1918. ACM (2013)
11. Henriksen, A.S., Nielsen, L., Hildebrandt, T.T., Yoshida, N., Henglein, F.: Trustworthy pervasive healthcare services via multiparty session types. In: Weber, J., Perseil, I. (eds.) FHIES 2012. LNCS, vol. 7789, pp. 124–141. Springer, Heidelberg (2013)
12. Honda, K., Yoshida, N., Carbone, M.: Multiparty asynchronous session types. In: POPL, pp. 273–284. ACM (2008)
13. Lanese, I., Bucchiarone, A., Montesi, F.: A framework for rule-dased dynamic adaptation. In: Wirsing, M., Hofmann, M., Rauschmayer, A. (eds.) TGC 2010. LNCS, vol. 6084, pp. 284–300. Springer, Heidelberg (2010)
14. Lanese, I., Guidi, C., Montesi, F., Zavattaro, G.: Bridging the gap between interaction- and process-oriented choreographies. SEFM, pp. 323–332. IEEE Computer Society, Washington, DC (2008)
15. Lanese, I., Montesi, F., Zavattaro, G.: Amending choreographies. In: WWV. EPTCS, vol. 123, pp. 34–48. Open Publishing Association (2013)
16. Lyng, K.M., Hildebrandt, T., Mukkamala, R.R.: From paper based clinical practice guidelines to declarative workflow management. In: ProHealth, BPM 2008 Workshops, pp. 36–43 (2008)
17. Mukkamala, R.R., Hildebrandt, T., Slaats, T.: Towards trustworthy adaptive case management with dynamic condition response graphs. In: EDOC, pp. 127–136. IEEE (2013)
18. OMG. Case management model and notation 1.0 - beta 1, January 2013
19. Swenson, K.D.: Mastering the Unpredictable - How Adaptive Case Management Will Revolutionize the Way That Knowledge Workers Get Things Done. Meghan-Kiffer, Tampa (2010)

A Concurrent Programming Language with Refined Session Types

Juliana Franco$^{(\boxtimes)}$ and Vasco Thudichum Vasconcelos

LaSIGE, Faculdade De Ciências, Universidade De Lisboa, Lisboa, Portugal
jfranco@lasige.di.fc.ul.pt

Abstract. We present SePi, a concurrent programming language based on the monadic pi-calculus, where interaction is governed by linearly refined session types. On top of the core calculus and type system, and in order to facilitate programming, we introduce a number of abbreviations and derived constructs. This paper provides a brief introduction to the language.

1 Introduction

Session types [12] are by now a well-established methodology for typed, message-passing concurrent computations. By assigning session types to communication channels, and by checking programs against session type systems, a number of important program properties can be established, including the absence of races in channel manipulation operations, and the guarantee that channels are used as prescribed by their types. As a simple example, a type of the form ! **string** .! **integer** .**end** describes a channel end on which processes may first output a string, then output an integer value, after which the channel provides no further interaction. The process holding the other end of the channel must first input a string, then an integer, as described by the complementary (or dual) type, ?**string** .?**integer** .**end**. If the string denotes a credit card number and the integer value the amount to be charged to the credit card, then we may further *refine* the type by requiring that the capability to charge the credit card has been offered, as in ?ccard : **string** .?amount:{x:**integer**|charge(ccard,x)}.**end**. The most common approach to handle refinement types is classical first-order logic which is certainly sufficient for many purposes but cannot treat formulae as resources. In particular it cannot guarantee that the credit card is charged with the given amount only once.

SePi is an exercise in the design and implementation of a concurrent programming language solely based on the message passing mechanism of the pi calculus [16], where process interaction is governed by (linearly refined) session types. SePi allows to explore the practical applicability of recent work on session-based type systems [1,25], as well as to provide a tool where new program idioms and type developments may be tested and eventually incorporated. In this respect, SePi shares its goal with Pict [19] and TyCO [22].

S. Counsell and M. Núñez (Eds.): SEFM 2013 Collocated Workshops, LNCS 8368, pp. 15–28, 2014.
DOI: 10.1007/978-3-319-05032-4_2, © Springer International Publishing Switzerland 2014

The SePi core language is the monadic synchronous pi-calculus [16] with replication rather than recursion [15], labelled choice [12], and with assume/assert primitives [1]. On top of this core we provide a few derived constructs aiming at facilitating code development. The current version of the language includes support for mutually recursive process definitions and type declarations, for polyadic message passing and session initiation, a **dualof** operator on types, and an abbreviation for shared types. The type system of SePi is that of linearly refined session types [1], the algorithmic rules for the refinement-free type language are adapted from [25], and those for refinements are described in this paper.

SePi is currently implemented as an Eclipse plug-in, allowing code development with the usual advantages of an IDE, such as syntax highlighting, syntactic and semantic validation, code completion and refactoring. It further includes a simple interpreter based on Turner's abstract machine [21]. There is also a command line alternative, in the form of a jar file. Installation details and examples can be found at http://gloss.di.fc.ul.pt/sepi.

The rest of this paper is structured as follows. The next Section reviews related work. Section 3 briefly introduces SePi based on a running example. Section 4 presents a few technical aspects of the language. Section 5 concludes the paper, pointing possible future language extensions.

2   Related Work

This section briefly reviews programming language *implementations* either based on the pi-calculus or that incorporate session types.

There are a few programming languages based on the pi-calculus, but none incorporate session types. Pict [19] is a language in the ML-tradition, featuring labelled records, higher-order polymorphism, recursive types and subtyping. Similarly to the SePi approach, Pict builds on a tiny core (a variant of the asynchronous pi-calculus [3,11]) by adding a few derived constructs. TyCO [23] is another language based on a variant of the asynchronous pi-calculus, featuring labelled messages (atomic select/output) and labelled receptors (atomic branch/input) [22], predicative polymorphism and full type inference. In turn, SePi is based on the monadic synchronous pi-calculus with labelled choice [12], explicitly typed and equipped with refined session types [1]. Polymorphism and subtyping are absent from the current version of SePi.

On the other hand, we find programming languages that feature session types or variants of these, but are based on paradigms other than the pi-calculus. For functional languages, we have those that take advantage of the rich system of Haskell, monads in particular, and those based on ML. Neubauer and Thiemann implemented session types on Haskell using explicit continuation passing [17]. Sackman and Eisenbach improve this work, augmenting the expressive power of the language [20]. Given that session types are encoded, the Haskell code for session-based programs can be daunting. SePi works directly with session types, thus hopefully leading to readable programs. Bhargavan et al. [2] present a ML-like language for specifying multiparty sessions [13] for cryptographic protocols, with integrity and secrecy support.

For object-oriented languages, Fähndrich et al. developed Sing# [6], a variant of C# that supports message-based communication via shared-memory where session types are used to describe communication patterns. Hu et al. introduced SJ [14], an extension of Java with specific syntax for session types and structured communication operations. Based on a work by Gay et al. [7], Bica [4] is an extension of the Java 5 compiler that checks conventional Java source code against session type specifications for classes. Type specifications, included in Java annotations, describe the order by which methods in classes should be called, as well as the tests clients must perform on results from method calls. Following a similar approach, but using session types with lin/un annotations [25], Mool [5] is a minimal object based language.

Finally, for imperative languages, Ng et al. developed Session C [18], a multi-party session-based programming environment for the C programming language and its runtime libraries [18]. Also using the theory of multiparty session types, we have the Scribble framework presented by Honda et al. [10], that supports bindings for several high-level languages such as ML, Java, Python, C# or C++, and whose purpose is to provide a formal and intuitive language and tools to specify communication protocols and their implementations. Neither of the works discussed above feature any form of refinement types, linear or classical.

3   A Gentle Introduction to the SePi Language

This section introduces the SePi language, its syntax, type system and operational semantics. The presentation is intentionally informal. Technical details can be found on the theoretical work the language builds upon, namely [25] for the base language and [1] for refinements.

Our running example is based on the online petition service [24] and on the online store [1]. An Online Donation Server manages donation campaigns. Clients seeking to start a donation campaign for a given cause begin by setting up a session with the server. The session is conducted on a channel on which the campaign related data is provided. The same channel may then be disseminated and used by different benefactors for the purpose of collecting the actual donations. Parties donating for some cause do so by providing a credit card number and the amount to be charged to the card. The type system makes sure that the exact amount specified by the donor is charged, and that the card is charged exactly once.

SePi is about message passing on bi-directional synchronous channels. Each channel is described by two end points. Processes may write on one end or else read from the other end, at each particular location in a program. Channels are governed by types that describe the sequence of messages a channel may carry. We start with *input/output types*. A type of the form !**integer**.**end** describes a channel end where processes may write an integer value, after which the channel offers no further interaction. Similarly, a type ?**integer**.**end** describes a channel end from which processes may read an integer value, after which the channel offers no further interaction.

To *create a channel* of the above type one writes

```
new w r: !integer.end
```

Such a declaration introduces two new program variables: w of type !**integer**.**end**, and r of type ?**integer**.**end**. A semantically equivalent declaration is **new** r w: ?**integer**.**end** . To *write* the integer value 2013 on the newly created channel, one uses w!2013. To *read* from the channel and let program variable x denote the value read, one writes r?x. For the purpose of printing integer values on the console, SePi provides the primitive channels printInteger and printIntegerLn , and similarly for the remaining base types: **boolean** and **string**. The Ln versions issue a newline after printing the value. Code such as channel writing or reading can be composed by *prefixing* via the dot notation. To read an integer value and then to print it, one writes r?x. printInteger !x. To run two processes in *parallel* one uses the vertical bar notation. Putting everything together one obtains our first complete program, composed of a channel declaration and two processes running in parallel while sharing the channel.

```
new w r: !integer.end
w!2013 | r?x.printInteger !x
```

Running such a program would produce 2013 on the console, after which the program terminates.

We now move on to *choice types*. The donation server allows clients to setup donation campaigns piece-wise. The required information (title, description, due date, etc.) may be introduced in any order, possibly more than once each. Once satisfied, the client "presses the commit" button. A channel end that allows a writer to *select* either the setDate option or the commit option is written as:

```
+{setDate:end, commit:end}
```

Conversely, a channel end that provides a menu composed of the two same choices can be written as &{setDate:end, commit:end}. To select the setDate option on a + channel end we write w **select** setDate. Conversely to branch on a & channel end one may write **case** r **of** setDate → ... commit → .... Putting everything together one obtains the following process.

```
new w r: +{setDate:end, commit:end}
w select setDate |
case r of setDate → printString !"Got setDate"
           commit → printString !"Got commit"
```

We have seen that types are composed by prefixing, using the dot notation: !**integer**.**end** means write an integer and then go on as **end**. We can compose the output and the select type we have seen above, so that the output of an integer is required after the setDate choice is taken. We leave to the reader composing the two programs above so that it interacts correctly on a channel whose client end is of type +{setDate:!**integer**.**end**, commit:**end**}.

The problem with this type is that it does not reflect the idea of "uploading the campaign information until satisfied, and then press the commit button". All a client can do is *either* set the date *or else* commit. What we would like to say is that after the setDate choice is taken the whole menu is again available. For this we require a *recursive* type of the form:

```
rec a.+{setDate :! integer.a , commit : end}
```

A client w may now upload the date two times before committing:

```
w select setDate. w!2012.
w select setDate. w!2013. w select commit
```

The donation server, when governed by type etDate:?integer.a, commit:endrec a.& s, needs to continuously offer the setDate and commit options. Such behaviour cannot be achieved with a finite composition of the primitives we have seen so far. We need some form unbounded behaviour, which SePi provides in the form a **def** process. The setup process below is the part of the donation server responsible for downloading the campaign information. To simplify the example, only the due date is considered and even this information, x, is immediately discarded. We will see that setup is a form of an input process that survives interaction, thus justifying its invocation with the exact same syntax as message sending: setup!r.

```
def setup r: rec a.&{setDate :? integer.a , commit : end} =
    case r of setDate → r?x. setup!r
              commit   → ...
```

Process definition, **def**, is the second form of declaration in SePi (the first is **new**). There is yet a third kind of declaration (rather, an abbreviation): **type**. Introducing the name Donation for the above recursive type, one may write:

```
type Donation = +{setDate : ! integer. Donation , commit : end}
```

thus foregoing the explicit use of the **rec** type constructor. Type, process and channel declarations may be mutually recursive. Keywords **type**, **def**, and **new** introduce a series of equations that are elaborated by the compiler, as described in Sect. 4.

There is a further handy abbreviation. Session types tend to be quite long; if a channel's end point is of type **rec** a.+{setDate:!**integer**.a, commit:**end**}, the other end is of type **rec** a.&{setDate:?**integer**.a, commit:**end**}. In this case we say that one type is *dual* to the other, a notion central to session types. Given that we abbreviated the first type to Donation, the second can be abbreviated to **dualof** Donation. Putting every together we obtain the following process.

```
type Donation = +{setDate : ! integer. Donation , commit : ...}
def setup r: dualof Donation =
    case r of setDate → r?x. setup!r
              commit   → ...
new w r : Donation        // the donation channel
w select setDate. w!2012. w select setDate. w!2013.
    w select commit |     // a client
setup!r                   // a server
```

Continuing with the example, after setup comes the promotion phase. Here the donation channel is used to collect donations from benefactors. Benefactors donate to a cause by providing a credit card number and the amount to be charged to the card. So we rewrite the donation type to:

type Donation = +{setDate :! **integer** . Donation , commit : Promotion }
type CreditCard = **string**

How does type Promotion look like? If we make it !CreditCard .! **integer**.**end**, then the server accepts a single donation. Clearly undesirable. If we choose **rec** a .! CreditCard .! **integer**.a, then we accept an infinite number of donations. And this is undesirable for two reasons: (a) regrettably, no campaign will ever receive an infinite number of donations, and (b) all these donations would have to be issued from the same thread (a process without parallel composition), one after the other. The first problem can be easily circumvented with a rec-choice combination, as in type Donation. The root of the second problem lies in the fact that types are *linear* by default, meaning that each channel end can be known, at any given point in the program, by exactly one thread. And this goes against the idea of disseminating the channel in such a way that any party may individually donate, by just knowing the channel. We need a means to say that channel ends can be shared by more than one process. Towards this end, we label *each prefix* as either **un** or **lin**. Shared types are qualified with **un** (for unrestricted); linear types with **lin**. It turns out that the **lin** qualifier is optional. For example, !**integer**.**end** abbreviates **lin** !**integer**.**end**.

The type system keeps track of how many threads know a channel end: if **lin** then exactly one, if **un** then zero or more. Linear channels are exempt from races: we do not want two threads competing to set up a donation campaign. Shared channels are prone to races: we do want many (as many as possible) simultaneous benefactors carrying out their donations. Care must however be exerted when using shared channels. Imagine that type Promotion looks like **rec** a.**un**!CreditCard.**un**!**integer**.a, and that we have two donors trying to interact with the server,

w!"2345".w!500 | w!"1324".w!2000 | r?x.r?y...

Further imagine that the first donor wins the race, and exchanges message "2345". We are left with a process of the form w!500 | w!"1324".w!2000 | r?y..., where the value transmitted on the next message exchange can be an integer value (500) or a string ("1324"), a situation clearly undesirable. To circumvent this situation we pass the two values in a single message, by making w of type **rec** a.**un**!(CreditCard, **integer**).a. This pattern, **rec** a.**un**!T.a, is so common that we provide an abbreviation for it: *!T, and similarly for input. So here is the new type for Promotion.

type Promotion = *!(CreditCard , **integer**)

Now a client can donate twice (in parallel); it may also pass the channel to all its acquaintances so that they may donate and/or further disseminate the channel. In the process below, notice the parallel composition operator enclosed in braces when used within a process.

```
w select setDate. w!2014. w select commit. {
    w!("2345", 500) | w!("1324", 2000) | acquaintance!w
}
```

The ability to define types that "start" as linear (e.g. Donation) and end up as unrestricted (Promotion) was introduced in [25].

So far our example is composed of one server and one client. What if we require more than one client (the plausible scenario for an online system) or more than one server (perhaps for load balancing)? If we add a second client, in parallel with the above code for the server and the client, the program does not compile anymore: there is a race between the two clients for the linear channel end w. On the one hand we have seen that the donation channel must be linear; on the other hand we want a donation server reading on a well-known, public, **un,** channel. We start by installing the server on a channel end of type *?Donation, and disseminate the client end of the channel (of type **dualof** *!Donation, that is *?Donation). Our main program with two clients looks as follows.

```
new c s: *?Donation     // create an Online Donation channel
donationServer!s |      // send one end to the Donation Server
client1!c | client2!c   // let the whole world know the other
```

To this pattern—create a channel, send one end to the server, keep the other—we call *session initiation*. We found it so common that we introduced an abbreviation for it. The above three lines of code can be replaced with the following process.

```
donationServer!(new c: *?Donation). { client1!c | client2!c }
```

Now the first output introduces a binding (for program variable c), hence we cannot use parallel composition anymore. Instead we use prefix. One of the advantages of the session initiation abbreviation is that it spares the programmer from coming up with two different identifiers; that for the server end becomes implicit. Notice however that, in a session initiation process of the form x!(**new** y:T).P the actual end point that is sent is of type **dualof** T.

We now concentrate on how the donation server charges credit cards. In general, merchants cannot directly charge credit cards. As such our donation server forwards the transaction details (the credit card number and amount to be charged) to the credit card issuer (a bank, for example). Assume the following definition for a bank: **def** bank (ccard: CreditCard, amount: **integer**). Well behaved servers receive the data and forward it to the bank:

```
r?(ccard, amount). bank!(ccard, amount)
```

Not so honest servers may try to charge a different amount (perhaps a hidden tax),

```
r?(ccard, amount). bank!(ccard, amount+10)
```

or to charge the right amount, but twice.

```
r?(ccard, amount).{bank!(ccard, amount)|bank!(ccard, amount)}
```

While types cannot constitute a general panacea for fraudulent merchants, the situation can be improved. The idea is that the bank is not interested in arbitrary (ccard,amount) pairs but on pairs for which a charge (ccard,amount) capability has been granted. We then *refine* the type of the amount in the bank's signature. We are now interested on amounts x of type integer for which the predicate charge (ccard,x) holds, that is, parameter amount becomes of type

```
{x:  integer  |  charge(ccard ,x)}
```

The capability of charging a given amount on a specific credit card is usually granted by the benefactor, by *assuming* an instance of the charge predicate, as in:

```
assume  charge("2345" ,  500)  |  w!("2345" ,  500)
```

The bank, in turn, makes sure that the transaction details were granted by the client, by *asserting* the same predicate:

```
def bank (ccard:  CreditCard ,
          amount:  {x:  integer  |  charge(ccard ,x)}) =
     assert  charge(ccard ,  amount) ...
```

Assumptions and assertions have no operational significance on well-typed programs. At the type system level, assumptions and assertions are treated *linearly*: for each asserted predicate there must be exactly one assumed, and conversely. In this way formulae are treated as resources: they are introduced in the type system via **assume** processes, passed around in refinement types, and consumed via **assert** processes. As such, the code for servers that try to charge twice the right amount (see above) does not type check, for the bank's "second" **assert** is not matched by any assumption. The code for servers that try to charge a different amount (see above) does not type check either. In this case the benefactor's assumption charge("2345", 500) would never be asserted, whereas the bank's assertion charge("2345", 510) would not have a corresponding assumption. Linearity also means that code for banks that forget to **assert** charge(ccard, amount) does not type check. We leave as an exercise writing a typeful server code that charges an amount different from that stated (and assumed) by the benefactor (or that charges twice the right amount), by careful manipulation of **assume**/**assert** *in the server code*.

Benefactors that wish to be charged twice, may issue two separate assumptions or join them on a single formulae, as in the code below.

```
assume  charge("2345" ,500)*charge("2345" ,500)  |
w!("2345" ,500)  |  w!("2345" ,500)
```

Likewise, multiple assertions can be conjoined in one, via the tensor (∗) formula constructor [9].

4   Technical Aspects of the Language

SePi is based on the synchronous monadic pi calculus (as in [25]) extended with **assert** and **assume** primitives (inspired by [1]). On top of this core calculus we added a few derived constructs. This section briefly describes the core language, the derived constructs in the SePi language and the type checking system.

The *core language* includes syntactic categories for formulae A, types T, values v, expressions e, and processes P. *Formulae* in the current version of the language are built from uninterpreted predicates (over values only), tensor ($*$) and unit. At the *type* level we have base types (**integer, boolean, string**, and **end**), prefix types (namely, input $q?x:T.U$, output $q!x:T.U$, branching $q\&\{l_1:T_1 ,..., l_n:T_n\}$ and selection $q+\{l_1:T_1 ,..., l_n:T_n\}$, where q is either **lin** or **un**), recursion (**rec** a.T and a) and refinement types ($\{x:T|A\}$). Prefix types are labelled with an optional identifier x that may be referred to in the continuation type (e.g., $!x:$**integer** $.!\{y:$**integer** $|p(x,y)\}$.**end**).

Values in SePi are program variables (standing for channel ends), as well as integer, boolean and string constants. At the level of *expressions* SePi includes the familiar operators on integer and boolean values. For *processes* we have channel creation (**new** $x_1 y_1:T_1 ...$ **new** $x_n y_n:T_n$ P), prefix processes (monadic input, replicated $x*?y.P$ or use-once $x?y.P$, monadic output $x!e.P$, selection x **select** $l.P$, and branching processes **case** x **of** $l_1{\to}P_1 ... l_n{\to}P_n$), conditional **if** e **then** P **else** Q, n-ary parallel composition($\{P_1 |...| P_n\}$), **assume** A and **assert** A.P. Mutually recursive channel creation **new** $x_1 y_1:T_1$ **new** $x_2 y_2:T_2$ allows for channel x_1 to occur in type T_2, and for x_2 to occur in type T_1.

Derived constructs at the *type* level include support for polyadic message passing ($q!(y_1:T_1 ,... y_n:T_n).U$ and $q?(y_1:T_1 ,... y_n:T_n).U$), the star syntax for unrestricted types ($*?T$, $*!T$, $*\&\{l_1 ,..., l_n\}$, and $*+\{l_1 ,..., l_n\}$), and the **dualof** type operator. Furthermore, the **lin** qualifier is optional.

Derived constructs at the *process* level include support for polyadic message passing ($x!(e_1 ,..., e_n).P$ and $x?(y_1 ,..., y_n).P$) and for session initiation (x $!(...,$ **new** $y:T ,...)$ .P). Furthermore the empty parallel composition is optional when used in the continuation of a prefix process ($x!e$ abbreviates $x!e.\{\}$).

Finally, there is one derived construct that mixes types and processes: mutually recursive declarations of the form $D_1 ... D_n$ P, where each declaration D_i is either a channel creation **new** x $y:T$, a process definition **def** $x(y_1:T_1 ,..., y_n: T_n) = P$, or a type abbreviation **type** $a = T$.

We now discuss the derived constructors in SePi, starting with those related to types. A type of the form $*?T$ is expanded into **rec** $b.$**un**$?T.b$ for b a fresh type variable, and similarly for output, branching and selection. The **dualof** type operator produces a new type where input ? is replaced by output !, branching & is replaced by selection +, and conversely in both cases. All other type constructors remain unchanged (except for **rec**). We use the co-inductive definition of Gay and Hole [8], extended to refinement types in the natural way.

In order to simulate interference-free polyadic message passing on shared (**un**) channels, we use a standard encoding for the send and receive operations (cf. [16,25]). For example, the pair-type (ccard: CreditCard, amount: $\{x:$ **integer**$|$ charge(ccard,x)$\}$) in the signature of the bank definition (Sect. 3) is equivalent to the refined linear session type

lin $?c:$ **CreditCard** . **lin** $?\{x:$**integer**$|$ **charge** $(c,x)\}$. **end**

where the prefix ?CreditCard is labelled with identifier c, so that it may be referred to in the continuation, namely in the predicate charge(c,x) for the amount to be charged. On the process side, the output process b!("2345",500).P abbreviates

new r w: **lin** ?c : CreditCard . **lin** ? { x : **integer** | charge (c , x) } . **end**
b ! r .w !" 2345 " .w ! 500 . P

and the input process b?(x,y).P abbreviates

b?z. z?x. z?y .P

All process constructors in the core language were introduced in Sect. 3, except for *replication*. A replicated input process behaves as an input process, except that it survives message reception. We use ? for a linear input and *? for a replicated input. For example:

new w r : ∗! **integer**
w!2013 | r∗?x. printInteger !x | w!2014

prints two integer values, while

new w r : ∗! **integer**
w!2013 | r?x. printInteger !x | w!2014

will print one only.

A *process definition* is expanded into a channel creation followed by a replicated input process. Each declaration of the form **def** p x : T = P introduces a new channel, as in **new** p p': ∗!T where p' is a fresh identifier, in the scope of which, we add a replicated process of the form p'*?x.P, in parallel with the rest of the program. Process definitions obviate in most cases the direct usage of replicated input processes, hiding one of the channel ends (p'), thus simplifying code development. They are also amenable to an optimisation in code interpretation [21].

Session initiation is discussed in Sect. 3. In general, a process x !(..., **new** y :T ,...) .P is expanded into a process of the form **new** $z_1 z_2$: T x !(..., z_2 ,...) .P', where variables z_1 and z_2 are fresh, and P' is obtained from P by replacing (free) occurrences of y by z_1. This substitution is also applied to the arguments of the output process to the right of the **new**. Fresh variables prevent the free variable capture that would occur in process x!(**new** x:end) or y!(x,**new** x:end). Our experience shows that process definition and session initiation account for the vast majority of channel creation, effectively dispensing the explicit declaration of one channel end.

A sequence of declarations followed by a process is a SePi process. Declarations may be mutually recursive. Below is an example that, when run, prints an infinite sequence of alternating **true/false** values. Notice the mutually recursive process (p and q) and type (T and U) definitions. Further notice that type T depends on process p, which depends on channel r, which depends on type T again.

```
type T = *!(boolean,{y:U | a(y,p)})
type U = dualof T
def p b: boolean = { assume a(r,p) | w!(not b,r). q!() }
def q () = r?(x,y). assert a(y,p). printBoolean!b. p!x
new w r: T
p!false | q!()
```

Declarations are elaborated in a few steps. In the first step, type names, channel names, and process names (which are after all channel names) are collected. This information allows us to check type formation (essentially that types do not contain free type and program variables). In the second pass, we check type formation and solve the system of equations. Systems of type equations are guaranteed to be solvable due to the presence of recursive types in the syntax of the language and to the fact that types are required to be contractive.[1] We defer to the next phase the elaboration of the **dualof** operator. For example, the solution to the system of equations above is $T = \mathbf{rec}\ u.!(\mathbf{boolean},\{y:\mathbf{dualof}\ u \mid a(y,p)\}).u$ and $U = \mathbf{dualof}\ T$.[2] The third step expands the occurrences of **dualof** (co-inductively, as explained above) to obtain:

```
T = rec u.un!(boolean,
              {y:rec v.un?(boolean,{z:v|a(z,p)}).u|a(y,p)}).u
U = rec u.un?(boolean,
              {y:rec v.un?(boolean,{z:v|a(z,p)}).u|a(y,p)}).u
```

At this point all types are resolved. The fourth step adds to the typing context entries for new channels (in **new** and **def** declarations) with the appropriate types. Finally, the last pass checks the replicated processes obtained from process definitions. Translating the example above into the core language yields the process below.

```
new p p': rec u.un!boolean.u
new q q': rec v.un!().v
new w r: T
p'*?b. { assume a(r,p) | w!(not b,r). q!() } |s
q'*?(). r?(b,x). assert a(x,p). printBoolean!b. p!b |
p!false | q!()
```

The type system of the SePi language is decidable. The algorithmic rules are those in [25], with minor adaptations in the rules for replicated input and **case** processes. Algorithmic typing systems crucially rely on the decidability of type equivalence. Type equivalence for the non-refined language is decidable [25]. Type equivalence for SePi is also decidable thanks to the extremely simple syntax of formulae. In essence, we keep separated a typing context and a multiset of predicates. An invariant of the type system states that context entries do not contain refinement types at the top level. The type equivalence procedure (basically, equality of regular infinite trees) may use (hence, remove) predicates from the multiset, if required.

---

[1] A type is contractive if it contains no sub-expression of the form **rec** a_1 ... **rec** $a_n.a_1$.

[2] To keep types manageable we did not expand polyadic message passing.

The rules for **assume** and **assert** in [1] are not algorithmic. Nevertheless, algorithmic rules are easy to obtain. Processes of the form **assume** A add A to the formulae multiset after breaking the tensors and eliminating occurrences of **unit**; processes of the form **assert** A try to remove the predicates in A from the multiset. Input processes of the form x?y.P eliminate the top-level refinements in the type for y; the resulting type is added to the typing environment, the predicates are added to the multiset. The remaining rules remain as in [25], except that they now work with the new procedure for type equivalence.

5   Conclusion and Future Work

We presented SePi, a concurrent programming language based on the monadic pi-calculus where communication between processes is governed by session types and where linearly refinement types may be used to specify properties about the values exchanged. In order to facilitate programming we added to SePi a few derived constructs, such as output and input of multiple values, mutually recursive process definitions and type declaration, session initiation, as well as the **dualof** type operator.

Our early experience with the language unveiled a few further constructs that may speed up code development, such as, a simple import clause allowing the inclusion of code in a different source file, thus providing for limited support for API development. In order to keep the language simple, the current version of SePi uses predicates over values only, thus preventing formulae containing expressions, such as p(x+1). We plan to add expressions to predicates, together with the appropriate theories (e.g., arithmetic), combining the current type checking algorithm with an SMT solver. Finally, we acknowledge that the current language of formulae is quite limited (essentially a multiset of uninterpreted formulae). We are working on a system that provides for the persistent availability of resources in a form of replicated (or exponential) resources. Polymorphism and subtyping may be incorporated in future versions of the language. We are also interested in extending the type system so that it may guarantee some form of progress for well typed processes.

Acknowledgements. This work was partially supported by project PTDC/EIA–CCO/1175 13/2010 and by LaSIGE (PEst-OE/EEI/UI0408/2011). We are grateful to Dimitris Mostrous, Hugo Vieira, and to anonymous referees for their feedback.

References

1. Baltazar, P., Mostrous, D., Vasconcelos, V.T.: Linearly refined session types. In: 2nd International Workshop on Linearity, vol. 101 of EPTCS, pp. 38–49 (2012)
2. Bhargavan, K., Corin, R., Deniélou, P.-M., Fournet, C., Leifer, J.J.: Cryptographic protocol synthesis and verification for multiparty sessions. In: Computer Security Foundations Symposium, pp. 124–140. IEEE (2009)

3. Boudol, G.: Asynchrony and the pi-calculus (note). Rapport de Recherche 1702, INRIA, Sophia-Antipolis (1992)
4. Caldeira, A., Vasconcelos, V.T.: Bica. http://gloss.di.fc.ul.pt/bica
5. Campos, J., Vasconcelos, V.T.: Channels as objects in concurrent object-oriented programming. In: 3rd International Workshop on Programming Language Approaches to Concurrency and Communication-cEntric Software, vol. 69 of EPTCS, pp. 12–28 (2011)
6. Fähndrich, M., Aiken, M., Hawblitzel, C., Hodson, O., Hunt, G., Larus, J.R., Levi, S.: Language support for fast and reliable message-based communication in singularity OS. Oper. Syst. Rev. **40**(4), 177–190 (2006)
7. Gay, S., Vasconcelos, V.T., Ravara, A., Gesbert, N., Caldeira, A.Z.: Modular session types for distributed object-oriented programming. In: Principles of Programming Languages, pp. 299–312. ACM (2010)
8. Gay, S.J., Hole, M.J.: Subtyping for session types in the pi calculus. Acta Inf. **42**(2/3), 191–225 (2005)
9. Girard, J.-Y.: Linear logic. Theor. Comput. Sci. **50**, 1–102 (1987)
10. Honda, K., Mukhamedov, A., Brown, G., Chen, T.-C., Yoshida, N.: Scribbling interactions with a formal foundation. In: Natarajan, R., Ojo, A. (eds.) ICDCIT 2011. LNCS, vol. 6536, pp. 55–75. Springer, Heidelberg (2011)
11. Honda, K., Tokoro, M.: An object calculus for asynchronous communication. In: America, P. (ed.) ECOOP 1991. LNCS, vol. 512, pp. 133–147. Springer, Heidelberg (1991)
12. Honda, K., Vasconcelos, V.T., Kubo, M.: Language primitives and type discipline for structured communication-based programming. In: Hankin, C. (ed.) ESOP 1998. LNCS, vol. 1381, pp. 122–138. Springer, Heidelberg (1998)
13. Honda, K., Yoshida, N., Carbone, M.: Multiparty asynchronous session types. In: Principles of Programming Languages, pp. 273–284. ACM (2008)
14. Hu, R., Yoshida, N., Honda, K.: Session-based distributed programming in Java. In: Vitek, J. (ed.) ECOOP 2008. LNCS, vol. 5142, pp. 516–541. Springer, Heidelberg (2008)
15. Milner, R.: Functions as processes. J. Math. Struct. Comput. Sci. **2**(2), 119–141 (1992)
16. Milner, R., Parrow, J., Walker, D.: A calculus of mobile processes, part I/II. Inf. Comput. **100**, 1–77 (1992)
17. Neubauer, M., Thiemann, P.: An implementation of session types. In: Jayaraman, B. (ed.) PADL 2004. LNCS, vol. 3057, pp. 56–70. Springer, Heidelberg (2004)
18. Ng, N., Yoshida, N., Honda, K.: Multiparty session C: safe parallel programming with message optimisation. In: Furia, C.A., Nanz, S. (eds.) TOOLS 2012. LNCS, vol. 7304, pp. 202–218. Springer, Heidelberg (2012)
19. Pierce, B.C., Turner, D.N.: Pict: a programming language based on the pi-calculus. In: Plotkin, G.D., Stirling, C.P., Tofte, M. (eds.) Proof, Language and Interaction: Essays in Honour of Robin Milner, pp. 455–494. MIT Press, Massachusetts (2000)
20. Sackman, M., Eisenbach, S.: Session types in Haskell: updating message passing for the 21st century. Technical report, Department of Computing, Imperial College (2008)(2008)
21. Turner, D.N.: The polymorphic Pi-calculus: theory and implementation. Ph.D. thesis, University of Edinburgh (1995)
22. Ng, N., Yoshida, N., Honda, K.: Multiparty session C: safe parallel programming with message optimisation. In: Pareschi, R. (ed.) ECOOP 1994. LNCS, vol. 821, pp. 202–218. Springer, Heidelberg (1994)

23. Vasconcelos, V.T.: TyCO gently. DI/FCUL TR 01–4, Faculty of Sciences, Department of Informatics, University of Lisbon (2001)
24. Vasconcelos, V.T.: Sessions, from types to programming languages. Bull. Eur. Assoc. Theor. Comput. Sci. **103**, 53–73 (2011)
25. Vasconcelos, V.T.: Fundamentals of session types. Inf. Comput. **217**, 52–70 (2012)

Behavioural Types Inspired
by Cellular Thresholds

Bogdan Aman and Gabriel Ciobanu[(✉)]

Romanian Academy, Institute of Computer Science,
Blvd. Carol I no.8, 700506 Iaşi, Romania
baman@iit.tuiasi.ro, gabriel@info.uaic.ro

Abstract. The sodium-potassium exchange pump is a transmembrane transport protein that establishes and maintains the appropriate internal concentrations of sodium and potassium ions in cells. This exchange is an important physiological process; it is critical in maintaining the osmotic balance of the cell. Inspired by the functioning of this pump, we introduce and study a threshold-based type system in a bio-inspired formalism. Such a system can avoid errors in the definition of the formal model used to model certain biologic processes. For this type system we prove a subject reduction theorem.

1 Introduction

Cell membranes are crucial to the life of the cell. Defining the boundary of the living cells, membranes have various functions, and participate in many essential cell activities including barrier functions, transmembrane signalling and intercellular recognition. The sodium-potassium exchange pump [12] is a transmembrane transport protein in the plasma membrane that establishes and maintains the appropriate internal ratio of sodium (Na^+) and potassium ions (K^+) in cells. By using energy from the hydrolysis of ATP molecules, the pump extrudes three Na^+ ions, in exchange for two K^+. This exchange is an important physiological process, critical in maintaining the osmotic balance of the cell, the resting membrane potential of most tissues and the excitability properties of muscle and nerve cells. Limitations on the values of the Na^+/K^+ ratio, together with their significance are described in [11]. If this ratio is unbalanced, it indicates physiological malfunctions within the cell: an unbalanced sodium-potassium ratio is associated with heart, kidney, liver, and immune deficiency diseases. The sodium-potassium ratio is also linked to adrenal gland function [8]. For example, the intracellular Na^+/K^+ ratios of the normal epithelial cells fall in a rather narrow range defined by certain thresholds [13].

The description of the sodium-potassium exchange pump given in Table 1 is known as the Albers-Post model of the pump. The two ions species, Na^+ and K^+, are transported sequentially. The Na-K pump essentially exists in two conformations, E_1 and E_2, which may be phosphorylated (E_1^P, E_2^P) or dephosphorylated (E_1, E_2). These conformations correspond to mutually exclusive

S. Counsell and M. Núñez (Eds.): SEFM 2013 Collocated Workshops, LNCS 8368, pp. 29–43, 2014.
DOI: 10.1007/978-3-319-05032-4_3, © Springer International Publishing Switzerland 2014

Table 1. Albers-Post model

$$E_1 + (Na_{in}^+)^3 \rightleftharpoons (Na^+)^3 \cdot E_1 \tag{1}$$
$$((Na^+)^3 \cdot E_1) + ATP \rightleftharpoons ((Na^+)^3 \cdot E_1^P) + ADP \tag{2}$$
$$(Na^+)^3 \cdot E_1^P \rightleftharpoons (Na^+)^3 \cdot E_2^P \tag{3}$$
$$(Na^+)^3 \cdot E_2^P \rightleftharpoons E_2^P + (Na_{out}^+)^3 \tag{4}$$
$$E_2^P + (K_{out}^+)^2 \rightleftharpoons (K^+)^2 \cdot E_2^P \tag{5}$$
$$(K^+)^2 \cdot E_2^P \rightleftharpoons ((K^+)^2 \cdot E_2) + P_i \tag{6}$$
$$(K^+)^2 \cdot E_2 \rightleftharpoons (K^+)^2 \cdot E_1 \tag{7}$$
$$(K^+)^2 \cdot E_1 \rightleftharpoons (K_{in}^+)^2 + E_1 \tag{8}$$

states in which the pump exposes ion binding sites alternatively on the intracellular (E_1) and extracellular (E_2) sides of the membrane. Transitions between these conformations mediate ion transport.

In Table 1 we use the following notations:

- $B + D$ means that B and D are present together and could react;
- $B \cdot D$ means that B and D are bound to each other non-covalently;
- E_2^P indicates that E_2 is covalently bound to the phosphoryl group P;
- P_i is the inorganic phosphate group;
- $(Na^+)^3$ indicates three Na^+ ions;
- since there is no explicit representation of the membrane containing the Na^+/K^+ pump, we use additional notations to represent ions:
  - Na^+ (K^+) indicates a Na^+ (K^+) ion placed inside the pump;
  - Na_{in}^+ (K_{in}^+) indicates a Na^+ (K^+) ion placed inside the cell;
  - Na_{out}^+ (K_{out}^+) indicates a Na^+ (K^+) ion placed outside the cell;
- $\rightleftharpoons$ indicates that the process can be reversible.

Figure 1 presents a graphical representation of the conformations and the functioning of the pump described in Table 1. Na^+ ions are pictured as small squares and K^+ ions as small circle; for simplicity, neither ATP and ADP molecules nor phospates are represented.

The traditional notion of types offers abstractions for data, objects and operations on them. The basic form of behavioural types articulates the ways in which interactions are performed. In this paper we introduce behavioural types inspired by cellular thresholds. We associate to each system a set of constraints that must be satisfied in order to assure that the application of the rules to a well-formed membrane system leads to a well-formed membrane system as well. We have a two-stage approach to the description of biological behaviours: the first describes reactions in an "untyped" setting, and the second rules out certain evolutions by imposing thresholds. This allows one to treat separately different aspects of modelling: which transitions are possible at all, and under which circumstances they can take place.

Membrane systems represent a formalism inspired by biological systems [14]. They are used to model the sodium-potassium pump [3]. The model uses compartments defined by membranes, floating objects, proteins associated with the

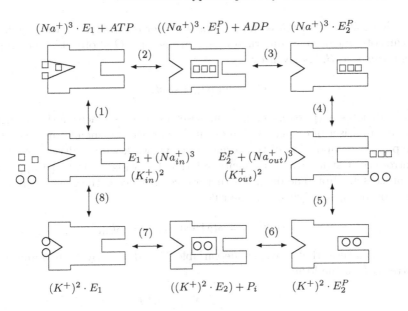

$(Na^+)^3 \cdot E_1 + ATP \qquad ((Na^+)^3 \cdot E_1^P) + ADP \qquad (Na^+)^3 \cdot E_2^P$

$(K^+)^2 \cdot E_1 \qquad ((K^+)^2 \cdot E_2) + P_i \qquad (K^+)^2 \cdot E_2^P$

Fig. 1. The sodium–potassium pump

internal and external surfaces of the membranes, and built-in proteins (the pump) that transport the chemical substances. Evolution rules represent the formal counterpart of chemical reactions, and are given in the form of rewriting rules that operate on the objects, as well as on the compartmentalised structure. A rule is applicable when all the objects appearing on its left hand side are available in the region where the rule is placed. In this paper we use a formalism inspired by such systems.

2   A Model of the Sodium-Potassium Pump

Given a finite set O of symbols, the set of all strings over O is denoted by O^*, and the set of all non-empty strings over O is denoted by $O^+ = O^*\backslash\lambda$, where λ is the empty string. A multiset over O [15] is a map $u : O \to \mathbb{N}$, where $u(a)$ denotes the multiplicity of the symbol $a \in O$ in the multiset u; $|u| = \sum_{a \in O} u(a)$ denotes the total number of objects appearing in a multiset u. A multiset u is included into a multiset v (denoted by $u \subseteq v$) if $u(a) \le v(a)$ for all $a \in O$. An object a is included into a multiset u (denoted by $a \in u$) if $u(a) > 0$. For $a \in O$, we write a instead of the multiset u if $u(a) = 1$ and $u(b) = 0$ for all $b \ne a$. The empty multiset is denoted by ϵ, and $\epsilon(a) = 0$ for all $a \in O$. For two multisets u and v, we define the sum uv by $(uv)(a) = u(a) + v(a)$ for all $a \in O$, and the difference $u - v$ by $(u - v)(a) = max\{0, u(a) - v(a)\}$ for all $a \in O$. More details and operations over multisets can be found in [15].

In what follows we work with terms ranged over by st, st_1, ..., that are built by means of a membrane constructor $[-]_-$, using a set O of objects. The syntax of the terms $st \in ST$ is given by

$$st ::= u \mid [st]_v \mid st\ st,$$

where u denotes a (possibly empty) multiset of objects placed inside a membrane, v a multiset of objects within or on the surface of a membrane, and $st\ st$ is the parallel composition of two terms. Since we work with multisets of terms, we introduce a structural congruence relation following a standard approach from process algebra. The defined structural congruence is the least congruence relation on terms satisfying also the rule:

$$\text{if } v_1 \equiv v_2 \text{ and } st_1 \equiv st_2 \text{ then } [st_1]_{v_1} \equiv [st_2]_{v_2}.$$

A pattern is a term that may include variables. We denote by $\mathcal{P}$ the infinite set of patterns P of the form:

$$P ::= st \mid [\,P\,X\,]_{v\ y} \mid P\,P.$$

We distinguish between "simple variables" (ranged over by x, y, z) that may occur only on the surface of membranes (i.e., they can be replaced only by multisets of objects) and "term variables" (ranged over by X, Y, Z) that may only occur inside regions (they can be replaced by arbitrary terms). Therefore, we assume two disjoint sets: V_{O^*} (set of simple variables) and V_{ST^*} (set of term variables). We denote by $V = V_{O^*} \cup V_{ST^*}$ the set of all variables, and with ρ any variable in V.

An instantiation is a partial function $\sigma : V \to ST^*$ that preserves the type of all variables: simple variables ($x \in V_{O^*}$) and term variables ($X \in V_{ST^*}$) are mapped into objects ($\sigma(x) \in O^*$) and terms ($\sigma(X) \in ST^*$), respectively. Given a pattern P, the term obtained by replacing all occurrences of each variable $\rho \in V$ with the term $\sigma(\rho)$ is denoted by $P\sigma$. The set of all possible instantiations is denoted by Σ, and the set of all variables appearing in P is denoted by $Var(P)$.

Formally, a rewriting rule r is a pair of patterns (P_1, P_2), denoted by $P_1 \to P_2$, where $P_1 \neq \epsilon$ (i.e., P_1 is a non-empty pattern) and $Var(P_2) \subseteq Var(P_1)$. A rewriting rule $P_1 \to P_2$ states that a term $P_1\sigma$ can be transformed into the term $P_2\sigma$, for some instantiation function σ.

Example 1. A description of the pump using membrane systems is presented in [3]. The authors model the sodium-potassium pump by using membrane systems with integral proteins. The inner and outer regions are characterised by multisets over the alphabet $O = \{Na, K, ATP, ADP, P, P_i, E_1, E_2, E_1^P, E_2^P\}$. The dephosphorylated conformations of the pump are denoted by the objects E_1 and E_2, while the phosphorylated conformations are denoted by the objects E_1^P and E_2^P. An important aspect of this system is given by the fact that an object P undergoes a structural modification by passing from being an object placed inside the membrane to being part of a membrane protein.

Let us consider a system $[Na^n K^m ATP^k]_{E_1} Na^r K^t$ given by the inner region consisting of n symbols Na of sodium, m symbols K of potassium, and k symbols ATP, together with the outer region consisting of r symbols Na and t symbols K. The membrane between the inner and outer regions is presented as a multiset containing initially only an object E_1. The description of the pump is given in Table 2, where the whole system is decomposed into a set of six rules. The smaller number of rules with respect to Table 1 is due to the fact that we combined the rules (3) with (4) and (6) with (7) of Table 1 into rules r_3 and r_5 of Table 2. The first rule (rule r_1) describes the conformation E_1 binding three Na^+ ions from the inner region of the cell to the pump which is in the membrane. This stimulates ATP hydrolysis and the release of ADP inside the cell, forming a phosphorylated enzyme intermediate E_1^P (rule r_2). Extrusion of the three Na^+ ions from the pump outside the cell is completed by a conformation change to E_2^P (rule r_3). In this conformation, the pump has a high affinity with K^+ ions: two K^+ ions outside the cell go to the pump in the membrane (rule r_4). The conformation is dephosphorylated and changes to E_1 (rule r_5). This is followed by the release of the two K^+ ions from the pump inside the cell (rule r_6). After this step, the pump is restored to its original configuration, and is capable to react again with Na^+ ions (rule r_1).

The notion of context is used to complete the definition of a rewriting semantics for our systems. This is done by enriching the syntax with a new object $\square$ representing a hole. By definition, a context is represented as a single hole $\square$. The infinite set $\mathcal{C}$ of contexts (ranged over by C) is given by:

$$C ::= \square \mid C\ st \mid [\,C\,]_v.$$

Given $C_1, C_2 \in \mathcal{C}$, $C_1[\,st\,]$ denotes the term obtained by replacing $\square$ with st in C_1, while $C_1[\,C_2\,]$ denotes the context obtained by replacing $\square$ with C_2 in C_1.

Given a set R of rewriting rules, a reduction semantics of the system is given by the least transition relation $\rightarrow$ closed with respect to $\equiv$ satisfying also the rule:

$$\frac{P_1 \rightarrow P_2 \in R \quad P_1\sigma \not\equiv \epsilon \quad \sigma \in \Sigma \quad C \in \mathcal{C}}{C[P_1\sigma] \rightarrow C[P_2\sigma]}.$$

$\rightarrow^*$ denotes the reflexive and transitive closure of $\rightarrow$.

Table 2. Rewriting rules for the Na-K pump

r_1	:	$[\,Na^3\,X\,]_{E_1}Y \rightarrow [\,X\,]_{E_1\,Na^3}Y$
r_2	:	$[\,ATP\,X\,]_{E_1\,Na^3} \rightarrow [ADP\,X\,]_{E_1^P\,Na^3}Y$
r_3	:	$[\,X\,]_{E_1^P\,Na^3}Y \rightarrow [\,X\,]_{E_2^P}Na^3\,Y$
r_4	:	$[\,X\,]_{E_2^P}K^2\,Y \rightarrow [\,X\,]_{E_2^P\,K^2}Y$
r_5	:	$[\,X\,]_{E_2^P\,K^2}Y \rightarrow [\,P_i\,X\,]_{E_1\,K^2}Y$
r_6	:	$[\,X\,]_{E_1\,K^2}Y \rightarrow [\,K^2\,X\,]_{E_1}Y$

Example 2 (cont.). Starting from the term

$$[\, Na^8 \; K^2 \; ATP^3 \,]_{E_1} \; Na^3 \; K^5$$

the system evolves by using twice all the rules of Table 2. In what follows we illustrate how the rules are applied; after each configuration we add on the same row which rule has been applied and the proper instantiations. When a set of rules is applied, then we ignore the instantiations.

$$
\begin{aligned}
& [Na^8 \; K^2 \; ATP^3]_{E_1} \; Na^3 K^5 \\
\rightarrow \; & [Na^5 K^2 ATP^3]_{E_1 Na^3} \; Na^3 K^5 && [r_1, \; X = Na^5 K^2 ATP^3, \; Y = Na^3 K^5] \\
\rightarrow \; & [Na^5 K^2 ATP^2 ADP]_{E_1^P Na^3} Na^3 K^5 && [r_2, \; X = Na^5 K^2 ATP^2, \; Y = Na^3 K^5] \\
\rightarrow \; & [Na^5 K^2 ATP^2 ADP]_{E_2^P} Na^6 K^5 && [r_3, \; X = Na^5 K^2 ATP^2 ADP, \; Y = Na^3 K^5] \\
\rightarrow \; & [Na^5 K^2 ATP^2 ADP]_{E_2^P K^2} Na^6 K^3 && [r_4, \; X = Na^5 K^2 ATP^2 ADP, \; Y = Na^3 K^2] \\
\rightarrow \; & [P_i Na^5 K^2 ATP^2 ADP]_{E_1 K^2} Na^6 K^3 && [r_5, \; X = Na^5 K^2 ATP^2 ADP, \; Y = Na^3 K^2] \\
\rightarrow \; & [P_i Na^5 K^4 ATP^2 ADP]_{E_1} Na^6 K^3 && [r_6, \; X = Na^5 K^2 ATP^2 ADP, \; Y = Na^3 K^2] \\
\rightarrow^* \; & [P_i^2 Na^2 K^6 ATP \; ADP^2]_{E_1} Na^9 K && [r_1, r_2, r_3, r_4, r_5, r_6]
\end{aligned}
$$

Unfortunately, some constraints over certain ratios (e.g., Na^+/K^+, ATP/ADP) described in [11] cannot be modelled using the above class of membrane systems. From a physiological point of view, these ratios are important, as well as the lower and upper bounds for the objects involved in the ion channel transport. For this reason we introduce a type system (for the above defined formalism) that is able to impose constraints on the pump evolution taking into consideration the ratios between objects, and also certain thresholds.

3   Threshold-Based Type System Over Multisets

An important idea of type theory is to provide the possibility of distinguishing between different classes of objects. Types are fundamental both in logic and computer science, and have many applications. Recently it has been used in biological formalisms in order to transfer the complexity of biological properties from evolution rules to types. The syntax of types is simple, easy to understand and use, and these aspects make types ideal for expressing general constraints. The type system could be also used to decrease the number of rules in some models by defining a limited number of generic rules as in [1].

The behaviour of typed terms can be controlled by a type system in order to avoid unwanted evolutions. According to [11], the evolution of a healthy cell ensures that the ratio between objects (e.g., Na^+/K^+) of a cell is kept between certain values. We investigate how to extend a type system such that to describe the change of evolution depending on the ratio between objects, and also specific thresholds.

Let T be a finite set of basic types ranged over by t. We classify each object in O with a unique element of T; we use Γ to denote this classification. In general, different objects a and b can have the same basic type t. When there is no ambiguity, we denote the type associated with an object a by t_a. For each ordered pair of basic types (t_1, t_2), we assume the existence of two functions, $min : T \times T \to (0, \infty) \cup \{\diamond\}$ and $max : T \times T \to (0, \infty) \cup \{\diamond\}$. These functions indicate the minimum and maximum ratio between the number of objects of basic types t_1 and t_2 that can be present inside a membrane.

For example, by taking the constraints $min(t_a, t_b) = 3$ and $max(t_a, t_b) = 5$, the number of objects of basic type t_a is larger than the number of objects of basic type t_b with a coefficient between three and five. $min(t_1, t_2) = \diamond$ and $max(t_1, t_2) = \diamond$ mean that these functions are undefined for the pair of types (t_1, t_2). Biologically speaking, the ratio between the types t_1 and t_2 is either unknown, or can be ignored.

We consider only local properties: the objects influence each other only if

- they are present inside the same membrane;
- they are integral on sibling membranes;
- one is present inside and the other is integral to the membrane;
- one is present outside and the other is integral to the membrane.

Definition 1 (Consistent Basic Types). *A system using a set of basic types T and the functions min and max is consistent if:*

1. *$\forall t_1, t_2 \in T$, $min(t_1, t_2) \neq \diamond$ iff $max(t_1, t_2) \neq \diamond$;*
2. *$\forall t_1, t_2 \in T$, $min(t_1, t_2) \neq \diamond$ iff $min(t_2, t_1) \neq \diamond$;*
3. *$\forall t_1, t_2 \in T$ if $min(t_1, t_2) \neq \diamond$, then $min(t_1, t_2) \leq max(t_1, t_2)$;*
4. *$\forall t_1, t_2 \in T$ if $min(t_1, t_2) \neq \diamond$ and $max(t_2, t_1) \neq \diamond$,*
   then $min(t_1, t_2) \cdot max(t_2, t_1) = 1$.

The meaning of these constraints is explained below:

1. the minimum ratio between the number of objects of basic types t_1 and t_2 is defined iff the corresponding maximum ratio is defined;
2. the minimum ratio between the number of objects of basic types t_1 and t_2 is defined iff the minimum ratio between the number of objects of basic types t_2 and t_1 is defined;
3. the minimum ratio between the number of objects of basic types t_1 and t_2 must be lower than the maximum ratio between the number of objects of basic types t_1 and t_2;
4. the maximum ratio between the number of objects of basic types t_2 and t_1 must be equal to the inverse of the minimum ratio between the number of objects of types t_1 and t_2.

Example 3. The system using the following set of basic types

$$T = \{t_a, t_b, t_c\}$$

and min, max defined by

$$
\begin{array}{cc}
min(t_1, t_2) & max(t_1, t_2) \\
\begin{array}{c|ccc}
t_1\backslash t_2 & t_a & t_b & t_c \\
\hline
t_a & \diamond & 0.4 & \diamond \\
t_b & 0.2 & \diamond & \diamond \\
t_c & \diamond & 3 & \diamond
\end{array}
&
\begin{array}{c|ccc}
t_1\backslash t_2 & t_a & t_b & t_c \\
\hline
t_a & \diamond & 5 & \diamond \\
t_b & 2.5 & \diamond & \diamond \\
t_c & \diamond & 6 & \diamond
\end{array}
\end{array}
$$

is consistent because each pair of basic types respects the previous definition.

Definition 2 Quantitative types *are triples* (L, Pr, U) *over the set* T *of basic types, where:*

- L *(lower) is the set of minimum ratios between basic types;*
- Pr *(present) is the multiset of basic types of present objects (the objects present at the top level of a pattern, i.e. in the outermost membrane);*
- U *(upper) is the set of maximum ratios between basic types.*

The number of objects of type t appearing in a multiset Pr is denoted by $Pr(t)$. In order to define well-formed types, given a multiset M of types, the sets RP_M (ratios of present types in M), L_M (lower bounds of present types in M) and U_M (upper bounds of present types in M) are required:

- $RP_M = \begin{cases} \emptyset & \text{if} |M| \leq 1 \\ \bigcup_{t,t' \in M} \left\{ t/t' : \dfrac{Pr(t)}{Pr(t')} \mid t \neq t', Pr(t') \neq 0 \right\} & \text{otherwise} \end{cases}$

- $L_M = \begin{cases} \emptyset & \text{if} |M| \leq 1 \\ \bigcup_{t,t' \in M} \{ t/t' : min(t, t') \mid t \neq t', min(t, t') \neq \diamond \} & \text{otherwise} \end{cases}$

- $U_M = \begin{cases} \emptyset & \text{if} |M| \leq 1 \\ \bigcup_{t,t' \in M} \{ t/t' : max(t, t') \mid t \neq t', max(t, t') \neq \diamond \} & \text{otherwise} \end{cases}$

These sets contain labelled values in order to be able to refer to them when needed: e.g., $t/t' : \dfrac{Pr(t)}{Pr(t')}$ denotes the fact that the ratio between the objects of types t and t' that are present in Pr has the label t/t', and the value is $\dfrac{Pr(t)}{Pr(t')}$.

Definition 3 (Well-Formed Types). *A type* (L, Pr, U) *is well-formed if*

$$L = L_{Pr}, U = U_{Pr} \text{ and } L \leq RP_{Pr} \leq U.$$

The constraints of this definition can be read as follows:

- $L = L_{Pr}$ contains the minimum ratio constraints for the present objects;
- $U = U_{Pr}$ contains the maximum ratio constraints for the present objects;

- $L \leq RP_{Pr}$ means that the ratio between present objects respects the minimum ratio from L: if for all $(t/t' : min(t,t')) \in L$ and $(t/t' : \frac{Pr(t)}{Pr(t')}) \in RP_{Pr}$, then

$$min(t,t') \leq \frac{Pr(t)}{Pr(t')};$$

- $RP_{Pr} \leq U$ means that the ratio between present objects respects the maximum ratio from U: if for all $(t/t' : \frac{Pr(t)}{Pr(t')}) \in RP_{Pr}$ and $(t/t' : max(t,t')) \in U$, then

$$\frac{Pr(t)}{Pr(t')} \leq max(t,t').$$

Remark 1. If the set T contains a large number of basic types, defining a type to be well-formed only if $L = L_{Pr}$ and $U = U_{Pr}$ reduces the amount of information encapsulated by a type. E.g., for $|T| = 100$, the number of entries in the *min* table is equal to 10000.

Example 4 (cont.). Let us assume a set of basic types $T = \{t_{Na}, t_K\}$, a classification $\Gamma = \{Na : t_{Na}, K : t_K\}$ and the functions *min*, *max* defined as:

$min(t_1,t_2)$			$max(t_1,t_2)$		
$t_1 \backslash t_2$	t_{Na}	t_K	$t_1 \backslash t_2$	t_{Na}	t_K
t_{Na}	$\diamond$	0.6	t_{Na}	$\diamond$	4
t_K	0.25	$\diamond$	t_K	$5/3$	$\diamond$

The term $Na^5 K^2$ is well-formed, while the term $Na^9 K$ is not, because the ratio between t_{Na} and t_K equals 9, and so it exceeds the maximum 4 indicated in *max* table.

From now on we work only with well-formed types. For instance, the two well-formed types (L, Pr, U) and (L', Pr', U') of the following two definitions are constructed by using specific ratio tables for *min* and *max*.

Definition 4 (Type Compatibility). *Two well-formed types (L_{Pr}, Pr, U_{Pr}) and $(L_{Pr'}, Pr', U_{Pr'})$ are compatible, written $(L, Pr, U) \bowtie (L_{Pr'}, Pr', U_{Pr'})$, if*

$$L_{Pr+Pr'} \leq RP_{Pr+Pr'} \leq U_{Pr+Pr'}$$

A **basis** Δ assigning types to simple and term variables is defined by

$$\Delta ::= \emptyset \mid \Delta, x : (L_t, t, U_t) \mid \Delta, X : (L, Pr, U).$$

A basis is well-formed if all types in the basis are well-formed.

A **classification** Γ maps each object in O to a unique element of the set T of basic types. The judgements are of the form $\Delta \vdash P : (L, Pr, U)$ indicating that a pattern P is well-typed having the type (L, Pr, U) relative to a typing environment Δ.

Table 3. Typing rules

$$\Delta \vdash \epsilon : (\emptyset, \emptyset, \emptyset) \quad (TEps) \qquad \frac{a : t \in \Delta}{\Delta \vdash a : (L_t, t, U_t)} \quad (TObj)$$

$$\Delta, \rho : (L, Pr, U) \vdash \rho : (L, Pr, U) \qquad (TVar)$$

$$\frac{\Delta \vdash v : (L, Pr, U) \quad \Delta \vdash P' : (L', Pr', U') \quad (L, Pr, U) \bowtie (L', Pr', U')}{\Delta \vdash [P']_v : (L, Pr, U)} \quad (TMem)$$

$$\frac{\begin{array}{c} \Delta \vdash P : (L_{Pr}, Pr, U_{Pr}) \quad \Delta \vdash P' : (L_{Pr'}, Pr', U_{Pr'}) \\ (L_{Pr}, Pr, U_{Pr}) \bowtie (L_{Pr'}, Pr', U_{Pr'}) \end{array}}{\Delta \vdash P \; P' : (L_{Pr+Pr'}, Pr + Pr', U_{Pr+Pr'})} \quad (TPar)$$

Types are assigned to patterns and terms according to the typing rules of Table 3. It is not difficult to verify that a derivation starting from well-formed bases produces only well-formed bases and well-formed types.

The rules are rather trivial, except for the rules $(TPar)$ and $(TMem)$. The type of a parallel composition given by the $(TPar)$ rule is derived from the types of the two sub-patterns; if two patterns P and P' are compatible, then the type of the obtained pattern $P \; P'$ is derived from the types (L_{Pr}, Pr, U_{Pr}) and $(L_{Pr'}, Pr', U_{Pr'})$ of the connected patterns where $Pr + Pr'$ is the multiset sum of the present types pr and Pr'. The type of rule $(TMem)$ is the type of the multiset of integral proteins v (because a membrane makes the objects inside it invisible to the outside). Since the objects on the membrane are influenced by the ones inside it, the type of the multiset placed on the membrane and the type of the pattern placed inside the membrane must be compatible in order to obtain the overall type of the membrane.

We define a typed semantics, since we are interested in applying reduction rules only to correct terms having well-formed types, and whose requirements are satisfied. More formally, a term st is correct if $\emptyset \vdash st : (L, Pr, U)$ for some well-formed type (L, Pr, U). An instantiation σ agrees with a basis Δ (denoted by $\sigma \in \Sigma_\Delta$) if $\rho : (L, Pr, U) \in \Delta$ implies $\emptyset \vdash \sigma(\rho) : (L, Pr, U)$.

In order to apply the rules in a safe way, we introduce a restriction on rules based on the context of application rather than on the type of patterns involved in the rule. In this direction, we characterise contexts by the types of terms that can fill their hole, and the rules by the types of terms produced by their application.

Definition 5 (Typed Holes). *Given a context C and a type (L, Pr, U) that is well-formed, the type (L, Pr, U) fits the context C if for some well-formed type (L', Pr', U') it can be shown that $X : (L, Pr, U) \vdash C[X] : (L', Pr', U')$.*

The above notion guarantees that we obtain a correct term filling a context with a term whose type fits the context: note that there may be more than one type (L, Pr, U) such that (L, Pr, U) fits the context C.

We can classify reduction rules according to the types that can be derived for the right hand sides of the rules, since they influence the type of the obtained term.

Definition 6 (Δ-(L, Pr, U) safe rules). *A rewriting rule $P_1 \rightarrow P_2$ is Δ safe if for some well-formed type (L, Pr, U) it can be shown that $\Delta \vdash P_2 : (L, Pr, U)$.*

To ensure correctness, each application of a rewriting rule must verify that the type of the right hand side of the rule fits the context. Using Definitions 5 and 6, if it is applied a rule whose right hand side has type (L, Pr, U) and this type fits the context, then a correct term is obtained.

Typed Semantics. Given a finite set R of rewriting rules (e.g., the one presented in Table 2), the typed semantics of a system is given by the least relation $\Rightarrow$ closed with respect to $\equiv$ and satisfying the following rule:

$$\frac{\sigma \in \Sigma_\Delta \quad C \in \mathcal{C} \quad \begin{array}{c} P_1 \rightarrow P_2 \in R \text{ is a } \Delta\text{-}(L, Pr, U) \text{ safe rule}, \quad P_1\sigma \not\equiv \epsilon \\ \text{and} \quad (L, Pr, U) \text{ fits } C \end{array}}{C[P_1\sigma] \Rightarrow C[P_2\sigma]} \quad (TSem)$$

4   Subject Reduction and Other Results

The type system presented in Table 3 satisfies weakening and other properties.

Proposition 1 (Weakening).

> *If $\Delta \vdash P : (L, Pr, U)$ and $\Delta \subseteq \Delta'$, then $\Delta' \vdash P : (L, Pr, U)$.*

Proposition 2. *If $\Delta \vdash C[P] : (L, Pr, U)$, then*

1. *$\Delta \vdash P : (L', Pr', U')$ for some (L', Pr', U');*
2. *$\Delta, X : (L', Pr', U') \vdash C[X] : (L, Pr, U)$;*
3. *if P' is such that $\Delta \vdash P' : (L', Pr', U')$ (i.e., P' has the same type as P), then $\Delta \vdash C[P'] : (L, Pr, U)$.*

The link between substitutions and well-formed bases guarantees type preservation, as expressed in the following result.

Proposition 3. *For all $\sigma \in \Sigma_\Delta$, $\emptyset \vdash P\sigma : (L, Pr, U)$ iff $\Delta \vdash P : (L, Pr, U)$.*

Proof ($\Leftarrow$): By induction on the depth of derivation $\Delta \vdash P : (L, Pr, U)$, considering the last applied rule.

- If the rule is $(TEps)$, it implies that $\emptyset \vdash \epsilon : (\emptyset, \emptyset, \emptyset)$ holds since the empty multiset is typable from the empty environment. Since ϵ is a term, yields that $\epsilon\sigma = \epsilon$, namely $\emptyset \vdash \epsilon\sigma : (\emptyset, \emptyset, \emptyset)$.
- If the rule is $(TObj)$, it implies that $\emptyset \vdash a : (L_t, t, U_t)$ holds since any element of Γ is typable from the empty environment. Since a is a term, yields that $a\sigma = a$, namely $\emptyset \vdash a\sigma : (L_t, t, U_t)$.

- If the rule is $(TVar)$, it implies that $\rho : (L, Pr, U) \in \Delta$ and $\Delta \vdash \rho : (L, Pr, U)$. Since $\sigma \in \Sigma_\Delta$, yields that $\emptyset \vdash \sigma(\rho) : (L, Pr, U)$.
- If the rule is $(TPar)$, it implies that $P = P'\ P''$ with $(L, Pr, U) = (L_{Pr'+Pr''}, Pr' + Pr'', U_{Pr'+Pr''})$, $\Delta \vdash P' : (L_{Pr'}, Pr', U_{Pr'})$, $\Delta \vdash P'' : (L_{Pr''}, Pr'', U_{Pr''})$ and $(L_{Pr'}, Pr', U_{Pr'}) \bowtie (L_{Pr''}, Pr'', U_{Pr''})$. By inductive hypothesis, it holds that $\emptyset \vdash P'\sigma : (L_{Pr'}, Pr', U_{Pr'})$ and $\emptyset \vdash P''\sigma : (L_{Pr''}, Pr'', U_{Pr''})$. Since $P'\sigma\ P''\sigma = (P'\ P'')\sigma$, by applying $(TPar)$, yields $\emptyset \vdash (P'\ P'')\sigma : (L, Pr, U)$.
- If the rule is $(TMem)$, it implies that $P = [P']_v$ with $\Delta \vdash v : (L, Pr, U)$, $\Delta \vdash P' : (L', Pr', U')$ and $(L, Pr, U) \bowtie (L', Pr', U')$. By inductive hypothesis, it holds that $\emptyset \vdash v\sigma : (L, Pr, U)$ and $\vdash P'\sigma : (L', Pr', U')$. Since $[P'\sigma]_{v\sigma} = ([P']_v)\sigma$, by applying $(TMem)$, we get $\emptyset \vdash ([P']_v)\sigma : (L, Pr, U)$.

$(\Rightarrow)$: By induction on the structure of P.

- If $P = \epsilon$ it means that $\emptyset \vdash \epsilon\sigma : (\emptyset, \emptyset, \emptyset)$, and since $\emptyset \subseteq \Delta$ and $\epsilon\sigma = \epsilon$, it implies (by weakening) that $\Delta \vdash \epsilon : (\emptyset, \emptyset, \emptyset)$.
- If $P = a$ it means that $\emptyset \vdash a\sigma : (L_t, t, U_t)$, and since $\emptyset \subseteq \Delta$ and $a\sigma = a$, it implies (by weakening) that $\Delta \vdash a : (L_t, t, U_t)$.
- If $P = \rho$ it means that $\emptyset \vdash \sigma(\rho) : (L, Pr, U)$, and from the fact that $\sigma \in \Sigma_\Delta$ it follows that $\rho : (L, Pr, U) \in \Delta$; by applying the rule $(TVar)$, it implies that $\Delta \vdash \rho : (L, Pr, U)$.
- For $P = P'\ P''$, we have that $(P'\ P'')\sigma = P'\sigma\ P''\sigma$ and $\emptyset \vdash (P'\ P'')\sigma : (L, Pr, U)$ implies that the last applied rule must be $(TPar)$. Then the following relations hold: $(L, Pr, U) = (L_{Pr'+Pr''}, Pr' + Pr'', U_{Pr'+Pr''})$, $(L_{Pr'}, Pr', U_{Pr'}) \bowtie (L_{Pr''}, Pr'', U_{Pr''})$, $\emptyset \vdash P'\sigma : (L_{Pr'}, Pr', U_{Pr'})$ and $\emptyset \vdash P''\sigma : (L_{Pr''}, Pr'', U_{Pr''})$. By inductive hypothesis on P and P', it holds that $\Delta \vdash P' : (L_{Pr'}, Pr', U_{Pr'})$ and $\Delta \vdash P'' : (L_{Pr''}, Pr'', U_{Pr''})$. By applying $(TPar)$, it follows that $\Delta \vdash P'\ P'' : (L, Pr, U)$.
- For $P = [P']_v$, from $([P']_v)\sigma = [P'\sigma]_{v\sigma}$ and $\emptyset \vdash ([P']_v)\sigma : (L, Pr, U)$ results that the last applied rule must be $(TMem)$. Then, the following relations hold: $(L, Pr, U) \bowtie (L', Pr', U')$, $\emptyset \vdash v\sigma : (L, Pr, U)$ and $\emptyset \vdash P'\sigma : (L', Pr', U')$. By inductive hypothesis on P' (and v), it holds that $\Delta \vdash v : (L, Pr, U)$ and $\Delta \vdash P' : (L', Pr', U')$. By applying $(TMem)$, it follows that $\Delta \vdash ([P']_v) : (L, Pr, U)$.

Starting from a correct term, all the terms obtained via Δ-(L, Pr, U) safe rules are correct, and thus we can avoid conditions over P_1 because they do not influence the type of the obtained term. As expected, typed reduction preserves correctness. The main result of the paper is given by the following subject reduction theorem.

Theorem 1 (Subject Reduction). *If $\emptyset \vdash st : (L, Pr, U)$ and $st \Rightarrow st'$, then $\emptyset \vdash st' : (L', Pr', U')$ for a well-formed type (L', Pr', U').*

Proof. The given typed semantics implies $st = C[P_1\sigma]$ and $st' = C[P_2\sigma]$, while Definition 6 implies $\Delta \vdash P_2 : (L, Pr, U)$. From Proposition 3 and $\sigma \in \Sigma_\Delta$ it follows that $\emptyset \vdash P_2\sigma : (L, Pr, U)$. Since (L, Pr, U) fits C (according to the given typed semantics), it means that $X : (L, Pr, U) \vdash C[X] : (L', Pr', U')$ for some well-formed type (L', Pr', U'). According to Proposition 3, it follows that $\emptyset \vdash C[P_2\sigma] : (L', Pr', U')$ for some well-formed type (L', Pr', U').

The next example illustrates the notions of context, instantiation, Δ-(L, Pr, U) safe rules, (L, Pr, U) fits a context C and application of $(TSem)$ rules.

Example 5. Let us assume the consistent system formed from a set of basic types $T = \{t_{Na}, t_K, t_{ATP}, t_{ADP}, t_P, t_E\}$, a classification $\Gamma = \{Na : t_{Na}; \ K : t_K; \ ATP : t_{ATP}; \ ADP : t_{ADP}; \ P, P_i : t_P; \ E_1, E_2, E_1^P, E_2^P : t_E\}$, and the functions min and max given by

$$min(t_1, t_2) = \begin{cases} 0.6 & \text{if } t_1 = t_{Na} \text{ and } t_2 = t_K \\ 0.25 & \text{if } t_1 = t_K \text{ and } t_2 = t_{Na} \\ \diamond & \text{otherwise} \end{cases}$$

$$max(t_1, t_2) = \begin{cases} 4 & \text{if } t_1 = t_{Na} \text{ and } t_2 = t_K \\ 5/3 & \text{if } t_1 = t_K \text{ and } t_2 = t_{Na}. \\ \diamond & \text{otherwise} \end{cases}$$

Using all of the rules of Table 2, the well-formed term

$$[ATP^3 \ Na^8 \ K^2]_{E_1} Na^9 \ K^5$$

is rewritten in several steps, by using $(TSem)$, in another well-formed term:

$$[ATP^3 \ Na^8 \ K^2]_{E_1} Na^9 \ K^5 \Rightarrow^* [ATP^2 \ ADP \ P_i \ Na^5 \ K^4]_{E_1} Na^{12} \ K^3.$$

It is worth to note that for this term there is no rule in Table 2 that can be selected in order to apply the $(TSem)$ rule. For instance, consider the rule $r_1 : [\ Na^3 \ X \ ]_{E_1} Y \ \rightarrow \ [\ X \ ]_{E_1} Na^3 Y$, the context $C = \square \ Na^{12} \ K^3$ and the instantiations $\sigma(X) = ATP^2 \ ADP \ P_i \ Na^2 \ K^4$, $\sigma(Y) = \epsilon$. Verifying the hypotheses of the $(TSem)$ rule, we have

- rule r_1 is a Δ-(L, Pr, U) safe rule, where $(L, Pr, U) = (L_{t_{Na}^3 t_{E_1}}, t_{Na}^3 t_{E_1}, U_{t_{Na}^3 t_{E_1}})$ is the type of $[\ X \ ]_{E_1} Na^3 Y = [ATP \ ADP^2 \ P_i \ Na^2 \ K^4]_{E^1} Na^3$;
- $[ATP^2 \ ADP \ P_i \ Na^5 \ K^4]_{E_1} \neq \epsilon$,
- but the type $(L_{t_{Na}^3 t_{E_1}}, t_{Na}^3 t_{E_1}, U_{t_{Na}^3 t_{E_1}})$ of $[ATP \ ADP^2 \ P_i \ Na^2 \ K^4]_{E^1} Na^3$ does **not** fit the context $C = \square \ Na^{12} \ K^3$; this happens since the term $C[[ATPADP^2 \ P_i \ Na^2 \ K^4]_{E^1} Na^3] = [ATPADP^2 \ P_i \ Na^2 \ K^4]_{E^1} Na^3 Na^{12} \ K^3$ has the type $(L_{t_{Na}^{15} t_{E_1} t_K^3}, t_{Na}^{15} t_{E_1} t_K^3, U_{t_{Na}^{15} t_{E_1} t_K^3})$ that is **not** well-formed (the ratio between t_{Na} and t_K is $(12 + 3)/3 = 5$ which is greater than 4).

Similar reasonings hold for all the rules from Table 2, thus the evolution stops.

5   Conclusion

Recent years have seen an increase in research on behavioural types, driven partly by the need to formalise and codify communication structures. Behavioural type systems go beyond data type systems in order to specify, characterise and reason about certain dynamic aspects of execution. Behavioural types encompass session types [9], multiparty session types [10] and other functional types for communications in distributed systems. Here we present a related view inspired by cellular biology, and introduce quantitative types based on ratio thresholds able to control the behaviour of some systems. The inspiration comes from sodium-potassium pump, which extrudes sodium ions in exchange for potassium ions. Such an exchange takes place only if the ratios of the elements are between certain thresholds (lower and upper bounds). To properly cope with such constraints, we introduce a threshold-based type system. We associate to each system a set of constraints, and relate them to the ratios between elements. If the constraints are satisfied, we prove that if a system is well-typed and an evolution rule is applied, then the obtained system is also well-typed.

The proposed typed semantics completely excludes the fact that sometimes biological constraints can be broken leading to a disease or even to the death of the biological system. However, the typed semantics can be modified in order to allow transitions that lead to terms that are not typable. In this case the type system should signal that some undesired event has been reached. In this way, it can be checked if a term breaks some biological property, or if the system has some unwanted behaviour.

We previously modelled the sodium-potassium pump using untyped membrane systems [3] and typed symport/antiport membrane systems [1]. The novelty of [1] is that it introduces types for the symport/antiport membrane systems, defining typing rules which control the passage of objects through the membranes. The sodium-potassium pump was also described by using the π-calculus [7]. The exchange pump was described step by step, and then software verification tools were applied [6]. This means that it would be possible to verify automatically some properties of the described systems, and so to use the verification software tools as a substitute for expensive lab experiments. A similar development for systems described by using membrane systems would be a useful achievement.

A formalism that is somewhat related to the systems considered in this paper is the calculus of looping sequences (CLS), a formalism based on term rewriting. An essential difference is that our formalism uses multisets to describe objects within or on membranes, while CLS terms use (looping) sequences. There are various type systems for CLS [2,4,5]. Our work is related to [4], where a type systems defined for the calculus of looping sequences is based on the number of elements (and not on the ratios between elements). The quantitative type system for CLS preserves some biological properties depending on the minimum and the maximum number of elements of some type; the author uses the number of elements in a system, a fact that is not so relevant in biology, where concentration and ratios are typical.

Acknowledgements. Many thanks to the reviewers for their useful comments. The work was supported by a grant of the Romanian National Authority for Scientific Research, project number PN-II-ID-PCE-2011-3-0919.

References

1. Aman, B., Ciobanu, G.: Typed membrane systems. In: Păun, G., Pérez-Jiménez, M.J., Riscos-Núñez, A., Rozenberg, G., Salomaa, A. (eds.) WMC 2009. LNCS, vol. 5957, pp. 169–181. Springer, Heidelberg (2010)
2. Aman, B., Dezani-Ciancaglini, M., Troina, A.: Type disciplines for analysing biologically relevant properties. Electron. Notes Theor. Comput. Sci. **227**, 97–111 (2009)
3. Besozzi, D., Ciobanu, G.: A P system description of the sodium-potassium pump. In: Mauri, G., Păun, G., Jesús Pérez-Jímenez, M., Rozenberg, G., Salomaa, A. (eds.) WMC 2004. LNCS, vol. 3365, pp. 210–223. Springer, Heidelberg (2005)
4. Bioglio, L.: Enumerated type semantics for the calculus of looping sequences. RAIRO - Theor. Inform. Appl. **45**, 35–58 (2011)
5. Bioglio, L., Dezani-Ciancaglini, M., Giannini, P., Troina, A.: Typed stochastic semantics for the calculus of looping sequences. Theoret. Comput. Sci. **431**, 165–180 (2012)
6. Ciobanu, G.: Software verification of the biomolecular systems. In: Modelling in Molecular Biology, Natural Computing Series, pp. 40–59. Springer, Heidelberg (2004)
7. Ciobanu, G., Ciubotariu, V., Tanasă, B.: A Pi-Calculus model of the Na/K pump. Genome Inf. **13**, 469–472 (2002). Universal Academy Press
8. Guyton, A., Hall, J.: Textbook of Medical Physiology, 12th edn. Elsevier (2010)
9. Honda, K., Vasconcelos, V.T., Kubo, M.: Language primitives and type discipline for structured communication-based programming. In: Hankin, C. (ed.) ESOP 1998. LNCS, vol. 1381, pp. 122–138. Springer, Heidelberg (1998)
10. Honda, K., Yoshida, N., Carbone, M.: Multiparty asynchronous session types, In: Proceedings POPL, pp. 273–284. ACM Press, New York (2008)
11. Kennedy, B.G., Lunn, G., Hoffman, J.F.: Effects of altering the ATP/ADP ratio on pump-mediated Na/K and Na/Na exchanges in resealed human red blood cell ghosts. J. Gen. Physiol. **87**, 47–72 (1986)
12. Lingrel, J.B., Kuntzweiler, T.: Na$^+$, K$^+$-ATPase. J. Biol. Chem. **269**, 19659–19662 (1994)
13. Zs.-Nagy, I., Lustyik, G., Zs.-Nagy, V., Zarandi, B., Bertoni-Freddari, C.: Intracellular N+/K+ ratios in human cancer cells as revealed by energy dispersive X-ray microanalysis. J. Cell Biol. **90**, 769–777 (1981)
14. Păun, G., Rozenberg, G., Salomaa, G. (eds.): Handbook of Membrane Computing. Oxford University Press, Oxford (2010)
15. Salomaa, A.: Formal Languages. Academic Press, Edinburgh (1973)

Ensuring Faultless Communication Behaviour in A Commercial Cloud

Ross Horne[1,2](✉) and Timur Umarov[2]

[1] Romanian Academy, Institute of Computer Science,
Blvd. Carol I, No. 8, 700505 Iaşi, Romania
[2] Faculty of Information Technology, Kazakh-British Technical University,
Tole Bi 59, Almaty, Kazakhstan
ross.horne@gmail.com, t.umarov@kbtu.kz

Abstract. For many Cloud providers, the backbone of their system is a Cloud coordinator that exposes a portfolio of services to users. The goal of this work is to ensure that a Cloud coordinator interacts correctly with services and users according to a specification of their communication behaviour. To accomplish this goal, we employ session types to analyse the global and local communication patterns. A session type provides an appropriate level of abstraction for specifying message exchange patterns between participants. This work confirms the feasibility of applying session types to protocols used by a commercial Cloud provider. The protocols are developed in SessionJ, an extension of Java implementing session-based programming. We also highlight that the same techniques can be applied when Java is not the development environment by type checking runtime monitors, as in Scribble. Finally, we suggest how our methodology can be used to ensure the correctness of protocols for Cloud brokers, that integrate services exposed by multiple Cloud coordinators, each of whom must correctly cooperate with the Cloud broker.

Keywords: Session types · Runtime monitors · Cloud · Intercloud

1 Introduction

Cloud providers typically offer a portfolio of services, where access and billing for all services are integrated in a single distributed system. The integration of services is done by a Cloud coordinator or controller [1–3] that exposes services to users. Services are made available on demand to anyone with a credit card, eliminating the up front commitment of users [4]. Furthermore, there is a drive for services to be integrated, not only within a Cloud, but also between multiple Cloud providers.

For a Cloud coordinator that integrates heterogeneous services with a single point of access and billing strategy, protocols can become complex. Thus we require an appropriate level of abstraction to specify and implement such protocols. Further to the complexity, the protocols are a critical component of the business strategy of a Cloud provider. Failure of the protocols could result in

S. Counsell and M. Núñez (Eds.): SEFM 2013 Collocated Workshops, LNCS 8368, pp. 44–55, 2014.
DOI: 10.1007/978-3-319-05032-4_4, © Springer International Publishing Switzerland 2014

divergent behaviour that jeopardises services, potentially leading to loss of customers and legal disputes. These risks can be limited by using techniques that statically prove that protocols are correct and dynamically check that protocols are not violated at runtime.

It is challenging to manage service interactions that go beyond simple sequences of requests and responses and involve large numbers of participants. One technique for managing protocols between multiple services is to specify the protocol using a choreography. A choreography specifies a global view of the interactions between participating services. However, by itself, a choreography does not determine how the global view can be executed.

The challenge of controlling interactions of participants motivated The WS-CDL working group to identify critical issues [5]. One issue is the need for tools to validate conformance of participants to a choreography specification, to ensure that participants cooperate according to the choreography. Another issue is the static design time verification of choreographies to analyse safety properties such as the absence of deadlock or livelock in a system.

The aforementioned challenges can be tackled by adopting a solid foundational model, such as session types [6,7]. Successful approaches related to session types include: SessionJ [8,9], Session C [10] and Scribble [11] due to the team lead by Honda and Yoshida; Sing# [12] that extends Spec# with choreographies; and UBF(B) [13] for Erlang.

In this paper, we present a case study where the interaction of process that integrate services in a commercial Cloud provider[1] are controlled using session types. Session types ensure communication safety by verifying that session implementations of each participant (the customers, services and Cloud coordinator), conform to the specified protocols. In our case study, we use SessionJ, an extension of Java supporting sessions, to specify protocols used by the Cloud coordinator that involve branching, iterative behaviour and higher order communication.

In Sect. 2 we describe a methodology for designing protocols in SessionJ. In Sect. 3, we introduce and refine a protocol used by a Cloud coordinator which is implemented using SessionJ. Finally, in Sect. 4, we suggest that session types can be used in the design of reliable Intercloud protocols, following the techniques employed in this work.

2   Methodology for Verifying Protocols in SessionJ

We chose SessionJ for the core of our application, since Java was already used for several services. SessionJ has a concise syntax that tightly extends Java socket programming. Furthermore, the overhead of runtime monitoring in SessionJ is low [8,9].

We briefly outline a methodology for using SessionJ to correctly implement protocols. Firstly, the global protocol is specified using a global calculus similar to sequence diagrams. Secondly, the global calculus is projected to sessions

---

[1] V3na Cloud Platform. AlmaCloud Ltd., Kazakhstan. http://v3na.com

types, which specify the protocol for each participant. Thirdly, the session is implemented using operations on session sockets. The correctness of the global protocol can be verified by proving that the implementation of each session conforms to the corresponding session type.

Protocol Specification. The body of a protocol is defined as a *session type*, according to the grammar in Fig. 1. The session type specifies the actions that the participant in a session should perform. The constructs in Fig. 1 can describe a diverse range of complex interactions, including message passing, branching and iteration. Each session type construct has its dual construct, because a typical requirement is that two parties implement compatible protocols such that the specification of one party is dual to another party.

Higher Order Communication. SessionJ allows message types to themselves be session types. This is called higher-order communication and is supported by using subtyping [14]. Consider the dual constructs $!\langle ?(\text{int})\rangle$ and $?(?(\text{int}))$. These types specify sessions that expect to respectively send and receive a session of type $?(\text{int})$. Higher order communication is often referred to as session delegation. Figure 2 shows a basic delegation scenario.

In Fig. 2, the left diagram represents the session configuration before the delegation is performed: the user is engaged in a session s of type $!\langle\text{int}\rangle$ with the Cloud, while the Cloud is also involved in a session s' with a service of type $!\langle ?(\text{int})\rangle$. So, instead of accepting the integer from the user, the Cloud delegates its role in session s to the service. The diagram on the right of Fig. 2

	$T ::= T \cdot T$	sequencing
L_1, L_2 label	| begin	session initiation
	| $!\langle M\rangle$	message send
p protocol name	| $?(M)$	message receive
	| $!\{L_1 : T_1, \ldots, L_n : T_n\}$	branching send
$M ::= Datatype \mid T$ message	| $?\{L_1 : T_1, \ldots, L_n : T_n\}$	branching receive
	| $![T]*$	iterative send
$S ::= p\{T\}$ protocol	| $?[T]*$	iterative receive
	| $@p$	protocol reference

Fig. 1. SessionJ protocol specification using session types (T).

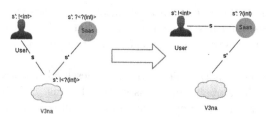

Fig. 2. Session delegation.

represents the session configuration after the delegation has been performed: the user now directly interacts with the service for the session s. The delegation action corresponds to a higher-order send type for the session s' between the Cloud and the service.

Protocol Implementation and Runtime Monitors. Session sockets represent the participants of a session. Each socket implements the session code according to the specified session type, using a vocabulary of session operations. The session is implemented within a session-try scope, which allows the implementation to respond to exceptions thrown by a runtime monitor.

The runtime monitor dynamically checks the types of messages received, since in a distributed system it is difficult to guarantee that other participants always send a message of the type specified. The runtime also detects the failure of any participant to enact its role in the session. Upon failure, a meaningful exception is raised that can be used to elegantly recover or close a failed session. At the scales which Cloud providers operate, unavoidable node failures are expected to frequently occur. For example, during a MapReduce job over a cluster of 130 nodes, it is expected that one node will fail [15]. Thus runtime monitors that raise meaningful exceptions when protocols diverge from the behaviour specified by the session type can help improve fault tolerance.

We argue that, for Cloud providers, the performance overhead due to runtime monitors is low compared to the potential cost of problems avoided. In Cloud computing, it is perfectly acceptable to slow down transactions to guarantee correctness. For example, in Google Spanner [16,17] transactions observe a commit wait that deliberately slows down transactions by a few milliseconds to guarantee globally meaningful commit timestamps.

3 Case Study: Protocols for a Cloud Coordinator

Our case study is a commercial Cloud provider, V3na, that provides integrated Software as a Service solutions for businesses. V3na provides a central access point to a portfolio of services, including document storage, document flow, and customer relations management. For comparison, market leading Cloud providers, such as Amazon or Rackspace, offer a portfolio of compute, storage and networking services that are exposed to users on demand. The central component in V3na is a Cloud coordinator that is responsible for exposing and integrating services that a user subscribes to, while managing user accounts and billing.

A typical scenario is when a user requires the document storage service. The user will first subscribe for the service either by registering to be billed or by entering a trial period. When the user has been successfully authenticated by the Cloud coordinator, requests to the API of the document store are delegated, by the Cloud coordinator, to the relevant document server for a renewable lease period. After delegation, the user interacts directly with the API of the document store until the session ends.

A major challenge was to automate the process of service integration as a reliable service. In particular, V3na implements protocols that address the following problems that can be addressed using sessions types:

- A customer can connect to a service for a trial period;
- A customer can connect to all services subscribed to through a single entry point;
- A subscription may be extended or frozen;
- Invoices and payment for use of services can be managed.

In this section we illustrate a naive first implementation and a more scalable refinement of a protocol that implements the first scenario above.

3.1 First Attempt: Forwarding and Branching

We specify a first attempt of a simple protocol for connecting to a service. The protocol is informally specified as follows:

1. The user begins a session with Cloud coordinator and sends the request "connect to service" as a JSON message.
2. The Cloud coordinator selects either:
   (a) FAIL, if the user has no active session (not signed in).
   (b) OK, if the user has logged in and the request is validated.
3. If OK is selected, then, instead of responding immediately to the user, the Cloud initiates a new session with the relevant service. In the new session, the Cloud forwards the JSON message from the user to the service and receives a response from the service. The session between the Cloud and the service closes successfully.
4. Finally, the original session resumes and the Cloud forwards the response from the service to the user. From the perspective of the user it appears that the Cloud coordinator responded directly.

Protocol 1.1: User

```
protocol p_uv {
  begin.
  !<JSONMsg>.
  ?{
    OK: ?(JSONMsg),
    FAIL:
  }
}
```

Protocol 1.2: Cloud

```
protocol p_vu {
  begin.?(JSONMsg).!{
    OK: !<JSONMsg>,
    FAIL:
  }
}

protocol p_vs {
  begin.!<JSONMsg>.
    ?(JSONMsg)
}
```

Protocol 1.3: Service

```
protocol p_sv {
  begin.
  ?(JSONMsg).!<JSONMsg>
}
```

Fig. 3. Protocol specifications for forwarding protocol.

In Fig. 3, we provide the protocol specifications for each participant — the user, Cloud coordinator and service. The protocols between the user and the Cloud and between the Cloud and the service are dual, i.e. the specification of interaction from one perspective is opposite to the other perspective. SessionJ employs `outbranch` and `inbranch` operations to implement the branching behaviour. The `outbranch` operation is an internal choice, since the sender has control over the message sent. The `inbranch` operation is an external choice, since the receiver does not have control of the message received.

There is a fatal problem with the above protocol, from the perspective of a Cloud provider. The Cloud coordinator is involved in servicing all requests to services. As the number of services and users increases, the load on the Cloud coordinator will increase. Soon, the Cloud coordinator will be unable to serve requests. The most basic economic advantage of Cloud computing, called elasticity [4], is that services can scale up and down to fulfil the demands of users. The above protocol cannot deliver elasticity.

3.2 Refined Protocol: Session Delegation and Iteration

We present a refined protocol that demonstrates iteration and session delegation. To avoid the Cloud coordinator becoming a bottleneck, the Cloud coordinator should delegate sessions to a service as soon as the user is authenticated for the service.

Figure 4 depicts two related sessions s and s'. Session s begins with interactions between the user and the Cloud coordinator. However, after authentication, s' delegates the rest of session s from the Cloud coordinator to the service. Session s is completed by exchanging messages between the user and the service directly. We informally describe the global protocol in more detail:

1. The user begins a request session (session s in Fig. 4) with the Cloud coordinator.
2. The user logs in by providing the Cloud with a user name and password.

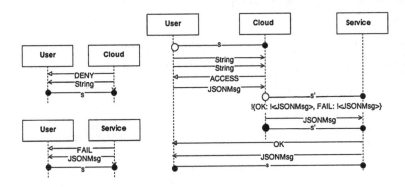

Fig. 4. Sequence diagram of interactions for delegationprotocol.

3. The Cloud coordinator receives the user credentials and verifies them. If the user is not authenticated and still has tries go back to step 2, otherwise continue.

4. If the user is not allowed to access the Cloud, the DENY branch is chosen and the session terminates. Otherwise, the ACCESS-branch is chosen and the session continues.

5. On the ACCESS branch, the user sends the connection request in a JSON message to the Cloud coordinator. The Cloud creates a new session with the service (session s' in Fig. 4). The new session delegates the remaining session with the user to the service, and also forwards relevant user request details to the service. Session s' is then terminated.

6. The service continues session s, but now interactions are between the user and the service. The service either responds to the user with OK or FAIL. In either case, the user receives the response directly from the service in a JSON message. Finally, session s is terminated.

In Fig. 5, the user appears to interact with the Cloud coordinator. The iterative login, and first connection message is a direct interaction between the user and the Cloud coordinator. However, instead of the Cloud coordinator responding to the connection request, the session in Fig. 6 is triggered.

The session in Fig. 6 delegates the part of the session where the response OK or FAIL is selected by the service. This delegation is enabled by a higher order session type, where a socket of session type $!\{\texttt{OK}: !\langle JSONMessage\rangle, \texttt{FAIL}: !\langle JSONMessage\rangle\}$ is sent from the Cloud coordinator in protocol p_vs and received by the service in protocol p_sv. Following the delegation, a JSON message is sent from the Cloud coordinator to the service, which forwards on the relevant details of the user request.

Once the delegation has taken place, the service is able to complete the session that was begun by the Cloud coordinator. The service can negotiate directly with the user and either choose the OK branch or the FAIL branch, followed by sending the appropriate JSON message. For more complex scenarios, this simple choice between an OK and a FAIL message could be replaced by a more complex session between the user and the service.

Protocol 2.1: User

```
protocol p_uv {
  begin.?[!<String>.!<String> ]*.
  ?{
   ACCESS: !<JSONMsg>.
      ?{
        OK: ?(JSONMsg),
        FAIL: ?(JSONMsg)
      },
   DENY: ?(String)
  }
}
```

Protocol 2.2: Cloud

```
protocol p_vu {
  begin.
    ![ ?(String).?(String) ]*. // login
    !{
     ACCESS: ?(JSONMsg).
       !{
         OK: !<JSONMsg>,
         FAIL: !<JSONMsg>
       },
     DENY: !<String>
    }
}
```

Fig. 5. User-Cloud interaction protocol specifications for delegation protocol.

Protocol 2.3: Cloud

```
protocol p_vs {
  begin.
  !<!{
    OK: !<JSONMsg>,
    FAIL: !<JSONMsg>
  }>.
  !<JSONMsg>
}
```

Protocol 2.4: Service

```
protocol p_sv {
  begin.
  ?(!{
    OK: !<JSONMsg>,
    FAIL: !<JSONMsg>
  }).
  ?(JSONMsg)
}
```

Fig. 6. Cloud-Service interaction protocol specifications for delegation protocol.

The protocol presented in this section is scalable. The Cloud coordinator is only involved in authenticating users for access to services. The amount of data exchanged during authentication is tiny compared to the amount of data exchanged by a service such as a document store.

3.3   Delegation Elsewhere: Payment for Services

Delegation is powerful elsewhere in the Cloud provider. At the end of each month, a user pays for the services used. The user may have multiple payment options. The two session types in Fig. 7 represent two different payment protocols. In the first protocol, the user pays with a credit card. In the second protocol, the user pays using a wallet, which is automatically recharged.

The user enters a session with the Cloud coordinator where, after authenticating, the payment option is selected then the payment is made. The session provided by the Cloud coordinator is presented on the left in Fig. 8.

However, the Cloud coordinator does not service either payment. One of the two delegation protocols on the right of Fig. 8 is invoked. The handling of the payment is delegated to either a bank or the wallet service within the Cloud provider. As in the previous example, delegation is performed by passing a higher order session type.

```
protocol p_payment {
  !<Goods>.?{
    VISA_MASTER: ?(CardDetails),
    TRANSFER: ?(TransferDetails)
  }.!{
    PAID: !<String>,
    DECLINED: !<String>,
    FAILED: !<String>
  }
}
```

```
protocol p_wallet {
  !<String>.?(Integer).?(Integer).!{
    PAYMENT_INACTIVE: !<OSMPMessage>,
    USER_NOT_FOUND: !<OSMPMessage>,
    OK: !<OSMPMessage>
  }
}
```

Fig. 7. Server side protocols for processing payments.

```
protocol p_vu {                    protocol p_vp {
  begin.![                           begin.!<String>.!<@p_payment>
    ?(String).?(String)            }
  ]*.!{
    ACCESS: ?{                     protocol p_vw {
      PAYMENT: @p_payment,           begin.!<String>.!<@p_wallet>
      WALLET: @p_wallet            }
    },
    DENY: !<String>
  }
}
```

Fig. 8. Delegating to chosen payment service.

4   Future Work: Runtime Monitors and Intercloud Protocols

4.1   Language Independent Runtime Monitors

A limitation with the work presented is that services in a Cloud provider are not implemented exclusively in Java, or any other single language. The initial design of V3na was conducted using session types in SessionJ according to the methodology presented. However, as the start up company scales up to take on more clients, the development team is diversifying. The team now operates mainly in the Python based Django framework.

Session types can still be used by Python developers. Scribble [11] offers an alternative to SessionJ, where language independent runtime monitors [18] are statically checked according to session types. The runtime monitors dynamically check that low level communication patterns are within the space of behaviours specified by a session type. Scribble has already been used to monitor Python code in related work [19,20]. We argue that the approach offered by Scribble has a more promising future than SessionJ, since distributed systems are typically heterogeneous.

4.2   Session Types for Intercloud Protocols

For Cloud users, there are considerable benefits when applications can be hosted on more than one Cloud provider [4,21,22]. Users can build applications based on services provided by multiple Cloud providers. Furthermore, if data is replicated across multiple Cloud providers, customers can avoid becoming locked in to one provider. Thus customers are less exposed to risks such as fluctuations in prices and quality of service at a single provider. If a Cloud provider goes out of business, then customers entirely dependent on that Cloud provider also risk going out of business.

Several visions have been proposed for Intercloud protocols [1,23,24]. The main components debated for an Intercloud architecture are a *Cloud coordinator*, for exposing services, and a *Cloud broker* for mediating between Cloud coordinators. In this work, we have touched on some aspects of Cloud coordinators. The Cloud broker is a mediator that sits between the user and the Cloud coordinators for several Cloud providers. Another component debated is a *Cloud exchange*, which acts as a market place for services exposed by Cloud providers.

Based on our experience in this work, we suggest that session types are appropriate for specifying and correctly implementing protocols between Cloud coordinators and Cloud brokers. Like the delegation protocols between the Cloud coordinator and services, a Cloud broker will delegate communications to the Cloud coordinator as early as possible in the session. The protocols between Cloud brokers and Cloud coordinators are a critical component of the business model of a Cloud broker; hence, we argue that the overhead of deploying type checked runtime monitors is small compared to the potential risk posed by faults in protocols.

5 Conclusion

This case study addresses the question of whether session types have a role in Cloud computing. Competitive Cloud providers are looking for ways to better manage risks on behalf of their customers. We argue that session types are one contribution that can help manage the risk posed by divergent critical components. In particular, we demonstrate that session types can be used to design, implement and verify protocols behind a Cloud coordinator that exposes services on demand to users.

Session type implementations such as SessionJ, as used in the work, and Scribble, as proposed for future work, involve some runtime monitoring. The runtime monitoring ensures that protocols stay within the space of behaviours permitted by a session type. We argue that the performance cost of dynamic runtime monitoring is small compared the risk managed. Divergent protocols can corrupt systems, while node failures are unavoidable at scale. Monitors can avoid divergence and help respond to node failures.

We found that session types provide an appropriate level of abstraction for quickly designing critical protocols. Session type implementations are accessible to programmers without background in formal semantics, including our industrial partners AlmaCloud Ltd. The level of abstraction provided by the SessionJ language, enabled effortless translation of business scenarios into verified implementations of protocols. We were able to refine our protocol from a simple forwarding protocol (Sect. 3.1) to a scalable delegation protocol (Sect. 3.2), due to support for higher-order message passing. The benefits of delegation are further highlighted by payment and wallet recharging transactions (Sect. 3.3).

We suggest that the methodology presented can be applied to emerging Intercloud protocols. In particular, protocols between Cloud brokers and Cloud coordinators delegate sessions similarly to protocols between Cloud coordinators and services. Furthermore, it is in the interest of Cloud brokers to minimise their exposure to risk due to divergent protocols or node failures. One approach to managing this risk is by using session types.

Acknowledgements. We thank the anonymous reviewers for their clear and constructive comments. We are particularly grateful to Ramesh Kini for his support for this project.

References

1. Buyya, R., Ranjan, R., Calheiros, R.N.: InterCloud: utility-oriented federation of cloud computing environments for scaling of application services. In: Hsu, C.-H., Yang, L.T., Park, J.H., Yeo, S.-S. (eds.) ICA3PP 2010, Part I. LNCS, vol. 6081, pp. 13–31. Springer, Heidelberg (2010)
2. Nurmi, D., Wolski, R., Grzegorczyk, C., Obertelli, G., Soman, S., Youseff, L., Zagorodnov, D.: The Eucalyptus open-source Cloud-Computing system. In: Cappello, F., Wang, C.L., Buyya, R. (eds.) CCGRID, pp. 124–131. IEEE Computer Society (2009)
3. Sotomayor, B., Montero, R.S., Llorente, I.M., Foster, I.T.: Virtual infrastructure management in private and hybrid clouds. IEEE Internet Comput. **13**(5), 14–22 (2009)
4. Armbrust, M., Fox, A., Griffith, R., Joseph, A.D., Katz, R., Konwinski, A., Lee, G., Patterson, D., Rabkin, A., Stoica, I., et al.: A view of cloud computing. Commun. ACM **53**(4), 50–58 (2010)
5. Barros, A., Dumas, M., Oaks, P.: A critical overview of the Web services choreography description language. BPTrends Newslett. **3**, 1–24 (2005)
6. Carbone, M., Honda, K., Yoshida, N., Milner, R., Brown, G., Ross-Talbot, S.: A theoretical basis of communication-centred concurrent programming. In: WS-CDL working report, W3C (2006)
7. Carbone, M., Honda, K., Yoshida, N.: Structured communication-centered programming for web services. ACM Trans. Program. Lang. Syst. **34**(2), 8 (2012)
8. Hu, R., Yoshida, N., Honda, K.: Session-Based distributed programming in java. In: Vitek, J. (ed.) ECOOP 2008. LNCS, vol. 5142, pp. 516–541. Springer, Heidelberg (2008)
9. Hu, R., Kouzapas, D., Pernet, O., Yoshida, N., Honda, K.: Type-safe eventful sessions in Java. In: D'Hondt, T. (ed.) ECOOP 2010. LNCS, vol. 6183, pp. 329–353. Springer, Heidelberg (2010)
10. Ng, N., Yoshida, N., Honda, K.: Multiparty session C: safe parallel programming with message optimisation. In: Furia, C.A., Nanz, S. (eds.) TOOLS 2012. LNCS, vol. 7304, pp. 202–218. Springer, Heidelberg (2012)
11. Honda, K., Mukhamedov, A., Brown, G., Chen, T.-C., Yoshida, N.: Scribbling interactions with a formal foundation. In: Natarajan, R., Ojo, A. (eds.) ICDCIT 2011. LNCS, vol. 6536, pp. 55–75. Springer, Heidelberg (2011)
12. Basu, S., Bultan, T., Ouederni, M.: Deciding choreography realizability. ACM SIGPLAN Notices **47**(1), 191–202 (2012)
13. Armstrong, J.: Getting Erlang to talk to the outside world. In: Proceedings of the 2002 ACM SIGPLAN Workshop on Erlang, pp. 64–72. ACM (2002)
14. Simon Gay, M.H.: Subtyping for session types in the pi calculus. J. Acta Inf. **42**(2–3), 191–225 (2005)
15. Dean, J., Ghemawat, S.: MapReduce: simplified data processing on large clusters. Commun. ACM **51**(1), 107–113 (2008)

16. Corbett, J.C., Dean, J., Epstein, M., Fikes, A., Frost, C., Furman, J., Ghemawat, S., Gubarev, A., Heiser, C., Hochschild, P., et al.: Spanner: Google's globally-distributed database. In: Proceedings of the 10th USENIX Conference on Operating Systems Design and Implementation, pp. 251–264. USENIX Association (2012)
17. Ciobanu, G., Horne, R.: Non-interleaving operational semantics for geographically replicated databases. In: 15th International Symposium on Symbolic and Numeric Algorithms for Scientific Computing. IEEE (2013, in press)
18. Bocchi, L., Chen, T.-C., Demangeon, R., Honda, K., Yoshida, N.: Monitoring networks through multiparty session types. In: Beyer, D., Boreale, M. (eds.) FORTE 2013 and FMOODS 2013. LNCS, vol. 7892, pp. 50–65. Springer, Heidelberg (2013)
19. Neykova, R.: Session types go dynamic or how to verify your Python conversations. In: PLACES'13, Rome, Italy, 23 March, pp. 34–39 (2013)
20. Hu, R., Neykova, R., Yoshida, N., Demangeon, R., Honda, K.: Practical interruptible conversations. In: Legay, A., Bensalem, S. (eds.) RV 2013. LNCS, vol. 8174, pp. 130–148. Springer, Heidelberg (2013)
21. Buyya, R., Yeo, C.S., Venugopal, S., Broberg, J., Brandic, I.: Cloud computing and emerging it platforms: vision, hype, and reality for delivering computing as the 5th utility. Future Gener. Comput. Syst. 25(6), 599–616 (2009)
22. Bernstein, D., Ludvigson, E., Sankar, K., Diamond, S., Morrow, M.: Blueprint for the Intercloud - protocols and formats for cloud computing interoperability. In: Perry, M., Sasaki, H., Ehmann, M., Bellot, G.O., Dini, O. (eds.) ICIW, pp. 328–336. IEEE Computer Society (2009)
23. Cavalcante, E., Lopes, F., Batista, T.V., Cacho, N., Delicato, F.C., Pires, P.F.: Cloud integrator: building value-added services on the cloud. In: NCCA, pp. 135–142 (2011)
24. Pawluk, P., Simmons, B., Smit, M., Litoiu, M., Mankovski, S.: Introducing STRATOS: a cloud broker service. In: Chang, R. (ed.) IEEE CLOUD, pp. 891–898. IEEE (2012)

A Typing System for Privacy

Dimitrios Kouzapas[1] (✉) and Anna Philippou[2]

[1] Department of Computing, Imperial College London, London, UK
dk208@doc.ic.ac.uk
[2] Department of Computer Science, University of Cyprus, Nicosia, Cyprus
annap@cs.ucy.ac.cy

Abstract. In this paper we report on work-in-progress towards defining a formal framework for studying privacy. Our framework is based on the π-calculus with groups [1] accompanied by a type system for capturing privacy-related notions. The typing system we propose combines a number of concepts from the literature: it includes the use of *groups* to enable reasoning about information collection, it builds on *read/write capabilities* to control information processing, and it employs *type linearity* to restrict information dissemination. We illustrate the use of our typing system via simple examples.

1   Introduction

The notion of privacy does not have a single solid definition. It is generally viewed as a collection of related rights as opposed to a single concept and attempts towards its formalization have been intertwined with philosophy, legal systems, and society in general. The ongoing advances of network and information technology introduce new concerns on the matter of privacy. The formation of large databases that aggregate sensitive information of citizens, the exchange of information through e-commerce as well as the rise of social networks, impose new challenges for protecting individuals from violation of their right to privacy as well as for providing solid foundations for understanding privacy a term.

A study of the diverse types of privacy, their interplay with technology, and the need for formal methodologies for understanding and protecting privacy is discussed in [7], where the authors base their arguments on the taxonomy of privacy rights by Solove [6]. According to [6], the possible privacy violations within a system can be categorized into four groups: *invasions, information collection, information processing,* and *information dissemination*. These violations are typically expressed within a model consisting of three entities: the *data subject* about whom a *data holder* has information and the *environment*, the data holder being responsible to protect the information of the data subject against unauthorized adversaries in the environment.

The motivation for this work stems from the need to provide a formal framework (or a set of different formal frameworks) for reasoning about privacy-related concepts, as discussed above. Such a framework would provide solid foundations

S. Counsell and M. Núñez (Eds.): SEFM 2013 Collocated Workshops, LNCS 8368, pp. 56–68, 2014.
DOI: 10.1007/978-3-319-05032-4_5, © Springer International Publishing Switzerland 2014

for understanding the notion privacy and it would allow to rigorously model and study privacy-related situations. Our interest for formal privacy is primarily focused on the processes of *information collection, information processing*, and *information dissemination* and how these can be controlled in order to guarantee the preservation of privacy within a system.

1.1 Privacy and the π-Calculus

The approach we follow in this paper attempts to give a correspondence between the requirements of the last paragraph and the theory and meta-theory of the π-calculus [4]. The π-calculus is a formal model of concurrent computation that uses message-passing communication as the primitive computational function. A rich theory of operational, behavioural and type system semantics of the π-calculus is used as a tool for the specification and the study of concurrent systems. Our aim is to use the π-calculus machinery to describe notions of privacy. Specifically, we are interested in the development of a meta-theory, via a typing system, for the π-calculus that can enforce properties of privacy, as discussed above.

The semantics for the $G\pi$-calculus, a π-calculus that disallows the leakage of information (secrets) is presented in [1]. That work proposes the *group type* along with a simple typing system that is used to restrict the scope of a name's existence, i.e., a name cannot exist outside its group scope. We find the semantics of the $G\pi$-calculus convenient to achieve the privacy properties regarding the *information collection* category. A data holder can use the group type to disallow unauthorized adversaries from collecting information about a data subject.

Consider for example the processes:

$$\mathsf{DBadmin} = \overline{a}\langle c\rangle.\mathbf{0}$$
$$\mathsf{Nurse} = a(x).\overline{b}\langle x\rangle.\mathbf{0}$$
$$\mathsf{Doctor} = b(x).x(y).\overline{x}\langle\mathsf{data}\rangle.\mathbf{0}$$

The database administrator process DBadmin sends a reference c to a patient's data to a doctor process Doctor using a nurse process Nurse as a delegate. Channel c is sent to the nurse via channel a and is then forwarded to the doctor via channel b by the nurse. The doctor then uses c to read and write data on the patient's records. The composition of the above processes under the fresh hospital group Hosp, and an appropriate typing of c, enforces that no external adversary will be able to collect the information exchanged in the above scenario, namely c: name c, belonging to group Hosp, is not possible to be leaked outside the defined context because (1) groups are not values and cannot be communicated and (2) the group Hosp is only known by the three processes (see [1] for the details).

$$(\nu\ \mathsf{Hosp})(((\nu c : \mathsf{Hosp}[])\mathsf{DBadmin})\mid \mathsf{Nurse}\mid \mathsf{Doctor})$$

Let us now move on to the concept of *information processing* and re-consider the example above with the additional requirement that the nurse should not be able to read or write on the patient's record in contrast to the doctor who is allowed both of these capabilities. To address this issue we turn to the input/output typing system for the π-calculus of Pierce and Sangiorgi, [5]. Therein, the input/output subtyping is used to control the input and output capabilities on names and it is a prime candidate for achieving privacy with respect to the requirement in question: A type system that controls read and write capabilities[1] can be used by a data holder to control how the information about a data subject can be processed. Thus, in the case of our example, the requirements may be fulfilled by extending the specification with a read/write typing system as follows:

$$T_{\text{data}} = \text{Hosp}[\text{MedicalData}]^{-}$$
$$T_c = \text{Hosp}[T_{\text{data}}]^{\text{rw}}$$
$$T_a = \text{Hosp}[\text{Hosp}[T_{\text{data}}]^{-}]^{\text{rw}}$$
$$T_b = \text{Hosp}[\text{Hosp}[T_{\text{data}}]^{\text{rw}}]^{\text{rw}}$$

where names a, b and c are of types T_a, T_b and T_c, respectively. The medical data are a basic type with no capability of read and write. Channel c can be used for reading and writing medical data. Channel a is used to pass information to the nurse without giving permission to the nurse to process the received information, while channel b provides read and write capabilities to the doctor. Nonetheless, the above system suffers from the following problem. Although the nurse acquires restricted capabilities for channel c via channel a, it is still possible for a nurse process to exercise its read capability on b and, thus, acquire read and write capability on the c channel. To avoid this problem, the system may be redefined as follows:

$$\text{DBadmin} = (\nu b : T_b) \, \overline{tonurse}\langle b \rangle.\overline{todoc}\langle b \rangle.\overline{a}\langle c \rangle.\mathbf{0}$$
$$\text{Nurse} = tonurse(z).a(x).\overline{z}\langle x \rangle.\mathbf{0}$$
$$\text{Doctor} = todoc(z).z(x).x(y).\overline{x}\langle\text{data}\rangle.\mathbf{0}$$

where channel $todoc$ has type $\text{Hosp}[T_b]^{\text{rw}}$ but channel $tonurse$ has type $\text{Hosp}[T_b']^{\text{rw}}$, where $T_b' = \text{Hosp}[\text{Hosp}[T_{\text{data}}]^{\text{rw}}]^{\text{w}}$. In other words, the nurse is not assigned read capabilities on channel b.

Note that the above typing is not completely sound: for instance the nurse process is expected to pass on to the doctor process more capabilities than those it acquires via channel a. Nevertheless in our theory we use a more complex type structure able to solve this problem.

Regarding the *information dissemination* category of privacy violations, we propose to handle information as a *linear resource*. Linear resources are resources that can be used for some specific number of times. A typing system for linearity was originally proposed in [3]. A linear typing system can be used by the data holder to control the number of times an information can be disseminated. In our

---

[1] The terminology for read and write capabilities is equivalent with input and output terminology.

example, we require from the nurse the capability of sending the reference of the patient only once, while we require from the doctor not to share the information with anyone else:

$$T_{\mathsf{data}} = \mathsf{Hosp}[\mathsf{MedicalData}]^{-*}$$
$$T_c = \mathsf{Hosp}[T_{\mathsf{data}}]^{\mathrm{rw}*}$$
$$T_a = \mathsf{Hosp}[\mathsf{Hosp}[T_{\mathsf{data}}]^{-1}]^{\mathrm{rw0}}$$
$$T_b = \mathsf{Hosp}[\mathsf{Hosp}[T_{\mathsf{data}}]^{\mathrm{rw0}}]^{\mathrm{rw0}}$$
$$T_b' = \mathsf{Hosp}[\mathsf{Hosp}[T_{\mathsf{data}}]^{\mathrm{rw0}}]^{\mathrm{w0}}$$

The $*$ annotation on the types above defines a shared (or unlimited) resource. Such resources are the patient's data and the reference to the patient's data. Channels a and b communicate values that can be disseminated one and zero times respectively. (Again there is a soundness problem solved by a more complex typing structure.) Furthermore channels a and b cannot be sent to other entities.

A central aspect of our theory is the distinction between the basic entities. The operational semantics of the π-calculus focuses on the communication between processes that are composed in parallel. Although a process can be thought of as a computational entity, it is difficult to distinguish at the operational level which processes constitute a logical entity. In our approach, we do not require any operational distinction between entities, since this would compromise the above basic intuition for the π-calculus, but we do require the logical distinction between the different entities that compose a system.

Finally, we note that our typing system employs a combination of i/o types and linear types, which are low-level π-calculus types, to express restrictions on system behavior. We point out that the expressivity of such ordinary π-calculus types has been studied in the literature and, for instance, in [2] the authors in fact prove that linear and variant types can be used to encode session types.

2   The Calculus

Our study of privacy is based on the π-calculus with groups proposed by Cardelli et al. [1]. In this section we briefly overview the syntax and reduction semantics of the calculus.

Beginning with the syntax, this is standard π-calculus syntax with the addition of the group restriction construct, $(\nu\,G)P$, and the requirement for typing on bound names (the definition of types is in Sect. 3).

$$P ::= x(y{:}T).P \;\mid\; \overline{x}\langle z\rangle.P \;\mid\; (\nu\,G)P \;\mid\; (\nu\,a{:}T)P \;\mid\; P_1 \mid P_2 \;\mid\; !P \;\mid\; \mathbf{0}$$

Free names $\mathtt{fn}(P)$, bound names $\mathtt{bn}(P)$, free variables $\mathtt{fv}(P)$, and bound variables $\mathtt{bv}(P)$ are defined in the standard way for π-calculus processes. We extend this notion to the sets of free groups in a process P and a type T which we denote as $\mathtt{fg}(P)$ and $\mathtt{fg}(T)$, respectively.

We now turn to defining the reduction semantics of the calculus. This employs the notion of *structural congruence* which allows the structural rearrangement of a process so that the reduction rules can be performed. Structural congruence is the least congruence relation, written $\equiv$, that satisfies the rules:

$$
\begin{array}{ll}
P \mid \mathbf{0} \equiv P & (\nu\ a{:}T)P_1 \mid P_2 \equiv (\nu\ a : T)(P_1 \mid P_2) \text{ if } a \notin \mathbf{fn}(P_2) \\
P_1 \mid P_2 \equiv P_2 \mid P_1 & (\nu\ a{:}T_1)(\nu\ b{:}T_2)P \equiv (\nu\ b{:}T_2)(\nu\ a{:}T_1)P \\
(P_1 \mid P_2) \mid P_3 \equiv P_1 \mid (P_2 \mid P_3) & (\nu\ G)P_1 \mid P_2 \equiv (\nu\ G)(P_1 \mid P_2) \text{ if } G \notin \mathbf{fg}(P_2) \\
!P \equiv P \mid !P & (\nu\ G_1)(\nu\ G_2)P \equiv (\nu\ G_2)(\nu\ G_1)P \\
\multicolumn{2}{c}{(\nu\ G_1)(\nu\ a{:}T)P \equiv (\nu\ a{:}T)(\nu\ G_1)P \text{ if } G \notin \mathbf{fg}(T)}
\end{array}
$$

We may now present the reduction relation $P \longrightarrow Q$ which consists of the standard π-calculus reduction relation extended with a new rule for group creation.

$$
\begin{array}{rcl}
\multicolumn{3}{c}{\overline{a}\langle b \rangle.P_1 \mid a(x : T).P_2 \longrightarrow P_1 \mid P_2\{b/x\}} \\[4pt]
P_1 \longrightarrow P_2 & \text{implies} & P_1 \mid P_3 \longrightarrow P_2 \mid P_3 \\[4pt]
P_1 \longrightarrow P_2 & \text{implies} & (\nu\ G)P_1 \longrightarrow (\nu\ G)P_2 \\[4pt]
P_1 \longrightarrow P_2 & \text{implies} & (\nu\ a : T)P_1 \longrightarrow (\nu\ a : T)P_2 \\[4pt]
P_1 \equiv P_1',\ P_1' \longrightarrow P_2',\ P_2' \equiv P_2 & \text{implies} & P_1 \longrightarrow P_2
\end{array}
$$

3   Types and Typing System

In this section we define a typing system for the calculus which builds upon the typing of [1]. The typing system includes: (i) the notion of groups of [1], (ii) the read/write capabilities of [5] extended with the empty capability, and (iii) a notion of linearity on the dissemination of names. The type structure is used for static control over the permissions and the disseminations on names in a process.

For each channel, its type specifies (1) the group it belongs to, (2) the type of values that can be exchanged on the channel, (3) the ways in which the channel may be used in input/output positions (permissions p below) and (4) the number of times it may be disseminated (linearity λ below):

$$
\begin{array}{lll}
T & ::= & G[]^{p\lambda} \mid G[T]^{p\lambda} \\
p & ::= & - \mid \mathbf{r} \mid \mathbf{w} \mid \mathbf{rw} \\
\lambda & ::= & * \mid i \qquad \text{where } i \geq 0
\end{array}
$$

For example, a channel of type $T = G[]^{\mathbf{r}\,2}$ is a channel belonging to group G that does not communicate any names, can be used in input position and twice in object position. Similarly, a name of type $G'[T]^{\text{rw}*}$ is a channel of group G' that can be used in input and output position for exchanging names of type T and can be sent as the object of a communication for an arbitrary number of times.

Subtyping. Our typing system makes use of a subtyping relation which, in turn is, based on two pre-orders, one for permissions p, denoted as $\sqsubseteq_p$, and one for linearities λ, denoted as $\sqsubseteq_\lambda$:

$$\sqsubseteq_p: \quad \text{rw} \sqsubseteq_p \text{w} \qquad \text{rw} \sqsubseteq_p \text{r} \qquad \text{rw}, \text{r}, \text{w} \sqsubseteq_p -$$
$$\sqsubseteq_\lambda: \quad * \sqsubseteq_\lambda i \ \text{ for all } i \qquad i \sqsubseteq_\lambda j \quad \text{if } i \geq j$$

The preorder for permissions is as expected with the empty capability being the greatest element. For linearities, *fewer* permissions are included in *larger* permissions and $*$ is the least element.

Let Type be the set of all types T. The subtyping relation, written $\leq$ as an infix notation, may be defined coinductively as the largest fixed point ($\mathscr{F}^\omega(\text{Type} \times \text{Type})$) of the monotone function:

$$\mathscr{F} : (\text{Type} \times \text{Type}) \longrightarrow (\text{Type} \times \text{Type})$$

where

$$
\begin{aligned}
\mathscr{F}(\mathscr{R}) = & \{(G[]^{-0}, G[]^{-0})\} \\
& \cup \{(G[T_1]^{p\lambda_1}, G[T_2]^{-\lambda_2})) \mid (T_1, T_2) \in \mathscr{R}, (T_2, T_1) \in \mathscr{R}, \lambda_1 \sqsubseteq_\lambda \lambda_2\} \\
& \cup \{(G[T_1]^{p\lambda_1}, G[T_2]^{r\lambda_2}) \mid (T_1, T_2) \in \mathscr{R}, p \sqsubseteq_p r, \lambda_1 \sqsubseteq_\lambda \lambda_2\} \\
& \cup \{(G[T_1]^{p\lambda_1}, G[T_2]^{w\lambda_2}) \mid (T_2, T_1) \in \mathscr{R}, p \sqsubseteq_p w, \lambda_1 \sqsubseteq_\lambda \lambda_2\} \\
& \cup \{(G[T_1]^{rw\lambda_1}, G[T_2]^{rw\lambda_2}) \mid (T_1, T_2), (T_2, T_1) \in \mathscr{R}, \lambda_1 \sqsubseteq_\lambda \lambda_2\}
\end{aligned}
$$

The first pair in the construction of $\mathscr{F}$ says that the least base type is reflexive. The next four cases define subtyping based on the preorders defined for permissions and linearities. According to the second case, the empty permission is associated with an invariant subtyping relation because the empty permission disallows for a name to be used for reading and/or writing. The read permission follows covariant subtyping, the write permission follows contravariant subtyping, while the read/write permission follows invariant subtyping. Note that linearities are required to respect the relation $\lambda_1 \sqsubseteq \lambda_2$ for subtyping in all cases. For example, according to the subtyping relation, the following hold: $G_1[G_2[]^{rw5}]^{rw*} \leq G_1[G_2[]^{w3}]^{r3}$, $G_1[G_2[]^{-3}]^{rw*} \leq G_1[G_2[]^{w3}]^{w0}$, and $G_1[G_2[]^{w5}]^{rw*} \leq G_1[G_2[]^{w5}]^{-1}$.

Typing Judgements. We now turn to the typing system of our calculus. This assigns an extended notion of a type on names which is constructed as follows:

$$T = (T_1, T_2)$$

In a pair T we record the current capabilities of a name, captured by T_1, and its future capabilities after its dissemination, captured by T_2.

Based on these extended types, the environment on which type checking is carried out in our calculus consists of the components Π and Γ. These declare the names (free and bound) and groups in scope during type checking. We define Γ-environments by $\Gamma ::= \emptyset \mid \Gamma \cdot x : T \mid \Gamma \cdot G$. The domain of an environment Γ, $\text{dom}(\Gamma)$, is considered to contain all names and groups recorded in Γ. We assume that any name and group in $\text{dom}(\Gamma)$ occurs exactly once in Γ. Then, a Π-environment is defined by $\Pi ::= \emptyset \mid \Pi \cdot x : T$, where $\text{dom}(\Pi)$ contains all variables in Π, each of which must exist in Π exactly once.

We define three typing judgements: $\Gamma \vdash x \triangleright T$, $\Pi \vdash x \triangleright T$, and $\Pi, \Gamma \vdash P$. The first two typing judgement say that under the typing environment Γ, respectively Π, variable x has type T. The third typing judgement stipulates that process P is well typed under the environments Π, Γ, where Γ records the groups and the types of the free names of P and Π the types of all bound names x that are created via a (νx) construct within P. We require that these bound names are uniquely named within P and, if needed, we employ α conversion to achieve this. In essence, this restriction requires for all freshly-created names to be recorded a-priori within the typing environment. If an unrecorded name is encountered, then the typing system will lead to failure as is implemented by the typing system. It turns out that recording this information on bound names of a process is necessary in order to control the internal processing of names that carry sensitive data.

Typing System. We now move on to the rules of our typing system. First, we present two auxiliary functions. To begin with we define the linearity addition operator $\oplus$ where $\lambda_1 \oplus \lambda_2 = *$, if $\lambda_1 = *$ or $\lambda_2 = *$, and $\lambda_1 \oplus \lambda_2 = \lambda_1 + \lambda_2$, otherwise. We may now lift this notion to the level of typing environments via operator $\odot$ which composes its arguments by concatenating their declarations with the exception of the common domain where linearities are added up via $\oplus$:

$$
\begin{aligned}
\Gamma_1 \odot \Gamma_2 \quad = \quad & \Gamma_1 \backslash \Gamma_2 \cdot \Gamma_2 \backslash \Gamma_1 \\
& \cdot \quad \{x : G[T]^{p\lambda_1 \oplus \lambda_2} \mid x : G[T]^{p\lambda_1} \in \Gamma_1, x : G[T]^{p\lambda_2} \in \Gamma_2\}
\end{aligned}
$$

At this point we make the implicit assumption that Γ_1 and Γ_2 are compatible in the sense that the declared types of common names may differ only in the linearity component.

We are ready now define the typing system:

$$(\text{Name}) \quad \frac{\begin{array}{c} x \notin \text{dom}(\Gamma \cdot \Gamma') \\ \mathtt{fg}(T) \subseteq \text{dom}(\Gamma \cdot \Gamma') \end{array}}{\Gamma \cdot x : T \cdot \Gamma' \vdash x \triangleright T} \qquad (\text{SubN}) \quad \frac{\Gamma \vdash x \triangleright (T_1', T_2'), T_1' \leq T_1, T_2' \leq T_2}{\Gamma \vdash x \triangleright (T_1, T_2)}$$

$$(\text{In}) \quad \frac{\begin{array}{c} \Pi, \Gamma \cdot y : (T_1, T_2) \vdash P \\ \Gamma \vdash x \triangleright (G[T_1]^{\mathtt{r}0}, G[T_2]^{\mathtt{r}0}) \end{array}}{\Pi, \Gamma \vdash x(y : T_1).P} \qquad (\text{Out}) \quad \frac{\begin{array}{c} \Pi, \Gamma \cdot y : (G_y[T_1]^{-\lambda}, T_2) \vdash P \\ \Gamma \vdash x \triangleright (G_x[T_2]^{\mathtt{w}0}, G_x[T_2]^{\mathtt{w}0}) \end{array}}{\Pi, \Gamma \cdot y : (G_y[T_1]^{-(\lambda \oplus 1)}, T_2) \vdash \overline{x}\langle y \rangle.P}$$

$$(\text{ResG}) \quad \frac{\Pi, \Gamma \cdot G \vdash P}{\Pi, \Gamma \vdash (\nu\, G)P} \qquad (\text{ResN}) \quad \frac{\Pi, \Gamma \cdot x : (T, T') \vdash P}{\Pi \cdot x : (T, T'), \Gamma \vdash (\nu\, x : T)P}$$

$$(\text{Par}) \quad \frac{\Pi_1, \Gamma_1 \vdash P_1 \quad \Pi_2, \Gamma_2 \vdash P_2}{\Pi_1 \odot \Pi_2, \Gamma_1 \odot \Gamma_2 \vdash P_1 \mid P_2} \qquad (\text{Rep}) \quad \frac{\begin{array}{c} \Pi, \Gamma \vdash P \\ \forall x \in \mathtt{fn}(P) \text{ if } \Gamma \vdash x \triangleright (G[T_1]^{p\lambda_1}, G[T_2]^{p\lambda_2}) \\ \text{then } \lambda_1 \in \{0, *\} \end{array}}{\Pi, \Gamma \vdash !P}$$

$$(\text{Nil}) \quad \Pi, \Gamma \vdash \mathbf{0} \qquad (\text{SubP}) \quad \frac{\Pi, \Gamma \cdot x : (T_1', T_2') \vdash P \quad T_1' \leq T_1, T_2' \leq T_2}{\Pi, \Gamma \cdot x : (T_1, T_2) \vdash P}$$

Rule (Name) is used to type names. Note that in name typing we require that all group names of the type are present in the typing environment. Rule (SubN) defines a subsumption based on subtyping for channels. Rule (In) types the input prefixed process. We first require that the input subject has at least permission for reading. Then, the type y is included in the type environment Γ with a type that matches the type of the input channel x. This is to ensure that the input object will be used as specified. The rule for the output prefix (Out) checks that the output subject has write permissions. Furthermore, x should be a channel that can communicate names up-to type T_2, the maximum type by which y can be disseminated. Then, the continuation of the process P, should be typed according to the original type of y and with its linearity reduced by one. Finally, the output object should have at least the empty permission.

In rule (ResG) we record a newly-created name in Γ. For name restriction (ResN) specifies that a process type checks only if the restricted name is recorded in environment Π. In this way is is possible to control the internal behavior of a process, in order to avoid possible privacy violations. Parallel composition uses the $\odot$ operator to compose typing environments, since we want to add up the linearity usage of each name. For the replication operator, axiom (Rep) we require that free names of P have either linearity zero (i.e. they are not sent by P) or infinite linearity (i.e. they can be sent as many times as needed). The inactive process can be typed under any typing environment (axiom (Nil)). Finally we have a subsumption rule, (SubP) that uses subtyping to control the permissions on processes.

Type Soundness. We prove that the typing system is sound through a subject reduction theorem. Before we proceed with the subject reduction theorem we state the basic auxiliary lemmas.

Lemma 1 (Weakening).

1. If $\Gamma \vdash x \rhd \mathsf{T}$ and $y \notin \mathrm{dom}(\Gamma)$ then $\Gamma \cdot y : \mathsf{T}' \vdash x \rhd \mathsf{T}$.
2. If $\Pi, \Gamma \vdash P$ and $y \notin \mathrm{dom}(\Gamma)$ then $\Pi, \Gamma \cdot y : \mathsf{T} \vdash P$.

Lemma 2 (Strengthening).

1. If $\Gamma \cdot y : \mathsf{T}' \vdash x \rhd \mathsf{T}$, $y \neq x$, then $\Gamma \vdash x \rhd \mathsf{T}$.
2. If $\Pi, \Gamma \cdot y : \mathsf{T} \vdash P$ and $y \notin \mathrm{fn}(P)$ then $\Pi, \Gamma \vdash P$.

Lemma 3 (Substitution). If $\Pi, \Gamma \cdot x : \mathsf{T} \vdash P$ and $\Gamma \vdash y \rhd \mathsf{T}$ then $\Pi, \Gamma \vdash P\{y/x\}$

Lemma 4 (Subject Congruence). If $\Pi, \Gamma \vdash P_1$ and $P_1 \equiv P_2$ then $\Pi, \Gamma \vdash P_2$.

We are now ready to state the Subject Reduction theorem.

Theorem 1 (Subject Reduction). Let $\Pi, \Gamma \vdash P$ and $P \longrightarrow P'$ then $\Pi, \Gamma \vdash P'$.

Proof. The proof is by induction on the reduction structure of P.
Basic Step:

$P = \overline{a}\langle b \rangle.P_1 \mid a(x).P_2 \longrightarrow P_1 \mid P_2\{b/x\}$ and $\Pi, \Gamma \vdash P$. From the typing system we get that

$$\Gamma = \Gamma_1 \odot \Gamma_2 \tag{1}$$
$$\Pi_1, \Gamma_1 \vdash \overline{a}\langle b \rangle.P_1 \tag{2}$$
$$\Pi_2, \Gamma_2 \vdash a(x).P_2 \tag{3}$$

From the typing system we get that $\Pi_1, \Gamma_1 \vdash P_1$ for (2) and $\Pi_2, \Gamma_2 \cdot x : \mathsf{T} \vdash P_2$ for (3). We apply the substitution lemma (Lemma 3) to get that $\Pi_2, \Gamma_2 \cdot b : \mathsf{T} \vdash P_2\{b/x\}$. We can now conclude that $\Pi, \Gamma \vdash P_1 \mid P_2\{b/x\}$.
Induction Step:

Case: Parallel Composition. Let $P_1 \mid P_2 \longrightarrow P_1' \mid P_2$ with $\Pi, \Gamma \vdash P_1 \mid P_2$. From the induction hypothesis we know that $\Pi_1, \Gamma_1 \vdash P_1$ and $\Pi_1, \Gamma_1 \vdash P_1'$. From these two results and the parallel composition typing we can conclude that $\Pi_1 \odot \Pi_2, \Gamma_1 \odot \Gamma_2 \vdash P_1 \mid P_2$ and $\Pi_1 \odot \Pi_2, \Gamma_1 \odot \Gamma_2 \vdash P_1' \mid P_2$ as required.

Case: Group Restriction. Let $(\nu\, G)P \longrightarrow (\nu\, G)P'$ with $\Pi, \Gamma \vdash (\nu\, G)P$. From the induction hypothesis we know that $\Pi, \Gamma \cdot G \vdash P$ and $\Pi, \Gamma \cdot G \vdash P'$. If we apply the name restriction rule on the last result we get $\Pi, \Gamma \vdash (\nu\, G)P'$.

Case: Name Restriction. Let $(\nu\, a : T)P \longrightarrow (\nu\, a : T)P'$ with $\Pi \cdot a : T, \Gamma \vdash P$. From the induction hypothesis we know that $\Pi, \Gamma \cdot a : T \vdash P$ and $\Pi, \Gamma \cdot a : T \vdash P'$. If we apply the name restriction rule on the last result we get $\Pi \cdot a : T, \Gamma \vdash (\nu\, a : T)P'$.

Case: Structural Congruence Closure. We use the subject congruence lemma (Lemma 4).

Let $P \equiv P_1, P_1 \longrightarrow P_2, P_2 \cong P'$ with $\Pi, \Gamma \vdash P$. We apply subject congruence on P to get $\Pi, \Gamma \vdash P_1$. Then we apply the induction hypothesis and subject congruence once more to get the required result. $\qquad \square$

4   Examples

In this section we show simple use cases that apply the theory developed. We also show how we tackle different problems that might arise.

4.1   Patient Privacy

Our first example revisits our example from the introduction and completes the associated type system. Recall the scenario where a database administrator (process DBadmin) sends a reference to the medical data of a patient to a doctor (process Doctor) using a nurse (process Nurse) as a delegate.

$$\mathsf{DBadmin} = (\nu b : T_b)\ \overline{\mathsf{tonurse}}\langle b \rangle.\overline{\mathsf{todoc}}\langle b \rangle.\overline{a}\langle c \rangle.\mathbf{0}$$
$$\mathsf{Nurse} = \mathsf{tonurse}(z).a(x).\overline{z}\langle x \rangle.\mathbf{0}$$
$$\mathsf{Doctor} = \mathsf{todoc}(z).z(x).x(y).\overline{x}\langle \mathsf{data} \rangle.\mathbf{0}$$

The processes are composed together inside the hospital (Hosp) group.

$$\mathsf{Hospital} = (\nu\ \mathsf{Hosp})(((\nu c : T_c)\mathsf{DBadmin})\ |\ \mathsf{Nurse}\ |\ \mathsf{Doctor})$$

Our prime interest is to avoid leakage of the data during their dissemination to the doctor. This means that the nurse should not have access to the patient's data. On the other hand the doctor should be able to read and update medical data, but not be able to send the data to anyone else. We can control the above permissions using the following typing.

We define the types

$$\begin{aligned}
T_{\mathsf{data}} &= \mathsf{Hosp}[]^{-*} \\
T_c &= \mathsf{Hosp}[T_{\mathsf{data}}]^{\mathsf{rw}*} \\
T_a &= \mathsf{Hosp}[\mathsf{Hosp}[T_{\mathsf{data}}]^{-1}]^{\mathsf{rw}0} \\
T_a' &= \mathsf{Hosp}[T_c]^{\mathsf{rw}0} \\
T_b &= \mathsf{Hosp}[\mathsf{Hosp}[T_{\mathsf{data}}]^{\mathsf{rw}0}]^{\mathsf{rw}2} \\
T_b^n &= \mathsf{Hosp}[\mathsf{Hosp}[T_{\mathsf{data}}]^{\mathsf{rw}0}]^{\mathsf{w}0} \\
T_b^d &= \mathsf{Hosp}[\mathsf{Hosp}[T_{\mathsf{data}}]^{\mathsf{rw}0}]^{\mathsf{r}0} \\
T_{td} &= \mathsf{Hosp}[T_b^n]^{\mathsf{rw}0} \\
T_{tn} &= \mathsf{Hosp}[T_b^d]^{\mathsf{rw}0}
\end{aligned}$$

to construct:

$$\begin{aligned}
D &= (T_{\mathsf{data}}, T_{\mathsf{data}}) \\
C &= (T_c, T_c) \\
A &= (T_a, T_a') \\
B &= (T_b, T_b) \\
TD &= (T_{td}, T_{td}) \\
TN &= (T_{tn}, T_{tn}).
\end{aligned}$$

We can show that:

$$b : B \cdot c : C, \mathsf{tonurse} : TN \cdot \mathsf{todoc} : TD \cdot a : A \cdot \mathsf{data} : D \vdash \mathsf{Hospital}$$

Now, let us consider the case where the nurse sends channel c on a private channel in an attempt to gain access on the patient's medical data:

$$\mathsf{Nurse}_2 \; = \;\; \mathsf{tonurse}(z).a(x).(\nu\ e : T_b)(\overline{e}\langle x\rangle.\mathbf{0} \mid e(y).y(w).\mathbf{0})$$

In this case, in order for the resulting system to type-check, the type of name e would be recorded in the environment Π, as in

$$e : B \cdot b : B \cdot c : C, \mathsf{tonurse} : TN \cdot \mathsf{todoc} : TD \cdot a : A \cdot \mathsf{data} : D$$
$$\vdash (\nu\ \mathsf{Hosp})(((\nu c : T_c)\mathsf{DBadmin}) \mid \mathsf{Nurse}_2 \mid \mathsf{Doctor})$$

This implies that, if we allow the creation of e, there is possibility of violation in a well-typed process. To avoid this, the administrator of the system should observe all names created and included in Π and, in this specific case, disallow the creation of e. In future work we intend to address this point by providing typing policies that capture this type of problems and to refine our type system to disallow such privacy violations, possibly by controlling the process of name creation.

4.2   Social Network Privacy

Social networks allow users to share information within social groups. In the example that follows we define a type system to control the privacy requirements of participating users. In particular, we consider the problem where a user can make a piece of information public (e.g. a picture), but require that only specific people (his friends) can see it (and do nothing else with it).

The example considers a user who makes public the address, paddr, of a private object, pic, and wishes only the friend Friend to be able to read pic through the public address paddr. To achieve this the user makes available through the typing of name public only the object capability for paddr. However, by separately providing the friend with name a, it is possible to extend the capabilities of paddr to the read capability. In this way, channel a acts as a key for Friend to unlock this private information. Assuming that notAFriend does not gain access to a name of type T_a, as in the process below, he will never be able to obtain read capability on channel paddr.

$$\mathsf{User} = (\nu a : T_a)(\overline{\mathsf{tofriend}}\langle a\rangle.(\nu\mathsf{paddr} : T_{paddr})(!\overline{\mathsf{public}}\langle\mathsf{paddr}\rangle.\mathbf{0} \mid !\overline{\mathsf{paddr}}\langle\mathsf{pic}\rangle.\mathbf{0}))$$
$$\mathsf{notAFriend} = \mathsf{public}(z).\mathbf{0}$$
$$\mathsf{Friend} = \mathsf{tofriend}(x).\mathsf{public}(y).(\overline{x}\langle y\rangle.\mathbf{0} \mid x(z).z(w).\mathbf{0})$$

The processes are composed together inside the SN group.

$$\mathsf{SocialNetwork} = (\nu\ \mathsf{SN})(\mathsf{User} \mid \mathsf{notAFriend} \mid \mathsf{Friend})$$

To achieve this, we define the types

$$T_{pic} = SN[]^{-*}$$
$$T_{paddr} = SN[T_{pic}]^{rw*}$$
$$T'_{paddr} = SN[T_{pic}]^{-1}$$
$$T_a = SN[T_{paddr}]^{rw*}$$
$$T_{tofriend} = SN[T_a]^{rw0}$$
$$T_{public} = SN[T_{paddr}]^{rw0}$$
$$T'_{public} = SN[T'_{paddr}]^{rw0}$$

which are combined into the following tuples

$$PIC = (T_{pic}, T_{pic})$$
$$A = (T_a, T_a)$$
$$PA = (T_{paddr}, T_{paddr})$$
$$TF = (T'_{tofriend}, T_{tofriend})$$
$$PB = (T'_{public}, T_{public})$$

We can show that:

$$a : A \cdot paddr : PA, tofriend : TF \cdot public : PB \cdot pic : PIC \vdash \mathsf{SocialNetwork}$$

whereas for $\mathsf{notAFriend'} = \mathsf{public}(z).z(w).\mathbf{0}$ and

$$\mathsf{SocialNetwork'} = (\nu\ \mathsf{SN})(\mathsf{User}\ |\ \mathsf{notAFriend'}\ |\ \mathsf{Friend})$$

the following judgment fails.

$$a : A \cdot paddr : PA, tofriend : TF \cdot public : PB \cdot pic : PIC \vdash \mathsf{SocialNetwork'}$$

5   Conclusions

In this paper we have presented a formal framework based on the π-calculus with groups for studying privacy. Our framework is accompanied by a type system for capturing privacy-related notions: it includes the use of *groups* to enable reasoning about information collection, it builds on *read/write capabilities* to control information processing, and it employs *type linearity* to restrict information dissemination. We illustrate the use of our typing system via simple examples.

In future work we would like to provide a safety criterion for our framework by developing a policy language for defining privacy policies associated to process calculus descriptions and subsequently to refine our type system so that it can check the satisfaction/violation of these policies. Furthermore, we would like to study the relation of our type system to other typing systems in the literature.

References

1. Cardelli, L., Ghelli, G., Gordon, A.D.: Secrecy and group creation. Inf. Comput. **196**(2), 127–155 (2005)
2. Dardha, O., Giachino, E., Sangiorgi, D.: Session types revisited. In: Proceedings of PPDP'12, pp. 139–150. ACM, New York (2012)
3. Kobayashi, N., Pierce, B.C., Turner, D.N.: Linearity and the pi-calculus. ACM Trans. Program. Lang. Syst. **21**(5), 914–947 (1999)
4. Milner, R., Parrow, J., Walker, D.: A calculus of mobile processes, parts I and II. Inf. Comput. **100**(1), 1–77 (1992)
5. Pierce, B.C., Sangiorgi, D.: Typing and subtyping for mobile processes. Math. Struct. Comput. Sci. **6**(5), 409–453 (1996)
6. Solove, D.J.: A taxonomy of privacy. Univ. PA Law Rev. **154**(3), 477–560 (2006)
7. Tschantz, M.C., Wing, J.M.: Formal methods for privacy. In: Cavalcanti, A., Dams, D.R. (eds.) FM 2009. LNCS, vol. 5850, pp. 1–15. Springer, Heidelberg (2009)

Compliance and Testing Preorders Differ

Giovanni Bernardi[(✉)] and Matthew Hennessy

School of Computer Science, Trinity College, University of Dublin, Dublin 2, Ireland
bernargi@tcd.ie

Abstract. Contracts play an essential role in the Service Oriented Computing, for which they need to be equipped with a *sub-contract relation*. We compare two possible formulations, one based on *compliance* and the other on the testing theory of De Nicola and Hennessy. We show that if the language of contracts is sufficiently expressive then the resulting *sub-contract relations* are incomparable.

However if we put natural restrictions on the contract language then the *sub-contract relations* coincide, at least when applied to servers. But when formulated for clients they remain incomparable, for many reasonable contract languages. Finally we give one example of a contract language for which the client-based *sub-contract relations* coincide.

1 Introduction

Contracts play a central role in the orchestration and development of web services, [CCLP06, LP07]. Existing services are advertised for use by third parties, which may combine these existing services to construct, and in turn advertise for further use, new services. The behavioural specification of advertised services is given via *contracts*, high-level descriptions of expected behaviour, which should come equipped with a *sub-contract* relation. Intuitively $\mathrm{CT}_1 \sqsubseteq_{\mathrm{CRT}} \mathrm{CT}_2$ means that a third party requiring a service to provide contract CT_1 may use one which already provides CT_2, so in this sense CT_2 is better than CT_1. The purpose of this short technical note is to compare and contrast two different approaches to defining this *sub-contract* relation.

The first method, [LP07, CGP09, Pad10], is based on a notion of *compliance* between two contracts, where one contract notionally formalises the behaviour offered by a server p, and the other one the behaviour offered by a client r. Contracts are interpreted as abstract processes, written in process algebras similar to CCS or CSP, [Mil89, Hoa85]. However, as pointed out by [Bd10, BH12] they can also be viewed as session types [THK94, GH05]. Intuitively p and r are in compliance, written $r \dashv p$, if when viewed as abstract processes they can continuously interact, and if this interaction ever stops then the client is in a *happy state*; the formal definition is co-inductive and is given in Definition 2.4. This leads to a natural comparison between server-oriented contracts: $p_1 \sqsubseteq_{\mathrm{SVR}}^{\mathrm{cpl}} p_2$ if every client which complies with p_1 also complies with p_2. As suggested in [Bd10],

---

Research supported by SFI project SFI 06 IN.1 1898.

S. Counsell and M. Núñez (Eds.): SEFM 2013 Collocated Workshops, LNCS 8368, pp. 69–81, 2014.
DOI: 10.1007/978-3-319-05032-4_6, © Springer International Publishing Switzerland 2014

client-oriented contracts can also be compared, but in terms of the servers with which they comply, $r_1 \sqsubseteq^{\mathsf{cpl}}_{\mathsf{CLT}} r_2$.

It has been pointed out by various authors [LP07, CGP09, Pad09, Pad10] that the server contract preorder, $\sqsubseteq^{\mathsf{cpl}}_{\mathsf{SVR}}$, bears a striking resemblance to the well-known *must-testing* preorders from [DH84]. For example, the axioms for the strong sub-contract relation in [Pad09, Table 1], are essentially the same for the testing preorder in [Hen85, Fig. 3.6]; and the behavioural characterisations of the sub-contract relation use *ready sets*, which were already in the behavioural characterisation of the *must-testing* preorder [DH84]. In this approach clients are viewed as *tests* for servers and servers are compared by their ability to guarantee that tests are satisfied. This is formalised as an *inductive* relation between tests and servers. Intuitively p MUST r if whenever the two abstract processes p, r are executed in parallel the test r is guaranteed to reach a *happy state*. This in turn leads to a second pair of *sub-contract* relations, which we denote by $p_1 \sqsubset^{\mathsf{tst}}_{\sim\mathsf{SVR}} p_2$ and $r_1 \sqsubset^{\mathsf{tst}}_{\sim\mathsf{CLT}} r_2$ respectively.

In this paper we contrast these two different approaches to the notion of *sub-contract* by comparing the relations $\sqsubseteq^{\mathsf{cpl}}_{\star}$ and $\sqsubset^{\mathsf{tst}}_{\sim\star}$, for both servers and clients. This study is of interest because the testing-based preorders have been thoroughly studied. In particular $\sqsubset^{\mathsf{tst}}_{\sim\mathsf{SVR}}$ has a behavioural characterisation, an axiomatisation (for finite terms) [DH84, Hen85], a logical characterisation [CH10], and an algorithm to decide it (on finite state LTSs) [CH93]; moreover the client preorder $\sqsubset^{\mathsf{tst}}_{\sim\mathsf{CLT}}$ has recently been investigated in [Ber13].

The outcome of the comparison depends on the expressive power of the language used to express contracts. We examine three different possibilities. The first is when there is no restriction on the contract language. We essentially allow any description of behaviour from the process calculus CCS; this includes infinite state and potentially divergent contracts. In this case the preorders are incomparable; see Sect. 3.1.

In the second case we restrict the contract language to what we call $\mathsf{CCS}_{\mathsf{web}}$; this only allows finite-state contracts, which can never give rise to divergent behaviour; this language includes all the contract languages used in the standard literature, such as [LP07, Bd10, Pad09] and the concrete one of [CGP09]. In this setting the two server-contract preorders coincide:

$$p_1 \sqsubseteq^{\mathsf{cpl}}_{\mathsf{SVR}} p_2 \text{ if and only if } p_1 \sqsubset^{\mathsf{tst}}_{\sim\mathsf{SVR}} p_2$$

However the client-contract preorders remain incomparable. This is discussed in Sect. 3.2.

It turns out that the difference in the formulation of the *compliance* relation between contracts and that based on *must-testing*, one co-inductive and the other inductive, has significant implications on the client-preorders, regardless of the expressivity of the contract language. This is explained via examples in Sect. 3.3. In particular it is difficult to think of a reasonable contract language in which they coincide. We provide one example, also in Sect. 3.3, which essentially coincides with the *finite session behaviours* of [Bd10]; one can think of these as *first-order* session types [THK94]. But, as we will see, introducing recursion into this contract language will once more enable us to differentiate between the two client-preorders.

The remainder of the paper is structured as follows. In the next section, Sect. 2, we provide formal definitions for the concepts introduced informally above, together with a description of the abstract language CCS, which is used as a general description language for contracts. Then the three different scenarios are discussed in turn in Sect. 3. Finally we discuss the related literature in Sect. 4.

2   LTS and Behavioural Preorders

A labelled transition system, LTS, consists of a triple $\langle P, \longrightarrow, \mathsf{Act}_{\tau\checkmark} \rangle$ where P is a set of processes and $\longrightarrow \subseteq P \times \mathsf{Act}_{\tau\checkmark} \times P$ is a transition relation between processes decorated with labels drawn from the set $\mathsf{Act}_{\tau\checkmark}$. We let λ range over $\mathsf{Act}_{\tau\checkmark}$, and μ range over Act_τ. We use the infix notation $p \xrightarrow{\lambda} q$ in place of $(p, \lambda, q) \in \longrightarrow$. Let CCS be the set of terms defined by the grammar

$$p, q, r \ ::= \ 1 \mid A \mid \mu.p \mid \sum\nolimits_{i \in I} p_i$$

where $\mu \in \mathsf{Act}_\tau$, I is a countable index sets, and $A, B, C, \dots$ range over a set of definitional constants each of which has an associated definition $A \overset{\text{def}}{=} p_A$. We use 0 to denote the empty external sum $\sum_{i \in \emptyset} p_i$ and $p_1 + p_2$ for the binary sum $\sum_{i \in \{1,2\}} p_i$. Note that we have omitted the parallel operator $\|$, as contracts, and their associated session types [Bd10,BH12], are normally expressed purely in terms of prefixing and choices.

The operational semantics of the language is given by the LTS generated by the relations $p \xrightarrow{\lambda} q$ determined by the rules given in Fig. 1. The *happy* or successful states mentioned in the Introduction are considered to be those CCS terms satisfying $p \xrightarrow{\checkmark}$.

We use standard notation for operations in LTSs. For example $\mathsf{Act}^\star_{\tau\checkmark}$, ranged over by t, denotes the set of *finite* sequences of actions from the set $\mathsf{Act}_{\tau\checkmark}$, and for any $t \in \mathsf{Act}^\star_{\tau\checkmark}$ we let $p \xrightarrow{t} q$ be the obvious generalisation of the single transition relations to sequences. For an infinite sequence $u \in \mathsf{Act}^\infty_{\tau\checkmark}$ of the form $\lambda_0 \lambda_1 \dots$ we write $p \xrightarrow{u}$ to mean that there is an infinite sequence of actions $p \xrightarrow{\lambda_0} p_0 \xrightarrow{\lambda_1} p_1 \dots$. These action relations are lifted to the weak case in the standard manner, giving rise to $p \overset{s}{\Longrightarrow} q$ for $s \in \mathsf{Act}^\star_\checkmark$ and $p \overset{u}{\Longrightarrow}$ for $u \in Act^\infty$. We write $\Longrightarrow$ in place of $\overset{\varepsilon}{\Longrightarrow}$, where ε denotes the empty string. Finally a process *diverges*, written $p \Uparrow$, if there is an infinite sequence of actions $p \xrightarrow{\tau} p_1 \xrightarrow{\tau} \dots \xrightarrow{\tau} p_k \xrightarrow{\tau} \dots$. Otherwise it is said to *converge*, written $p \Downarrow$.

To model the interactions that take place between the server and the client contracts, we introduce a binary composition of contracts, $r \| p$, whose operational semantics is in Fig. 2.

Definition 2.1. [Compliance]
Let $\mathcal{F}^{\dashv} : \mathcal{P}(CCS^2) \longrightarrow \mathcal{P}(CCS^2)$ be the rule functional defined so that $(r, p) \in \mathcal{F}^{\dashv}(\mathcal{R})$ whenever the following conditions are true:

(a) if $p \Uparrow$ then $r \xrightarrow{\checkmark}$
(b) if $r \parallel p \overset{\tau}{\nrightarrow}$ then $r \xrightarrow{\checkmark}$
(c) if $r \parallel p \xrightarrow{\tau} r' \parallel p'$ then $r' \mathcal{R} p'$

If $X \subseteq \mathcal{F}^{\dashv}(X)$, then we say that X is a *co-inductive* compliance *relation*. The monotonicity of $\mathcal{F}^{\dashv}$ and the Knaster-Tarski theorem ensure that there exists the greatest solution of the equation $X = \mathcal{F}^{\dashv}(X)$; we call this solution the *compliance relation*, and we denote it $\dashv$. That is $\dashv = \nu X.\mathcal{F}^{\dashv}(X)$. If $r \dashv p$ we say that the client r *complies with* the server p. □

Thanks to its co-inductivenature, the compliance admits everlasting computations, even if the client side never reaches a happy state. This is a typical feature of the compliance relation.

Example 2.2. Let $C \overset{def}{=} \tau.\alpha.C$ and $S \overset{def}{=} \bar{\alpha}.S$. Even if C can not reach a happy state, it complies with S, for $\{ (C, S), (\alpha.C, S) \}$ is a co-inductive compliance. This set enjoys the properties required by Definition 2.1: Point (a) is trivially true for S converges, point (b) is true because $C \parallel S \xrightarrow{\tau}$ and $\alpha.C \parallel S \xrightarrow{\tau}$. A routine check shows that also point (c) is true. □

Another property of $\dashv$ is that it is preserved by the interactions of contracts.

$$\frac{}{1 \xrightarrow{\checkmark} 0} \text{ [A-Ok]} \qquad \frac{}{\mu.p \xrightarrow{\mu} p} \text{ [A-Pre]}$$

$$\frac{p \xrightarrow{\lambda} p'}{p + q \xrightarrow{\lambda} p'} \text{ [R-Ext-l]} \qquad \frac{q \xrightarrow{\lambda} q'}{p + q \xrightarrow{\lambda} q'} \text{ [R-Ext-r]}$$

$$\frac{p \xrightarrow{\lambda} p'}{A \xrightarrow{\lambda} p'} A \overset{def}{=} p; \text{ [R-Const]}$$

Fig. 1. The operational semantics of CCS

$$\frac{q \xrightarrow{\lambda} q'}{q \parallel p \xrightarrow{\lambda} q' \parallel p} \text{ [P-Left]} \qquad \frac{p \xrightarrow{\lambda} p'}{q \parallel p \xrightarrow{\lambda} q \parallel p'} \text{ [P-Right]}$$

$$\frac{q \xrightarrow{\alpha} q' \quad p \xrightarrow{\bar{\alpha}} p'}{q \parallel p \xrightarrow{\tau} q' \parallel p'} \text{ [P-Synch]}$$

Fig. 2. The operational semantics of contract composition

Lemma 2.3. If $r \dashv p$ and $r \parallel p \xrightarrow{\tau}^{*} r' \parallel p'$ then $r' \dashv p'$.

Proof. It follows from induction on the number of reduction steps in $\xrightarrow{\tau}^{*}$, and point (c) of Definition 2.1. □

Definition 2.4. [Compliance preorders]
In an arbitrary LTS we write

(1) $p_1 \sqsubseteq_{\mathrm{SVR}}^{\mathrm{cpl}} p_2$ if for every r, $r \dashv p_1$ implies $r \dashv p_2$
(2) $r_1 \sqsubseteq_{\mathrm{CLT}}^{\mathrm{cpl}} r_2$ if for every p, $r_1 \dashv p$ implies $r_2 \dashv p$ □

Note that our compliance relation is slightly different than that of [LP07]; we require that a client that complies with a divergent server report success immediately, whereas in [LP07] the client may report success in the future, and cannot engage in any interaction. This does not affect the resulting *sub-contract* relations on the language of contracts discussed in [CGP09, Pad10].

We also briefly recall the notion of *must-testing* from [DH84]. A *computation* consists of series of τ actions of the form

$$r \parallel p = r_0 \parallel p_0 \xrightarrow{\tau} r_1 \parallel p_1 \xrightarrow{\tau} \ldots \xrightarrow{\tau} r_k \parallel p_k \xrightarrow{\tau} \ldots \tag{1}$$

It is *maximal* if it is infinite, or whenever $r_n \parallel p_n$ is the last state then $r_n \parallel p_n \xrightarrow{\tau}\!\!\!\!\!/$. A computation may be viewed as two processes p, r, one a server and the other a client, co-operating to achieve individual goals. We say that (1) is *client-successful* if there exists some $k \geq 0$ such that $r_k \xrightarrow{\checkmark}$.

Definition 2.5. [Testing preorders]
In an arbitrary LTS we write p MUST r if every maximal computation of $r \parallel p$ is *client-successful*. Then

(1) $p_1 \sqsubset_{\sim \mathrm{SVR}}^{\mathrm{tst}} p_2$ if for every r, p_1 MUST r implies p_2 MUST r
(2) $r_1 \sqsubset_{\sim \mathrm{CLT}}^{\mathrm{tst}} r_2$ if for every p, p MUST r_1 implies p MUST r_2 □

Before comparing the testing and the compliance preorders, we highlight the differences between $\dashv$ and MUST . We use standard examples [LP07, Ber13]. The discussion on the preorders will mirror the differences shown in these examples.

Example 2.6. [Meaning of livelocks]
In this example we prove that $r \dashv p$ does not imply p MUST r. Recall the contracts C and S from Example 2.2. In that example we have seen that since $\{(C, S), (\alpha.C, S)\}$ is a co-inductive compliance, $C \dashv S$.

The fact that S MUST C is true because C does not perform $\checkmark$, and so no computation of $C \parallel S$ is client-successful.   □

The previous example shows that while the compliance admits livelocks where clients do not report success, the must testing does not. The testing relation requires clients to reach a successful state in every (maximal) computation.

Example 2.7. [Meaning $\checkmark$]

In this example we prove that p MUST r does not imply $r \dashv p$. Let $r = 1 + \tau.0$. For every p, p MUST r because $r \xrightarrow{\checkmark}$, so all the computations of $r \parallel p$ are client-successful. For every p, the proof that $r \not\dashv p$ relies on the following computation,

$$r \parallel p \xrightarrow{\tau} 0 \parallel p \xrightarrow{\tau} \ldots$$

Since $0 \not\dashv p$, Lemma 2.3 implies that $r \not\dashv p$.   □

In the must testing, the behaviour of a client that has reported success is completely disregarded; that is p MUST r and $r \parallel p \xrightarrow{\tau} r' \parallel p'$ does not imply p' MUST r'. For the compliance it is the contrary, as we have seen in Lemma 2.3.

3   Examples

We have three sub-sections, each examining one of the scenarios for contracts alluded to in the Introduction.

3.1   General Contracts

Here we assume that contracts may be any term in the language CCS defined above. First we show that the server-contract preorders are incomparable.

Example 3.1. [Infinite traces and servers]

Here we prove that $p \sqsubseteq_{\text{SVR}}^{\text{cpl}} q$ but $p \not\sqsubseteq_{\sim\text{SVR}}^{\text{tst}} q$ where these terms are depicted in Fig. 3.

The symbol p_k denotes a process which performs a sequence of k α actions and then becomes 0; so the process p performs every finite sequence of αs. In contrast, the process q performs also an infinite sequence of αs.

To prove that $p \sqsubseteq_{\text{SVR}}^{\text{cpl}} q$, we have to show that $r \dashv p$ then $r \dashv q$. It suffices to prove that the following relation is a co-inductivecompliance,

$$\mathcal{R} = \{ (r', q) \mid r \dashv p, r \xLongrightarrow{\overline{\alpha}^k} r', \text{ for some } k \in \mathbb{N} \text{ and } r \in \mathsf{CCS} \}$$

We have to show that if $r' \mathcal{R} q$ then the pair (r', q) satisfies the conditions given in Definition 2.1.

Pick a pair (r', q) in the relation $\mathcal{R}$. By construction of $\mathcal{R}$ and of q, we know that $r \xLongrightarrow{\overline{\alpha}^k} r'$ for some $k \in \mathbb{N}$ and some r such that $r \dashv p$.

Condition (a) is trivially true, because q converges. We discuss condition (b) and (c). Suppose that $r' \parallel q \xrightarrow{\tau} \!\!\!\!\!\!/\;$; this implies that $r' \xrightarrow{\tau} \!\!\!\!\!\!/\;$. By construction $p \xRightarrow{\alpha^k} 0$, so we infer $r \parallel p \Longrightarrow r' \parallel 0 \xrightarrow{\tau} \!\!\!\!\!\!/\;$. Now $r \dashv p$ and Lemma 2.3 imply that $r' \dashv 0$; Definition 2.1 ensures that $r' \xrightarrow{\checkmark}$.

Suppose that $r' \parallel q \xrightarrow{\tau} r'' \parallel q'$; we prove that $r'' \mathcal{R} q'$. The argument is a case analysis on the rule used to infer the reduction. In every case $q = q'$. If rule

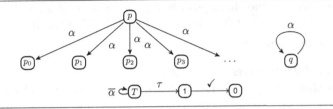

Fig. 3. While $p \sqsubseteq^{\mathsf{cpl}}_{\mathsf{SVR}} q$, the test T witnesses that $p \not\approx^{\mathsf{tst}}_{\mathsf{SVR}} q$ (see Example 3.1)

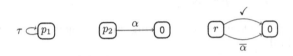

Fig. 4. While $p_1 \approx^{\mathsf{tst}}_{\mathsf{SVR}} p_2$, the client r lets us prove that $p_1 \not\sqsubseteq^{\mathsf{cpl}}_{\mathsf{SVR}} p_2$ (see Example 3.2)

[P-LEFT] was applied then $r' \xrightarrow{\tau} r''$; as $r \xRightarrow{\overline{\alpha}^k} r''$ the definition of $\mathcal{R}$ implies that $r'' \mathcal{R} q'$. Rule [P-RIGHT] cannot have been applied, for $q \xnrightarrow{\tau}$. If rule [P-SYNCH] was applied, then the reduction is due to an interaction. As q engages only in α, it follows $r \xRightarrow{\overline{\alpha}^{k+1}} r''$. The definition of $\mathcal{R}$ implies that $r'' \mathcal{R} q'$.

We have proven that the relation $\mathcal{R}$ is a co-inductivecompliance, so $p \sqsubseteq^{\mathsf{cpl}}_{\mathsf{SVR}} q$. Now we prove that $p \not\approx^{\mathsf{tst}}_{\mathsf{SVR}} q$; we define a test that is passed by p and not by q. Let $T \stackrel{\text{def}}{=} \tau.\,1 + \overline{\alpha}.T$. The LTS of T is depicted in Fig. 3. Every computation of $T \parallel p$ is finite and successful, so p MUST T. However when q is run as a server interacting with T, there is the possibility of an indefinite synchronisation on α, which is not a successful computation; $q \not\!\!\text{MUST } T$. □

Example 3.2. [Convergence of servers]

In this example we prove that $p_1 \sqsubset^{\mathsf{tst}}_{\mathsf{SVR}} p_2$ but $p_1 \not\sqsubseteq^{\mathsf{cpl}}_{\mathsf{SVR}} p_2$, where $p_1 = \tau^{\infty}$ and $p_2 = \alpha.\,0$. The LTS of these processes is in Fig. 4.

We prove that $p_1 \sqsubset^{\mathsf{tst}}_{\mathsf{SVR}} p_2$. First note that $p_1 \Uparrow$, so if p_1 MUST r, then $r \xrightarrow{\checkmark}$; this is because of the infinite computation due only to the divergence of p_1. It follows that if p_1 MUST r then p_2 MUST r.

Now we define a client that lets us prove $p_1 \not\sqsubseteq^{\mathsf{cpl}}_{\mathsf{SVR}} p_2$. Let $r = 1 + \overline{\alpha}.\,0$. To prove that $r \dashv p_1$ Definition 2.1 requires us to show a co-inductive compliance that contains the pair (r, p_1). The following relation $\{(r, p_1)\}$ will do, because the only state ever reached by $r \parallel p_1$ is itself. We have to prove that $r \not\dashv p_2$.

Consider the computation $r \parallel p_2 \Longrightarrow 0 \parallel 0 \xnrightarrow{\tau}$. Since $0 \xnrightarrow{\checkmark}$, Definition 2.1 ensures that $0 \not\dashv 0$. An application of Lemma 2.3 leads to $r \not\dashv p_2$. □

Let us now consider the client preorders in this setting of general contracts. The fact that $\sqsubseteq^{\mathsf{tst}}_{\sim\mathrm{CLT}} \not\subseteq \sqsubseteq^{\mathsf{cpl}}_{\mathrm{CLT}}$ will follow from Example 3.5. One final example is needed to show the converse.

Example 3.3. [Infinite traces and clients]
Here we prove that $\sqsubseteq^{\mathsf{cpl}}_{\mathrm{CLT}} \not\subseteq \sqsubseteq^{\mathsf{tst}}_{\sim\mathrm{CLT}}$. Let us define r as the process p of Example 3.1, but with a $\checkmark$ transition after each finite sequence of αs. Recall also the process T of Example 3.1. To see why $r \sqsubseteq^{\mathsf{cpl}}_{\mathrm{CLT}} T$, it is enough to check that the relation

$$\mathcal{R} = \{\, (T, p') \mid r \dashv p, \, p \overset{\overline{\alpha}^k}{\Longrightarrow} p' \text{ for some } k \in \mathbb{N} \text{ and } p \in \mathsf{CCS} \,\}$$
$$\cup \{\, (1, p) \mid p \in \mathsf{CCS} \,\}$$

is a co-inductivecompliance. To prove this, an argument similar to the one of Example 3.1 will do.

Now we show that $r \not\sqsubseteq^{\mathsf{tst}}_{\sim\mathrm{CLT}} T$; to see why, consider the server $S \overset{\text{def}}{=} \overline{\alpha}.S$. All the maximal computations of $r \parallel S$ are client-successful, so S MUST r; while $T \parallel S$ performs an infinite computation with no client-successful states. □

The two essential differences in how servers are treated by the compliance relation and the testing relation are crystallised Example 3.1 and Example 3.2. In the former we see that a server may fail a test because of the presence of an infinite sequence of actions, although this does not impede the test, or client, from complying with the server. In the latter we see that divergent computations affect the preorders differently. The relation $\sqsubseteq^{\mathsf{tst}}_{\sim\mathrm{SVR}}$ is sensitive to the divergence of servers: any server that diverges is a least element of $\sqsubseteq^{\mathsf{tst}}_{\sim\mathrm{SVR}}$. So if $p_1 \sqsubseteq^{\mathsf{tst}}_{\sim\mathrm{SVR}} p_2$ and p_1 diverges, the traces that p_2 performs need not be matched by the traces of p_1. This is not the case if $p_1 \sqsubseteq^{\mathsf{cpl}}_{\mathrm{SVR}} p_2$; the traces of p_2 have to be matched suitably by the traces of p_1, regardless of the divergence of p_1.

3.2   Contracts for Web-Services

There are natural constraints on the contract language which avoid the phenomena described above. We say that a process p *converges strongly* if for every $s \in Act^\star$, $p \overset{s}{\Longrightarrow} p'$ implies $p' \Downarrow$. Then let $\mathsf{CCS}_{\mathsf{web}}$ denote the subset of processes in CCS which both strongly converge and are finite-state. Note that Konigs Lemma ensures that for every $p \in \mathsf{CCS}_{\mathsf{web}}$, p can perform an infinite sequence of actions u whenever it can perform all finite subsequences of u. Thus neither Example 3.1 nor Example 3.2 can be formulated in $\mathsf{CCS}_{\mathsf{web}}$. Nevertheless it is still a very expressive contract language. It encompasses (via an interpretation) first-order session types [Bd10, BH12], and, up to syntactic differences, the LTSs of contracts for web-services used in [LP07, CGP09, Pad10] are contained in the LTS $\langle\, \mathsf{CCS}_{\mathsf{web}}, \longrightarrow, Act_{\tau\checkmark} \,\rangle$.

Theorem 3.4. In $\mathsf{CCS}_{\mathsf{web}}$, $p_1 \sqsubseteq^{\mathsf{tst}}_{\sim\mathrm{SVR}} p_2$ if and only if $p_1 \sqsubseteq^{\mathsf{cpl}}_{\mathrm{SVR}} p_2$.

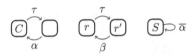

Fig. 5. In any LTS that contains C and r, and where $\overline{\alpha} \neq \overline{\beta}$, S witnesses that $C \not\sqsubseteq_{\text{CLT}}^{\text{cpl}} r_2$. However $C \lesssim_{\text{CLT}} r$ (see Example 3.5)

Proof. See Proposition 5.1.21 of [Ber13]. The proof relies on the behavioural characterisation of the two preorders, which is the same relation $\lesssim_{\text{SVR}}$. Roughly speaking, $p_1 \lesssim_{\text{SVR}} p_2$ if and only if for every trace $s \in Act^*$, the potential deadlocks of p_2 after s are matched the potential deadlocks[1] of p_1 after s. These properties characterise both $\sqsubseteq_{\sim\text{SVR}}^{\text{tst}}$ and $\sqsubseteq_{\text{SVR}}^{\text{cpl}}$, that is $\sqsubseteq_{\sim\text{SVR}}^{\text{tst}} = \lesssim_{\text{SVR}}$ and $\sqsubseteq_{\text{SVR}}^{\text{cpl}} = \lesssim_{\text{SVR}}$. The theorem follows from these equalities. $\qquad\square$

However even in $\mathsf{CCS_{web}}$ the client sub-contract preorders remain different. In Examples 3.5 and 3.6 below we prove that the client preorders are not comparable; Theorem 3.4 is false for the client preorders. and Also the converse (negative) inequality is true; we prove it in Example 3.6 below.

Example 3.5. [Client preorders and livelocks]
In this example we prove that in $\mathsf{CCS_{web}}$, $\sqsubseteq_{\sim\text{CLT}}^{\text{tst}} \not\sqsubseteq \sqsubseteq_{\text{CLT}}^{\text{cpl}}$. Suppose that for two actions α, β we have $\overline{\alpha} \neq \overline{\beta}$, recall the processes C, S of Example 2.6. Their LTS are depicted in Fig. 5 along with the LTS of a process r.

We prove that $C \sqsubseteq_{\sim\text{CLT}}^{\text{tst}} r$ and that $C \not\sqsubseteq_{\text{CLT}}^{\text{cpl}} r$. The inequality $C \sqsubseteq_{\sim\text{CLT}}^{\text{tst}} r$ is trivially true, because C does not perform $\checkmark$, so p ᴍᴜѕᴛ C for every C.

To show that $C \not\sqsubseteq_{\text{CLT}}^{\text{cpl}} r$ we have to exhibit a server with which C complies, while r does not. This server is S. In Example 2.2 we have already proven that $C \dashv S$. On the other hand, since $\overline{\alpha}$ cannot interact with β, we have $r' \parallel S \xrightarrow{\tau} \not\rightarrow$. As $r' \xrightarrow{\checkmark} \not\rightarrow$, Definition 2.1 and Lemma 2.3 ensure that $r \not\dashv S$. $\qquad\square$

3.3 Finite Session Behaviours

Underlying Example 3.5 is the treatment of *livelocks*. These are catastrophic for the testing based preorder, but can be accommodated by the compliance based one. However, there is another completely independent reason for which the two client preorders are different. Both are sensitive to the presence of the $\checkmark$ action, but in different ways.

In the examples below, Examples 3.6 and 3.7, we prove that because of this difference, even for finite clients, with no recursion, the client preorders are incomparable. These examples show that any test which immediately performs

---

[1] More precisely, the acceptance sets.

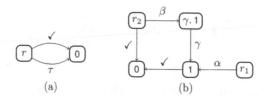

Fig. 6. Clients that let us prove that the client preorders are not comparable even in the finite fragment of CCS$_{web}$ (see Examples 3.6 and 3.7)

✓ is a top element in the testing based preorder, even if it subsequently evolves to a state in which ✓ is no longer possible. On the other hand for the compliance relation the action ✓ matters only in the stuck states of the client; its presence in all other states is immaterial.

Example 3.6. [1 and internal moves]
Here we prove that $\sqsubseteq_{\text{CLT}}^{\text{cpl}} \not\subseteq\ \sqsubseteq_{\underset{\sim \text{CLT}}{}}^{\text{tst}}$ even for finite clients (without recursion).
Recall the client r of Example 2.7; its LTS is depicted in column (a) of Fig. 6.

On the one hand, $r \sqsubseteq_{\text{CLT}}^{\text{cpl}} 0$. This is true because for every p, $r \parallel p \xrightarrow{\tau} 0 \parallel p$; thus $r \dashv p$ and Lemma 2.3 imply that $0 \dashv p$. On the other hand $r \not\sqsubseteq_{\underset{\sim \text{CLT}}{}}^{\text{tst}} 0$, because 0 MUST r (as $r \xrightarrow{\checkmark}$). However 0 $\cancel{\text{MUST}}$ 0. □

Example 3.7. [1 and interactions]
Here we show that $\sqsubseteq_{\underset{\sim \text{CLT}}{}}^{\text{tst}} \not\subseteq \sqsubseteq_{\text{CLT}}^{\text{cpl}}$. Let $r_1 = \alpha.\,1$ and $r_2 = 1 + \beta.\gamma.\,1$; their LTS is in column (b) of Fig. 6.

Regardless of the server p we have p MUST r_2 because $r_2 \xrightarrow{\checkmark}$. It follows trivially that $r_1 \sqsubseteq_{\underset{\sim \text{CLT}}{}}^{\text{tst}} r_2$. However, $r_1 \not\sqsubseteq_{\text{CLT}}^{\text{cpl}} r_2$; a typical server which distinguishes the two clients is $p = \overline{\alpha}.\,0 + \overline{\beta}.\,0$. The proof that $r_1 \dashv p$ amounts to checking that the relation $\{\,(r_1, p),\ (1, 0)\,\}$ is a co-inductivecompliance. The fact that $r_2 \not\dashv p$ is due to Lemma 2.3 and the computation $r_2 \parallel p \xrightarrow{\tau} \gamma.\,1 \parallel 0 \xrightarrow{\tau}\!\!\!/$. □

A further restriction of CCS$_{web}$ provides a language in which this difference in the treatment of ✓ does not materialise. Let SB^f be the language given by the following grammar,

$$p, q, r \ ::= \ 1 \ \mid\ \sum_{i \in I} \alpha_i.p_i \ \mid\ \sum_{i \in I} \tau.\overline{\alpha_i}.p_i$$

where $\alpha \in Act$, I is a finite non-emptyset, and the actions α_is are pairwise distinct. This language gives rise to the LTS $\langle$ SB^f, $\longrightarrow$, Act$_\tau\,$✓ $\rangle$ in the usual manner. The language SB^f is essentially the finite part of the session behaviours of [Bd10], which we can think of as the *first-order* part of the session types used in [GH05].

Here the language is finite so as to avoid duplicating Example 3.5. But the finiteness of the language implies also that the computations are finite. This is sufficient to show that a client and a server in compliance are related by the MUST testing as well.

Lemma 3.8. If SB^f if $r \dashv p$ then p MUST r.

Proof. Suppose that $r \dashv p$. We have to show that all the maximal computations of $r \parallel p$ are successful. Fix such a computation. Since r and p are finite, the computation must have a terminal state, say $r' \parallel p' \overset{\tau}{\nrightarrow}$. The hypothesis $r \dashv p$ and the reductions $r \parallel p \Longrightarrow r' \parallel p'$ imply that $r' \dashv p'$. As this state is stable, the definition of compliance ensures that $r' \overset{\checkmark}{\longrightarrow}$; thus the maximal computation we picked is successful. □

Thanks to the restrictive syntax of SB^f, the converse of Lemma 3.8 is also true. This is due to two reasons. One is a general property of MUST borne out by Lemma 3.10. The other reason is the next lemma, which explains why the different treatment of $\checkmark$ does not materialse in SB^f.

Lemma 3.9. In SB^f, if $p \overset{\checkmark}{\longrightarrow}$ then $p = 1$.

Proof. In principle $p \overset{\checkmark}{\longrightarrow}$ may be proven by using one of the rules [A-OK], [R-EXT-L], and [R-EXT-R]. But the last two rules can be used only on external sums, and in SB^f these sums do not engage in $\checkmark$. It follows that $p \overset{\checkmark}{\longrightarrow}$ must be due to rule [A-OK], hence $p = 1$. □

The previous lemma is not true for CCS. For instance the client r of Example (2.7) performs the action $\checkmark$, but $r \neq 1$.

Lemma 3.10. In CCS if p MUST r, $r \parallel p \overset{\tau}{\longrightarrow} r' \parallel p'$ and $r' \overset{\checkmark}{\nrightarrow}$ then p' MUST p'.

Proof. (Outline) To prove the result it suffices to add to every maximal computation of $r' \parallel p'$ the suffix $r \parallel p \overset{\tau}{\longrightarrow} r' \parallel p'$, and then use the hypothesis p MUST r and $r \overset{\checkmark}{\nrightarrow}$. □

Lemma 3.11. In SB^f, if p MUST r then $r \dashv p$.

Proof. We show that the next relation is a co-inductive compliance,

$$\mathcal{R} = \{ (r, p) \mid p \text{ MUST } r \}$$

Pick a pair $r \mathcal{R} p$. Suppose $r \parallel p \overset{\tau}{\nrightarrow}$. Then the definition of MUST ensures that $r \overset{\checkmark}{\longrightarrow}$. Suppose $r \parallel p \overset{\tau}{\longrightarrow} r' \parallel p'$. If $r \overset{\checkmark}{\longrightarrow}$ then Lemma 3.9 lets us prove that $r' \overset{\checkmark}{\longrightarrow}$. In turn this ensures that p' MUST r'. If $r \overset{\checkmark}{\nrightarrow}$, then Lemma 3.10 implies that p' MUST r'. □

Theorem 3.12. In SB^f,

(1) $p_1 \sqsubseteq^{\mathsf{tst}}_{\underset{\sim}{\mathsf{SVR}}} p_2$ if and only if $p_1 \sqsubseteq^{\mathsf{cpl}}_{\mathsf{SVR}} p_2$

(2) $r_1 \sqsubseteq^{\mathsf{tst}}_{\underset{\sim}{\mathsf{CLT}}} r_2$ if and only if $r_1 \sqsubseteq^{\mathsf{cpl}}_{\mathsf{CLT}} r_2$

Proof. This is a direct consequence of Lemmas 3.11 and 3.8.

4   Conclusion

In this paper we have shown the differences between the sub-contract preorders [CGP09, Pad10, Ber13] and the testing preorders [DH84, BH13]. Another study of sub-contract relations is [BMPR10], There different compliances are used; two similar to ⊣, and a fair one.

The sub-contract relation was first proposed in [CCLP06], and further developed in [LP07, CGP09, Pad10]. For instance, the latter papers show how to adapt the behaviour of contracts by applying filters, or orchestrators; thereby defining weak sub-contracts, whose elements can be forced (by filtering) into the sub-contract. Reference [CGP09] also shows an encoding of WS-BPEL activities into the language of contracts. A result similar to Theorem 3.4 was already established in [LP07], and it has been referenced by , [Pad09, Pad10, Proposition 2.7], and [CGP09, pag. 13]. The sub-contract for clients was proposed first in [Bd10], and it is instrumental in modelling the subtyping for first-order session types [GH05]. The preorder that models the subtyping coincides with a combination of the client sub-contract and a server one. This model was proven sound in [Bd10], fully-abstract in [BH12], and extended to higher-order session types in [Ber13].

References

[Bd10]   Barbanera, F., de'Liguoro, U.: Two notions of sub-behaviour for session-based client/server systems. In: Kutsia, T., Schreiner, W., Fernández, M. (eds.) PPDP, pp. 155–164. ACM (2010)

[Ber13]   Bernardi, G.: Behavioural equivalences for web services. Ph.D. thesis, Trinity College Dublin. https://www.scss.tcd.ie/~bernargi (2013)

[BH12]   Bernardi, G., Hennessy, M.: Modelling session types using contracts. In: Ossowski, S., Lecca, P. (eds.) SAC, pp. 1941–1946. ACM (2012)

[BH13]   Bernardi, G., Hennessy, M.: Mutually testing processes (extended abstract). In: D'Argenio, P.R., Melgratti, H. (eds.) CONCUR 2013. LNCS, vol. 8052, pp. 61–75. Springer, Heidelberg (2013)

[BMPR10]   Bugliesi, M., Macedonio, D., Pino, L., Rossi, S.: Compliance preorders for web services. In: Laneve, C., Su, J. (eds.) WS-FM 2009. LNCS, vol. 6194, pp. 76–91. Springer, Heidelberg (2010)

[CCLP06]   Carpineti, S., Castagna, G., Laneve, C., Padovani, L.: A formal account of contracts for web services. In: Bravetti, M., Núñez, M., Zavattaro, G. (eds.) WS-FM 2006. LNCS, vol. 4184, pp. 148–162. Springer, Heidelberg (2006)

[CGP09] Castagna, G., Gesbert, N., Padovani, L.: A theory of contracts for web services. ACM Trans. Program. Lang. Syst. **31**(5), 1–61 (2009). (Supersedes the article in POPL '08)

[CH93] Cleaveland, R., Hennessy, M.: Testing equivalence as a bisimulation equivalence. Formal Asp. Comput. **5**(1), 1–20 (1993)

[CH10] Cerone, A., Hennessy, M.: Process behaviour: Formulae vs. tests (extended abstract). In: Fröschle, S.B., Valencia, F.D. (eds) EXPRESS'10. EPTCS, vol. 41, pp. 31–45 (2010)

[DH84] De Nicola, R., Hennessy, M.: Testing equivalences for processes. Theoret. Comput. Sci. **34**, 83–133 (1984)

[GH05] Gay, S.J., Hole, M.: Subtyping for session types in the pi calculus. Acta Inf. **42**(2–3), 191–225 (2005)

[Hen85] Hennessy, M.: Algebraic Theory of Processes. MIT Press, Cambridge (1985)

[Hoa85] Hoare, C.A.R.: Communicating Sequential Processes. Prentice-Hall, Hardcover (1985)

[LP07] Laneve, C., Padovani, L.: The must preorder revisited. In: Caires, L., Vasconcelos, V.T. (eds.) CONCUR 2007. LNCS, vol. 4703, pp. 212–225. Springer, Heidelberg (2007)

[Mil89] Milner, R.: Communication and Concurrency. PHI Series in Computer Science. Prentice Hall, Upper Saddle River (1989)

[Pad09] Padovani, L.: Contract-based discovery and adaptation of web services. In: Bernardo, M., Padovani, L., Zavattaro, G. (eds.) SFM 2009. LNCS, vol. 5569, pp. 213–260. Springer, Heidelberg (2009)

[Pad10] Padovani, L.: Contract-based discovery of web services modulo simple orchestrators. Theor. Comput. Sci. **411**(37), 3328–3347 (2010)

[THK94] Takeuchi, K., Honda, K., Kubo, M.: An interaction-based language and its typing system. In: Halatsis, C., Philokyprou, G., Maritsas, D., Theodoridis, S. (eds.) PARLE 1994. LNCS, vol. 817. Springer, Heidelberg (1994)

Scalable Session Programming for Heterogeneous High-Performance Systems

Nicholas Ng[(✉)], Nobuko Yoshida, and Wayne Luk

Imperial College London, London, UK
{nickng,n.yoshida,w.luk}@imperial.ac.uk

Abstract. This paper introduces a programming framework based on the theory of session types for safe and scalable parallel designs. Session-based languages can offer a clear and tractable framework to describe communications between parallel components and guarantee communication-safety and deadlock-freedom by compile-time type checking and parallel MPI code generation. Many representative communication topologies such as ring or scatter-gather can be programmed and verified in session-based programming languages. We use a case study involving N-body simulation, dense and sparse matrix multiplication to illustrate the session-based programming style. Finally, we outline a proposal to integrate session programming with heterogeneous systems for efficient and communication-safe parallel applications by a combination of code generation and type checking.

1 Introduction

Software programs that utilises parallelism to increase performance is no longer an exclusive feature of high performance applications. Modern day hardware, from multicore processor in smartphones to multicore multi-graphics card gaming systems, all take advantage of parallelism to improve performance. Message-passing is a scalable programming model for parallel programming, where the user has to make communication between components explicit using the basic primitives of message *send* and *receive*.

However, writing correct parallel programs is far from straightforward – blindly parallelising components with data dependencies might leave the overall program in an inconsistent state; arbitrary interleaving of parallel executions combined with complex flow control can easily lead to unexpected behaviour, such as blocked access to resources in a circular chain (i.e. deadlock) or mismatched send-receive pairs. These unsafe communications are a source of non-termination or incorrect execution of a program. Thus tracking and avoiding communication errors of parallel programs is as important as ensuring their functional correctness.

This work focuses on a programming framework which can automatically ensure deadlock-freedom and communication-safety i.e. matching communication pairs, for message-passing parallel programs based on the theory of *session*

S. Counsell and M. Núñez (Eds.): SEFM 2013 Collocated Workshops, LNCS 8368, pp. 82–98, 2014.
DOI: 10.1007/978-3-319-05032-4_7, © Springer International Publishing Switzerland 2014

types [6,7]. Towards the end of this paper, we discuss how this session-based programming framework can fit in heterogeneous computing environments with reconfigurable acceleration hardware such as Field Programmable Gate Arrays (FPGAs).

To illustrate how session types can track communication mismatches, consider the parallel program in Fig. 1 that exchanges two values between two processes.

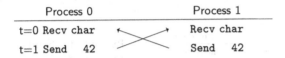

Process 0		Process 1
t=0 Recv char		Recv char
t=1 Send 42		Send 42

Fig. 1. Mismatched communication.

In this notation, the arrow points from the sender of the message to the intended receiver. Both `Process0` and `Process1` start by waiting to receive a value from the other processes, hence we have a typical deadlock situation.

Process 0		Process 1
t=0 Send 42	⟶	Recv char
t=1 Recv char	⟵	Send 42

Fig. 2. Communication order swapped.

A simple solution is to swap the order of the receive and send commands for one of the processes, for example, Process 0, shown in Fig. 2.

However, the above program still has mismatched communication pairs and causing type error. Parallel programming usually involves debugging and resolving these communication problems, which is often a tedious task.

Using the session programming methodology, we can not only statically check that the above programs are incorrect, but can also encourage programmers to write safe designs from the beginning, guided by the information of types. Session types [6,7] have been actively studied as a high-level abstraction of structured communication-based programming, which are able to accurately and intelligibly represent and capture complex interaction patterns between communicating parties.

The two examples above have session types shown in Figs. 3 and 4 respectively.

In the session types above, Send `int` stands for output with type `int` and Recv `int` stands for input with type `int`. The session types are used to check that the communications between `Process 0` and `Process 1` are *incompatible* (i.e. incorrect) because one process must have a *dual type* of the other.

Process 0: Recv char; Send int   Process 0: Send int; Recv char
Process 1: Recv char; Send int   Process 1: Recv char; Send int

Fig. 3. Session types for original exam-   **Fig. 4.** Session types for swapped
ple.   example.

On the other hand, the following program is correct, having neither deadlock nor type errors, since it has a *mutually dual* session types shown on the right hand side:

Process 0		Process 1
t=0 Send 'a'	⟶	Recv char
t=1 Recv int	⟵	Send 42

Process 0: Send char; Recv int
Process 1: Recv char; Send int

In the session types theory, Recv type is dual to Send type, hence the type of Process 0 is dual of the type of Process 1.

The above compatibility checking is simple and straightforward in the case of two parties. We can extend this idea to multiparty processes (i.e. more than two processes) based on multiparty session type theory [7]. Type-checking for parallel programs with multiparty processes is done statically and is efficient, with a polynomial-time bound with respect to the size of the program.

Below we list the contributions of this paper.

– Novel programming languages for communications in parallel designs and two session-based approaches to guarantee communication-safety and deadlock freedom (Sect. 2)
– Implementations of advanced communication topologies for parallel computer clusters by session types (Sect. 3)
– Case studies including N-body simulation, dense and sparse matrix multiplication to illustrate session programming for parallel computers (Sect. 4)

2   Session-Based Language Design

2.1   Overview

As a language independent framework for communication-based programming, session types can be applied to different programming languages and environments. Previous work on Session Java (SJ) [8,14] integrated sessions into the object-oriented programming paradigm as an extension of the Java language, and was applied to parallel programming [14]. Session types have also been implemented in different languages such as OCaml, Haskell, F#, Scala and Python. This section explains session types and their applications, focussing on an implementation of sessions in the C language (Session C) as a parallel programming framework. Amongst all these different incarnations of session types, the key idea remains unchanged. A session-based system provides (1) a set of predefined primitives or interfaces for session communication and (2) a session typing system which can verify, at compile time, that each program conforms to its session type. Once the programs are type checked, they run correctly without deadlock nor communication errors.

2.2 Multiparty Session Programming

Session C [12,21] implements a generalised session type theory, *multiparty session types* (MPST) [7]. The MPST theory extends the original binary session types [6] by describing communications across multiple participants in the form of *global protocols*. Our development uses a Java-like protocol description language Scribble [5,16] for describing the multiparty session types. Figure 5 explains two design flows of Session C programming. In the type checking approach, the programmer writes a global protocol starting from the keyword `protocol` and the protocol name. In the first box of Fig. 5, the protocol named as P contains one communication with a value typed by `int` from participant A to participant B. For Session C implementation, the programmer uses the *endpoint protocol* generated by the projection algorithm in Scribble. For example, the above global protocol is projected to A to obtain `int to B` (as in the second box) and to B to obtain `int from A`. Each endpoint protocol gives a template for developing safe code for each participant and as a basis for static verification. Since we started from a correct global protocol, if endpoint programs (in the third box) conform to the induced endpoint protocols, it automatically ensures deadlock-free, well-matched interactions. This endpoint projection approach is particularly useful when many participants are communicating under complex communication topologies. Due to space limitation, this paper omits the full definition of global protocols, and will explain our framework and examples using only endpoint protocols introduced in the next subsection.

2.3 Protocols for Session Communications

The endpoint protocols include types for basic message-passing and for capturing control flow patterns. We use the endpoint protocol description derived from Scribble to algorithmically specify high-level communication of distributed parallel programs as a library of network communications. A protocol abstracts away the contents but keeps the high level structures of communications as a series of type primitives.

The syntax of Scribble is described in details in [5,16], and can be categorised to three types of operations: *message-passing*, *choice* and *iteration*.

Message Passing. It represents that messages (or data) being communicated from one process to another; in the language it is denoted by the statements `datatype to P1` or `datatype from P0` which stands for sending/receiving data of `datatype` to the participant identified by P0/P1 respectively. Notice that the protocol does not specify the value being sent/received, but instead designate the

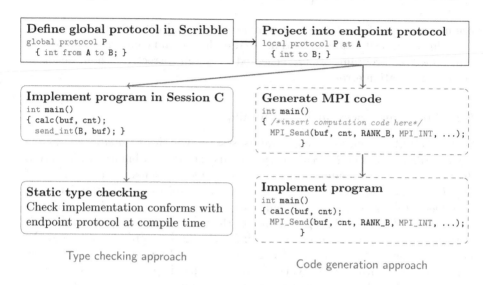

Fig. 5. Session C design flows.

datatype (which could be primitive types such as `int` or composite types), indicating its nature as a high-level abstraction of communication.

Choice. It allows a communication to exhibit different behavioural flows in a program. We denote a choice by a pair of primitives, `choice from` and `choice to`, meaning a distributed choice receiver and choice maker, respectively. A choice maker first decides a branch to take, identified by its `label`, and executes its associated block of statements. The chosen label is sent to the choice receiver, which looks up the label in its choices and execute the its associated block of statements. This ensures the two processes are synchronised in terms of the choice taken.

Iteration. It can represent repetitive communication patterns. We represent recursion by the `rec` primitive (short for recursion), followed by the block of statements to be repeated, enclosed by braces. The operation does not require communication as it is a local recursion. However two communicating processes have to ensure both of their endpoint protocols contains recursion, otherwise their protocols will not be compatible.

2.4   Session C

We present two approaches to session programming in C, using the Session C framework. The first approach is by type checking of user written code, using a simple session programming API we provided. The second approach is by MPI code generation from protocols.

Type Checking Approach In the type checking approach, a user implements a parallel program using the simple API provided by the library, following communication protocols stipulated in Scribble. Once a program is complete, the type checker verifies that the program code matches that of the endpoint protocol description in Scribble to ensure that the program is safe. The core runtime API corresponds the endpoint protocol as described below.

Message Passing Primitives in Session C are written as `send_datatype` (`participant, data`) for message send, which is `datatype to participant` in the protocol, and `recv_datatype (participant, &data)` for message receive (`datatype from participant` in the protocol).

Choice in Session C is a combination of ordinary C control-flow syntax and session primitives. For a choice maker, each if-then or if-else block in a session-typed choice starts with `outbranch(participant, branchLabel)` to mark the beginning of a choice. `inbranch(participant, &branchLabel)` is a choice receiver, used as the argument of a switch-case statement, and each case-block is distinguished by the `branchLabel` corresponding to a choice in the `choice from` block in the protocol.

Iteration in Session C corresponds to `while` loops in C. As no communication is required, the implementation simply repeats a block of code consisting of above session primitives in a `rec` recursion block.

Code Generation Approach In the code generation approach, given a Scribble protocol, we generate an MPI parallel program skeleton. The program skeleton contains all the MPI code needed, the user inserts code that performs computation on the input data (e.g. for scientific calculation) between the MPI primitives, completing the program.

This approach is part of a larger extension of the Scribble language to support parameterised session types [2]. The extension, *Parameterised Scribble*, or Pabble [11], uses indices to parameterise participants. Participants can be defined and accessed in an array-like notation, in order to denote logical groupings of related participants. For example, a parallel algorithm that uses many parallel workers, can define a group of participants using `role participant[1..N]`, and a pipeline of message passing is written in Pabble as `datatype from participant[i:1..N-1] to participant[i+1]`. Pabble protocols can be written once, and a protocol with different number of participants can be instantiated by changing the value of N. MPI code generated from Pabble protocols can also take advantage of this feature and will be scalable over different number of processes.

These two approaches to session programming complement each other and cover different use cases: critical applications can use the type checking approach to ensure that the written program is communication and type safe; whereas scalable and parametric applications can use the MPI code generation capability to create communication safe and type safe parallel programs.

3   Advanced Communication Topologies for Clusters

This section shows how session endpoint protocols introduced in Sect. 2.3 can be used to specify advanced, complex communications for clusters. Consider a heterogeneous cluster with multiple kinds of acceleration hardware, such as GPUs or FPGAs, as Processing Elements (PEs). To allow a safe and high performance collaborative computation on the cluster, we can describe communications between PEs by our communication primitives. The PEs can be abstracted as small computation functions with a basic interface for data input and result output, hence we can easily describe high-level understanding of the program by the session types.

We list some widely used structured communication patterns that form the backbones of implementations of parallel algorithms. These patterns were chosen because they exemplify representative communication patterns used in clusters. Computation can interleave between statements if no conflict in the data dependencies exists. The implementation follows the theory of the optimisation for session types developed in [10], maximising overlapped messaging.

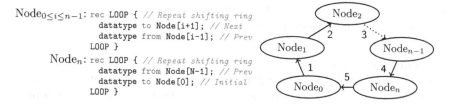

```
Node0≤i≤n-1: rec LOOP { // Repeat shifting ring
               datatype to Node[i+1]; // Next
               datatype from Node[i-1]; // Prev
             LOOP }
      Noden: rec LOOP { // Repeat shifting ring
               datatype from Node[N-1]; // Prev
               datatype to Node[0]; // Initial
             LOOP }
```

Fig. 6. Endpoint protocols of Ring.   **Fig. 7.** n-node ring pipeline.

Ring Topology. pology, as depicted in Fig. 7, processes or PEs are arranged in a pipeline, where the end of the node of the pipeline is connected to the initial node. Each of the connections of the nodes is represented by an individual endpoint session. We use N-body simulation as an example for ring topology. Note that the communication patterns between the middle $n - 1$ Nodes are identical. The endpoint protocol is shown in Fig. 6.

Map-Reduce Pattern. Map-reduce is a common scatter-gather pattern used to parallelise tasks that can be easily partitioned with few dependencies between the partitioned computations. The endpoint protocol and the topology is shown in Figs. 8 and 9 respectively. It combines the map pattern which partitions and distributes data to parallel workers by a Master coordination node, and the reduce pattern which collects and combines completed results from all parallel workers. At the end of a map-reduce, the Master coordination node will have a copy of the final results combined into a single datum. All Workers in a map-reduce topology share a simple communication pattern, where they only interact with the Master coordination node. The Master node will have a communication pattern containing all known Workers. The MPI operation `MPI_Alltoall` is a communication-only instance of the map-reduce pattern for all of the nodes, and only applies memory concatenation to the collected set of data. Our endpoint types can represent this topology with more fine-grained primitives so that we can obtain performance gain by communication-computation overlap. Although collective operations are more efficient in cases where the implementations take advantage of the underlying architectures, fine-grained primitives can more readily allow partial data-structures to be distributed, without the need to create new copies of data or calculating offsets (as in `MPI_Alltoallv`) for transmission.

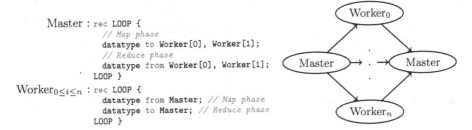

Master : `rec LOOP {`
      `// Map phase`
      `datatype to Worker[0], Worker[1];`
      `// Reduce phase`
      `datatype from Worker[0], Worker[1];`
      `LOOP }`
Worker$_{0 \le i \le n}$: `rec LOOP {`
      `datatype from Master; // Map phase`
      `datatype to Master; // Reduce phase`
      `LOOP }`

Fig. 8. Endpoint protocols of Map-reduce.

Fig. 9. Map-reduce pattern.

4 Case Studies

This section presents case studies of using Scribble protocols in parallel programming. All of these examples are representative patterns from common parallel patterns known as Dwarfs [1]. The Dwarf evaluation metric was proposed as a collection of high-level, core parallel communication patterns from important scientific and engineering methods. Each of these patterns is called a *Dwarf*, which represents one category of patterns and covers a broad range of concrete algorithm implementations. Dwarfs are used to evaluate our session-based protocol language and our programming methodology because they are not language or optimisation specific, being able to express the Dwarfs confirms that our approach is general enough to be extended to more practical use cases.

We have chosen N-body simulation, an example of particle methods dwarf, dense matrix-vector multiplication, a dense linear algebra dwarf, and sparse matrix-vector multiplication, a sparse linear algebra dwarf, to show how Scribble and MPI can be used together for parallel programming from either of our two session-based approaches.

4.1 N-Body Simulation

We implemented a 2-dimension N-body simulation using a ring topology. Each Worker is initially assigned to a partition of the input data. In every round of the ring propagation, each Worker receives a set of partitioned input from a neighbour, and pipelines the input data received from the previous round to the other neighbour. This propagation continues until the set of particles have been received by all Workers once. The algorithm will then perform one step of global update to calculate the new positions of the particles after one time step of the simulation.

Listing 1 is the protocol specification of the Worker participant of our N-body simulation implementation, and Listing 2 is the automatically generated endpoint version, both written in the syntax of parameterised Scribble.

```
1   global protocol Nbody(role Worker[0..N] {
2     rec RING {
3       // Workers 0 to N: Worker[i] -> [i+1]
4       int from Worker[i:1..N-1] to Worker[i+1];
5
6       // Data from Worker[N] -> [0]
7       int from Worker[N] to Worker[0];
8
9       continue RING;
10    }
11  }
```

```
1   local protocol Nbody at Worker[0..N] {
2     rec RING {
3       // Workers 0 to N: Worker[i] -> [i+1]
4       if Worker[i:1..N] int from Worker[i-1];
5       if Worker[i:0..N-1] int to Worker[i+1];
6       // Data from Worker[N] -> r[0]
7       if Worker[0] int from Worker[N];
8       if Worker[N] int to Worker[0];
9       continue RING;
10    }
11  }
```

Listing 1. Protocol of N-body simulation. **Listing 2.** Worker endpoint of N-body protocol.

The block rec RING {} means recursion, and represents the repeating ring propagation in the algorithm. The line if Worker[i:1..N] int from Worker[i-1] stands for receiving a message from my previous neighbour Worker[i-1] with a message of type int, given that the current participant is one of Worker[1], ..., or Worker[N]. The protocol generates MPI code equivalent to Listing 3.

```
1   while (i++<N) {
2     if (1<=rank && rank<=N) MPI_Recv(rbuf, count, rank-1, MPI_INT, ..);
3     // (Sub-compute) Send received data to FPGA to process ..
4     if (0<=rank && rank<=N-1) MPI_Send(sbuf, count, rank+1, MPI_INT, ..);
5     if (rank==0) MPI_Recv(rbuf, count, N, MPI_INT, ..);
6     // (Sub-compute) Send received data to FPGA to process ..
7     if (rank==N) MPI_Send(sbuf, count, 0, MPI_INT, ..); }
8   // Perform global update after round
```

Listing 3. MPI implementation of Worker endpoint.

In MPI, all processes share the same source code and compiled program file, and they are only distinguished at runtime by their assigned process id. The process id is stored in the rank variable, and is available throughout the program to calculate participants addresses. In the above MPI code, MPI_Send and MPI_Recv are the primitives in the MPI library to send and receive data, and all the lines are guarded by a rank check. The variables sbuf and rbuf stand for send buffer and receive buffer respectively, and count is the number of elements to send/receive (i.e. array size); MPI_INT is an MPI defined macro to indicate the data being sent/received is of type int.

The ring topology above is a simple yet powerful topology to distribute data between multiple participants in small chunks. This allows more sub-computation and will potentially allow more overlapping between communication and computation.

A Scribble protocol contains the interaction patterns (i.e. the session typing) for a set of participants. It contains sufficient information to generate the MPI code shown above.

4.2 Dense Matrix-Vector Multiplication

Dense matrix-vector multiplication takes a $M \times N$ matrix and multiply it by a N dimensional vector to get a N dimensional vector result. The multiplication can be parallelised by partitioning the input matrix to N segments by row-wise block striping shown in Fig. 10 and distributed to N processes. Each process gets a copy of the vector, and each elements in the vector can be calculated by the processes in parallel.

Listing 4 shows a protocol for our dense matrix-vector multiplication. The Worker[0] is the coordinator which distributes the partitions to each Workers. The primitive foreach (i:1..N) is a foreach-loop, which iterates from 1 to N using the index variable i. Inside the foreach, Worker[1..N] sends the offset and length of the partitions to each Worker (Line 4 and 5)respectively, followed by the actual matrix elements (Line 6).Vector B, which is of size N, is broadcasted to all processes by the coordinator on Line 9. Finally, the results of each Workers are gathered by the coordinator and combined to get the result of the matrix multiplication (Line 14).

```
1   global protocol DenseMatVec(role Worker[0..N]){
2     // Scatter Matrix A
3     foreach (i:1..N) {
4       LBound(int) from Worker[0] to Worker[i];
5       UBound(int) from Worker[0] to Worker[i];
6       Data(double) from Worker[0] to Worker[i];
7     }
8     // Scatter Vector B
9     (double) from Worker[0] to Worker[1..N];
10    // --- Perform calculation ---
11    // Gather data
12    (double) from Worker[1..N] to Worker[0];
13  }
```

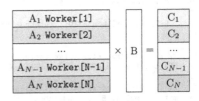

Listing 4. Global protocol of dense matrix-vector multiplication.

Fig. 10. Partitioning of input matrix.

An MPI implementation following above protocol has the code structure shown below. In the initial phase of the calculation, the coordinator, the process of rank 0 (Line 5–17), uses a `for` loop to iterate through the worker process ids (processes with ranks above 0, up to the total number of processes `size`) and calculates the `lbound` and `ubound` for each of the participants, where `lbound` is the first row of the partition, and `ubound` is the last. The partition is then sent to the corresponding `Worker[i]`. Other `Worker` processes receive the values and store locally.

This is followed by a broadcast on Line 25 using an `MPI_Bcast` with root `Worker[0]` for the workers to receive the input vector. A partial result, `C`, is then calculated on each worker, and the result collected by the coordinator using `MPI_Gather`. `MPI_Gather` collects the partial results, then combines them in the `Result` N dimensional array.

The implementation show how our session protocol descriptions can also correspond to collective operations, such as `(double)from Worker[0] to Worker[1..N]` and `MPI_Bcast`, or `(double)from Worker[1..N] to Worker[0]` and `MPI_Gather`.

```
1    double A[A_ROWS][A_COLS]; // Matrix A
2    double B[B_COLS]; // Vector B
3    double C[B_COLS]; // Partial result
4    ...
5    if (rank == 0) {
6      for (i = 1; i < size; i++) { // Calculate then send to each Worker
7        // Calculate LowerBound and UpperBound for each Worker
8        lbound = (i - 1) * partition_size;
9        ubound = lbound + partion_size;
10
11       MPI_Send(&lbound, 1, MPI_INT, Worker[i], LBound, ...);
12       MPI_Send(&ubound, 1, MPI_INT, Worker[i], UBound, ...);
13
14       // Send partition of matrix A
15       MPI_Send(&A[lbound][0], (ubound-lbound) * A_COLS, MPI_DOUBLE, Worker[i], Data, ...);
16     }
17   } else if (rank > 0) { // Workers, receiving work
18     MPI_Recv(&lbound, 1, MPI_INT, Worker[0], LBound, ...);
19     MPI_Recv(&ubound, 1, MPI_INT, Worker[0], UBound, ...);
20
21     MPI_Recv(&A[lbound][0], (ubound-lbound) * A_COLS, MPI_DOUBLE, Worker[0], Data, ...);
22   }
23
24   // All Workers receive the vector B
25   MPI_Bcast(&B, B_ROWS, MPI_DOUBLE, Worker[0], ...);
26   ...
27   // Calculate matrix multiplication
28   mat_vec_mul(A, B, lbound, ubound, C);
29   ...
30   // ... Gather results to Worker[0] ...
31   MPI_Gather(C, 1, MPI_DOUBLE, Result, 1, MPI_DOUBLE, Worker[0], ...);
32
```

Listing 5. MPI implementation of dense matrix-vector multiplication.

4.3   Sparse Matrix-Vector Multiplication

Finally we show an implementation of a direct sparse matrix-vector multiplication. Sparse matrices are often used for data representation that are too large to fit in memory as an array, but the content is sparse and can be efficiently compressed to a more compact format. Our implementation uses a $M \times N$ sparse matrix input stored in a compressed sparse row (CSR) format, where the data are represented by three arrays.

- `vals`: a contiguous array containing all values of the sparse matrix in a left-to-right, top-to-bottom order. This compact storage of the matrix skips all empty (or zero) cells in the matrix and only contains cells with a value.
- `row_ptr`: an array containing indices for the `vals` array, each element contains the accumulated total of elements in each row. For example, [1, 3, 4, 8] means that row 0 has 1 element, row 1 has 2 elements, row 2 has 1 element and row 3 has 4 elements. This array has the same size as the total number of rows.
- `col_ind`: the column indices for each of the values in `vals`. This array has the same size of `vals`.

The three arrays combined is sufficient to represent a sparse matrix, or a partition of the sparse matrix.

The protocol to perform a sparse matrix-vector multiplication is shown in listing 6. In the protocol, the partitioned matrix rows in CSR format are sent to each worker as separate row, col and values arrays (Line 3,4 and 5). The N dimensional vector is then sent to all workers. The results of the calculation by each `Workers` are sent back to `Worker[0]` (Line 8).

```
1   global protocol SparseMatVec(role PE[0..N]) {
2       /* Distribute data */
3       (int) from W[0] to W[1..N]; // row_ptr
4       (int) from W[0] to W[1..N]; // col_ind
5       (double) from W[0] to W[1..N]; // vals
6       (double) from W[0] to W[1..N]; // vector
7       /* Output vector */
8       (double) from W[1..N] to W[0];
9   }
```

Listing 6. Global protocol of sparse matrix-vector multiplication.

A corresponding implementation for the above protocol may look like the MPI code below:

```
1    MPI_Comm_size(MPI_COMM_WORLD, &size);
2    int nr_of_rows=MATRIX_ROWS/size;
3    ...
4    MPI_Scatter(row_ptr, nr_of_rows, MPI_INT,..);
5    ...
6    // calculate number of indices for each process
7    ...
8    MPI_Scatterv(col_ind, nr_of_elems, MPI_INT, ...);
9    MPI_Scatterv(vals, nr_of_elems, MPI_DOUBLE, ...);
10   ...
11   MPI_Bcast(vector, MATRIX_ROWS, MPI_DOUBLE, Worker[0], ...); // Distribute vector
12   ...
13   // Calculate matrix multiplication
14   mat_vec_mul(row_ptr, col_ind, vals, vector, C);
15   ...
16   MPI_Gather(C, 1, MPI_DOUBLE, Result, 1, MPI_DOUBLE, Worker[0], ...);
```

Listing 7. MPI implementation of sparse matrix-vector multiplication.

Each process starts by calculating the expected number of rows it will be owner of, and we assume that the number of rows for each process is the same and the total number of rows can divide exactly by the total number of processes. Next we use MPI_Scatter to distribute segments of the row_ptr array to each worker process, which sends segments of a given input memory to other processes based on their rank and the segment position in the memory (Line 4).

nr_of_elems is an array containing the number of elements to be sent to each worker. Since in a sparse matrix the number of elements in each row is not fixed, the nr_of_elements array contains the number of matrix elements each worker receives. The indices of the array correspond to the rank of the workers and the column index col_ind is distributed to each worker process by MPI_Scatterv (Line 8), a variant of the MPI_Scatter, where the v stands for variable size as opposed to fixed size in MPI_Scatter. Similarly, the actual matrix element values are distributed to all workers by a call to MPI_Scatterv on Line 9, using the same nr_of_elems to specify the number of elements for each worker.

Once the workers have received the matrix partitions, the coordinator distributes the N dimension vector by MPI_Bcast to all workers to perform the matrix-vector calculation for the rows of the sparse matrix each processor has.

Finally, as in the dense matrix-vector multiplication example, the results are collected by the root worker Worker[0] using a MPI_Gather. In this implementation, we use exclusively collective operations to distribute and collect results as it is more efficient with the CSR data format. Notice that the protocol does not distinguish between different modes of MPI_Scatter, in particular, the Scribble statement (int) Worker[0] to Worker[1..N]; corresponds to both MPI_Scatter and MPI_Scatterv. Hence a single protocol statement can map to multiple implementations, and without external information about the implementation, a code generation tool cannot choose a suitable implementation, and this use case is more suitable for our type checking approach.

5   Related Work and Conclusion

ISP [3,20] and the distributed DAMPI [19] are formal dynamic verifiers which apply model-checking techniques to standard MPI C source code to detect deadlocks using a test harness. The tool exploits independence between thread actions to reduce the state space of possible thread interleavings of an execution, and checks for potentially violating situations. TASS [3,17] is another suite of tools for formal verification of MPI-based parallel programs by model-checking. It constructs an abstract model of a given MPI program and uses symbolic execution to evaluate the model, which is checked for a number of safety properties including potential deadlocks and functional equivalences.

Compared to the test-based and model-checking approaches which may not be able to cover all possible states of the model, the session type-based approach does not depend on external testing or extraction of models from program code for safety. It encourages designing communication-correct programs from the start, especially given the high level communication structure which session types captures.

Recent works [4,9] used annotated MPI code and a software verifier to check the annotated MPI code for compliance against session types. Their bottom-up approach focusses on accurately representing MPI primitives and datatypes, whereas Session C treats them as high level abstractions, ignoring details such as send/receive data payload size.

There are a lot of challenges of verifying real-world MPI source code. MPI is a standardised and platform independent message-passing API, the ubiquitous nature in supercomputing makes it a convenient abstraction layer between software and underlying hardware. In cases such as [15], it was used as a programming model for FPGAs. Hence its specification is intentionally vague, in order to allow different implementations to take advantage of any platform-specific optimisations. For example, there are a number of message transport modes such as the more commonly used `MPI_Send`/`MPI_Recv` (standard mode) or `MPI_Isend`/`MPI_Irecv` (immediate/non-blocking). The modes do not correspond directly to standard synchronous or asynchronous communication modes as one would expect. The different communication modes in MPI have subtle differences in their semantics. Care must be taken when making assumptions and correspondences with high-level Scribble protocols. In addition to standard point-to-point communication primitives, MPI also includes a huge number of primitives such as collective operators, topology construction and process management. A complete session type checking framework will be able to consider these additional information to extract the session types from the source code. Combining the flexibility of the host language (C) and the large number of MPI primitives makes our approach more challenging compared to model checking based approaches. This is because MPI model checkers work by observing the behaviours of the programs, which the same behaviour can be implemented in many different ways; whereas our type based approach requires us to understand the consequences of each primitive because we construct a type model without executing the program.

Furthermore, to apply our approach on low-level host languages, it is important to define a concise and simple correspondence between a Scribble and Pabble protocol to practical implementation, but offer enough flexibility to cope with conventional programs. This correspondence is important to both type checking and code generation: for type checking, the ability to support different programming styles would enable the type checker to check more existing code, and for code generation, the generated code will have a more natural style. For example, MPI uses process IDs (or ranks) to identify processes, and it is valid to perform numeric operations on the ranks to efficiently calculate target processes. A more concrete example is instead of conventional conditional statements, `MPI_Send(buf, cnt, MPI_INT, rank` may be used and the process ID, `rank`, is being used as a boolean to perform a choice, thus a straightforward analysis of `rank` usages would not be sufficient. These are valid programs that exploit the C language features and will require much more extensive analysis.

This paper is an extension of our previous works on Session C [12,13]. In both of the works, parametric protocols and MPI code generation were not explored, this work is a short insight into the benefits of using parametric protocols and potentials of integrating with specialised accelerators, as the framework was evaluated on [18], a heterogeneous cluster with FPGAs.

6 Future Work

Integration with Heterogeneous Workflow. Immediate future works includes refining our MPI code generation tool to better integrate with APIs of specialised hardware. This includes streamlining the data received/sent from MPI directly into input/output buffers of acceleration hardware. Tighter integration between MPI and acceleration hardware will achieve better overall performance of the heterogeneous system.

Type-Directed Optimisations. Extending our type checker to support inferring parameterised MPST from MPI code is a prerequisite for type-directed optimisations. Once parameterised MPST can be extract from MPI code, Session C framework can then extend the support of asynchronous message optimisation [10] described in Session C framework [12] to expressive parameterised protocols. The theoretical and engineering challenges of this future work will be keeping type checking process decidable and representing most, if not all, of the common MPI primitives in Scribble.

Assertion and Error Recovery. We propose the use of runtime assertions for session-based programming in the Session C framework. Assertions are properties that are expected to hold during runtime, and they can complement static type checking. Error recovery is also a topic of interest, as large scale high performance parallel applications often need to gracefully handle unexpected errors such as hardware failures. Type-based approach to error handling and recovery will be explored as part of ongoing research on Scribble.

Adapting to Other Programming Models. Our session-based approach is based on the message passing communication model, which can be used for coordination between heterogeneous nodes. Heterogeneous accelerators all use different programming and communication models, for example, General Purpose computing on GPU (GPGPU) uses a streaming model, and some reconfigurable hardware uses data-flow programming model. Adapting the high-level Scribble and Pabble language to these models will enable session types to be a common language to describe communication behaviour for parallel applications. We are aiming to achieve this by generalising our code generation to generate different target code.

Acknowledgement. The research leading to these results has received funding from EPSRC EP/F003757/01, EP/G015635/01 and the European Union Seventh Framework Programme under grant agreement number 257906, 287804 and 318521. The support by the HiPEAC NoE, the Maxeler University Program, and Xilinx is gratefully acknowledged.

References

1. Asanovic, K., Bodik, R., Demmel, J., Keaveny, T., Keutzer, K., Kubiatowicz, J., Morgan, N., Patterson, D., Sen, K., Wawrzynek, J., Wessel, D., Yelick, K.: A view of the parallel computing landscape. Commun. ACM **52**(10), 56–67 (2009)
2. Deniélou, P.M., Yoshida, N., Bejleri, A., Hu, R.: Parameterised multiparty session types. LMCS **8**(4), 1–47 (2012)
3. Gopalakrishnan, G., Kirby, R.M., Siegel, S., Thakur, R., Gropp, W., Lusk, E., De Supinski, B.R., Schulz, M., Bronevetsky, G.: Formal analysis of mpi-based parallel programs. CACM **54**(12), 82–91 (2011)
4. Honda, K., Marques, E.R.B., Martins, F., Ng, N., Vasconcelos, V.T., Yoshida, N.: Verification of MPI programs using session types. In: Träff, J.L., Benkner, S., Dongarra, J.J. (eds.) EuroMPI 2012. LNCS, vol. 7490, pp. 291–293. Springer, Heidelberg (2012)
5. Honda, K., Mukhamedov, A., Brown, G., Chen, T.-C., Yoshida, N.: Scribbling interactions with a formal foundation. In: Natarajan, R., Ojo, A. (eds.) ICDCIT 2011. LNCS, vol. 6536, pp. 55–75. Springer, Heidelberg (2011)
6. Honda, K., Vasconcelos, V.T., Kubo, M.: Language primitives and type discipline for structured communication-based programming. In: Hankin, C. (ed.) ESOP 1998. LNCS, vol. 1381, p. 122. Springer, Heidelberg (1998)
7. Honda, K., Yoshida, N., Carbone, M.: Multiparty asynchronous session types. In: POPL08. vol. 5201, p. 273 (2008)
8. Hu, R., Yoshida, N., Honda, K.: Session-based distributed programming in java. In: Vitek, J. (ed.) ECOOP 2008. LNCS, vol. 5142, pp. 516–541. Springer, Heidelberg (2008)
9. Marques, E., Martins, F., Vasconcelos, V., Ng, N., Martins, N.: Towards deductive verification of MPI programs against session types. In: Proc. PLACES 2013 EPTCS 137, pp. 103–113 (2013)
10. Mostrous, D., Yoshida, N., Honda, K.: Global principal typing in partially commutative asynchronous sessions. In: Castagna, G. (ed.) ESOP 2009. LNCS, vol. 5502, pp. 316–332. Springer, Heidelberg (2009)
11. Ng, N., Yoshida, N.: Pabble: Parameterised scribble for parallel programming. In: PDP 2014 (2014) (to appear)
12. Ng, N., Yoshida, N., Honda, K.: Multiparty session C: safe parallel programming with message optimisation. In: Furia, C.A., Nanz, S. (eds.) TOOLS 2012. LNCS, vol. 7304, pp. 202–218. Springer, Heidelberg (2012)
13. Ng, N., Yoshida, N., Niu, X.Y., Tsoi, K.H., Luk, W.: Session types: towards safe and fast reconfigurable programming. SIGARCH Comput. Archit. News **40**(5), 22–27 (2012)
14. Ng, N., Yoshida, N., Pernet, O., Hu, R., Kryftis, Y.: Safe parallel programming with session java. In: De Meuter, W., Roman, G.-C. (eds.) COORDINATION 2011. LNCS, vol. 6721, pp. 110–126. Springer, Heidelberg (2011)
15. Saldaña, M., Patel, A., Madill, C., Nunes, D., Wang, D., Chow, P., Wittig, R., Styles, H., Putnam, A.: MPI as a programming model for high-performance reconfigurable computers. ACM TRETS **3**(4), 1–29 (2010)
16. Scribble homepage, http://www.jboss.org/scribble
17. Siegel, S.F., Zirkel, T.K.: Automatic formal verification of MPI-based parallel programs. In: PPoPP'11, p. 309. ACM Press (2011)
18. Tsoi, K.H., Luk, W.: Axel: A Heterogeneous Cluster with FPGAs and GPUs. In: FPGA'10, pp. 115–124. ACM (2010)

19. Vo, A., Aananthakrishnan, S., Gopalakrishnan, G., de Supinski, B.R., Schulz, M., Bronevetsky, G.: A Scalable and Distributed Dynamic Formal Verifier for MPI Programs. In: SC'10, pp. 1-10. IEEE (2010)
20. Vo, A., Vakkalanka, S., DeLisi, M., Gopalakrishnan, G., Kirby, R.M., Thakur, R.: Formal verification of practical MPI programs. In: PPoPP'09, pp. 261-270 (2009)
21. Session C homepage, http://www.doc.ic.ac.uk/~cn06/sessionc/

WS-FMDS 2013

A Supervisor Synthesis Tool for Finite Nondeterministic Automata with Data

Aleksandar Kirilov[1], Darko Martinovikj[1], Kristijan Mishevski[1],
Marija Petkovska[1], Zlatka Trajcheska[1], and Jasen Markovski[1,2(✉)]

[1] University Ss. Cyril and Methodius, PB 393, 1000 Skopje, Republic of Macedonia
[2] Eindhoven University of Technology, PB 513,
5600 MB Eindhoven, The Netherlands
j.markovski@tue.nl

Abstract. Supervisory control theory deals with automated synthesis of models of supervisory controllers based on the models of the unsupervised systems and the control requirements. The models of the supervisory controllers are referred to as supervisors. We present a supervisor synthesis tool for finite nondeterministic automata with data-based control requirements. The tool implements a process-theoretic approach to supervisory control theory, which employs the behavioral preorder partial bisimulation to characterize the notion of a supervisor. To illustrate the tool, we remodel an industrial case study dealing with coordination of maintenance procedures of a printing process of a high-tech printer.

1 Introduction

Development of control software with high quality has become a major bottleneck in design and production of high-tech systems [9]. Traditional techniques that employ (re)coding-testing loops struggle to satisfactorily cope with this challenge due to ever-increasing system complexity and frequent design changes in the (informal) control requirements, which results in a large amount of expensive iterations. These issues gave rise to supervisory control theory of discrete-event systems [4,16], which studies automated synthesis of models of supervisory control software that ensure safe and nonblocking coordination of discrete-event behavior of the concurrent components of the system.

Supervisory controllers observe the discrete-event behavior of the system, typically given by sensory information, as depicted in Fig. 1(a). Based upon the made observations, the controllers decide upon activities that are allowed to be carried out safely, avoiding potentially dangerous or otherwise undesired situations, and send back control signals to the hardware actuators. We work under the standard assumption that the supervisory controller timely reacts on system input and we model this *supervisory control feedback loop* as a pair of synchronizing processes [4, 16]. We refer to the model of the uncontrolled system as *plant*, whereas the model of the supervisory controller is referred to as *supervisor*. The supervisory control

Supported by Dutch NWO project ProThOS, no. 600.065.120.11N124.

S. Counsell and M. Núñez (Eds.): SEFM 2013 Collocated Workshops, LNCS 8368, pp. 101–112, 2014.
DOI: 10.1007/978-3-319-05032-4_8, © Springer International Publishing Switzerland 2014

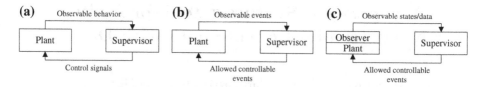

Fig. 1. (a) Generic supervisory control loop; (b) Loop with event-based observations; (c) Loop with an observer and state- or data-based observations

loop in which the system is coupled with the controller is modeled by the synchronization of the plant and the supervisor, resulting in the *supervised plant*, which specifies the behavior of the controlled system.

The activities of the system are traditionally modeled by means of discrete events. The supervisor is synthesized as a process that synchronizes with the plant, employing the synchronization to enable or disable available events in the plant [4]. Traditionally, the events are split into *controllable* and *uncontrollable events*, where the former usually model interaction with the actuators and the latter model user and environment interaction or observation of sensory information. Consequently, the supervisor is allowed to disable controllable events, but it cannot disable any available uncontrollable events, which is an important structural restriction [16]. In addition, the supervised plant must satisfy a set of *control requirements* that model the allowed behavior of the system by restrictions, typically given as safety properties.

Based on the type of observations, we distinguish between control loops with event-based control requirements or state- or data-based control requirements, which depend on the type of available observations from the system. The former situation is depicted in Fig. 1(b), where the allowed behavior is typically specified in terms of allowed languages. Some synthesis tools that allow this type of specifications are TCT [6], UMDES [4], or Supremica [1]. In the latter situation, the supervision relies on state- or data-based observations, that are usually supplied by an auxiliary process to the plant, known as an observer, which provides the supervisor with observation information of interest. An example of a state-based tool is NBC [10], whereas Supremica [1] also admits data-based control requirements in a restricted structural form. There also exist synthesis tools that admit temporal logic specifications, like extensions of the model checker NuSMV [19], but they usually suffer from high computational complexity.

Our contribution is a supervisor synthesis tool with data-based requirements for finite nondeterministic automata with data. Admittedly, the synthesis tool Supremica supports this model, but the control requirements must be specified as automata as well, which leads to certain structural restrictions. We specify the control requirements with respect to the data, independent of the structure of the plant. In addition, we employ a different type of controllability condition: Supremica relies on state-controllability [15], whereas we employ the behavioral relation termed partial bisimulation. It has been shown that partial bisimulation is a coarser notion of controllability that exhibits desirable algebraic properties, unlike state controllability that is not a preorder relation [12]. Extensions of supervisory control theory with data have a two-fold gain. They allow for a more concise specification due to parametrization of the systems [5,15] and they provide for a greater expressiveness and modeling convenience [7,18].

In the remainder of this paper, we define the model and the corresponding notion of controllability that relies on the partial bisimulation preorder. Then, we discuss the synthesis algorithm and the extraction of a supervisory controller. We illustrate the synthesis tool by revisiting an industrial case study that deals with coordination of maintenance procedures of a printing process of an Océ prototype printer [14]. Due to confidentiality issues, we can only present an obfuscated part of the case study. The goal of the case study is to synthesize a supervisory coordinator that ensures that quality of printing is uncompromised by timely performing maintenance procedures, while interrupting ongoing print jobs as little as possible.

2   Finite Automata with Variables

We model the unsupervised system by means of finite nondeterministic automata with data. For a complete process-theoretic treatment to supervisory control theory, we refer to [2,3,11] for event-, state-, and data-based supervision, respectively. We introduce some preliminary notation.

The set of finite data variables is denoted by V, where given a variable $X \in V$, its finite domain is denoted by $\text{dom}(X)$. We keep track of the data assignments by employing a function $\delta \in \Delta(V)$, where $\Delta(V) = V \to \text{dom}(V)$. Standard arithmetical expressions, like addition $+$ or subtraction $-$, over a set of variables $V \subset V$ are denoted by $E(V)$ and they can be evaluated by a function $\text{evar}_\delta \colon E(V) \to \text{dom}(V)$. For the sake of clarity and compactness, we do consider invalid expressions that evaluate outside the variable domain. We note that such inconsistent processes can be treated by a straightforward extension of the approach of [3]. We denote Boolean expressions over the set of variables $V \subseteq V$ by $B(V)$. The atomic propositions are formed by comparison predicates over variables induced by $\{<, =, >\}$ together with the logical constants false F and true T. To form the Boolean expression, we employ the standard set of logical operators $\{\neg, \wedge, \vee, \Rightarrow\}$ denoting logical negation, conjunction, disjunction, and implication. The Boolean expressions are evaluated with respect to a valuation function $\text{evbl}_\delta \colon B(V) \to \{F, T\}$ that depends on the current data assignments. The set of actions is denoted by A.

We define a finite nondeterministic automaton with data as a tuple $G = (S, A, V, \longmapsto, \gamma, \upsilon, (s_0, \delta_0))$, where

- S is a finite set of states;
- $A \subseteq A$ is a finite set of event labels;
- $V \subseteq V$ is a finite set of variables;
- $\longmapsto \subset S \times A \times S$ is a labeled transition relation;

- $\gamma \colon \longmapsto \ \to \mathsf{B}(V)$ are transition guards;
- $v \colon (\longmapsto \times V) \to \mathsf{E}(V)$ is a partial variable updating function; and
- (s_0, δ_0) is the initial state $s_0 \in S$ and initial data assignment $\delta_0 \in \Delta$.

We employ infix notation and we write $s \xrightarrow{a} s'$ for $(s, a, s') \in \longmapsto$.

The dynamics of the finite automaton with variables G is induced by the instantiated labeled transition system $\longrightarrow \subseteq S \times \Delta(V) \times A \times S \times \Delta(V)$ that depends on the valuation of the transition guards with respect to the current data assignments. Its semantics is given by the instantiated labeled transition system $T(G)$, which is defined by the tuple $T(G) = (S \times \Delta(V), A, \longrightarrow, (s_0, \delta_0))$, where the set of states is coupled with the valuation of the data variables, the initial state is induced by the initial state s_0 of the automaton with the initial data assignment δ_0, and the dynamics of the instantiated labeled transition relation is captured by operational rule (1), where (s, δ) denotes the state $s \in S$ in the data assignment environment given by δ:

$$\frac{s \xrightarrow{a} s', \ \mathrm{evbl}_\delta(\gamma(s, a, s')) = \mathrm{T},}{(s, \delta) \xrightarrow{a} (s', \delta')} \text{for all } X \in V \colon \delta'(X) = \begin{cases} \mathrm{evar}_\delta(v((s, a, s'), X)), & \text{if } ((s, a, s'), X) \in \mathrm{dom}(v) \\ \delta(X), & \text{otherwise} \end{cases}$$

$$(1)$$

Rule (1) states that labeled transitions are instantiated when such transition is defined in the automaton, the guard of that transition evaluates to true, whereas the variables are updated according to the variable updating function. We note that if the set of variables V of the automaton G is empty, i.e., $V = \emptyset$, then $\longmapsto$ and $\longrightarrow$ coincide, provided that the (then trivial) transition guards are set to be true, and G reduces to a standard automaton. By $\xrightarrow{t}^*$, we denote the multistep labeled transition relation for $t \in A^*$. We define it inductively as $(s, \delta) \xrightarrow{\varepsilon}^* (s, \delta)$ for the empty trace ε, and $(s, \delta) \xrightarrow{ta}^* (s', \delta')$ if there exists $(s'', \delta'') \in S \times \Delta(V)$ such that $(s, \delta) \xrightarrow{t}^* (s'', \delta'')$ with $t \in A^*$ and $(s'', \delta'') \xrightarrow{a} (s', \delta')$ with $a \in A$.

To model the behavior of the supervised system, we need to define a synchronous composition of two finite nondeterministic automata with variables. In general, this composition cannot be consistently defined due to conflicts induced by the partial assignment functions v. For example, if two automata synchronize on transitions that update the same variable to two different values, then this synchronization leads to a conflict as the data assignment cannot be consistently executed [18]. Again, for the sake of clarity, we do not consider these conflicting situations, which are easily detectable as none of the conditions for the synchronization from below apply. Moreover, the synchronization of the plant and the supervisor is always well-defined as the supervisor does not update any shared variables with the plant, so these conflicting situations are not of importance in the setting of this paper.

By $f|_D$ we denote the restriction of the function f to the domain $\mathrm{dom}(f) \cap D$. By $f[g] = f|_{\mathrm{dom}(f) \setminus \mathrm{dom}(g)} \cup g$ we denote the replacement of the function f by g on their common domain. Given two automata $G_1 = (S_1, A_1, V_1, \longmapsto_1, \gamma_1, \upsilon_1, (s_{01}, \delta_{01}))$ and $G_2 = (S_2, A_2, V_2, \longmapsto_2, \gamma_2, \upsilon_2, (s_{02}, \delta_{02}))$ such that $\delta_{01}|_{\mathrm{dom}(\delta_{02})} = \delta_{02}|_{\mathrm{dom}(\delta_{01})}$, we define their synchronous composition as $G_1 \parallel G_2 = (S_1 \times S_2, A_1 \cup A_2, V_1 \cup V_2, \longmapsto, \gamma, \upsilon, ((s_{01}, s_{02}), \delta_0))$, where $\delta_0 = \delta_{01}[\delta_{02}] = \delta_{02}[\delta_{01}]$, $\longmapsto$, γ, and υ are defined by Eqs. (2)–(4) as follows.

$$(s_1, s_2) \overset{a}{\longmapsto} \begin{cases} (s'_1, s_2), & \text{if } s_1 \overset{a}{\longmapsto}_1 s'_1, a \in A_1 \setminus A_2 \\ (s_1, s'_2), & \text{if } s_2 \overset{a}{\longmapsto}_2 s'_2, a \in A_2 \setminus A_1 \\ (s'_1, s'_2), & \text{if } s_1 \overset{a}{\longmapsto}_1 s'_1, s_2 \overset{a}{\longmapsto}_2 s'_2, a \in A_1 \cap A_2 \end{cases} \tag{2}$$

$$\gamma((s_1, s_2), a, (s'_1, s'_2)) = \begin{cases} \gamma_1(s_1, a, s'_1), & \text{if } s_1 \overset{a}{\longmapsto}_1 s'_1, a \in A_1 \setminus A_2 \\ \gamma_2(s_2, a, s'_2), & \text{if } s_2 \overset{a}{\longmapsto}_2 s'_2, a \in A_2 \setminus A_1 \\ \gamma_1(s_1, a, s'_1) \wedge \\ \gamma_2(s_2, a, s'_2) \end{cases}, \text{if } s_1 \overset{a}{\longmapsto}_1 s'_1, s_2 \overset{a}{\longmapsto}_2 s'_2, a \in A_1 \cap A_2 \tag{3}$$

$$\upsilon(((s_1, s_2), a, (s'_1, s'_2)), X) = $$
$$\begin{cases} \upsilon_1((s_1, a, s'_1), X), & \text{if } ((s_1, a, s'_1), X) \in \mathrm{dom}(\upsilon_1), ((s_2, a, s'_2), X) \notin \mathrm{dom}(\upsilon_2) \\ \upsilon_2((s_2, a, s'_2), X), & \text{if } ((s_2, a, s'_2), X) \in \mathrm{dom}(\upsilon_2), ((s_1, a, s'_1), X) \notin \mathrm{dom}(\upsilon_1) \\ \upsilon_1((s_1, a, s'_1), X), & \text{if } \begin{array}{l} ((s_1, a, s'_1), X) \in \mathrm{dom}(\upsilon_1), ((s_2, a, s'_2), X) \in \mathrm{dom}(\upsilon_2), \\ \upsilon_1((s_1, a, s'_1), X) = \upsilon_2((s_2, a, s'_2), X) \end{array} \end{cases} \tag{4}$$

Unlike [18] that defines the synchronous parallel composition in terms of the instantiated labeled transition systems, we define the synchronous parallel composition directly in terms of automata. We note that both definition are compatible [12], i.e., they induce the same labeled transition systems.

To capture the notion of controllability, we employ the behavioral relation termed partial bisimulation, originally proposed in [17] as a suitable relation to capture controllability of deterministic discrete-event systems. The notion was lifted in [2] to a process theory for supervisory control of nondeterministic discrete-event systems. Here, we provide a variant for finite nondeterministic automata with data.

Partial bisimulation is parameterized by a so-called bisimulation action set $B \subseteq A$. Intuitively, this relation states that all transitions of the first automaton should be simulated by the second automaton, whereas the transitions with labels in the bisimulation action set should be bisimulated in the sense of [8]. In the supervisory control setting, the bisimulation action set comprises the uncontrollable actions that must always be enabled both in the original and the supervised plant, whereas controllable events are only simulated as they are possibly restricted by the supervisor.

Let $T_1 = (Q_1, A_1, \longrightarrow_1, s_{01})$ and $T_2 = (Q_2, A_2, \longrightarrow_2, s_{02})$ be two transition systems. We say that a relation $R \subseteq Q_1 \times Q_2$ is a partial bisimulation with respect to a bisimulation action set $B \subseteq A_2$, if for all $(q_1, q_2) \in R$, it holds that:

1. if $q_1 \xrightarrow{a} q_1'$ for $a \in A_1$ and $q_1' \in Q_1$, then there exists $q_2' \in Q_2$ such that $q_2 \xrightarrow{a} q_2'$ and $(q_1', q_2') \in R$;
2. if $q_2 \xrightarrow{b} q_2'$ for $b \in B$ and $q_2' \in Q_2$, then there exists $q_1' \in Q_1$ such that $q_1 \xrightarrow{a} q_1'$ and $(q_1', q_2') \in R$;

If R is a partial bisimulation relation such that $(q_{01}, q_{02}) \in R$, then T_1 is partially bisimilar to T_2 with respect to B and we write $T_1 \leq_B T_2$. If $T_2 \leq_B T_1$ holds as well, we write $T_1 =_B T_2$.

We note that due to the first condition, it must hold that $A_1 \subseteq A_2$, whereas due to the second condition, it holds that $B \subseteq A_1$ as well. It can be shown that partial bisimilarity is a preorder [2]. Moreover, following the guidelines of [17], it can be shown that $\leq_B$ is a partial bisimulation relation with respect to B. Thus, we obtain standard results for the partial bisimulation preorder and equivalence, similarly as for simulation preorder and equivalence [8]. Moreover, the partial bisimulation preorder is a precongruence with respect to the most prominent process operations [2]. Finally, we note that $T_1 =_{A_1 \cup A_2} T_2$ amounts to bisimulation, whereas $T_1 \leq_\emptyset T_2$ reduces to simulation preorder and $T_1 =_\emptyset T_2$ reduces to simulation equivalence [2].

3   Supervisor Synthesis

As discussed above, we split the action set A to set of controllable C and uncontrollable U actions such that $C \cap U = \emptyset$ and $C \cup U = A$. The plant is typically modeled by a set of synchronizing components, ultimately resulting in automaton $P = (S_P, A_P, V_P, \longmapsto_P, \gamma_P, \upsilon_P, (s_{0P}, \delta_0))$. We note that we assume that the parallel composition of the components is well-defined and that there are no restrictions regarding nondeterministic behavior inside the plant.

We require, however, that the supervisor is a deterministic process that sends unambiguous feedback to the plant. Moreover, the supervisor cannot alter the internal state of the plant as it only observes its discrete-event behavior, i.e., it does not comprise any variable assignments [11]. In the setting of this paper, the supervisor relies on data observations from the plant to make supervision decisions in the vein of [11,15]. Its behavior is given as an deterministic automaton $S = (S_S, A_S, V_S, \longmapsto_S, \gamma_S, \emptyset, (s_{0S}, \delta_0))$, where $V_S \subseteq V_P$, and the labeled transition function $\longmapsto_S$ is such that if $s \xrightarrow{a}_S s'$ and $s \xrightarrow{a}_S s''$, then $s' = s''$ for every $s, s', s'' \in S_S$ and $a \in A_S$. The supervisor does not necessarily synchronize on all events from the plant, i.e., in general $A_S \subseteq A_P$, implying that the events in the set $A_P \setminus A_S$ are unconditionally enabled. As the supervisor does not update any variables, i.e., $\upsilon_S = \emptyset$, there arise no conflicts in Eq. (4) for the update function of the synchronization, and the synchronous composition $P \parallel S$ is always well-defined.

The composition $P \parallel S$ models the supervised plant, i.e., the behavior of the controlled system as given by the supervisory feedback loop of Fig. 1(c). To state that the supervisor has no control over the uncontrollable actions, i.e., all available uncontrollable actions in the reachable states should be enabled, we employ the partial bisimulation preorder. We express this controllability condition by requesting that the transition system of the supervised plant is partially bisimulated by the transition system of the original plant with respect to the uncontrollable events, i.e.,

$$T(P \parallel S) \leq_U T(P). \tag{5}$$

It can be shown that for deterministic processes, relation (5) reduces to the original notion of controllability of [12,16,17].

The set of control requirements R comprises control requirements with the following form R:

$$R ::= \phi \mid \xrightarrow{a} \Rightarrow \phi,$$

where $\phi \in B$ and $a \in A$. A given instantiated state (s, δ) satisfies a requirement $R \in R$, notation $(s, \delta) \models R$, if the following is satisfied:

- $(s, \delta) \models \phi$ if and only if $\text{evbl}_\delta(\phi) = T$; and
- $(s, \delta) \models \xrightarrow{a} \Rightarrow \phi$ if and only if for all $(s, \delta) \in S \times \Delta$ such that $(s, \delta) \xrightarrow{a}$ it holds that $(s, \delta) \models \phi$.

The first form of control requirements enforces an invariant on the data assignments that must hold for all states of the instantiated transition system $T(P \parallel S)$, whereas the second form restricts the possible occurrences of events, i.e., outgoing events are conditioned by the data assignments.

In addition to conforming to the control requirements, we also require that the supervisor is nonblocking, i.e., it prevents deadlock and livelock behavior in the system. Deadlock behavior occurs in states where no outgoing transitions are possible, whereas livelocks occur when the system remains in a set of states in which it cannot successfully execute its tasks, nor leave this set of states. We model successful termination by marking certain states as final, referred to as marked states in the literature [4,16], denoted by $M \subseteq S$ for a given state set S. The supervisor must assure that a marked state is reachable from all reachable states in the supervised plant.

The synthesis algorithm is an adaptation of the synthesis algorithms of [4,15,16], which employ backtracking from the marked states in order to ensure nonblocking behavior, whereas controllability is ensured by eliminating all blocking states and their predecessors that are reachable by (inverse) uncontrollable transitions. To this end, we define the notion of an inverse uncontrollable reach. Given an instantiated state (s, δ), we inductively define its reverse uncontrollable reach $\text{UR}(s, \delta)$ as follows. Initially, $\text{UR}(s, \delta) = \{(s, \delta)\}$. For every state (s', δ') such that $(s', \delta') \xrightarrow{a} (s, \delta)$ for some $a \in U$, we put $\text{UR}(s, \delta) = \text{UR}(s, \delta) \cup \text{UR}(s', \delta') \cup \{(s', \delta')\}$. Note that given a state (s, δ), all incoming transitions to its uncontrollable reach $\text{UR}(s, \delta)$ from states outside $\text{UR}(s, \delta)$ are labeled by controllable actions.

We summarize the synthesis algorithm of the maximal supervised behavior in Alg. 1. Line 1 instantiates the labeled transition system. Lines 2–10 eliminate the states or transitions that do not conform to the control requirements. When

---

Alg. 1: An algorithm for computing a maximal supervised behavior for a given finite automaton with data $G = (S, A, V, \longmapsto, \gamma, \upsilon, (s_0, \delta_0))$, a set of final states $M \subseteq S$, and a set of control requirements R

---

1   Compute the instantiated labeled transition system $\mathrm{T}(G) = (Q, A, \longrightarrow, (s_0, \delta_0)$, $Q = S \times \Delta(V)$;

2   **for** $\phi \in R$ *and* $(s, \delta) \in (S \times \Delta(V))$ **do**

3   **if** $(s, \delta) \not\models \phi$ **then**

4   Eliminate $\mathrm{UR}(s, \delta)$ from $\mathrm{T}(G)$, $Q = Q \setminus \mathrm{UR}(s, \delta)$;

5   **for** $\xrightarrow{a} \Rightarrow \phi \in R$ *and* $(s, \delta) \in (S \times \Delta(V))$ **do**

6   **if** $(s, \delta) \not\models \xrightarrow{a} \Rightarrow \phi$ **then**

7   **if** $a \in \mathsf{U}$ **then**

8   Eliminate $\mathrm{UR}(s, \delta)$ from $\mathrm{T}(G)$, $Q = Q \setminus \mathrm{UR}(s, \delta)$;

9   **else**

10   Eliminate all transitions $(s, \delta) \xrightarrow{a}$;

11 **repeat**

12    $B = \emptyset$;

13   **for** $(s, \delta) \in Q$ **do**

14   **if** $\nexists t \in A^*$ *and* $(s', \delta') \in Q$ *such that* $s' \in M$ *and* $(s, \delta) \xrightarrow{t}{}^* (s', \delta')$ **then**

15        $B = B \cup \{(s, \delta)\}$;

16   **for** $(s, \delta) \in B$ **do**

17   Eliminate $\mathrm{UR}(s, \delta)$ from $\mathrm{T}(G)$, $Q = Q \setminus \mathrm{UR}(s, \delta)$;

18 **until** $B = \emptyset$;

---

a state is eliminated, then its complete inverse uncontrollable reach must be eliminated from the labeled transition system. The elimination of these states, actually requires that controllable transitions are disabled by the supervisor. Lines 2–4 only consider the data-based invariants, whereas lines 5–10 take care of restrictions of labeled transitions. We note that if the transition is controllable, then it can be safely disabled, whereas if it is uncontrollable, then the whole state with its inverse uncontrollable reach must be eliminated.

Once the control requirements are applied, we iteratively ensure nonblockingness by eliminating states that cannot reach marked states in lines 13–17 and checking if by eliminating their inverse uncontrollable reach, we have made some other states blocking, given as the end condition of the repeat loop $B = \emptyset$, where B is the set that holds the blocking states. The end result of Alg. 1 is the maximal restriction of the instantiated labeled transition system of the plant that conforms to the control requirements. By comparison with the original system, we compute the supervisor as a function $\sup \colon \delta \rightarrow 2^{(A \cap C)}$ in the vein of [15]. The correctness of the algorithm with respect to our notion of controllability is by construction as the uncontrollable reach is preserved for every state in the supervised plant. This directly implies partial bisimulation with respect to the uncontrollable events on the controllable restriction of the plant. As an adaptation of the synthesis algorithms of [4,15,16], our algorithm has a comparable polynomial worst-case complexity in the number of transitions of the system.

We note that the internal representation of the instantiated labeled transition system can be optimized by employing binary decision diagrams see, e.g., [15]. We decided to keep the state space explicit as a preparation for future work, where we intend to employ parallel algorithms for supervisor synthesis that will harness the computing power of modern multicore processors. To implement the synthesis tool, which is available from [13], we employed Java and the supporting software package JFLAP, see http://www.jflap.org/, that enables libraries for manipulation of formal languages and automata.

4   Supervisory Coordination of Maintenance Procedures

We illustrate the modeling process on a case study involving coordination of maintenance procedures of a printing process of a high-end Océ printer of [14]. We abstractly depict a printing process function in Fig. 2, where the control architecture of the printer is given to the left. Once a user initiates a print job, the job is forwarded to the printer controller that coordinates different parts of the printer. Here, we coordinate the function responsible for the printing process, which applies the toner image onto the toner transfuse belt and fuses it onto the paper sheet. This function coordinates the power mode of the printer with the maintenance procedures. Namely, the printer executes print jobs in run mode of operation. However, to maintain high printing quality, several maintenance operations have to be carried out, e.g., coarse toner particles removal operation that ensures high quality prints. However, to perform a maintenance operation, the printing process needs to switch to standby mode of operation. Moreover, maintenance operations are scheduled based on the amount of prints since the last performed maintenance. There are two types of deadlines: soft deadlines, which denote that a maintenance operation can be scheduled, and hard deadlines, which denote that the maintenance must be scheduled. Maintenance procedures with expired soft deadlines can be postponed if there is an ongoing print job, but hard deadlines must be respected not to compromise print quality.

A printing process function comprising one maintenance operation in depicted in Fig. 2. The supervisory control problem is to synthesis a model of the Status Procedure, which is responsible for coordinating the other procedures given input from the controllers. The plant that models the printing process function is given in Fig. 2. Uncontrollable events are underscored, whereas variable updates are placed below transitions labels. Initial states have incoming arrows, whereas marked states are gray. The plant is formed by the synchronization of the automata in Fig. 2. Current Power Mode sets the power mode to run or standby using *Stb2Run* and *Run2Stb*, respectively, and sends back feedback by employing *_InRun* and *_InStb*, respectively. Maintenance Operation either carries out a maintenance operation, started by *OpStart* or it is idle. The confirmation is sent back by the event *_OpFin*, which synchronizes with Maintenance Scheduling and Page Counter. Page Counter announces when soft or hard deadlines are reached using *_SoftDln* and *_HardDln*, respectively. The page counter

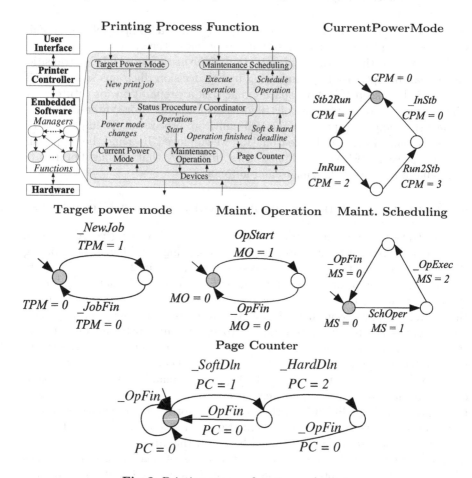

Fig. 2. Printing process function and plant

is reset, triggered by the synchronization on _OpFin_, each time the maintenance is finished. The controller Target Power Mode sends signals regarding incoming print jobs to Status Procedure by _NewJob_, which should set the printing process to run mode for printing and standby mode for maintenance and power saving. When the print job is finished, the signal _NoJob_ is sent. Maintenance Scheduling receives a request for maintenance with respect to expiration of Page Counter from Status Procedure, by the signal _SchOper_ and forwards it to the manager. The manager confirms the scheduling with the other functions and sends a response back to the Status Procedure, using _ExOper_. It also receives feedback from Maintenance Operation that the maintenance is finished in order to reset the scheduling, again triggered by _OpFin_.

The coordination is performed according to the following requirements:

1. Maintenance operations can be performed only when Printing Process Function is in standby;

2. Maintenance operations can be scheduled only if soft deadline has been reached and there are no print jobs in progress, or a hard deadline is passed;
3. Only scheduled maintenance operations can be started;
4. The power mode of the printing process must follow the power mode dictated by the managers, unless overridden by a pending maintenance operation.

For a detailed account of the model-based systems engineering process and specification and formalization of the control requirements, we refer to [14].

1. To model this requirement, we consider the states from Current Power Mode and Maintenance Operation, identified by $CPM = 1$ and $MO = 2$, respectively. We require that it must always hold

$$MO = 2 \Rightarrow CPM = 1. \tag{6}$$

2. The states identified by $PC = 1$ and $PC = 2$ indicate when soft and hard deadline is reached, respectively. State with $TPM = 1$ of Target Power Mode states that there is a print job in progress. The event $SchOper$ is responsible for scheduling maintenance procedures. We specify the requirement as follows:

$$\xrightarrow{SchOper} \Rightarrow (PC = 2 \wedge \neg TPM = 2) \vee PC = 3. \tag{7}$$

3. The maintenance operation can be started when the maintenance scheduling is completed, which is modeled as:

$$\xrightarrow{OpStart} \Rightarrow MS = 3. \tag{8}$$

4. The last condition is modeled by two separate requirements for switching from Run to Standby mode, and vice versa. We can change from run to standby mode if this is required by the manager, i.e., identified by $TPM = 2$, and there is no need to start a maintenance operation, identified by $MS \neq 3$. The transitions labeled by $Stb2Run$ are enabled as follows:

$$\xrightarrow{Stb2Run} \Rightarrow TPM = 2 \wedge \neg MS = 3. \tag{9}$$

In the other direction, we have:

$$\xrightarrow{Run2Stb} \Rightarrow TPM = 1 \vee MS = 3. \tag{10}$$

Employing the control requirements of Eqs. (6)–(10), we synthesize a supervisor equivalent to the one of [14].

5   Concluding Remarks

We presented a tool for supervisor synthesis based on a process-theoretic approach to supervisory control for finite nondeterministic automata with data. The approach relies on the partial bisimulation preorder to capture controllability of nondeterministic discrete-event systems. To illustrate the modeling process, we revisited an industrial case study dealing with supervisory coordination maintenance procedures of a high-tech printer.

References

1. Akesson, K., Fabian, M., Flordal, H., Malik, R.: Supremica - an integrated environment for verification, synthesis and simulation of discrete event systems. In: Proceedings of WODES 2006. pp. 384–385. IEEE (2006)
2. Baeten, J.C.M., van Beek, D.A., Luttik, B., Markovski, J., Rooda, J.E.: A process-theoretic approach to supervisory control theory. In: Proceedings of ACC 2011, pp. 4496–4501. IEEE (2011)
3. Baeten, J., van Beek, D., van Hulst, A., Markovski, J.: A process algebra for supervisory coordination. In: Proceedings of PACO 2011. EPTCS, vol. 60, pp. 36–55. Open Publishing Association (2011)
4. Cassandras, C., Lafortune, S.: Introduction to discrete event systems. Kluwer Academic, Dordrecht (2004)
5. Chen, Y.L., Lin, F.: Modeling of discrete event systems using finite state machines with parameters. In: Proceedings of CCA 2000, pp. 941–946 (2000)
6. Feng, L., Wonham, W.M.: TCT: a computation tool for supervisory control synthesis. In: Proceedings of WODES 2006, pp. 388–389. IEEE (2006)
7. Gaudin, B., Deussen, P.: Supervisory control on concurrent discrete event systems with variables. In: Proceedings of ACC 2007, pp. 4274–4279 (2007)
8. van Glabbeek, R.J.: The linear time – branching time spectrum I. In: Bergstra, J.A., Ponse, A., Smolka, S.A. (eds.) Handbook of Process Algebra, pp. 3–99. Elsevier, Amsterdam (2001)
9. Leveson, N.: The challenge of building process-control software. IEEE Softw. 7(6), 55–62 (1990)
10. Ma, C., Wonham, W.M.: Nonblocking Supervisory Control of State Tree Structures. LNCIS, vol. 317. Springer, Heidelberg (2005)
11. Markovski, J.: Communicating processes with data for supervisory coordination. In: Proceedings of FOCLASA 2012. EPTCS, vol. 91, pp. 97–111. Open Publishing Association (2012)
12. Markovski, J.: Controllability for nondeterministic finite automata with variables. In: Proceedings of ICSOFT 2013. CCIS, Springer (2013) (To appear)
13. Markovski, J.: Supervisor synthesis tool and demo models. http://sites.google.com/site/jasenmarkovski (2013)
14. Markovski, J., Jacobs, K.G.M., van Beek, D.A., Somers, L.J.A.M., Rooda, J.E.: Coordination of resources using generalized state-based requirements. In: Proceedings of WODES 2010. pp. 300–305. IFAC (2010)
15. Miremadi, S., Akesson, K., Lennartson, B.: Extraction and representation of a supervisor using guards in extended finite automata. In: Proceedings of WODES 2008, pp. 193–199. IEEE (2008)
16. Ramadge, P.J., Wonham, W.M.: Supervisory control of a class of discrete-event processes. SIAM J. Control Opt. 25(1), 206–230 (1987)
17. Rutten, J.J.M.M.: Coalgebra, concurrency, and control. In: Boel, R., Stremersch, G. (eds.) Proceedings of WODES 2000, pp. 31–38. Kluwer, Dotretch (2000)
18. Skoldstam, M., Akesson, K., Fabian, M.: Modeling of discrete event systems using finite automata with variables. In: Proceedings of CDC 2007, pp. 3387–3392. IEEE (2007)
19. Ziller, R., Schneider, K.: Combining supervisor synthesis and model checking. ACM Trans. Embed. Comput. Syst. 4(2), 331–362 (2005)

SMT-Constrained Symbolic Execution for Eclipse CDT/Codan

Andreas Ibing[(⊠)]

TU München, Chair for IT Security, Arcisstr. 21, 80333 München, Germany
ibing@sec.in.tum.de

Abstract. This paper presents a symbolic execution plug-in extension for Eclipse CDT/Codan, which serves to reason about satisfiable paths of C programs. Programs are translated into the SMT-LIB sublogic of arrays, uninterpreted functions and nonlinear integer and real arithmetic (AUFNIRA), and path satisfiability is automatically examined with an SMT solver. The presented plug-in can serve as a basis for path-sensitive static bug detection with bounded or unrestricted context, where the presence of bugs is decided with the solver. An interface provides notifications and context information for checker classes. With a buffer bound checker the symbolic execution plug-in is shown capable of accurately detecting bugs with currently 36 of the 39 C flow variants of the NSA's Juliet test suite for static analyzers.

1 Introduction

Software weaknesses cause high follow-up cost both for developers and users. The C language is on the one hand widely used, with currently rank 2 in the TIOBE index of programming language popularity (March 2013). On the other hand C is especially prone to certain weaknesses [1], and the estimatated average defect density for C code in the software industry is according to [2] about 1 defect per 1000 lines of code. Software vulnerabilities are registered if detected and reported, and classified according to the common weakness enumeration (CWE, [3]). The detection of weaknesses is difficult, because unlike in their 'baseline' version, the weaknesses in programs occur in conjunction with any control and data flow variants the language offers, and accurate detection needs to consider enough context depth.

Static detection on the source code level is an attractive approach, and methods with different context consideration exist [4]. They offer a trade-off between complexity and detection (in)accuracy. An overview of methods on the more complex and accurate side is given in [5]. Symbolic execution was first described in [6]. The reasoning about symbolic values uses a constraint solver [7,8] as backend. While previously SAT solvers were predominant, more recent tools rather rely on Satisfiability Modulo Theories (SMT) solvers [8,9]. SMT solvers offer a more convenient word-level interface and can decide many problems faster. A standardized interface is defined by the SMT-LIB [10]. A path-sensitive checker

S. Counsell and M. Núñez (Eds.): SEFM 2013 Collocated Workshops, LNCS 8368, pp. 113–124, 2014.
DOI: 10.1007/978-3-319-05032-4_9, © Springer International Publishing Switzerland 2014

for C with a SAT solver backend is described in [11]. Reference [12] uses a linear integer arithmetic solver, while [13–15] use an SMT backend with the SMT-LIB sublogic of arrays, uninterpreted functions and bit-vectors (QF_AUFBV).

Comparisons of static analysis tools for C are given in [16,17]. Checkers are compared by the number of false negative and false positive detections on a test suite and the needed detection times. While several other test suites like e.g. [18] have been used, the most comprehensive one is currently the NSA's Juliet test suite for C/C++ [19]. It covers over 100 CWEs with about 1500 'baseline' bugs. The 'baseline' bugs are combined with 47 data/control flow variants (of which 8 are only relevant for C++), resulting in about 57000 test cases. Each test case contains 'good' as well as 'bad' functions to provide enough possibilities for false positive detections. The maximum context depth spanned by a flow variant is five functions in five different source files.

In order to detect weaknesses as early as possible, the integration of bug checkers into the development environment is desirable. The Eclipse IDE is of special interest because it is open source, widely used and designed for extensibility. References [13,20] provide plug-ins for Eclipse, which start the tools as external processes and parse their output, [21] comes with its own GUI. The tools mentioned above are in most cases written in languages other than Java (e.g. [11,21] are written in O'Caml), and rely on yet other external tools for their analysis ([11,21] analyse CIL [15,22] analyses LLVM [23] intermediate code). These properties don't fit well to Eclipse's architecture and complicate both installation and updating (Eclipse features its own update management). Eclipse CDT on the other hand includes the code analysis framework Codan [24] since version 7.0 as optional feature. Codan currently does not support path-sensitive analyses.

This paper presents a plug-in extension of Eclipse CDT/Codan for symbolic execution, which is implemented as symbolic tree-based interpretation on abstract syntax trees (AST) generated by the CDT parser. The remainder is organized as follows: Sect. 2 describes the functionality of the plug-in, Sect. 3 describes its design. The path sensitivity is evaluated in Sect. 4 with a few test cases from the Juliet test suite, and a discussion is given in Sect. 5.

2   Functionality

2.1   Unrestricted Context Depth

The symbolic execution supports interprocedurally path-sensitive analyses with a call string approach [4,25]. The path sensitivity is based on per-function control flow graphs (no inlining), and a function's call context is represented by a program path leading to its call. The symbolic execution can be run either without restriction, which on the negative side includes the possibility of non-termination (for endless loops). Or it can be run with a context bound for e.g. the number of loop iterations (which in general incurs accuracy degradation).

2.2 Separation of Path Generation and Symbolic Interpretation

With the reasoning that path generation is fast while symbolic interpretation is slow, and with the intention to support different code coverage criteria, the generation of program paths for analysis is separated from the symbolic interpretation. A program path can be represented as the sequence of decision branches it contains. An unsatisfiable decision branch is detected during symbolic interpretation and reported, to avoid generation of further unsatisfiable path extensions. Satisfiable program paths can be enumerated by backtracking.

2.3 Automatic Slicing

Only the logic equations which are relevant for a certain verification condition are passed to the solver, which keeps the equation systems for satisfiability checks small. This corresponds to automatic slicing [26] over the control flow (for separate analysis of different program paths) and over the data flow (for verification conditions on a program path). Tracking the data flow on one path during symbolic interpretation is straightforward. Logic formulas are assigned to (symbolic) variables, and in case of consecutive assignments to one variable the different formulas may be needed to correctly generate the equation system for a verification condition. Therefore different variable versions are generated, i.e. single assignments on a program path. Dependencies of variables are also tracked. This allows for garbage collection (removal of dead variable versions) and slicing by resolving dependencies.

2.4 Context Sharing for Different Checkers

Symbolic path interpretation is separated from any specific checkers to allow them to share the contexts, i.e. to perform all checks with one enumeration of satisfiable paths. An interface allows checkers to register for notifications (triggers) and to query context equations. When triggered, a checker queries the symbolic interpreter to resolve dependencies of the variables at the trigger location into the relevant equation system slice and adds the verification condition formula for a satisfiability query.

2.5 Logic Representation

In order to use a high-level logic that is automatically decidable, the SMTLIB sublogic of arrays, uninterpreted functions and nonlinear integer and real arithmetic (AUFNIRA) has been chosen. Pointers are internally handled by the interpreter as symbolic pointers with a target and a symbolic integer as offset formula. They are output as logic formula only when dereferenced. Composites (structs and in case of C++ also classes) are also not translated, but rather treated like scopes. Symbolic variables are created for their fields.

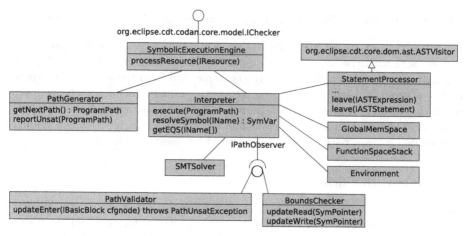

Fig. 1. Class diagram with an overview of the main classes.

3   Design

3.1   Main Classes

An overview of the main classes is given in Fig. 1. They are:

– SymbolicExecutionEngine: can be run by the Codan framework on a project, controls the cycle of path generation and symbolic interpretation, and reports results back to Codan.
– PathGenerator: generates the next path to check as a list of control flow graph (CFG) nodes, and supports backtracking and changing decision branches.
– Interpreter: handles the translation into logic on a per CFG node basis, which usually corresponds to a statement-wise translation; provides a symbolic program state to checkers.
– SMTSolver: allows queries with logic equation systems according to the SMTLIB.
– PathValidator: is triggered for branch nodes, forms branch satisfiability queries and reports unsatisfiable branches.
– BoundsChecker: one example checker which triggers on memory access with (symbolic) pointers, forms bounds violation satisfiability queries and reports buffer overflows, underflows etc.

These classes are described in more detail in the following subsections.

3.2   Eclipse Extension

The SymbolicExecutionEngine implements Codan's IChecker interface and plugs in at the extension point org.eclipse.cdt.codan.core.checkers. Configuration can be done through the Codan property pages. While the available Codan checkers

---

Function 1

```
void simplified_memcpy_17_bad() {
  for(int j=0; j<1; j++) {
    charvoid cv_struct;
    cv_struct.y = (void *)SRC_STR;
    /* FLAW: Use the sizeof(cv_struct) which will overwrite the pointer y */
    memcpy(cv_struct.x, SRC_STR, sizeof(cv_struct));
  }
}
```

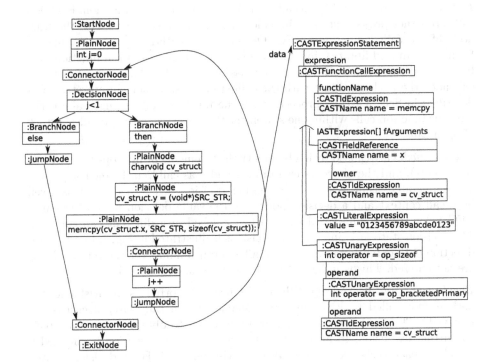

Fig. 2. CFG (left) for Function 1, and part of the AST referred to by one plain node (right).

are normally configured to be 'run as you type' or 'run with build', the symbolic execution engine is only run 'on demand' e.g. with a GUI command or as JUnit plug-in tests, due to the higher complexity and larger runtime of path-sensitive analysis. A further distinction is that the symbolic execution runs only on complete projects instead of smaller units. Detected errors are reported through Codan to the marker framework. The plug-in uses the CDT parser(s) to generate abstract syntax trees (AST) for translation units, and uses the CDT index (persisted document object model) for certain lookups. The plug-in further uses Codan's ControlFlowGraphBuilder to generate CFGs for parts of an AST which are rooted in a function definition. CFG and AST are illustrated in the object diagram Fig. 2, which corresponds to the example C function shown in Function 1.

3.3   Path Generation

The PathGenerator supports path enumeration through backtracking, so that the next path can be generated from its predecessor. A program path is a sequence of CFG nodes, and can be represented as the decision branches contained in the path. Of special interest for path generation and backtracking are function calls and decision nodes.

Function calls are interesting because CFGs are generated per function. Function calls are either project-internal, in which case the path continues with the start node of the called function's CFG. Or the call is external (e.g. to a function from the standard library), in which case a symbolic model of the function may be provided through the Environment class (compare Fig. 1). After a function's exit node the path continues with the calling node (statement interpretation as described in Sect. 3.4 then proceeds with the function call's return value). For multiple function calls within one statement the PathGenerator provides a stack of open calls.

Decision nodes are caused by if/else or switch statements or by loops (for or while statements), and they have several branch nodes as children. Branch sequences are enumerated using a state machine per decision, where a decision is given by a call context and a decision node (i.e. the same decision node object in a CFG belongs to a different decision when reached in a different call context). The decision state machine for loop decisions is illustrated in Fig. 3. In a forward direction path extension always the smallest branch number is chosen, and loops are not entered. This is indicated by the 'next' branch in Fig. 3.

Backtracking and backrolling. When a branch is reported as unsatisfiable, the path is first rolled back to this unsatisfiable branch (any later decisions are removed). Then one decision needs to be changed to obtain a new start path for further extension. In an iteration the respective last decision is changed if possible ('backtrack-next' in Fig. 3), otherwise removed. For a decision related to an if/else or switch statement the 'backtrack-next' branch is simply the next higher branch number if existent. For loop decisions it is referred to Fig. 3.

3.4   Translation and Symbolic Interpretation

The symbolic interpreter follows the tree-based interpreter pattern [27]. It tracks symbols with a memory system with global and function scopes (compare Fig. 1). A program path for interpretation comes as a CFG node sequence with references to the corresponding C statements as AST subtrees (compare Fig. 2).

Symbolic variables are objects which are resolved using their AST name or index name. For an assignment a new version is created which has a logic equation (single assignments). For each version the direct dependencies are tracked, i.e. other symbolic variable versions which are part of the equation.

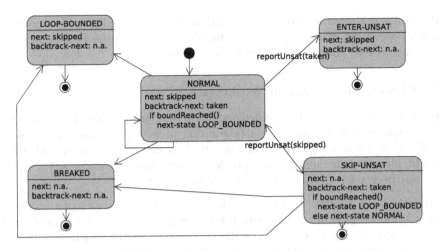

Fig. 3. Decision state machine for loop decisions. 'next' gives the next branch for path extension, and 'backtrack-next' for backtracking.

Interpretation proceeds CFG node by CFG node, which basically means statement-wise processing. The Interpreter therefore uses a StatementProcessor class, which extends CDT's ASTVisitor (Fig. 1). The translation works by bottom up traversal of a statement's AST part with the leave() functions from the visitor pattern. Information can be passed upwards as attributes. One possible attribute is a symbolic variable which has been generated as intermediate result. Translation has to consider type promotion depending on operators. Boolean variables for example are represented as integers in C, while in SMT logics boolean and integer are different sorts. Symbolic variables are implicitly generated not only as intermediate results, but also as symbolic input from the environment. An example are calls to the standard library (rand(), fgets() etc.).

In some cases the translation proceeds not strictly statement-wise with tracking and resolving of symbolic variables. One such case are function call expressions, where call parameters and return value have to be evaluated (i.e. entering the function) before proceeding with that statement's evaluation. Another case are path decisions (CFG decision nodes and branch nodes), for which symbolic boolean variables are generated. The formula for a 'default' branch in a switch statement for example includes the labels from all 'case' branches as context (siblings in the CFG).

3.5 Path Validation

The PathValidator class is triggered for branch nodes. It uses the same interface as checkers do (Fig. 1). It queries the equation system slice for all path decisions up to the current branch, with resolution of variable dependencies. It then adds the satisfiability check. If the solver answers with 'unsatisfiable', the

PathValidator throws a PathUnsatException, which is caught by the Symbol-icExecutionEngine (which reports the unsatisfiable path to the PathGenerator, and symbolic execution proceeds with the next path).

3.6   Checking for Common Weaknesses

Any number of checkers can be added and share the symbolic execution contexts. The Codan extension point supports addition of new problems and problem detail views. Detected problems are reported to the marker framework with their Id, file name, line number and problem description. Currently only a buffer overflow checker has been written as path-sensitive checker.

Buffer Overflow Checks: The bounds checker is notified for memory accesses, with a symbolic pointer variable which includes a symbolic target variable and an offset formula. The checker queries the slice of equations on which the memory access depends, and adds two satisfiability checks. The first one checks if an access with offset smaller than the lower bound (zero) is satisfiable. The second one checks for an access with offset larger than the upper bound. If the solver answers 'satisfiable' to one of the queries, the problem is reported. In principle CWEs 121-127 are detectable, which includes stack-based buffer overflow (121), heap-based buffer overflow (122), buffer underwrite (124), over-read (126) and under-read (127).

3.7   SMT Solving

The common Eclipse distributions come with a SAT solver plug-in [28], but an SMT solver plug-in is unfortunately not (yet) available. Therefore the SMT solver described in [29] (version 5.2.3) is used as a temporary replacement. It is wrapped by the SMTSolver class and started as external process.

4   Evaluation

This section evaluates to which extent the symbolic execution implementation can follow C language constructs for control and data flow. For this purpose test cases from the Juliet test suite [19] are used. Its test cases are combinations of 'baseline' bugs with different flow variants. The 39 flow variants for C are listed in Table 1. The flow numbering is not consecutive, and not all 'baseline' bugs can be combined with all flow variants. The maximum context depth is five functions in five source files (flow 54).

The path sensitivity is tested with the bounds checker, by evaluating false negative and false positive detections. Juliet test cases for a few stack-based buffer overflows with the different flow variants are imported as JUnit plug-in tests, and run with the Eclipse GUI. The tests assert that the correct number of problem markers is set at the correct positions and measure the runtime.

The tests are run in Eclipse 4.2 on a Core 2 Quad CPU Q9550, on 64-bit Linux kernel 3.2.0. The runtimes for correct detection are shown in Fig. 4 for two

Table 1. The 39 flow variants for C from [19] (the numbering is not consecutive to allow for later insertions).

Flow nr.	Flow variant
1	Baseline Simplest form of the flaw
2	if(1) and if(0)
3	if(5==5) and if(5!=5)
4	if(static_const_t) and if(static_const_f)
5	if(static_t) and if(static_f)
6	if(static_const_five==5) and if(static_const_five!=5)
7	if(static_five==5) and if(static_five!=5)
8	if(static_returns_t()) and if(static_returns_f())
9	if(global_const_t) and if(global_const_f)
10	if(global_t) and if(global_f)
11	if(global_returns_t()) and if(global_returns_f())
12	if(global_returns_t_or_f())
13	if(global_const_five==5) and if(global_const_five!=5)
14	if(global_five==5) and if(global_five!=5)
15	switch(6) and switch(7)
16	while(1) and while(0)
17	for loops
18	goto statements
19	Dead code after a return
21	Flow controlled by value of a static global variable. All functions contained in one file.
22	Flow controlled by value of a global variable. Sink functions are in a separate file from sources.
31	Data flow using a copy of data within the same function
32	Data flow using two pointers to the same value within the same function
34	Use of a union containing two methods of accessing the same data (within the same function)
41	Data passed as an argument from one function to another in the same source file
42	Data returned from one function to another in the same source file
44	Data passed as an argument from one function to a function in the same source file called via a function pointer
45	Data passed as a static global variable from one function to another in the same source file
51	Data passed as an argument from one function to another in different source files
52	Data passed as an argument from one function to another to another in three different source files
53	Data passed as an argument from one function through two others to a fourth; all four functions are in different source files
54	Data passed as an argument from one function through three others to a fifth; all five functions are in different source files
61	Data returned from one function to another in different source files
63	Pointer to data passed from one function to another in different source files
64	void pointer to data passed from one function to another in different source files
65	Data passed as an argument from one function to a function in a different source file called via a function pointer
66	Data passed in an array from one function to another in different source files
67	Data passed in a struct from one function to another in different source files
68	Data passed as a global variable in the class from one function to another in different source files

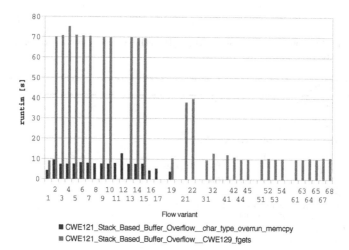

Fig. 4. Runtimes for two 'baseline' bugs with different flow variants, as JUnit plug-in tests with Eclipse GUI.

'baseline' bugs with the flow variants. The symbolic execution implementation currently supports accurate detection with 36 of the 39 flows. Flow 34 results in a false negative, because the translation does not (yet) support unions. Flow 18 results in a false negative, because the goto statements cause an exception during CFG construction. Flow 66 causes a false positive because the current solver version gives a wrong satisfiability answer for the corresponding mixture of array logic and arithmetic. Another property of the solver is that it currently supports division only with constant arguments. For the investigated test cases this limitation did not cause inaccuracies, because the translation could use symbolic constant propagation for dividend and divisor (implemented with a solver query and the 'get-value' command). The runtime measurements show a strong dependence on the presence of loops with high satisfiable iteration numbers.

5 Discussion

This paper presented a symbolic execution extension for Eclipse CDT/Codan, which might serve as a basis for path-sensitive detection of common weaknesses with unrestricted or bounded context. The plug-in has been shown to support detection of buffer overflows with about 90 % of the C flow variants of the Juliet test suite. The percentage of the currently detectable 'baseline' buffer overflows on the other hand is yet unsatisfying, because only a small part of the standard library functions is interpreted. The test programs were tiny, the "biggest" one consisted only of about 54000 AST nodes (sum over six .c files, AST nodes in headers were not counted). While the usage of array logic offers no advantage for the current functionality, it might be beneficial for a future checker for user assertions, potentially with a smooth transition to verification of functionality. Future work includes the symbolic interpretation of larger parts of the standard library, a more coherent solver integration, evaluation of scaling behaviour to bigger programs, and the development of checkers for further common weaknesses.

Acknowledgement. This work has been partially funded by the German Ministry for Education and Research (BMBF) under grant 01IS13020.

References

1. Seacord, R.: The CERT C secure coding standard. Addison-Wesley, Reading (2009)
2. Coverity Scan: 2011 open source integrity report (2011). www.coverity.com/library/pdf/coverity-scan-2011-open-source-integrity-report.pdf
3. Martin, R., Barnum, S., Christey, S.: Being explicit about security weaknesses. In: Blackhat DC (2007)
4. Khedker, U., Sanyal, A., Karkare, B.: Data Flow Analysis. CRC Press, Boca Raton (2009)
5. Jhala, R., Majundar, R.: Software model checking. J. ACM Comput. Surv. **41**(4), 21–74 (2009)
6. King, J.: Symbolic execution and program testing. Commun. ACM **19**(7), 385–394 (1976)
7. Dechter, R.: Constraint Processing. Morgan Kaufmann, San Francisco (2003)
8. Harrison, J.: Handbook of Practical Logic and Automated Reasoning. Cambridge University Press, Cambridge (2009)
9. Armando, A., Mantovani, J., Platania, L.: Bounded model checking of software using SMT solvers instead of SAT solvers. Int. J. Softw. Tools Technol. Transf. **11**(1), 69–83 (2009)
10. Barrett, C., Stump, A., Tinelli, C.: The SMT-LIB Standard Version 2.0. (Dec. 2010) online http://goedel.cs.uiowa.edu/smtlib/papers/smt-lib-reference-v2.0-r10.12.21.pdf
11. Xie, Y., Aiken, A.: Scalable error detection using Boolean satisfiability. In: Principles of Programming Languages (POPL) (2005)
12. Xie, Y., Chou, A., Engler, D.: Archer: Using symbolic, path-sensitive analysis to detect memory access errors. In: SIGSOFT Softw. Eng. Notes. pp. 327–336 (2003)
13. Clarke, E., Kroning, D., Lerda, F.: A tool for checking ANSI-C programs. In: Jensen, K., Podelski, A. (eds.) TACAS 2004. LNCS, vol. 2988, pp. 168–176. Springer, Heidelberg (2004)
14. Cordeiro, L., Fischer, B., Marques-Silva, J.: SMT-based bounded model checking for embedded ANSI-C software. In: The International Conference on Automated Software Engineering (2009)
15. Cadar, C., Dunbar, D., Engler, D.: KLEE: unassisted and automatic generation of high-coverage tests for complex systems programs. In: USENIX Symposium on Operating Systems Design and Implementation (2008)
16. Emanuelsson, P., Nilsson, U.: A comparative study of industrial static analysis tools. In: Electronic Notes in Computer Science (ENTCS). Number 217, pp. 5–21 (2008)

17. Chatzieleftheriou, G., Katsaros, P.: Test-driving static analysis tools in search of C code vulnerabilities. In: IEEE Computer Software and Application Conference Workshops (COMPSACW), pp. 96–103 (2011)
18. Ku, K., Hart, T., Chechik, M., Lie, D.: A buffer overflow benchmark for software model checkers. In: IEEE/ACM International Conference on Automated Software Engineering (2007)
19. United States National Security Agency, Center for Assured Software: Juliet Test Suite v1.1 for C/C++ (Dec. 2011). http://samate.nist.gov/SRD/testCases/suites/Juliet_Test_Suite_v1.1_for_C_Cpp.zip
20. Duprat, S., Velten, M.: FCDT: Using Eclipse CDT + FRAMA-C for advanced C static analysis in industrial context. In: Eclipse Day Toulouse (2012). http://gforge.enseeiht.fr/projects/fcdt/
21. L. Correnson et al.: FRAMA-C User Manual, release oxygen-20120901. CEA LIST (2012). http://frama-c.com/download/frama-c-user-manual.pdf
22. Necula, G., McPeak, S., Rahul, S., Weimer, W.: CIL: Intermediate language and tools for analysis and transformation of C programs. In: International Conference Compiler Construction, pp. 213–228 (2002). http://dl.acm.org/citation.cfm?id=647478.727796
23. Lattner, C., Adve, V.: LLVM: A compilation framework for lifelong program analysis and transformation. In: International Symposium Code Generation and Optimization (2004)
24. Laskavaia, A.: Codan- C/C++ static analysis framework for CDT. In: EclipseCon. (2011)
25. Sharir, M., Pnueli, A.: Two approaches to interprocedural data flow analysis. In: Muchnik, S., Jones, N. (eds.) Program Flow Analysis: Theory and Applications, pp. 189–233. Prentice-Hall, Englewood Cliffs (1981)
26. Tip, F.: A survey of program slicing techniques. J. Program. Lang. 3(3), 121–189 (1995)
27. Parr, T.: Language Implementation Patterns. Pragmatic Bookshelf, Raleigh (2010)
28. LeBerre, D.: The SAT4J library, release 2.2, system description. J. Satisfiability Boolean Model. Comput. (JSAT) 7, 59–64 (2010)
29. Cimatti, A., Griggio, A., Schaafsma, B., Sebastiani, R.: The MathSAT5 SMT solver. In: TACAS (2013)

IOCO as a Simulation

Luis Llana and Rafael Martínez-Torres(✉)

Departamento Sistemas Informáticos y Computación, Universidad Complutense de
Madrid, Madrid, Spain
llana@ucm.es, rmartine@fdi.ucm.es

Abstract. Since ioco (input output conformance) is a linear semantics,
it cannot distinguish the local execution context in a system. We have
defined iocos (input output conformance simulation): an ioco inspired
semantics defined with simulation techniques. In this way iocos is able
to capture the natural non-determinism of reactive systems. The original definition ioco deals only with input-enabled implementations while
iocos have been defined in a more general context where input-enabled
implementations are not required. In this paper we prove that ioco and
iocos coincide in the natural domain of ioco, i.e., when implementations
are input-enabled.

Keywords: Model based testing · Input output conformance · Simulation · Formal methods

1 Introduction and Related Work

Model Based Testing (MBT) [2,7–9] is an active research area where the main
goal is the study of *correctness* of a given system with respect to a set of requirements. The main component of MBT theory is a formal implementation relation
for which a procedure to generate *tests* from a given specification is provided.
The procedure is expected to be sound and complete.

For every concrete case study and industrial application, selecting a suitable conformance relation is a decision that may depend on many factors: The
costs of implementation, security considerations, performance, context of application, etc. It would be desirable to have a theory with the capacity to express
conformance at different levels.

The research we present in this paper is a small step in that direction. Instead
of the classic approach based on linear semantics, we have used a conformance
relation based on simulation semantics. The reason for this decision is that some
recent research on process theory has shown [3,4] that the group of simulation
semantics forms the backbone on a spectrum of semantics from which a hierarchy
of layers of linear semantics can be derived in a systematic way.

Research partially supported by the Spanish MEC projects TIN2009–14312-C02-01
and TIN2012–36812-C02-01.

S. Counsell and M. Núñez (Eds.): SEFM 2013 Collocated Workshops, LNCS 8368, pp. 125–134, 2014.
DOI: 10.1007/978-3-319-05032-4_10, © Springer International Publishing Switzerland 2014

In recent years ioco [8] has emerged as one of the most important MBT theories. Summing up, an implementation is considered sound with respect to a specification when the outputs produced by the former are among those prescribed by the latter after any interaction allowed by the specification. As expected, a complete testing framework is presented, including a test generating algorithm and the proof of its completeness.

Nevertheless, the implementation under testing (IUT) must fulfill an important requirement: It must be input-enabled, that is, it must react to any possible action demanded by the environment. Although this assumption maybe natural in some contexts is not so in others. For instance, in a vending machine, a slot, for a credit card or parking ticket, can only be enabled if a card is not inserted; as with of graphical interfaces which do not need to consider any possible event on a window, they just code the response for the interesting events, etc.

Let us focus on Fig. 1: the specification gives the implementation relative freedom to serve either a soda or a snack after the client inserts a coin. However, as the implementation does not always react to coin insertion, it is discarded as a *valid* implementation, even when the specification does not prescribe any thing in this respect. Though simple, this example highlight a weakness in ioco rationale, namely, that implementations are forced to react to any possible action by the environment. It also prevents ioco relation from having a desirable property: as implementation and specification lie in different domains, ioco is not a transitive relation, so it can be difficult to use ioco as a *refinement* implementation relation.

In a previous paper [6], we decided to drop this hypothesis and in order to extend the analysis within a more general framework. However, in many cases adopting such an approach has immediate consequences: we fall in the area of *linear* semantics, where implementation relation cannot distinguish the local execution context. Therefore we propose iocosas an implementation relation in the spirit of ioco. This new relation is based on simulation techniques, so it overcomes that fault, and it also enriches iocos in more subtle aspects. As a result, we obtained a refinement for ioco in the general case.

The iocos relation has a related testing framework. This testing framework is inspired by the one defined by Abramsky [1]. The main difference with respect to the original framework of Abramsky is the distinction between input and output actions: while the former are given by the environment, the latter are generated

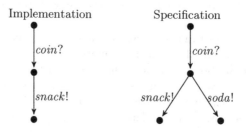

Fig. 1. Non input-enabled implementation

by the system. In this way the iocos relation can be seen as a link between the framework defined by Tretmans and the theory defined by Abramsky.

The main goal of this paper is to measure how far the iocos relation is from the original ioco relation. As we have already mentioned the iocos relation is stronger than the ioco relation. So in this paper we study which are the conditions make ioco as strong as iocos. These conditions will be the input-enabled requirement for the implementations. It is not because the ioco relation gains in expressiveness, but because of the reduction in the space of possible implementations.

The rest of the paper is organized as follow: First, in Sect. 2, we collect widely known concepts as well as other interesting theorems necessary for our purpose whose detailed proof can be found in other sources. Next, in Sect. 3 we will show some examples that differentiate ioco and iocos, we will also show how these differences disappear if the implementations are input-enabled. In Sect. 4 we present the main result of the paper stating that ioco is indistinguishable from iocos in the case of input-enabled implementations. Finally in Sect. 5, we present the conclusions of the paper and we outline some future research lines.

2 Preliminaries

A common formalism used in MBT to represent not only the models but also the implementations and even the tests are labelled transition systems. In order to deal with input-output behaviours we are going to consider two disjoint finite sets of actions: inputs I and outputs O. Output actions are those initiated by the system, they will be annotated with an exclamation mark, $a!, b!, x!, y! \in O$. Input actions are initiated by the environment and will be annotated with a question mark, $a?, b?, x?, y? \in I$. In many cases we want to name actions in a general sense, inputs and outputs indistinctly. We will consider the set $L = I \cup O$ and we will omit the exclamation or question marks when naming generic actions, $a, b, x, y \in L$.

A state with no output actions cannot autonomously proceed, such a state is called *quiescent*. Quiescence is an essential component of the ioco theory. For the sake of simplicity and without lost of generality (see for instance [8], p. 12), we directly introduce the event of quiescence as a special action denoted by $\delta!$ into the definition of our models.

Definition 1. A *labelled transition system with inputs and outputs* is a 4-tuple (S, I, O, T) such that

- S is a set of states or behaviours.
- I and O are disjoint sets of input and output actions respectively. We define $L = I \cup O$ and consider a new symbol $\delta! \notin L$ for *quiescence*. We will consider also the sets $L_\delta = L \cup \{\delta!\}$ and $O_\delta = O \cup \{\delta!\}$.
- $T \subseteq S \times L_\delta \times S$. As usual we write $p \xrightarrow{a} q$ instead of $(p, a, q) \in T$ and $p \xrightarrow{a}$, for $a \in L_\delta$, if there exists $q \in S$ such that $p \xrightarrow{a} q$. Analogously, we will write $p \xrightarrow{a}\!\!\!/$, for $a \in L_\delta$, if there is no q such that $p \xrightarrow{a} q$.

In order to allow only coherent quiescent systems the set of transitions T should also satisfy:

- if $p \xrightarrow{\delta!} p'$ then $p = p'$. A quiescent transition is always reflexive.
- if $p \xslashedarrow{o!}$ for any $o! \in O$, then $p \xrightarrow{\delta!} p$. A state with no outputs is quiescent.
- if there is $o! \in O$ such that $p \xrightarrow{o!}$, then $p \xslashedarrow{\delta!}$. A quiescent state performs no output actions.
- We say that system is *input-enabled* if at any $s \in S$ for every $a? \in I$ we have $s \xrightarrow{a?}$.   □

For the sake of simplicity, we will denote the set of labelled transition systems with inputs and outputs just as LTS. In general we use $p, q, p', q' \ldots$ for states or behaviours, but also i, i', s and s' when we want to emphasise the concrete role of a behaviours as implementations or specifications.

Without losing generality, we will consider implementations and specifications, or, more in general, behaviours under study, as states of the same LTS[1]. This modification simplifies the coinductive definition we are going to present and the reasoning behind the proof.

Traces play an important role in gathering basic information for behaviours. A trace is a finite sequence of symbols of L_δ. We will normally use the symbol σ to denote traces, that is, $\sigma \in L_\delta^*$. The empty trace is denoted by ϵ and we juxtapose, $\sigma_1 \sigma_2$, to indicate concatenation of traces. The transition relation of labelled transition systems can naturally be extended using traces instead of single actions.

Definition 2. Let $(S, I, O, T) \in LTS$, $p, q \in S$ and $\sigma \in L_\delta^*$. We inductively define $p \xrightarrow{\sigma} q$ as follows:

- $p \xrightarrow{\epsilon} p$
- $p \xrightarrow{a\sigma} q$ for $a \in L_\delta$, $\sigma \in L_\delta^*$ and $p' \in S$ such that $p \xrightarrow{a} p'$ and $p' \xrightarrow{\sigma} q$.   □

Next we introduce some definitions and notation that will be frequently used throughout the paper.

Definition 3. Let $(S, I, O, T) \in LTS$, and $p \in S$, $S' \subseteq S$, and $\sigma \in L_\delta^*$, we define:

1. $\mathsf{init}(p) = \{a \mid a \in L_\delta, p \xrightarrow{a}\}$, the set of initial actions of p.
2. $\mathsf{traces}(p) = \{\sigma \mid \sigma \in L_\delta^*, p \xrightarrow{\sigma}\}$, the set of traces from p.
3. $p \text{ after } \sigma = \{p' \mid p' \in S, p \xrightarrow{\sigma} p'\}$, the set of reachable states from p after the execution of trace σ.
4. $\mathsf{outs}(p) = \{x \mid x \in O_\delta, p \xrightarrow{x}\}$, the set of outputs of a state p or the quiescent symbol $\delta!$.
5. $\mathsf{outs}(S') = \bigcup_{p \in S'} \mathsf{outs}(p)$, the set of outputs of a set of states S'.
6. $\mathsf{ins}(p) = \{x? \mid x? \in I, p \xrightarrow{x?}\}$, the set of inputs of a state p.   □

---

[1] If we had two different $LTSs$, one for a specification and one for the implementation, we could always consider a larger LTS that is the disjoint union of the original $LTSs$.

Definition 4. Let $(S, I, O, T) \in LTS$, the relation ioco $\subseteq S \times S$ is defined as follows: i ioco $s \Leftrightarrow_{def} \forall \sigma \in$ traces(s) : outs$(i$ after $\sigma) \subseteq$ outs$(s$ after $\sigma)$ □

The ioco relation we use keeps the spirit of the original in [8], but while the original imposed implementations to be input enabled, our definition has been extended to the more general domain of input-output labelled transition systems. Also, the original definition used suspension traces while we can consider just traces because the quiescence symbol has already been introduced in the description of the behaviours.

Now we can give the formal definition of iocos. Since it is a simulation relation, it cannot be defined directly. So first we give the notion of an iocos-relation. Then the iocos relation would be the union of all iocos-relations.

Definition 5. Let $(S, I, O, T) \in LTS$, we say that a relation $R \subseteq S \times S$ is a iocos-relation iff for any $(p, q) \in R$ the following conditions hold

1. ins$(q) \subseteq$ ins(p)
2. For all $a? \in$ ins(q) such that $p \xrightarrow{a?} p'$ there exists $q' \in S$ such that $q \xrightarrow{a?} q'$ and $(p', q') \in R$.[2]
3. For all $x \in$ outs(p) such that $p \xrightarrow{x} p'$ there exists $q' \in S$ such that $q \xrightarrow{x} q'$ and $(p', q') \in R$.

We define the *input-output conformance simulation* as

$$\text{iocos} = \bigcup \{R \mid R \subseteq S \times S, \ R \text{ is a iocos -relation}\}$$

and we write p iocos q instead of $(p, q) \in$ iocos. □

Intuitively, the definition above highlights the fact that any action by implementation must be within the limits considered by specification. As a vestige from ioco rationale, in some contexts this is referred to as *final* semantics. Taking advantage of simulation techniques, we enrich ioco by forcing to implement at least one of the input-action leaded behaviour, thus avoiding tricky implementations, as the empty one. Inclusion of $\delta!$ as an special output symbol (quiescence) has a special meaning: a system is allowed to remain silent just in case specification does. To conclude this Section we recall a result proved in [6]: iocos is stronger than ioco.

Theorem 1. Let $(S, I, O, T) \in LTS$; then iocos $\subseteq$ ioco. That is, for any $p, q \in S$, if p iocos q then p ioco q. □

3 ioco vs. iocos Through Examples

In this section we will show the similarities differences between ioco and iocos. In order to simplify the reading of the examples, we are going to mark the quiescent states as ○, these kind of nodes are shorthands for ●⇌δ.

---

[2] Let us note that the Condition 2 does not imply Condition 1.

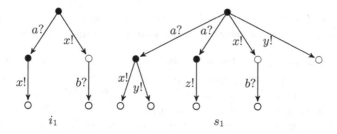

Fig. 2. ioco vs. iocos: i_1 iocos s_1.

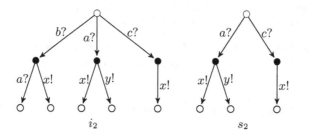

Fig. 3. ioco vs. iocos: i_2 iocos s_2.

Let us begin explaining the similarities between ioco and iocos. The examples in Figs. 2 and 3 are paradigmatic cases where ioco and iocos coincide (despite the fact the implementations are input-enabled or not). The example in Fig. 2 indicates that the specification establishes a limit on the output actions that the implementation can execute. In this case, the implementation only responds with $x!$ after the execution of the input action $a?$, while the specification indicates that it could respond with $x!$, $y!$ or $z!$. On the contrary, the example in Fig. 3 shows that the implementation does not limit the set of input actions that an implementation must perform. In other words, the implementation is free to react to more inputs than the specification indicates. In this case, the implementation can react to the input action $b?$ which is not prescribed by the specification.

The main differences between ioco and iocos is their behavior in the presence of non-determinism and their behavior with respect to input actions. The first difference is presented in Fig. 4. In the implementation (left tree) there is a non-deterministic choice between the two branches so, after producing output $x!$ we are not sure about what input actions ($c?$ or $b?$) are available. While the specification indicates that both ($b?$ and $c?$) input actions must be enabled. In Fig. 5 there is an example showing the different behavior of ioco and iocos with respect to the input actions. In this example, the specification establishes that the implementation must react (and how to react) to input $b?$. Instead, the implementation does not react to the input $b?$.

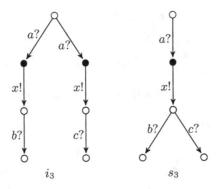

Fig. 4. ioco vs. iocos: i_3 iocȱ s_3

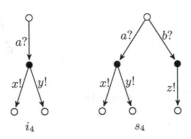

Fig. 5. ioco vs. iocos: i_4 iocȱs s_4

From this point we are going to consider the case where the implementations must be input-enabled. At first glance, the transition from general labelled transition systems to input-enabledness ones may seem trivial. In fact, a systematic procedure - called *angelic completion* is described at [8]. It basically consists of completing the given transition system by looping every state with a missing entry. Under a certain *categorical* perspective, we could look at it as the most conservative solution to the problem of finding out how an input-enabled system differs from a given one. However, by proceeding in this way, there is no guarantee that the previous relation still holds: systems previously stated to be ioco may no longer be related after the completion. In the following examples we are going to denote the angelic completion with a star: ✦ for ordinary states and ✩ for quiescent states. So, considering the set of inputs $\{a?, b?, c?\}$, the graphs in Fig. 6 represent the same system.

The angelic completion of the implementations of Figs. 4 and 5, they are in Fig. 7. i'_1 is the angelic completion of i_1 and i'_2 is the angelic completion of i_2. In this figure we have made explicit the angelic completion in one critical state in i'_1 and i'_2. Let us recall that i_1 iocȱs s_1 is just because the state we have made the angelic completion explicit in i_1 does not have the action $b?$ available. But in i'_1 the action $b?$ is now available and we can easily prove that i'_1 iocos s_1. In this case it is as if the non-determinism at the top of the tree has disappeared

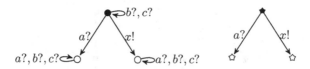

Fig. 6. Angelic completion shortcut

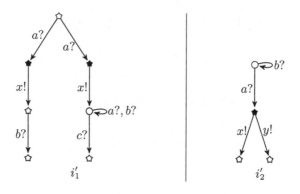

Fig. 7. Angelic completion of Figs. 4 and 5.

because the angelic completion makes the input action $b?$ available in that state. The angelic completion transforms i_1 into i_1' such that i_1' iocos s_1.

The case of i_2 and i_2' is just the opposite. In this case i_2' has a new trace that corresponds to the execution of $b?$ at the top of the system, and we obtain $\mathsf{outs}(i_2' \text{ after } b?) = \{\delta!\}$ while $\mathsf{outs}(s_2 \text{ after } b?) = \{z!\}$ and then i_2' ioc̸o s_2. Let us note that $\mathsf{outs}(i_2 \text{ after } b?) = \varnothing$ and i_2 ioco s_2.

4   IOCO as a Simulation

In the previous section we have seen that the input-enabled condition is very strong indeed. The differences between ioco and iocos vanish. In Figs. 4 and 5 we have presented two examples where i_1 ioco s_1 and i_2 ioco s_2 but i_1 ioc̸os s_1 and i_2 ioc̸os s_2. When making the angelic completion of the implementations we obtained two systems i_1' and i_2' that are related to the corresponding specifications in a different way. In the first case we obtain i_1' iocos s_1 while in the second i_2' ioc̸o s_2. But what could be surprising is that in both cases ioco and iocos coincide. This result is generalized in the following theorem stating that ioco and iocos coincide when the implementation (the left side of the relation) is input enabled.

Theorem 2. Let i be an input-enabled LTS and $s \in LTS$ such that i ioco s, then i iocos s.

Proof. In order to prove that i iocos s, we have to find R a iocos-relation that $(i, s) \in R$. Let us consider the following:

$$R = \{(p_1, p_2) \mid \exists \sigma \in traces(s) : \ p_1 \in i \text{ after } \sigma, p_2 \in s \text{ after } \sigma, \}$$

It is clear that $(i, s) \in R$ by taking the empty trace $\epsilon \in traces(s)$. So let us consider $(p_1, p_2) \in R$ and let us to check that R meets the requirements from Definition 5. First of all let us note that there is a trace $\sigma \in traces(s)$ such that $p_1 \in i$ after σ and $p_2 \in s$ after σ because $(p_1, p_2) \in R$.

- $\mathsf{ins}(p_1) \supseteq \mathsf{ins}(p_2)$. Since i is input enabled we obtain: $\mathsf{ins}(p_1) = I \supseteq \mathsf{ins}(p_2)$
- Now let us consider $a? \in ins(p_2)$ (i.e., there exists p_2' such that $p_2 \xrightarrow{a?} p_2'$) and $p_1 \xrightarrow{a?} p_1'$. Under these conditions we obtain $\sigma a? \in traces(s)$, $p_2' \in s$ after $\sigma a?$ and $p_1' \in i$ after $\sigma a?$. So $(p_1', p_2') \in R$ because of the construction of R.
- Now let us consider $x! \in O_\delta$ such that $p_1 \xrightarrow{x!} p_1'$. Then $x! \in \mathsf{outs}(p_1) = \mathsf{outs}(i \text{ after } \sigma)$. As i iocos s and $\sigma \in traces(s)$, then $\mathsf{outs}(i \text{ after } \sigma) \subseteq \mathsf{outs}(s \text{ after } \sigma)$. So $x! \in \mathsf{outs}(s \text{ after } \sigma) = \mathsf{outs}(p_2)$, that is, there exists p_2' such that $p_2 \xrightarrow{x!} p_2'$. From this we obtain that $\sigma x! \in traces(s)$. Then $p_1' \in i$ after σx and $p_2' \in i$ after σx, so $(p_1', p_2') \in R$ by the construction of R. $\qquad \square$

From Theorem 1 and Theorem 2 we obtain the simulation characterization of ioco: when an implementation is input enabled, then ioco can be defined as simulation.

Corollary 1. Let i be an input-enabled LTS and $s \in LTS$ then i ioco s iff i iocos s. $\qquad \square$

5   Conclusions and Future Work

In this paper we have studied the relation between ioco [8] and iocos [6]. We had already proved [6] that in the general case iocos is a refinement of ioco. In this paper we have investigated the context where ioco was originally defined: input-enabled implementations. Through some examples we have shown that this condition is quite strong. The behavior of both ioco and iocos change dramatically. In fact, we have proved that in this case both relations coincide. This fact has important implications for both implementation relations. On the one hand, it confirms that iocos is a natural extension of ioco when considering non input-enabled implementations. On the other hand, it opens the broad field of simulation to the ioco relation.

Regarding the iocos relation, there are still well known issues in MBT that we need to address in our proposal. We are specially interested in test selection and on-the-fly, or on-line, testing [10] which does not need to generate a priori test suites, but instead try to check dynamically the implementation under test.

It is well known that simulations can be efficiently implemented [5, 11]. This fact can be very interesting to both ioco and iocos. In order to find an efficient implementation of iocos, it should be enough to reduce its current definition to the context of a generic simulation as defined in [5, 11].

References

1. Abramsky, S.: Observational equivalence as a testing equivalence. Theoret. Comput. Sci. **53**(3), 225–241 (1987)
2. Chow, T.S.: Testing software design modeled by finite-state machines. IEEE Trans. Softw. Eng. **4**(3), 178–187 (1978)
3. de Frutos-Escrig, D., Gregorio-Rodríguez, C., Palomino, M.: On the unification of process semantics: equational semantics. Electron. Notes Theoret. Comput. Sci. **249**, 243–267 (2009)
4. de Frutos-Escrig, D., Gregorio-Rodríguez, C.: (Bi)simulations up-to characterise process semantics. Inf. Comput. **207**(2), 146–170 (2009)
5. Gentilini, R., Piazza, C., Policriti, A.: From bisimulation to simulation: coarsest partition problems. J. Autom. Reasoning **31**(1), 73–103 (2003)
6. Gregorio-Rodríguez, C., Llana, L., Martínez-Torres, R.: Input-output conformance simulation (iocos) for model based testing. In: Beyer, D., Boreale, M. (eds.) FORTE 2013 and FMOODS 2013. LNCS, vol. 7892, pp. 114–129. Springer, Heidelberg (2013)
7. Tretmans, J.: Test generation with inputs, outputs and repetitive quiescence. Softw. - Concepts Tools **17**(3), 103–120 (1996)
8. Tretmans, J.: Model based testing with labelled transition systems. In: Hierons, R.M., Bowen, J.P., Harman, M. (eds.) FORTEST. LNCS, vol. 4949, pp. 1–38. Springer, Heidelberg (2008)
9. Tretmans, J., Ed Brinksma, H.: Torx: automated model-based testing. In: Hartman, A., Dussa-Ziegler, K. (eds.) First European Conference on Model-Driven Software Engineering, pp. 31–43, Dec 2003
10. Utting, M., Pretschner, A., Legeard, B.: A taxonomy of model-based testing approaches. Softw. Test. Verif. Reliab. **22**(5), 297–312 (2012)
11. van Glabbeek, R.J., Ploeger, B.: Correcting a space-efficient simulation algorithm. In: Gupta, A., Malik, S. (eds.) CAV 2008. LNCS, vol. 5123, pp. 517–529. Springer, Heidelberg (2008)

Modeling and Simulating Interaction Protocols Using Nested Petri Nets

Mirtha Lina Fernández Venero[✉] and Flávio Soares Corrêa da Silva

Department of Computer Science, University of São Paulo,
São Paulo 05508-090, Brazil
{mirtha,fcs}@ime.usp.br

Abstract. This paper is concerned with the problem of analyzing inter-action protocols in a coordination platform called JamSession. We use nested Petri nets to provide a formal model for simulating the protocols and predicting conflicts on the system behavior.

1 Introduction

The notion of mobility has been increasingly used in areas such as communication protocols, multi-agent and intelligent systems, web and business applications, virtual environments, computers games, etc. This notion has introduced the need of designing location-dependent and context-aware software components whose complexity demands the unavoidable use of formal models (e.g. process calculi, Petri nets, Markov chains and automata-based techniques) for their development. In this article we use Petri nets (PNs) to provide a formal framework for simulating the interaction protocols of a coordination platform called JamSession. The platform was proposed in [3] for coordinating distributed, heterogeneous and mobile agents and resources. It uses a notion of location similar to the one provided in *Multilayered Multi-Agent Situated Systems* [1], where sites are related by pathways to form a directed graph. Agents inhabit these sites and can move from site to site to look for specific resources to accomplish their goals. Services are modeled using predicates attached to locations. Interaction protocols for coordinating agents are also linked to locations and are built from basic logic constructions. The language is simple but other notions such as norms and roles from *Electronic Institutions* [5] and the *Lightweight Coordination Calculus* (LCC) [11] can be modeled as well.

JamSession was recently used for coordinating inter-organizational workflows [4]. In that work, it was shown how hierarchical protocols can be verified using colored Petri nets (CPNs). This paper formalizes and extends that previous model for protocols involving recursive calls. Furthermore, we explain how to specify the dynamic behavior of concurrent interactions. Our aim is to provide a formal ground for the construction of a visualization tool for JamSession that supports the simulation and analysis of the agents movements. Here, we use

This work was supported by the São Paulo Research Foundation (FAPESP) under the grant 2010/52505-0.

S. Counsell and M. Núñez (Eds.): SEFM 2013 Collocated Workshops, LNCS 8368, pp. 135–150, 2014.
DOI: 10.1007/978-3-319-05032-4_11, © Springer International Publishing Switzerland 2014

nested Petri nets (NPNs), a class of high-level Petri nets where tokens can also be Petri nets [8]. As classical tokens, the net tokens can be added to or removed from places, but they can also fire their transitions, synchronizing them with other net tokens. The idea of using nets within nets has been effectively applied to multi-agent systems and mobile agents [2,7,10]. To model mobility, locations are encoded as places and the possible movements are encoded as transitions. Mobile agents are modeled as net tokens which can be moved from one place to another. Nevertheless, few methodologies have been proposed for modeling the rules that coordinate a sequence of agents movements [2]. In JamSession, these rules can be defined by means of interaction protocols. Therefore, in this article we provide a systematic approach for translating a JamSession specification into a NPN. For simplicity and due to the fact that in JamSession agents may be just passive entities, we represent the environment (agents, locations and feasible movements) as a color set and protocol calls as net tokens. However, the method can be easily adapted for dealing with agents nets. We model the system behavior as a Workflow Net [12] and define a property for its correctness which can be used for the early detection of interactions in conflict.

The paper has the following structure. Section 2 summarizes JamSession syntactical features and its computation rules. Section 3 presents an informal description of the translation of JamSession protocols into NPNs. The formal translation and the model for the dynamics of concurrent interactions are described in Sects. 4, 5 respectively. We draw some conclusions in Sect. 6.

2   The JamSession Platform

The coordination mechanism of JamSession is based on a directed graph where nodes represent locations that are inhabited by agents. The arcs of the graph characterize the admissible movements that agents can perform across locations. The agents provide services that are represented as first-order predicates. Each predicate is associated to a pair [$Agent, Location$] and may also have *Input* and *Output* parameters. An agent stays in a location until it receives an order to move. Predicates and movements are combined in JamSession using interaction protocols which are linked to locations. A JamSession specification is a tuple $J = \langle Loc, Path, Ag, Var, D, Pred, Prot, \phi, \psi \rangle$ where

- $Loc \neq \emptyset$ is a set of locations and $Path \subseteq Loc \times Loc$ is a set of directed arcs between locations. The pair ($Loc, Path$) is called the graph of locations;
- $Ag, Var, D, Pred, Prot$ are non-empty sets of agents, variables, domain values, predicate and protocol symbols respectively;
- $\phi : Pred \times Ag \times Loc \rightarrow (T_D \rightarrow \{\bot, \top\} \times T_D)$ characterizes the predicates definitions. Hereafter, T_C denotes the set of tuples over a set C;
- $\psi : Prot \times Loc \rightarrow \Sigma \times T_{Var} \times T_{Var}$ characterizes the protocols definitions and Σ is the language generated by the next rules, where $pd \in Pred$, $pt \in Prot$, $a \in Ag$, $l, l_1, l_2 \in Loc$, $V \in T_{Var}$ and $P \in T_{Var \cup D}$

$$Disj := Disj \vee Disj \mid Conj$$
$$Conj := Conj \wedge Conj \mid Entity$$
$$Entity := \bot \mid \top \mid \mathbf{move}(a, l_1, l_2) \mid [a, l]pd(P, V) \mid [l]pt(P, V)$$

Given a predicate symbol pd, an agent a and a location l, the function $\phi(pd, a, l)$ takes a list of domain values as input and returns a list of output domain values and the result of the evaluation ($\perp$ or $\top$). Given a protocol symbol pt and a location l, the protocol definition $\psi(pt, l) = (F, V_i, V_o)$ is written as $[l]\ pt(V_i, V_o):: = F$. The formula F has the structure of a disjunctive normal form in which literals may be move orders and predicate or protocol calls. Some of the variables occurring in F are considered as input (V_i) or output (V_o) variables in the protocol definition. The conjunction denotes the sequential evaluation of the atoms and the disjunction an alternative computation branch.

In JamSession, several protocols may be executed in parallel. The concurrent processes share the same configuration of the graph but they do not share variables. Besides, an agent can be used by just one predicate or move order at any given time. Predicates calls and move orders are suspended until the involved agent reaches the appropriate location. During the evaluation of a predicate, the agent is locked at the location. A move order is executed as an atomic operation.

Example 1. We illustrate the functioning of Jam-Session by means of two protocols (*buyerP* and *shopkeeperP*) describing an interaction for a basic shopping. The graph of locations is shown in the right. The agent tokens *askMsg*, *buyMsg*, *priceMsg* and *soldMsg* represent messages to be exchanged between the protocols. The protocols correspond-ing to the roles are shown below. We have used c, b and sh to abbreviate the location names *customer*, *buyer*, *shopkeeper* respectively.

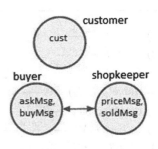

The *buyerP* protocol has a client B and an item X as input parameters and no output variable. The input data is verified by means of an agent *cust* at c. The *updateAsk* predicate stores the required data for the *askMsg* token and the message is moved to the sh location. After that, the *getPrice* predicate waits until *priceMsg* reaches the b location. When this occurs, the message *priceMsg* is sent back to the sh. After checking that X is affordable, the *buyMsg* token is updated and sent, and the *getConf* predicate waits for *soldMsg*. Once it is received, it is sent back and the purchase is confirmed to the client using the *chkConf* predicate. The behavior of *shopkeeperP* protocol is similar but it has a recursive call at the end, in order to wait for another buyer.

$[c]\ buyerP((B, X), ()):: = [cust, c]\ need((B, X), ()) \land$
$\quad [askMsg, b]\ updateAsk((B, X), ())\ \land\ \mathbf{move}(askMsg, b, sh)\ \land$
$\quad [priceMsg, b]\ getPrice((V), (P))\ \land\ \mathbf{move}(priceMsg, b, sh)\ \land\ [cust, b]\ afford((X, P), ())\ \land$
$\quad [buyMsg, b]\ updateBuy((X, B), ())\ \land\ \mathbf{move}(buyMsg, b, sh)\ \land$
$\quad [soldMsg, b]\ getConf((), (C))\ \land\ \mathbf{move}(soldMsg, b, sh)\ \land\ [cust, c]\ chkConf((C), ()).$

$[sh]shopkeeperP():: = [askMsg, sh]\ getAsk((), (X, B))\ \land\ \mathbf{move}(askMsg, sh, b)\ \land$
$\quad [priceMsg, sh]\ instock((X), (P))\ \land\ \mathbf{move}(priceMsg, sh, b)\ \land$
$\quad [buyMsg, sh]\ getBuy((), (X, B))\ \land\ \mathbf{move}(buyMsg, sh, b)\ \land$
$\quad [soldMsg, b]\ setConf((X, B, P), ())\ \land\ \mathbf{move}(soldMsg, sh, b)\ \land$
$\quad [soldMsg, sh]\ closeSale()\ \land\ [sh]\ shopkeeperP().$

A state in the computation of a JamSession formula consists of a formula, the distribution of agents over the graph (represented as a function $st : Ag \rightarrow Loc$) and a substitution θ holding the values of instantiated variables. The transition relation between the states ($\rightarrow$) is defined by the rules in Table 1. We write $F \xrightarrow{st,\theta,st',\theta'} F'$ instead of $(F, st, \theta) \rightarrow (F', st', \theta')$ to improve readability. The notation $st(a) \uparrow l$ indicates that the state of the graph has changed by the movement of a to l. Furthermore, we use $\theta \uparrow v = d$ to denote a new substitution obtained from θ where the variable v has been updated with the domain value d. As usual, the application of a substitution θ to a formula F is written as $F\theta$. The replacement of all occurrences of a variable x in F by the a value or variable v is denoted as $F[v/x]$. These notations are extended to tuples of variables and values in a straightforward way.

Table 1. JamSession computation rules

---

1) $\perp \vee F \xrightarrow{st,\theta,st,\theta} F\theta$ 2) $\top \vee F \xrightarrow{st,\theta,st,\theta} \top$

3) $\perp \wedge F \xrightarrow{st,\theta,st,\theta} \perp$ 4) $\top \wedge F \xrightarrow{st,\theta,st,\theta} F\theta$

5) $F_1 \diamond F_2 \xrightarrow{st,\theta,st,\theta} F \diamond F_2$ $if \diamond \in \{\vee, \wedge\}, F_1 \xrightarrow{st,\theta,st,\theta} F$

6) $\mathbf{move}(a, l_1, l_2) \xrightarrow{st,\theta,st,\theta} \perp$ $if\ st(a) = l_1, (l_1, l_2) \notin Path$

7) $\mathbf{move}(a, l_1, l_2) \xrightarrow{st,\theta,st(a)\uparrow l_2,\theta} \top$ $if\ st(a) = l_1, (l_1, l_2) \in Path$

8) $[a, l]\, pd(P, V) \xrightarrow{st,\theta,st,\theta\uparrow V=O} b$ $if\ st(a) = l, \phi(pd, a, l)(P\theta) = (b, O)$

9) $[l]\, pt(P, V) \xrightarrow{st,\theta,st,\theta} F_1$ $if\ \psi(pt, L) = (F, V_i, V_o), F_1 = F[P\theta/V_i][V/V_o]$

The first three rows of Table 1 describe the rules for conjunction and disjunction. The left-hand side of these operators must be reduced to a truth value before the right-hand side can be rewritten. This is enforced by the fifth rule. The sixth rule states that a move order fails in case the agent inhabits a location with no direct arc to the intended destination. On the contrary, a move order holds (rule 7) if l_1 is the current location of a and (l_1, l_2) is an arc of the graph. If a has not reached l_1, the move order is postponed until it can be evaluated. Predicate calls have a similar behavior with respect to agents and locations. If a is already situated at l, the function $\phi(pd, a, l)$ is evaluated for the input values, the formula is reduced, and the output variables are updated. Finally, a protocol call is unfolded by applying the function ψ to obtain its body definition. W.l.o.g we assume that each time a fresh copy is obtained from ψ (i.e. with a fresh set of variables). Furthermore, the input/output variables of the new formula are replaced by the parameters of the call. The substitution θ is initially empty and it is updated by the rules 6,7,8 and 10. It is applied to the remaining atoms of the formula using rules 1 and 4. We write $F \rightarrow^* F'$ if F reduces to F' in 0 or more steps. We write $F \xrightarrow{st,st_f} F'$ when no further step can be done from F'.

3   PN-Based Semantics for JamSession

In [4], it was shown how to model non-recursive protocols in JamSession using hierarchical CPNs [6]. CPNs are PNs in which each place has a type (color set) that describes the tokens it may store. The state of a CPN, called a marking, is a function relating each place to the multiset of tokens that inhabit it. Transitions represent actions or events that may change the marking of the net. An incoming (respectively outgoing) arc of a transition indicates that it may remove (respectively add) tokens from the corresponding place. The number and color of tokens to be removed or added is determined by the arc expressions which may contain variables. A transition is enabled in a marking if there is a binding of the variables which satisfies the expressions on the input arcs. In this case, the transition may fire, consuming and producing the input and output tokens respectively.

In this section we present an informal description of the translation of Jam-Session protocols into colored and nested PNs. As in [4], three basic color sets are used: Ag, $AgTok = Ag \times Loc$ and $Bool = \{\bot, \top\}$. The state of the graph of locations is represented by means of a special place of $AgTok$ type, denoted as SGL. In addition, the CPN associated to a JamSession formula has two special places of $Bool$ type: one with no incoming arc (*source node*) and the other one with no outgoing arc (*sink node*). These places are denoted as In and Out respectively. The CPNs corresponding to a move order and a predicate call have a single transition relating In, Out and SGL (see Fig. 1 a and b). In case of a predicate call, after firing t_p, the content of SGL remains the same and a $Bool$ token is produced at Out. The latter is represented by a variable (x) that indicates any token value belonging to the type. In the net corresponding to a move order, the firing of t_m produces a (possibly new) token at SGL and a $Bool$ token at Out. The color of these tokens depends on the existence of an arc between the involved locations. To this end, we use the function s to represent adjacency relation of the graph and the conditional operator ($\_?\_:\_$).

The structure of the net for either $A \wedge B$ or $A \vee B$ is depicted in Fig. 1c. The substitution transitions A and B represent the nets for the operands. The input (respectively output) place of the substitution transition is fused with the input (respectively output) place of the associated CPN. The output token of the CPN for A enables an intermediary transition $t_\diamond$ that controls the activation of the CPN for B. For the CPN of the conjunction, the outgoing arcs of $t_\diamond$ are labeled by the expressions (1) $x = \top?\top : \emptyset$ and (2) $x = \bot?\bot : \emptyset$. Here, $\emptyset$ indicates that no token should be added to the output place[1]. For the CPN of a disjunction, the expressions are defined as (1) $x = \bot?\top : \emptyset$ and (2) $x = \top?\top : \emptyset$. Note that this is not the usual (non-deterministic) PN representation of an alternative. This is because JamSession disjunction evaluates the right-hand side only if the left-hand side was previously reduced to $\bot$.

If the protocol definitions are not recursive, then a hierarchical CPN can be used to represent a formula. However, a more powerful formalism is required

---

[1] This arc inscription is allowed e.g. by CPN Tools.

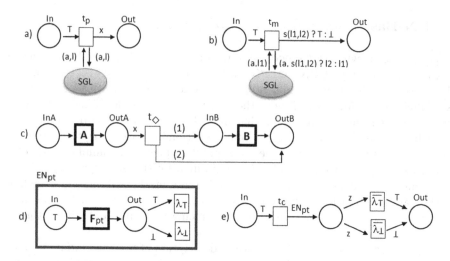

Fig. 1. PNs for JamSession constructions: a) $[a, l]\ pd(P, V)$; b) $move(a, l1, l2)$; c) $A \diamond B$; d) protocol definition and e) protocol call.

for protocols that are recursively defined. In this paper we use NPNs [9], an extension of CPNs in which tokens can be also nets. These net tokens may be added or removed as ordinary ones. In addition, they are allowed to change the marking by firing their own internal transitions. More precisely, a NPN is formed by several CPNs $(SN, EN_1, \ldots, EN_n)$, one of them called *system net* (SN) and the rest *element nets*. Each EN_i is considered as a type whose values are marked nets of the form (EN_i, M). The firing of a transition t, in SN or a marked net, may be performed according to the classical PN rules. In addition, a net token may synchronize the firing with another net token at the same place (*horizontal synchronization step*) or with the parent net (*vertical synchronization step*). The synchronization is performed by means of two disjoint sets of labels, respectively Lab_h and Lab_v, which are attached to transitions. It is assumed that for each label $l \in Lab_v$ there is a complementary label $\bar{l} \in Lab_v$.

In our model, we associate an element net to each protocol definition. The net (say EN_{pt}) is built by adding two sink transitions at the *Out* place of the protocol formula, as shown in Fig. 1d. These transitions represent the two possible results of a protocol call and they are labeled for vertical synchronization. A protocol call is modeled as depicted in Fig. 1e. After the *In* node, the net has a transition which creates a net token of EN_{pt} type (say nt) at an intermediary place (pc). The initial marking of nt has a token $\top$ at the source place and the remaining places are empty. The child net may perform several steps, corresponding to the reduction sequence of the protocol call. Once nt reaches a final marking (i.e. a *Bool* token at its *Out* place) the execution of the protocol call terminates and one of the sink transitions gets enabled. The complementary transition at the parent net will be also enabled by the binding $z = nt$. Hence, a vertical synchronization occurs, the transitions fire, nt is removed from pc and a *Bool* token is added at the *Out* place of the parent net.

4   Formal Translation of Jamsession Protocols into NPNs

In the later we provide the formal translation of Jamsession protocols into NPNs. To this end, firstly we adapt the definition of NPN from [9] for sharing some places of the system net. Besides, we restrict ourselves to autonomous steps and the vertical steps that remove the net tokens involved. As usual in CPNs, we have a set of finite basic types and a set of basic constants belonging to these types. The element nets represent types and constants. We assume that the arc expressions are multisets over the constants and typed variables. However, we will omit the braces for multisets of a single element.

Definition 1. *A NPN is a tuple* $N = (\Sigma, P_s, L, (EN_0, EN_1, \ldots, EN_n))$ *s.t.* Σ *is a finite set of non-empty basic types,* P_s *is a finite set of shared places and* L *is a set of labels s.t. for each* $l \in L$, *there is a complementary label* $\bar{l} \in L$ *s.t.* $\bar{\bar{l}} = l$ *and for all* $l_1, l_2 \in Lab_v$, $l_1 \neq l_2$ *implies* $\bar{l}_1 \neq \bar{l}_2$. *Furthermore, for all* $i = 0 \ldots n$, $EN_i = (P, C, I, T, \Lambda, A, W)$ *(called net component) is a colored Petri Net where*

- *P is a finite set of places s.t.* $P_s \subset P$ *if* $i = 0$ *and* $P \cap P_s = \emptyset$ *if* $i > 0$,
- $C : P \to \Sigma \cup \{\{EN_1\}, \ldots, \{EN_n\}\}$ *is a type function s.t. for all* $p \in P_s$, $C(p) \in \Sigma$,
- *I is the initial function defined from P into closed expressions over* Σ,
- *T is a finite set of transitions s.t.* $P \cap T = \emptyset$,
- Λ *is a partial function from T to L,*
- $A \subseteq ((P_s \cup P) \times T) \cup (T \times (P_s \cup P))$ *is a set of arcs,*
- *W is an arc expression function defined from A to expressions s.t.*
  - *there are no net constants in input arc expressions;*
  - *every variable has at most one occurrence in each input arc expression;*
  - *given two arcs* (p_1, t) *and* (p_2, t), $Var(W(p_1, t)) \cap Var(W(p_2, t)) = \emptyset$;
  - *for each net variable* $x \in Var(W(t, q))$ *there should be one input arc of t s.t.* $x \in Var(W(p, t))$; *and*
  - *if* $\Lambda(t)$ *is defined and* $x \in Var(W(p, t)) \cap Var(W(t, q))$ *then* $C(x) \in \Sigma$.

The net components share a set of places of basic types belonging to EN_0. The remaining places and transitions of the net components are pairwise disjoint. A *marking* of an element net is inductively defined as follows.

- A marking of EN_i over N, $1 \leq i \leq n$, is a function M, mapping each place p in EN_i to a finite multiset over Σ. The pair (EN_i, M) is called a marked net component or a net token of EN_i.
- Let $\bar{\Sigma}$ be a set of marked net components. Then a function M, mapping each place in a net component EN_i to a finite multiset over $\bar{\Sigma} \cup \Sigma$, is also marking of EN_i over N.

Let $\bar{\Sigma}$ denote the set of net tokens of NPN N. A marking of N is a function M, mapping each place in the net component EN_0 to a finite multiset over $\bar{\Sigma} \cup \Sigma$. Any marking must respect the type definition of the place. Hence, for all $p \in P$, if $C(p) \in \Sigma$, then $M(p)$ is a multiset over $C(p)$; otherwise $M(p)$ is a multiset of net tokens of $C(p)$. The initial marking of any net component is the marking obtained from the initialization expressions. The constant EN_i represents the marked net (EN_i, I_i). The initial marking of N is denoted as I_0. By definition, all places with net type are initially empty.

Given a transition t in a net component EN_i, we write $W(t)$ for the set $\{W(a)|a = (p,t) \in A\}$. A *binding* for t is a function b assigning to each variable $v \in W(t)$ a value from $\bar{\Sigma} \cup \Sigma$ (of the corresponding type). It is extended in a straightforward way to set of expressions. A transition t may fire in a marking M if it is *enabled* w.r.t. a binding b, i.e. for all $a = (p,t) \in A$, $b(W(a)) \subseteq M(p)$. If so, after the firing, it is obtained a new marking M' s.t. for any place p, $M'(p) = (M(p) - b(W(p,t))) \cup b(W(t,p))$. This is denoted as $M[t\rangle M'$. The set $\{b(x) \notin \Sigma \mid x \in W(p,t)\}$ are the net tokens involved in the firing of t.

An *autonomous step* is the firing of an unlabeled transition in SN or in a net token, according to the above rule. A *vertical step* is the firing of a transition t, labeled as $l = \Lambda(t)$ and the firing of a transition labeled as $\bar{l}$ in all net tokens involved in the firing of t. Due to the restrictions on the arc expressions, any vertical step removes the involved net tokens. We say that M' is *directly reachable* from M, denoted as $M[\rangle M'$, if there is an autonomous or vertical step s.t. $M[t\rangle M'$. A marking M is called *dead* if there is no directly reachable marking from it. It is called *reachable* if there is a sequence of zero or more steps $I_0[\rangle M_1[\rangle \ldots [\rangle M_k$ s.t. $M_k = M$. This is denoted as $I_0[*\rangle M$. A NPN terminates if there is no infinite sequence of steps starting from I_0.

The next definition provides the formal translation of a JamSession formula F into a NPN. As we mentioned in the previous section, the element nets are obtained from the protocols definitions and the system net is the net associated to F. Case I.1.a of the definition deals with the translation of $\top$ and $\bot$. Cases I.1.b, I.1.c, I.2, I.3 and II correspond to the nets in Fig. 1a, b, c, d and e respectively. The initial marking of SN has a token $\top$ at the source and the SGL place with the initial state of the graph of locations.

Definition 2. *Let* $J = \langle Loc, Path, Ag, Var, D, Pred, \phi, Prot, \psi \rangle$ *be a JamSession specification,* F *be a JamSession formula and st an initial configuration of the graph. The NPN associated to* J *and* F *is* $N = (\{Bool, Ag, AgTok\}, \{SGL\}, \{\lambda_\top, \bar{\lambda}_\top, \lambda_\bot, \bar{\lambda}_\bot\}, (EN_F, EN_{pt_1}, \ldots, EN_{pt_k}))$ *where*

I- $EN_F = (\{SGL\} \cup P, C, I, T, \Lambda, A, W)$ *is s.t.* $C(SGL) = AgTok$, $I(SGL)$ *is the multiset obtained from st and*

    1. *If* $F \in \{\top, \bot\}$ *or* $F = move(a, l_1, l_2)$ *or* $F = [a, l]$ $pd(\ldots)$ *then* $P = \{In, Out\}$, $C(In) = C(Out) = Bool$, $I(In) = \top$ *and* $\Lambda = \emptyset$. *Besides,*

        a. *If* $F \in \{\top, \bot\}$ *then* $T = \{t_F\}$, $A = \{a_1 = (In, t_F), a_2 = (t_F, Out)\}$, $W(a_1) = \top$ *and* $W(a_2) = F$.

      b. If $F = [a,l]\ pd(\ldots)$ then $T = \{t_p\}$, $A = \{a_1 = (In, t_p), a_2 = (t_p, Out), a_3 = (SGL, t_p), a_4 = (t_p, SGL)\}$, $W(a_1) = \top$, $W(a_2) = x$ is a Bool variable, $W(a_3) = W(a_4) = (a,l)$.

      c. If $F = move(a, l_1, l_2)$ then $T = \{t_m\}$, $A = \{a_1 = (In, t_m), a_2 = (t_m, Out), a_3 = (SGL, t_m), a_4 = (t_m, SGL)\}$, $W(a_1) = \top$, $W(a_2) = s(l_1, l_2)?\top : \bot$, $W(a_3) = (a, l_1)$ and $W(a_4) = (a, s(l_1, l_2)?l_2 : l_1)$.

   2. If $F = F_1 \diamond F_2$ with $\diamond \in \{\vee, \wedge\}$, let N_1 and N_2 the nets constructed for F_1 and F_2. Then $P = P_1 \cup P_2$, $C = C_1 \cup C_2$, $I = I_1$, $T = T_1 \cup T_2 \cup \{t_\diamond\}$, $\Lambda = \Lambda_1 \cup \Lambda_2$, $A = A_1 \cup A_2 \cup \{a_1 = (Out_1, t_\diamond), a_2 = (t_\diamond, In_2), a_3 = (t_\diamond, Out_2)\}$ and $W = W_1 \cup W_2 \cup \{W(a_1) = x\} \cup W_\diamond$. If $F = F_1 \wedge F_2$, then $W_\diamond = \{W(a_2) = x = \top?\top : \emptyset, W(a_3) = x = \bot?\bot : \emptyset\}$; otherwise $F = F_1 \vee F_2$ and $W_\diamond = \{W(a_2) = x = \bot?\top : \emptyset, W(a_3) = x = \top?\top : \emptyset\}$.

   3. If $F = [l]\ pt(\ldots)$ then $P = \{In, Out, p_c\}$, $C(p_c) = \{EN_{pt}\}$, $T = \{t_c, t_\top, t_\bot\}$, $\Lambda(t_\top) = \bar{\lambda}_\top$, $\Lambda(t_\bot) = \bar{\lambda}_\bot$, $A = \{a_1 = (In, t_c), a_2 = (t_c, p_c), a_3 = (p_c, t_\top), a_4 = (p_c, t_\bot), a_5 = (t_\top, Out), a_6 = (t_\bot, Out)\}$, $W(a_1) = \top$, $W(a_2) = EN_{pt}$, $W(a_3) = W(a_4) = z$ is a variable of EN_{pt} type, $W(a_5) = \top$ and $W(a_6) = \bot$.

II- There is one component net EN_{pt_i} for each protocol definition $\psi(pt, l) = (F_1, V_i, V_o)$. The net $EN_{pt} = (P, C, I, T, \Lambda, A, W)$ is constructed from the net $N_1 = (P_1, C_1, I_1, T_1, \Lambda_1, A_1, W_1)$ corresponding to F_1. This way, we have $P = P_1 - \{SGL\}$, $C = C_1 - \{C_1(SGL)\}$, $I = I_1$, $T = T_1 \cup \{tr_\top, tr_\bot\}$, $\Lambda = \Lambda_1 \cup \{\Lambda(tr_\top) = \lambda_\top, \Lambda(tr_\bot) = \lambda_\bot\}$, $A = A_1 \cup \{a_1 = (Out, tr_\top), a_2 = (Out, tr_\bot)\}$ and $W = W_1 \cup \{W(a_1) = \top, W(a_2) = \bot\}$.

In Appendix A, Proposition 1, we prove that this translation preserves the semantics of Table 1, i.e, any reduction sequence of F can be simulated by a firing sequence of N. If the computation of F is finite the firing sequence is also finite and ends with the same state of the graph. If F leads to an infinite execution then the net has also an infinite firing sequence. Furthermore, if we label each reduction step and each autonomous step of the net with the involved operation ($[a,l]pd, move(a, l_1, l_2), \vee, \wedge, [l]pt$), then we can show that the resulting sequences of labels are the same. The translation models all possible reduction sequences of the formula, abstracting away from input/output parameters and even the initial configuration of the graph. Therefore, the behavior of the net may include firing sequences corresponding to infeasible execution sequences. But these sequences may become feasible when F becomes part of an interaction or some predicate definition changes.

5   The Dynamic Behavior of Concurrent Protocols

Workflow definitions provide an effective method for specifying the execution flow of a set of tasks. They can be modeled by PNs where the tasks are represented by transitions and the places represent causal dependencies. These nets are called *Workflow Nets* (WF-nets) [12] and they have a unique source place i and a unique sink place o. Furthermore, every other place or transition is on a path from i to o. The initial and final markings of the net have a single token at i and o resp and are denoted in the same way.

The dynamic behavior of a JamSession interaction can be specified by means of a NPN where the system net models the execution flow of a set of concurrent formulas. The net SN can be obtained from a WF-net (say WN) by replacing each transition corresponding to a task (say T) with the JamSession net associated to a formula (say NF). Let In and Out be the source and the sink of NF respectively. Then, the next rules can be used for the replacement of T by NF:

1. Add transitions it and ot and arcs (it, In) and (Out, ot) labeled as $\top$ and z respectively, where z is a $Bool$ variable.
2. Replace each arc (p, T) or (T, p) by (p, it) or (ot, p) respectively.

As an alternative, the formula may be defined as an element net instead of embedding it in the WF-net. In this case the rules are:

1. Add a sink transition t to NF with a label for vertical synchronization, e.g. λ. Furthermore, add an arc (Out, t) with a $Bool$ variable as the label and define the resulting net as an element net, say EN_F.
2. Add a place pF of EN_F type to the WF-net and two transitions it and ot s.t. ot is labeled as $\bar{\lambda}$. Furthermore, add the arcs (it, pF) and (pF, ot) labeled as EN_F and z respectively, where z is a variable of EN_F type.
3. Replace each arc (p, T) or (T, p) by (p, it) or (ot, p) respectively.

In both cases, the last rule must preserve the arc labels. The latter replacement is more suitable for interactions that require the parallel composition of multiple instances of the same formula. In such a case, the expression of the arcs (it, pF) and (pF, ot) should be defined with a number of constants and variables according to number of required instances.

Example 2. The interaction of Example 1 can be modeled using the WF-net for the parallel composition of two tasks (shown on the right). In Fig. 2, the tasks have been replaced (using the two approaches above) by the nets corresponding to each protocol call. The net

tokens are represented as black dots with an arrow pointing to the marked net. The starts stand for a net of a predicate call or a move order.

A workflow is correct if its WF-net is *sound* [12]. Three conditions are required to satisfy this property. First, from the initial marking, it is always possible to reach the final state. Second, the final marking is the only marking reachable with a token at o. Finally, every task must be performed for at least one execution of the workflow. We use this property to define the correctness of a JamSession interaction. Note that the net resulting from the above rules is also a WF-net and preserves all the nodes from WN. Therefore, we may assume that any marking of WN is also a marking of N (the remaining places of SN are empty, except SGL). In a sound interaction there should be no conflict in the use of agents, i.e, if the evaluation of a predicate or mover order is required then

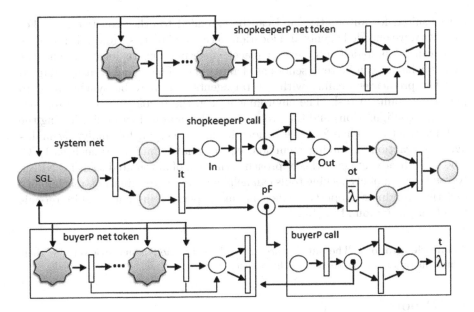

Fig. 2. A system net for the JamSession interaction of Example 1

it will be eventually completed. Furthermore, the interaction should terminate by reducing all formulas along a workflow path to a truth value. The soundness of WN ensures that if there exists a dead state other than o, then it is due to a transition in the net of a formula, in particular a predicate or move transition.

Definition 3. *Let $SF = \{F_1, \ldots, F_n\}$ be a set of formulas over a JamSession specification J. Let WN be a sound WF-net over the tasks $T_1, \ldots, T_n$ where for all $1 \leq i \leq n$, T_i is associated to F_i. Furthermore, let N be the NPN obtained from J, SF and WN. The interaction N is sound for an initial marking I_0 if and only if N terminates and for any marking M, $I_0[*\rangle M$ implies $M[*\rangle o$.*

The NPNs in which the vertical synchronization consumes the child nets are called NPNs *with autonomous elements*. For these nets, a finite coverability tree can be effectively constructed [9]. The leaves of this tree allow to decide termination and investigate properties of infinite sequences and dead markings. The nets defined in Sect. 4 are NPNs with autonomous elements in which the net tokens may share a set of basic places belonging to SN. This extension has little influence on the construction of the coverability tree. Therefore, the soundness property for a JamSession interaction can be decided by inspecting the leaves of this tree. See Appendix A, Proposition 2 for further details.

6   Conclusions

The NPN approach provided a suitable framework for modeling and simulating the interaction protocols in JamSession. The translation presented in this work is well-suited for automation and can be extended to other constructions. For simplicity, we encoded agents and locations as colored tokens. However, the place SGL can be unfolded into several places corresponding to locations and the agents behavior can be represented as element nets. The model is easily adapted to allow predicates dealing with several agents that may be synchronized to perform a common task. The environment (e.g. the topology of the graph and its initial configuration) and the protocols can be modified without affecting the system structure. Therefore, we believe it can be helpful for analyzing multi-agent interactions involving recursion, e.g. in related initiatives such as LCC. The main disadvantage of this approach is the lack of automated tools for NPNs. Nevertheless, model checking tools can help in verifying termination, reachability and the soundness property defined in this paper. Preliminary results on this direction can be found in [13].

Acknowledgments. The authors are grateful to the anonymous reviewers for their comments on an earlier version of this paper.

A   Proofs

In this section we prove that, given a JamSession formula F and an initial configuration of the graph, the NPN obtained from Definition 2 has a firing sequence that simulates the reduction sequence of F (Proposition 1). Furthermore, we show that the soundness property defined for a JamSession interaction is decidable (Proposition 2). In the later we say that a marking M_f of a NPN associated to a JamSession formula is final if there is a single token c at the sink place and all other places, but SGL, are empty. This is denoted as M_f^c. We will assume that a marking may contain empty places not belonging to the net.

Lemma 1. *Let J be a JamSession specification, F be a JamSession formula, st an initial configuration of the graph of locations and N be the NPN associated to J and F. If $F \xrightarrow{st,st_f} c$ with $c \in Bool$ then there is M_f s.t. $I_0[*\rangle M_f^c$ and $M_f^c(SGL) = st_f$.*

Proof. The property trivially holds if $F \in \{\top, \bot\}$: the only transition in net (t_F) is enabled in I_0 and, after it fires, the final marking M_f^F is obtained. Hence, we have $I_0[t_F\rangle M_f^c$ with $F = c$ and $I_0(SGL) = M_f^c(SGL) = st = st_f$. If $F = move(a, l_1, l_2)$ then $F \xrightarrow{st,st_f} c$ either by rule 6 or 7. In both cases we have $st(a) = l_1$ and, by definition of N, I_0 has a token (a, l_1) at SGL. Since $I_0(In) = \top$, the transition t_m is enabled and an autonomous step occurs. After that, the In place is empty, the Out place has a token which coincides with c and SGL is updated according to the rule applied. Hence, $I_0[t_m\rangle M_f^c$ and $M_f^c(SGL) = st_f$ holds. When $F = [a, l] \, pd(\ldots)$ then $F \xrightarrow{st,st_f} c$ by rule 8 and hence $st(a) = l$. Therefore, $(a, l) \in I_0(SGL)$, the transition t_p is enabled and an autonomous step occurs. After that, the In place is empty, SGL remains unchanged and the

Out place has a token c using the binding $x = c$. Thus, we have $I_0[t_p\rangle M_f^c$ and $I_0(SGL) = M_f^c(SGL) = st = st_f$.

For the remaining cases, we use induction on the length of the sequence $F \xrightarrow{st, st_f} c$. If $F = F_1 \wedge F_2$, then by rules 3–5, we have that $F_1 \xrightarrow{st, st_f^1} c_1$ with $c_1 \in \{\top, \bot\}$. Note that I_0 can be considered as an initial marking for the net obtained from F_1, say N_1. By induction, there is a final marking $M_{f,1}$ s.t. $I_0[*\rangle M_{f,1}^{c_1}$ and $M_f^c(SGL) = st_f^1$. This marking for N_1 also enables the transition $t_\wedge$ which, after firing, removes c_1 from Out_1. If $c_1 = \bot$ then $F \xrightarrow{st, st_f^1} c_1$ using rule 3 and $t_\wedge$ adds $c_1 = c$ to Out_2 which is also the sink place of N. Hence, we have $I_0[*\rangle M_{f,1}^{c_1}[t_\wedge\rangle M_f^c$ and $M_f^c(SGL) = st_f^1 = st_f$. On the contrary, if $c_1 = \top$ then $F \rightarrow^* \top \wedge F_2 \xrightarrow{st_f^1, \theta, st_f^1, \theta} F_2\theta$ by rule 4. Besides, c_1 is added at In_2 by $t_\wedge$, leading to a marking M'. The net N_2 for F_2 coincides with net for $F_2\theta$ (say N_2') and M' is an initial marking for N_2'. Using induction, we have that if $F_2\theta \rightarrow^1 c$ then there is $M'[*\rangle M_f^c$ and $M_f^c(SGL) = st_f$. Since M_f^c is also a final marking for N, we obtain $I_0[*\rangle M_{f,1}^{c_1}[t_\wedge\rangle M'[*\rangle M_f^c$. The proof is analogous in case $F = F_1 \vee F_2$.

When $F = [l]\ pt(\ldots)$ we have $F \xrightarrow{st, \theta, st, \theta} F_1$ by rule 9. Let N_1 be the net associated to F_1. By the induction hypothesis, if $F_1 \xrightarrow{st, st_f} c$ then there is $M_{f,1}$ s.t. $I_1 = M_{11}[\rangle M_{21}[*\rangle M_{k1} = M_{f,1}^c$ and $M_{f,1}^c(SGL) = st_f$. Note that, in N, the transition t_c is enabled and we have the autonomous step $I_0[t_c\rangle M_1$ where $M_1(In) = M_1(Out) = \emptyset$ and $M_1(p_c) = (EN_{pt}, I_{pt})$. By Definition 2, the element net EN_{pt} has the same structure as N_1, except for SGL and the two sink transitions at the end. Hence, the marking $I_{pt} \cup I_0(SGL)$ coincides with I_1. Furthermore, for every marking M_{i1} in the sequence $I_1[*\rangle M_{f,1}^c$ we obtain a marking M_i in N by defining $M_i(In) = M_i(Out) = \emptyset$, $M_i(SGL) = M_{i1}(SGL)$ and $M_i(p_c) = (EN_{pt}, M_{i1} - M_{i1}(SGL))$ with $1 \leq i \leq k$. Thus, we obtain a sequence $M_1[\rangle M_2[*\rangle M_k$ of autonomous steps in N. The marking M_k enables the transition tr_c in the net token at pc. At the same time, the transition t_c in N gets enabled. Therefore, by a vertical step, the net token is removed from pc and a token c is added at Out reaching desired final marking. All in all, we obtain the sequence $I_0[\rangle M_1[*\rangle M_k[\rangle M_f^c$ s.t. $M_f^c(SGL) = st_f$. $\qquad\square$

Lemma 2. *Let J be a JamSession specification, F be a JamSession formula, st an initial configuration of the graph of locations and N be the NPN associated to J and F. If $F \xrightarrow{st, st'} F'$ with $F' \notin Bool$ then there is a dead marking M s.t. $I_0[*\rangle M$, $M(SGL) = st'$ and $M(Out) = \emptyset$.*

Proof. If $F = F'$ then either $F = move(a, l_1, l_2)$ or $F = [a, l]\ pd(\ldots)$ none of the rules can be applied. This is due to the fact that $st(a) \neq l_1$ and hence in the initial marking I_0, there is no token (a, l_1) at SGL. Therefore, the only transition in net is not enabled, the initial marking is dead and we obtained $I_0[*\rangle I_0 = M$, $M(Out) = \emptyset$ and $M(SGL) = st = st'$.

We proceed using induction on the length of the sequence $F \xrightarrow{st, st'} F'$ and the size of the formula. If $F = F_1 \diamond F_2$ with $\diamond \in \{\vee, \wedge\}$ then we have the next two cases. Let N_1 and N_2 be the nets obtained from F_1 and F_2 respectively. If $F_1 \xrightarrow{st,st_1} F_1'$ with $F_1' \notin Bool$ then $F' = F_1' \diamond F_2$ and $st_1 = st'$. Using induction we have that, for N_1 there is a dead marking M_1' s.t. $I_0[*\rangle M_1'$ and $M_1'(SGL) = st_1$. Since Out_1 (the sink place of N_1) is empty, the transition $t_\diamond$ is not enabled and the marking is also dead for N. Otherwise, $F_1 \xrightarrow{st,st_1} c$ and $F \rightarrow^* c \diamond F_2 \xrightarrow{st_1,\theta,st_1,\theta} F_2\theta \xrightarrow{st_1,st'} F'$. Then, by Lemma 1, $I_0[*\rangle M_{f,1}^c$ for N_1. The same firing sequence can be considered for N leading to the firing of the transition $t_\diamond$. The marking obtained is an initial marking for N_2 (which coincides with the net for $F_2\theta$). Let denote this marking as I_1. Now, using induction, we have that $I_1[*\rangle M$, M is dead, $M(SGL) = st'$ and $M(Out_2) = \emptyset$. The required result holds since $I_0[*\rangle M_{f,1}^\top[t_\diamond\rangle I_1[*\rangle M$ and M is also a dead for N.

Finally, if $F = [l] \, pt(...)$ we have $F \xrightarrow{st,\theta,st,\theta} F_1$ by rule 9. By the induction hypothesis, the net N_1 corresponding to F_1 has a firing sequence s.t. $I_1[*\rangle M_1$, M_1 is a dead marking, $I_1(SGL) = st$, $M_1(SGL) = st'$ and the sink place of N_1 is empty. For the net N we have $I_0[t_c\rangle M'$ where $M'(In) = M'(Out) = \emptyset$ and $M'(p_c) = (EN_{pt}, I_{pt})$. Since EN_{pt} has the same set of places as N_1 except for SGL, the sequence $I_1[*\rangle M_1$ can be considered as the inner sequence of the net token at p_c. Hence, we obtain a sequence $I_0[*\rangle M'[*\rangle M$ of autonomous steps in N s.t. $M(SGL) = st'$. However, since M_1 is dead and the Out place of the net token is empty, the transitions for vertical synchronization will never fire. Therefore M is also dead in N.   □

Proposition 1. *Let J be a JamSession specification, $F \in \Sigma$ be a JamSession formula, st an initial configuration of the graph of locations and N be the NPN associated to J and F. Then, there is a firing sequence of N simulating the reduction sequence of F.*

Proof. When the reduction sequence of F is finite, the result follows from Lemmas 1 and 2. It remains to show that, if there is an infinite sequence of reductions starting from F and st then there is also an infinite firing sequence with N. Note that, all rules of Table 1 reduce the size of the formula w.r.t the number of operations and entities, but the last one. Hence, if there is an infinite reduction sequence from F, there is also an infinite reduction sequence from a protocol call which is a subterm of F. Therefore, we may assume that $F = F_1 \diamond [l]pt(...) \diamond F_2 \rightarrow^* [l]pt(...) \diamond F_2$ and $[l]pt(...)$ leads to an infinite reduction sequence. Since $F_1 \rightarrow^! c$, we use Lemma 1 to obtain a firing sequence of N till the creation of the net token corresponding to $[l]pt(...)$. Using induction on the marking structure we obtain an infinite firing sequence corresponding to the reduction sequence of $[l]pt(...)$. From that firing sequence, we construct an infinite sequence of autonomous steps for N which completes the proof.   □

Proposition 2. *Soundness is decidable for JamSession interactions.*

Proof. The coverability tree for a NPN with autonomous elements is constructed in [9] as follows. The nodes of the tree are labeled with markings of N. The root of the tree is labeled as I_0 and any internal node labeled by M has a child node labeled M' for each M' s.t. $M[\rangle M'$. The leaves of the tree are classified as final (dead markings), covering (markings leading to infinite cycles) and iterative (markings leading to infinite recursion). A node labeled as M' is called covering if it has an ancestor labeled as M s.t. $M \preceq M'$, where $\preceq$ is a quasi-ordering based on the tree structure of the markings. A node labeled as M' is called iterative if it has an ancestor labeled as M s.t. both markings are obtained from the firing of a transition t that generates the same net token, and the last token is nested in the first one. The net is terminating if all leaves are final.

The extension introduced in Definition 1 does not affect the tree structure of the markings. This is due to the fact that the shared places belong to SN and no net token is created for this net component. Therefore, for these nets, the quasi-ordering $\preceq$ and the covering nodes can be defined as in [9]. Nevertheless, a further condition is required in order to ensure that an iterative node leads to an infinite recursive sequence. Since the transition t may have shared places as input, we should also demand that M' covers the marking of the shared places in M, i.e. $M(P_s) \preceq M'(P_s)$. This relation can be effectively computed for places of basic type (or even for multi-level nets). Therefore, the coverability tree is finite. In order to decide the soundness of Definition 3 it is enough to check that all leaves of the tree are labeled by markings with a single token at o and the remaining places empty, except SGL. These markings are dead because o is a sink and there is no transition in N having SGL as the only input place. $\square$

References

1. Bandini, S., Manzoni, S., Vizzari, G.: Multi-agent approach to localization problems: the case of multilayered multi-agent situated system. Web Intell. Agent. Syst. **2**(3), 155–166 (2004)
2. Chang, L., He, X., Shatz, S.M.: A methodology for modeling multi-agent systems using nested Petri nets. Int. J. Softw. Eng. Knowl. Eng. **22**(7), 891–925 (2012)
3. Corrêa da Silva, F.S.: Knowledge-based interaction protocols for intelligent interactive environments. Knowl. Inf. Syst. **30**, 1–24 (2012)
4. Corrêa da Silva, F.S., Venero, M.L.F., David, D.M., Saleemb, M., Chung, P.W.H.: Interaction protocols for cross-organisational workflows. Knowl. Based Syst. **37**, 121–136 (2013)
5. Esteva, M., Rodríguez-Aguilar, J.A., Sierra, C., Garcia, P., Arcos, J.L.: On the formal specification of electronic institutions. In: Sierra, C., Dignum, F.P.M. (eds.) AgentLink 2000. LNCS (LNAI), vol. 1991, pp. 126–147. Springer, Heidelberg (2001)
6. Jensen, K.: Coloured Petri Nets. Basic Concepts, Analysis Methods and Practical Use. Springer, Heidelberg (1992)
7. Köhler, M., Moldt, D., Rölke, H.: Modelling mobility and mobile agents using nets within nets. In: van der Aalst, W.M.P., Best, E. (eds.) ICATPN 2003. LNCS, vol. 2679, pp. 121–139. Springer, Heidelberg (2003)
8. Lomazova, I.A., Schnoebelen, P.: Some decidability results for nested Petri Nets. In: Bjorner, D., Broy, M., Zamulin, A.V. (eds.) PSI 1999. LNCS, vol. 1755, pp. 208–220. Springer, Heidelberg (2000)
9. Lomazova, I.A.: Recursive nested Petri nets: analysis of semantic properties and expessibility. Program. Comput. Softw. **27**(4), 183–193 (2001)

10. Lomazova, I.A.: Modeling dynamic objects in distributed systems with nested Petri nets. Fundam. Informaticae **51**(1–2), 121–133 (2002)
11. Robertson, D.: Multi-agent coordination as distributed logic programming. In: Demoen, B., Lifschitz, V. (eds.) ICLP 2004. LNCS, vol. 3132, pp. 416–430. Springer, Heidelberg (2004)
12. van der Aalst, W.M.P.: Interorganizational workflows: an approach based on message sequence charts and Petri nets. Syst. Anal. Model. Simul. **34**(3), 335–367 (1999)
13. Fernández Venero, M.L., Corrêa da Silva, F.S.: On the use of SPIN for studying the behavior of nested Petri Nets. In: Iyoda, J., de Moura, L. (eds.) SBMF 2013. LNCS, vol. 8195, pp. 83–98. Springer, Heidelberg (2013)

PetriCode: A Tool for Template-Based Code Generation from CPN Models

Kent Inge Fagerland Simonsen[1,2(✉)]

[1] Department of Computing, Bergen University College, Bergen, Norway
[2] DTU Compute, Technical University of Denmark, Kongens Lyngby, Denmark
kifs@hib.no, kisi@imm.dtu.dk

Abstract. Code generation is an important part of model driven methodologies. In this paper, we present PetriCode, a software tool for generating protocol software from a subclass of Coloured Petri Nets (CPNs). The CPN subclass is comprised of hierarchical CPN models describing a protocol system at different levels of abstraction. The elements of the models are annotated with code generation pragmatics enabling PetriCode to use a template-based approach to generate code while keeping the models uncluttered from implementation artefacts. PetriCode is the realization of our code generation approach which has been described in previous works.

Keywords: Model-driven development · Implementation of platforms and tools · Formal methods for software engineering · Coloured Petri Nets

1 Introduction

Coloured Petri Nets (CPNs) [5] is a graphical modelling language combining Petri Nets and the programming language Standard ML. CPNs have been widely used for modelling and validation of concurrent systems. CPN Tools [6] provides tool support for construction, simulation and analysis of CPN models but does not provide tool support for automatic code generation from CPN models. The contribution of this paper is to present PetriCode which complements CPN Tools by providing tool support for automatic code generation from CPN models. PetriCode implements the approach presented in [19].

In contrast to previous works [16,18,19], this paper focuses on the technical software realization of our approach whereas earlier work has focused on the conceptual and theoretical aspects of our modelling and code generation methods. The intended use of PetriCode is to generate software for network protocols in a flexible way based on annotated and descriptive protocol CPN models [18] and for different target languages and platforms.

PetriCode takes a template-based approach to code generation based on CPN models annotated with *pragmatics*. Pragmatics are syntactic annotations on CPN model elements that are used to direct the code generation procedure.

S. Counsell and M. Núñez (Eds.): SEFM 2013 Collocated Workshops, LNCS 8368, pp. 151–163, 2014.
DOI: 10.1007/978-3-319-05032-4_12, © Springer International Publishing Switzerland 2014

Pragmatics are associated with code templates that are invoked for code generation. Our code generation approach [19] consists of three main steps. The first step is to parse the CPN model and automatically derive additional pragmatics for the CPN model. The derived pragmatics are used to provide the code generator with additional information of what is represented by the various CPN structures. The second step is to construct an Abstract Template Tree (ATT) which is used as an intermediary structure for code generation. The ATT provides a platform independent data structure that simplifies the final step of the code generation. The third and final step is the actual code generation where the ATT, using a series of visitors and templates, is transformed into code by invoking the templates associated with pragmatics.

The rest of this paper is organized as follows. Section 2 shows, by an example, how PetriCode can be used to generate code for a simple framing protocol. Section 3 provides an overview of the software architecture and design of Petri-Code. Section 4 describes the pragmatics module which is responsible for parsing and deriving pragmatics. Section 5 describes the ATT module which is responsible for generating the ATTs. Section 6 describes the code generation module which is responsible for generating code based on ATTs and templates. Section 7 contains a discussion of related work. Concluding remarks and future work are presented in Sect. 8.

We assume that the reader is familiar with the basic concepts of Petri Nets (places, transitions, enabling and occurrence/firing). Due to space limitations we only provide a high-level introduction to CPNs. The reader is referred to [5] for a detailed introduction to CPNs.

Details on how to download and operate PetriCode are available at the Petri-Code project website [15]. Due to space limitations we cannot present all details of PetriCode in this paper. For a more detailed presentation, we refer the reader to the technical report [17].

2   Example Model and Usage

In order to present the workings of PetriCode, we use a simple framing protocol as a running example. The protocol is described in detail in the technical report [19]. The model is divided into three hierarchical layers: the protocol system, principal, and service layers. The protocol system layer, depicted in Fig. 1, shows the principal agents of the protocol system as well as the connections between them. In the example, those are the Sender, Receiver and the Channel connecting them. In Fig. 1, the substitution transitions Sender and Receiver (rectangles with double-lined borders) are both annotated with a ⟨⟨principal⟩⟩ pragmatic. This conveys to the code generator that the sub-modules represented by each of these substitution transitions represent principal agents of the system. The third substitution transition in the protocol system module, Channel, is annotated with the pragmatic ⟨⟨channel⟩⟩ specifying that the underlying module defines the channel. The ⟨⟨channel⟩⟩ pragmatic, in addition, has some attributes describing the service provided by the channel. In the rest of this paper, we focus

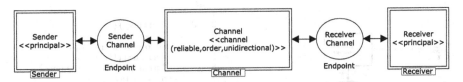

Fig. 1. The protocol system level

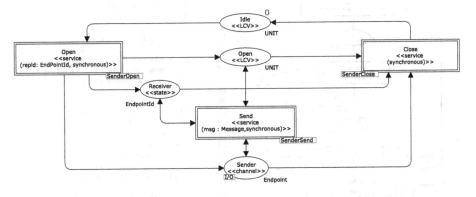

Fig. 2. Example of a principal level module: The Sender module

on the Sender principal of the protocol. Figure 2 shows the principal level of the sender which is the sub-module of the substitution transition Sender in Fig. 1. The principal level contains the services provided by each principal as well as *life cycle variables* which control when the various services can be called and places which hold global data for the principal. The Open and Close services (represented by substitution transitions with a ⟨⟨service⟩⟩ pragmatic) opens and, respectively, closes the channel to the Receiver while the Send service sends a message over the channel. To illustrate the models of the services, we provide details on the Send service. The Send service, shown in Fig. 3(left), contains the sending part of the protocol. The Send service divides a message into smaller fragments called frames. Each frame is sent together with a bit (flag) that is set if the current frame is the last frame of the message, and unset otherwise. In the model, the message, which is a parameter to the Send service, is broken up into frames by the transition Partition. Then the fragments are sent one by one in a loop (from the Start place to the PacketSent place) until all the fragments have been sent. The ⟨⟨service⟩⟩ pragmatic is used on transition Send (top) to indicate the entry point of the service. At the bottom of Fig. 3, the pragmatic ⟨⟨return⟩⟩ on the Completed transition indicates the termination of the service.

Usage Example. In order to generate code from the CPN model, PetriCode is invoked with appropriate arguments. An example of such an invocation is shown in Listing 1. The first step of the program is to parse the model and automatically add *derived pragmatics*. It is also possible, as part of the command-line arguments, to give further pragmatics and rules for deriving them as will be

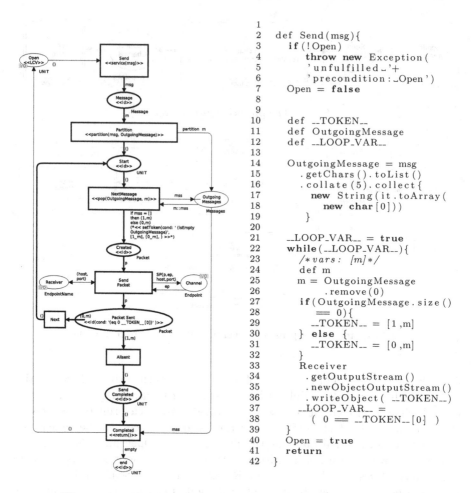

```
1
2    def Send(msg){
3       if (!Open)
4          throw new Exception(
5             'unfulfilled '+
6             'precondition: Open')
7       Open = false
8
9
10      def __TOKEN__
11      def OutgoingMessage
12      def __LOOP_VAR__
13
14      OutgoingMessage = msg
15         .getChars().toList()
16         .collate(5).collect{
17            new String(it.toArray(
18               new char[0]))
19         }
20
21      __LOOP_VAR__ = true
22      while(__LOOP_VAR__){
23         /*vars: [m]*/
24         def m
25         m = OutgoingMessage
26            .remove(0)
27         if(OutgoingMessage.size()
28            == 0){
29            __TOKEN__ = [1,m]
30         } else {
31            __TOKEN__ = [0,m]
32         }
33         Receiver
34            .getOutputStream()
35            .newObjectOutputStream()
36            .writeObject( __TOKEN__)
37         __LOOP_VAR__ =
38            ( 0 == __TOKEN__[0] )
39      }
40      Open = true
41      return
42   }
```

Fig. 3. The Sender Send module (left) and generated code (right)

discussed in Sect. 4. The second step is to generate the ATT which is discussed further in Sect. 5. The third and final phase is the code generation where the -o option provides the output directory where the generated code is placed and the -b option takes a *binding descriptor* file as an argument. The binding descriptor file provides a set of bindings of pragmatics to code generation templates for the specific platform under consideration. These bindings (known as *template bindings*) are described in further detail in Sect. 6. In this case binding descriptors for the Groovy platform are used. One thing that is not visible in the listing is a reference to pragmatics descriptors which describes the available pragmatics. This is because a core set of pragmatics, which contains most of the pragmatics used in this particular example, are defined in the tool and available by default.

Listing 1. Command to run PetriCode for the simple framing protocol example.

```
petriCode -o . -b ./groovy.bindings ./FramingProtocol.cpn
```

After running the command shown in Listing 1, two files will be generated in the output directory. Each of these files contain a single Groovy class, one for the Sender principal and one for the Receiver principal. For the Sender class there will be exactly three methods, one for each of the services that the principal provides (see Fig. 2). The generated code for the Send service is shown in Fig. 3 (right).

3   Architecture and Design of PetriCode

PetriCode is divided into three functional modules corresponding to the three main steps in our code generation approach. These are the Pragmatics, ATT, and Code generation modules.

When designing and implementing PetriCode, there was a number of key requirements that needed to be addressed and which affected the choice of software technologies used for the implementation. An important feature of Petri-Code is the ability to read, parse and write CPN models stored in the format of CPN Tools [6] which is one of the most widely used tools for construction and analysis of high-level Petri Nets. The Java library Access/CPN [21] provides this capability for the Java platform. Therefore, in order to use Access/CPN it is necessary to choose a platform with good integration with Java. Furthermore, in order to accommodate pragmatics it is required to be able to refine the meta-model underlying Access/CPN without introducing a complicated translation layer. Another important requirement was to easily be able to create Domain Specific Languages (DSLs) for defining pragmatics descriptors and template bindings. The Groovy programming language [3], which runs on the Java Virtual Machine, was chosen since it has a seamless integration with all Java libraries including Access/CPN. Groovy also has a simple mechanism (not available to Java) to manipulate classes at runtime and also has good support for many types of DSLs. Finally, Groovy has additional useful features such as a command-line interface options builder and a powerful template engine that can be used for code generation purposes.

Overall Architecture. Figure 4 provides an architectural overview of PetriCode. PetriCode is controlled by its main class PetriCode which makes up the Command Line Interface of the application. PetriCode parses the command-line arguments and calls the modules shown directly below the Command Line Interface in Fig. 4 as appropriate. PetriCode uses the CliBuilder included in Groovy to parse command line arguments. All the modules depend on Access/CPN for reading and manipulating CPN models. As explained above, PetriCode is implemented using the Groovy language and builds upon the Groovy and Java platforms. All modules are dependent on the data model for Pragmatics. The ATT and Generation modules also share a data model for ATTs.

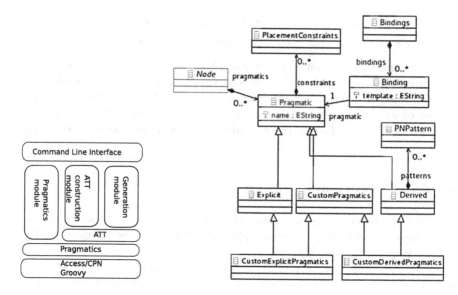

Fig. 4. PetriCode architecture   **Fig. 5.** Data model for the Pragmatics module

4 Pragmatics Module

The Pragmatics module has three main responsibilities: reading and parsing CPN
models, parsing *pragmatics descriptors*, and computing derived pragmatics for
CPN models. The pragmatics derivation process is driven by a DSL which is used
to parse the pragmatics descriptor files containing information about the pragmatics used in a model. A class diagram showing the meta-model for pragmatics
is provided in Fig. 5. In the diagram, pragmatics are separated via two cate-
gorizations. One categorization is whether the pragmatic is explicit or derived,
where explicit pragmatics must be added to the CPN model by the modeller, and
derived pragmatics are computed automatically based on structural patterns.
This categorization is represented in Fig. 5 by the Derived class. The second
categorization is whether the pragmatic is supplied by the user (a custom pragmatic) or is part of the built-in core pragmatics of PetriCode. This is represented
by the CustomPragmatics class.

The pragmatics description language is a builder language that describes
the available pragmatics. Listing 2 gives an example of a pragmatic descriptor
for an explicit pragmatic (⟨⟨principal⟩⟩) and a derived pragmatic (⟨⟨endLoop⟩⟩).
A core set of pragmatics is provided by PetriCode while others can be provided
by the user using the pragmatics description language. The language consists of
descriptors that each describe a pragmatic. Each descriptor consists of a name
(which is the name of the pragmatic) followed by a pair of parenthesis. Inside the
parenthesis, the parameters of the pragmatics definition are given in the form of
key-value pairs. The possible parameters for a pragmatics descriptor are origin

and `derivationRules`. The `origin` parameter indicates whether the pragmatic is explicitly given by the modeller or should be automatically derived. The origin field of ⟨⟨Principal⟩⟩ indicates that this is an explicit pragmatic meaning that it will not be generated automatically. The `derivationRules` parameter gives structural patterns that is used to find the elements of a CPN model where a derived pragmatic should be added. In addition, both ⟨⟨Principal⟩⟩ and ⟨⟨endLoop⟩⟩ have some constraints on where they may reside in the model which is supplied via the `constraints` field.

Listing 2. Examples of the core pragmatics for PetriCode.

```
principal(origin: 'explicit', constraints: [levels: 'protocol',
         connectedTypes: 'SubstitutionTransition'])
endLoop(origin: 'derived', derviationRules:
        ['new PNPattern(pragmatics: [\'Id\'],
         minOutEdges: 2, backLinks: 1)'],
        constraints: [levels: 'service', connectedTypes:'Place'])
```

Pragmatics Derivation. The method for deriving pragmatics is based on traversing each service module and checking each node (i.e., place or transition) against structural patterns described by the pragmatic descriptors. The last pragmatic descriptor in Listing 2 is the ⟨⟨endLoop⟩⟩ pragmatic. ⟨⟨endLoop⟩⟩ is a derived pragmatic with a structural pattern on the field *derivationRules*. An important concept for pragmatics derivation and indeed the entire code generation approach is the *control flow path*. The control flow path consists of all the nodes annotated with the ⟨⟨Id⟩⟩ pragmatic where the first node would be the node of a service annotated with ⟨⟨service⟩⟩ pragmatic and the last is annotated with ⟨⟨return⟩⟩ (see Fig. 3). Each of the ⟨⟨Id⟩⟩, ⟨⟨service⟩⟩ and ⟨⟨return⟩⟩ pragmatics are explicit and must be added by the modeller. For derived pragmatics, a list of patterns are supplied. Each pattern, will be matched against each node on the control-flow path. If a pattern matches, the corresponding pragmatic is added to the node.

5   ATT Construction Module

The ATT module is responsible for generating ATTs and the main classes that make up the ATTs are shown in Fig. 6. An ATT is an internal temporary data structure of PetriCode. Its purpose is to simplify the code generation process and make it more flexible by organizing so-called control flow blocks at the service modules in an ordered tree. When this tree has been constructed, code generation is performed by traversing the tree. The tree is built up according to the hierarchical structure of the considered subclass of CPN models down to the service level. At the service level, the control flow structure of the service is reflected in the structure of the ATT.

The ATT generation is done by the ATTFactory class which produces an instance of the class AbstractTemplateTree. The AbstractTemplateTree has as its

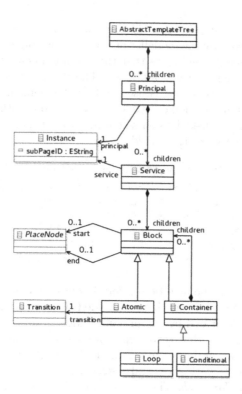

Fig. 6. Classes of the ATT

descendants instances of the classes Atomic, Conditional, Loop, Principal and Service corresponding to the different kinds of control flow blocks. The Principal and Service classes each have a link going to the Instance class of the Access/CPN model which represents substitution transitions. The Block class has two outgoing associations with Place nodes from Access/CPN. The Atomic block has an association with transitions.

An ATT is implemented as an ordered tree. Each non-leaf element in the tree has a list of children. The root element of an ATT is an instance of the AbstractTemplateTree class. Each child of the root element is expected to be of the class Principal. The Principal class has as its children the services of the principal. The Service class represents a service, its children are the control flow blocks of the service according to the block structure introduced in [19].

The ATT of the Sender side of the example in Sect. 2 is shown in Fig. 7. The tree has a single root representing the entire protocol system. At the next level, the principals are represented. For brevity, only the principal Sender of the protocol is shown. The children of the principal nodes are the services, and their children represent the control flow block structure of the services. Looking specifically at the Send service of the Sender principal, we see that the service has three direct descendants. These descendants represent the loop in the service and

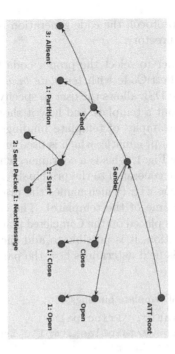

Fig. 7. Example ATT

one atomic block on each side of the loop. The first of the nodes is the partition atomic block which contains the partition pragmatic which is where the message sent by the framing protocol is divided into smaller fragments. The second node is the loop, and the final node is the atomic block after the loop which does not have any pragmatics and as such does not produce any code.

6   Code Generation Module

The generation module is responsible for generating code from ATTs. In order to generate code from CPNs annotated with pragmatics, the pragmatics must be connected to code generation templates. This is done using the Binding class which is connected to Pragmatics (see Fig. 5). The bindings are produced by another DSL which parses user provided template bindings and returns an object structure for the template bindings. The code generation phase can be divided into two separate sub-phases. The first sub-phase is the code generation for each element in the ATT. A visitor visits each element in the ATT in no particular order. The second sub-phase in the code generation phase is to stitch together the generated code for each ATT node. This is done by a depth-first traversal of the ATT. For each node, when all the sub-nodes have been visited, the %%yield%% tag in the code generated for the node is replaced by the concatenation of the text field of all the immediate descendants of the node. When this has been done for each principal in the protocol, the code generation is complete and the code is written to the output directory.

Template bindings. In order to select the proper code template for each pragmatic, the user supplies PetriCode with *template bindings*. These bindings are supplied using a DSL. The DSL allows the user to specify the template and other necessary information about a template and how it should be applied.

Listing 3 shows two examples of template bindings. The first binding is a binding for the ⟨⟨Principal⟩⟩ pragmatic, which is used on the Sender and Receiver substitution transitions in Fig. 1. This is a container, which means that the generator should add the code generated to the principals children in the ATT to it. The other fields are `pragmatic` (which names the pragmatic) and `template` (which contains the file-name of the template). The second template binding binds ⟨⟨endLoop⟩⟩, which is placed on the Completed place (see Fig. 3) after pragmatics derivation. In addition, it is possible to add the field parameterStrategy to template bindings. This field determines how the parameters of the template should be constructed.

Listing 3. Two examples of template bindings.

```
classTemplate(pragmatic: 'Principal',
    template: './groovy/mainClass.tmpl', isContainer: true)
endLoop(pragmatic: 'endLoop',
    template: './groovy/endLoop.tmpl')
```

7 Related Work

Many tools exist for generating software from models. Most of the tools, however, support only the generation of static parts of the code and, partly, standard behaviour [7]. This does less than it could to help create robust software since the non-trivial parts are still written manually. However, some tools allow for generating more than structural parts of software. In the discussion on related work below, we consider only tools and approaches that do full code generation where no manual coding is necessary.

Process-Partitioned CPNs (PP-CPNs) [9] have been used to automatically generate code for several purposes including protocol software. PP-CPNs are a restricted sub-class of CPNs. Code is generated from PP-CPNs by first translating the PP-CPN into a control flow graph (CFG), then translating the CFG into an abstract syntax tree for an intermediate language. The CFG is translated into another intermediary representation which is dependent on the target platform, and from this representation code is generated. In [9], PP-CPNs are used to model and obtain an implementation for the DYMO routing protocol using the Erlang programming language and platform. Both PP-CPNs and our modelling language are subclasses of CPNs. However, where we rely on pragmatics to control code generations, PP-CPNs rely on restricted colour sets and CPN structure to allow the generator to deduce the needed information. Our approach also models the environment of the services while PP-CPNs are geared to modelling only the intents of the services. This allows us to represent the protocol at higher levels of abstraction on the protocol and principal levels as well as on the service level. It also allows us to define how the services should be called in a structured way by third-party software.

There are several tools for modelling and generating protocol software based on the Specification and Description Language (SDL) [2,4]. SDL is created for the purpose of modelling protocols, and is extensively used in the telecommunications industry. The IBM Rational SDL Suite (previously Tau SDL Suite and SDT) is among the most well known proprietary tools for SDL. The Rational SDL Suite supports code generation for SDL models to C and C++ code and also supports verification through model checking. Another SDL tool is Jade [14] that supports editing and analysis/verification of SDL models. Code generation for JADE is still in development. SDL Integrated Tool Environment (SITE) supports editing of SDL models and code generation to Java and C++ code. SITE also supports some analysis of SDL models. SDL is a graphical language based on Finite State Machines (FSMs). This allows verification of protocols using model checking techniques. Compared to our approach, SDL is not as easily extensible as our approach.

Renew [12] is a tool that allows creation and execution of object-oriented Petri Nets. Renew supports several modelling formalisms based on various forms of Petri Nets. Renew supports Reference nets which can be annotated with Java code and can be executed using a built-in simulator engine. The simulator can execute the nets incorporating the Java annotations in a headless mode so that no visualization will occur. This means that the simulations can be used as stand-alone programs. The simulation approach is in contrast to our code generation approach where code is generated and can be inspected and compiled as computer programs created with traditional programming languages.

The Unified Modelling Language, and in particular state charts and sequence diagrams, has been used to model and generate code for protocols in several approaches [1,10,11,13,20]. Several tools exists for UML which support analysis and code generation in various ways. Since our approach is based on CPNs, verification is directly supported using CPN Tools [8]. This may be more challenging with UML-based approaches. Also, our pragmatics- and template-based approach allows us to give the user a great deal of flexibility by supporting the definition of custom pragmatics and templates.

8   Conclusions and Future Work

In this paper we have described a tool that can generate code from CPNs annotated with pragmatics. We have shown how this tool works by using the example of a simple communication protocol. The goal of our tool is to be able to generate code that is complete in the sense that no further coding should be required to use the services our code provides. Another important goal has been to generate code that is readable and analysable for human programmers.

The input of the tool is an instance of a specific class of CPN models. A main goal of the tool, and of our approach in general, is that these models should be descriptive in the sense that they can be used to convey the operation of the modelled protocol at several levels of abstraction.

In the future, we will use the tool to evaluate our approach using a larger and more realistic examples, and expand the range of available templates to other languages and platforms. Another future work item we are currently working on is to make our approach more flexible by allowing the users to easily add custom pragmatic patterns and placement conditions. Finally, we aim at integrating PetriCode with other popular software development tools such as Eclipse and IntelliJ IDEA.

References

1. Alanen, M., Lilius, J., Porres, I., Truscan, D.: On Modeling Techniques for Supporting Model Driven Development of Protocol Processing Applications, pp. 305–328. Springer, Heidelberg (2005)
2. Babich, F., Deotto, L.: Formal methods for specification and analysis of communication protocols. IEEE Commun. Surv. Tutor. **4**(1), 2–20 (2002)
3. Groovy. Project Web Site. http://groovy.codehaus.org
4. ITU-T. Recommendation Z.100 (11/99) Specification and Description Language (SDL) (1999)
5. Jensen, K., Kristensen, L.M.: Coloured Petri Nets - Modelling and Validation of Concurrent Systems. Springer, Heidelberg (2009)
6. Jensen, K., Kristensen, L.M., Wells, L.: Coloured Petri Nets and CPN Tools for modelling and validation of concurrent systems. Int. J. Softw. Tools Technol. Transf. **9**(3–4), 213–254 (2007)
7. Kindler, E.: Model-based software engineering: the challenges of modelling behaviour. In: Proceedings of BM-FA '10, pp. 4:1–4:8. ACM Electronic Libraries (2010)
8. Kristensen, L.M., Simonsen, K.I.F.: Applications of coloured Petri Nets for functional validation of protocol designs. In: Jensen, K., van der Aalst, W.M.P., Balbo, G., Koutny, M., Wolf, K. (eds.) ToPNoC VII. LNCS, vol. 7480, pp. 56–115. Springer, Heidelberg (2013)
9. Kristensen, L.M., Westergaard, M.: Automatic structure-based code generation from Coloured Petri Nets: a proof of concept. In: Kowalewski, S., Roveri, M. (eds.) FMICS 2010. LNCS, vol. 6371, pp. 215–230. Springer, Heidelberg (2010)
10. Kroiss, C., Koch, N., Knapp, A.: UWE4JSF: a model-driven generation approach for web applications. In: Gaedke, M., Grossniklaus, M., Díaz, O. (eds.) ICWE 2009. LNCS, vol. 5648, pp. 493–496. Springer, Heidelberg (2009)
11. Kukkala, P., Helminen, V., Hannikainen, M., Hamalainen, T.D.: UML 2.0 implementation of an embedded WLAN protocol. In: Proceedings of PIMRC '04, vol. 2, pp. 1158–1162 (2004)
12. Kummer, O., Wienberg, F., Duvigneau, M., Schumacher, J., Köhler, M., Moldt, D., Rölke, H., Valk, R.: An extensible editor and simulation engine for Petri Nets: renew. In: Cortadella, J., Reisig, W. (eds.) ICATPN 2004. LNCS, vol. 3099, pp. 484–493. Springer, Heidelberg (2004)
13. Parssinen, J., von Knorring, N., Heinonen, J., Turunen, M.: UML for protocol engineering-extensions and experiences. In: Proceedings of TOOLS '00, pp. 82–93 (2000)

14. Pereira, C.L., da Silva, D.C., Jr., Duarte, R.G., Fernandes, A.O., Canaan, L.H., Coelho, C.J.N., Ambrosio, L.L.: Jade: an embedded systems specification, code generation and optimization tool. In: Proceedings of SBCCI '00, pp. 263–268 (2000)
15. PetriCode. Project Web Site. http://kentis.github.io/petriCode/
16. Simonsen, K.I.F.: On the use of pragmatics for model-based development of protocol software. In: Proceedings of PNSE '11, vol. 723 of CEUR Workshop Proceedings, pp. 179–190. www.CEUR-WS.org (2011)
17. Simonsen, K.I.F.: PetriCode: a tool for template-based code generation from CPN models. Technical Report DTU Compute-Technical Reports-2013-11, PetriCode (2013)
18. Simonsen, K.I.F., Kristensen, L.M.: Towards a CPN-based modelling approach for reconciling verification and implementation of protocol models. In: Machado, R.J., Maciel, R.S.P., Rubin, J., Botterweck, G. (eds.) MOMPES 2012. LNCS, vol. 7706, pp. 106–125. Springer, Heidelberg (2013)
19. Simonsen, K.I.F., Kristensen, L.M., Kindler, E.: Code generation for protocol software from CPN models annotated with pragmatics. In: Proceedings of SBMF'13. LNCS. Springer (2013, to appear)
20. Wehrmeister, M.A., Freitas, E.P., Pereira, C.E., Rammig, F.: Genertica: a tool for code generation and aspects weaving. In: Proceedings of ISORC '08, pp. 234–238. IEEE Computer Society, Washington, DC (2008)
21. Westergaard, M., Kristensen, L.M.: The access/CPN framework: a tool for interacting with the CPN tools simulator. In: Franceschinis, G., Wolf, K. (eds.) PETRI NETS 2009. LNCS, vol. 5606, pp. 313–322. Springer, Heidelberg (2009)

FM-RAIL-BOK 2013

Twenty-Five Years of Formal Methods and Railways: What Next?

Alessandro Fantechi[✉]

DINFO - University of Florence, Via S. Marta 3, Firenze, Italy
`fantechi@dsi.unifi.it`

Abstract. Since more than 25 years, railway signalling is the subject of successful industrial application of formal methods in the development and verification of its computerized equipment.

However the evolution of the technology of railways signalling systems in this long term has had a strong influence on the way formal methods can be applied in their design and implementation. At the same time important advances had been also achieved in the formal methods area. The scope of the formal methods discipline has enlarged from the methodological provably correct software construction of the beginnings to the analysis and modelling of increasingly complex systems, always on the edge of the ever improving capacity of the analysis tools, thanks to the technological advances in formal verification of both qualitative and quantitative properties of such complex systems.

The thesis we will put forward in this paper is that the complexity of future railway systems of systems can be addressed with advantage only by a higher degree of distribution of functions on local interoperable computers - communicating by means of standard protocols - and by adopting a multi-level formal modelling suitable to support the verification at different abstraction levels, and at different life-cycle times, of the safe interaction among the distributed functions.

1 Introduction

Despite the quite long story of successful application of formal methods in the railway domain, it cannot be yet said that a single mature technology has emerged. The evolution of the technology of railways signaling systems in this long term has had a strong influence on the way formal methods can be applied in their design and implementation, and at the same time important advances had been also achieved in the formal methods area.

The evolution of railways signalling systems has seen railways moving from a protected market based on national railway companies and national manufacturers to an open market based on international standards for interoperability, in which systems of systems are providing more and more complex automated operation, but maintaining, and even strengthening, demanding safety standards.

The scope of the formal methods discipline has enlarged from the methodological provably correct software construction of the beginnings to the analysis

S. Counsell and M. Núñez (Eds.): SEFM 2013 Collocated Workshops, LNCS 8368, pp. 167–183, 2014.
DOI: 10.1007/978-3-319-05032-4_13, © Springer International Publishing Switzerland 2014

and modelling of increasingly complex systems, always on the edge of the ever improving capacity of the analysis tools, thanks to the technological advances in formal verification of both qualitative and quantitative properties of such complex systems.

In spite of these advances, the verification of complex railway signalling systems is still a main challenge and an important percentage of the cost in the development of these systems. We can maybe speak of a "grand challenge", that is, where progress with regards to this challenge would contribute to advance the whole field of verification of complex computer-based systems.

The thesis we will put forward in this talk is that the complexity of future railway *systems of systems* can be addressed with advantage only by a higher degree of distribution of functions on local interoperable computers - communicating by means of standard protocols - and by adopting a multi-level formal modelling suitable to support the verification at different abstraction levels, and at different life-cycle times, of the safe interaction among the distributed functions. A vision that can make railway applications closer to the emerging field of the so called *cyber-physical systems*, made of collaborating computational elements controlling physical entities, that will pervade the human activities in the future.

The paper is organized as follows: after recalling the first applications of formal methods to railway signalling equipments in Sect. 2, we briefly introduce model checking and direct code verification in Sects. 3 and 4 respectively. Section 5 discusses the Model Based development approach, also in connection with the CENELEC safety guidelines. Section 6 discusses a series of challenges put forward by the evolution of the domain. Section 7 discusses the possibility, offered by recent advance in the quantitative evaluation technology, to model and evaluate dependability issues as well. Section 8 concludes the paper.

2   Early Applications of Formal Methods to Railway Signalling

In its more general definition, the term *formal methods* encompasses all notations having a precise mathematical semantics, together with their associated analysis and development methods, that allow to describe and reason about the behaviour and functionality of a system in a formal manner, with the aim to produce an implementation of the system that is provably free from defects – although actually the aim of a complete proof can be only partially achieved, for example because correctness of the actually executed code requires the proof of correctness of the compiler as well, which is not normally available.

A general but comprehensive definition is given by the safety standard Def Stan 00–55 [47], where a formal method is said to be composed of the following three ingredients: "a software specification and production method that comprises:

- a collection of mathematical notations addressing the specification, design and development phases;

- a well-founded logical inference system in which formal verification proofs and other properties can be formulated;
- a methodological framework within which software can be developed from the specification to the implementation in a formally verifiable manner."

Railway signalling has been traditionally considered as one of the most fruitful areas of intervention for formal methods [23]. Already since the end of the eighties, a series of railway signalling products have benefited from the application of the B formal method [1] in the design process. This method targets software development from specification through refinement, down to implementation and automatic code generation, with formal verification at each refinement step: writing and refining a specification produces a series of proof obligations that need to be discharged by formal proofs. The B method is accompanied by support tools, which include tools for the derivation of proof obligations, theorem provers, and code generation tools. Hence it fits perfectly the definition of formal method that we have cited above.

The SACEM system for the control of a line of Paris RER [16] is the first acclaimed industrial application of B. Since then, B has been adopted for many later designs of similar systems by Matra (now part of Siemens). One of the most striking application has been the Paris automatic metro line 14: the report on the verification activities in [6], tells that indeed several errors were found and corrected during proof activities conducted at the specification and refinement stages. By contrast, no further bugs were detected by the various testing activities at system level that followed the code generation and integration.

The success of B has had a major impact in the sector of railway signalling by influencing the definition of the EN50128 guidelines [20], issued by the European Committee for Electrotechnical Standardization (CENELEC). These guidelines address the development of Software for Railway Control and Protection Systems, and constitute the main reference for railway signalling equipment manufacturers in Europe, with their use spreading to the other continents and to other sectors of the railway (and other safety-related) industry. The EN50128 document is part of a group of documents regarding the safety of railway control and protection systems, in which the key concept of Safety Integrity Level (SIL) is defined, a number ranging from 0 to 4, where 4 indicates a high criticality, 0 gives no safety concern. The SIL is actually a property of the system, related to the damage a failure of the system can produce, and is usually apportioned to subsystems and functions at system level in the preliminary risk assessment process. Also software functions are associated a level (Software SIL); assigning different SILs to different components helps to concentrate the efforts (and therefore the production costs) on the critical components. The EN50128 guidelines however dictate neither a precise development methodology for software, nor any particular programming technique, but classify a wide range of commonly adopted techniques in terms of a rating with respect to the established SIL of the component. Formal methods are rated as highly recommended for the software requirements specification and software design of systems/components with the higher levels of SIL. Formal proof is also highly recommended as a verification activity. The norm however does not dictate any process in which formal methods take a role, but just gives a list of the most common formal methods at the time of writing. Moreover, other combinations of highly recommended techniques, not including formal methods can be chosen: for example, testing combined to full traceability to requirements is a compliant, commonly used, approach to software verification of highest SIL software components.

Anyway, we can see that B-based methods have not so spread in railway software development, as one could have expected by their impressing record of successful applications in the domain. Indeed, methods like B end up to require a substantial change to the traditional software development life cycle already adopted in an industrial setting. The related investment cost is often perceived as not justified in the light of the forecast benefits, and their adoption is not welcome both to managers, and to development teams more skilled in programming than in theorem proving. On the other hand, accompanying the traditional life cycle with formal specification and verification techniques has often proved to have less impact and has gained a better acceptance by managers and development teams pushed by the need to show compliance to CENELEC norms, sometimes as a tradeoff with respect to the promise of a full formal proof of correctness achievable with a method that encompasses the whole development, like B.

The SACEM and similar systems are examples of ATP/ATC (Automatic Train Protection/Control) systems that guarantee safe speed and braking control for trains, along the line, where the main safety criterion is to guarantee that two trains travelling at speed in the same direction stay a safe distance apart.

The basic concept in ATP/ATC is the *braking curve*: safety is guaranteed if the speed is always below the line, should the speed be above the line, emergency braking is enforced. These systems, which accommodate both train distancing and protection of singular points of the line, are constituted by on-board components that receive information from wayside components. In the early computer-based systems of this kind, this communication is rather simple and occurs at specific points of the line. As a consequence, the safety enforcing algorithms were not excessively complex and were directly amenable to formal specification.

The other main class of signalling systems, that of *interlocking*, exhibits instead complex logic relations and event-based behaviour that were not conveniently encoded in assertion-centric formalisms as the plain B method (and indeed this class has prompted evolutions of B itself).

3   Railway Signalling Equipments - The Model Checking Advent

Model checking [14] has raised the interest of many railway signalling industries, being the most lightweight from the process point of view, and being rather promising in terms of efficiency.

Interlocking systems have immediately called for a direct application of model checking, since their safety properties are quite directly expressed in temporal logic, and their specifications by means of *control tables* can be directly formalized. An *interlocking* is the safety critical system that controls the movement of the trains in a station and between adjacent stations. The interlocking monitors the status of the objects in the railway yard and allows or denies the routing of the trains in accordance with safety and operational rules. In most computer based interlocking systems the instantiation of such rules on a station topology is stored in a *control table*, that is iteratively read and executed by an appropriate interpretation engine.

However, due to the high number of boolean variables involved, automatic verification by model checking of sufficiently large stations typically incurs in combinatorial state space explosion problem. The first applications of model checking have therefore attacked portions of an interlocking system [7,29], but even recent works [27,48] show that routine verification of interlocking designs for large stations is still a challenge. SAT-based Bounded Model Checking [8] is currently the most promising option and is used in industrial solutions.

We leave the discussion of this particular application domain and the related extensive bibliographic references to the companion papers [9,32,39,40].

We can observe that model checking is used in this context as a side verification and validation activity inside a more traditional, and domain dependent, development cycle: a completely formal development cycle along the definition of formal methods given above is not respected, but the approach concentrates on the formal verification of the most sensitive and complex kernel of such systems.

On the basis of such extensive usage in this domain, Model checking has indeed gained a mention in the 2011 revision of the EN50128 guidelines [21], as one of the recommended formal methods.

4   Code Formal Verification

The cited guidelines [21] recognize that most of the industrial application of model checking regards hardware design verification. Direct application of model checking to software code verification is considered to be still a challenge, because the correspondence between a piece of code and a finite state model on which temporal logic formulae can be proved is not immediate: in many cases software has, at least theoretically, an infinite number of states, or at best, the state space is just huge. This discipline, commonly named *software model checking* [41], has in the last years developed to gain a spread application in several industrial domains; some software model checkers, such as CBMC [12], hide the formality to the user by providing built-in default properties to be proven: absence of division by zero, safe usage of pointers, safe array bounds, etc. On this ground, such tools are in competition with tools based on Abstract Interpretation, that we discuss next. It is likely that software model checking will in the next years gain a growing industrial acceptance also in the railway domain, due to its ability to prove the absence of typical software bugs, not only for proving safety properties, but also to guarantee correct behaviour of non safety related software. An interesting application of CBMC to automatic test generation in the railway domain is reported in [3].

Another technique for code formal verification is the assertion-based formal proof: the code is annotated at various locations with assertions that predicate over variables'values. The assertions are used as pre- and post- conditions to various operations in the code. The proof consists of showing that the execution of the included program fragment when preconditions hold, implies that post-conditions hold when the fragment terminates.

Assertion-based formal proof, referred as highly recommended in the 2011 revision of the EN50128 guidelines [21], finds its most prominent industrial application within the SPARK subset of the Ada language and associated proof tools, which in the railway sector is considered inside the OpenETCS initiative [43].

Abstract interpretation is based on the theoretical framework developed by Patrick and Radhia Cusot in the seventies [15]. However, due to the absence of effective analyses techniques and to the lack of sufficient computer power, only after twenty years software tools have been developed to support it so that applications of the technology at industrial level could take place. The focus of the application of the technology is mainly on the analysis of source code for runtime error detection, which means detecting variables overflow/underflow, division by zero, dereferencing of non-initialized pointers, out-of-bound array access.

Since the correctness of the source is not in general decidable at the program level, the tools implementing abstract interpretation work on a conservative and sound approximation of the variable values in terms of intervals, and consider the state space of the program at this level of abstraction. The problem boils down to solve a system of equations that represent an over-approximate version of the program state space. Finding errors at this higher level of abstraction does not imply that the bug also holds in the real program. The presence of false positives after the analysis is actually the drawback of abstract interpretation, that hampers the possibility of fully automating the process. Uncertain failure states (i.e., statements for which the tool cannot decide whether there will be an error or not) have normally to be checked manually and several approaches have been put into practice to automatically reduce these false alarms. The process developed at General Electric Transportation Systems [28] for the verification of railway signalling software includes abstract interpretation analysis, employing the Polyspace tool [17] and handles false positives through a step of abstraction refinement.

Abstract interpretation is not explicitly listed among recommended techniques in CENELEC 50128, although static analysis is, and most sophisticated static analysis tools include abstract interpretation. It is not often referred as a formal methods either, although it provides the three ingredients of a formal method of the Def Stan 00–55 definition. In our opinion, this technique is one way the decades of research on formal methods have infiltrated industrial embedded software development.

5   Model Based Design and the CENELEC Guidelines

The adoption of modelling technologies into the different phases of development of software products is constantly growing within industry. Designing model abstractions before getting into hand-crafted code helps highlighting concepts that can hardly be focused otherwise, enabling greater control over the system under development.

Indeed, the 2011 revision of EN50128 recognizes the usefulness of modelling at several stages of the development cycle. EN50128 lists recommended techniques in a series of tables that follow the different stages of the software development cycle. In the 2011 version we see that there are two techniques that are cross-cutting over the main development phases, namely Formal Methods and Modelling. Indeed, both can be adopted as a paradigm to shape the complete software development cycle. The example of the B method is a good representative of the former, although the list of formalisms cited in the standard include other assertional techniques, such as Z and VDM, process algebras, algebraic specification, temporal logic and model checking.

About modelling, the norm lists a series of techniques that include formally based ones, such as Finite State Machines, Statecharts and Petri Nets. In the norm, the term modelling refers mainly to the description of some aspects of a system in support for its development and verification, but a recent trend in industry, and in particular in the industry of embedded systems, has seen modelling as a way of defining a *model-based* development cycle. This is particularly true in the case of embedded safety-critical applications industry which has been the first in line to adopt so called Model Based Development or Model Based Design (MBD), that employs modelling and simulation platforms like Simulink/Stateflow (toolboxes of Matlab from Mathworks) [46] or the SCADE Suite (from Esterel Technologies) [45] for lower-level design, to support the development of embedded applications. The adoption of automatic code generation, or automatic test cases generation, is also growingly followed in software production for safety critical systems. A typical notation for modelling the discrete behaviour of a system is that of Statecharts, hierarchical extended finite state machines: introduced by Harel [30], they have specialized in various dialects, supported by formal specification environments: among the most adopted commercial environments we can find the mentioned Stateflow and SCADE. UML State Diagrams as well are essentially Statecharts, and are supported by several free and commercial tools.

One example from the railway signalling domain is the model based development cycle defined by General Electric Transportation Systems (GETS), The company employed modelling first for the development of prototypes [4] and afterwards for requirements formalization and automatic code generation [24]. The production process for Automatic Train Protection (ATP) Systems has been based on modelling by means of Simulink/Stateflow descriptions. Extensive simulation of Stateflow diagrams with scenarios taken from the field was conducted, aiming at 100 % structural coverage of the diagrams'states. After automatic code generation from the diagrams, back-to-back model/code testing is conducted automatically with the same simulation scenario. Back-to-back testing has the main aim of confirming that the code generator has not introduced flaws in the code [26].

The kind of testing described above is one of the techniques that are encompassed by so called Model Based Testing (MBT). Another common MBT technique is Automatic Test Generation (ATG) in which test cases are automatically generated from the model in order to guarantee an extensive coverage of the system functionalities as described by the model.

The SCADE suite as well has been widely adopted in the railway field: its usage is reported by several companies. The activities that are supported by the suite are essentially the same as for Stateflow, but one point in favour of SCADE is that the suite includes a C Code Generator certified according the EN50128 guidelines. This allows to eliminate from the development process those steps that in the previous example were aimed at guaranteeing safety of the code generator.

Model Based Design is often not numbered among formal methods, essentially for one of two main reasons (or for both): the first is that some modelling frameworks are not based on a formal semantics, and they allow designers to write non precise or non completely defined models (that is, the mathematical notations ingredient is missing); the second reason is that in many cases no formal proof technique is given to demonstrate that the code is a correct concretization of the abstract specifications (that is, the inference system ingredient is missing). This is not always the rule, and indeed models can be made precise by using semantically sound description formalisms. Formal verification of models can be conducted with the aid of model checking techniques, as it happens for the two main tool frameworks mentioned above, that both include Design Verifier, a SAT based model checker, especially when one wants to verify that given safety properties are satisfied.

Hence, having a formally based modelling formalism in which system functions are described and proved to satisfy given properties, with automatic code generation, by means of a certified code generator, is another way the three ingredients of formal description, formal proof and software production, are assembled in a full formal method [25].

6 New Challenges

Railway signalling is a rapidly evolving domain, with different evolution driving forces, such as:

- the quest for more performant equipment in order to increase the capacity of lines;
- the need of decreasing operational costs;
- the European interoperability regulations;
- the evolution of the railway market;
- the technology improvements, which include contrasting supporting features, such as increasing computing power, which allows more functions to be concentrated in one platform, and more performant (wireless) communication, which favours distribution of functionalities over several distributed computing units.

In the following sections we briefly discuss these different evolution lines, from the point of view of the application of formal methods.

6.1 Evolution of ATP Systems: ETCS and CBTC

One major innovation in ATP systems is the shift from *Fixed block* to *Moving block*. In the Fixed block a line is topologically segmented into blocks, and appropriate sensors tell whether a block is free or not. The occupancy of the leading train includes the whole block which the train is located on; the following train is allowed to move only up to the last unoccupied block's border. In the Moving block, the train position and its braking curve is continuously calculated by the trains, and then communicated via radio to the wayside equipment, which establish protected areas for each train, each one called Limit of Movement Authority (LMA), or simply Movement authority (MA), up to the nearest obstacle (tail of the train in front).

The ERTMS/ETCS (European Rail traffic Management Systems / European Train Control System) [18] has been proposed to become the single train control system for the future transeuropean railway network. The project plans to gradually install the ERTMS/ETCS equipment side by side to the traditional national equipment, also exploiting the three successive ERTMS/ETCS levels, with increasing degree of information flowing from way-side to on-board equipment. In level 2 and 3, GSM-R (GSM radio communication specific to the railway industry) is adopted to continuously transfer information to the train on the status of the line ahead. Moving block is adopted in level 3, of which anyway no implementation currently exist yet.

ERTMS/ETCS makes use of standardized components (European Vital Computer on board, Radio Block Center, Eurobalise,...) and protocols (Euroradio), produced by a consortium of the main European signalling manufacturers. Specifications issued by ERTMS/ETCS are structured as a natural language requirement document, including tables, state diagrams and sequence charts to add some formality.

Several formal modelling and verification studies have been conducted regarding ETCS protocols and components; the most systematic approach to the formalization of ETCS natural language requirements has been the EuRailCheck project by the European Railway Agency [11] where UML diagrams augmented with constraints in a Controlled Natural Language have been exploited to produce formalized requirement fragments. Automated validation analysis of such fragments has then been possible by means of a customization of the NuSMV model-checker. The OpenETCS project [31] is now working at providing a full, open formal specification of ETCS protocols and components.

In the case of ETCS, the attention of the formal methods community has shifted from the consolidated train control logic (the braking curve principle), to the safety and real-time performance of radio-based control, which is going to be the sole mean by which the conditions of the track ahead are communicated to the train, since even signals will no more be present on the line [19].

In the domain of metro signalling equipments, An emerging standard is CBTC (Communication-Based Train Control) [44], where the train's *exact* position (which is not a trivial issue to determine), is continuously communicated to the Radio Block Center (RBC) via GSM-R, which in its turn continuously communicates the LMA to the following train. So CBTC can provide a continuous automatic train protection as well as improved performance, system availability and operational flexibility. CBTC is mostly installed in (automatic) metro lines, and includes not only ATP functions, but other higher level functions as well, such as ATO (Automatic Train Operation), ATS (Automatic Train Supervision), and interlocking. As opposed to the interoperability-oriented ETCS systems, CBTC is standardized at a very high level of abstraction: international standards only define systems functions and subsystems at a very high level [37]. Every CBTC vendor has its own solutions: the trend is to provide turnkey, proprietary and closed systems, facilitated by the fact that metros are closed environments. This may produce vendor lock-in phenomena, especially with respect to long-term maintenance.

CBTC can be classified as a *Systems of Systems* (SoS), that is, large-scale systems composed from the combination of several, often pre-existing, communicating systems to provide some functionality that cannot be provided by a single system. The research on SoS engineering needs to address the challenges posed by the increasing complexity of the requirements mapped to the complexity of the underlying constituent systems, in particular for what concerns formal verification of overall safety properties.

6.2 Integrating ATC/ATP and Interlocking Systems

The interface between ATC/ATP systems, which span over a full length line, and Interlocking Systems, which are mostly concentrated within a station, is subject to several solutions and studies. A common choice at this regard is to define a proper interface between the two separate systems. The INESS project has addressed the formal definition of the interface of ERTMS with interlocking systems [35].

An approach that exploits a tighter integration is to define a chain of distributed ATP components that act both as a sensor (axle counter) for occupancy of a section and as control over occupancy of next section to achieve fixed block distancing. Interlocking functions on (small) stations insisting on some section are included in the interested component.

An opposite trend is to concentrate in a *multistation* interlocking many functions, either ATP on a line, interlocking for the interested stations and ATS, in one centralized computer or network of computers.

We want also mention the formal verification process adopted by Ansaldo STS, that include Software model checking [13], applied to the ERTMS/ETCS RBC system that control train separation on a section of line that includes points (such as in a forking junction), and hence include interlocking functions on a small number of entities.

6.3 The Evolution of the Market

At the dawn of formal methods introduction in the railway signalling arena the market was a protected one, based on national railway companies and national manufacturers. Nowadays, the market is open and the national manufacturers have been merged in large multi-national companies.

However, most experiences in formal method applications to even complex systems have been carried on till now by a single manufacturer, or single railway operator on single systems.

New challenges are provided by the quest for interoperability. For what concerns interoperability of trains across national borders, a full solution by ERTMS/ETCS is still far from sight. Currently, and for many years from now on, an interoperable train travelling over Europe should be able to switch from ETCS lev. 2 to many national systems, until a complete deployment of ETCS is accomplished on all lines that maybe of interest for the market of train transport (a complete deployment that, for economic reasons, it is quite unlikely in the next future for secondary lines). In principle, it could be cheaper to equip trains with Multistandard systems that adopt well-defined *(that is, formalized)* transition procedures.

On the other hand, the partial ETCS implementation can raise the risk of new, virtual, barriers to interoperability, As an example, Italy requires all trains running on the national main network to be equipped by SCMT, essentially an ETCS Level 1 ATP. The cost of such equipment has represent an obstacle to trains from other countries to enter Italy; in particular, this is one of the reasons why at the time of writing there is no through passenger railway service between Italy and Slovenia, although the Slovenian infrastructure is fully compatible with the Italian one, for what concerns electric traction power (3kV DC), for historical reasons, and through Intercity trains were running till few years ago.

Interoperability of trains has stressed the standardization of board to ground communication: trains equipped with on-board systems produced by different vendors do travel on infrastructures equipped by different vendors: this is the main target of the standard definition of ETCS. Still, national variants (introduced for special needs) exist that may impede full interoperability across nation borders; moreover, the standard leaves implementation freedom to some other aspects. For example, the (ground-based, fixed) RBC to RBC communication is less strictly standardized: in Italy, the Milano-Bologna and the Bologna-Firenze high speed lines are equipped with ETCS level 2 by different manufacturers. In Bologna, the two lines were connected till recently through the old station, equipped with traditional signalling. Since June 2013, a new through underground station directly connects the two lines; a specific interface, implemented on a dedicated computer, between the last and first RBCs of the two lines, produced by different vendors, was needed to let them communicate.

Lowering costs and closing the standardization gaps are the objective of the openETCS initiative [31], which aims to create a new open standard for formal functional requirement specifications and open proof for ETCS systems.

Vendor lock-in phenomena can be raised also in the case of interlocking systems, for what concerns certification aspects: the configuration and verification process is expensive, monolithic and not easily repeatable. Moreover, certification has to be repeated for every deployed system, since the track layout changes from station to station. Hence, in case of modifications to the layout, reconfiguring the system on a new layout may be very expensive also for small layout changes. The configuration and verification process itself is often proprietary, and therefore an infrastructure company can become locked to the vendor for any modification of the track layout.

6.4   The Evolution of Interlocking Systems

As already said, formal verification of IXL control tables has been studied since years, SAT-based Bounded Model Checking verification currently being the most promising direction. However, control tables are a legacy of the relay-based equipments.

Formal methods, and software design disciplines in general, have inspired a different approach to interlocking design: in the Geographic approach [5] the interlocking logic is made up by composition of small elements (or objects, if the object oriented paradigm is chosen) that take care each of the control of a physical element (point, track circuit, signal), connected by means of predefined composition rules, mimicking the topology of the specific layout. Several interlocking equipments are now developed following this paradigm, that has been followed in the INESS project [35] to provide a full formal UML-based specification.

Pushing further the concept, with the aim to study alternative paradigms for the formal verification of interlocking systems, in [22] a distributed architecture is envisaged: elements of the geographic approach configured as a set of distributed communicating processes: each process controls a given layout element. The route is instead a global notion: a route has to be established by proper cooperation of the distributed elements. The communication among processes follows the physical layout of the station/yard and a route is established by the status of the elements that lie along the route.

Indeed, [33] already made the case for distributing interlocking functions: the concept of [22] can in principle be pushed to the design of a new kind of distributed railway interlocking system. The logic of the interlocking will be fine-grained and distributed on processors deployed at each sensor/actuator, along the track layout, and communicating with the adjacent controllers by means of safe, possibly wireless, communication. This is in contrast to the current systems with centralized logics. Distributed computing elements would autonomously collaborate in order to initialize, configure, monitor and reconfigure - for fault tolerance or in case of modifications to the layout -, without a centralized logic, but still guaranteeing the absolute safety of the train transit through the track layout. There are a number of motivations that can push the technological bar towards distribution for interlockings, such as:

- Easy deployment and maintenance
- Plug-and-play reconfiguration
- Copper-free communication if wireless links are adopted
- Simpler interface with ERTMS/ETCS or ATP/ATC equipments
- Vendor lock-in avoidance by means of an open interlocking protocol stack

A so fine-grained distributed interlocking, including configuration and reconfiguration, is not something that is currently in practice nor in the foreseeable future (5–10 years) of the railway industry, but the general trend to distribute intelligence in scattered locations will probably push in this direction. Formal verification that safety guarantees are enforced will play an essential role; this verification will be the basis of the definition of certified plug-in components: if such components are assembled according to a track layout and respecting the interlocking protocol, the entire system safety is guaranteed, hence sparing on costly recertification processes. The future standardisation of the interlocking protocol will aid independence of certification with respect to the interlocking rules of a particular country.

7 Beyond Safety

In the discussion above, we have mostly focused on the ability of formal methods to prove that a given system is safe. However, liveness properties are often of interest as well: at the level of the internal working of an equipment, proving that a particular system is live or responsive is often achieved by testing in the railway industry, not recurring to formal proof, since the higher costs of formal proof are reserved to the safety-related issues, according to safety guidelines. Formal methods can be a more cost effective way to guarantee liveness as well (INESS recommends, for example, livelock and deadlock absence verification [36]).

At the system level, we observe that, as a general principle, railway safety is in the end achieved at the cost of availability: halting trains is the basic form of safety enforcement. As the number of controlling elements increase, safety mechanisms that simply tend to halt trains at any single element failure could easily lower availability, capacity and QoS.

Quantitative modelling at a high abstraction level of the working of the system and of anticipated fault scenario, can be adopted for availability or capacity evaluation. Many works in the railway research literature focused on capacity analysis with the objective of optimizing the use of railway infrastructure, especially in consideration of the growth of the entire transport sector in consequence of globalization of the economy and the increasing integration of the international economies; an overview of several techniques and methodologies can be found, e.g., in [2,10,42]. They range from analytical methods, mainly based on mathematical formulae or algebraic expressions, to more complex optimization solutions, e.g. based on heuristics to obtain optimal saturated timetables, to simulation methods. Model-based analysis has been widely applied in the last two decades to assess performance and dependability indicators in the railway domain, exploiting a Markov-chain based modelling, or Petri-net based formalism. The potential of *probabilistic model checking* in an area still dominated by simulation-based engines has to be evaluated.

Anyway, quantitative analysis is carried on at a higher level of abstraction, namely at the system level, with respect to formal verification of safety, that act on the logic inside a subsystem or on the communication between subsystems. The key is hence to adopt a multi-level modelling approach to address the complexity of a railway system. The ongoing SafeCap project [34] develops modelling techniques and tools for improving railway capacity [38] while ensuring that safety standards are maintained with a multi-level modelling approach.

8 Conclusions

Formal Methods *are* used for industrial railway signalling applications. The evolution of systems require companies to adopt automatic verification tools to attack their complexity, which makes verification by testing only unfeasible, especially for high SIL systems. The evolution of formal methods and formal verification tools themselves opens new possibilities to tackle the complexity of these systems, not only for safety certification, but also for other dependability issues. Formal modelling can even act as a facilitator for railway signalling innovations.

In the discussion above, we can envisage two main research directions that will need to be pursued in the next year, namely i) multi-level modelling to cope with the increasing complexity of systems and of their dependability requirements and ii) formal description and verification of complex distributed systems of systems. These two directions are not actually orthogonal, but can be seen as two facets of the same vision: only extensive formal description and verification tools will have the potential to master the exponentially growing complexity of railway control applications of the future.

References

1. Abrial, J.R.: The B-Book. Cambridge University Press, New York (1996)
2. Abril, M., Barber, F., Ingolotti, L., Salido, M.A., Tormos, P., Lova, A.: An assessment of railway capacity. Transp. Res. Part E-Logist. Transp. Rev. **44**, 774–806 (2008)
3. Angeletti, D., Giunchiglia, E., Narizzano, M., Puddu, A., Sabina, S.: Using bounded model checking for coverage analysis of safety-critical software in an industrial setting. J. Autom. Reason. **45**, 397–414 (2010)
4. Bacherini, S., Fantechi, A., Tempestini, M., Zingoni, ò: A story about formal methods adoption by a railway signaling manufacturer. In: Misra, J., Nipkow, T., Sekerinski, E. (eds.) FM 2006. LNCS, pp. 179–189. Springer, Heidelberg (2006)
5. Banci, M., Fantechi, A.: Instantiating generic charts for railway interlocking systems. In: Tenth International Workshop on Formal Methods for Industrial Critical Systems (FMICS 2005), Lisbon, 5–6, September 2005

6. Behm, P., Benoit, P., Faivre, A., Meynadier, J.-M.: Météor: a successful application of B in a large project. In: Wing, J.M., Woodcock, J. (eds.) FM 1999. LNCS, vol. 1708, pp. 369–387. Springer, Heidelberg (1999)

7. Bernardeschi, C., Fantechi, A., Gnesi, S., Larosa, S., Mongardi, G., Romano, D.: A formal verification environment for railway signaling system design. Formal Methods Syst. Des. **12**(2), 139–161 (1998)

8. Biere, A., Cimatti, A., Clarke, E., Zhu, Y.: Symbolic model checking without BDDs. In: Cleaveland, W.R. (ed.) TACAS 1999. LNCS, vol. 1579, pp. 193–207. Springer, Heidelberg (1999)

9. Bonacchi, A., Fantechi, A., Bacherini, S., Tempestini, M., Cipriani, L.: Validation of railway interlocking systems by formal verification, a case study. In: Counsell, S., Núñez, M. (eds.) SEFM 2013 Workshops. LNCS, vol. 8368, pp. XX–XY (2013)

10. Burdett, R., Kozan, E.: Techniques for absolute capacity determination in railways. Transp. Res. Part B: Methodol. **40**, 616–632 (2006)

11. Cavada, R., Cimatti, A., Mariotti, A., Mattarei, C., Micheli, A., Mover, S., Pensallorto, M., Roveri, M., Susi, A., Tonetta, S.: EuRailCheck: tool support for requirements validation. In: ASE 2009, Auckland, New Zealand, 16–20, November 2009

12. CBMC. http://www.cprover.org/cbmc/

13. Cimatti, A., Corvino, R., Lazzaro, A., Narasamdya, I., Rizzo, T., Roveri, M., Sanseviero, A., Tchaltsev, A.: Formal verification and validation of ERTMS industrial railway train spacing system. In: Madhusudan, P., Seshia, S.A. (eds.) CAV 2012. LNCS, vol. 7358, pp. 378–393. Springer, Heidelberg (2012)

14. Clarke, E.M., Grumberg, O., Peled, D.A.: Model Checking. MIT Press, Cambridge (1999)

15. Cousot, P., Cousot, R.: Abstract interpretation: a unified lattice model for static analysis of programs by construction or approximation of fixpoints. In: Proceedings of 4th ACM SIGACT-SIGPLAN Symposium on Principles of Programming Languages, POPL '77, pp. 238–252. ACM, New York (1977)

16. DaSilva, C., Dehbonei, B., Mejia, F.: Formal specification in the development of industrial applications: subway speed control system. In: Proceedings 5th IFIP Conference on Formal Description Techniques for Distributed Systems and Communication Protocols (FORTE'92), Perros-Guirec, North-Holland, pp. 199–213 (1993)

17. Deutsch, A.: Static verification of dynamic properties. Polyspace, White Paper (2004)

18. http://www.ertms.net

19. Esposito, R., Lazzaro, A., Marmo, P., Sanseviero, A.: Formal verification of ERTMS Euroradio safety critical protocol. In: 4th Symposium on Formal Methods for Railway Operation and Control Systems (FORMS'03). L'Harmattan, Budapest, Hongrie (2003)

20. European Committee for Electrotechnical Standardization: EN50128, Railway Applications - Software for Railway Control and Protection Systems. CENELEC, Brussels (1997)

21. European Committee for Electrotechnical Standardization: EN50128, Railway Applications - Communication, Signalling and Processing Systems - Software for Railway Control and Protection Systems. CENELEC, Brussels (2011)

22. Fantechi, A.: Distributing the challenge of model checking interlocking control tables. In: Margaria, T., Steffen, B. (eds.) ISoLA 2012, Part II. LNCS, vol. 7610, pp. 276–289. Springer, Heidelberg (2012)

23. Fantechi, A., Fokkink, W., Morzenti, A.: Some trends in formal methods applications to railway signaling. In: Gnesi, S., Margaria, T. (eds.) Formal Methods for Industrial Critical Systems: A Survey of Applications. IEEE Computer Society Press, Los Alamitos, pp. 63–84 (2013)

24. Ferrari, A., Fantechi, A., Bacherini, S., Zingoni, N.: Modeling guidelines for code generation in the railway signaling context. In: Proceedings of 1st Nasa Formal Methods Symposium, pp. 166–170 (2009)

25. Ferrari, A., Fantechi, A., Gnesi, S., Magnani, G.: Model-based development and formal methods in the railway industry. IEEE Softw. **30**(3), 28–34 (2013)

26. Ferrari, A., Grasso, D., Magnani, G., Fantechi, A., Tempestini, M.: The Metro Rio case study. Sci. Comput. Program. **78**(7), 828–842 (2013)

27. Ferrari, A., Magnani, G., Grasso, D., Fantechi, A.: Model checking interlocking control tables. In: Proceedings of the 8th FORMS/FORMAT Symposium, pp. 98–107 (2010)

28. Ferrari, A., Magnani, G., Grasso, D., Fantechi, A., Tempestini, M.: Adoption of model-based testing and abstract interpretation by a railway signalling manufacturer. IJERTCS **2**(2), 42–61 (2011)

29. Groote, J.F., van Vlijmen, S., Koorn, J.: The safety guaranteeing system at station Hoorn-Kersenboogerd. In: Logic Group Preprint Series 121. Utrecht University (1995)

30. Harel, D.: Statecharts: a visual formalism for complex systems. Sci. Comput. Program. **8**, 231–274 (1987)

31. Hase, K.R.: Open proof for railway safety software - a potential way-out of vendor lock-in advancing to standardization, transparency, and software security. In: Proceedings of the 8th FORMS/FORMAT Symposium, pp. 4–37 (2010)

32. Haxthausen, A.E., Peleska, J., Pinger, R.: Applied bounded model checking for interlocking system designs. In: Counsell, S., Núñez, M. (eds.) SEFM 2013 Workshops. LNCS, vol. 8368, pp. XX–YY (2013)

33. Haxthausen, A.E., Peleska, J.: Formal development and verification of a distributed railway control system. IEEE Trans. Softw. Eng. **26**(8), 687–701 (2000)

34. Iliasov, A., Romanovsky, A.: SafeCap domain language for reasoning about safety and capacity. Newcastle University, Computing Science, Technical Report Series, CS-TR-1352 (2012)

35. FP7 Project INESS - Deliverable D.1.5 Report on translation of requirements from text to UML (2009)

36. FP7 Project INESS - Deliverable D.4.1 Documented strategy for Verification and Validation, Report (2009)

37. Institute of Electrical and Electronics Engineers: IEEE Standard for Communications Based Train Control (CBTC) Performance and Functional Requirements. IEEE Std 1474.1-2004

38. Isobe, Y., Moller, F., Nguyen, H.N., Roggenbach, M.: Safety and line capacity in railways - an approach in timed CSP. In: Derrick, J., Gnesi, S., Latella, D., Treharne, H. (eds.) IFM 2012. LNCS, vol. 7321, pp. 54–68. Springer, Heidelberg (2012)

39. James, P., Lawrence, A., Moller, F., Roggenbach, M., Seisenberger, M., Setzer, A., Kanso, K., Chadwick, S.: Verification of solid state interlocking programs. In: Counsell, S., Núñez, M. (eds.) SEFM 2013 Workshops. LNCS, vol. 8368, pp. XX–YY (2013)

40. James, P., Moller, F., Nguyen, H.N., Roggenbach, M., Schneider, S., Treharne, H., Trumble, M., Williams, D.: Verification of Scheme Plans using CSP∥B. In: Counsell, S., Núñez, M. (eds.) SEFM 2013 Workshops. LNCS, vol. 8368, pp. XX–YY (2013)

41. Jhala, R., Majumdar, R.: Software model checking. ACM Comput. Surv. **41**(4), 21:1–21:54 (2009)

42. Kontaxi, E., Ricci, S.: Railway capacity analysis; methodological framework and harmonization perspectives. In: Proceedings of the 12th World Conference on Transportation Research, Lisboa, July 2010

43. Mentre, D.: Evaluation model of ETCS using GNATprove, openETCS Technical Report June 2013

44. Pascoe, R.D., Eichorn, T.N.: What is Communication-Based Train Control? IEEE Vehicular Technology Magazine (2009)

45. Sauvage, S., Bouali, A.: Development approaches in software development. In: Proceedings of ERTS, Toulouse (2006)

46. Simulink. http://www.mathworks.com/products/simulink/

47. UK Ministry of Defence: Def Stan 00–55: Requirements for Safety Related Software in Defence Equipment, August 1997

48. Winter, K., Johnston, W., Robinson, P., Strooper, P., van den Berg, L.: Tool support for checking railway interlocking designs. In: Proceedings of the 10th Australian workshop on Safety critical systems and software, pp. 101–107 (2006)

What IS a BoK? Large
– Extended Abstract –

Tom Maibaum[✉]

McMaster Centre for Software Certification, McMaster University, 1280 Main St W,
Hamilton, ON L8S 4K1, Canada
tom@maibaum.org

1 Main Points

Software engineering is different from traditional engineering disciplines in certain crucial ways. But software engineering *is* an engineering discipline. However, software engineering fails to meet the requirements of an engineering discipline, as commonly conceived by conventional engineers. Software Engineering Books of Knowledge (BoKs) fail spectacularly in organising engineering knowledge as understood in classical engineering disciplines.

"The SWEBOK Guide:

- characterizes the contents of the software engineering discipline
- promotes a consistent view of software engineering worldwide
- clarifies software engineering's place with respect to other disciplines
- provides a foundation for training materials and curriculum development, and
- provides a basis for certification and licensing of software engineers."

We will "show" below that this is nothing like classical engineering knowledge and, in particular, like the so called cookbooks well known in engineering.

2 What is Engineering?

So, what characterises classical engineering disciplines? The following books have been immensely helpful in understanding engineering:

- GFC Rogers, The Nature of Engineering, The Macmillan Press Ltd, 1983
- WG Vincenti, What Engineers Know and How They Know It, The Johns Hopkins University Press, 1990

We have also been inspired by various papers of Michael Jackson [Jac10]. That software engineering is an engineering discipline is a simple consequence of the fact that: "engineering refers to the practice of organising the design and construction of any artifice which transforms the physical world around us to meet some recognised need" [Rog83]. Vincenti [Vin90] argues that engineering is different, in epistemological terms and, consequently, as praxis, from science or even applied science: "In this view, technology, though it may apply science, is not the

S. Counsell and M. Núñez (Eds.): SEFM 2013 Collocated Workshops, LNCS 8368, pp. 184–188, 2014.
DOI: 10.1007/978-3-319-05032-4_14, © Springer International Publishing Switzerland 2014

same as or entirely applied science". Rogers argues the same view on the basis of what he calls the teleological distinction concerning the aims of science and technology: "In its effort to explain phenomena, a scientific investigation can wonder at will as unforeseen results ... The essence of technological investigations is that they are directed towards serving the process of designing and constructing particular things whose purpose has been clearly defined." "We have seen that in one sense science progresses by virtue of discovering circumstances in which a hitherto acceptable hypothesis is falsified, and that scientists actively pursue this situation. Because of the catastrophic consequences of engineering failures - whether it be human catastrophy [sic] for the customer or economic catastrophy [sic] for the firm - engineers and technologists must try to avoid falsification of their theories. Their aim is to undertake sufficient research on a laboratory scale to extend the theories so that they cover the foreseeable changes in the variables called for by a new conception. The scientist seeks revolutionary change - for which he may receive a Nobel Prize. The engineer too seeks revolutionary conceptions by which he can make his name, but he knows his ideas will not be taken up unless they can be realised using a level of technology not far removed from the existing level" [Rog83].

So, science is different from engineering. We can ask what the praxis of engineering is. Vincenti [Vin90] defines engineering activities in terms of *design*, *production* and *operation* of artefacts. Of these, design and operation are highly pertinent to software engineering. In the context of discussing the focus of engineers activities, he then talks about *normal design* as comprising "the improvement of the accepted tradition or its application under new or more stringent conditions". He goes on to say: "The engineer engaged in such design knows at the outset how the device in question works, what are its customary features, and that, if properly designed along such lines, it has good likelihood of accomplishing the desired task." Jackson discusses this concept of normal design, although he does not use this phrase himself: "An engineering handbook is not a compendium of fundamental principles; but it does contain a corpus of rules and procedures by which it has been found that these principles can be most easily and effectively applied to the particular design tasks established in the field. The outline design is already given, determined by the established needs and products." "In this context, design innovation is exceptional. Only once in a thousand car designs does the designer depart from the accepted structures by an innovation like front-wheel drive or a transversely positioned engine. True, when a radical innovation proves successful it becomes a standard design choice for later engineers. But these design choices are then made at a higher level than that of the working engineer: the product characteristics they imply soon become well understood, and their selection becomes as much a matter of marketing as of design technology. Unsuccessful innovations - like the rotary internal combustion engine - never become established as possible design choices." "The methods of value are micro-methods, closely tailored to the tasks of developing particular well-understood parts of particular well-understood products."

Another important aspect of engineering design is the organising principle of hierarchical design: "Design, apart from being normal or radical, is also multi-level and hierarchical. Interesting levels of design exist, depending on the nature of the immediate design task, the identity of some component of the device, or the engineering discipline required" [Vin90]. It is quite clear from the engineering literature that engineering normally involves the use of multiple technologies. The observation that software engineering requires knowledge of other domains and that its teaching should be application oriented is not as perspicacious as its proponents would have us believe. This is part of the essence of engineering, whatever the discipline. An implied but not explicitly stated view of engineering design is that engineers normally design devices as opposed to systems, in the sense of Vincenti. A device, in this sense, is an entity whose design principles are well defined, well structured and subject to normal design principles. (See also Michael Polanyis operational principle of a device [Pol58]). A system, in this sense, is an entity that lacks some important characteristics making normal design possible. "Systems are assemblies of devices brought together for a collective purpose." Examples of the former given by Vincenti are airplanes, electric generators, turret lathes; examples of the latter are airlines, electric-power systems and automobile factories. The software engineering equivalent of devices may include compilers, relational databases, PABXs, etc. Software engineering examples of systems may include air traffic control systems, automotive software, the internet, etc. It would appear that systems become devices when their design attains the status of being normal. That is, the level of creativity required in their design becomes one of systematic choice, based on well defined analysis, in the context of standard definitions and criteria developed and agreed by engineers.

3   Engineering Knowledge

Is the knowledge used by software engineers different in character from that used by conventional engineers? The latter is underpinned by mathematics and some physical science(s), providing models of the physical universe in terms of which artefacts must be understood. What about software engineering? I would claim that logic (in its widest sense) fulfills these roles, although from different perspectives in computer science and software engineering. Software engineering is distinguished from conventional engineering because the artefacts constructed by the former are conceptual, while those built by the latter are physical. For the latter, the "real world" is a fixed constraint, whereas it is not clear that there are the same limitations on the "computational world". There is an existing track record of working with concepts and abstractions in mathematics and logic, particularly philosophical logic.

What distinguishes software engineering is the day to day invention of theories (descriptions) by engineers and the problems of size and structure induced by the nature of the artefacts. Can we successfully apply the analogy between conventional engineering and its use of mathematical techniques and scientific analyses, on the one hand, and software engineering and its use of ideas from the relevant mathematics and logic based analyses, on the other?

An example that may be used in this context is program construction. The well understood underlying mathematics was developed over 25 years (in the sequential case), starting in the 1960s. Thus, we might have expected the SE equivalent of the engineering CAD tool to appear at the end of this time. Instead, we have CASE tools with no relation to the underlying mathematics, or formal methods, which offer a relaxation of the exhaustiveness requirement of the scientific/theoretical viewpoint. There is no equivalent of the conventional engineering disciplines available in industrial software engineering settings.

4   Categories of Engineering Knowledge

Software engineering is distinct in character from conventional disciplines of engineering. However, it has enough in common with them to look for the same categories of knowledge [Vin90]:

1. Fundamental design concepts
2. Criteria and specifications
3. Theoretical tools
4. Quantitative data
5. Practical considerations
6. Design instrumentalities

Fundamental design concepts include the operational principle of their device. According to Polanyi, this means knowing for a device "how its characteristic parts ... fulfill their special functions in combining to an overall operation which achieves the purpose" [Pol58]. A second principle taken for granted is the normal configuration for the device, i.e., the commonly accepted arrangement of the constituent parts of the device. These two principles (and possibly others) provide a framework within which normal design takes place. Criteria and specifications allow the engineer using a device with a given operational principle and normal configuration to "translate general, qualitative goals couched in[to] concrete technical terms". That the development of such criteria may be problematic is clear. However, the development and acceptance of such criteria is an inherent part of the development of engineering disciplines.

Engineers require theoretical tools to underpin their work, including intellectual concepts for thinking about design, as well as mathematical methods and theories for making design calculations. Both conceptual tools and mathematical tools may be devised specifically for use by the engineer and be of no particular value to a scientist/mathematician. "...the most useful context for the precision and reliability that formality can offer is in sharply focused micro-methods, supporting specialised small-scale tasks of analysis and detailed design" [Jac10]. Engineers also use quantitative data as well as tabulations of functions in mathematical models. (A good example in software engineering of this thoroughness in providing data useful for design is the work of Knuth on sorting and searching.)

There are also practical considerations in engineering. These are not usually subject to systematisation in the sense of the categories above, but reflect pragmatic concerns. For example, a designer will use various trade-offs which are the result of general knowledge about the device, its use, its context, its cost, etc. Design instrumentalities include "the procedures, ways of thinking, and judgmental skills by which it [design] is done" [Vin90]. This is clearly what the Capability Maturity model has in mind when it refers to well defined and repeatable processes in software engineering.

According to Vincenti, as noted above, the day to day activities of engineers consist of normal design, as comprising "the improvement of the accepted tradition or its application under new or more stringent conditions". This is the combination of discipline and a little bit of creativity encapsulated in engineering cookbooks! He goes on to say: "The engineer engaged in such design knows at the outset how the device in question works, what are its customary features, and that, if properly designed along such lines, it has a good likelihood of accomplishing the desired task."

5   In Summary

"An engineering handbook is not a compendium of fundamental principles; but it does contain a corpus of rules and procedures by which it has been found that these principles can be most easily and effectively applied to the particular design tasks established in the field. The outline design is already given, determined by the established needs and products" [Jac10].

Systems become devices when their design attains the status of being normal, i.e., the level of creativity required in their design becomes one of systematic choice, based on well defined analyses, in the context of standard definitions and criteria developed and agreed by the relevant engineers ([Vin90], definition of normal design). This is exactly what engineering BoKs should be about!

References

[Jac10] Jackson, M.: The operational principle and problem frames. In: Roscoe Bill, A.W., Jones, C.B., Wood, K.R. (eds.) Reflections on the Work of CAR Hoare, pp. 143–165. Springer, London (2010)

[Pol58] Polanyi, M.: Personal Knowledge: Towards a Post-critical Philosophy. Routledge & Kegan Paul, London (1958). Reprinted by University of Chicago Press (1974)

[Rog83] Rogers, G.F.C.: The Nature of Engineering: A Philosophy of Technology. Macmillan Press, London (1983)

[Vin90] Vincenti, W.G.: What Engineers Know and How They Know It: Analytical Studies from Aeronautical History. The Johns Hopkins University Press, Baltimore (1990)

Verification of Scheme Plans Using CSP||B

Philip James[1], Faron Moller[1], Hoang Nga Nguyen[3]([✉]), Markus Roggenbach[1], Steve Schneider[2], Helen Treharne[2], Matthew Trumble[2], and David Williams[4]

[1] Swansea University, Swansea, UK
[2] University of Surrey, Surrey, UK
[3] University of Nottingham, Nottingham, UK
Hoang.Nguyen@nottingham.ac.uk
[4] VU University Amsterdam, Amsterdam, The Netherlands

Abstract. The paper presents a tool-supported approach to graphically editing scheme plans and their safety verification. The graphical tool is based on a Domain Specific Language which is used as the basis for transformation to a CSP||B formal model of a scheme plan. The models produced utilise a variety of abstraction techniques that make the analysis of large scale plans feasible. The techniques are applicable to other modelling languages besides CSP||B. We use the ProB tool to ensure the safety properties of collision, derailment and run-through freedom.

1 Introduction

In a series of papers [1–7] we have been developing a new modelling approach for railway interlockings. This work has been carried out in conjunction with railway engineers drawn from our industrial partner. By involving the railway engineers from Siemens Rail Automation, we benefit twofold: they provide realistic case studies, and they guide the modelling approach, ensuring that it is natural to the working engineer.

We base our approach on CSP||B [8], which combines event-based with state-based modelling. This reflects the double nature of railway systems, which involves events such as train movements and – in the interlocking – state based reasoning. The formal models are by design close to the domain models. To the domain expert, this provides traceability and ease of understanding. The validity of this claim was demonstrated in particular in [3] where a non-trivial case study – a complex double junction – was provided, a formal model of which was understandable and usable by our industrial partners.

In the UK, the development of interlockings follows prescribed processes from Railway Authorities such as the *Governance for Railway Investment Projects* (GRIP) process from Network Rail. In this process, the development of an interlocking consists of five phases where the first four phases are responsible for defining a track plan and determining routes to be used while, in the last phase, a contractor such as Siemens Rail Automation participates and is responsible for designing a control table for the track plan, implementing the interlocking

S. Counsell and M. Núñez (Eds.): SEFM 2013 Collocated Workshops, LNCS 8368, pp. 189–204, 2014.
DOI: 10.1007/978-3-319-05032-4_15, © Springer International Publishing Switzerland 2014

and choosing appropriate track equipment. To this end, our paper offers a work flow which enables safety to be validated in each of these phases.

In [4,5] we addressed how to *effectively* and *efficiently* verify safety properties within our CSP||B models. The properties of interest are collision, derailment and run-through freedom. To this end we developed a set of abstraction techniques for railway verification that allow the transformation of complex CSP||B models into less involved ones; we proved that these transformations are sound; and we demonstrated that they allow one to verify a variety of railway systems via model checking. The first set of abstractions reduces the number of trains that need to be considered in order to prove safety for an unbounded number of trains. Their correctness proof involves slicing of event traces. Essentially, these abstractions provide us with finite state models. The second set of abstractions simplifies the underlying track topology. Here, the correctness proof utilizes event abstraction specific to our application domain similar to the ones suggested by Winter in [9]. These abstractions make model checking faster.

Still present in our approach from the aforementioned papers was the need to write the formal models by hand. In [6] we described our OnTrack toolset[1], an open tool environment allowing graphical descriptions to be captured and supported by formal verification. This enables an engineer to visually represent the tracks and signals etc., within a railway network.

In this paper we continue the dissemination of our modelling approach which now also incorporates multi-directional tracks. We demonstrate that when changes are made to the models they are systematic and traceable; again this addition will be incorporated within our OnTrack tools.

The paper is organised as follows. In Sect. 2 we introduce our modelling language CSP||B so that we have the basis for discussing our workflow and provide examples. In Sect. 3 we introduce concepts in railway systems. In Sect. 4 we describe the workflow for our CSP||B modelling approach and summarise where the different abstraction techniques fit into the workflow. In Sect. 5 we introduce the modelling concepts of multi-directional travel and provide two illustrative examples. The application of our approach is presented in Sect. 6 via verification of our example scenarios. In Sect. 7 we put our work in the context of related approaches and finally conclude with future plans for the approach.

2   Background to CSP||B

The CSP||B approach [8] allows us to specify communicating systems using a combination of the B-Method [10] and the process algebra CSP (Communicating Sequential Processes) [11]. The overall specification of a combined communicating system comprises two separate specifications: one given by a number of CSP process descriptions and the other by a collection of B machines. Our aim when using B and CSP is to factor out as much of the "data-rich" aspects of a system as possible into B machines. The B machines in our CSP||B approach are classical B machines, which are components containing state and operations on that

---

[1] OnTrack available for download from http://www.csp-b.org.

state. The CSP||B theory [8] allows us to combine a number of CSP processes Ps in parallel with machines Ms to produce $Ps \parallel Ms$ which is the parallel combination of all the controllers and all the underlying machines. Such a parallel composition is meaningful because a B machine is itself interpretable as a CSP process whose event-traces are the possible execution sequences of its operations. The invoking of an operation of a B machine outside its precondition within such a trace is defined as divergence [12]. Therefore, our notion of consistency is that a combined communicating system $Ps \parallel Ms$ is *divergence-free*. We do not consider deadlock-freedom in this paper as it is concerned with liveness, and the focus of the paper is on safety.

A B MACHINE clause declares a machine and gives it a name. The VARIABLES of a B machine define its state. The INVARIANT of a B machine gives the type of the variables, and more generally it also contains any other constraints on the allowable machine states. There is an INITIALISATION which determines the initial state of the machine. The machine consists of a collection of OPERATIONS that query and modify the state. Besides this kind of machine we also define static B machines that provide only sets, constants and properties that do not change during the execution of the system.

The language we use to describe the CSP processes for B machines is as follows:

$$P ::= e?x!y \rightarrow P(x) \mid P_1 \square P_2 \mid P_1 \sqcap P_2 \mid$$
$$\textbf{if } b \textbf{ then } P_1 \textbf{ else } P_2 \textbf{ end} \mid N(exp) \mid$$
$$P_1 \parallel P_2 \mid P_1 \,_A\|_B\, P_2 \mid P_1|||P_2$$

The process $e?x!y \rightarrow P(x)$ defines a channel communication where x represents all data variables on a channel, and y represents values being passed along a channel. Channel e is referred to as a *machine channel* as there is a corresponding operation in the controlled B machine with the signature $x \longleftarrow e(y)$. Therefore the input of the operation y corresponds to the output from the CSP, and the output x of the operation to the CSP input. Here we have simplified the communication to have one output and one input but in general there can be any number of inputs and outputs. The other CSP operators have the usual CSP semantics.

In this paper we omit a detail discussion of the semantic models used for reasoning of CSP||B models. In [5] we discuss that the traces models is enough to deal with the safety properties of railway interlockings.

3   Railway Systems

Together with railway engineers we developed a common view on the information flow in railways. In physical terms a railway consists of, at least, four different components as illustrated in Fig. 1:

- The *Controller* selects and releases routes for trains.
- The *Interlocking* serves as a safety mechanism with regards to the Controller and, in addition, controls and monitors the Track equipment.

– The *Track equipment* consists of elements such as signals, points, and track circuits. Signals can show the different aspects to indicate when trains can proceed; points can be in normal position (leading trains straight ahead) or in reverse position (leading trains to a different line) and track circuits detect if there is a train on a track.

– Finally, *Trains* have a driver who determines their behaviour.

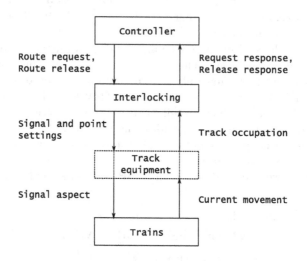

Fig. 1. Information flow.

For the purposes of modelling, we simplify the signals in railway systems to have only two aspects. We also make a further assumption that track equipment reacts instantly and is free of defects.

The information flow shown in Fig. 1 is as follows: the controller sends a request message to the interlocking to which the interlocking responds; the interlocking sends signalling information to the track equipment and receives information from track sensors on whether a track element is occupied. The interlocking and the trains interact indirectly via the track equipment only. The interlocking serves as the system's clock: in a cycle the status of all the track sensors are read then the interlocking reacts to all of them with one change of state. Routes cannot be in conflict since requests to select and release routes are sequentialised. In our modelling we will abstract away from modelling the track equipment explicitly.

Each railway system is provided from the railway industry as a *scheme plan* which consists of a track plan (describing the topological relation between elements of the track equipment such as which tracks are connected and where signals are), a control table (determining how the interlocking of the railway system sets signals, moves points and lock points where, for each signal, there is one or more rows describing the condition under which the signal can show proceed) and a number of release tables (specifying when locks on points can be released). More details about control tables and release tables can be found in [3]. To this end, our task is to provide models which faithfully capture the behaviour associated with these railways systems.

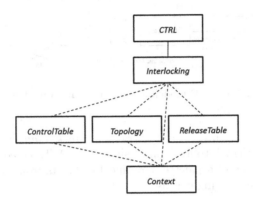

Fig. 2. CSP‖B architecture.

In this setting, we consider three safety properties:

1. collision freedom excludes two trains occupying the same track;
2. run-through freedom says that whenever a train enters a point, the point is set to cater for this;
3. no-derailment says that whenever a train occupies a point, the point does not move.

Our modelling approach of railway systems in CSP‖B, presented in [3], is restated in Fig. 2. The centralised control logic is represented in the *Interlocking* machine, whereas the train behaviour is controlled by CSP processes defined in the *CTRL* script. These process and machine synchronise on common events. In the next sections we illustrate some aspects of the CSP processes and machines via examples[2] and focus on how multi-directional travel of trains on tracks is modelled.

4   Workflow

In this section, we present the workflow that we employ in our methodology in order to verify safety properties of railway systems. Figure 3 demonstrates the essential steps of the workflow which makes use of two tools: OnTrack [6] and the ProB model checker [13]. Here, OnTrack is implemented in a typical EMF/GMF/Epsilon[3] architecture [14,15] where a graphical editor realised in GMF is the front-end for the user.

---

[2] Examples available for download from http://www.csp-b.org.
[3] EMF and GMF stand for Eclipse Modeling Framework and Graphical Modeling Project, respectively.

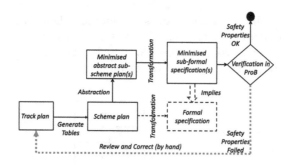

Fig. 3. CSP∥B modelling and verification workflow.

In this workflow, a user initially draws a *Track Plan* using the graphical front-end in the OnTrack tool. Figure 4 shows the OnTrack editor that consists of a drawing canvas and a palette. Graphical elements from the palette can be positioned onto the drawing canvas.

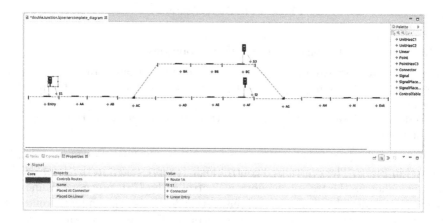

Fig. 4. A screenshot of "OnTrack" modelling a track plan.

Then the first transformation, *Generate Tables* leads to a *Scheme Plan*, which is a track plan and its associated control and release tables. Track plans and scheme plans are models formulated relative to a modified version of the DSL developed by Bjørner [16]. The concepts of such a DSL can be easily captured within an ECORE meta-model which underlies our toolset. A small excerpt of topological concepts within our meta-model is given in Fig. 5. In this DSL, a *Railway Diagram* is built from *Units*, *Connectors* and *Signals*. *Units* come in two forms: *Linear* representing straight tracks, or *Point* representing a splitting track. All *Unit(s)* are attached together via *Connector(s)*. Finally, *Signals* can be placed on *Linear* units and at *Connectors*. To this end, the implementation of the GMF front-end for this meta-model involves selecting the concepts of

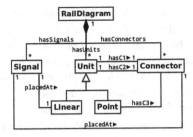

Fig. 5. Static concepts from Bjørner's DSL.

the meta-model that should become graphical constructs within the editor and assigning graphical images to them.

A scheme plan is the basis for subsequent workflows that support its verification. Scheme plans can be captured as formal specifications. The simplest transformation, indicated by the *Transformation* dashed arrow, is to produce one *Formal specification* that is a faithful representation of the scheme plan. This transformation is a mapping from the railway DSL meta-model to the CSP‖B meta-model and its subsequent representation as CSP‖B script files that can be inputted into ProB. This automated transformation makes use of the finitisation theory in order to be able to perform bounded model checking of the formal specification [4,7]. The finitisation theory allows us to reduce the problem of verifying of scheme plans for safety (i.e., freedom from collision, derailment, and run-through) for any number of trains to that of a two-train scenario.

Nonetheless, even when examining a reduced number of trains the formal specifications of realistic examples will inevitably contain too many states for safety analysis. Thus, our methodology enables us to carry out two forms of abstraction on a scheme plan:

(1) Covering Abstraction supports the decomposition of a scheme plan with a set of smaller sub-scheme plans. Any particular track in a scheme plan has a 'zone of influence': the other tracks which need to be considered to see what will happens on that track (e.g., when routes including it are enabled, when trains are approaching it, etc.). In particular, we only need to look at the zone of influence in order to see if a collision is possible on that track. To analyse if a collision, derailment or run-through is possible on that track, it is enough just to analyse the behaviour of trains within the zone of influence. We can do this for all the tracks, in each case just analysing for collisions, derailment or run-through within its zone of influence. This is called a covering. In general each zone of influence is much smaller than the overall track plan, so the analyses will be much quicker, and in practice can be done efficiently.

(2) Topological Abstraction supports the collapsing of tracks of a scheme plan to minimise the number of superfluous tracks in a plan, i.e., ones which do not impact on safety. Thus, for a particular track plan we take a sequence of tracks, and think of them as one single track. We do this for a number of sequences of tracks along the way. It is a topological abstraction if we can match moves around the original track plan with moves around the smaller one, so changes such as routes being enabled, points being released, trains being on particular routes, points being set, trains being at lights must still match for this collapsing to be a topological abstraction. If this is true then it means that we can analyse the behaviour of trains on the smaller scheme plan (which is easier because there are fewer positions to consider) and the results that we get will still be true for the original larger scheme plan.

We have proved the soundness of these abstractions in [4,7]. In our methodology we first apply covering abstraction to generate sub-scheme plans and then apply topological abstraction to each of them. Using these abstractions we follow the *Abstraction* vertical workflow from the scheme plan to produce one or more *Minimised abstract sub-scheme plan(s)*. One or more such plans may be produced because as we shall see in our examples, in Sect. 5, it may not always be possible to perform covering, and in which case the only abstraction that may yield a reduction in the number of tracks in the plan will be topological abstraction. Applying these abstractions is done at the DSL level and is independent of the formalism being used to represent the abstract CSP∥B specification. Currently, the covering abstraction is not fully automated but is ongoing development work within the OnTrack tool.

Following abstraction (top left box on the diagram) the *Transformation* workflow, described earlier, can be applied to the minimised abstract sub-scheme plans to produce corresponding sub-formal specifications. All of the transformations that are performed by the OnTrack tool are validated via manual review. The verification of all of these sub-formal specifications implies the safety of the formal specification, as illustrated by the *Implies* arrow workflow; this result has been formally proved [4,7].

Once OnTrack produces the sub-formal specifications they are all systematically verified using the ProB model checker to ensure that the models are collision- and derailment-free and contain no run-throughs. Successful checks verify that the safety properties hold for the particular scheme-plan. The workflow has the potential for round-trip engineering where the counter examples produced from unsuccessful model checking are automatically fed back into the OnTrack tool. This has not, as yet, been incorporated into the tool but it would provide an improved tool-supported workflow; this is illustrated using the dotted *Review and Correct* arrow on the workflow.

5 Modelling of Multi-Directional Examples of CSP∥B Railway Models

In this section we provide details of the extension to our modelling approach in CSP∥B which allows for multi-directional railway systems.

5.1 Tunnel Example

Consider the track plan in Fig. 6 where tracks AB, AC and AD are bi-directional tracks. For route $R1$ associated with signal $S1$ their direction is left to right,

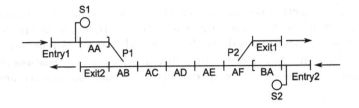

Fig. 6. Track plan for the tunnel example.

whereas for route $R2$ associated with signal $S2$ their direction is right to left. The CSP process that controls the movement of trains is $TRAIN\_CTRL$. Figure 7 illustrates the fragment of it controlling the movement of a train from a track that is neither an *exit* one or one which has a signal on it. The *move* event is parameterised with the train identifier t and its current position p. This event is a synchronisation with a *move* B operation which returns its new position *newp*. Therefore, moving from track AC to AD corresponds to the event *move.t.AC.AD* for a particular train t.

```
1    TRAIN_CTRL(t, pos) = ...
2    □ pos ∉ EXIT ∧ pos ∉ SIGNALHOMES &
3           move!t.pos?newp → TRAIN_CTRL(t, newp)
4    □ ...
```

Fig. 7. Fragment of the CSP control process for trains.

Note, there is no information in the CSP event that corresponds to the direction of travel. All this information is contained in the *Topology* machine and used in the *move* operation within the *Interlocking* machine. In the *Topology* machine there are three relations which define the direction of tracks. For example, the relation *direction* shown in Fig. 8 shows that the model needs to contain details of the way tracks are connected together, and this is explicitly done via the notion of identified *connectors* — the glue between tracks and points.

```
1    direction ∈ TRACK ↔ CONNECTOR * CONNECTOR ∧
2    direction = {...,
3           AA ↦ (C1, C2), ..., /* uni-directional tracks */
4           AC ↦ (C3, C4), AC ↦ (C4, C3), ... /* bi-directional tracks */ }
```

Fig. 8. Fragment of the *direction* relation from *Topology*.

As we saw above the notion of a train's position in the CSP was captured using two parameters (t, pos). In the INVARIANT of the *Interlocking* machine a similarly named function *pos* also includes information about the connectors, as shown in Fig. 9. In its INITIALISATION $pos := \emptyset$ since there are no trains on the tracks. The *move* operation updates the track and connectors related to train t in *pos* each time the train moves. (In earlier papers, e.g., [3], *pos* was simply a partial function between trains and tracks and *direction* was not required.)

1	$pos \in TRAIN \rightarrow ALLTRACK *$
2	$(ALLCONNECTOR * ALLCONNECTOR)$

Fig. 9. *pos* function from *Interlocking*.

In addition to B operations which define the behaviour of movement, granting and releasing of route requests the OnTrack tool automatically produces B operations to support the verification of safety properties. Three B operations are produced, *collision*, *derailment* and *run-through*. Collision is encoded as follows:

```
1  collision =
2  SELECT
3    ∃t₁, t₂ ∈ TRAIN ∧ t₁ ≠ t₂∧
4    t1 ∈ dom(pos) ∧ t2 ∈ dom(pos)
5    (dom(pos(t₁))) − (EXIT ∪ ENTRY)) ∩
6    (dom(pos(t₂))) − (EXIT ∪ ENTRY)) = ∅
7  THEN skip
8  END;
```

Here collision is detected when two different trains t_1 and t_2 occupy the same track segment (different from the $EXIT$ and $ENTRY$ tracks). The collision condition will be enabled when the two trains are at the same position.

Collision freedom can then be established by model checking the validity of the following CTL formula:

$$AG(not(e(collision)))$$

This formula is false if *collision* is enabled. In the CTL variant of PROB AG, stands for "on all paths it is globally true that", and $e(a)$ stands for "event a is enabled".

5.2   Buffer Example

Our next example is also multi-directional as shown in Fig. 10. Interestingly, track BC has three directions, i.e., $\{BC\} \triangleleft direction = \{(C12, C11), (C11, C12), (C7, C12)\}$, where $C7$ is the connector between tracks AC and BC, $C11$ is between BB and BC, and $C12$ is between BC and BD, respectively.

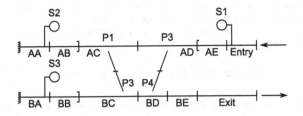

Fig. 10. Track plan for the buffer example.

It also serves to illustrate how additional complexity can easily be traced within a formal specification. We model the behaviour of buffers, i.e., tracks where trains can turn around; in our example the buffers are AA and BA. Two routes are associated with signal $S1$, i.e., route $R1A$ is associated with AE, AD, AC, AB and AA and $R1B$ is associated with AE, AD, BD, BC, BB and BA. Thus, when a train is on route $R1A$ and is on track AA it can change direction and then follow route $R2$ which is associated with signal $S2$. Similarly, for route $R3$ associated with signal $S3$.

This additional behaviour requires three additions to the CSP processes and B machines:

- The additional definition of $BUFFER = \{AA, BA\}$ in the *Context* machine and similarly in the CSP types.
- A new *changeDirection* operation as shown in Fig. 11. The purpose of this operation is to simply modify the direction of the connectors for the particular buffer track on which the train t currently resides. Hence, changing the direction of train t on track AA means changing the maplet $(t \mapsto AA, (C1, C0))$ to $(t \mapsto AA, (C0, C1))$ within the *pos* function. This means that we can leave the *move* operation unchanged.
- Within the CSP, rather than disturb the existing processes, we define a new process, $BUFFER_P(b, t)$ in Fig. 12 which defines that after a train moves

```
1   changeDirection(t, currp) =
2   PRE t ∈ TRAIN ∧ t ∈ dom(pos)∧
3       {currp} = dom({pos(t)}) ∧ currp ∈ BUFFER
4   THEN
5     movedPoints := {} ||
6     LET(track, d) BE (track, d) = pos(t) IN
7      LET(d1, d2) BE (d1, d2) = d IN
8       pos(t) := (track, (d2, d1))
9      END
10    END
11  END;
```

Fig. 11. *changeDirection* method from *Interlocking*.

$$
\begin{array}{ll}
1 & BUFFER_P(b,t) = move!t?p!b \rightarrow changeDirection.t.b \\
2 & \qquad\qquad\qquad \rightarrow move.t.b?newp \rightarrow BUFFER_P(b,t)
\end{array}
$$

Fig. 12. $BUFFER_P$ process in $CTRL$.

onto the buffer track b it must change direction before it can move off it. In the model there will be a separate buffer process for each buffer and they are independent of each other. These new processes are combined to reformulate the overall CSP processes contained in the $CTRL$ script.

6   Experimental Results

In this section, we present the experiment results when verifying safety properties of the tunnel and buffer examples presented in the previous section. These experiments are carried out by following the verification workflow defined in Sect. 4.

In order to verify the tunnel example, an engineer first uses the OnTrack tool to draw the track plan as depicted on Fig. 6. Then the safety properties of the example can be verified by loading the formal specification produced by OnTrack into the ProB tool and performing this check. Here, a total of 1,516 distinct states were examined in order to determine that no collision was possible. Our methodology currently requires us to do this loading by hand but automating this as a batch process for all the safety properties could easily be done.

Similarly, verification of the buffer example can be carried out by using the OnTrack tool to draw the track plan as depicted on Fig. 10. The state space of the formal specification produced by OnTrack required by ProB to model check the safety properties for the formal specification of the Buffer example was 18,510 states, significantly more than in the tunnel example. In Sect. 4 we noted that it may not always be feasible to model check a complex scenario but our methodology supports the systematic generation of all the sub-scheme plans for a particular scheme plan. The track plan for one of the sub-scheme plans of the buffer example is shown in Fig. 13. It illustrates the plan for the track AC constructed using the covering abstraction. The highlights from this plan are as follows:

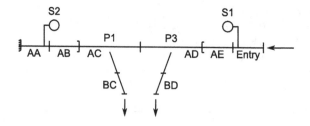

Fig. 13. Sub-track plan for track AC of the buffer example

- The point BC in the overall buffer example can now be considered as an *exit* track and after which we do not need to consider the behaviour of subsequent linear tracks and points. The reason being is that all that needs to be captured is what happens to the state when a train moves off the point AC and that this can be represented using a simple linear track rather than a point.
- The point BD is similarly converted to an *exit* track.
- The current version of our covering technique has not considered the impact of buffers on the abstraction of the scheme plans. Therefore, we must include them in the zone of influence. Therefore, both tracks AA and AB retain their bi-directional properties in the sub-scheme plan. We shall of course examine in future work whether such tracks can be further reduced.
- Notice also that we need not consider the path along $Entry$, AE, AD, BD, BC, BB, BA because it does not belong to the zone of influence as it does not contain the track AC, but of course $Entry$, AE and AD are included because they are on the normal route $R1A$ and BD is included for the above reason.

Running the formal specification of the sub-scheme plan for AC through ProB gives a state space of 3,995 compared to 18,510 states for the full specification. We have also verified that the three important safety properties hold for this sub-scheme plan. Methodologically, we would then be required to run all the sub-scheme plans through ProB and by appealing to our theoretical results we would conclude that the overall buffer example from Fig. 10 preserves the safety properties.

7 Related Work

The railway interlocking problem has long been studied by the Formal Methods community, and our work builds upon prior approaches to the modelling and verification of railways. Prominent studies from the B community include [17, 18] whilst [19,20] are classical contributions from process algebra and [21] uses techniques from Algebraic Specification. On a lower abstraction layer, [22–25] verify the safety of interlocking programs with logical approaches.

Our modelling is most related to Winter's uni-directional approach in CSP [26] and Abrial's bi-directional modelling in Event-B [27], which however excludes that trains can turn around at end stations. Winter [26] presents a generic, event-based railway model in CSP as well as generic formulations of two safety properties: CollisionFreedom and NoMovingPoints. Overall, this results in a generic architecture and a natural representation of two safety properties. Traceability, however, is limited. There are relations in the model which are *derived* from the control table. For example, the driving rule "trains stop at a red signal" is distributed over different parts of the model: it is a consequence of the fact that (1) the event "move to the first track protected by a signal" belongs to a specific synchronziation set and (2) a red signal does not offer this event. Purely event-based modelling leads to such decentralized control. Consequently,

the model has no interlocking cycle. Chapter17 of the book by Abrial [27] gives
an excellent detailed description and analysis of the railway domain, deriving
a total of 39 different requirements. The modelling approach is generic, even
though no concrete model is proven to be correct. Traceability in a tower of
specifications can be complex for various reasons. For instance, a requirement
can be the consequence of invariants from different levels. The relation between
intended properties and the model remains an informal one. This is in contrast
to other approaches (including Winter's and our own) which directly represent
the intended property in the formal world and then prove that the modelled
property is a mathematical consequence of the formal model. Furthermore, the
approach is monolithic: behaviour is not attached to different entities to which
they relate.

To put our work into context we must first clarify that railway verification
falls into two categories: the verification of railway designs prior to their implementation and the verification of the implementation descriptions themselves.
Our work is in the first area. A comparison using different model checkers in the
analysis of control tables has been conducted by Ferrari *et al.* [28] and falls into
the first category. Winter in a recent paper [29] considers different optimising
strategies for model checking using NuSMV and demonstrates the efficiency of
their approach on very large models. These analyses also fall into the first category but the models are flat in structure compared to our models as they are
defined in terms of boolean equations and do not focus on providing behavioural
models. The analysis of interlocking tables (cf. control tables) by Haxthausen [30]
also falls into the first category and is supported by automated tools that generate the models. Cimatti *et al.* [25] also have had considerable success using
NuSMV but their analysis is focussed on the implementation descriptions.

8   Conclusion

In this paper we provided an overview of our methodology that uses the OnTrack
tool to provide a graphical front-end for the automatic generation of formal specifications. The formal specifications are then separately model checked using the
ProB tool. We described the architecture of a CSP∥B formal specification of
a scheme plan giving details of the new aspects that allow the modelling of
multi-directional travel. We appreciate the absolute necessity to include these
aspects in our CSP∥B formal specifications and recognise that the majority of
the related work includes such detail, for example [30]. Our aim by demon-
strating its inclusion incrementally was to show the robustness of the CSP∥B
architecture and the ease by which new modelling aspects can be included. Similarly, additional development of the OnTrack tool-support can also be achieved
incrementally. We are currently completing the implementation of the covering
abstractions and the integration of the output from ProB model checking with
OnTrack in order to provide round-trip engineering to the graphical editor. This
will mean that the engineer is not required to manipulate the formal specifications when safety properties are violated. Instead, the engineer will be able to

change a graphical scheme plan, re-generate the formal specifications and re-run the model checking in order to verify that the amended scheme plan preserves safety (i.e., freedom from collision derailment and run-through).

Heitmeyer in [31] discusses the importance of complete abstractions. Our abstractions are sound. It is future theoretical work to investigate if completeness can be established. Furthermore, we also would like to extend our methodology so that capacity and safety of large-scale railway systems can be studied simultaneously. One way to obtain this goal is to combine our modelling approach with others which take capacity into account such as presented in [32].

Acknowlegements. Thanks to S. Chadwick and D. Taylor from the company Siemens Rail Automation for their support and encouraging feedback.

References

1. Moller, F., Nguyen, H.N., Roggenbach, M., Schneider, S., Treharne, H.: Combining event-based and state-based modelling for railway verification. Technical report CS-12-02, University of Surrey (2012)
2. Moller, F., Nguyen, H.N., Roggenbach, M., Schneider, S., Treharne, H.: Using ProB and CSP||B for railway modelling. In: Proceedings of IFM 2012 and ABZ 2012 Posters and Tool Demos Session, pp. 31–35 (2012)
3. Moller, F., Nguyen, H.N., Roggenbach, M., Schneider, S., Treharne, H.: Railway modelling in CSP||B: The double junction case study. Electron. Commun. EASST **53** (2012)
4. Moller, F., Nguyen, H.N., Roggenbach, M., Schneider, S., Treharne, H.: Defining and model checking abstractions of complex railway models using CSP||B. In: Biere, A., Nahir, A., Vos, T. (eds.) HVC 2013. LNCS, vol. 7857, pp. 193–208. Springer, Heidelberg (2013)
5. James, P., Moller, F., Nguyen, H.N., Roggenbach, M., Schneider, S., Treharne, H.: On modelling and verifying railway interlockings: tracking train lengths. Technical report CS-13-03, University of Surrey (2013)
6. James, P., Trumble, M., Treharne, H., Roggenbach, M., Schneider, S.: OnTrack: an open tooling environment for railway verification. In: Brat, G., Rungta, N., Venet, A. (eds.) NFM 2013. LNCS, vol. 7871, pp. 435–440. Springer, Heidelberg (2013)
7. James, P., Moller, F., Nguyen, H.N., Roggenbach, M., Schneider, S., Treharne, H.: Techniques for modelling and verifying railway interlockings. STTT (to appear)
8. Schneider, S., Treharne, H.: CSP theorems for communicating B machines. Formal Asp. Comput. **17**(4), 390–422 (2005)
9. Winter, K., Robinson, N.: Modelling large railway interlockings and model checking small ones. In: Proceedings of the 26th Australasian Computer Science Conference, pp. 309–316. Australian Computer Society, Inc. (2003)
10. Abrial, J.R.: The B-Book: Assigning Programs to Meanings. Cambridge University Press, Cambridge (1996)
11. Hoare, C.A.R.: Communicating Sequential Processes. Prentice-Hall, Upper Saddle River (1985)
12. Morgan, C.: Of wp and CSP. In: Beauty is our business: a birthday salute to E. W. Dijkstra, pp. 319–326 (1990)

13. ProB: The ProB animator and model checker (ProB 1.3.6-final). http://www.stups. uni-duesseldorf.de/ProB. Accessed 1 May 2013
14. Gronback, R.C.: Eclipse Modeling Project: A Domain-Specific Language (DSL) Toolkit. Addison-Wesley Professional, Upper Saddle River (2009)
15. Kolovos, D., Rose, L., Paige, R., García-Domínguez, A.: The Epsilon Book. The Eclipse Foundation (2012)
16. Bjørner, D.: Formal software techniques for railway systems. In: CTS 2000 (2000)
17. Leuschel, M., Falampin, J., Fritz, F., Plagge, D.: Automated property verification for large scale B models with ProB. Formal Asp. Comput. 23(6), 683–709 (2011)
18. Sabatier, D., Burdy, L., Requet, A., Guéry, J.: Formal proofs for the NYCT line 7 (flushing) modernization project. In: Derrick, J., Fitzgerald, J., Gnesi, S., Khurshid, S., Leuschel, M., Reeves, S., Riccobene, E. (eds.) ABZ 2012. LNCS, vol. 7316, pp. 369–372. Springer, Heidelberg (2012)
19. Simpson, A., Woodcock, J., Davies, J.: The mechanical verification of solid-state interlocking geographic data. In: Formal Methods Pacific 97. Springer, Heidelberg (1997)
20. Morley, M.J.: Safety in railway signalling data: a behavioural analysis. In: 6th International Workshop on HOLTPA, pp. 464–474. Springer, Heidelberg (1993)
21. Haxthausen, A.E., Peleska, J.: Formal development and verification of a distributed railway control system. IEEE Trans. Softw. Eng. 26(8), 687–701 (2000)
22. Ferrari, A., Magnani, G., Grasso, D., Fantechi, A.: Model checking interlocking control tables. In: FORMS/FORMAT 2010, pp. 107–115 (2011)
23. Kanso, K., Moller, F., Setzer, A.: Automated verification of signalling principles in railway interlockings. ENTCS 250, 19–31 (2009)
24. James, P., Roggenbach, M.: Automatically verifying railway interlockings using SAT-based model checking. Electr. Commun. EASST 35 (2010)
25. Cimatti, A., Corvino, R., Lazzaro, A., Narasamdya, I., Rizzo, T., Roveri, M., Sanseviero, A., Tchaltsev, A.: Formal verification and validation of ERTMS industrial railway train spacing system. In: Madhusudan, P., Seshia, S.A. (eds.) CAV 2012. LNCS, vol. 7358, pp. 378–393. Springer, Heidelberg (2012)
26. Winter, K.: Model checking railway interlocking systems. Aust. Comput. Sci., Commun. 24(1), 303–310 (2002)
27. Abrial, J.R.: Modeling in Event-B. Cambridge University Press, Cambridge (2010)
28. Ferrari, A., Magnani, G., Grasso, D., Fantechi, A.: Model checking interlocking control tables. In: FORMS/FORMAT, pp. 107–115 (2010)
29. Winter, K.: Optimising ordering strategies for symbolic model checking of railway interlockings. In: Margaria, T., Steffen, B. (eds.) ISoLA 2012, Part II. LNCS, vol. 7610, pp. 246–260. Springer, Heidelberg (2012)
30. Haxthausen, A.E.: Automated generation of safety requirements from railway interlocking tables. In: Margaria, T., Steffen, B. (eds.) ISoLA 2012, Part II. LNCS, vol. 7610, pp. 261–275. Springer, Heidelberg (2012)
31. Heitmeyer, C.L., Kirby, J., Labaw, B.G., Archer, M., Bharadwaj, R.: Using abstraction and model checking to detect safety violations in requirements specifications. IEEE Trans. Softw. Eng. 24(11), 927–948 (1998)
32. Isobe, Y., Moller, F., Nguyen, H.N., Roggenbach, M.: Safety and line capacity in railways - an approach in timed CSP. In: Derrick, J., Gnesi, S., Latella, D., Treharne, H. (eds.) IFM 2012. LNCS, vol. 7321, pp. 54–68. Springer, Heidelberg (2012)

Applied Bounded Model Checking
for Interlocking System Designs

Anne E. Haxthausen[1]([⊠]), Jan Peleska[2], and Ralf Pinger[3]

[1] DTU Compute, Technical University of Denmark, Kongens Lyngby, Denmark
aeha@dtu.dk
[2] Department of Mathematics and Computer Science, Universität Bremen,
Bremen, Germany
jp@informatik.uni-bremen.de
[3] Siemens AG, Braunschweig, Germany
Ralf.pinger@siemens.com

Abstract. In this paper the verification and validation of interlocking systems is investigated. Reviewing both geographical and route-related interlocking, the verification objectives can be structured from a perspective of computer science into (1) verification of static semantics, and (2) verification of behavioural (operational) semantics. The former checks that the plant model – that is, the software components reflecting the physical components of the interlocking system – has been set up in an adequate way. The latter investigates trains moving through the network, with the objective to uncover potential safety violations. From a formal methods perspective, these verification objectives can be approached by theorem proving, global, or bounded model checking. This paper explains the techniques for application of bounded model checking techniques, and discusses their advantages in comparison to the alternative approaches.

Keywords: Railways · Interlocking systems · Formal methods · Verification · Bounded model checking · Temporal logic

1 Introduction

Formal methods have been applied for years in the railway domain and reached a level that enables the compilation of the body of knowledge in the form of an engineering handbook (in the style of [1]), recording case-based "best practices". To this end, this paper contributes knowledge concerning verification and validation (V&V) of interlocking system designs. First we outline the state-of-the-art of V&V tasks and formal methods for performing them. Then techniques for applying one of these methods (bounded model checking) are explained in more detail.

1.1 Interlocking V&V – State-of-the-art

Software controlling interlocking systems has to be verified on two levels. The first level focuses on the correctness of configuration data specifying how the

S. Counsell and M. Núñez (Eds.): SEFM 2013 Collocated Workshops, LNCS 8368, pp. 205–220, 2014.
DOI: 10.1007/978-3-319-05032-4_16, © Springer International Publishing Switzerland 2014

topology of the railway network controlled by the interlocking system is reflected by re-usable software objects, their interfaces, and their instantiation data. Correctness of the configuration data ensures that the software has adequate control over the electro-mechanical components of the physical interlocking system. In terms of computer science, physical railway network layout may be regarded as formal models conforming to some graph grammar. The associated software configurations are correct if they conform to a similar grammar where physical language objects – e.g., a point – have been replaced by language objects representing software components – e.g., the software instance representing a point. Apart from grammatical well-formedness, additional rules concerning proper parameterisation of objects apply. All in all, checking the correctness of interlocking configurations corresponds to checks of model syntax and static semantics. The second verification level investigates the safety of trains passing through the controlled network area. The verification objective is to prove the absence of hazardous situations in the network, provided that all trains follow the restrictions (signals, speed limitations) imposed by the interlocking system. Extending the object attributes of the static software configuration by dynamic state information – e.g., whether trains reside on track elements, or the switch state of a signal or a point – the object configuration is turned into a model with both static and behavioural semantics. The latter specifies the potential dynamic changes of the interlocking system configuration – e.g., a train leaving one track segment and entering another.

Interlocking systems are designed according to different paradigms [21, Chapter 4]. Two of the most widely used ones are (a) *geographical interlocking systems* and (b) *route-based interlocking systems* using interlocking tables. For design type (a), routes through the railway network can be allocated dynamically by indicating the starting and destination points of trains intending to traverse the railway network portion controlled by the interlocking system under consideration. In the original technology, electrical relay-based circuits were applied, whose elements and interconnections where designed in one-to-one correspondence with those of the physical track layout. The electric circuit design ensured dynamic identification of free routes from starting point to destination, the locking of points and setting of signals along the route, as well as on neighbouring track segments for the purpose of flank protection. In today's software-controlled electronic interlocking systems, instances of software components "mimic" the elements of the electric circuit. Typically following the object-oriented paradigm, different components are developed, each corresponding to a specific type of physical track element, such as points, track sections associated with signals, and others with axle counters or similar devices detecting trains passing along the track. Similar to connections between electric circuit elements, instances of these software components are connected by communication channels reflecting the track network. The messages passed along these channels carry requests for route allocation, point switching and locking, signal settings, and the associated responses acknowledging or rejecting these requests. The software components are developed for re-use, so that novel interlocking software designs can be realised by means of configuration data, specifying which instances of software components are required, their attribute values, and how their communication channels shall be connected. The geographical approach to interlocking system design induces a separate verification and validation (V&V) step which is called *data validation*. Its objective is to check whether the instantiation of software components is complete, each component is equipped with the correct attribute values, and whether the channel interconnections are adequate. The data validation objectives are specified by means of rules, and the rules collection is usually quite extensive (several hundred), so that manual data validation is a cumbersome, costly, and error-prone task. Moreover, the addition of new rules often required expensive extensions of manually programmed checking software. Data validation investigates only the static semantics of the network of software components. A second V&V step is required to check whether the design will ensure the safety properties required, so that – at least under certain boundary conditions stating that train engine drivers have to respect signals and speed restrictions, as far as not automatically enforced by the underlying technology – trains moving concurrently through the railway network are protected against derailing and collisions.

Route-based interlocking (system type (b)) is less flexible than geographical interlocking, since it fixes all train routes through the railway network a priori, using route tables specifying the sequences of track segments to be allocated for each route. This loss of flexibility is compensated by the advantage that configuration data is considerably simpler. The route table is complemented by interlocking tables specifying the point positions and signal states to be enforced when allocating routes. The interlocking tables fix these positions both for the track elements which are part of the actual route, and the elements which are outside the route, but contribute to its safety by guaranteeing flank protection. Finally, a route conflict table identifies the routes which may never be simultaneously allocated, due to utilisation of common track elements [17]. Route-related interlocking offers simpler means for data validation, since the control software does not need to be based on communicating software instances related to each track element. Instead, a control algorithm monitors a dynamic plant model (each track element with its free/occupied status, and the locked/unlocked states of points). Route allocation decisions can made by means of these element states and their compatibility with the interlocking table restrictions. Data validation is only concerned with choosing the proper software components (e.g., the correct types of signals and points), and their consistency with the physical network. V&V of the dynamic behaviour now has the objective to verify both the correctness of the control algorithm and the correctness of the interlocking tables. Even in presence of a completely correct algorithm, a safety violation may occur if these tables are not adequately specified; e.g., if a conflict between two routes has not been properly documented in the tables. As a consequence, the data validation activities concerning static semantics of the software components is simpler and less critical than in the case of geographical interlocking systems, but only V&V of the dynamic behaviour can verify the crucial safety properties of the interlocking tables.

1.2 State-of-the-art Formal Methods for Interlocking V&V

The European CENELEC standards applicable for the development of software in railway control systems require the application of formal specification and design models and formalised, justified V&V activities to be performed for software of the highest criticality, as applicable for interlocking systems [9]. The objective of such formalizations is to ensure that potential safety breaches caused by invalid configuration data or erroneous control algorithms can be identified in a systematic way. If formal methods application can also be "mechanised" by means of suitable tools, it contributes to the efficiency of V&V for interlocking system designs in a considerable way. As of today, three methods are applied for formal interlocking V&V: formal verification by theorem proving, by global model checking, or by bounded model checking (BMC). Each of these methods depends on the existence of models describing the static semantics of the interlocking systems, and their dynamic behaviour in combination with trains traversing the railway network.

While – just like theorem proving – global model checking may result in complete correctness proofs of data correctness and safety properties, experience (see for instance [12]) has shown that complex interlocking systems cannot be verified by means of global model checking, since this would lead to state explosions for all but the simplest interlocking systems. In contrast to this, bounded model checking investigates model properties in the vicinity of a given state only, and can therefore be applied to models of considerable size. In this contribution we describe first how BMC is applied to data validation. This is performed by checking the compliance of the data with correctness rules that may be expressed formally by some temporal logic. Next, for the verification of safety properties, BMC can be combined with inductive reasoning, and again, this results in a global proof of the desired safety properties. The bounded model checking techniques to be applied are sufficiently mature today to be applied in an industrial context.

1.3 BMC as Best Practice for Interlocking V&V

The bounded model checking solution to data validation is explained for geographical interlocking systems, since there the requirements for this validation are far more complex than for route-related interlocking. We describe how the software components instantiated according to the given configuration data can be formalised by means of a Kripke Structure whose state space is given by the software component instances, where the transition relation is induced by the communication channels connecting neighbouring objects, and the labelling function specifies the attributes associated with each instance. It is explained how typical pattern of data validation rules can be expressed by means of Linear Temporal Logic (LTL) including existential quantification of specific variable values. A trace of states fulfilling such a formula identifies a witness for a *violation* of the validation rule. Application of LTL model checking allows for easy extendability of the rule base, by simply adding new LTL formulae representing violations of the new rules. No further software extensions are required, as long as a sufficiently powerful bounded model checker for LTL exists. We further describe how the BMC approach can be rightfully applied, because each data validation rule only applies to a finite trace through the Kripke structure (while LTL property checking in general refers to infinite computations). A bounded LTL property checking algorithm is sketched which can be efficiently applied for performing the data validation activities.

In [16] we have described a formal, model-driven method for efficient development and verification of product lines of re-configurable route-related interlocking systems. This method is based on many years of research of which the most recent publications include [14,15] and [17]. According to this method the development and verification of an interlocking system should be made in a number of steps including the following ones: (1) Specify application-specific parameters in a domain-specific railway language, and (2) from the domain-specific specification, generate a formal, behavioural model of the interlocking system and formal specification of the required safety properties. This generation should be fully automated by tools developed for the purpose. For this setting we describe how BMC may be applied in combination with inductive reasoning, in order to verify global safety properties of the interlocking system software and configuration data generated from these models. This combination of BMC and induction is well-established today in many domains, and it is known to scale up for complex "real-world" applications.

1.4   Related Work

An overview of trends in formal methods applications to railway signalling can be found in [5,11]. Many other research groups have been using model-checking for the verification of interlocking systems. In [12] a systematic study of applicability bounds of the symbolic model-checker NuSMV and the explicit model checker SPIN showed that these popular model checkers could only verify small railway yards. Several domain-specific techniques to push the applicability bounds for model checking interlocking systems have been suggested. Here we will just mention some of the most recent ones. In [25] Winter pushes the applicability bounds of symbolic model checking (NUSMV) by optimizing the ordering strategies for variables and transitions using domain knowledge about the track layout. Fantechi suggests in [10] to exploit a distributed modelling of geographical interlocking systems and break the verification task into smaller tasks that can be distributed to multiple processors such that they can be verified in parallel. In [20], it is suggested to reduce the state space using abstraction techniques reducing the number of track sections and the number of trains.

For the alternative approach to interlocking V&V based on theorem proving, the B-Method and its variants, such as Event-B, seem to be the formal methods most strongly favoured for railway control applications in Europe. The formal verification of behavioural properties is described, and the methods' applicability on an industrial scale has been established, for example, in [2]. In [6,18], the application of Event-B to data validation is described. Further verification approaches using theorem proving have been based on the RAISE method, as described in [13].

An introduction into LTL can be found in [7]. The existential quantification operator for LTL, which plays a crucial role in our concept of automated data validation, has been originally introduced in [19]. Its adaptation to finite trace semantics has been performed by the authors. The original semantics and algorithms for verifying LTL formulae against finite trace segments have been devised in [3,4]. On these finite segments only a subclass of LTL formulae can be verified, this class has been identified in [24]. Fairness properties, for example, which can be expressed in the complete LTL with infinite computations as models, are not part of this class. Our data validation properties, however, as well as the safety properties to be fulfilled by the behavioural interlocking system semantics, are all part of the so-called *Safety LTL* subset which is expressible on finite trace segments.

1.5   Paper Overview

Sections 2 and 3 describe our methods for data validation and for verifying system safety, respectively. In Sect. 4, the presented methods are discussed.

2   Data Validation

2.1   Kripke Structure Encodings of Static Plant Model

As sketched above, the software controlling geographical interlocking systems consists of instances communicating over channels, each instance representing a physical track element in the plant model. A subset of these channels – called primary channels in the following – reflect the physical interconnection between neighbouring track elements which are part of possible routes, to be dynamically allocated when a request for traversal from some starting point to a destination is given (Fig. 1). Other channels – called secondary channels – connect certain elements s_1 to others s_2, such that s_1 and s_2 are never neighbouring elements on a route, but s_2 may offer flank protection to s_1, when some route including s_1 should be allocated. Since geographical interlocking is based on request and response messages, each channel for sending request messages from some instance s_1 connected to an instance s_2 is associated with a "response channel" from s_2 to s_1. Primary channels are subsequently denoted by variable symbols a, b, c, d, while secondary channels are denoted by e, f, g, h.

All software instances are associated with a unique *id*. Depending on the track element type they are representing in the plant model, software instances carry an element type t. Depending on the type, a list of further attributes $a_1, \ldots, a_k$ may be defined for each software instance. By using a default value 0 for attributes that are not used for a certain component type, each element can be associated with the same complete list of attributes, where the ones which are

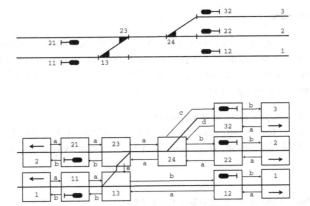

Fig. 1. Physical layout, associated software instances and channel connections.

not applicable are set to 0. Each valuation of a channel variable contains either a default value 0, meaning "no connection on this channel", or the instance identification $id > 0$ of the destination instance of the channel.

We will now formalise the static design of geographical interlocking systems as a Kripke Structure $K = (S, S_0, R, L, AP)$, with state space S, set of initial states $S_0 \subseteq S$, transition relation $R \subseteq S \times S$ and labelling function $L : S \to 2^{AP}$, where AP is a set of atomic propositions and 2^{AP} denotes its power set [7]. To this end, define a set V of variable names as introduced above, $V = \{id, t, a, b, c, d, e, f, g, h, a_1, \ldots, a_k\}$. The state space S consists of one valuation function $s : V \to \mathbf{N}_0$ for each software component. Each function maps the variables to integers identifying the associated software component (id is mapped to its unique id, t to its type, etc.). The set of initial states S_0 is defined to be the set of all states S. This allows us to start data validations at arbitrary track elements. The transition relation R defines each instance s_2 reachable from some instance s_1 via any of the channels $a, \ldots, h$ to be a possible post-state of s_1.

$$R = \{(s_1, s_2) \mid s_1(v) = s_2(id) \wedge v \in \{a, \ldots, h\}\} \tag{1}$$

The set of atomic propositions AP is defined as the collection of all propositions stating equality of some attribute $v \in V$ to one of its possible values, $AP = \{v = \xi \mid v \in V \wedge \xi \in \mathbf{N}_0\}$. The labelling function L maps each state s to the set $L(s)$ of propositions which hold true in s, that is, $\forall s \in S : L(s) = \{v = s(v) \mid v \in V\}$.

Now the violation of any data validation rule may be defined as a LTL formula specifying witnesses of such an unwanted sequence of neighbouring elements. This will be illustrated in the following by a collection of validation examples.

2.2   LTL Syntax

The LTL formulae specifying witnesses for rule violations use symbols from V as free variables. The atomic propositions involved may consist of arithmetic expressions and comparison operators $=, <, >, \leq, \geq, \neq$. The valid LTL formulae are constructed according to the following rules.

– Every atomic proposition is a LTL formula.
– If φ, ψ are LTL formulae, then[1] $\neg\varphi$, $\phi \wedge \psi$, $\phi \vee \psi$, $(\exists b : \varphi)$, $\mathbf{F}\varphi$, $\mathbf{G}\varphi$, $\mathbf{X}\varphi$, $(\varphi\mathbf{U}\psi)$ are LTL formulae. It is assumed that bound variable symbol b is not contained in V.

2.3   Bounded Trace Semantics forLTL

The semantic rules for evaluating LTL formulae on finite trace segments $s_i \ldots s_k$ are specified using notation $\langle\varphi\rangle_i^k$. The recursive rules for evaluating the truth value of $\langle\varphi\rangle_i^k$ can be directly transformed into an algorithm unrolling $\langle\varphi\rangle_i^k$ into a proposition no longer involving any temporal operators ($\mathbf{F}, \mathbf{G}, \mathbf{X}, \mathbf{U}$), but referring to variable valuations in states $s_i, s_{i+1}, \ldots, s_k$ and Boolean operators $\neg, \wedge, \vee$ only. Observe that we omit the semantics for $\mathbf{G}$ here, because our witnesses violating data rules are always represented by finite trace segments $s_i.s_{i+1} \ldots s_k$ without loops, whereas $\mathbf{G}\varphi$ only holds true if the trace segment has a lasso shape, where previous state on the segment is re-visited, thereby creating a cycle. The BMC semantics of $\mathbf{G}$ is discussed in detail in [3,4].

The remaining transformation rules applicable for data validation are (symbols p denote atomic propositions)

$$\langle\varphi\rangle_i^k = \text{false} \quad \text{if} \quad i > k \tag{2}$$

$$\langle p\rangle_i^k \quad \text{iff} \quad p[s_i(v)/v \mid v \in var(p)] \tag{3}$$

$$\langle\neg\varphi\rangle_i^k \quad \text{iff} \quad neg \ \langle\varphi\rangle_i^k \tag{4}$$

$$\langle\varphi \wedge \psi\rangle_i^k \quad \text{iff} \quad \langle\varphi\rangle_i^k \wedge \langle\psi\rangle_i^k \tag{5}$$

$$\langle\varphi \vee \psi\rangle_i^k \quad \text{iff} \quad \langle\varphi\rangle_i^k \vee \langle\psi\rangle_i^k \tag{6}$$

$$\langle(\exists b : \varphi)\rangle_i^k \quad \text{iff} \quad \langle\varphi\rangle_i^k \wedge \bigwedge_{j=i}^{k-1} (s_j(b) = s_{j+1}(b)) \tag{7}$$

$$\langle\varphi\mathbf{U}\psi\rangle_i^k \quad \text{iff} \quad \langle\psi\rangle_i^k \vee (\langle\varphi\rangle_i^k \wedge \langle\varphi[b'/b \mid b \in \text{bound}(\varphi)]\mathbf{U}\psi\rangle_{i+1}^k) \tag{8}$$

$$\langle\mathbf{X}\varphi\rangle_i^k \quad \text{iff} \quad \langle\varphi\rangle_{i+1}^k \tag{9}$$

$$\langle\mathbf{F}\varphi\rangle_i^k \quad \text{iff} \quad \bigvee_{j=i}^{k} \langle\varphi\rangle_j^k \tag{10}$$

In this specification of semantic transformations, Eq. (2) describes a termination condition: if $i > k$, the formula is evaluated on an empty trace segment, and this

---

[1] We do not need to consider the weak until operator $\mathbf{W}$, or the release operator $\mathbf{R}$.

is false by definition. Equation (3) associates truth value true with an atomic proposition if it evaluates to true after having replaced all variables v by their actual value $s_i(v)$ in the initial state s_i of the trace segment under consideration. In Eq. (7) it is shown how a formula using existential quantification with bound variable b is transformed into a proposition. Note that b occurs free in right-hand side formula, and extends domain of $s_j, s_{j+1}, \ldots, s_k$ by b. The conjunction over terms $s_j(b) = s_{j+1}(b)$ specifies that, once the value of b has been fixed for some state s_j, the same value has to be used in all states along the trace segment. The recursive definition of the until operator in Eq. (8) requires to use fresh bound variable symbols in each transformation step of the formula. This is illustrated in Example 1.

Example 1. Consider the BMC evaluation of property $(\exists b : y = b \wedge \mathbf{X}(y = b + 1))\mathbf{U}(x > 10)$ on trace segment $s_0.s_1.s_2$, that is $\langle(\exists b : y = b \wedge \mathbf{X}(y = b + 1))\mathbf{U}(x > 10)\rangle_0^2$. Applying the rules above, this is unrolled to

$$\langle(\exists b : y = b \wedge \mathbf{X}(y = b + 1))\mathbf{U}(x > 10)\rangle_0^2 \equiv$$
$$\langle(x > 10)\rangle_0^2 \vee$$
$$((\langle(\exists b : y = b \wedge \mathbf{X}(y = b + 1))\rangle_0^2 \wedge$$
$$\langle(\exists b' : y = b' \wedge \mathbf{X}(y = b' + 1))\mathbf{U}(x > 10)\rangle_1^2) \equiv$$
$$(s_0(x) > 10) \vee$$
$$((\langle(y = b) \wedge \mathbf{X}(y = b + 1))\rangle_0^2 \wedge$$
$$\bigwedge_{j=0}^{1} (s_j(b) = s_{j+1}(b)) \wedge$$
$$\langle(\exists b' : y = b' \wedge \mathbf{X}(y = b' + 1))\mathbf{U}(x > 10)\rangle_1^2) \equiv$$
$$(s_0(x) > 10) \vee$$
$$((s_0(y) = s_0(b)) \wedge (s_1(y) = s_1(b) + 1)) \wedge$$
$$\bigwedge_{j=0}^{1} (s_j(b) = s_{j+1}(b)) \wedge$$
$$((s_1(x) > 10) \vee$$
$$(s_1(y) = s_1(b') \wedge s_2(y) = s_2(b') + 1) \wedge (s_1(b') = s_2(b')) \wedge$$
$$\langle(\exists b'' : y = b'' \wedge \mathbf{X}(y = b'' + 1))\mathbf{U}(x > 10)\rangle_2^2) \equiv$$
$$(s_0(x) > 10) \vee$$
$$((s_0(y) = s_0(b)) \wedge (s_1(y) = s_1(b) + 1)) \wedge$$
$$\bigwedge_{j=0}^{1} (s_j(b) = s_{j+1}(b)) \wedge$$
$$((s_1(x) > 10) \vee$$
$$((s_1(y) = s_1(b')) \wedge (s_2(y) = s_2(b') + 1) \wedge (s_1(b') = s_2(b')) \wedge$$
$$((s_2(x) > 10) \vee ((s_2(y) = s_2(b'')) \wedge \text{false})))$$

2.4 Data Validation by Bounded Model Checking

Bounded model checking in general is concerned with the solution of so-called *bounded model checking instances*, that is, constraints of the form

$$J(s_0) \wedge \bigwedge_{i=1}^{k} R(s_{i-1}, s_i) \wedge G(s_0, \ldots, s_k) \tag{11}$$

For solving these constraints, SMT solvers are used. When applied in the context of BMC, $J(s_0)$ is a proposition specifying the starting state from where a witness should be found within a bounded number of steps k. For the purpose of data validation, $J(s_0)$ admits any track element – respectively, its software instance – s_0 as a starting point, since all validation rules have to be applied to track segments starting at any element s_0 in the interlocking system area. Therefore $J(s_0)$ can be expressed by

$$J(s_0) \equiv \bigvee_{s \in S} \left(\bigwedge_{v \in V} s_0(v) = s(v) \right) \tag{12}$$

This initial condition states that any initial valuation[2] of variables $v \in V$ must coincide with any of the software instances $s \in S$ representing track elements.

Proposition $G(s_0, \ldots, s_k)$ specifies the unwanted property of the trace segment of length k to be found, that is, a sequence of track element-related software instances $s_0, \ldots, s_k$ violating some validation rule $\neg G$. As described in Sect. 2.5, such an unwanted property G to be uncovered will be specified in LTL. Therefore bounded LTL model checkers parse the original LTL formulae and apply the transformation rules specified in formulae (2–10), in order to produce an equivalent propositional formula G, as illustrated in Example 1 above.

The conjuncts $R(s_{i-1}, s_i)$ enforce that only solutions of $G(s_0, \ldots, s_k)$ are considered that correspond to trace segments whose elements are related by the transition relation. For our purpose of data validation this means, that each pair (s_{i-1}, s_i) of a solution trace $s_0, \ldots, s_k$ is connected by some primary or secondary channel $a, \ldots, h$. Therefore the conjunction is expressed by (see Eq. (13))

$$\bigwedge_{i=1}^{k} R(s_{i-1}, s_i) \equiv \bigwedge_{i=1}^{k} \left(\bigvee_{c \in \{a, \ldots, h\}} s_{i-1}(c) = s_i(id) \right) \tag{13}$$

Summarising, data validation for geographical interlocking requires to solve BMC instances of the form

$$\bigvee_{s \in S} \left(\bigwedge_{v \in V} s_0(v) = s(v) \right) \wedge \bigwedge_{i=1}^{k} \left(\bigvee_{c \in \{a, \ldots, h\}} s_{i-1}(c) = s_i(id) \right) \wedge \text{Trans}(\phi) \tag{14}$$

where ϕ specifies a violation of some validation rule in LTL, and $\text{Trans}(\phi)$ denotes the transformation of LTL formulae into propositional formulae according to the rules specified in formulae (2–10).

If the bounded model checker is able to calculate a witness, that is, a solution of Formula (14) within k steps, an error has been found, so the bounded model checker is a valuable tool for *bug finding*. If, however, no witness can be found

---

[2] Recall from Sect. 2.1 that V contains the variable symbols for element identification (id), element type (t), channels connecting to neighbouring elements ($a, \ldots, h$), and additional type-specific attributes ($a_1, \ldots, a_k$). For some $v \in V$, notation $s_0(v)$ denotes the value of variable v to be determined by the SMT solver for the initial state s_0.

within k steps, it remains to be determined whether some witness might be found if k is increased. This question has been answered for the general case of arbitrary Kripke Structures and LTL formulae in [3,4]. If k corresponds to the so-called *diameter* of the Kripke Structure under consideration, and no solution could be found for this k, bounded model checking provides a global *proof* of non-existence for such a witness. While the diameter is often too large to be applied for BMC in practice, it is of feasible size in the case of data validation, because it roughly corresponds to the maximal length of track segments from some element to the boundary of the interlocking system area.

2.5 Applications

We will now describe several examples illustrating the expressiveness of LTL for the verification of data validation rules.

Example 2. The simplest validation rules state that instances representing elements of a certain type $t = \tau$ must have certain attributes with values in a specific range, such as $a_i \in [x_0, x_1]$. A violation of this property is readily expressed by LTL formula $\mathbf{F}(t = \tau \wedge (a_i < x_0 \vee x_1 < a_i))$.

Example 3. The following rule checks the correctness of channel connections. *"If there exists a channel from s_1 to s_2, there must exist a channel in the reversed direction"*. A violation of this rule can be specified in natural language as *"There exists an instance s_1 which is not the auxiliary initial state, so that s_1 is connected to some instance s_2, but all channels emanating from s_2 lead to instances different from s_1"*. In LTL this is expressed as

$$\mathbf{F}(\exists i : id = i \wedge id > 0 \wedge \mathbf{X}(a \neq i \wedge b \neq i \wedge \ldots \wedge h \neq i))$$

A witness for such a rule violation reaches an element s with positive id (so it does not equal s_0) and at least one of its reachable neighbours (which, by definition of R, are only reachable if there is a connecting channel from s to this neighbour) has no channel with destination s.

Example 4. The following rule pattern frequently occurs when checking configuration data with respect to software component instances representing illegal sequences of track elements along a route. *"Following a track element of type τ_1 along its a-channel, and only regarding primary channel connections, an element of type τ_2 must occur, before an element of type τ_3 is found"*. The violation of this rule is specified by *"Find a track element of type τ_1 and follow it along its a-channel, so that only elements of type $t \neq \tau_2$ may be found along its primary channel directions, until an element of type τ_3 is encountered"*.

$$\mathbf{F}(t = \tau_1 \wedge \exists x : (a = x \wedge \mathbf{X}(id = x \wedge ((t \neq \tau_2 \wedge \\ \exists y : ((a = y \vee b = y \vee c = y \vee d = y) \wedge \mathbf{X}(id = y))) \\ \mathbf{U}(t = \tau_3)))))$$

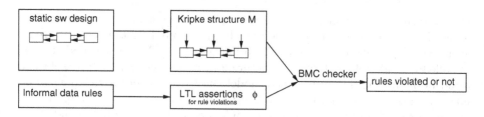

Fig. 2. Tool support for data validation work flow.

2.6   Tool Support

In principle, data validation by means of LTL can be performed with any LTL model checker that is able to encode the Kripke Structure representing the static semantics of the geographical interlocking system as described in Sect. 2.1. A reference implementation has been performed by the authors using the model-based testing and bounded model checking tool RT-Tester, described in more detail in [22]. RT-Tester performs automated test data generation or calculation of BMC witnesses by solving constraints of the form specified in Eq. (11), with the help of the SONOLAR SMT solver described in [23].

Figure 2 shows the data validation work flow and indicates the interaction between tool components.

- The static software design of the geographical interlocking system is represented by encodings $s \in S$ of software instances corresponding to track elements. In the reference implementation described here, this is encoded in XML.
- A parser front-end of RT-Tester developed for this XML encoding reads the design and transforms it into the internal model representation of the tool. This is an abstract syntax tree data structure that allows for syntactic representation of a wide variety of formalisms, such as UML/SysML, Matlab/Simulink, process algebras, and the proprietary interlocking system format described here.
- RT-Tester allows for utilisation of different transition relation generators, associated with the semantics of each supported modelling formalism. One of these generators creates the initial state condition and transition relation for the Kripke Structure introduced in Sect. 2.1, according to Eqs. (12) and (13).
- The data validation rules are transformed by experts into LTL formulae ϕ representing rule violation.
- The LTL parser of RT-Tester reads the formulae, and they are transformed by the tool into propositional formulae.
- The diameter k of the track network is determined.
- The SMT solver tries to find a solution for the BMC instance shown in Eq. (14). If a solution can be found, a violation of rule $\neg\phi$ has been uncovered. If no solution can be found, it has been *proven* that this rule is nowhere violated, because k is the diameter of the network.

3   Verification of System Safety

This section describes our method for formally verifying safety of an interlocking system.

3.1   Formalization of the Verification Task

According to our method, the input of this verification step should consist of: (1) a formal, state-based, behavioural model $\mathcal{M}$ of the interlocking system and its physical environment and (2) safety conditions Φ expressed as a conjunction of propositions over the state variables in $\mathcal{M}$. The verification goal is then to verify that the safety conditions Φ hold for any reachable state in $\mathcal{M}$.

As will be explained below, a model checker tool should be used for automated verification of such a goal. Therefore, the model $\mathcal{M}$ and the formula Φ should be expressed in the input language of the chosen model checker.

3.2   Verification Strategy

There is an established approach to apply bounded model checking in combination with inductive reasoning, in order to prove global system properties; this approach is called *k-induction*. For proving that safety condition Φ holds for all reachable states of $\mathcal{M}$, this method proceeds as follows.

1. First prove that $\Phi \wedge \Psi$ holds for the $k > 0$ first execution cycles after initialisation, i.e. $\Phi \wedge \Psi$ holds for $k > 0$ successive[3] states $\sigma_0, \dots, \sigma_{k-1}$ of which σ_0 is the initial state of $\mathcal{M}$.
2. Next prove the following for an arbitrary execution sequence of $k+1$ successive states $\sigma_t, \dots, \sigma_{t+k}$ of which the first σ_t is an arbitrary state (reachable or not from the initial state σ_0): if $\Phi \wedge \Psi$ holds in the k first states $\sigma_t, \dots, \sigma_{t+k-1}$, then $\Phi \wedge \Psi$ must also hold for the $k + 1^{st}$ state σ_{t+k}.

Here Ψ is an auxiliary property that holds for reachable states. (Note that Ψ is simultaneously proven by the given induction principle.) The proofs of the base case and the induction step should be performed by a bounded model checker tool. An example of such a tool is described in [8]. This tool treats the two proof obligations by exploring corresponding propositional satisfiable problems and solving these by a SAT solver. Note that the induction steps argue over an execution sequence of k+1 states of which the first state, σ_t, may be unreachable, although it would have been sufficient only to consider sequences for which σ_t is reachable. For sequences starting at an unreachable state, the induction step may fail and the property checker produces a *false negative*. To avoid this, the desired property Φ is strengthened with auxiliary property Ψ that is false for those unreachable states, σ_t, for which the induction step would otherwise fail.

---

[3] Two states σ_i and σ_{i+1} are successive, if there is a transition from σ_i to σ_{i+1} according to $\mathcal{M}$.

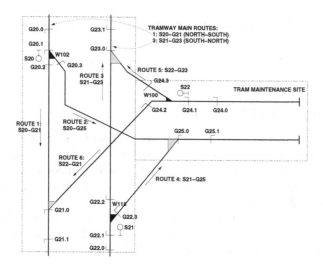

Fig. 3. A tramway network.

3.3   Case Study

A reference publication for this verification technique has been published in [8]. It describes a real-world route-related tramway control system. For the network in Fig. 3, the model of the tramway control system was verified to be safe, using k-induction. The safety conditions Φ was a conjunction of 15 conditions ensuring no collisions and no derailments of trams, and the auxiliary condition Ψ was a conjunction of conditions expressing state relations needed as assumptions in the induction step, in order to rule out unreachable states that would have given rise to false negatives otherwise. It turned out that a value of $k = 3$ sufficed to carry out the induction. The proofs of the base case and the induction step were performed by a bounded model checker, which used 392 s to perform the proofs. For more details about the case study, see e.g. [8,17].

4   Conclusion

In this paper the application of bounded model checking for verification and validation of interlocking systems has been described. In contrast to global model checking which usually leads to state space explosions when applied to complex interlocking systems, bounded model checking allows for application in large and complex interlocking system layouts. It has been shown how the technique can be applied on two levels. First, in the form of LTL property checking, for the purpose of configuration data validation. Next, in combination with inductive reasoning, for the purpose of verifying safety properties for the dynamic behaviour of trains traversing the track network. Tool applications and measurements show that both application scenarios scale up for application in an industrial context.

Acknowledgments. The first author has been supported by the RobustRailS project funded by the Danish Council for Strategic Research. The second and third authors have been supported by the openETCS project funded by the European ITEA2 organisation.

References

1. Guide to the software engineering body of knowledge. Technical report, IEEE Computer Society (2004). http://www.computer.org/portal/web/swebok/htmlformat
2. Behm, P., Benoit, P., Faivre, A., Meynadier, J.-M.: Météor: a successful application of B in a large project. In: Wing, J.M., Woodcock, J., Davies, J. (eds.) FM 1999. LNCS, vol. 1708, pp. 369–387. Springer, Heidelberg (1999)
3. Biere, A., Cimatti, A., Clarke, E., Zhu, Y.: Symbolic model checking without BDDs. In: Cleaveland, W.R. (ed.) TACAS 1999. LNCS, vol. 1579, pp. 193–207. Springer, Heidelberg (1999)
4. Biere, A., Heljanko, K., Junttila, T., Latvala, T., Schuppan, V.: Linear encodings of bounded LTL model checking. Log. Meth. Comput. Sci. **2**(5), 1–64 (2006)
5. Bjørner, D.: New results and current trends in formal techniques for the development of software for transportation systems. In: Proceedings of the Symposium on Formal Methods for Railway Operation and Control Systems (FORMS'2003). L'Harmattan Hongrie, Budapest, 15–16 May 2003
6. Clabaut, M., Metayer, C., Morand, E.: 4B-2 formal data validation - formal techniques applied to verification of data properties. In: Embedded Real Time Software and Systems ERTS (2010)
7. Clarke, E.M., Grumberg, O., Peled, D.A.: Model Checking. The MIT Press, Cambridge (1999)
8. Drechsler, R., Große, D.: System level validation using formal techniques. IEE Proc. - Comput. Digit. Tech. **152**(3), 393–406 (2005)
9. European Committee for Electrotechnical Standardization: EN 50128:2011 - Railway Applications - Communications, Signalling and Processing Systems - Software for Railway Control and Protection Systems. CENELEC, Brussels (2011)
10. Fantechi, A.: Distributing the challenge of model checking interlocking control tables. In: Margaria, T., Steffen, B. (eds.) ISoLA 2012, Part II. LNCS, vol. 7610, pp. 276–289. Springer, Heidelberg (2012)
11. Fantechi, A., Fokkink, W.J., Morzenti, A.: Some trends in formal methods applications to railway signaling. In: Formal Methods for Industrial Critical Systems, pp. 61–84. Wiley, Hoboken (2012)
12. Ferrari, A., Magnani, G., Grasso, D., Fantechi, A.: Model checking interlocking control tables. In: Schnieder, E., Tarnai, G. (eds.) Proceedings of Formal Methods for Automation and Safety in Railway and Automotive Systems (FORMS/FORMAT 2010). Springer, Braunschweig (2011)
13. Haxthausen, A.E., Peleska, J.: Formal development and verification of a distributed railway control system. IEEE Trans. Softw. Eng. **26**(8), 687–701 (2000)
14. Haxthausen, A.E.: Towards a framework for modelling and verification of relay interlocking systems. In: Calinescu, R., Jackson, E. (eds.) Monterey Workshop 2010. LNCS, vol. 6662, pp. 176–192. Springer, Heidelberg (2011)
15. Haxthausen, A.E.: Automated generation of safety requirements from railway interlocking tables. In: Margaria, T., Steffen, B. (eds.) ISoLA 2012, Part II. LNCS, vol. 7610, pp. 261–275. Springer, Heidelberg (2012)

16. Haxthausen, A.E., Peleska, J.: Efficient development and verification of safe railway control software. In: Railways: Types, Design and Safety Issues, pp. 127–148. Nova Science Publishers Inc, New York (2013)

17. Haxthausen, A.E., Peleska, J., Kinder, S.: A formal approach for the construction and verification of railway control systems. Formal Aspects Comput. **23**(2), 191–219 (2011)

18. Lecomte, T., Burdy, L., Leuschel, M.: Formally checking large data sets in the railways. CoRR, abs/1210.6815 (2012)

19. Manna, Z., Pnueli, A.: The Temporal Logic of Reactive and Concurrent Systems. Springer, New York (1992)

20. Moller, F., Nguyen, H.N., Roggenbach, M., Schneider, S., Treharne, H.: Defining and model checking abstractions of complex railway models using CSP||B. In: Biere, A., Nahir, A., Vos, T. (eds.) HVC. LNCS, pp. 193–208. Springer, Heidelberg (2013)

21. Pachl, J.: Railway Operation and Control. VTD Rail Publishing, Mountlake Terrace (2002)

22. Peleska, J: Industrial-strength model-based testing - state of the art and current challenges. In: Petrenko, A.K., Schlingloff, H. (eds.) Proceedings Eighth Workshop on Model-Based Testing, Rome, 17 March 2013. Electronic Proceedings in Theoretical Computer Science, vol. 111, pp. 3–28. Open Publishing Association (2013)

23. Peleska, J., Vorobev, E., Lapschies, F.: Automated test case generation with SMT-solving and abstract interpretation. In: Bobaru, M., Havelund, K., Holzmann, G.J., Joshi, R. (eds.) NFM 2011. LNCS, vol. 6617, pp. 298–312. Springer, Heidelberg (2011)

24. Sistla, A.P.: Liveness and fairness in temporal logic. Form. Aspects Comput. **6**(5), 495–512 (1994)

25. Winter, K.: Optimising ordering strategies for symbolic model checking of railway interlockings. In: Margaria, T., Steffen, B. (eds.) ISoLA 2012, Part II. LNCS, vol. 7610, pp. 246–260. Springer, Heidelberg (2012)

Formal Implementation of Data Validation for Railway Safety-Related Systems with OVADO

Robert Abo and Laurent Voisin$^{(\boxtimes)}$

Systerel, Les Portes de l'Arbois - Bâtiment A, 1090 rue Descartes,
13857 Aix-en-Provence Cedex 3, France
{robert.abo,laurent.voisin}@systerel.fr
http://www.systerel.fr

Abstract. This paper describes the process of data validation for railway safety-critical computer-based systems formally implemented by Systerel as supplier of railway industry's companies. More precisely, it describes the validation of data against the requirements it has to meet to ensure systems safety. International standards, especially CENELEC EN 50128, recommend the use of formal methods for designing the most critical safety-related systems. We use the OVADO formal tool to perform data validation. For that, we model data requirements by using the specification language of the B method, namely the B language, before using OVADO that automatically checks that data meet requirements. This tool integrates two independent components that must give the same results when they are applied on the same data, according to the principle of redundancy. An example of data validation for a CBTC system is also given.

Keywords: Railway systems · CBTC · Data validation · B language · Ovado

1 Introduction

Saying that present-day railway systems implement computer-based components, moreover as most industrial systems (objects of our everyday life, cars, planes, plants, nuclear power stations, weapons, etc.), is obvious, almost a commonplace, as computer-science controls our modern industries. But it is not trite to note that some of them implement a safety function, so that their malfunction or failure may have dramatic consequences on them and their users. This is the reason why their development requires a lot of rigor and discipline, leading to its own branch of computing known as *safeware* [1]. Otherwise, each electrical and/or electronic system is characterized by a *Safety Integrity Level* (SIL) which, as defined in IEC 61508 standard [2], denotes the risks involved in the system application by using a scale of 1 (the lowest risks) to 4 (the highest ones). Failures of SIL 3 or SIL 4 systems, aka *safety-critical systems*, may cause environmental harms, severe damages or the destruction of expensive pieces of equipment and human casualties.

S. Counsell and M. Núñez (Eds.): SEFM 2013 Collocated Workshops, LNCS 8368, pp. 221–236, 2014.
DOI: 10.1007/978-3-319-05032-4_17, © Springer International Publishing Switzerland 2014

Standards. In Europe, the development of railway systems is governed by the legislation in force in a specific country and by international CENELEC[1] standards, which define objectives in terms of safety and security and the methods to reach them. These standards, which are all variations of IEC 61508 [2], are: EN 50126 [3] (for the methods to implement to demonstrate RAMS[2] of applications), EN 50128 [4] (dedicated to the safety of software components[3]), and EN 50129 [5] (devoted to the safety of hardware components). They are completed by EN 50159 dedicated to safety-related communications in closed (part 1) and in open transmission systems (part 2) [6].

CBTCs. Among the safety-related railway systems, we find *Communication-Based Train Controls* (CBTCs), on which we focus in this paper, i.e. railway signalling systems that use telecommunications between trains and trackside equipment [7]. They aim at safely managing trains on an entire line, while absorbing the passenger traffic in particular during peak hours. There may be some differences depending on the technologies implemented by the different suppliers. But, basically, a railway signalling system has a pyramidal structure made of five layers as illustrated in Fig. 1. And, of course, like most of the systems with a layered structure, each sub-layer uses the services provided by the layer which is located just below it, in order to provide services to that located just above it by using specific interfaces.

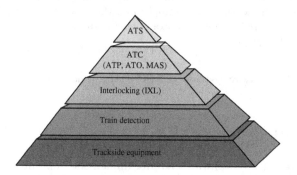

Fig. 1. The pyramidal structure of a railway signalling system

At the base of the structure, the first layer is composed of the trackside equipments (i.e. rails, balises, points, signals, etc.). Just above, we find the pieces of equipment in charge of detecting a train on the track, i.e. track circuits mainly. The first of the higher layers consists of *Interlocking* (IXL) which is in charge

---

[1] This is the *European Committee for Electrotechnical Standardization*, which is responsible for European standardization in the area of electrical engineering.

[2] RAMS stands for *Reliability, Availability, Maintainability* and *Safety*.

[3] This standard defines the notion of *Software SIL* inherited from that of IEC 61508 with a first level, SSIL 0, which denotes a non-safety-related software component.

of safely establishing and monitoring the train routes without any risks of collisions, catching up, and other traffic conflicts, for example with cars at crossings.
Interlocking is SIL 4. The layer above is the *Automatic Train Control* (ATC)
whose purpose is running a train while protecting it from dangerous situations.
For that, it is composed of *Automatic Train Protection* (ATP) in charge of super-
vizing the train speed (ATP is SIL 4), and *Automatic Train Operation* (ATO)
which automatically drives the train. A *Maintenance Aid System* (MAS) complements this layer. Finally, the *Automatic Train Supervision* (ATS) heads up
the whole structure, and allows operators to remotely control railway traffic on
an entire line.

The Crucial Role of Data. Besides, many railway safety-related systems, including CBTCs, are wholly or partially composed of generic software elements,
which are adapted to a particular application by means of application algorithms and/or *configuration data* ([4], Sect. 8). This static data describes the
geographical arrangement of equipment and capability of the rail infrastructure
and, therefore, it never changes, contrarily to dynamic data, which describes the
current state of equipment along the track. Each software component of a CBTC,
in particular the most critical ones, loads at runtime static data to perform its
aim. This is why static configuration data plays a *crucial role* in ensuring the
safe operations of trains: if it is wrong, the safety-related components perform
their functions by using wrong data as input, and thus fail, even if they are
well designed and programmed and the electronic boards where they are stored
are well manufactured. Therefore data needs to be validated in the same way
as safety-related hardware and software components. This is usually done in
the earliest stages of a CBTC's life cycle by a dedicated team. In addition, for
safety-critical software components including IXL and ATP, EN 50128 standard
"highly recommends" the use of formal methods for their development process.
This recommendation has influenced the data validation process introduced in
the following sections.

Systerel. This paper describes this process as it is done by Systerel. It does not
address another important task generally performed by prime contractors as
part of data validation, which is that static data used by safety-related systems
really correspond to the used physical railway. The core business of Systerel, a
medium-sized enterprise both located in Aix-en-Provence, Lyon, Toulouse and
Paris in France, is the development of safety-critical embedded systems for rail
transportation, aeronautics, space industry, energy, etc. It provides an expertise
in the use of formal methods throughout the development cycle of a system, i.e.
its design, its development and its validation[4].

Organization of the Paper. This paper is organized as follows. Section 1 introduces data validation in the railway sector. Section 2 outlines its basics. Section 3
is entirely dedicated to the OVADO data validation tool used by Systerel in order

---

[4] For further information, please visit http://www.systerel.fr.

to conduct its projects. Section 4 presents a real example of data validation of a CBTC. Finally, Sect. 5 concludes this article.

2   Background

In the introduction, we have highlighted the necessity of validating data as a process of the design of a CBTC. But, what do we exactly mean by "validating data"? In this section, we define data validation before describing a process that implements it independently of any CBTC.

2.1   Definition

Usually, when we validate hardware and software components, we check that they meet their requirements by testing them or by proving it using formal methods. Similarly, we define data validation as *the process consisting in ensuring that data used by a safety-critical computer-based system conforms to a collection of requirements which define its usefulness, correctness and completeness for this system.*

   In other words, data validation consists in checking that data meets the requirements defined for this system. Generally, due to its high cost, this validation concerns the safety-related requirements only.

2.2   A Semiautomatic Process Based on the B Method

Methodology. In the railway sector, data validation has been done entirely manually for a long time, leading to a tricky, fastidious, error-prone and long-term activity. For example, the authors note in [8], that it took more than six months to check that one hundred thousand data items were in accordance with two hundred properties representing requirements. Great R&D efforts have induced the design of industrial practical tools that now allow the semiautomatisation of data validation. This process is not fully automatic because, while the validation is automatically performed by a tool, the requirements still need to be manually modeled and these models need to be checked by dedicated engineers. Nevertheless, semiautomatisation has undoubtedly increased the speed and level of confidence of data validation [8]. As mentioned in Sect. 4.4, let us note now that the way of modelling requirements has got a great influence on the performance of the tool.

B Language. On the other hand, known as a success story in software engineering for the railway sector, the *B method* is a formal method designed in the nineties by Jean-Raymond Abrial [9]. Let us briefly recall that software development with B consists in successively refining the models of a specification until obtaining an implementation which is automatically translated into source code. Each refinement step consists in introducing details in abstract models, and then in proving the consistency and compliancy of refined models with the abstract ones they refine. More recently designed, *Event-B* enlarges the scope of the B method with the purpose of studying and specifying whole systems, not only its software components [10]. We use a subset of the specification language of the B method, namely the *B language*[5], to model data requirements specified in natural language. The choice of the B language is explained by the implementation of B in software engineering for railways, its ease of use (although models are not always easy to write), and also its ease of learning. Let us note that a data validation process relying on Event-B has been also developed [11]. The B method and OVADO were chosen because they are part of the expertise and know-how of Systerel. Other formal languages and tools exist: for example, let us quote SCADE based on the synchronous language Lustre[6]. This is another approach of formal data validation which is not described in this paper. Ontologies for railway systems constitute a promising R&D axis [12,13].

2.3   An Iterative Process

Principle. The principle of data validation is illustrated in Fig. 2.

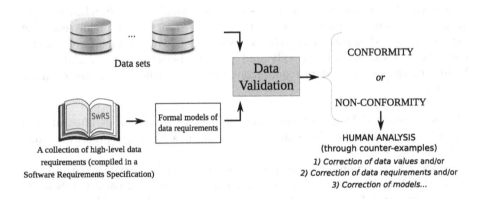

Fig. 2. Principle of data validation

Firstly, high-level data requirements are modelled as predicates of set-theory and first order logic that use data sets. These predicates are expressed using the B language. Secondly, a tool automatically evaluates their truthfulness (true or false). In these conditions, data falls into two categories: on the one hand, the correct data that meet the requirements and for which predicates are true, and on the other hand the incorrect data that do not meet them and for which predicates are false. For the latter, an analysis is performed to determine the origin of the non-conformity before restarting the process from its beginning.

---

[5] A useful summary of the syntax of the B language can be found at http://www.stups.uni-duesseldorf.de/ProB/index.php5/Summary_of_B_Syntax.

[6] Further information about Lustre or model checking is available at http://www-verimag.imag.fr/Synchrone,30?lang=en.

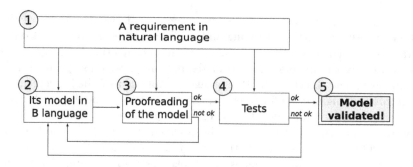

Fig. 3. Validation of the models

In effect, this is an iterative process in the sense that it is repeated after corrections are made until all data are compliant with the requirements. The origin of an error may be: the value of data itself; the requirements in natural language that have not been updated; or the model! Because, they can be wrong too and wrong models may validate faulty data!

Indeed, data validation is a great source of errors[7] especially when requirements are difficult to model[8]. We must highlight wrong data by really ensuring that data marked as correct is really correct. This is why the models of requirements need themselves to be validated prior to being able to validate data. Validating the models of data requirement aims at ensuring that wrong data are detected.

Models Validation. Therefore, the principle of data validation as illustrated in Fig. 2 has to be refined. Modelling requirements is a five-stage process as illustrated in Fig. 3.

Stage #1 corresponds to the specification of a requirement in a natural language (English, French, etc.) by system engineers. Stage #2 corresponds to its translation into a formal model. Several properties can be provided to cover a single requirement of the informal specification, with the purpose of simplifying the model. In order to reduce the risk of errors previously mentioned, each model is proofread by a reviewer who is different from the specifier who has written it, as required by EN 50128 Sects. 5 and 6 (stage #3). Then, the proofread model is tested by using a set of deliberately wrong data (stage #4). Again, as required by EN 50128, the tester is different from the designer who wrote the model. Moreover, he (or she) performs black-box testing, i.e. he (or she) can only access the specification in natural language of the requirement, not the model under test.

---

[7] *Cuiusvis hominis est errare, nullius nisi insipientis in errore perseverare* i.e. "Any man can make mistakes: nobody but a fool will persist in error (Cicero, Philippicae XII, ii, 5)".

[8] Let us quote an encountered real example of an indivisible requirement described in nineteen pages of a document. Its model has five hundred lines of predicates written in the B language.

If an error is discovered, the model is corrected and the whole validation cycle restarts (return to stage #2). Finally, when no error is found anymore, the model is approved and thus can be used to validate data (stage #5).

Proofreading consists in tracking down what we could call "over-specification" errors (i.e. the model specifies more things than the informal specification), and "under-specification" errors (i.e. the model specifies less things than the informal specification)[9]. These kinds of errors are usually due to a lack of understanding of the requirements, repetitions, oversights, non-updated models after changes, sometimes minor, of the informal specification and so on.s Let us add that the designer is not compelled to follow the proofreader's comments by justifying his (her) choice.

Verifying the models aims at checking that they translate well into the B language a requirement in natural language, and that the specifier does not make any foolish mistakes. But, tests are also performed to track tautologies i.e. predicates which are always true, whatever data is. For example, A, B and C being some predicates, $((A \wedge B) \Rightarrow C) \Leftrightarrow (A \Rightarrow (B \Rightarrow C))$ is a tautology. This kind of error is difficult to highlight by proofreading. Only one test is carried out for each property: we aims at checking out that the property can be false at least once, and we do not perform a total coverage as it is done for unit tests of safety-critical systems [2,4]. If it is impossible that a property becomes false with wrong data, then it is a tautology and it must be corrected.

When completed, stages 2 to 4 produce some deliverables: the *proofreading report*, which summarizes the proofreads of all models; the *test report*, which aims at doing the same thing for the tests of models; and, of course, the *documentation of the models* which summarizes the models with their description and justification in natural language, and also a traceability matrix in order to show that all the informal requirements are covered by at least one property written in the B language.

Finally, to increase confidence in the results, data validation is done by using two independent tools that must draw the same conclusion of data compliancy when they are used to validate the same data. For data validation done at Systerel, these tools, *PredicateB* and *ProB*, are integrated in the OVADO platform which is the subject of the next section.

Let us note that other data validation tool exist, such as Alstom's *DTVT* [8] not presented in this paper. Doing a comparison between the existing data validation tools of the market is quite difficult, almost impossible, due to the lack of information published by industrials. That is the reason why this paper does not include any paragraph on this subject.

---

[9] A systematic proofreading method is described in chapter 17, "Rigorous Review", of the book by Shaoyin Liu, "Formal Engineering for Industrial Software Development using the SOFL Method" [14].

2.4   A New Kind of Job

To conclude this section, we would like to stress that data validation process as previously introduced, has lead to a new specialized job in engineering: the "data validator".

He (or she) is in charge of modelling data requirements specified in natural language by using the choosen formalism, and then analyzing the non-conformity cases of data. This job differs from the system engineer who identifies and specify the requirements in natural language, and also who helps to check formal properties. It also differs from the computer scientist in charge of designing tools implementing by data validation. All are a necessity for the design of safety-related systems.

3   The OVADO Tool

3.1   Overview

The RATP[10] initiated the development of OVADO[11], a formal tool in order to validate static data of the Paris's metro line 13 that was being automated.

This tool parses datasets (XML, Excel, text-based, or binary formats), loads properties and checks compliancy of data with respect to the loaded properties. The development of OVADO is now subcontracted to Systerel. It is composed of two different tools that form the basis of two independent data validation workflows:

- The *PredicateB* predicate evaluator is in charge of checking the truthfulness of predicates modeling data requirements in the B language as explained in Sect. 2); and
- ProB[12] [15], is an animator and model checker for the B Method. It can be used to check a specification for a range of errors. The constraint-solving capabilities of ProB can also be used for model finding, deadlock checking and test-case generation. ProB is currently developed by Michael Leuschel's team at the University of Düsseldorf in Germany, while its commercial support is provided by Formal Mind. Data and the models of requirements are converted into B models that are fed to the tool to validate data. This tool has been used with success on several projects (Roissy-Charles de Gaulle airport shuttle, Paris line 1, Barcelona line 9, Algiers line 1, etc.).

Data validation with OVADO is organized as follows. Data and formal properties of data requirements are fed into the tool. Properties are modelled as

---

[10] The *Régie Autonome des Transports Parisiens* is the firm in charge of the public transports in Paris, France.

[11] This acronym stands for *Outil de VAlidation de DOnnées* which means "Data Validation Tool" in French.

[12] The ProB website is http://www.stups.uni-duesseldorf.de/ProB/

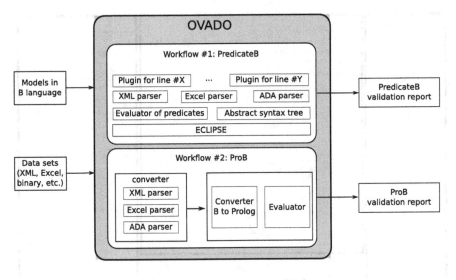

Fig. 4. Architecture of OVADO

predicates in the B language. The conformance of the input data with the input requirements is independently validated by the two validation workflows of the tool. Each of them produces a validation report for each analysed property. The results of two reports relating to the same property must be equal. If not, the model or one of the tool is likely wrong and must be corrected. Let us add that OVADO has been applied with suceess to data validation of Paris lines 1, 3, 5, 13, and also Lyon's line B, etc.

3.2 Architecture

As shown in Fig. 4, OVADO is a generic platform combining PredicateB and ProB, and can be completed by specific project plugins, such as the adaptation of OVADO for the acquisition of data described in a customer-specific format. Thus OVADO is able to be tailored to specific projects of industrials. OVADO can be used on a computer equiped with Microsoft Windows or Linux, and Java 6.

3.3 User Interface

The user interface of OVADO is illustrated in Fig. 5 that shows the three main parts needed to write the models, perform data validation and analyse the results. Their organization within Eclipse depends entirely on how an engineer wants to organize his workspace. As shown in the figure:

- Part 1 displays the project tree.
- Part 2 shows different tabs where a designer can specify definitions and properties as explained in Sect. 4.2.

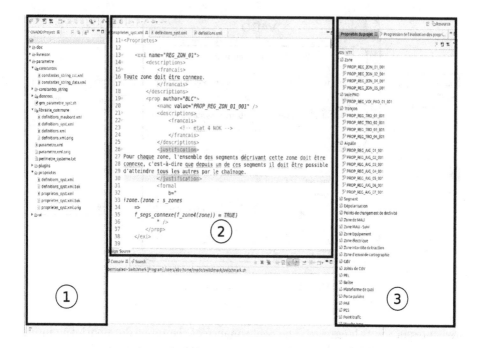

Fig. 5. The user interface of OVADO based on Eclipse

- Finally, Part 3 shows the "project properties" tab that lists all the specific properties of a system.

By right-clicking on one of them, it is possible to launch its validation on the fly. A tab named "evaluation progress" shows the progress of the evaluation of a property. An example of the implementation of OVADO for validating data of a CBTC is detailed in the next section.

4 Applying OVADO

This section describes a project conducted by Systerel to validate the static data of a metro line. All names have been changed to respect the confidentiality of information.

4.1 Data

Datasets and models are structured in XML (*eXtensible Markup Language*) files. Each requirement is modeled by one or more properties. The decomposition of requirements in one or more properties is left to the discretion of a designer.

4.2   Models

In order to understand the model of this section, let us recall that a useful summary of the syntax of the B language can be found at http://www.stups. uni-duesseldorf.de/ProB/index.php5/Summary_of_B_Syntax.

Interface Constants. The first step of the modelling activities consists in interfacing data with B constants used in the models. The following types can be defined to link the elements of datasets with constants of the properties written in the B language:

- carrier sets and their subsets;
- scalar data (mostly integers and character strings);
- relations between a scalar type and another scalar type;
- functions from a scalar type to another scalar type; and
- functions from a scalar type to functions of the previous type.

Each of them has a name, a predicate that specifies it (except for carrier sets) and a value, or a set of values, which is the result of a XPath request, or several XPath requests in case of relations and functions, applied on the XML file defining real data as presented in Sect. 4.1.

- *Carrier sets* define the different objects of the datasets used by a CBTC corresponding to the trackside equipment, the train detection equipment but also the organisation of the line according to a one-dimensional Cartesian coordinate system, such as balises, signals, points, track circuits, blocks, etc. A block is an elementary portion of a railroad track, which has two extremities. Its origin extremity is at abscissa 0, while the abscissa of its destination extremity corresponds to its length. We also define four types of *zones* i.e. collections of blocks corresponding to four carrier sets: oriented (t_zoneori), non-oriented (t_zonenori), with two oriented extremities (t_zone2extrori) and, finally, with two non-oriented extremities (t_zone2extr). Oriented zones have *singularities* i.e. oriented extremities, while non-oriented zones have only extremities.
- *Scalar sets* define constant numbers of the system such as abscissae, distances, speeds, temporary speed limits, delays, etc.
- *Relations* and *functions* specify links between these objects such as the length of a block, the block where a particular object is located, its abscissa in millimeters on the block (an integer), the block which follows the current one in a particular direction, etc.

Definitions. In order to simplify the expression of properties, several libraries of definitions are defined prior to the modelling of properties themselves. These definitions are quite different from the macros one can define in a DEFINITIONS clause of a classical B machine. In the B method, our definitions would rather be declared as ABSTRACT CONSTANTS. A definition has a unique name, a description in natural language and an expression in the B language. They ease writing and understanding of properties, and checking them when proofreading.

For the project under consideration, a library of useful definitions was used to model graph functions. In effect, a railway network is represented by an oriented graph. Thus, the following r_zone2extr_extr relation gives the extremities of a zone with two extremities:

$$
\begin{aligned}
&\texttt{dom}(\{\texttt{zone}, \texttt{extr}, \texttt{numabsextr} \mid \\
&\quad \texttt{zone} \mapsto \texttt{numabsextr} : \\
&\qquad \texttt{t\_zone2extr} \lhd (\texttt{f\_TabZones2Extr\_NumAbsExtr1} \\
&\qquad\qquad\qquad \cup \texttt{f\_TabZones2Extr\_NumAbsExtr2}) \ \wedge \\
&\quad \texttt{extr} \mapsto \texttt{numabsextr} : \\
&\qquad \texttt{t\_extremite} \lhd \texttt{f\_TabExtremities\_NumAbsolu}\})
\end{aligned}
$$

And, for each extremity, the f_extr_segdirabs function gives the triplet formed by its block, its direction and its abscissa on its block:

$$
\begin{aligned}
&\texttt{ran}(\{\texttt{extr}, \texttt{seg}, \texttt{dir}, \texttt{abs}, \texttt{res} \mid \\
&\quad \texttt{xtr} \mapsto \texttt{seg} : \texttt{f\_extr\_seg} \ \wedge \\
&\quad \texttt{extr} \mapsto \texttt{dir} : \texttt{f\_extr\_dir} \ \wedge \\
&\quad \texttt{extr} \mapsto \texttt{abs} : \texttt{f\_extr\_abs} \ \wedge \\
&\quad \texttt{res} = \texttt{extr} \mapsto (\texttt{seg} \mapsto \texttt{dir} \mapsto \texttt{abs})\})
\end{aligned}
$$

In the same manner, the r_zone2extrori_singu relation gives the singularities of a zone with two oriented extremities:

$$
\begin{aligned}
&\texttt{dom}(\{\texttt{zone}, \texttt{sing}, \texttt{numabssing} \mid \\
&\quad \texttt{zone} \mapsto \texttt{numabssing} : \\
&\qquad \texttt{t\_zone2extrori} \lhd (\texttt{f\_TabZones2ExtrOri\_NumAbsSing1} \\
&\qquad\qquad\qquad \cup \texttt{f\_TabZones2ExtrOri\_NumAbsSing2}) \ \wedge \\
&\quad \texttt{sing} \mapsto \texttt{numabssing} : \\
&\qquad \texttt{t\_singularite} \lhd \texttt{f\_TabSingu\_NumAbsolu}\})
\end{aligned}
$$

And, the f_singu_segdirabs function gives, for each singularity, the triplet formed by its block, its direction and its abscissa on its block:

$$
\begin{aligned}
&\texttt{ran}(\{\texttt{singu}, \texttt{seg}, \texttt{dir}, \texttt{abs}, \texttt{res} \mid \\
&\quad \texttt{singu} \mapsto \texttt{seg} : \texttt{f\_singu\_seg} \ \wedge \\
&\quad \texttt{singu} \mapsto \texttt{dir} : \texttt{f\_singu\_dir} \ \wedge \\
&\quad \texttt{singu} \mapsto \texttt{abs} : \texttt{f\_singu\_abs} \ \wedge \\
&\quad \texttt{res} = \texttt{singu} \mapsto (\texttt{seg} \mapsto \texttt{dir} \mapsto \texttt{abs})\})
\end{aligned}
$$

The following r_zonenori_extr relation gives the extremities of a non-oriented zone. The absolute number of an "extremity" (numabsextr) is different from -1, which denotes a non-representative element of the f_TabExtremities_NumAbsolu function:

$$\text{ran}(\{\text{zone}, \text{extr}, \text{numabsextr}, \text{ind}, \text{res} \mid$$
$$\text{zone} \mapsto \text{ind} \mapsto \text{numabsextr} :$$
$$(\text{t\_zonenori} \times \text{INTEGER}) \lhd \text{f\_TabZonesNOri\_NumAbsExtremites} \quad \wedge$$
$$\text{numabsextr}/ = -1 \quad \wedge$$
$$\text{extr} \mapsto \text{numabsextr} :$$
$$\text{t\_extremite} \lhd \text{f\_TabExtremities\_NumAbsolu} \quad \wedge$$
$$\text{res} = \text{zone} \mapsto \text{extr}\})$$

The following r_zoneori_singu relation gives the singularities associated with a particular oriented zone:

$$\text{ran}(\{\text{zone}, \text{singu}, \text{numabssingu}, \text{index}, \text{res} \mid$$
$$\text{zone} \mapsto \text{index} \mapsto \text{numabssingu} :$$
$$(\text{t\_zoneori} \times \text{INTEGER}) \lhd \text{f\_TabZonesOri\_ListSingZone} \quad \wedge$$
$$\text{numabssingu}/ = -1 \quad \wedge$$
$$\text{singu} \mapsto \text{numabssingu} :$$
$$\text{t\_singularite} \lhd \text{f\_TabSingu\_NumAbsolu} \quad \wedge$$
$$\text{res} = \text{zone} \mapsto \text{singu}\})$$

Properties. Each property has a name, a tag recalling the requirement it refers to, a description in natural language and a formal description in the B language. The requirement tags are used for the sake of traceability, in order to ensure that all requirements that must be modelled have been effectively modelled. Models should not be too complex to be easily proofread. In particular, definitions should be intensively used.

Let us consider the informal requirement "each zone must be connected". It means that for each zone, all blocks describing it (a zone is a collection of blocks) should be connected, meaning that from one of these blocks it should be possible to reach any other block by connection. With the previous interface constants and definitions, except the definition of the f_zone_connexe which is not given in this paper, the model of this requirement is specified as follows:

$$\forall(\text{typezone}, \text{r\_zone\_extr}, \text{zone}, \text{extrs}).(\quad$$
$$\text{typezone} : 0..3 \quad \wedge$$
$$\text{r\_zone\_extr} =$$
$$\{ 0 \mapsto (\text{r\_zone2extr\_extr}; \text{f\_extr\_segdirabs})$$
$$, 1 \mapsto (\text{r\_zone2extrori\_singu}; \text{f\_singu\_segdirabs})$$
$$, 2 \mapsto (\text{r\_zonenori\_extr}; \text{f\_extr\_segdirabs})$$
$$, 3 \mapsto (\text{r\_zoneori\_singu}; \text{f\_singu\_segdirabs})$$
$$\}(\text{typezone}) \quad \wedge$$
$$\text{zone} : \text{dom}(\text{r\_zone\_extr}) \quad \wedge$$
$$\text{extrs} = \text{r\_zone\_extr}[\{\text{zone}\}]$$
$$\Rightarrow$$
$$\text{f\_zone\_connexe}(\text{extrs}) = \text{TRUE})$$

Table 1. Results of data validation with PredicateB (a component of OVADO)

Component (and quantity (of it in the system)	Number of properties	Number of lines in B	Validation time in minutes for a component (and total)
#1 (13)	39	2050	<1 (<10)
#2 (4)	28	1177	<1 (<4)
#3 (4)	369	19613	180 (720 i.e. 12 h)
#4 (1)	62	2741	< 1
#5 (34)	159	12400	15 (510 i.e. 8.5 h)
#6 (1)	26	1641	6

The automatic treatment performed by OVADO has demonstrated us that initial data sets did not meet this requirement: four oriented zones were not connected, i.e. there was no communication channel between them. Data sets were therefore corrected by the team in charge of the definition of data before being successfully validated, in particular against this requirement, by the validation team.

4.3   Final Results

We have modelled the data requirements for six components of a CBTC both carborne and trackside. Table 1 summarizes the results obtained with PredicateB only. To preserve confidentiality, the component names have been changed. The last column represents the validation time for a component and, in parenthesis, the total obtained by adding all the validation time of all components of the same kind.

4.4   Influence of Models on Performance

Figure 6 shows two model patterns that look quite similar.

$$
\begin{array}{ll}
\forall\,(x,y,z)\,\cdot & \forall\,(x,y,z)\,\cdot \\
(& (\\
\quad x \in 0\,..\,100 \quad \wedge & \quad x \in 0\,..\,100 \quad \wedge \\
\quad y \in 0\,..\,100 \quad \wedge & \quad y \in 0\,..\,100 \quad \wedge \\
\quad z \in 0\,..\,100 \quad \wedge & \quad z = f(x \mapsto y) \quad \wedge \\
\quad z = f(x \mapsto y) & \quad z \in 0\,..\,100 \\
\quad \Rightarrow & \quad \Rightarrow \\
\quad Predicate & \quad Predicate \\
) &) \\
\quad\quad (a) & \quad\quad (b)
\end{array}
$$

Fig. 6. The design of models influences performance of OVADO

But, in fact, if we specify the model shown in Fig. 6a, OVADO checks the rule $z = f(x \mapsto y) \Rightarrow$ Predicate for each triplet (x, y, z) verifying $x \in [0..100]$ and $y \in [0..100]$ and $z \in [0..100]$. That is to say that OVADO creates one million triplets before checking that this rule is right, or wrong, for each of them. On the contrary, when we specify the model shown in Fig. 6b, OVADO checks the rule $z : 0..100 \Rightarrow$ Predicate for each triplet (x, y, z) verifying $x \in [0..100]$ and $y \in [0..100]$ and $z = f(x \mapsto y)$. That is to say that OVADO only creates ten thousand triplets and only performs ten thousand checks. Thus, model 6b is much more efficient in terms of performance than model 6a while being practically the same. This is also true for properties that use existantial quantifiers and/or sets defined by comprehension.

This simple example shows that modelers must keep in mind and apply some simple rules of model design in order to perform data validation: validating data is a necessity, but it must not be done in any way but in an efficient manner in terms of validation time and memory usage, i.e. in terms of performance of OVADO.

5   Conclusion

In this paper we have described the process for validating data used for safety-related railway systems. This process, which relies on the B method, presents several benefits: using formal methods is recommanded by international standards, the B language is quite easy to learn and to use, it is well suited for modelling requirements of CBTCs, large datasets can be used while the validation time is reasonable. On the contrary, let us face it is ill-suited for proving performance requirements and, unfortunately, applied mainly in the railway industry at the moment, while nothing prevents users from using it for other applications that CBTCs.

Acknowledgment. The authors would like to thank their teammates involved in data validation both based in Aix-en-Provence and Paris. This paper summarizes their work. Their gratitude is also addressed to Mr. François Bustany, President of Systerel, for allowing the writing of this paper.

References

1. Leveson, N.G.: Safeware - System Safety and Computers: A Guide to Preventing Accidents and Losses Caused by Technology. Addison-Wesley, Reading (1995)
2. International Electrotechnical Commission (IEC): Functional safety of electrical/electronic/programmable electronic safety-related systems (IEC 61508)
3. European Committee for Electrotechnical Standardization (CENELEC): Railway applications - The specification and demonstration of Reliability, Availability, Maintainability and Safety (RAMS) (EN 50126)
4. European Committee for Electrotechnical Standardization (CENELEC): Railway applications - Communication, signalling and processing systems - Software for railway control and protection systems (EN 50128)

5. European Committee for Electrotechnical Standardization (CENELEC): Railway applications - Communication, signalling and processing systems - Safety related electronic systems for signalling (EN 50129)
6. European Committee for Electrotechnical Standardization (CENELEC): Railway applications - Communication, signalling and processing systems - Safety-related communication in transmission systems (EN 50159)
7. Institute of Electrical and Electronics Engineers (IEEE): IEEE Standard Method for CBTC Performance and Functional Requirements (IEEE Std 1474.1-2004)
8. Lecomte, T., Burdy, L., Leuschel, M.: Formally checking large data sets in the railways. CoRR abs/1210.6815 (2012)
9. Abrial, J.R.: The B-Book: Assigning Programs to Meanings. Cambridge University Press, Cambridge (1996)
10. Abrial, J.R.: Modeling in Event-B - System and Software Engineering. Cambridge University Press, Cambridge (2010)
11. Badeau, F., Doche-Petit, M.: Formal data validation with Event-B. The Computing Research Repository (CoRR) abs/1210.7039 (2012)
12. Lodemann, M., Luttenberger, N.: Ontology-based railway infrastructure verification - planning benefits. In: KMIS, pp. 176–181 (2010)
13. Hoinaru, O., Mariano, G., Gransart, C.: An ontology for complex railway systems; application to the ERTMS/ETCS system. DTU Compute-Technical Report-2013 Towards a Formal Methods Body of Knowledge for Railway Control and Safety Systems (FM-RAIL-BOK Workshop), pp. 7–13 (2013)
14. Liu, S.: Formal Engineering for Industrial Software Development using the SOFL Method. Springer, Heidelberg (2004)
15. Leuschel, M., Butler, M.: ProB: A model checker for B. In: Araki, K., Gnesi, S., Mandrioli, D. (eds.) FME 2003. LNCS, vol. 2805, pp. 855–874. Springer, Heidelberg (2003)

Validation of Railway Interlocking Systems by Formal Verification, A Case Study

Andrea Bonacchi[1]([✉]), Alessandro Fantechi[1], Stefano Bacherini[2],
Matteo Tempestini[2], and Leonardo Cipriani[2]

[1] Università di Firenze, Dipartimento di Ingegneria dell'Informazione, Florence, Italy
{a.bonacchi, alessandro.fantechi}@unifi.it
[2] General Electric Transportation Systems, Florence, Italy
{stefano.bacherini, matteo.tempestini, leonardo.cipriani}@ge.com

Abstract. Notwithstanding the large amount of attempts to formally verify them, railway interlocking systems still represent a challenging problem for automatic verification. Interlocking systems controlling sufficiently large stations, due to their inherent complexity related to the high number of variables involved, are not readily amenable to automatic verification, typically incurring in state space explosion problems. The study described in this paper aims at evaluating and experimenting the industrial application of verification by model checking for this class of systems. The choices made at the beginning of the study, also on the basis of specific requirements from the industrial partner, are presented, together with the advancement status of the project and the plans for its completion.

1 Introduction

In the railway signalling domain, an *interlocking* is the safety critical system that controls the movement of the trains in a station and between adjacent stations. The interlocking monitors the status of the objects in the railway yard and allows or denies the routing of the trains in accordance with the railway safety and operational regulations that are generic for the region or country where the interlocking is located. The instantiation of these rules on a station topology is stored in the part of the system named *control table*. Control tables of modern computerized interlockings are implemented by means of iteratively executed software controls over the status of the yard objects.

One of the most common way to describe the interlocking rules given by control tables is through boolean equations or, equivalently, ladder diagrams which are interpreted either by a PLC or by a proper evaluation engine over a standard processor. A first concern in the history of computerized interlockings has been the automatic generation of such boolean equation sets starting from generic signalling principles and from the topology of the layout of the station [14].

On the other hand, the certification activities for an interlocking include the verification that the implemented control tables actually satisfy safety rules.

S. Counsell and M. Núñez (Eds.): SEFM 2013 Collocated Workshops, LNCS 8368, pp. 237–252, 2014.
DOI: 10.1007/978-3-319-05032-4_18, © Springer International Publishing Switzerland 2014

Verification of correctness of control tables has been a prolific domain for formal methods practitioners, and the literature counts the application of several techniques to the problem, namely the Vienna Development Method (VDM) [16], property proving [7,13], Colored Petri Nets (CPN) [24] and model checking [23,25]. This last technique in particular has raised the interest of many railway signalling industries, being the most lightweight from the process point of view, and being rather promising in terms of efficiency.

However, due to the high number of boolean variables involved, automatic verification of sufficiently large stations typically incurs in combinatorial state space explosion problem.

The first applications of model checking have therefore attacked portions of an interlocking system [4,15]; but even recent works [12,26] show that routine verification of interlocking designs for large stations is still out of reach for symbolic model checker NuSMV [9] and explicit model checker SPIN [19], although specific optimizations can help [26]. As we argument later, SAT-based model checking appear to be more promising at this respect.

We want however to notice that control tables may have two main roles (not always both present) in the development of these systems: either as specifications of the interlocking rules [18], often issued by a railway infrastructure company, or as implementations, when they come encoded in some (typically proprietary) executable language. Hence also verification may address different problems, such as the consistency of the former, or the correctness of the latter w.r.t. the former, or the check of safety properties on the latter. In the study presented in this paper, we address the last mentioned verification problem. Anyway, a typical issue of any of these verification tasks is the choice of how to express control tables in a language suitable for the verification tool adopted.

Indeed, commercial solutions exist for the production of interlocking software, such as Prover Technology's (Ilock), that includes formal proof of safety conditions as well, by means of a SAT solving engine. Industrial acceptance of such "black-box" solutions is however sometimes hindered by the fear of vendor lock-in phenomena and by the loss of control over the production process.

In the Safety and Validation Laboratory (S&V Lab) of General Electric Transportation System (GETS), with the final aim of reducing the costs of verifying the safety requirements of the produced interlocking systems, a feasibility study has been started, conducted in collaboration with the Ph.D School of Information Engineering of the University of Florence, on the verification of legacy control tables that control a portion of a railway yard.

Indeed, the S&V Lab is acting (according to CENELEC 50128 standard [1]) as an independent verifier of the interlocking systems produced by other branches of the company, with little insight of the followed process, and focusing on the final product. Actually, the only information available on the implemented control tables can be extracted from the binary files, that are written in the target using a proprietary format, by means of libraries, that we will refer from now on as *legacy libraries*, provided by the interlocking developers.

In a previous exploratory work [12] the control tables were modelled as finite state machines and safety properties were proved by means of NuSMV. In this case, the choice of the tool and hence of the modelling language was taken instead according to specific constraints posed by the S&V Lab of GETS: in order to smoothly adopt this verification technique inside the internal production process, it was required that the verification tool is a commercial tool, already known within the company. Moreover, the difficulties encountered in dealing with medium and large size interlocking systems by means of BDD-based verification pointed to the alternative of adopting a SAT-based model checker, in order to exploit at best the native boolean coding coming from the control tables [20]. The conjunction of these constraints has favoured the choice of Matlab *Design Verifier* [2], which is based on a SAT solver, using boolean functions with logical gates as the language in which to translate the legacy control tables.

The commercial constraints posed by the company are due to a precise industrial policy, that is, minimizing additional investment, minimizing dependency from external suppliers, especially if not yet already known, while internally mastering the overall verification process.

This paper describes the current advancement of the feasibility study concentrating on the modelling phase [6]. First we introduce the reader to the CENELEC 50128 standard and to *Model Checking* techniques. In Sect. 4 we describe the ladder logic, that is, the industrial standard graphical language to represent boolean functions involved in control tables. In Sect. 5 we introduce the modelling process and in particular the algorithm *LLD Parser* that allows the control tables to be translated into boolean functions that will be implemented in a Simulink model. The algorithm has been used to extract the Simulink models fo several stations. Model checking has been experimented on such models, and the results of one of them that are shown in Sect. 6 confirm the initial intuition about using SAT-based verification tools.

2   CENELEC Standard

CENELEC 50128 is the standard that specifies the procedures and the technical requirements for the development of programmable electronic devices to be used in railway control and signalling protection. This standard is part of a family, and it refers only to the software components and to their interaction with the whole system. The basic concept of the standard is the SIL (Safety Integrity Level). Integrity levels range is defined from 0 to 4, where 0 is the lowest level, which refers to software with no effects on the safety of system and on the people; 4 is the maximum level: a failure in the software has effects on the safety of system, resulting in possible loss of human life [1].

The CENELEC 50128 however dictate neither a precise development methodology for software, nor any particular programming technique, but classifies a wide range of commonly adopted techniques in terms of a rating with respect to the established SIL of a component.

Formal methods are rated as *highly recommended* for the software requirements specification and software design of systems with the higher levels of SIL. Formal proof is also highly recommended as a verification activity. The standard however does not dictate any process in which formal methods take a role, but just gives a list of the most common formal and semiformal methods. Moreover, other combinations of highly recommended techniques, not including formal methods can be chosen.

3   Model Checking

A formal verification technique that has recently acquired popularity also in industrial applications is *Model Checking* [11] an automated technique that, given a finite-state model of a system and a property stated in some appropriate logical formalism (*temporal logic*), checks the validity of this property on the model.

Formal verification by means of model checking consists in verifying that a *Kripke structure* M, modelling the behaviour of a system, satisfies a temporal logic formula ϕ, expressing a desired property for M. A model checking basic algorithm labels each state of M with the subformulae of ϕ that hold in that state, starting with the ones having length 0, that is with atomic propositions, then with those of length 1, where a logic operator is used to connect atomic propositions, then to increasing length subformulae. This algorithm requires a navigation of the state space, and can be optimized to achieve a linear complexity with respect to the number of states of M. When a formula is found not to be satisfied, the subformulae labelling the states can then be used to provide a *counterexample*, that is, an execution path that leads to the violation of the property, thus helping the debugging of the model.

The basic model checking algorithm, that explores the entire state space, is affected by the so called *exponential state space explosion*, since the state space can have a size exponential in the number of independent variables of the system.

Many techniques have been developed to attack this problem: among them, symbolic model checking, where the state space is encoded by means of boolean functions, compactly represented by Binary Decision Diagrams (BDD) [8], is able to reduce memory consumption in many cases. Other approaches try to consider only a part of the state space that is sufficient to verify the formula, such as local model checking and Bounded Model Checking (BMC): the latter generates a counterexample of fixed length. The basis idea of the BMC is to evaluate only the paths of fixed length k: to define the length k is necessary to know the system and how it works to guarantee that the k-length chosen represents a good candidate to solve the verification problem.

BMC has shown itself as particularly efficient since the problem of checking a formula over a finite depth computation tree can be encoded as a satisfiability problem, and hence efficiently solved by current *SAT-solvers* [5].

4   Ladder Logic Diagrams

In Relay Interlocking Systems (RIS), still operating in several sites, the logical rules of the control tables were implemented by means of physical relay connections. With Computer Interlocking Systems (CIS), in application since 30 years, the control table becomes a set of software equations that are executed by the interlocking. Since the signaling regulations of the various countries were already defined in graphical form for the RIS, and also in order to facilitate the representation of control tables by signaling engineers, the design of CISs has usually adopted traditional graphical representations such as *Ladder Logic Diagrams* (LLD) [21] and relay diagrams [17]. These graphical schemata, usually called *principle schemata*, are instantiated on a station topology to build the control table, that is then translated into a program for the interlocking.

Correctness of control tables depends also on their model of execution by the interlocking software. In building CISs, the manufacturers adopt the principle of *as safe as the relay based equipment* [24], and often the implemented model of execution is very close to the hardware behaviour.

Ladder Logic is a graphical language which can represent a set of boolean equations and the execution order (*control cycle*) of them can be detailed as the following equation system:

$$y_1 = f_1(x_{i_{11}}, x_{i_{12}}, \ldots x_{i_{1k_1}});$$
$$y_2 = f_2(x_{i_{21}}, x_{i_{22}}, \ldots x_{i_{2k_2}});$$
$$\ldots$$
$$y_n = f_n(x_{i_{n1}}, x_{i_{n2}}, \ldots x_{i_{nk_n}});$$

where y_i are either output or latch variables, and $x_{i_{jk}}$ are either input or latch variables; each f_i is the function that computes the next value of each variable y_i and is applied to a different set of input or state variables.

Ladder Logic represents the working of relay-based control systems. For this reason the variables on the right expression of the equation are also named *contacts*, while the variables in the left hand are named *coils*. Variables can be distinguished in:

– *Input variables*: the value is assigned by sensor readings or operator commands. These variables are defined in the expressions e_i and cannot be used as coil.
– *Output variables*: can be only coils and their value is determined by means of the assignments of the diagram and is delivered to actuators.
– *Latch variables*: the value is calculated by means of the assignments, but is used only for internal computation of the values of other variables. A latch variable is used as coil in an assignment and is an input variable in other assignments.

With these three kinds of variables, a Ladder Logic Diagram describes a state machine whose memory is represented by the latch variables and the evolution is described by the assignment set. An execution of this state machine, named *control cycle*, involves:

1. Reading input variables; the values of these variables are assumed to be constant for the entire duration of the control cycle.

2. Computation of the current values for the output variables and for the latch variables starting from the values of the input variables and the values of the latch variables at the previous control cycle.
3. Transmission of the values of the output variables.

In this way, the equations can be seen as interpreted by a reasoner engine. The reasoner engine is the same for every plant; the control table is coded as data, actually boolean equations, for the reasoner. Behind this choice is the minimization of certification efforts: the reasoner is certified once for all, the data are considered "easier" to certify if they can be related in some way to the standard principle schemata adopted by railway engineers in the era of relay-based interlockings. For this reason, this approach is also referred as "data-driven".

In order to give a metric to the dimension of the problem in terms of parameters of the control tables, [12] defines the *size* of a control table as the couple *(m, n)*, where *m* is the maximum number of inter-dependent equations involved, that means equations that, taken in pairs, have at least one variable in common, and *n* is the number of inputs of the control table. Another used metric is just the size of the layout, given as the number of physical entities that constitute the layout (points, track circuits, signals, ...) and the number of routes that are established on the layout.

An example of a single row of a Ladder Logic Diagram is reported in Fig. 1, expressing the boolean equation:

$$y = x \wedge (w \vee \neg z)$$

In this graphical language, if x is a boolean variable, an expression e can be defined in inductive way by means of following syntax:

$- --]$ $[--$ represents an un-negated variable.
$- --]/[--$ represents a negated variable.
$- - - (\ \ )$ represents a coil.

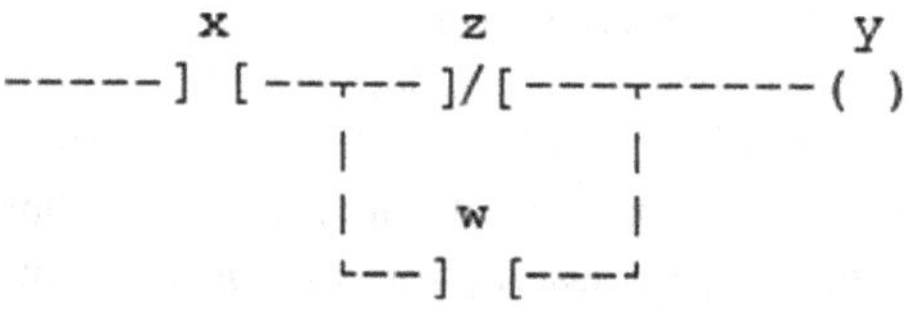

Fig. 1. Example of ladder logic diagram

In general, a Ladder Logic Diagram expresses a set of boolean equations that can be written:

$$\tilde{x} = f(\tilde{x}, \tilde{y})$$

where $\tilde{x}, \tilde{y}$ are boolean variable vectors representing respectively state/output variables and input variables: these equations are cyclically executed. Let us call

$\tilde{x}_i, \tilde{y}_i$ the vectors of values taken by such variables in successive executions. From the equations we can define $F(\tilde{x}_i, \tilde{x}_{i+1}, \tilde{y}_i)$ as a boolean function that is true iff $\tilde{x}_{i+1} = f(\tilde{x}_i, \tilde{y}_i)$, representing one execution of the equations. Let be $Init(\tilde{x})$ a predicate which is true for the initial vector value of state and output variables. If $P(\tilde{x})$ is a predicate telling that a desired (safety) property is verified by the vector $\tilde{x}$, then the following expression:

$$\Phi(k) = Init(\tilde{x}_0) \wedge \bigwedge_{i=0}^{k-1} F(\tilde{x}_i, \tilde{x}_{i+1}, \tilde{y}_i) \wedge \bigvee_{i=0}^{k} \sim P(\tilde{x}_i)$$

is a boolean formula that tells that P is not true for the state/output vector for some of the first k execution cycles. According to the BMC principles [5], using a SAT-solver to find a satisfying assignment to the boolean variables ends up either in unsatisfiability, which means that the property is satisfied by the first k execution cycles, or in an assignment that can be used as a counterexample for P, in particular showing a k-long sequence of input vectors that cause the safety problem with P.

In the next section we focus on the representation in a format suitable for Design Verifier of the legacy control tables that are loaded, in the form of LLDs, in the analysed interlocking systems.

5   Model Extraction

The first activity in the feasibility study has therefore addressed the definition of a process that allows a model of a station to be obtained from the analysed implementation in three steps:

1. **Import Station Data**: all data about a station (equations, timers, interfaces, ...) are imported in Matlab by means of the legacy libraries that read the binary files loaded on the interlocking system.
2. **Model Station Data**: the equations and the links between them are modelled in a Simulink model by means of the *LLD-Parser*.
3. **Model Properties**: safety properties are modelled with reference to the station model and are proved by means of Design Verifier.

Before to talk of the entire process of model extraction we describe briefly the Simulink environment, the core of our framework.

5.1   Simulink Enviroment

Simulink is a data flow graphical programming language tool for modeling, simulating and analyzing multidomain dynamic system, developed by *MathWorks* [3]. Its primary interface is a graphical block diagramming tool and a customizable set of block libraries. It offers tight integration with the rest of the MATLAB environment and can either drive MATLAB or be scripted from it. Simulink is widely used in control theory and digital signal processing for multidomain simulation and Model Based Design.

A number of MathWorks and third-party products hardware and software design are available for use with Simulink. For example, *Stateflow* extends Simulink with a design environment for developing state machines and flow charts.

Simulink can automatically generate C source code for real-time implementation of systems. As the efficiency and flexibility of the code improves, this is becoming more widely adopted for production in addition to being a popular tool for embedded system design work because of its flexibility and capacity for quick iteration.

Simulink Verification and Validation enables systematic verification and validation of models through modeling style checking, requirements traceability and model coverage analysis. Simulink Design Verifier uses SAT-based model checking to identify design errors like integer overflow, division by zero and dead logic, and generates test case scenarios for model checking within the Simulink environment.

5.2   Importing Data Station

As discussed in Sect. 4 the boolean equations of an interlocking are represented in a ladder logic diagram (Fig. 1), which is encoded in a proprietary binary format for the diagram interpreter engine.

In order to extract this information from the binary code, we use those proprietary interpretation routines that we have called "legacy libraries". These libraries allow each boolean equation to be read as a matrix $M^{n \times k}$. The matrix is just a one to one representation of the ladder diagram with numeric codes. The code values in the matrix can be either positive, representing variables, or negative, representing either a connector or the polarity of a variable (see Table 1).

Table 1. Symbol translation

Symbol	Value	Symbol	Value
∟	-1	--] [--	-10
⌐	-2	--]/ [--	-20
⊥	-3	--( )	-30
⊤	-4	Blank space	-40
⊦	-5	Horizontal line	-50
⊣	-6	Vertical line	-70
+	-7		

The LLD in Fig. 1 is for example encoded by the following matrix M:

$$\begin{bmatrix} -40 & 100 & -40 & 200 & -40 & 500 \\ -50 & -10 & -4 & -20 & -4 & -30 \\ -40 & -40 & -70 & 300 & -70 & -40 \\ -40 & -40 & -1 & -10 & -2 & -40 \end{bmatrix}$$

The values 100, 200, 300 and 500 are respectively associated to the variables x, z, w and y.

5.3 LLD Parser

The extracted matrix needs to be interpreted in order to define the boolean function it implements, expressed in a format suitable for Design Verifier. Three alternative ways to describe these functions are possible in Matlab, that is, using boolean gates in a Simulink diagram, using truth tables, or, by taking into account the typical cyclic execution of the equations as well, using a State-flow state machine. Some preliminary experiments have suggested that the latter choice was employing the less direct correspondence with the boolean equations, and hence less prone to be efficiently handled by Design Verifier. We have for the moment chosen the first alternative, leaving a more accurate efficiency comparison as a future work.

We have hence designed an algorithm that translates the matrix into Simulink boolean and/or/not gates.

If we focus on the graphical format of LLD, we recognize one or more *connectors* which belong to the following set:

$$C = \{\llcorner \ \lrcorner \ \perp \ \top \ \vdash \ \dashv \ +\}$$

Considering specific pairs of connectors, in the set C, it is possible to define a *connection relation* (CR) between them, which defines a particular conjunction/disjunction between the variables in a LLD:

$$CR = \{(\llcorner, \lrcorner), (\perp, \lrcorner), (\llcorner, \perp)\}$$

The connection relation is the basis to provide semantics to a LLD. By means of this relation we can classify LLDs in a few *Families of Equations* (FoE).

A FoE is a set of Ladder Logic Diagrams that share some common graphical features. Definition of the families is done on the basis of the order of the connectors that are found during a depth first search fo the graph. For example, the diagram in Fig. 2 represents the boolean equation:

$$y_1 = x_1 \wedge \neg x_2 \wedge ((x_3 \wedge \neg x_4) \vee (x_5 \wedge \neg x_6 \wedge x_7) \vee (y_1 \wedge x_8))$$

and belongs to the same FoE of the diagram in Fig. 1 because in both equations and operators are found first followed by inner or operators; the difference

Fig. 2. Example of ladder logic diagram

between this two members of the family is that in the second equation, the *or gate* has three inputs (three *and gates*), while the first equation has two variables in input.

We need to find these patterns (pairs) to model the equations by means of logical gates. In fact, the LLD Parser (reported in Algorithm 1) visits four times the matrix M; the first time it discovers all the input/output variables (positive values in the odd rows of M), then it reads the even rows of M, which contain the polarity of the variables (that is if they are asserted and/or negated in the equation).

Finally, if there is at least a logic *or*, that is, the value corresponding to the symbol $\top$ is present in the equation matrix M (*line* 3), the LLD Parser looks for the FoE to which the matrix M belongs and then runs a *Depth First Search* (DFS) on the connectors that are in the equation; otherwise this means that all the variables in the equation are in logic *and* (*line* 15).

Algorithm 1 LLD Parser

Require: M equation matrix
Ensure: Model of the equation
 1: $var \leftarrow$ GetVariables(M)
 2: $syntax \leftarrow$ GetVariablePolarity(M,var)
 3: **if** $\top \in M$ **then**
 4:     $family \leftarrow$ GetFoE(M)
 5:     **switch** $(family)$
 6:     **case 1:**
 7:         $DFS_1(M, var, syntax)$
 8:     **case 2:**
 9:         $DFS_2(M, var, syntax)$
         $\vdots$
10:     **case N:**
11:         $DFS_N(M, var, syntax)$
12:     **default:**
13:     **end switch**
14: **else**
15:     $LogicAnd(var)$
16: **end if**

The Algorithm 2 is the DFS for the LLDs reported in Figs. 1, 2 and the subrelations defined are: $CR_1 = \{\lfloor, \rfloor\}$, $CR_2 = \{\vdash, \dashv\}$ and $CR_3 = \{\top, \top\}$.

Sorting connectors (lines 2-3): the connectors in the matrix (C_M) are sorted from the deepest (greatest row and column in M) to the shallowest (C_{MO}).

Main Loop (lines 4–16): from the set C_{MO} a connectors pair (c_1, c_2) is extracted and if the pair belongs to a connection subrelation the variables are linked accordingly. In particular:

Create a new or gate (lines 5–10): if (c_1, c_2) belongs to CR_1 an *or* gate is created and the variables $var_{pattern}$ between the connectors (c_1, c_2) are connected (w.r.t. them syntax), possibly through an *and* gate, to the new *or* gate; this construction is done by the function *LinkVariables*. At last, the variables in $var_{pattern}$ are deleted from the set *var* which contains all not yet connected variables.

Link other variables (lines 11–15): the case in which (c_1, c_2) belongs to CR_2 or CR_3 is similar to the previous cases, but no new *or* gate is built and the $var_{pattern}$ variables are connected to the most recently created *or* gate by the function *LinkVariables*. *Create final and gate (lines 17–19):* if there are still variables in the set *var* (see the example of variable x for the LLD in Fig. 1 and variables x_1, x_2 in Fig. 2), they are linked with the most recently created *or* gate to a final *and* gate; otherwise the most recently created *or* gate is the final gate. The question of the correctness of the proposed traslation has been addressed by running the same test suites on the original target and on the model, obtaining the same results apart from some timing issues.

Algorithm 2 Depth First Search

Require: M equation matrix, *var* set of variables, *syntax* syntax of variables
Ensure: Build correctly the equation model

1: $numOrGate \leftarrow 0$
2: $C_M \leftarrow C \in M$
3: $C_{MO} \leftarrow Order(C_M)$
4: **for all** $(c_1, c_2) \in C_{MO}$ **do**
5:   **if** $(c_1, c_2) \in CR_1$ **then**
6:     $numOrGate \leftarrow numOrGate + 1$
7:     $var_{pattern} \leftarrow var \in (c_1, c_2)$
8:     $LinkVariables(var_{pattern}, M, syntax)$
9:     $var \leftarrow DeleteVariables(var_{pattern}, var)$
10:   **end if**
11:   **if** $(c_1, c_2) \in CR_2 \| (c_1, c_2) \in CR_3$ **then**
12:     $var_{pattern} \leftarrow var \in (c_1, c_2)$
13:     $LinkVariables(var_{pattern}, M, syntax)$
14:     $var \leftarrow DeleteVariables(var_{pattern}, var)$
15:   **end if**
16: **end for**
17: **if** $var \in var_{pattern}$ **then**
18:   $CreateAndFinal(var, numOrGate)$
19: **end if**

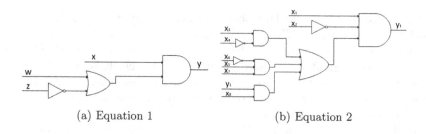

(a) Equation 1   (b) Equation 2

Fig. 3. LLDs translated in logic equations

After the parsing of the matrix M the output of the equation can: (1) activate a timer, (2) be input to the same equation. In the first case a timer is modelled and the output of the equation is linked to the timer, in the second case a delay block is created. The Simulink diagrams with boolean gates for the two equations depicted in this paper are reported in Fig. 3.

All the equations are then linked between them by means of the latch variables, or by timers when needed; in this way the model of a station is completed (see left part of Fig. 5). The model has as input and output the input/output variables of the equations.

6   Verification with Design Verifier

The algorithm proposed in the previous section has been used by the S&V Laboratory to extract the Simulink model of several production station equipments. We show in the following the verification performed on a network of four Computer Interlocking Subsystems: $(CIS_1, CIS_2, CIS_3, CIS_4)$ that controls a small railway station.

The network has 2625 equations, 717 inputs and 915 outputs; each equation can have from one input to a maximum of 25 inputs. The number of equations, inputs and outputs, apportioned to single CISs is reported in Table 2.

An example of property P that has been defined is the following:
Under the preconditions:

1. The input from a track circuit A gives it as *unoccupied*.
2. A predefined time period (e.g. 2 s) has elapsed.

Table 2. Data of single CIS

CIS	Number of equations	Number of inputs	Number of outputs
CIS_1	77	44	52
CIS_2	1608	370	522
CIS_3	430	151	157
CIS_4	511	152	184

3. The input from the adjacent track circuit B, in accordance with the driving direction, is *occupied*.

the modelled state of A passes from *occupied* to *unoccupied*.

The property P can be written, using a *real-time version* of LTL logic [22] as:

$$(p_1 \wedge \mathbf{G}^{[2,2]}p_3) \Rightarrow p_4$$

where p_4 is the event "the state of A passed from occupied to unoccupied", p_1 the event "the input of track circuit A is unoccupied", p_3 is "the input of B is occupied" and $\mathbf{G}^{[2,2]}$ represents that after 2 s my model verifies the condition p_3 is true.

The verification with Design Verifier requires the property P to be expressed as a Simulink "observer". The property P above is modelled in Simulink by the diagram in Fig. 4. To prove the property P a small number of input/output variables was used (see Fig. 5); indeed the property is relative to CIS_3 but, the behaviour of this system, depends from the interaction with the other CISs and for this reason it has been necessary to prove the property on the entire station model.

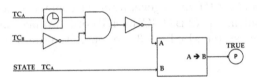

Fig. 4. Property P

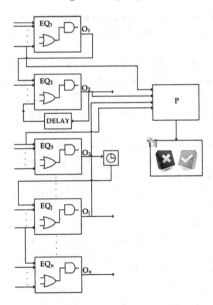

Fig. 5. Prove property

Table 3. Times

Phase	Time (s)
Import data	60,334
Model station	2506,271
Prove property	2,000
Total	2568,605

Design Verifier has generated a counterexample; that is an input variables assignment that does not satisfy the property P. Each input variable in the counterexample assumes the values: *true* (1), *false* (0) or *don't care* (-). Due to the high complexity of the interlocking logic, interpretation of the counterexample is not immediate, and requires the help of signalling engineers, who are able to distinguish real counterexamples from unfeasible combinations of inputs. At the current stage of the project, this particular activity has not yet been started. The run experiments were rather aimed at testing the capability of Design Verifier to deal with models of this size.

The entire process of importing data from the binaries, modelling the station and proving the property P (with a generation of a counterexample) has been run on an AMD Athlon(tm) II X2 B24 3GHz, 4GB of RAM machine with Windows 7, 32 bits, operating system. In Table 3, we report the times (in seconds) of the three phases.

7   Conclusion

In this paper we have reported a solution to extract a model from the implementation of an interlocking system and to prove the correctness of safety properties P on the model.

We have implemented an algorithm that: (1) reads the station data by the binary files, that is loaded on the target, by means of legacy library; (2) parses the boolean equations, that are written in ladder logic, and generates a model which contains the equations and the station interfaces towards the adjacent stations.

To model the boolean equations we have defined the semantic of the ladder logic. The algorithm runs a depth first search in the ladder logic diagram to find out the connection patterns and by means of these patterns the algorithm builds the equation model. Finally all equation models are linked between them and the station model is created.

We have shown the application of the algorithm on an interlocking system of 2625 equations, 717 input and 915 output interfaces that controls a portion of a railway station, obtaining the station modelling in less than one hour; finally the verification of safety properties has been addressed by means of Design Verifier, raising the problem of the interpretation of counterexamples obtained by verification, which may require the help of signalling engineers, to distinguish real counterexamples from unfeasible combinations of inputs. In order to rule out such unfeasible counterexamples, we are studying to shape our verification process according to the CEGAR (CounterExample Guided Abstraction Refinement) paradigm [10], in order to provide an automated method adoptable in an industrial context.

The current experiments are focused on providing verification results on a set of production interlocking cases of different sizes. We will then address a deeper analysis of these results, focusing in particular on the optimization of the model to better exploit the underlying SAT solver of Design Verifier. At this regard, the possible alternative choices (state machine, truth tables) for modelling the control tables will be compared w.r.t. the verification performance of the tool.

Moreover, we shall investigate the application of other verification tools, such as NuSMV, to the extracted data, in order to compare results and performance issues. This activity, although a change of the verification engine in the defined verification process is not planned by the company, will help to consolidate it, and will provide interesting compared data about the application of formal verification tools on industrial production case studies.

References

1. European Committee for Electrotechnical Standardization, CENELEC EN50128, Railway applications-Communication signalling and processing system software for railway control and protection systems
2. Simulink®: Design Verifier R2012b. MathWorks (2012)
3. Simulink®: User Guide R2012b. MathWorks (2012)
4. Bernardeschi, C., Fantechi, A., Gnesi, S., Larosa, S., Mongardi, G., Romano, D.: A formal verification environment for railway signaling system design. Formal Methods Syst. Des. **12**, 139–161 (1998)
5. Biere, A., Cimatti, A., Clarke, E., Zhu, Y.: Symbolic model checking without BDDs. In: Cleaveland, W.R. (ed.) TACAS 1999. LNCS, vol. 1579, pp. 193–207. Springer, Heidelberg (1999)
6. Bonacchi, A.: Formal safety proof: a real case study in a railway interlocking system. In: ISSTA, pp. 378–381. ACM (2013)
7. Borälv, A.: Case study: formal verification of a computerized railway interlocking. Formal Asp. Comput. **10**, 338–360 (1998)
8. Bryant, R.E.: Graph-based algorithms for boolean function manipulation. IEEE Trans. Comput. **35**(8), 677–691 (1986)
9. Cimatti, A., Clarke, E., Giunchiglia, E., Giunchiglia, F., Pistore, M., Roveri, M., Sebastiani, R., Tacchella, A.: NuSMV 2: an OpenSource tool for symbolic model checking. In: Brinksma, E., Larsen, K.G. (eds.) CAV 2002. LNCS, vol. 2404, pp. 359–364. Springer, Heidelberg (2002)
10. Clarke, E.M., Grumberg, O., Jha, S., Lu, Y., Veith, H.: Counterexample-guided abstraction refinement. In: Emerson, E.A., Sistla, A.P. (eds.) CAV 2000. LNCS, vol. 1855, pp. 154–169. Springer, Heidelberg (2000)
11. Clarke, E.M., Grumberg, O., Peled, D.A.: Model Checking. MIT Press, Cambridge (1999)
12. Ferrari, A., Magnani, G., Grasso, D., Fantechi, A.: Model checking interlocking control tables. In: FORMS/FORMAT, pp. 98–107 (2010)

13. Fokkink, W., Hollingshead, P.: Verification of interlockings: from control tables to ladder logic diagrams. In: FMICS'98, pp. 171–185 (1998)
14. Fringuelli, B., Lamma, E., Mello, P., Santocchia, G.: Knowledge-based technology for controlling railway stations. IEEE Expert: Intell. Syst. Appl. **7**, 45–52 (1992)
15. Groote, J.F., van Vlijmen, S., Koorn, J.: The Safety Guaranteeing System at Station Hoorn-Kersenboogerd. In: Logic Group Preprint Series 121. Utrecht University (1995)
16. Hansen, K.M.: Formalising railway interlocking systems. In: Proceedings of the 2nd FMERail, Workshop (1998)
17. Haxthausen, A.E.: Developing a domain model for relay circuits. Int. J. Softw. Inf. **3**(2–3), 241–272 (2009)
18. Haxthausen, A.E., Le Bliguet, M., Kjær, A.A.: Modelling and verification of relay interlocking systems. In: Choppy, C., Sokolsky, O. (eds.) Monterey Workshop 2008. LNCS, vol. 6028, pp. 141–153. Springer, Heidelberg (2010)
19. Holzmann, G.: Spin Model Checker, The Primer and Reference Manual. Addison-Wesley Professional, Reading (2003)
20. James, P., Roggenbach, M.: Automatically verifying railway interlockings using SAT-based model checking. In: AVOCS, pp. 141–153 (2010)
21. Kanso, K., Moller, F., Setzer, A.: Automated verification of signalling principles in railway interlocking systems. Electron. Notes Theor. Comput. Sci. **250**(2), 19–31 (2009)
22. Kristoffersen, K.J., Pedersen, C., Andersen, H.R.: Runtime verification of timed LTL using disjunctive normalized equation systems. Electr. Notes Theor. Comput. Sci. **89**(2), 210–225 (2003)
23. Mirabadi, A., Yazdi, M.: Automatic generation and verification of railway interlocking control tables using FSM and NuSMV. Transport Prob.: Int. Sci. J. **4**, 103–110 (2009)
24. Vanit-Anunchai, S.: Modelling railway interlocking tables using coloured petri nets. In: Clarke, D., Agha, G. (eds.) COORDINATION 2010. LNCS, vol. 6116, pp. 137–151. Springer, Heidelberg (2010)
25. Winter, K., Johnston, W., Robinson, P., Strooper, P., van den Berg, L.: Tool support for checking railway interlocking designs. In: Proceedings of the 10th Australian Workshop on Safety Critical Systems and Software, pp. 101–107 (2006)
26. Winter, K., Robinson, N.J.: Modelling large railway interlockings and model checking small ones. In: Twenty-Sixth Australasian Computer Science Conference (ACSC2003), Adelaide, South Australia, pp. 309–316 (2003)

Verification of Solid State Interlocking Programs

Phillip James[1], Andy Lawrence[1], Faron Moller[1], Markus Roggenbach[1(✉)],
Monika Seisenberger[1], Anton Setzer[1], Karim Kanso[2], and Simon Chadwick[3]

[1] Swansea Railway Verification Group, Swansea University, Wales, UK
csmarkus@swan.ac.uk
[2] Critical Software Technologies, Southampton, England, UK
[3] Invensys Rail, Chippenham, England, UK

Abstract. We report on the inclusion of a formal method into an industrial design process. Concretely, we suggest carrying out a verification
step in railway interlocking design between programming the interlocking and testing this program. Safety still relies on testing, but the burden of guaranteeing completeness and correctness of the validation is
in this way greatly reduced. We present a complete methodology for
carrying out this verification step in the case of ladder logic programs
and give results for real world railway interlockings. As this verification
step reduces costs for testing, Invensys Rail is working to include such a
verification step into their design process of solid state interlockings.

1 Introduction

Solid state interlockings represent one of many safety measures implemented in
railways. In Vincenti's terminology [27], interlockings are *normal* designs: railway
engineers have a clear understanding of their workings and customary features,
and it is standard practice to design them and to bring them into operation.

The formal method we propose is a verification step between programming
the interlocking using ladder logic [11] and testing of this program. The method
we suggest is first to automatically translate the program as well as its desired
properties and then to apply standard model checking approaches and tools to
the resulting model checking problem.

Our work has been inspired by [7,8]. Reference [8] gives a detailed description of model checking railway interlockings and highlights the use of program
slicing. Reference [7] presents an approach to translate ladder logic programs
into propositional logic and formulates model checking for sliced ladder logic
programs. Alternative approaches include [28] who apply timed automata and
UPPAAL or [9] who present a development framework for ladder logic, including
verification by port-level simulation. Ladder logic programs for programmable
logic controllers in general have been verified using the symbolic model checker
SMV [23]. Another type of interlocking program developed in so called "Safety
Logic" has been verified using the SPIN model checker [3]. In [10], Haxthausen
extracts a transition system (a SAL model) from circuit diagrams which are

S. Counsell and M. Núñez (Eds.): SEFM 2013 Collocated Workshops, LNCS 8368, pp. 253–268, 2014.
DOI: 10.1007/978-3-319-05032-4_19, © Springer International Publishing Switzerland 2014

reminiscent of ladder logic programs. Reference [15] verifies interlockings by interactive theorem proving, reducing the gap between verification of safety and safety in the real world.

This paper's contribution is, besides giving a precise formalisation of the translation from ladder logic into a model checking problem, to put known verification approaches into the context of a concrete engineering problem and, by providing a prototypical implementation, demonstrate that they work.

We first define interlockings and describe their design exemplified by the GRIP process and the realisation of GRIP's Detailed Design phase at Invensys Rail. We then detail our formal method, i.e., the verification step, and compile different technologies upon which the verification can be based. Finally, we present comparative results in terms of an industrial case study. This paper summarises results published in [15–18,20].

2 Designing Solid State Interlockings

In railway systems, solid state interlockings provide a safety layer between the controller and the track. In order to move a train, the controller issues a request to set a route. The interlocking uses rules and track information to determine whether it is safe to permit this request: if so, the interlocking will change the state of the track (move points, set signals, etc.) and inform the controller that the request was granted; otherwise the interlocking will not change the track state. In this sense, an interlocking is like a Programmable Logic Controller (PLC). The standard IEC 61131 [11] identifies programming languages for such controllers, including the visual language ladder logic discussed below.

Interlockings applications are developed according to processes prescribed by Railway Authorities, such as Network Rail's *Governance for Railway Investment Projects* (GRIP) process. The first four GRIP phases define the track plan and routes of the railway to be constructed, while phase five – the detailed design – is contracted to a signalling company such as Invensys which chooses appropriate track equipment, adds control tables to the track plan, and implements the solid state interlocking. It is for part of this phase, namely for the correct implementation of a control table in a solid state interlocking, that our paper offers support in terms of a formal method.

Signalling handbooks (e.g. [21]) describe how to design control tables for the routes of a track plan. Technical data sheets provide information of how to control the selected hardware such as points, signals and track circuits. It is a complex programming task to implement the control tables for the selected hardware elements. For a larger railway station, the resulting program can involve thousands of tightly coupled variables, so thorough testing for safety is a must. To this end, programs are run on a rig which simulates the physical railway, and it can take any number of iterations of testing and debugging for a program to pass all prescribed tests. This testing cycle is cost intensive, as it is hardly automated due to its interactive nature and concerns about the safety integrity of any automated testing environment: the tester has to run the program through various scenarios developing over time. Furthermore, debugging is time consuming as there is little support for producing counter examples.

It is at this point that the formal method described below is able to reduce costs in the design process. Rather than testing an interlocking program, we automatically transform the program and the safety property that the test shall establish into a model checking problem. Tool support then allows to automatically check if the property is fulfilled. In case it is not, a counter example is produced, possibly in the form of a trace of controller requests and train movements. This allows the programmer to obtain intelligible feedback. This process is fast and far less involved than testing the program. For these reasons, based on our research, Invensys Rail is working to include such a verification step into their design process of solid state interlockings.

3   From Ladder Logic to Model Checking

We first introduce the programming language ladder logic, show how ladder logic programs can be represented in propositional logic, and give them a semantics in terms of transition systems. We then discuss how typical safety properties from the railway domain expressed in first order logic can be specialised to propositional logic. These two steps result in a model checking problem: is the specialisation of a safety property satisfied w.r.t. the labelled transition system gained from the ladder logic program? We discuss how to apply standard model checking approaches to this question and address the problem of false positives.

3.1   Ladder Logic

Ladder logic gets its name from its graphical "ladder"-like form (see Fig. 1) reminiscent of relay circuits. Each rung of the ladder computes the current value of an output. A ladder logic program is executed top-to-bottom, and an interlocking executes such a program indefinitely.

A ladder logic rung consists of the following entities. *Coils* represent boolean values that are stored for later use as output variables from the program. A coil is always the right most entity of the rung and its value is computed by executing the rung from left to right. *Contacts* are the boolean inputs of a rung, with *open* and *closed* contacts representing the values of un-negated and negated variables, respectively. The value of a coil is calculated when a rung fires, making use of the current set of inputs – input variables, previous output variables, and output variables already computed for this cycle – following the given connections. A horizontal connection between contacts represents logical conjunction and a vertical connection represents logical disjunction. For example:

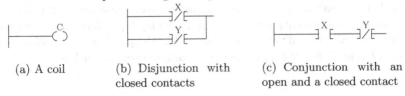

(a) A coil   (b) Disjunction with closed contacts   (c) Conjunction with an open and a closed contact

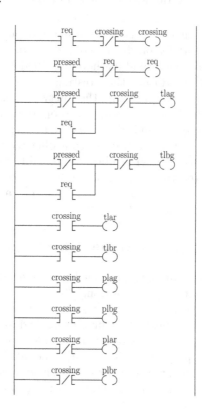

Fig. 1. The ladder logic program for the pelican crossing

As a running example we model a Pelican crossing, consisting of: two buttons at each side of a road, allowing pedestrians to make a request to cross; and four sets of lights (2 pedestrian lights, pla and plb, and 2 traffic lights, tla and tlb) controlling the flow of pedestrians and traffic. This is modelled by a boolean input variable *pressed* and 8 variables *plar*, *plag*, *plbr*, *plbg*, *tlar*, *tlag*, *tlbr*, *tlbg*, modelling the aspect of the light, 'r' for 'red', 'g' for 'green'. We also have two internal variables: *req* represents whether one of the pedestrian buttons has been pressed in a previous iteration of the program and whether there is already a request to cross; and *crossing* models the fact that a pedestrian is allowed to cross the road. Figure 1 presents a ladder logic program for such a Pelican crossing. The execution model for a ladder logic program is an infinite repetition of the *sense-think-act* cycle common in the design of embedded systems. *Sense:* all inputs are read; *think:* the program is executed; *act:* the outputs are all written. It thus makes sense to speak about consecutive execution cycles; and we discuss program execution for the current cycle, depending on the values of the input and the internal variables at the end of the previous cycle. We explain our use of ladder logic by considering the example program in Fig. 1.

- If the state variable "crossing" becomes true in Rung 1, then as a consequence, at the end of the cycle the pedestrian lights will be green and the traffic lights will be red (by Rungs 3-10).
- For "crossing" to become true, a request "req" to cross must have been made and in the previous cycle pedestrians could not cross (see Rung 1).
- The state variable "req" is true if and only if at (the beginning of) the previous cycle the button was pressed and at (the end of) the previous cycle the pedestrian lights were red i.e. "req" was previously false (see Rung 2)
- Rungs 5 and 6 control the setting of the red light for the traffic depending on on the state variable "crossing". Rungs 6-9 control the pedestrian lights depending on the state variable "crossing".
- Rungs 3 and 4 deliberately use a complicated encoding in order to demonstrate later the difference between model checking approaches. However, they still encode the correct behaviour: namely, setting the green light for traffic exclusively to setting the green light for pedestrians.

3.2   From Ladder Logic to Propositional Logic

From an abstract perspective, ladder logic diagrams represent propositional formulae. However, the process of obtaining these requires special care. In [14] we detail of how to use the Tseitin Transformation [26] in order to prevent a blow-up in formula size regarding nested disjunctions. This avoids bad performance when translating formulae into CNF, which is the usual input format of SAT solvers, the verification technology we intend to use.

The Tseitin Transformation traverses the formula from left to right, building up sub-formulae, each of which consisting of a conjunction or disjunction. The efficient use of sub-formulae requires the introduction of auxiliary variables. Figure 2 shows an example and locations where variables are introduced. Here, a new variable is introduced for each step in the computation: After every contact x a new variable x_i is introduced (where i is fresh for x), and for each vertical connection (disjunction) a new variable $\vee_j$ is introduced (where j is fresh). The rung is then broken at each of the intermediate variables, resulting in a simplified ladder. Each rung in the simplified ladder consists of only conjunction or disjunction and at most one negation. By following the above procedure, applied to the ladder in Fig. 2, the below assignments and formulae are obtained:

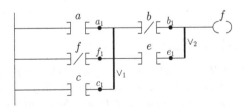

Fig. 2. Tracing back from coil f: Without auxiliary variables, the nested disjunction results in the large formula $f' \leftrightarrow (\neg b \wedge (a \vee \neg f' \vee c)) \vee (e \wedge (a \vee \neg f' \vee c))$.

$$a_1 := a \qquad\qquad (\ a_1' \leftrightarrow a \qquad\qquad)$$
$$f_1 := \neg f \qquad\qquad \wedge \ (\ f_1' \leftrightarrow \neg f \qquad\qquad)$$
$$c_1 := c \qquad\qquad \wedge \ (\ c_1' \leftrightarrow c \qquad\qquad)$$
$$\vee_1 := a_1 \vee f_1 \vee c_1 \qquad\qquad \wedge \ (\ \vee_1' \leftrightarrow a_1' \vee f_1' \vee c_1' \ )$$
$$b_1 := \vee_1 \wedge \neg b \qquad\qquad \wedge \ (\ b_1' \leftrightarrow \vee_1' \wedge \neg b \qquad)$$
$$e_1 := \vee_1 \wedge e \qquad\qquad \wedge \ (\ e_1' \leftrightarrow \vee_1' \wedge e \qquad)$$
$$\vee_2 := b_1 \vee e_1 \qquad\qquad \wedge \ (\ \vee_2' \leftrightarrow b_1' \vee e_1' \qquad)$$
$$f := \vee_2 \qquad\qquad \wedge \ (\ f' \leftrightarrow \vee_2' \qquad\qquad)$$

(a) Assignments of Fig. 2.   (b) Translation of Fig. 2.

The ladder logic of the Pelican logic Fig. 1 translates (for readability without the optimisation) into the conjunction of these formulae:

$$crossing' \leftrightarrow req \wedge \neg \, crossing,$$
$$req' \leftrightarrow pressed \wedge \neg \, req,$$
$$tlag' \leftrightarrow (\neg \, pressed \vee req') \wedge \neg \, crossing',$$
$$tlbg' \leftrightarrow (\neg \, pressed \vee req') \wedge \neg \, crossing',$$
$$tlar' \leftrightarrow crossing', \qquad\qquad tlbr' \leftrightarrow crossing',$$
$$plag' \leftrightarrow crossing', \qquad\qquad plbg' \leftrightarrow crossing',$$
$$plar' \leftrightarrow \neg \, crossing', \qquad\qquad plbr' \leftrightarrow \neg \, crossing'$$

3.3   Ladder Logic Formulæ and Their Semantics

A ladder logic program is constructed in terms of disjoint finite sets I and C of input and output variables, where internal variables are subsumed in C. In our example in Fig. 1, we have $I = \{pressed\}$ and $C = \{crossing, req, tlag, tlbg, tlar,$ $tlbr, plag, plbg, plar, plbr\}$. We define $C' = \{c' \mid c \in C\}$ to be a set of new variables (intended to denote the output variables computed in the current cycle). In addition, we need a function unprime : $C' \to C$, unprime$(c') = c$.

Definition 1 (Ladder Logic Formulae). *A ladder logic formula ψ is a propositional formula of the form*

$$\psi \equiv (c_1' \leftrightarrow \psi_1) \wedge (c_2' \leftrightarrow \psi_2) \wedge \cdots \wedge (c_n' \leftrightarrow \psi_n)$$

such that the following holds for all $i, j \in \{1, \ldots, n\}$:

- $c_i' \in C'$;
- $i \neq j \to c_i' \neq c_j'$; *and*
- $\mathrm{Vars}(\psi_i) \subseteq I \cup \{c_1', \ldots, c_{i-1}'\} \cup \{c_i, \ldots, c_n\}$.

Remark 1. *Note that the output variable c_i' of each rung ψ_i, may depend on $\{c_i, \ldots, c_n\}$ from the previous cycle, but not on c_j with $j < i$, due to the imperative nature of the ladder logic implementation. Those values are overridden.*

Remark 2. *In the formulae extracted from a ladder logic program equivalences $(c_1' \leftrightarrow \psi_1) \wedge \cdots$ can be replaced by $(c_1' = \psi_1) \wedge \cdots$. Both formulae are equivalent.*

Definition 2 (Semantics of Ladder Logic Formulae). *Let* $\{0,1\}$ *represent the set of boolean values and let*

$$\text{Val}_I = \{\mu_I \mid \mu_I : I \to \{0,1\}\} = \{0,1\}^I$$
$$\text{Val}_C = \{\mu_C \mid \mu_C : C \to \{0,1\}\} = \{0,1\}^C$$

be the sets of valuations for input and output variables. The semantics of a ladder logic formula ψ *is a function that takes the two current valuations and returns a new valuation for output variables:*

$$[\psi] \ : \ \text{Val}_I \times \text{Val}_C \to \text{Val}_C$$
$$[\psi](\mu_I, \mu_C) \ = \ \mu'_C$$

where

$$\mu'_C(c_i) = [\psi_i](\mu_I, (\mu_C)_{\restriction\{c_i,...,c_n\}}, (\mu'_C \circ \text{unprime})_{\restriction\{c'_1,...,c'_{i-1}\}})$$
$$\mu'_C(c) = \mu_C(c) \ \textit{if } c \notin \{c_1, \ldots, c_n\}$$

and $[\psi_i](\cdot, \cdot, \cdot)$ *denotes the usual value of a formula under a valuation.*

3.4   Labelled Transition Systems

We turn this into a transition system representing the ladder logic program.

Definition 3 (Labelled Transition System, Reachability). *A Labelled Transition System (LTS)* M *is a four tuple* (S, T, R, S_0) *where*

– S *is a finite set of states;*
– T *is a finite set of transition labels;*
– $R \subseteq S \times T \times S$ *is a labelled transition relation; and*
– $S_0 \subseteq S$ *is the set of initial states.*

We write $s \xrightarrow{t} s'$ *for* $(s, t, s') \in R$. *A state* s *is called* reachable *if*

$$s_0 \xrightarrow{t_0} s_1 \xrightarrow{t_1} \ldots \xrightarrow{t_{n-1}} s_n = s,$$

for some states $s_0, \ldots, s_n \in S$, *and labels* $t_0, \ldots, t_{n-1} \in T$ *where* $s_0 \in S_0$.

Definition 4 (Ladder Logic Labelled Transition System). *We define the labelled transition system* $\text{LTS}(\psi)$ *for a ladder logic formula* ψ *to be the four tuple* $(\text{Val}_C, \text{Val}_I, \to, \text{Val}_0)$ *where*

– $\mu_C \xrightarrow{\mu_I} \mu'_C \ iff \ [\psi](\mu_I, \mu_C) = \mu'_C$
– $\text{Val}_0 \ = \ \{\mu_C \mid \mu_C \text{ inital valuation}\}$

Remark 3. *The standard initial valuation in the railway domain sets all red lights to 1, and all other variables to 0, i.e. this results in exactly one initial state. A variant proceeds as follows: First, all output variables are set to 0 and then all possible transitions are performed.* Val_0 *is then defined as the set of states obtained after this first transition. In the Pelican crossing example (see Fig. 3 below) this would lead to two initial states rather than one. In both cases, a formula Init characterises* Val_0.

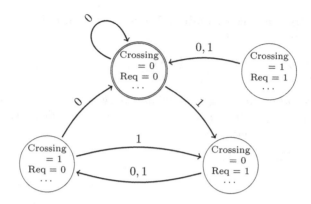

Fig. 3. Pelican crossing transition system

3.5   Producing Verification Conditions

In order to guarantee safety, companies such as Invensys ensure through testing that interlockings fulfil certain properties. We formulate them as logical formulae, and call the result *safety conditions*. These conditions are the main example of *verification conditions*, which are formulae, for which we check using our tools whether they hold in an interlocking system. In our setting verification conditions are first-order formulae, with variables ranging over entities such as points, signals, routes, track segments, while referring to predicates. An example of a safety condition is the formula

$$\forall rt, rt' \in \text{Route}.\forall ts \in \text{Segment}.$$
$$\left(rt \neq rt' \ \wedge \ \text{part\_of}(ts, rt) \ \wedge \ \text{part\_of}(ts, rt')\right)$$
$$\longrightarrow \neg\left(\text{routeset}(rt) \ \wedge \ \text{routeset}(rt')\right)$$

expressing the property: *for all pairs of routes that share a track segment, at most one of them can be set to proceed.*

Note there are two kinds of predicates: *State* and *Topology*. State predicates express the state of entities at a given time; e.g., routeset($rt26$) expresses that route $rt26$ has been set. These predicates will unfold into variables in the ladder logic program, so in the previous example the predicate would—depending on the actual naming scheme—unfold to the variable $rt26ru$. *Topology* predicates express meta information relating to the topology of the railway yard. E.g. part_of($ts54, rt26$) expresses that the track segment $ts54$ is part of route $rt26$. These predicates unfold to *true* or *false*, depending on whether the property holds; thus, the previous example unfolds to *true* when $ts54$ is actually part of $rt26$, otherwise *false*.

Some topology predicates are atomic and stated explicitly as true or false for given arguments. Other predicates can be computed in terms of these atomic predicates. E.g., signal $ms1$ is a main signal guarding access to route rt, if there exists track segments *ts1* and *ts2* such that *ts1* is before route *rt*, *ts1* is connected with *ts2*, *ts2* is part of the route *rt*, and *ms1* is located directly between *ts1* and *ts2*. This can be expressed as follows:

$$\text{route\_main\_signal}(ms1, rt) \leftrightarrow \exists ts1, ts2 \in \text{Segment}.$$
$$\text{before}(ts1, rt) \wedge \text{connected}(ts1, ts2) \wedge \text{part\_of}(ts2, rt)$$
$$\wedge \text{ infrontof}(ts1, ms1) \wedge \text{inrearof}(ts2, ms1)$$

In [14,16] Kanso introduces a translation of such formulae to propositional formulae which can then be verified using either SAT solving or model checking. This approach takes the following steps:

1. We first express the topology using a Prolog program that determines the truth of the topology predicates. The program consists of clauses such as
   - mainsignal(*ms1*) – signifying that *ms1* is a main signal, and
   - infrontof(*ts0a*, *ms1*) – signifying that signal *ms1* is in front of track segment *ts0a*.

   The above predicate route_main_signal(*ms1*, *rt*) is defined in Prolog as:
   route_main_signal(*ms1*, *rt*) :−

   $$\text{before}(ts, rt), \text{connected}(ts, tss),$$
   $$\text{part\_of}(tss, rt), \text{infrontof}(ts, ms1), \text{inrearof}(tss, ms1).$$

2. We then translate the formula into prenex form – i.e., a formula consisting of a block of quantifiers followed by a quantifier free formula – using standard techniques from logic.
3. Finally, we replace each occurrence of $\forall x \in A.\varphi(x)$ by $\varphi(a_1) \wedge \cdots \wedge \varphi(a_n)$ and each occurrence of $\exists x \in A.\varphi(x)$ by $\varphi(a_1) \vee \cdots \vee \varphi(a_n)$, where $a_1, \ldots, a_n$ are the elements of set A in the topology. φ is now instantiated to closed instances. Therefore the topological predicates evaluate to truth values that can then easily be omitted from the formula. Safety formulae can usually be translated into universally quantified formulae in prenex normal; the universally quantified formula is replaced by conjunctions, where most conjuncts reduce to false, since topology predicates such as connected(*ts1*, *ts2*) are false for most choices of arguments. Finally state predicates are replaced by the Boolean variables of the ladder logic. In the case of safety conditions we obtain a conjunction of instantiations of ψ. Since safety conditions usually become conjunctions, the validity of the conjuncts can be checked separately. This allows to identify problems relating specific objects of the railway yard.

A typical verification condition for our Pelican crossing example would for instance ensure that the traffic lights and the pedestrian lights are not green at the same time:

$$\varphi \equiv (tlag \wedge tlbg \wedge \neg plag \wedge \neg plbg) \vee (\neg tlag \wedge \neg tlbg \wedge plag \wedge plbg)$$

3.6 The Model Checking Problem

We want to speak about the properties of the system that ensure safety – the so-called safety conditions – and then define what it means for a safety condition to hold in a labelled transition system. The following definition is motivated by the fact that safety conditions (tend to) describe properties which hold for two consecutive cycles of the ladder logic program.

Definition 5 (Safety Condition for a Ladder Logic Program). *Given a ladder logic formula ψ over the variables in $I \cup C$, a **verification condition** is a propositional formula formed from the variables in $I \cup C \cup C'$.*

Having defined the model of our system and the type of properties we want to speak about in that model, we must answer the following question: Given a model of our system and a safety condition, how do we check that the safety condition holds in that model. This motivates the following definition.

Definition 6 (Verification Problem for Ladder Logic Programs). *We define (and denote) the verification problem for a ladder logic formula ψ for a verification condition ϕ as follows:*

$$\text{LTS}(\psi) \models \phi \quad \textit{iff} \quad \textit{for all reachable transitions of the LTS – that is, triples}$$
$$\mu_C, \; \mu_I, \; \mu'_C \; \textit{such that } \mu_C \xrightarrow{\mu_I} \mu'_C, \textit{ and } \mu_C \textit{ is reachable}$$
$$\textit{in } \text{LTS}(\psi) \textit{ – we have } [\phi](\mu_C, \mu_I, \mu'_C) = 1.$$

Note that in most cases, as in our Pelican crossing, the verification condition ϕ only consists of variables in C, thus, the model checking problem simplifies to considering individual states, i.e. whether $[\phi](\mu_C) = 1$ at all times. Figure 3 shows the labelled transition system for the Pelican crossing example. We have included one unreachable state in which both **required** and **crossing** are true.

3.7 Model Checking Approaches

Target technology for the first three algorithms is SAT-solving; in the algorithms, execution terminates after a "return" statement has been performed.

Bounded Model Checking (BMC). BMC, see, e.g., [5], restricts the depth of the search space. Let the formulae ψ_n^{Init}, $n \geq 1$, be the unrolled transition relations which encode n steps with ψ from an initial state of the transition system. The following algorithm explores the transition system to a depth of up to K steps (we assume that ϕ uses the variables concerning the last transition):

```
if ¬(Init → φ) is satisfiable, return error state
n ← 1
while n ≤ K do
    if ¬(ψₙᴵⁿⁱᵗ → φ) is satisfiable, return error trace
    n ← n + 1
return "K-Safe"
```

As BMC produces a counter example trace if the verification fails, it is especially interesting for debugging purposes.

Inductive Verification (IV). IV checks if an over approximation of the reachable state space is safe. In the following algorithm we assume that ϕ uses the variables concerning the current transition and ϕ' those concerning the last transition:

---

if $\neg(Init \rightarrow \phi')$ is satisfiable, return error state
if $\neg(\psi \wedge \phi \rightarrow \phi')$ is satisfiable, return pair of error states
return "Safe"

The over approximation happens in the second line of the algorithm: here one considers all safe transitions rather than the *reachable* ones. This idea makes IV a very efficient approach involving at most two calls to a SAT solver [14, 16].

Temporal Induction (TI). TI, see, e.g., [6], combines BMC and IV to allow for both complete verification and counter example production. For $n \geq 0$, let ψ_n be the unrolled transition relation encoding n steps with ψ; let LF_n be a formula encoding that all transitions of a sequence of n transitions are pairwise different; and $safe_n$ be a formula encoding that all these transitions fulfil the verification condition. Define

$Base_n \equiv Init \wedge \psi_n \rightarrow \phi,$ and
$Step_n \equiv \psi_{n+1} \wedge LF_{n+1} \wedge safe_n \rightarrow \phi,$ where ϕ uses the variables concerning the last transition.

We then have the following procedure.

$n \leftarrow 0$
while true do
    if $\neg Base_n$ is satisfiable, return error trace
    if $\neg Step_n$ is unsatisfiable, return "Safe"
    $n \leftarrow n + 1$

Stålmarck's Algorithm. This algorithm has been developed and patented by Stålmarck [24]. It generally works well on industrial problems as – despite often being of a considerable size – they typically have a simple underlying structure.

Optimisation via Slicing. Usually, the verification condition ϕ does not use all variables of the ladder logic formula ψ. This opens up the possibility to slice ψ with respect to ϕ, i.e., to compute a formula ψ_ϕ with $\psi \models \phi \Leftrightarrow \psi_\phi \models \phi$ where ψ_ϕ involves fewer variables and rungs than ψ. Reference [7, 8] present an algorithm to compute ψ_ϕ, [12,13] give a correctness proof. Here is the sliced ladder logic program of the Pelican crossing example for the condition $(tlag \lor tlar) \land \neg(tlag \land tlar) \land (tlbg \lor tlbr) \land \neg(tlbg \land tlbr)$:

$$
\begin{aligned}
crossing' &\leftrightarrow req \land \neg crossing, \\
req' &\leftrightarrow pressed \land \neg req, \\
tlag' &\leftrightarrow (\neg\, pressed' \lor req') \land \neg\, crossing' \\
tlbg' &\leftrightarrow (\neg\, pressed' \lor req') \land \neg\, crossing' \\
tlar' &\leftrightarrow crossing', \\
tlbr' &\leftrightarrow crossing'
\end{aligned}
$$

Such slicing can be applied as a pre-processing step for all discussed approaches.

3.8   Excluding False Positives by Invariants

When verifying interlockings, often false positives are obtained. When discussing such false positives arising from the models with railway experts, they often state that in the physical system these situations do not occur because the specific value combination of the false positive is impossible, i.e., the false positive violates a system invariant. In [14] we identify two types of invariants.

Physical invariants are due to the fact that certain combinations of input variables are physically impossible. A typical example of this is a three way switch, modelled by 3 variables where each variable i indicates whether the switch is in position i or not. Physically it is impossible that such switch is in two positions simultaneously. This insight can be added to the system model as an invariant. However, in the real system it might happen that wet leaves fall on the three way switch and connect two of its contacts. This now puts the physical controller into a state that in the model was excluded by the physical invariant. Here, one has to decide if the system design and therefore its verification shall cater for such situations or not, i.e., physical invariants need to be carefully considered and validated by domain experts.

Mathematical invariants. In the case of IV, unreachable states may hinder verification through causing false positives. In this case one can identify invariants that hold in all reachable states. An example of such an invariant would be the equivalence $tlar \leftrightarrow tlbr$, which holds for the program given in Fig. 1.

3.9   Graphical Representation

In order to investigate counter examples a graphical representation of the error states was given. For our prototype, Kanso [14,16] develops a latex document, which contains a scheme plan with signals, sets of points and routes, together with tables listing the state of all variables in question. The state of signals (red or green) and points and of all tables listed is determined by macros. It is now easy to compute from an error state a document setting these macros to the values in this state, and therefore present an easy to view document.

4   Technology & Case Studies

4.1   SAT Solving with Open Software

An initial—successful—feasibility study was conducted using the open-source OKLibrary as underlying SAT solving framework to automate IV in order to establish safety properties. To this end, we used the Dimacs format as a target language. Note that this requires a representation in CNF.

Extending this implementation, we produced a framework of automatic translations of the formulae ψ, written in Haskell (about 8000 lines of code), and ϕ, written in Java (about 1000 lines of code), into the formulae required for the algorithms BMC, IV, and TI. As target format we chose TPTP [25], which is the input language of the Paradox tool [4]. Internally, the open source tool Paradox is based on the SAT solver Minisat [22], which is open source as well. Using Paradox has the advantage that the tool takes care of the translation into Dimacs format. The framework also includes a Haskell implementation of slicing (about 500 lines of code).

Using this framework, experiments on our Pelican crossing example with the above verification condition showed: with BMC the program is K safe for all $K \geq 0$ we tried; with IV, we obtain a pair of error states; TI gives the result "Safe". This example demonstrates that though IV is sound, it is not complete.

4.2   The *SCADE* Suite as an Industrial Tool

For comparison, we applied a tool widely used in industry, where however no control over the method applied is available. In *SCADE* (Safety Critical Applications Development Environment) [1] programs are verified using the *SCADE* language and Prover Technology based on Stalmarck's algorithm. The program to translate ladder logic programs into *SCADE* is based on the framework described above, it has a length of approximately 8000 lines of Haskell code [19].

The *SCADE* language is based on the synchronous dataflow language Lustre [2]. The flows which constitute a Lustre program are infinite sequences of values which describe how a variable changes over time. Flows are combined together to form nodes which can be seen as the Lustre equivalent of a function or procedure. There are two main temporal operations which can be applied to flows:

- The unary operator **pre** allows one to consider the previous value of a flow.
- The binary operator **->** allows one to express an initial value using the first operand and all subsequent values are computed using the second operand.

The following is the result of the automatic translation of the pelican crossing ladder logic to *SCADE*.

```
node PelicanLadderLogic1(pressed: bool) returns (req, crossing,
tlag, tlar, tlbg, tlbr, plag,
                       plar, plbg, plbr: bool)
```

```
let crossing = false -> pre req and (not (pre crossing));
    req = false -> (not pre req) and pressed;
    tlag = false -> ((not pressed) or req) and (not crossing);
    tlbg = false -> ((not pressed) or req) and (not crossing);
    tlar = true -> crossing;
    tlbr = true -> crossing;
    plag = false -> crossing;
    plbg = false -> crossing;
    plar =  true -> not crossing;
    plbr =  true -> not crossing;
tel
```

4.3 Industrial Case Study

Using the approaches described above we automatically translated real world railway interlockings and safety properties into the Dimacs format (for IV), the TPTP language (for BMC, IV, and TI) and the *SCADE* language. The verification results gained have been positive. For every safety condition the tools have either given a successful verification, or a counter example (trace). All results have been obtained within the region of seconds.

In the following we report on the verification of a small, but real world interlocking which actually is in use on the London Underground. The ladder logic program consists of approximately six hundred variables and three hundred and fifty rungs. Concerning typical verification conditions, slicing reduces the number of rungs down to 60 rungs, i.e., the program size is reduced by a factor of 5. All experiments reported have been carried out on a computer with the operating system Ubuntu 9.04, 64-bit edition, an Intel Q9650, Quad core CPU with 3GHz, and a System Memory of 8GB DDR2 RAM.

Evaluation with an Open Source Tool. The first condition encodes that if a point has been moved, it must have been free before. Here, the verification actually fails. IV yields a pair of states within 0.75 s, while BMC produces an error trace of length 3 in 0.81 s, TI produces the same trace. The rail engineers were able to exclude this counter example as a false positive. By adding justifiable invariants we could exclude this false positive. The second condition excludes that the program gives an inconsistent command, namely, that a point shall be set to normal and to reverse at the same time. IV proves this property in 0.71s; BMC yields K-safety for up to 1000 steps, after which we ran out of memory; BMC on the slided program is possible up to 2000 steps; TI does not terminate, neither for the original nor for the sliced version. Our experience is that IV can deal with real world examples. Slicing yields an impressive reduction of the size of the ladder logic program. It is beneficial when producing counter examples with BMC as it reduces the runtime and also helps with error localisation.

Verifying the Industrial Case Study Using *SCADE*. All above safety conditions take times less than 1 s [19]. We attempted the verification of 109 safety conditions out of these 54 were valid and 55 produced counter examples. The latter are false positives and were eliminated by adding invariants as described above. The total time for the verification and production of counter examples for all of these safety conditions was under 10 s. This may be in part due to some support for multi-core processors allowing the *SCADE* suite to dispatch multiple verification tasks efficiently. Generally, in the process of removing false positives approximately one hundred invariants were added. Overall, this shows that *SCADE* is a viable option for the verification of railway interlockings.

5 Conclusion

The overall result is that the verification step described works out: the required translations can be automated, the current tools scale up to real world problems, the gained benefits are convincing enough for the company Invensys to change its practice. Concerning proof technology, it is a matter of taste / philosophy / further constraints if one prefers open software or commercial products.

Acknowledgments. Our thanks go to Ulrich Berger for advice on the semantics of ladder logic formulae.

References

1. Abdulla, P.A., Deneux, J., Stålmarck, G., Ågren, H., Åkerlund, O.: Designing safe, reliable systems using scade. In: Margaria, T., Steffen, B. (eds.) ISoLA 2004. LNCS, vol. 4313, pp. 115–129. Springer, Heidelberg (2006)
2. Caspi, P., Pilaud, D., Halbwachs, N., Plaice, J.A.: LUSTRE: a declarative language for real-time programming. In: Proceedings of POPL'87, pp. 178–188 (1987)
3. Cimatti, A., Giunchiglia, F., Mongardi, G., Romano, D.: Formal verification of a railway interlocking system using model checking. FACS **10**(4), 361–380 (1998). Springer
4. Claessen, K., Sorensson, N.: New techniques that improve mace-style finite model finding. In: Proceedings of CADE'03 Workshop: Model Computation (2003)
5. Clarke, E., Biere, A., Raimi, R., Zhu, Y.: Bounded model checking using satisfiability solving. Formal Meth. Syst. Des. **19**(1), 7–34 (2001). Kluwer
6. Een, N., Sörensson, N.: Temporal induction by incremental SAT solving. ENTCS **89**(4), 543–560 (2003)
7. Fokkink, W., Hollingshead, P.: Verification of interlockings: from control tables to ladder logic diagrams. In: Proceedings of FMICS'98, pp. 171–185 (1998)
8. Groote, J., Koorn, J., Van Vlijmen, S.: The safety guaranteeing system at station Hoorn-Kersenboogerd. In: Proceedings of Compass'95, pp. 57–68 (1995)
9. Han, K., Park, J.: Object-oriented ladder logic development framework based on the unified modeling language. In: Lee, R., Hu, G., Miao, H. (eds.) Computer and Information Science 2009. SCI, vol. 208, pp. 33–45. Springer, Heidelberg (2009)
10. Haxthausen, A.: Automated generation of formal safety conditions from railway interlocking tables. STTT. Springer (to appear)
11. IEC 61131-3 edition 2.0 2003-01. International standard. Programmable controllers. Part 3: Programming languages (January 2003)

12. James, P.: SAT-based model checking and its applications to train control software. MRes Thesis, Swansea University (2010)
13. James, P., Roggenbach, M.: Automatically verifying railway interlockings using SAT-based model checking. In: Proceedings of AVoCS'10. Electronic Communications of EASST **35** (2010)
14. Kanso, K.: Formal verification of ladder logic. MRes Thesis, Swansea University (2009)
15. Kanso, K.: Agda as a platform for the development of verified railway interlocking systems. Ph.D Thesis, Swansea University (2012)
16. Kanso, K., Moller, F., Setzer, A.: Automated verification of signalling principles in railway interlocking systems. ENTCS **250**, 19–31 (2009)
17. Kanso, K., Setzer, A.: Specifying railway interlocking systems. In: Proceedings of AVoCS'09, pp. 233–236 (2009)
18. Kanso, K., Setzer, A.: Integrating automated and interactive theorem proving in type theory. In: Proceedings of AVoCS'10 (2010)
19. Lawrence, A.: Verification of railway interlockings in SCADE. MRes Thesis, Swansea University (2011)
20. Lawrence, A., Seisenberger, M.: Verification of railway interlockings in SCADE. In: Proceedings of AVoCS'10 (2010)
21. Leach, M. (ed.): Railway Control Systems: A Sequel to Railway Signalling. A & C Black, London (1991)
22. Minisat. http://minisat.se
23. Rausch, M., Krogh, B.: Formal verification of PLC programs. In: Proceedings of the American Control Conference. IEEE (1998)
24. Stålmarck, G.: System for determining propositional logic theorems by applying values and rules to triplets that are generated from boolean formula. US patent: 5,276,897 (1994)
25. The TPTP problem library for automated theorem proving. http://www.cs.miami.edu/tptp/
26. Tseitin, G.S.: On the complexity of derivation in propositional calculus. In: Ina Structures in Constructive Mathematics and Mathematical Logic, Steklov Mathematical Institute (1968)
27. Vincenti, W.G.: What Engineers Know and How They Know It. The Johns Hopkins University Press, Baltimore (1990)
28. Zoubek, B., Roussel, J.-M., Kwiatkowska, M.: Towards automatic verification of ladder logic programs. In: Proceedings of CESA'03. Springer (2003)

MoKMaSD 2013

Towards Knowledge Modeling
for Sustainable Transport

Paloma Cáceres$^{(\boxtimes)}$, Carlos E. Cuesta, José María Cavero, Belén Vela,
and Almudena Sierra-Alonso

VorTIC3 Research Group, Rey Juan Carlos University, C/Tulipán, s/n,
28933 Móstoles, Madrid, Spain
{paloma.caceres,carlos.cuesta,josemaria.cavero,
belen.vela,almudena.sierra}@urjc.es

Abstract. The paradigm shift from the current energy consumption model towards a sustainable model requires to develop new behaviors and strategies. This is particularly relevant in domains like the public transport. Many providers are currently offering services to assist passengers to plan their routes. However, these approaches are often restricted to some specific area or transport medium. We suggest using a Linked Data perspective, which makes simpler to combine data from different sources, as well as extending and managing them. Moreover, it makes possible to enrich the basic model to the extent of developing a knowledge model, able to use semantic techniques to unfold even better strategies. In this paper we present a proposal in the transport domain, which refines a basic model into a Transmodel specification and later adds more information according to the IFOPT model. This defines a knowledge model, which can be used to develop sustainable transport strategies.

Keywords: Sustainable development · Knowledge management · Semantic web · Transmodel · IFOPT · RDF

1 Introduction

Sustainable development makes reference to a mode of human development in which the use of resources aims to meet human needs while ensuring the sustainability of natural systems and the environment, so that these needs can be met not only in the present, but also for generations to come [1].

In this context, transport represents a significant proportion of global energy consumption. Sustainable mobility essentially emerges from the disadvantages caused by the current transport model, in which the central element is the private car. These include pollution and its effects on health and the environment, inefficient use of resources, traffic congestion, etc. These disadvantages have triggered different efforts to search for alternatives, trying to overcome the limitations of this model. In many cases, energy consumption can be significantly

S. Counsell and M. Núñez (Eds.): SEFM 2013 Collocated Workshops, LNCS 8368, pp. 271–287, 2014.
DOI: 10.1007/978-3-319-05032-4_20, © Springer International Publishing Switzerland 2014

reduced by an efficient use of transport media. In this way, there are many reasons to promote the use of public transport as environmental and economic arguments [2].

It is important, not only choosing the right path within the transport network, but also being to share a vehicle (including private vehicles) with others. There are several initiatives assisting people in sharing transport, the most popular being *carpooling*: more than one person sharing a car. However, no existing solution combines private transport sharing with the use of public transport, which would make it more flexible.

Having this in mind, we aim to apply information technologies to the task of improving citizen mobility – considering the case of citizens, both in usual or specific trips, and trying to optimize their intended routes by using any available means of transport: both public transport and the rational sharing of private transport. We have designed an IT platform, called CoMobility [3], to assist in intermodal transport sharing, integrating the use of carpooling with public transport, as well as other private transport media. To be accessible anytime and anywhere, we have taken into account mobile computing. Mobile systems are not only useful in their ability to provide pervasive access to computing systems (i.e. enabling computer access anywhere), but they also provide the inputs of a mobile and dynamic environment into a computational system; it is now possible to perform computations that, until recently, were simply impossible. A classic example is geolocation: it is now easy to provide the physical location of a user, and to use these data for a variety of purposes.

It is provided on the Internet "as a service", where both public transport information and data provided by users themselves are stored and accessed "in the cloud". The cloud approach is necessary as *scalability* is one of the most important requirements of this kind of wide-range service architecture. The platform also needs to access *a great amount of data*, which is also stored in the cloud – both the private data of carpoolers, and the public data accessed in a linked open data approach. Users are able to access their information in several formats, particularly in mobile devices (currently, Android devices) and web applications. Through these devices, they are able to plan their paths in the transport network, moving from a shared car to the underground, and from there to a bus line; and at the same time receiving an estimation of the saving of both money and energy. For this purpose, our CoMobility platform has "customized" analytics on savings and energy consumption, to make individuals aware of the benefits of this new way of travelling. These data are obtained from energy-aware institutions.

This work focuses on how to incorporate new knowledge into open data about transport, provided by its original sources. The format of public data within the open data initiatives prevents non-experts from using them directly, and thus it requires additional semantics, as provided by *"Linked Open Data"* [4,5]. In this way, our proposal in this paper focuses on modeling the knowledge of transport public data for sustainable transport. To do that, it is necessary: first, analyzing the original data formats and identifying the data semantics; second, matching these data with the vocabulary of the transport metamodels Transmodel [6] and IFOPT [7], and adding the relevant information; and finally, representing them as linked open data.

The paper is structured as follows: in Sect. 2, we briefly introduce the resource description framework (RDF). Section 3 outlines the public transport data providers (in this case, the public bus company of Madrid) and the transport specification standards Transmodel and IFOPT. Section 4 describes our specific proposal about a knowledge management architecture for Public Transport; in Sect. 5 we provide an example based on our proposal; and finally, the main conclusions are shown in Sect. 6.

2   A Brief Introduction to RDF

The Resource Description Framework (RDF) [8] provides an extremely simple data model in which entities (also called resources) are described in the form of triples (subject, predicate, object). For instance, consider a meteorology system consisting on several sensors, and a given sensor identified as Sensor_4UT; its description could comprise the following triples:

```
(Sensor_4UT, rdf:type, om-owl:System)
(Sensor_4UT, om-owl:parameter, weather:_AirTemperature)
(Sensor_4UT, om-owl:parameter, weather:_RelativeHumidity)
(Sensor_4UT, om-owl:parameter, weather:_WindDirection)
(Sensor_4UT, om-owl:parameter, weather:_WindSpeed)
```

The first triple states that Sensor_4UT is a particular class of system (hence the object om-owl:System), and the remaining four triples say that Sensor_4UT reports measurements about air temperature, relative humidity and wind direction and speed.

An RDF dataset can be seen as a graph of knowledge in which entities and values are linked via labeled edges. These labels (the predicates in the triples) own the semantics of the relation, hence it is highly recommendable to use standard vocabularies or to formalize new ones as needed. Figure 1 represents the previous RDF excerpt as a labeled graph in which the nodes (and edges between them) depict the mentioned triples, modeling a weather observation about the wind speed.

RDF has been gaining momentum since its inception thanks to its adoption in diverse fields, such as bioinformatics, social networks, or geographical data. The Linked Open Data project plays a crucial role in the RDF evolution [4]. It leverages the Web infrastructure to encourage the publication of such semantic data [7], providing global identity to resources using HTTP URIs. Moreover, integration between data sources is done at the most basic level of triples, that is, to connect two data sources can be as easy as making connection between those resources.

This philosophy pushes the traditional document-centric perspective of the Web to a data-centric view, emerging a huge interconnected cloud of data-to-data hyperlinks: the *Web of Data*. Latest statistics pointed out that more than

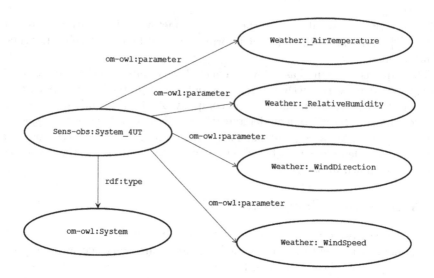

Fig. 1. Example of a RDF graph modeling weather data

31 billion triples were published and more than 500 million links established cross-relations between datasets. Although each piece of information could be particularly small (the so-called Big Data's *long tail*), the integration within a subpart of this Web of Data can also be seen as an example of Big Semantic Data.

It is worth noting that RFID labels, Web processes (crawlers, search engines, recommender systems), smartphones and sensors are potential sources of RDF data, such as in our previous use cases. These are the main players in the so-called *Internet of Things*, in which the Linked Data philosophy can be applied naturally by simply assigning URIs to the real-world things producing RDF data about them via Web. As a result, the activity of all involved devices is recorded and linked between them, enabling large projects (such as the emergent notion of smart-cities) to be successfully implemented.

3   Using Knowledge Modeling for Sustainable Transport

This work is focused on modeling public transport data in Linked Open Data (LOD). In this way, our work aims to study the source of the public transport data and the existing standard models related to public transport, to analyze them and to enrich this information adding semantic knowledge of the public transport data. The final data will be published in RDF.

3.1   A Modeling Approach to Public Transport

In this paper, we work with the public transport data of the public bus network in Madrid as open data source. EMT Madrid [9] is the public bus company of

Madrid, and follows an open data initiative with regard to its information. It provides the specification of the geographical services public platform, which includes these three parts: a customer-oriented SOA architecture [10], a public information services infrastructure architecture –described in a detailed way–, and the description of their information services. These services can be accessed by different kinds of devices.

EMT Madrid allows accessing its platform by means of the explicit authentication of users. This method is implemented in each Web Service. Moreover, it provides a specific set of output information about the bus line and the bus stop, as a set of fixed schemas into the services structure:

o With regard to the bus line, EMT Madrid offers a piece of basic information which can be shown on any device screen: Number of bus line, first/last bus stop and last/first bus stop (depending on the direction followed by the bus), type of the day in which the bus operates (to indicate working day, holiday and Saturday), direction, start and finish time of the bus line (in that direction), maximum and minimum frequency of the bus line (in that direction).
o With regard to the bus stop, EMT Madrid also offers a piece of basic information which can be shown on any screen, including those from mobile devices: code, name, postal address, geographical coordinates.

We have studied the standard transport models Transmodel [6] and IFOPT [7], to match the existing open data about the bus public network of EMT Madrid with them. Transmodel is an European Reference Data Model for Public Transport Information which provides a model of public transport concepts and data structures that can be useful to build information systems related to the different types of public transport. It includes information about real time data, journey planning, timetables, operational management, routes, etc. The present version (V5.0) uses an Entity-Relationship modeling approach and covers the following domains:

o Tactical Planning,
o Personnel Disposition,
o Operations Monitoring and Control,
o Passenger Information,
o Fare Collection and
o Management Information/Statistics

Transmodel establishes a consistent terminology for describing public transport concepts, providing definitive equivalents for use in the National Languages of each participant nation. Where public transport (PT) related words in vernacular use may span a number of different concepts and lead to differences of interpretation, it establishes a more precise technical terminology for unambiguous use by PT information system developers. For example the terms "trip", "journey", "service", are overlapping concepts that in Transmodel are used only in some more specific usages.

Sometimes, we need more descriptive information about the objects related to public access to Public Transport than the offered by Transmodel. Let's see an example: a Transmodel CONNECTION LINK represents the possibility of interchange between two Scheduled Stop Points used by different journeys, *without necessarily having a precise indication of place*. In contrast, a PATH LINK (from the IFOPT metamodel) represents a different information layer: a STOP PATH LINK and an ACCESS PATH LINK represent the possibility of navigation between specific located nodes of a STOP PLACE. A Transmodel ACCESS LINK is the physical (spatial) possibility for a passenger to access or leave the PT system: the walking movement of a passenger from a place (origin of the trip) to a stop point (the origin of the PT trip); the walking movement of a passenger from a stop point (the destination of the PT trip) to a place (destination of the trip.

For this reason, we have studied the IFOPT metamodel. It defines a model and identification principles for the main fixed objects related to public access to Public Transport (e.g. stop points, stop areas, stations, connection links, entrances, etc.). The IFOPT Standard builds on the TransModel Standard to define four related submodels:

- *Stop Place Model*: Describes the detailed structure of a STOP PLACE (that is station, airport, etc.) including physical points of access to vehicles and the paths between the points, including mobility hazards.
- *Point of Interest Model*: Describes the structure of a POINT OF INTEREST including physical points of access, i.e. ENTRANCEs.
- *Gazetteer Topographical Model*: Provides a topographical representation of the settlements (cities, towns, villages etc.) between which people travel. It is used to associate Stop and Station elements with the appropriate topographic names and concepts to support the functions of journey planning, stop finding, etc.
- *Administrative Model*: Provides an organizational model for assigning responsibility to create and maintain data as a collaborative process involving distributed stakeholders. Includes namespace management to manage the decentralised issuing of unique identifiers.

Our study focuses on the Stop Places model of IFOPT.

3.2   IFOPT: Modeling Stop Places

What type of information can be better modeled using IFOPT instead of using Transmodel? In the previous subsection, we introduced an example of related information between both metamodels and their differences. Now, we will show the differences graphically, explaining them in depth.

In Fig. 2, we show a route from a starting point (numbered as 1) to a destination (numbered as 6). This route is composed by three pedestrian subroutes (1-2, 3-4 and 5-6) and two PT subroutes (2-3 and 4-5). The pedestrian subroutes 1-2 and 5-6 are identified as ACCESS LINKs (paths to access to PT) in Transmodel. The pedestrian subroute 3-4 is a Transmodel CONNECTION LINK (to connect different PT routes).

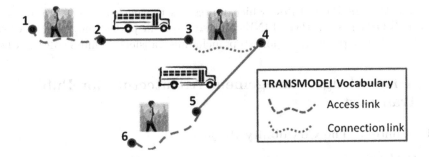

Fig. 2. Transmodel access and connection links

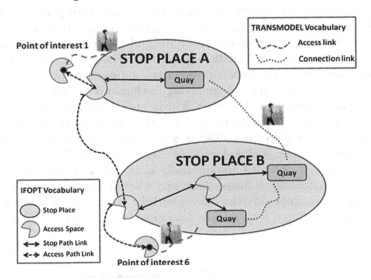

Fig. 3. Differences between transmodel and IFOPT elements

IFOPT is more specific describing fixed objects. It models STOP PLACEs, ACCESS PATH LINKs and STOP PATH LINKs. STOP PLACEs are related with a place where users can get on public transport. A STOP PLACE includes an ACCESS SPACE which provides the entrance to the place. The place could also be a POINT OF INTEREST, for example. STOP PATH LINKS represent the path between stops of public transport, within a STOP PLACE. ACCESS PATH LINKs represent the path to access to an ACCESS SPACE from another ACCESS SPACE.

Figure 3 shows POINTs OF INTEREST (numbered as 1 and 6), STOP PLACEs (labelled as A and B), ACCESS PATH LINKS and STOP PATH LINKS, which are represented as arrows. Each STOP PLACE and POINT OF INTEREST has an ACCESS PLACE which represents the entrance to these places. We want to emphasize that the STOP PLACE B also includes an ACCESS SPACE which could represent the space where users could change the journey or the public transport. We can also see in the figure that a Transmodel ACCESS LINK is less descriptive than an ACCESS PATH LINK, which represents the path through an ACCESS PLACE. IFOPT's STOP PATH LINKs represent specific paths from/to an ACCESS SPACE to/from a public transport stop, including transfers within STOP PLACES.

4 A Knowledge Management Architecture for Public Transport

4.1 Context: The CoMobility Project

The CoMobility Project [3] defines a multimodal architecture based on linked open data for a sustainable mobility. Its main goals are improving the citizen mobility, optimizing their trips combining both public transport and sharing private transport (i.e. car sharing or carpooling), providing accessible trips when necessary and saving energy and reducing the pollution (Fig. reff.comobility).

We have developing a systematic approach to (i) accessing open, integrated and semantically annotated transportation data and street maps, (ii) combining them with private data, and (iii) supplying mechanisms to allow the actors to share and search these data. Therefore, its conceptual architecture provides the means to perform the following tasks: First, the platform can identify, select, extract and integrate data from different and heterogeneous sources, stemming from the transportation, geographical and energy domains. Second, data from public institutions is obtained automatically in the form of open data. Third, these data are annotated as linked data, and a set of heuristics generate links between data items from different sources without human intervention. Fourth, these data are integrated with private data provided by users themselves. And

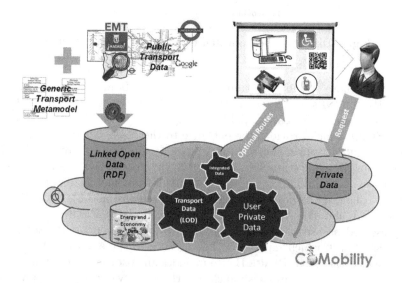

Fig. 4. The CoMobility Project

finally, CoMobility provides intuitive and customized data analytics and visualization, allowing individuals to become aware of the environmental impact of their transport choices. Next figure shows a general idea about the project.

Project CoMobility is supported by the Spanish Economy and Competitiveness Ministry and some companies have expressed their interest in their results. The most representative are: the public bus company from Madrid (EMT Madrid), the Public Regional Consortium of Transports of Madrid (CRTM) [11], the Chair of EcoTransport, Technology and Mobility of the Rey Juan Carlos University [12] and the Spanish National Society of Blind People (ONCE) [13].

4.2   Knowledge Management Architecture

In this paper we briefly describe the knowledge management architecture that supports the bus public transport data from EMT Madrid as linked data in RDF. To carry out this process we need: first, to provide the required mechanism to parse the XML [14] information from the source and to obtain the necessary data about the network transport (i.e. bus lines and bus stops); second, to mach these data with the IFOPT model; and finally, to publish them as RDF resources. Next subsections show the requirements of the architecture which supports this process.

4.3   Data Architecture for the Original Data

EMT Madrid provides an open data platform of its urban bus network, supported by a technological infrastructure which exports them as a Service-Oriented Architecture (SOA) to any requesting consumer (any consumer that requires it). In this way, the data can be accessed using Web services, which answer to the request by returning some specific XML files. EMT Madrid offers a set of open web services which clients can invoke according to their information needs: bus routes, pedestrian routes, bus stops, transfers, etc. The figure below shows the concrete architecture that support this kind of information interchange (Fig. reff.emt).

Each web service returns a different XML file which contains the information about the requested data by the client. It is then necessary to parse and translate the XML information into a readable information to the client. Figure 6 shows an XML example of a bus line. To preserve the confidentiality, we have hidden some data from the original information, or changed the specific formatting, in the following examples.

The code shows a generic description about the bus line 174 and its headers. First, the labels `<BusLine>` ... `</BusLine>` indicate that the information is about a bus line. The bus line number is 174: `<IdBusLine>174</IdBusLine>` and the first and last stops are Plaza de Castilla and Sanchinarro Este: that is, `<BusLineHeadA>` `PLAZA DE CASTILLA </BusLineHeadA>`, and then `<BusLineHeadB> SANCHINARRO ESTE` `</BusLineHeadB>`, respectively.

Figure 7 shows an XML example of a bus stop. The code shows the bus line number to which the bus stop belongs: `<IdBusLine>174</IdBusLine>`. Then, the bus stop number, `<Node>5611</Node>`; the distance from the first (initial) stop, `<Distance> 456 </Distance>`; and the distance from the previous stop `<DistancePrev> 147 </DistancePrev>`; and then the bus stop name, `<BusStopName> INTERCAMBIADOR PZA. DE CASTILLA </BusStopName>`. Finally, it also specifies the geographical coordinates, i.e. latitude `<GeoCoorX>40,4695235553361 </GeoCoorX>` and longitude `<GeoCoorY>-3,68778542580241</GeoCoorY>`.

4.4 Superposing Data Architectures

We need to identify which data from the source are corresponded with the structured of IFOPT. As mentioned before, IFOPT defines a model and identification principles for the main fixed objects related to public access to Public Transport (e.g. stop points, stop areas, stations, connection links, entrances, etc.). In this paper, we only work with the Stop Place Model, because it describes the detailed structure of a STOP PLACE (that is station, airport, etc.) including physical points of access to vehicles and the paths between the points, including mobility hazards.

As we will see in the next section (by developing an example), we actually need not to define a set of different models to later combine them – instead of that, we have information (models) from several sources which can be easily combined using specific *join points*. We begin with a simple model (i.e. bus

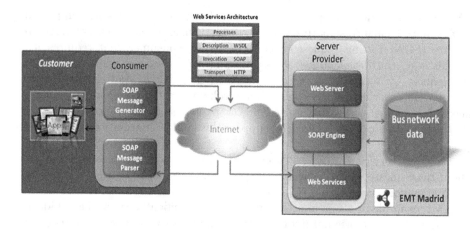

Fig. 5. SOA-based EMT infrastructure

```
<BusLine>
  <IdBusLine>174</IdBusLine>
  <BusLineHeadA>PLAZA DE CASTILLA</BusLineHeadA>
  <BusLineHeadB>SANCHINARRO ESTE</BusLineHeadB>
</BusLine>
```

Fig. 6. Example of a XML-based bus line description

```
<BusStop>
  <IdBusLine>174</IdLine>
  <Order>1</Order>
  <Node>5611</Node>
  <Distance>456</Distance>
  <DistancePrev>147</DistancePrev>
  <BusStopName>INTERCAMBIADOR PZA.DE CASTILLA</BusStopName>
  <GeoCoorX>40,4695235553361</GeoCoorX>
  <GeoCoorY>-3,68778542580241</GeoCoorY>
</BusStop>
```

Fig. 7. Example of a XML-based bus stop description

lines), where the fixed points are described as simple bus stops; and we enrich this model, step by step, adding the information provided by the different model, until these simple stops are transformed into complex structured STOP PLACEs.

5 Exporting the Transport Model as Linked Data

As already noted, we simply enrich the original model. The process can be described as the stepwise refinement of the original dataset provided by our original sources (EMT Madrid), simply provided as or translated to Linked Data (RDF) format, and then enriched with additional semantic information – in the first stage, identifying relevant sections according to the key concepts in Transmodel; then in a second stage, attaching additional information as described by the IFOPT model.

5.1 Representing the Original Information

First, consider the original source structure as provided by EMT Madrid, described in RDF terms. As already noted, as EMT Madrid is a bus service, it provides information in terms of bus lines, bus stops, etc. This can be simply described as Linked Data, essentially by represented the provided information as a graph, and thus reordering some elements in the structure as required.

The most important notion in the Bus model is still that of *route*, i.e. the path which must be followed by a passenger to reach his destination from some starting point. However, for the sake of simplicity, in the remainder of this example we will focus in a small part of the model – specifically, the one which refers to bus stops (and hence to bus lines, and to related pedestrian walks).

The first notion that we need to define is that of a *bus line*, which describes the first intuitive concept as provided by EMT Madrid. In RDF terms, a bus line is described as a resource in a certain URI, with a number of triples defining a number of attributes (line identifier, origin name, destination name), and also a number of relationships or connections (prominently, to the bus stops locating the start and the end of the line). Figure 8 depicts this structure in the usual graphical form, for EMT Madrid line 174.

Of course, both the predicates defining attributes (att:x) and those defining connections (conn:x) are already defined in RDF terms. Both abbreviations are defined as alias for longer URIs – for instance, the prefix att in the Figure is the short form for http://vortic3.com/rdf/attributes#.

Connection definitions show that bus lines need to refer to bus stops to locate their heads – and even more, any stops within the line. Therefore, bus stops define the obvious connection between lines. Indeed, bus stops can be considered as a key notion in the Bus model, and they provide a starting point to traverse the whole graph of bus lines – i.e. the triplestore.

In RDF terms a bus stop is again described as a resource, with certain attributes (name of the stop, e.g. the direction; spatial coordinates, etc.), and also a number of relationships (prominently, the crossing with bus lines, i.e. the set of lines which stop at this bus stop). This is depicted in the first part of Fig. 9, which shows part of the dataset describing the stop at "Intercambiador Plaza de Castilla".

Of course a stop is able to simultaneously participate in several bus lines – this is the case of the aforementioned "Intercambiador" (i.e. a transport hub). To be able to capture this, the auxiliary resource known as *node* (or crossing) is defined. A node describes the role of a certain bus stop in a certain line. For instance, the second half of Fig. 9 describes the node 1000A4, which represents the role of the bus stop at "Intercambiador Plaza de Castilla" in the already mentioned bus line 174 (see Fig. 8). Hence the attributes of the node describe the name of the stop, its position in the bus line (it is the first stop), its distance to the previous stop, etc. The node has also relationships, prominently the connection linking it to the corresponding bus line. As depicted in the lower part of the Figure, bus lines have separate definitions when they are considered in the opposite direction

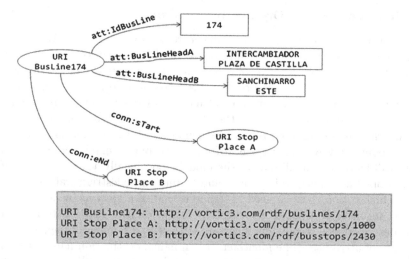

Fig. 8. RDF example for the bus line 174: bus line

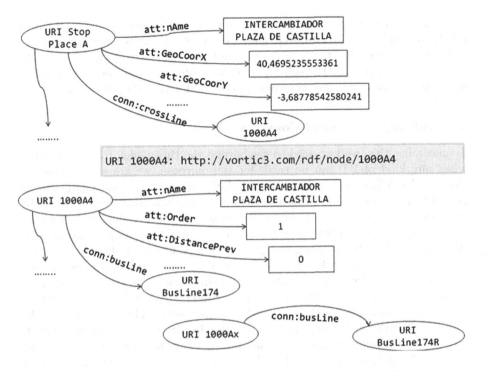

Fig. 9. RDF example for the bus line 174: bus stops and nodes

– and hence, if the same stop participates in this reverse line, the connection is described as a different node (that is, node 1000Ax in the Figure).

5.2 Exploring Connections in the Network

As already noted, we are particularly interested in the concept of *transfer*. Within the Bus model (and therefore in the bus lines domain) a transfer refers just to a change of bus line – the passenger steps off a certain bus line, and gets into another one. In this model, the number of transfers equals the number of changes – i.e. the number of bus lines in the route equals the number of transfers plus one.

In the initial conception, a transfer can happen when a certain stop crosses two lines, i.e. when it has at least two nodes. That is the simplest transfer: the passenger just leaves the first line, and in the same stop, he takes a different bus line. However, things are often more complicated – the passenger is able to walk to a different stop in the nearby, to do a different transfer as described in Figs. 2, 3. This notion of a *pedestrian walk* implies a different connection between two bus stops, and can be also modeled as a RDF resource, which starts in (i.e. connects to) one stop, covers a distance and (optionally) an average duration (attributes) and ends in (again, connects to) another stop.

So far we have used information from the Bus model as provided (and translated) by EMT Madrid. However, once we are out of the bus for a pedestrian walk, we can generalize the situation: if the passenger is able to walk or to take the bus, he can also use the subway – i.e. we might consider not only transfers between bus lines, but also movements between different PT providers.

5.3   Adding Transmodel Concepts

To generalize this, we just need to get beyond the Bus model, to go to a model when any kind of PT can be used; for this purpose, we are able to use the Transmodel definition to refer to any kind of transport, as already indicated in Sect. 3.1. Therefore the existing bus definitions are substituted by their equivalent (and more general) version in Transmodel. Instead of bus stops we have STOP POINTS, which could refer to any sort of stop, including Metro or train stations as well as bus stops. The definition of a pedestrian walk in Transmodel terms is summarized as described in Fig. 2. We consider all stop points from a certain origin to a certain destination, and pedestrian walks are captured either as ACCESS LINKS (i.e. the way we access a certain stop point) or as CONNECTION LINKS (i.e. a non-fixed path between two stop points). The notion of transfer corresponds to an *interchange* in Transmodel. In summary, the original data in the Bus model fulfills the requirements from a Transmodel specification, hence it can be immediately translated to these terms – and this means that it can be safely extended to include information about other PT media.

Therefore, the original structure is easily translated to a Transmodel specification, including all its data without any modification. Now these data can be easily extended to include e.g. the stop point which describes a Metro station, and hence we can use the connection link between this station and any other stop point to describe how to move from the bus to the subway – or vice versa. The notion of transfer between buses is now generalized to any kind of connection between PT media.

Note that the model is not required to be complete: we can have the full definition of bus lines and stops as provided by EMT Madrid, but we can add only a few Metro stations at the beginning – the connection links would be used wherever they are present, but the semantic model is perfectly able to work in the presence of partial information. That is, we need not to have the full definition of the Metro network to describe a partial combination.

5.4   Introducing the IFOPT Basic Model

However, this is not enough: as already indicated (Sect. 3.1, up to the comparison in Fig. 3), there are many details and attributes, related to different PT media which cannot be adequately described as Transmodel stop points. The Transmodel definition does not provide enough information to be able to handle the most complex reasoning related to simple bus transfers – even more for generic interchanges. Therefore we need to extend this information – hence the need for refinement, and the use of the IFOPT model, the standard which complements Transmodel providing information about fixed points. In particular, the notion of *stop point* is generalized to the concept of STOP PLACE, as already noted before (note also that even in Fig. 9, we have already modeled the bus stop actually as a stop place).

As already indicated (see again the comparison in Fig. 3) the notion of stop place is more general than a stop point, as it can also include generic POINTS OF INTEREST. The concept of *access link* is refined into a more structured ACCESS SPACE, and *connection links* are considered either "internal" (STOP PATH LINKS) or "external" (ACCESS PATH LINKS). Therefore, we can still represent, using the same structure, a bus transfer – i.e. two stop places and the access path link between them; but we are also able to describe how the passenger moves into a communication hub. For instance, the same stop place already described in Fig. 9 ("Intercambiador Plaza de Castilla") includes several bus stops (such as the connection to line 174, described as a *node* in the same Figure), but also a Metro station. This is part of the *same* stop place, but refers to a different *quay*, which would have its own access spaces. Therefore, the transfer between bus 174 and Metro line 10 at Plaza de Castilla can described here as a *stop path link*, as the passenger needs not to go out of the stop place to change the PT media.

5.5   Using Linked Data Information

Obvioulsy, all these notions are described as RDF resources. Bus stops are defined as stop places, as they already were. Metro lines are described similarly to bus lines, according to Transmodel definitions. Stop places are refined into *quays* (generalizing nodes); and instead of having "bus transfers" (which were not described in RDF terms), we actually have *access path links* between access spaces, and *stop path links* between the quays in the same stop place. All these elements are directly modeled as RDF resources with their own attributes, and these links take the form of connections between these resources.

Using the rich semantic model as provided by IFOPT, we are able to model all kinds of situations within this context. Specifically, we are particularly interested in aspects related to sustainable transport or to accessibility of disabled people. For instance, with regard to the first, IFOPT provides the concept of *CheckPoint* as a component of the stop place; attributes related to this checkpoint include estimates about the duration of the delays it might cause (*CheckPointDelay*), and the possibility of *Congestion*. With regard to the second, it is even more apparent, as according to IFOPT, any stop place element can include a validation related to its potential *AccesibilityLimitation*; which is described in turn as a resource with such attributes as *WheelchairAccess* or *VisualSignsAvailable*. Therefore, now we are not just able to tell if there is an access path link from stop place A to stop place B; but also if this path can be safely used by blind or disabled people.

6   Conclusions

This paper exposes two main arguments. First, that it is both simple and convenient to either design or translate the information from different sources –in our case, from the transport domain– to be managed as Linked Data. The generality and flexibility of the RDF format makes possible to express data from almost any source, and to easily translate to it information from varied origins – in the presented example, our data was originally provided as XML files and private services; and in both cases it is simple to encapsulate it as RDF triples. The generic nature of this format makes easy to integrate the information from many sources.

The second thesis is that it is possible to elaborate the information step by step, in a refinement process, starting with the most basic ("raw") data and to enrich these data adding information from semantically rich models – in our context, first the Transmodel specification for transport media, and then the IFOPT model to describe fixed points. The open nature of the Linked Data approach makes possible to perform this stepwise refinement in a seamless way, adding RDF triples without the need to modify the existing ones. The result is a semantically rich model, describing all available knowledge about PT media and the related places, which allows for a sophisticated form of reasoning. The ultimate purpose of our system –to find optimal routes in the PT network– is fulfilled to the extent of being able to optimize these routes considering not only traversability, but also sustainability and accessibility.

Acknowledgements. This work has been supported by the project CoMobility (TIN2012-31104), funded by the Spanish Ministry of Economy and Competitiveness; and it has also been supported by the Chair of Ecotransport, Technology and Mobility (http://www.catedraetm.es/) at Rey Juan Carlos University.

References

1. Sustainable development - Wikipedia. http://en.wikipedia.org/wiki/Sustainable_development (2013). Accessed 21 Nov 2013
2. Essortment Home Page. Advantages of Using Public Transportation. http://www.essortment.com/advantages-using-public-transportation-19689.html (2012). Accessed 22 June 2012
3. Cuesta, C.E., Cáceres, P., Vela, B., Cavero, J.M.: CoMobility: a mobile platform for transport sharing. ERCIM News 93 (2013)
4. Linked Open Data. http://linkeddata.org/
5. Heath, T., Bizer, C.: Linked Data: Evolving the Web into a Global Data Space. Morgan & Claypool, Seattle (2011)
6. Transmodel: European Reference Data Model for Public Transport. http://www.transmodel.org/index.html (2001)
7. Identification of Fixed Objects in Public Transport (IFOPT). http://www.dft.gov.uk/naptan/ifopt/ (2013)
8. Klyne, G., Carroll, J.: Resource Description Framework (RDF): Concepts and Abstract Syntax. W3C Recommendation. http://www.w3.org/RDF/ (2004)

9. EMT Madrid Home Page. http://www.emtmadrid.es/ (2012)
10. Service Oriented Architecture (SOA) - W3C Web Open Standards. http://www.w3.org/2008/11/dd-soa.html (2008)
11. Public Regional Consortium of Transports of Madrid Home Page. http://www.ctm-madrid.es/ (2013)
12. Chair of EcoTransport, Technology and Mobility of the Rey Juan Carlos University. http://www.catedraetm.es/
13. Spanish National Society of Blind People. http://www.once.es/ (2013)
14. eXtensible Markup Language (XML) - W3C. http://www.w3.org/XML/ (2013)

XBRL-Driven Business Process Improvement: A Simulation Study in the Accounting Domain

Martin Kloos[1], Joris Hulstijn[2(✉)], Mamadou Seck[3], and Marijn Janssen[2]

[1] Q-TC, Rotterdam, The Netherlands
[2] Faculty of Technology, Policy and Management, Delft University of Technology, Delft, The Netherlands
[3] Old Dominion University, Virginia, USA
emkloos@gmail.com,
{j.hulstijn,m.f.w.h.a.Janssen}@tudelft.nl, mseck@odu.edu

Abstract. The eXtensible Business Reporting Language (XBRL) has been developed to standardize financial reporting. It could also improve internal business processes. Yet there is no scientific research to substantiate this claim. In this paper we use discrete-event simulation to determine the impact of XBRL on internal business processes. Simulation models of the existing and possible new situation are developed in a case study within the accounting domain. The redesigned processes are validated in a workshop. XBRL allows the merging of accounting and fiscal reporting processes resulting in a reduction of the duplication of activities and higher information quality. In particular, it is demonstrated that information quality, efficiency and lead-time can be improved by adoption of XBRL. In addition to technology-standardization on XBRL, data-standardization is a necessary precondition for realizing benefits.

Keywords: XBRL · Standardization · Accounting · Simulation

1   Introduction

Information Technology is recognized as an enabler for process improvement [3,6]. The eXtensible Business Reporting Language (XBRL) is a technology aimed at creating a standard representation format for exchanging financial information [28]. XBRL is an XML-based standard for internal and external reporting, including financial, statistical, taxation, and inspection reports. XBRL is a freely available international standard that enables gathering and dissemination of business information [9]. XBRL provides a standardized way to describe system-to-system information exchange. XBRL therefore enables a high level of semantic and syntactic interoperability [5].

Use of XBRL is claimed to lead to benefits like greater efficiency and improved accuracy and reliability in financial reporting [8]. However there is little empirical evidence that XBRL is indeed creating added value [1] and what the conditions are for accomplishing these benefits. Time savings, reduced effort, improved

S. Counsell and M. Núñez (Eds.): SEFM 2013 Collocated Workshops, LNCS 8368, pp. 288–305, 2014.
DOI: 10.1007/978-3-319-05032-4_21, © Springer International Publishing Switzerland 2014

communication are mentioned frequently as possible benefits, but hardly any research to validate these claims could be recognized [25].

In the Netherlands, adoption of XBRL is embedded in the Standard Business Reporting program (SBR), which provides users with a unified meaning of financial concepts, such as income or revenue, made available in a taxonomy maintained by the Dutch government (http://www.sbr-nl.nl/english/). Although XBRL is originally developed for financial reporting to regulators it also offers opportunities for standardizing the internal business processes. Yet the actual adoption and usage of the standard is limited and many accounting firms are unsure how to adapt XBRL and specifically how to best apply XBRL in their own internal business processes to reap the benefits.

In this paper we report on a study of a simulation-based process improvement project at a medium-sized accounting firm in the Netherlands. A so called 'built-in' XBRL adoption strategy is modelled and simulated (see Sect. 2). In particular, we focus on the internal business processes for (i) compiling and submitting the annual financial statements of a client and (ii) preparing the tax returns for corporate income tax of a client. Both processes are affected by the adoption of XBRL. We conducted the following research activities. First we modelled the business processes in Business Process Model and Notation (BPMN) and analysed the existing software application landscape. We decided on definitions for measuring performance in this domain, such as duration and quality of outcomes. We then simulated the current processes in a discrete event simulation tool (ARENA). Based on literature, we identified opportunities for process improvement driven by XBRL and also simulated these expected process improvements. The outcomes of the modelling and simulation exercise were validated in a workshop with experts and end users.

The remainder of the paper is structured as follows. We start by explaining XBRL (Sect. 2) and by characterizing the accounting domain (Sect. 3). Thereafter we present the case background and simulation study (Sect. 4), followed by the relevant process improvements (Sect. 5) and the simulated studies (Sect. 6). The paper ends with a discussion and suggestions for future research (Sect. 7).

2 XBRL

The Extensible Business Reporting Language (XBRL) provides a foundation for the exchange of reports and data [9]. XBRL consists of four major components: XML standard, XBRL taxonomy, instance documents and XBRL specification. The actual data is represented in an instance document. Using link-bases, meaning is provided to this data by means of meta-data tags that refer to definitions from an official XBRL taxonomy. XBRL taxonomies for the accounting domain can have three categories: general-purpose financial reporting taxonomies (XBRL-FR), special purpose regulatory reporting taxonomies, and the general ledger taxonomy (XBRL-GL) [4]. XBRL is report oriented, but it enables to drill down to individual information items [17]. As XBRL is XML-based, instance documents are both human and machine-readable, and transferable between different software platforms. This means that once data has been collected and labelled with meaningful XBRL-tags, it can be re-used for different reporting purposes. In the context of the SBR programme, this philosophy is called 'store once, report many' [5]. Official extensions to the basic Netherlands Taxonomy (NT) exist for accounting, for various fiscal reports, and for statistical reporting. These extensions are maintained by experts. A related application concerns credit applications by banks. Recently, there are developments to standardize meta-data concerning assurance over XBRL instances [16].

The working assumption is that XBRL adoption would produce efficiency gains [1,9,28]. Why? In principle, XBRL and SBR taxonomies can lower the costs of compliance, improve efficiency and improve information quality for the following reasons: (i) at the individual firm level, standardization and improved interoperability between software packages reduce the need to re-enter information, reduce processing time (remove superfluous controls), improve the audit-trail and improve information quality [5,25], (ii) for a community of users, this may lead to increased comparability, transparency and accuracy of reporting, improved systems flexibility and inter-operability, and ultimately improved market efficiency [5,25].

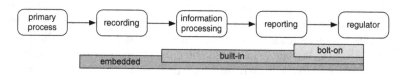

Fig. 1. Scope of XBRL adoption strategies: bolt-on, built-in and embedded [13]

These benefits are only potential. The way in which XBRL is utilized has an large impact on the benefits that can ultimately be achieved. Three different XBRL adoption strategies can be distinguished [13–15], illustrated in Fig. 1.

1. The *bolt-on* strategy only uses XBRL at the very end of the information processing chain. XBRL is not used within the client organization, but only for reporting to external regulators. One could argue that this will already produce some of the community benefits listed under (ii) above, but the process improvement impact on individual organizations is small: only the final PDF documents are being replaced by XBRL.
2. The *built-in* strategy integrates XBRL into the financial application landscape of both the client organization and its financial service providers, like accountants and tax consultants. This strategy requires adaptations to the software. Therefore it does involve a significant investment by clients and especially by the intermediaries. However, in the long run, this strategy is expected to reap most benefits.
3. The *embedded strategy* is most radical. Here XBRL is used for standardizing the way transactions are recorded in the primary process by the client, for instance into the general ledger. The version of XBRL that would allow such recording at the source is therefore called XBRL-GL. This makes it possible to

trace and verify transactions at the level of individual information items. We do see a purpose for this strategy, in particular in situations where assurance is required over specific limited subsets of data, such as credit reports for banks [16]. However, in the general case this vision would require a redesign of the core of ERP systems and financial software packages. This poses huge risks to the continuity and reliability of financial reporting. Currently, financial software vendors are reluctant to enter this market. They have often built their business models around a proprietary data representation standard.

3   Accounting Domain

In the following paragraphs we characterize the accounting domain by means of general observations: O1, O2, etc. These observations will be used in Sect. 3 to evaluate the feasibility of possible process improvements.

Accounting is the process of recording financial information about a business entity, analysing that information, and reporting the results to stakeholders, such as management, shareholders, creditors, and regulators [20]. Accountants must provide some form of assurance that the reported financial information is correct, complete and timely. The activities of an accountant are therefore subject to intensive regulation and professional standards. This means that the people in accounting firms are traditionally more focused on *information quality* and *compliance*, rather than on operational efficiency (O1). Please note that in our case study, we looked at the process for compilation of financial statements, for relatively small clients, which strictly speaking does not involve assurance. Therefore it is not as heavily regulated as the official accounting processes. However, like all processes, also these are subject to professional standards of conduct.

Many process improvement techniques have been pioneered in manufacturing [27]. An important difference between manufacturing and accounting, is the intangibility of services compared to the tangibility of products. Intangible products are known to be people intensive in production and delivery [21]. This makes for *large lead times* and explains the importance of *planning and control* (O2).

Intangible products typically are information intensive [22]: they require large amounts of data. Accounting is no exception. Moreover, decisions require knowledge and professional expertise, for example about business risks in different sectors, or about financial standards and regulations. Therefore specialized and trained professionals must execute the business processes. Accounting is a *knowledge-intensive* domain (O3).

We also find a high degree of *customization to clients* (O3), a characteristic that is specific to all services [30]. Accounting firms tend to serve a large variety of clients, each demanding different solutions for the financial issues they face. Fahy et al. [12] state "although there are reasonably homogeneous participants in the financial information supply chain, the clients demand a high degree of data customization" (p. 128). Because of client specificity, much time and effort is required for professionals to understand a new client. The dominant business model for accounting, is based on billable hours. So the time needed to understand a client is paid for by themselves. For these reasons, clients will not easily switch accountants.

Accounting firms can be characterized as a professional bureaucracy [24]. They typically have a decentralized structure. Usually, there is a head office with staff departments, such as an IT department and a professional standards office. The real power resides with individual departments, headed by a managing partner. Innovations are dependent on support from the managing partners; they need to be convinced. XBRL adoption requires IT adaptations and standardization of processes, which may trigger resistance. The decentralized structure, often grown during a series of mergers and acquisitions, has also resulted in a highly *complex application landscape* (O5). Adoption of XBRL, especially in the beginning of the information processing chain (built-in or embedded strategy), is likely to reduce the complexity of the application landscape.

Given the specialized nature of their tasks, employees rarely collaborate across department boundaries, even when that would be beneficial to the client. As we argued above, being a standardization effort XBRL is supposed to improve *information sharing* (O6), both internally between separate departments (e.g. between tax and accounting) and externally with regulators and government agencies.

4   Case

A medium sized accounting firm in the Netherlands, hereafter called BCD, was studied. The firm deals mostly with small and medium sized enterprises as clients. Like most accounting firms, the organizational structure of BCD reflects the most important activities: assurance, tax advisory, and various consultancy services. Although there is a centralized head office with support staff, individual departments are free to choose how to conduct their business. Traditionally assurance and tax advisory are separated.

The case study focuses on improvements to two processes performed for clients: the process for compiling and submitting the annual financial statements (FS), and the process for preparing the tax returns for corporate income tax (TR). Both processes are affected by the adoption of XBRL. The Standard Business Reporting (SBR) program of the Dutch Government provides an official taxonomy containing the meanings of financial concepts. In particular, the taxonomy has harmonized the fiscal and accounting perspectives on concepts like income or revenue. According to the Harmonization Act of 2008, small entities are allowed to compile their annual financial statement based on fiscal grounds (Dutch: Wet Samenval). Large parts of the TR process can therefore be based on results of the FS process. This opportunity triggered BCD to start a project to re-design their internal processes and application landscape around XBRL. Our research was done in the context of this project. For more background see also [19].

Data about the processes was collected by interviews with our informants, by document reviews, and by data obtained from the central 'hour registration files'

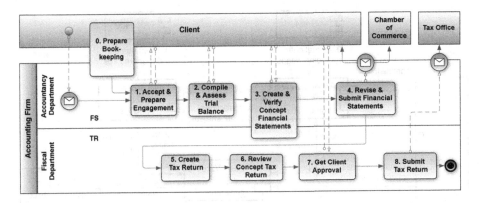

Fig. 2. Simplified process overview for compilation of annual financial statements (FS), and preparation of tax returns for corporate income tax (TR)

of BCD, where all billable and non-billable hours for employees are recorded. Our informants are members of the XBRL project management team, located within the centralized staff department. The validation workshop was carried out with experts and end users from various sub-departments and offices.

A simplified BPMN model of the FS and TR processes is shown in Fig. 2. A more detailed overview can be found in [19]. Interaction with the client and external stakeholders (chamber of commerce for filing annual financial statements, tax office for tax returns) is shown at the top. The accountancy department handles the FS process (upper swim lane) and tax specialists handle the TR process (lower swim lane).

Suppose a client has entered into an engagement with an accounting firm. In principal, a client performs its own bookkeeping, with some assistance by the accountant (task 0). The administration is transferred to the accounting firm, who must decide whether the quality is good enough to accept it, and prepare the activities involved in the engagement (task 1). The next step is the compilation of a trial balance on the basis of the data being provided and an assessment of the accuracy of the data (task 2). Each of these steps requires consultation with the client, indicated by dashed lines. In task 3 the accounting firm then creates a concept financial statement, and verifies it by consulting the client. Based on these checks the concept statement is revised, finalized by the client and submitted to the Chamber of Commerce (task 4). That concludes the FS process. Similar steps are followed for the TR process: task 5 creates a concept tax return, which is being reviewed (task 6) and approved by the client (task 7), after which the tax return is submitted to the tax office (task 8).

Next an overview was made of the software application landscape and how the different process steps are supported. The result is schematically shown in Fig. 3. Numbers refer to the steps in Fig. 2. The BPMN and software application landscape models were validated with our informants. As you can see, the

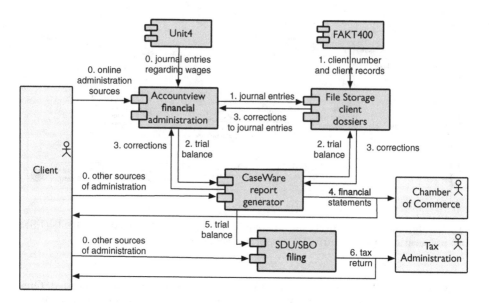

Fig. 3. Schematic software application landscape supporting the FS and TR processes

application landscape does contain redundancies. Some functionality is offered by several applications.

On the basis of the process model a simulation model was made of the FS process. A screen shot of the animation of the simulation model is shown in Fig. 4. The simulation model is more detailed than the process in Fig. 2. The different phases of the process are indicated as columns: planning and preparation, execution, verifying concept, client validation and approval, finalizing. Below you can see the subtasks for the different roles: accountants (yellow), distinguishing the assistant accountant, the engagement leader and the responsible accountant, client (green), secretary (orange), fiscal experts (dark orange), distinguishing responsible and assistant fiscal experts. Note that activities related to the client often involve waiting.

The structure of the simulation model was validated beforehand with process experts. The simulation model was tested by feeding it realistic input data and comparing the outcomes with actual data. In general, simulation studies depend on the quality of input data. It turned out that the accounting firm's hour registration that served as input data, was much less reliable than was initially believed. For instance, there are differences in the way separate departments record data, and therefore data turned out to be incomparable. Some categories of activities are not separately recorded. For instance, time spend on corrections was not recorded separately, so we could not quantitatively assess the impact of process improvements on quality. We could however make a qualitative assessment, as we expect that the number of corrections was reduced.

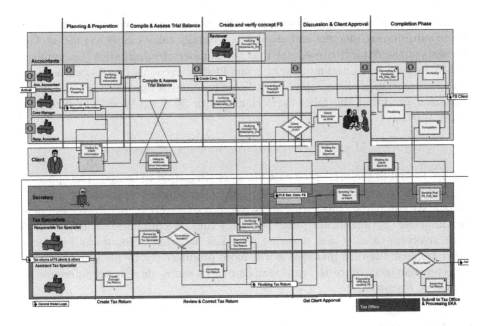

Fig. 4. Screenshot of the animation of the simulation model, to give an impression (Colour figure online)

How should can the effect of the proposed interventions be measured? Concerning input into the process, the most important resource is *human labour*, measured in hours spent by employees. Through their salaries, this is directly related to the costs. The organizational role of the employee is also noted. This information was obtained from the centralized hour registration. A natural unit of work is a client dossier. Information itself is not modelled as a separate resource in this type of process-based simulation.

Concerning output we decided that *lead-time* (in days), and *customer satisfaction* (on a 1 − 5 scale) are the most important variables. In addition, we also considered measures of *quality*, as this is essential in the accounting domain. However, it is hard to find a good measure of information quality. One could say that quality is inversely proportional to the number of errors per dossier. But what counts as an error in this case? Errors are professionally unacceptable: work must comply with accounting standards and procedures. We decided to approximate output quality by the number of additional corrections that were needed to complete a dossier. Compare [11] who use corrections to approximate deficiencies in internal control. Unfortunately, time spent on corrections and adjustments is not separately recorded in the hour registration. Therefore this quality variable turned out to be intractable.

We studied the empirical data collected from the hour registrations to find trends and correlations before starting the simulation studies.

An important variable is client complexity, as a more complex client structure due to subsidiaries, mergers and acquisitions usually takes longer to process. On the basis of the data, it turned out that the number of subsidiaries (i.e. number of dossiers per client) and number of general ledger accounts (GLA) can be used as approximation of client complexity. These predict the amount of work. Linear regression produced the following formula, with 50 % explained variance and $Sig. < 0,01$.

$$Hours = 51 + 28 * NumberofDossiers + 4,9 * Average\ GLA.$$

We also looked at the role of the case manager (Principle 4d below). The opposed suggestion is to 'empower' employees by giving them more responsibility (Principle 5c). We compared offices with and without a relatively large involvement of a case manager. No significant difference was found. We did find that offices with large involvement of a case manager used less assistant accountants per case, either because the case manager works more productively, or because the work is better managed. Since the case manager earns more, there is no difference in the use of resources.

5   Process Improvements

There has been a lot of research on process improvements. We mention Business Process Reengineering, e.g. [18], which suggests radical changes, often based on new business models or on clever use of IT. There are also continuous improvements schemes like Lean [7], which tries to identify and reduce 'wastage', those activities that do not add value for the customer, Six Sigma, e.g. [2], which tries to improve predictability of the process, and the Theory of Constraints, e.g. [10], which tries to remove or reduce the impact of bottlenecks. These approaches have been widely discussed in the literature. Therefore we take an existing overview by Reijers and Mansar [27], who have formulated best practices specifically for improving administrative processes.

The principles in Table 1 are mostly based on the best practices of Reijers and Mansar [27] and are also clustered according to the categorization they use. We did not use practices in their category 'Products', as the accounting domain is based on services. We didn't use their category 'External Environment' either, because that is about trusted third parties and outsourcing, which do not apply here.

In our case study, we identified those process improvement principles which made sense in the accounting domain, and which are facilitated or related to the possibilities offered by the adoption of XBRL. In particular, we looked at the characteristics of the accounting domain studied in Sect. 2. We use the following notation: a '+' in Table 1 means that the principle applies because of the specified domain characteristic, and a '−' that the principle is disqualified by the characteristic. Thereafter the usefulness of the principles was evaluated by actually applying them to the BPMN process models.

Table 1. Impact of domain characteristics on recommended process improvements, based on [27]

Clusters	Improvement principles	Quality and compliance (O1)	Planning an control (O2)	Knowledge intensive (O3)	Customization (04)	Application landscape (O5)	Information sharing (O6)
1. Customers	a. Control relocation: move control to the customer	+	+			+	+
	b. Contact reduction: reduce the number of points of contact with customer		+				
	c. Integration: integrate system and processes with customer systems and processes	+	+		−	+	+
2. Operation view	a. Task elimination: eliminate unnecessary tasks ('wastage')	−				+	+
	b. Triage: divide a general task into two or more alternative tasks, or combine several alternative tasks into a more general task		−	−	−	+	
	c. Task composition: combine small tasks into larger composite tasks and divide large tasks into workable smaller tasks		−	−	−	+	
3. Behavioural view	a. Parallelism: execute independent tasks in parallel, if possible		−			+	+
	b. Exception: optimize business processes for the normal flow and fork-off exceptions to specialists				+	+	
4. Organization: structure	a. Order assignment: let workers perform as many steps as possible for a single order			+	+		
	b. Customer teams: assign specific persons or teams to specific customers			+	+		
	c. Numerical Involvement: minimise the number of departments, groups and persons involved		−	+	+	+	
	d. Case manager: make one person (case manager) responsible for handling each type of order	+	+	+	+		
5. Organization: population	a. Specialist generalist (tasks): distinguish specialists and generalists for specific tasks				−	−	
	b. Specialist generalist (domains): distinguish specialists and generalists for customer domains				+	+	
	c. Empower: give people more decision rights and reduce middle management		−	−	+	+	
6. Information	a. Control addition: check completeness and correctness of input before processing, and check output before it is sent to customers	+		−	−	+	+
	b. Buffering (batch): instead of immediately asking for information, buffer requests		+				
7. Technology	a. Task automation: replace manual tasks by automated tasks	+		−	−	+	+
	b. Integrated technology: avoid constraints in the process by using integrated technology	+				+	+

Cluster 1. *Customers.* The first improvement principles refer to the customer. Re-allocation of controls to the customer may improve data quality. Data quality drives many other improvements [26]. When potential errors are caught early in the process, this will reduce repeated correction efforts later. In particular, we tested the principle to only start working on a dossier when it is known that all data is present. Incomplete dossiers lead to additional work, collecting, asking and verifying the missing data. Further benefits are expected from reducing the number of interactions with the client, and in general by better integration with the client's processes and systems. Note that XBRL standards make such systems integration relatively more feasible, as it facilitates software interoperability.

Cluster 2. *Operation view.* These principles refer to the design of the business process. Redundant tasks may be eliminated. In the Lean philosophy, tasks that do not directly add value for the customer are called 'wastage' [7]. Typical cases of wastage in this case are the numerous quality controls. Triage refers to the practice of identifying tasks into a specific categories, which must be handled in a specific way, e.g. by specialists. Composition refers to the practice of clustering tasks into larger units which need not be handled by a specific resource (person). The merging of FS and TR processes is an instance of composition.

Cluster 3. *Behavioural view.* The following principles are about choices made during execution of a business process. When possible, tasks should be executed in parallel. Because of the harmonization of fiscal and accounting concepts, some of the FR and TR processes can now be executed in parallel, on the basis of the same financial data ('store once, report many'). Task 4 can for example be done in parallel to task 5, 6 and 7, which are independent. The Exception principle refers to the practice of optimizing a business process for the most common flow, and fork off exceptions that require special treatment. This does make sense in the accounting domain, because of the large client variability, although it is hard to find a flow which is common to a majority of cases. In fact, deciding on these exceptions is part of the task of the case manager (see below).

Cluster 4. *Organization: structure.* These principles affect the way the work is being organized. Order assignment means that a case is preferably allocated to a single person, who has already worked on the same case before. This is common practice in accounting. Eventually, this practice leads to specialized customer teams. This corresponds to Observation 4. Numerical involvement seeks to minimize the number of departments, groups or persons involved in a single business process in order to reduce coordination overhead. However, accountants value segregation of duties to ensure quality control. According to this principle, no single person may both execute and approve a major decision. A case manager is appointed to manage all tasks related to a specific engagement. The converse idea of removing case managers to stimulate self-steering teams, is also tested in the simulation. We expect it will not lead to improvements, because case managers also have much experience about the content of the various engagements.

Cluster 5. *Organization: population.* This cluster is about resource allocation. An important principle is to distinguish specialists and generalists and only assign specific tasks to specialists. This frees up (expensive) specialist resources and also reduces waiting for a specific resource. In the case study we see a move towards generalists, especially now that FR and TR are harmonized. There is no longer a need for specific fiscal or accounting expertise. However, it does make sense to specialize in specific customer domains (e.g. healthcare; construction; financial services; manufacturing, etc.). In fact this is already the case, as is reflected by the names of the departments and the existence of customer teams. Empower refers to the practice of giving employees more decision rights and the ability to organize their own work. This should reduce the need for middle management, which strictly speaking does not add value. However, in the accounting domain, the partner (responsible accountant) must supervise quality of the work (Observation 1). We expect the partner to be a bottleneck. That would suggest planning the process to optimize their utilization, for instance, by adding a planner.

Cluster 6. *Information*. Control addition tries to improve information quality, by verifying outgoing materials to reduce potential complaints, and by checking the completeness and correctness of incoming materials, before processing. This makes a lot of sense as incomplete or sloppy client evidence is a well-known source of delays in the accounting domain. BCD does in fact try to convince clients to take responsibility for the quality of data, partly by price incentives. Clients who have a reliable bookkeeping system that can be easily interfaced with BCDs systems pay reduced fees. In this case, buffering means that instead of always requesting information from clients when needed (by telephone) it is better to cluster such requests and handle them all in one go. This reduces fragmentation of efforts and thereby also improves information quality.

Cluster 7. *Technology*. Task automation clearly makes sense for the data collection and processing steps, as manual errors can be avoided, especially since most data is already available electronically. Integrated technology is required to improve interoperability. Witness the overlaps between functionalities of applications in Fig. 2. This is one of the expected benefits of XBRL standardization.

6 Simulation Studies and Evaluation

The principles in Table 1 are generic. They must be translated into specific adjustments to the processes underlying Fig. 2. Each of these adjustments corresponds to a kind of hypothesis to be tested. However, some adaptations depend on each other; they cannot be tested independently. Therefore it makes sense to cluster these adaptations in the simulation experiments. Many adjustments could not be meaningfully implemented in the simulation model, for various reasons: lack of data, limitations of the software or of the analyst. Of the list of 35 adjustments proposed by Kloos [19], we will now discuss those that could be implemented and tested.

- As-Is: The situation as sketched in Fig. 2, before merging FS and TR.
- VII: Assign the most specialized resources (available) to the corresponding tasks.

Table 2. Lead time changes as a result of simulation experiments; resources are kept constant

Variable	As-Is	VII, IVa	XI	I	V, XIX	IX	XXI
Lead time concept FS	52,5	58,1 10,8 %	58,3 11,1	54,3 3,5 %	41,5 −20,9 %	72,6 38,4 %	47,8 −8,9 %
Lead time FS	63,0	70,5 11,8 %	70, 12,1 %	71,4 13,2 %	55,3 −12,3 %	80,9 28,4 %	58,6 −7,1 %
Lead time both	64,8	58,2 −10,3 %	75,5 16,4 %	82,6 27,4 %	62,0 −4,4 %	82,4 27,01 %	64,1 −1,2 %
Lead time concept TR	3,9	6,6 69,3 %	3,6 −7,9 %	4,0 3,4 %	3,9 −0,1 %	3,8 −0,98 %	4,1 5,0 %

IVa: Combine discussing with the client for the concept tax return with discussing the concept financial statements. These adjustments are already part of the running improvement project, which is why they are combined in the experiments.
- XI: Let the review of the tax position by the tax specialist be either performed by someone of the accountancy department or eliminate this review.
- I: Relocate checking completeness and accuracy of input data towards the customer.
- V: Prevent having to request additional or missing data.
  XIX: Always perform an intensive check on the input data.
- IX: Combine various planning and preparation tasks into one composite task.
- XXI: Collect input data from the customer on a more frequent basis.

First, the adapted processes were implemented and a series of simulation experiments were executed to test the influence of the adaptations on the only two performance measures that were tractable: lead-time and use of resources.

Second, we invited an expert panel consisting of 7 employees with different function levels (assistant accountant, case manager, responsible accountant) from different disciplines (tax and fiscal). Participants filled in an individual questionnaire. After that, we showed the process model and the simulation model, and discussed the expected influence of recommended process improvements on the performance indicators. According to the panel the expected benefits from the principles could be confirmed [19].

The simulation experiments display observable effects. These outcomes were later confirmed by the experts in the individual questionnaires and discussion session.

- *Decrease in lead time*: by having less process steps, less corrections, more parallel execution, less specialists and therefore less waiting time, the total lead time decreases. In particular the integration of FS and TR (VII, IVa) decreases total lead-time by 10 % (approximately 6 days). However, it increases the lead-time of FS. The decrease in total lead-time is less than originally expected by business experts. However, currently there is a large waiting time between the two processes, which was not modelled in the simulation. This explains the expectation gap.

The simulation model also shows a decrease in lead-time, when processing only starts after the required information is known to be complete. A 20 % decrease in the time needed before sending a concept version to the client is found for improvements V and XIX, and a decrease of 12 % for the time to complete a financial statement. For improvement XXI, collecting data more frequently, these reductions are respectively 9 % and 7 %.

- *Improved efficiency*: by avoiding data re-entry, reduction of control activities, and better deployment of people (mixed specialist teams; case manager) more work can be done with the same resources, while also maintaining the same quality level.

However, the simulation model lacks some predictive capability. For improvement XI (remove the separate tax review) we found an increase in lead-time of 11 %, while this is not logical. For improvement IX (combine tasks within the planning and preparation phase) an increase of 30–40 % (20 days) was found. Therefore, the simulation model is falsified regarding the effects of elimination (or combination) of tasks; apparently this changes the structure of the simulation model to such an extent that it leads to significantly different results.

In addition, there are a number of XBRL-related benefits that could not be quantitatively studied or simulated, but they could be qualitatively confirmed by the expert panel.

- *Improved data quality*: as data is not re-entered any more, and data definitions have been standardized, data quality is improved, which is itself a driver for other process benefits (less corrections; less customer contacts).
- *Improved assurance*: due to an increase of the data quality, the assurance level of the services might be improved too, although this depends on the business model. This is crucial in the domain (Observation 1)
- *Customer satisfaction*: although this is not easy to measure, experts expect that customer satisfaction will increase due to the overall higher quality of services (faster response times; less effort; less corrections). They thought that on the short term the use of XBRL could create an important competitive advantage.
- *Agility*: XBRL standardization enables reuse of data and aids configurability of systems. This makes it easier to create new business processes and adapt existing processes to new regulations.
- *Maintainability*: in the long run, the reduced complexity of the application landscape will make the software cheaper and easier to maintain.

In the expert validation session, we asked participants to cluster sets of related process improvements, resulting in four relatively independent categories that are meaningful for both experts and users. In the following description, the tasks refer to Fig. 2; individual numbers refer to the principles of Reijers and Mansar in Table 1.

- Category 1. *Rely on the customer* (task 0 and 1): improve data quality of the dossiers being provided by the client, by using XBRL-based software and improved software interoperability (7b), and by making the client responsible for the quality of the bookkeeping, possibly by price incentives (1).

- Category 2. *Merge the FR and TR process* (task 4 and 5, 6, 7), as much as possible, using the opportunities of XBRL standardization and SBR harmonization (2b,c). This leads to less dependencies, better utilization of resources, more parallel execution and less specialists to wait for (3a)(5ab).
- Category 3. *Remove quality controls* (2a), especially for smaller clients, by giving assistant accountants more responsibility (5b) and by building reconciliation checks into the software (task 3, 4, 6, 7a). XBRL makes these automated controls easier to set up and maintain.
- Category 4. *Simplify the application landscape.* Use only a few multi-purpose software applications instead of many traditional single-purpose applications, in order to reduce the complexity of the application landscape (Fig. 3) and avoid re-keying of crucial data (7b).

These alterations will have a large impact. Category 1 and 2 affect the way the accounting firm makes money from its services. Category 1 could involve a reduction in fees for customers with a reliable bookkeeping. Category 2 means that compilation services and tax advice are no longer offered as separate services. Likely the efficiency gains will be relatively more visible in a business model based on subscription, where the customer pays a fixed fee, than in the current business model based on billable hours. After all, efficiency gains reduce the number of billable hours. However, there was consensus among the experts that customers of accountancy firms are increasingly critical and demand more value for money, partly due to the credit crisis. They are no longer willing to pay for re-keying the information they provide electronically. Future research can look into the effect of business models on process improvements.

7   Related Research and Research Limitations

Alles et al. [1] provide an overview of research about XBRL adoption. They note that till now, most XBRL research has been technology-driven, and that proper empirical validation has been lacking. In particular, they call for a better analysis of the nature and benefits of XBRL adoption, and for field-based studies.

Concerning principles for process improvement, there has been a lot of research. Increasingly this also extends to the domain of administrative services [7,27], of which accounting services are only a part. Accounting is somewhat special in the sense that it concerns a highly regulated domain. Therefore, traditionally accountants have focused on compliance and information quality, rather than operational efficiency. In further research, it would be interesting to compare our findings with process improvements for other legal professions, such as notaries and lawyers. Note however that the mortgage industry, which is also about financial services, did in fact make a huge transition as the result of the adoption of inter-organizational systems and standards [23].

Not all simulation experiments were successful. Some adjustments concerning the elimination or combination of tasks show counter intuitive results. Moreover, the research is limited in scope. We studied a single case, which concerns a medium sized accounting firm and two internal processes targeting SMEs, so we can only draw limited conclusions. In particular, in future research we would like to look at larger accounting firms and we would like to investigate the auditing processes themselves, to find more empirical evidence of internal benefits of XBRL related to assurance, beyond interoperability and reporting functionality.

8 Conclusions

XBRL is a representation standard for information exchange, which is hailed for bringing many benefits. Yet there is little empirical evidence that XBRL creates these benefits and how they can be accomplished. In this paper we analysed the possibilities and implications of XBRL for improving the internal business processes of an accounting firm by simulating the effects of improvements. The XBRL-based improvements can be clustered into four main improvement categories: 1. Rely on the customer, 2. Merging the financial reporting and the tax reporting streams of the process, made possible by the semantic harmonisation of the financial and fiscal concepts, 3. Reducing unnecessary controls, and 4. Simplifying the complex application landscape. The benefit originates mostly from not having to re-enter information and from the standardization effects. XBRL shows precisely which data fields are mapped onto each other. This results in higher data quality, integrated processes, and efficiency. A decrease in lead-time was directly observable in the simulation studies.

In addition, benefits mentioned by the experts include improved data quality, improved assurance, increased customer satisfaction, increased agility and maintainability. The standardization of information exchange is a necessarily pre-condition for obtaining many of these advantages. The XBRL standard itself creates technological interoperability; this will facilitate a simplified application landscape. The data standardization of the SBR program creates semantic interoperability: shared meanings of financial concepts. The latter facilitates advantages like reduction of the number of manual controls and faster lead-time. An example is the harmonization of the fiscal and accounting concepts of income. Therefore, teams can be merged and resources are better allocated as there no need to wait for either fiscal or accounting specialists.

In this case study a built-in strategy towards XBRL adoption was followed, resulting in the before mentioned benefits. A more radical approach is the embedded strategy, which might result in more long-term benefits related to standardization and improved data quality. However, because the embedded strategy would require a redesign of the core of financial packages, with clear implications for the reliability of financial reporting, this approach is much more risky. We recommend more research in the different XBRL adoption strategies and the benefits that can be accomplished. In a sense, the XBRL standard with the taxonomies, their users and the various governance structures, can best be seen as a kind of information infrastructure, compare [29]. An infrastructure enables all kinds of improvement, but it requires users to apply it. Such an infrastructure may also provide opportunities for offering new services. Therefore more research is needed to test new business models for the accounting domain, based on improved interoperability and standardization, rather than billable hours.

References

1. Alles, M., Debreceny, R.: The evolution and future of XBRL research. Int. J. Account. Inf. Syst. **13**(2), 83–90 (2012)
2. Antony, J., Antony, F., Kumar, M., Cho, B.: Six sigma in service organisations: benefits, challenges and difficulties, common myths, empirical observations and success factors. Int. J. Qual. Reliab. Manag. **24**, 294–311 (2007)
3. Attaran, M.: Exploring the relationship between information technology and business process re-engineering. Inf. Manag. **41**, 585–596 (2004)
4. Baldwin, A., Brown, C., Trinkle, B.: XBRL: an impacts framework and research challenge. J. Emerg. Technol. Acc. **3**, 97–116 (2006)
5. Bharosa, N., Janssen, M., van Wijk, R., de Winne, N., van der Voort, H., Hulstijn, J., Tan, Y.H.: Tapping into existing information flows: the transformation to compliance by design in business-to-government information exchange. Gov. Inf. Q. **30**(1), S9–S18 (2013)
6. Blasini, J., Leist, S.: Success factors in process performance management. Bus. Process Manag. J. **19**(3), 477–495 (2013)
7. Bonaccorsi, A., Carmignani, G., Zammori, F.: Service value stream management (SVSM): developing lean thinking in the service industry. J. Serv. Sci. Manag. **4**(4), 428–429 (2011)
8. Burnett, R.D., Friedman, M., Murthy, U.: Financial reports: Why you need XBRL. J. Corp. Account. Finance **17**(5), 33–40 (2006)
9. Debreceny, R., Felden, C., Ochocki, B., Piechocki, M.: XBRL for Interactive Data: Engineering the Information Value Chain. Springer, Berlin (2009)
10. Dettmer, H.: Goldratts Theory of Constraints: A Systems Approach to Continuous Improvement. ASQC Quality Press, Milwaukee (1997)
11. Doyle, J., Ge, W., McVay, S.: Determinants of weaknesses in internal control over financial reporting. J. Account. Econ. **44**, 193–223 (2007)
12. Fahy, M., Feller, J., Finnegan, P., Murphy, C.: Co-operatively re-engineering a financial services information supply chain: a case study. Can. J. Adm. Sci. **26**(2), 125–135 (2009)
13. Garbellotto, G.: XBRL implementation strategies: the bold-on approach, the built-in approach, the deeply embedded approach. Strateg. Finance **90**(11) (2009)
14. Garbellotto, G.: XBRL implementation strategies: the bold-on approach, the built-in approach, the deeply embedded approach. Strateg. Finance **91**(2), 56–57 (2009)
15. Garbellotto, G.: XBRL implementation strategies: the bold-on approach, the built-in approach, the deeply embedded approach. Strateg. Finance **91**(5), 56–61 (2009)
16. Geijtenbeek, W., Lucassen, H.: Dutch approach to SBR assurance. In: Cohen, E. (ed.) Proceedings of the 25th XBRL International Conference, Yokohama, Japan, p. ASSR1. XBRL International (2012)
17. Grey, G.: XBRL: potential opportunities and issues for internal auditors. Technical report, The Institute of Internal Auditors Research Foundations (IIARF) (2005)
18. Hammer, M.: Reengineering work: Dont automate, obliterate. Harv. Bus. Rev. **68**(4), 104–112 (1990)
19. Kloos, M.: Business process management in an accounting firm. Msc, Delft University of Technology (2012)

20. Knechel, W., Salterio, S., Ballou, B.: Auditing: Assurance and Risk, 3rd edn. Thomson Learning, Cincinatti (2007)
21. Levitt, T.: Marketing intangible products and product intangibles. Harvard Bus. Rev. **59**(3), 94–102 (1981)
22. Loebbecke, C.: Electronic trading in on-line delivered content. In: Proceedings of the 32nd Hawaii International Conference on Systems Sciences, vol. 5, pp. 5009- (1999)
23. Markus, M.L., Steinfield, C.W., Wigand, R.T., Minton, G.: Industry-wide is standardization as collective action: the case of the us residential mortgage industry. MIS Q. **30**(1), 439–465 (2006)
24. Mintzberg, H.: Structure in Fives: Designing Effective Organizations. Prentice Hall Business Publishing, New Jersey (1983)
25. Müller-Wickop, N., Schultz, M., Nüttgens, M.: XBRL: impacts, issues and future research directions. In: Rabhi, F.A., Gomber, P. (eds.) FinanceCom 2012. LNBIP, vol. 135, pp. 112–130. Springer, Heidelberg (2013)
26. Orr, K.: Data quality and systems theory. Commun. ACM **41**(2), 66–71 (1988)
27. Reijers, H., Mansar, S.L.: Best practices in business process redesign: an overview and qualitative evaluation of successful redesign heuristics. Omega: Int. J. Manag. Sci. **33**(4), 283–306 (2005)
28. Roohani, S., Xianming, Z., Capozzoli, E.A., Lamberton, B.: Analysis of XBRL literature: a decade of progress and puzzle. Int. J. Digit. Account. Res. **10**, 131– 147 (2010)
29. Steinfield, C., Markus, M.L., Wigand, R.T.: Through a glass clearly: standards, architecture, and process transparency in global supply chains. J. Manag. Inf. Syst. **28**(2), 75–107 (2011)
30. Tyagi, R.K.: Measurement in service businesses: challenges and future directions. In: Demirkan, H., Spohrer, J.C., Krishna, V. (eds.) Service Systems Implementation. Service Science: Research and Innovations in the Service Economy, pp. 237–251. Springer, Heidelberg (2011)

The Role of Linked Data
and Semantic-Technologies
for Sustainability Idea Management

Alain Perez[1]([⊠]), Felix Larrinaga[1], and Edward Curry[2]

[1] Mondragon Unibertsitatea, Arrasate-Mondragon, Gipuzkoa, Spain
{aperez,flarrinaga}@mondragon.edu
[2] Digital Enterprise Research Institute, National University of Ireland,
Galway, Ireland
ed.curry@deri.org

Abstract. Idea Management Systems (IMS) manage the innovation life-cycle from the moment of invention until ideas are implemented in the market. During the life-cycle the IMS supports collaboration, allows idea enrichment with comments, contextual data, or connected to other relevant ideas. Semantic technologies can improve the knowledge management capabilities of IMSs allowing relevant information to be easily linked to ideas.

Many Enterprises concerned with sustainability encourage employee's participation as a means to boost creative innovation within their Sustainability Initiatives. However little work has examined the role of an IMS within Sustainability. In this paper we analyse the impact of a semantic-enabled IMS within a sustainability innovation process. In particular, how ideas can be enriched with contextual Linked Open Data (LOD), especially Life-Cycle Assessment (LCA) data, to improve the understanding, implication and value of the idea from the sustainability perspective.

Keywords: Idea management systems · Semantic web · Linked data · Sustainability · Life-cycle assessment

1 Introduction

Sustainability is the responsible management of resources encompassing the triple bottom line of environmental, economic, and social dimensions. Many organisations are starting to make serious commitments towards incorporating sustainability into their own organizational logics [1] to maximise profits in an environmentally and socially responsible manner. Sustainability is not only about Corporate Social Responsibility, Sustainability is an important business issue, affecting new products and services, compliance, cost reduction opportunities, the organization's reputation, and revenue generation often derived from technological innovation [2]. Porter recognises the role sustainability can play as

S. Counsell and M. Núñez (Eds.): SEFM 2013 Collocated Workshops, LNCS 8368, pp. 306–312, 2014.
DOI: 10.1007/978-3-319-05032-4_22, © Springer International Publishing Switzerland 2014

part of an organization's Competitive Strategy with the concept of "innovation offsets" where companies can "not only lower the net costs of meeting environmental regulations, but can lead to absolute advantages" over competitors [3].

Sustainability requires information on the use, flows and destinies of energy, water, and materials including waste, along with monetary information on environment-related costs, earnings, and savings. This type of information is critical if we are to understand the causal relationships between the various actions that can be taken, and their impact on sustainable performance.

Innovation is key to articulate knowledge management by means of effective processes and methodologies. The phase of the innovation process where idea management is developed is one of the most critical stages [4]. IMSs support this stage providing the necessary tools to collect, enrich, store, present and select ideas. IMS manage ideas through their life-cycle from the time of creation until they are selected for implementation. During this life-cycle it is crucial to gather as much relevant information as possible in order to collect quality-relevant ideas. Users can enrich ideas with opinions, other ideas and additional content. This task can be cumbersome and its automation is fundamental.

This paper aims to define how sustainability in enterprises can benefit from IMS. The hypothesis is that more precise relations among ideas and richer content can be automatically achieved if Semantic Web and Linked Data technologies are employed in IMS, linking sustainability ideas with data from different data sources. Managing innovation for sustainability needs to address some major challenges; the emergence of radical new technologies and markets, constant shift in the regulatory conditions, the involvement or participation of many agents, the large volume of ideas for screening and evaluation, and in particular the need to acquire, assimilate and exploit new knowledge [5].

An increasing number of organizations worldwide have adopted innovation contests not only for innovation purposes, but also for other reasons such as promoting sustainability [6]. A proof to this can be seen in the annual reports and sites of several energy providers and enterprises. In some of these experiences IMS have proven beneficial. IMS provide the workflow tools necessary to launch and manage innovation contest or waves, a common platform where different agents can collaborate, a repository where ideas are gathered and tools for editing, commenting or voting upon ideas. IMSs also encourage collaboration among people and enterprises.

One of the biggest problems in IMS is the difficulty of enriching these ideas. It is a manual and time consuming task that includes the searching and gathering of additional knowledge in different sources. Most of the time ideas are not linked with other data the enterprises may have in their systems or data available outside the company [7]. This causes disinformation and generates duplicates or poor quality ideas. A system that links generated ideas to stored data automatically may be an improvement. Semantic Web and Linked Data technologies propose a set of good practices to publish and link structured data in the Web.

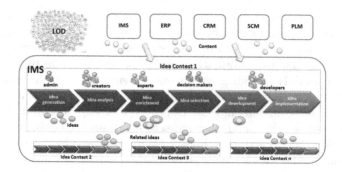

Fig. 1. IMS architecture

Many datasets and repositories are already available adopting this philosophy enabling machines in the 'understanding' of the data they store.

2 The Role of Knowledge Management and Idea Management in Sustainability

2.1 Reference Architecture

IMS are software platforms or applications that provide repositories and tools to gather, search for, edit, comment, and vote upon ideas. They accommodate different idea contests or campaigns and stakeholders; idea operators, experts, decision makers and administrators. Dependencies between ideas from different campaigns must be addressed. Figure 1 shows a standard IMS architecture.

IMS must provide workflows to manage the interactions between the different innovation process stages: Idea generation, analysis, enrichment, selection, development and implementation.

2.2 Linked Data and Linked Open Data (LOD)

Emerging from research into the Semantic Web, Linked Data proposes an approach for information interoperability based on creation of a global information space. Linked data leverages the existing open protocols and standards of the World Wide Web architecture for sharing structured data on the web. Linked data technology uses web standards in conjunction with four basic principles for exposing, sharing and connecting data. These principles are:

1. Use URIs as names for things.
2. Use HTTP URIs so that people can look up those names.
3. When someone looks up a URI, provide useful information using the standards.
4. Including links to other URIs so that people can discover more things.

Linked Data is facilitating the publishing of large amounts of structured data on the web. The resulting Web of Data can be considered as a web scale data space supported by Semantic Web technologies. The Linked Open Data represents a large number of interlinked datasets that are being actively used by industry, government and scientific communities.

2.3 Sustainability IMS and Semantic Web/Linked Data

A common problem with IMS is idea assessment due to data overflow, noisy data, bursty nature of idea contests and difficult in rating innovation [8]. This translates into difficulties such as the detection of similar or duplicated ideas. Several studies propose the application of Semantic Web technologies on the innovation process and more specifically for IMSs to overcome these issues [9, 10]. The GI2MO ontology, for instance, is a project that tries to improve current Idea Management Systems by offering an ontology that models the innovation process. The ontology lays foundations for knowledge management based on interlinking of enterprise systems and web assets to increase information awareness and help in innovation assessment [11]. Although GI2MO ontology provides coverage for most of the properties included in IMS, it lacks of explicitly capturing the contextual knowledge for the idea.

To boost interoperability among heterogeneous systems, some IMS platforms present ideas in RDF format and work as SPARQL endpoints so third parties can place idea or innovation process related queries [12]. In the reference architecture Sustainability datasets will be interlinked to IMS as external knowledge to enhance IMS content.

3 Examples of Ontologies for Use Cases

This section describes 3 different sustainability use cases that can benefit from the linking of ideas with external information. The first use case aims to enrich ideas for energy reduction. The second one addresses products life cycle and how data can be linked. The last use case shows how similar ideas can be identified helping administrators management tasks.

Energy Reduction: Imagine a user involved in an idea contest oriented to sustainability that proposes a new idea (graphically on Fig. 2): *I would change the incandescent bulb in desk #333 for a LED bulb in order to save energy.*

The system could identify the concepts **incandescent bulb in desktop #333** and **LED bulb** find on the data space (external to the IMS) information about the bulb in that desktop and led bulbs and show it in a widget or block next to the idea. If the system is able to identify the domain of the idea and annotate it semantically, the idea can be linked to data stored in a data space [13] (results on grey and blue widgets in Fig. 2) or searched on some data sources [14]. That way, the user would create an idea with automatically added information. If someone reads the idea will know if it is worth the effort of changing it or not. The reader could comment on the idea and discuss about it.

Life-cycle Assessment: This use case links IMSs with LCA data stored in a data space. Imagine a user concerned about the Greenhouse Gas emissions (GHG emissions) discovers that new laptops are going to be bought. He could write the following idea (graphically in Fig. 2):*If we buy 13-Inch MacBook Air laptops instead of 13-Inch MacBook Pro, we can reduce the amount of GHG emissions in the manufacture of our devices.*

If we can identify that the idea talks about 2 different laptops and their GHG emissions, we could link the idea with that data and show the amount of GHG emissions each laptop has and the savings of the idea.

In order to link the data we have to annotate it semantically, for example using The Resource Description Framework (RDF). In RDF, the statement *LCA Idea mentions MacBook Air* is expressed in triple format as:

$$(Subject\ \textbf{-\ LCA\ Idea}) \Rightarrow (Predicate\ \textbf{-\ mentions}) \Rightarrow (Object\ \textbf{-\ MacBook\ Air})$$

Using this semantic annotations some links can be found between different data in the system. That data can be found in the IMS or in some internal and external data spaces. Below, on Fig. 3, a graphical representation of those links can be seen.

Taking the LCA use case as an example, we can see the different links the data have (Fig. 3). Using these links we can extract some data and see what is the actual impact of the idea. For example, we can see how much greenhouse gas each mentioned laptop emits to the atmosphere on their manufacturing process.

Fig. 2. Energy reduction and LCA ideas (automatically added data widgets)

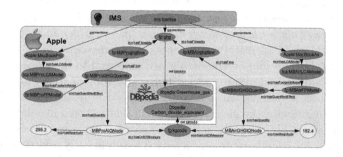

Fig. 3. Data links example

Similar Ideas Recognition: We can imagine an enterprise that has an innovation process for new idea gathering. Sometimes ideas can be repeated in the same or past waves. Having a system that identifies similarities can help innovation administrators in identifying relations or knowing the reason of rejection.

For instance in a previous wave the idea of changing an incandescent bulb for a led one was rejected because the led bulb was too expensive. If someone generates a similar idea it can be linked to the previous one, and see the reasons for the previous rejection. If now the led bulbs are cheaper, that idea may be interesting.

In order to perform that task the identification of main concepts of the idea is needed. If the system can find similarities in those main concepts, the ideas should be linked. The idea with mentioned concepts can be compared with the other ones and similar ideas can be identified and presented to the users.

4   Potential Benefits

Firstly, IMS ideas would be enriched automatically with relevant data provided by LOD/SW repositories. Sustainability impact will be included among that content. This could help users and administrators to see how important an idea could be. Secondly, the tools should help users in order to understand the context of the ideas. With additional data and related information users could understand some issues that the idea itself does not explain explicitly. And finally, the tools are expected to help administrator to perform their task faster and in an easier way. On one hand showing them the relations of the ideas can help them identifying in what are the users concerned and see if there are repeated ideas. On the other hand, measuring their possible impact could help them recognizing the most important ideas and select the best ones, helping even more if there is a big amount of data.

5   Summary and Future Challenges

The main innovation strives in the application of semantic web and LOD technologies to interlink Sustainability repositories with IMS in such a way that ideas are enriched with relevant content. SW technologies are also proposed in the detection of similar ideas. Some use cases have been defined describing the advantages semantic annotations and linked data might bring. Moreover, some possible benefits for users and system administrators have been outlined. Linking ideas with related data can be a powerful approach, but it can be a difficult task for the user. A future challenge can be identifying the data automatically in order to help users linking the idea. The system could make some recommendations based on what the user has written. Identifying the domain of the idea can be helpful too if additional information is wanted to be added. Knowing the domain of the idea can help recognizing specific data sources where more data can be found and linked. Finally, some case studies should be implemented in order to obtain results that validate the hypothesis of this paper.

References

1. Curry, E., Guyon, B., Sheridan, C., Donnellan, B.: Developing a sustainable IT capability: lessons from Intel's journey. MIS Q. Executive **11**(2), 61–74 (2012)
2. Watson, R.T., Lind, M., Haraldson, S.: The Emergence of sustainability as the new dominant logic: implications for information systems. In: International Conference on Information Systems, ICIS 2012 (2012)
3. Porter, M.E., Linde, C.V.D.: Toward a new conception of the environment-competitiveness relationship. J. Econ. Perspect. (JSTOR) **9**(4), 97–118 (1995)
4. Errasti, N., Santos, I., Lizarralde, O.: Social Software in Support of Collaborative Innovation. In: Erima (2010)
5. Seebode, D., Jeanrenaud, S., Bessant, J.: Managing innovation for sustainability. R&D Manag. **42**(3), 195–206 (2012)
6. Adamczyk, S., Bullinger, A.C., Mslein, K.M.: Innovation contests: a review, classification and outlook. Creativity Innov. Manag. **21**(4), 335–360 (2012)
7. Curry, E., Hasan, S., ul Hassan, U., Herstand, M., O'Riain, S.: An entity-centric approach to green information systems. In: Proceedings of the 19th European Conference on Information Systems (ECIS 2011) Helsinki (2011)
8. Westerski, A.: Semantic technologies in idea management systems: a model for interoperability, linking and filtering. Ph.D. thesis (2013)
9. Riedl, C., May, N., Finzen, J., Stathel, S., Kaufman, V., Krcmar, H.: An idea ontology for innovation management. Int. J. Seman. Web Inform. Syst. **5**(4), 1–18 (2009)
10. Lorenzo, L., Lizarralde, O., Santos, I., Passant, A.: Structuring e-brainstorming to better support innovation processes (2011)
11. Westerski, A., Iglesias, C.A., Rico, F.T.: A model for integration and interlinking of idea management systems. In: 4th International Conference on Metadata and Semantic Research, MTSR 2010, 20–22 October 2010, pp. 183. Springer, Alcala de Henares, Spain (2010)
12. Perez, A., Larrinaga, F., Lizarralde, O., Santos, I.: INNOWEB: gathering the context information of innovation processes with a collaborative social network platform. In: International Conference on Concurrent Enterprising (ICE) (2013)
13. Curry, E., Hasan, S., O'Riain, S.: Enterprise energy management using a linked dataspace for energy intelligence. In: The Second IFIP Conference on Sustainable Internet and ICT for Sustainability (SustainIT 2012). IEEE, Pisa,Italy (2012)
14. Curry, E., O'Donnell, J., Corry, E., Hasan, S., Keane, M., O'Riain, S.: Linking building data in the cloud: integrating cross-domain building data using linked data. Adv. Eng. Inform. **27**(2), 206–219 (2013)

Stochastic Modelling of Seasonal Migration Using Rewriting Systems with Spatiality

Suryana Setiawan[1,2(✉)] and Antonio Cerone[2(✉)]

[1] Dipartimento di Informatica, Università di Pisa, Pisa, Italy
setiawan@di.unipi.it
[2] UNU-IIST — International Institute for Software Technology, United Nations University, Macau SAR, China
ceroneantonio@gmail.com, setiawan@iist.unu.edu

Abstract. Seasonal migration is the long-distance movement of a large number of animals belonging to one or more species that occurs on a seasonal basis. It is an important phenomenon that often has a major impact on one or more ecosystem(s). It is not fully understood how this population dynamics phenomenon emerges from the behaviours and interactions of a large number of animals. We propose an approach to the modelling of seasonal migration in which dynamics is stochastically modelled using rewriting systems, and spatiality is approximated by a grid of cells. We apply our approach to the migration of a wildebeest species in the Serengeti National Park, Tanzania. Our model relies on the observations that wildebeest migration is driven by the search for grazing areas and water resources, and animals tend to follow movements of other animals. Moreover, we assume the existence of dynamic guiding paths. These paths could either be representations of the individual or communal memory of wildebeests, or physical tracks marking the land. Movement is modelled by rewritings between adjacent cells, driven by the conditions in the origin and destination cells. As conditions we consider number of animals, grass availability, and dynamic paths. Paths are initialised with the patterns of movements observed in reality, but dynamically change depending on variation of movement caused by other conditions. This methodology has been implemented in a simulator that visualises grass availability as well as population movement.

1 Introduction

Computer scientists have taken inspiration from natural processes to build new computing paradigms/formalisms. Their motivation is either for solving general computing problems or helping natural scientists in modelling and analysing natural phenomena [1,3,10,13,15,17–19,21,22]. In our work a formalism is being developed, the Grid Systems [2]. It is intended for modelling the dynamics of populations and their interactions with ecosystems. This formalism has taken inspiration from several existing formalisms, especially Cellular Automata [1] and Membrane P Systems [4–6,16,18].

S. Counsell and M. Núñez (Eds.): SEFM 2013 Collocated Workshops, LNCS 8368, pp. 313–328, 2014.
DOI: 10.1007/978-3-319-05032-4_23, © Springer International Publishing Switzerland 2014

In our previous work [2] the syntax and the semantics of the Gird Systems is elaborated and our approach for modelling the population growth of *Aedes albopictus* sp using the formalism is presented. In the model population dynamics were affected by external events: temperature fluctuation and rainfall. Behaviour was also modelled to vary spatially. The model was analysed by using a simulator that was developed based on the semantics of the Grid Systems and results were compared to real data.

In this paper a new feature for expressing the dynamic movement of the population around its habitat is introduced. This feature is expected to enable further analysis of the movement patterns, resulting from the changes in the ecosystem. To examine this feature the migration of wildebeests in Serengeti National Park, Tanzania, was used as our case study. The migration is massive since it involves about 1.2 million wildebeests together with hundreds of thousands of zebras, gazelles, impalas, and other herbivores. The route typically ranges about 1400 km from Ngorongoro crater in the south to Grumeti reserve in the west, then to Masai Mara reserve in the north and finally back to Ngorongoro, covering an area over 30,000 km^2. The main variables affecting the movement of the wildebeest are grass availability and the dynamic pathways that are formed by geographical boundaries (rivers and hills) and the communal memorisation of the route.

In the following sections the Grid Systems, and *links*, the new feature, will be discussed. They will be followed by the case study, its model, its simulation results and a short discussion of the results.

2   Grid Systems

Grid Systems are a formalism for modelling the dynamics of ecosystems [2]. They consist of biotic and abiotic components defined as the objects of the system.

2.1   Reaction Rules

The behaviour of the system is defined by reaction rules that rewrite a given multiset of objects into a new multiset of objects. In reaction rule

$$\alpha \rightarrow \beta$$

multiset α represents the objects that are consumed, called *reactants*, and multiset β represents the objects that are produced, called *products*. Some objects, called *promoters*, may be required for the reaction to occur although they are not consumed when the reaction occurs; other objects, called *inhibitors*, may instead inhibit the reaction.

Reaction rule includes promoters ψ and inhibitors χ:

$$\alpha \rightarrow \beta \; [\psi \mid \chi]$$

2.1.1   Reaction Rate and Duration

The frequency with which a reaction occurs is specified by a rate c as follows.

$$\alpha \xrightarrow{c} \beta \ [\psi \mid \chi].$$

In this case the duration of the reaction is implicitly given by $1/c$. This supports the high-level modelling of natural processes whose duration is inversely proportional to the frequency of their termination. For example, at population level life expectancy is inversely proportional to natural death rate.

When modelling at lower-level, for instance at individual level, there may be short duration processes that overlap longer duration processes and cause their early termination. For example, death due to predation concludes a very fast predation process that causes the early termination of the life of an individual. In this case the duration of the predation process is independent of its frequency. It is therefore necessary to explicitly specify duration d of such processes as follows.

$$\alpha \xrightarrow[d]{c} \beta \ [\psi \mid \chi].$$

2.1.2   Object States

Once a reaction starts, reactants can no longer be used by any other reactions but can still act as promoters or inhibitors of other reactions. Therefore, a reactant cannot be removed until the reaction is completed; instead it changes its state from "available" to "committed" when the reaction starts.

2.2   Principles in Conducting the Reactions

The Grid System evolves through reactions. During the reactions the system obeys three principles that are also typical in nature: parallelism, stochasticity and spatiality.

2.2.1   Maximal Parallelism

Reactions must be applied immediately and maximally whenever the required reactants are available and the conditions related to the promoters and the inhibitors are satisfied. Reactions must also be performed in a parallel (simultaneous) manner.

2.2.2   Stochasticity

In Grid Systems distinct rules may require the same reactants at the same time. This non-determinism is resolved stochastically based on the propensity of each rule using Gillespie's SSA [9].

Stochasticity is also manifested by varying the duration of the reactions. The duration is exponentially distributed with mean $1/c$ when duration d is not specified. Otherwise, the duration is exponentially distributed with mean d. To specify a rule having this stochastic property, mark M is placed after c for the former case,

$$\alpha \xrightarrow{c,M} \beta \ [\psi \mid \chi]$$

or after d for the later case, as written as

$$\alpha \xrightarrow[d,M]{c} \beta \ [\psi \mid \chi]$$

2.2.3   Spatiality

Grid Systems also consider the spatial dynamics of the objects that are distributed in the space. For instance, their behaviours (rules or parameters) might vary in different locations. A Grid system divides the space discretely into cells. Each cell is "associated" with a set of rules. Also, they define those rules which can only take the objects in the cell as the reactants. However, the objects from some other cells could be referenced as promoters or inhibitors in a reaction in that cell and the products can be placed in other cells. This referencing to other cells can be defined by any of two methods: relative addressing or absolute addressing. Relative addressing specifies the referenced cell's address as the column-row distance from the cell which the rule is associated with. Absolute addressing specifies the referenced cell's address as the referenced cell's actual row-column numbers. The address of object a in a cell will be expressed as the subscript to a. To differentiate their notations the absolute ones are placed within squared brackets "[.,.]" as in $a_{[3,4]}$, and relative ones within curved brackets "(.,.)", as in $a_{(-1,1)}$.

Grid Systems provide a method to address objects located in the "environment", by subscripting respective objects with "[E]", as in $a_{[E]}$. As to the cells the rules can be associated with the environment.

2.3   Formal Definition of Grid Systems

Definition 1. *A Grid System $G(N, M, \Sigma, R, A, C^{(0)})$ is defined as follows:*

- *G is the grid name;*
- *N and M are two integers indicating that G has $N \times M$ cells, also called local membranes;*
- *Σ is the alphabet of object types;*
- *R is a set of transition rules;*
- *A is the set of associations of the rules with the membranes, i.e.*

$$A = \{(\rho, \gamma) \mid \rho \in R, \ \gamma \in \{G_{i,j} | 0 \le i < N, \ 0 \le j < M\} \cup \{G_E\}\};$$

   where
   - *$G_{i,j}$, with $0 \le i < N$ and $0 \le j < M$, denotes the cell in position (i, j);*
   - *G_E is the global membrane surrounding the cells;*
- *$C^{(0)}$ is the initial configuration of the grid.*

Definition 2. *A transition rule $\rho : \alpha \xrightarrow[d]{c} \beta \; [\psi \mid \chi]$ is defined as follows:*

- *ρ is the unique identifier of the rule;*
- *α is a non-empty multiset of reactants;*
- *β is a multiset of products;*
- *ψ is a multiset of promoters;*
- *χ is a multiset of inhibitors;*
- *$c \in \mathbb{R}^+$ is the rate with which the rule may be applied to perform a reaction, $d \in \mathbb{R}^+$ is the duration of the reaction. When d is not specified, the duration will take $1/c$. When either c or d is marked by a 'M', it indicates that the duration time is an exponentially distributed random variable with parameter $1/d$ (or with parameter c, when d is not specified).*

3 Links

Living species have been given by nature the ability to sense and to follow the pathways for movements. Namely, wood ants can memorize snapshot views and landmarks [8], salmon fishes can sense geomagnetic fields [14], and sperm cells can sense chemotaxes to locate the ovum [12]. The pathways are either given by nature (as for salmon and sperm), created by themselves dynamically (as by ant), or a combination of both. Therefore, the model of the pathways might be more complex than just random walks (Brownian motion) as for chemical particles.

Pardini in his thesis reports the use of Spatial P Systems to imitate the movement of schooling fishes [16] which is based on the Boid flock model. This model determines the movement direction of each individual fish by a weighted-averaging computation from other fishes' directions inside its viewing space. Such heavy computations are originally intended for computer graphics animation rather than for biological simulation [20].

By using the basic definition of the Grid Systems movement may need to be expressed as a large number of rules. Instead, an extended definition of objects, termed 'links', is introduced which enables the pathways being modelled to function as pointers.

3.1 Basic Idea

A link is defined as a 'special object' that carries pointers, information which provides the address of a destination cell. The pointers can be used by rules in referring the objects in another cell. This is a third addressing method in addition to the relative addressing and the absolute addressing. Being used as an addressing method, different pointers carried by a link introduce another form of non-determinism into the system. In order to resolve this further non-determinism decision will be made stochastically based on the weighing of each pointer. Weights are real numbers between 0 and 1.0, and the total weights in the same cell is 1.0. Like objects, the number of links in a cell can be increased or decreased by applying its related rule.

3.2   Formal Definition of Links

3.2.1   Links as Special Objects

Let G be a Grid System whose object set is Σ. Moreover, P is the set of links and $P \subseteq \Sigma$. An object p is a link, if p carries one pointer η or more. The notation $p : \eta$ indicates that link p is carrying pointer η. When p carries more than one pointers in a cell, the pointers are weighted by $w_1, w_2, \ldots, w_k$ respectively, with $0 \leq w_i \leq 1.0$ and $\Sigma w_i = 1.0$.

3.2.2   Addressing by the Links

Pointer η can be expressed as either (dr, dc) or $[r, c]$. When p is the link existing in cell G_{r_0,c_0}, pointer $[r_1, c_1]$ carried by p points to the cell G_{r_1,c_1}, and pointer (dr, dc) carried by p points to the cell G_{r_0+dr,c_0+dc}. Also, regarding link p in G_{r_0,c_0}, pointer $[r_1, c_1]$ equals pointer (dr, dc) if and only if $r_0 + dr = r_1$, and, $c_0 + dc = c_1$.

Given that $p : \eta$, specifying a_p indicates object a in the cell pointed by η. For instance, if in $G_{5,6}$ there exists link $p : (2, -1)$ (a link with only one pointer), a rule containing a_p^m indicates that the number of a objects is m and they are located in $G_{7,5}$.

If link p has pointers $\eta_1, \eta_2, \ldots, \eta_k$ whose weights are $w_1, w_2, \ldots, w_k$ respectively with rule r specifies object A subscripted by link p as A_p, then in applying r, η_i will be chosen randomly weighted by w_i.

3.2.3   Rules for Changing the Weights

If in a cell link p^n has k distinct pointers labelled $\eta_1, \eta_2, \ldots, \eta_k$, and weighings $w_1, w_2, \ldots, w_k$ respectively, then,

- adding $p^m : \eta_i$ into that cell changes its overall weighing:
  $w_j' = \frac{nw_j}{(n+m)}$, for $\eta_i \neq \eta_j$, or
  $w_j' = \frac{(nw_j+m)}{(n+m)}$, for $\eta_i = \eta_j$, or
  $w_i' = \frac{m}{(n+m)}$, for $\eta_i \notin \{\eta_1, \eta_2, \ldots, \eta_k\}$ and $k > 0$, or
  $w_i' = 1$, for $k = 0$.
- adding p^m (without a pointer) into that cell will not affect the weights as they behave as ordinary objects.
- removing $p^m : \eta_i$, from that cell, where $m \leq nw_i$, changes its overall weighing:
  $w_j' = \frac{nw_j}{(n-m)}$, for $\eta_i \neq \eta_j$, or
  $w_j' = \frac{(nw_j-m)}{(n-m)}$, for $\eta_i = \eta_j$.
- removing p^m (without a pointer) will not affect the weighing, as they behave as ordinary objects, except in the case of $m = n$, all pointers will be removed.
- When a rule performs both adding and removing, adding will be done before removing to maintain the weighing properly.

3.3   Links as Objects in the Rules

Let p^n be a link p having quantity n in the cell and r be a rule applied to that cell. When link p appears in r without a pointer, as in p^m, it will be handled as an ordinary object. On the other hand, when it appears in a rule with a pointer η_i, as in $p^m : \eta_i$, it will be handled according to its role in the rule.

- As reactants, the rule can be applied when $mw_i \leq n$ and the changes will follow Sect. 3.2.3.
- As promoters, the rule can be applied when $mw_i \leq n$.
- As inhibitors, the rule can not be applied when $mw_i \geq n$.
- As products, the rule will be applied and the number of link p will change accordingly and the changes will follow Sect. 3.2.3.

4   Experimental Works on Seasonal Migration

Many hypotheses have been proposed to describe the migration phenomenon. Boone et al. report that at least 16 explanations have been given for the cause or timing of the migration in Serengeti [7]. Furthermore, they have observed that the main reason driving the direction of the wildebeest migration is the search for a grazing rather than following the rainfall. By using evolutionary programming they approximated a proportion of 75 % to 25 % for the above reasons. By using dynamic model fitting, Holdo *et al.* report a different result, namely, an opposing rainfall and fertility gradient as the main reason for the migration [11]. They go on to conclude that the rainfall affects the availability of the grass. However, the conclusions of both studies focussed on grass availability and except in the latter, rainfall also played an additional role as the external factor affecting grass availability. The route of migration is likely related by the topographics of the area as shown in Fig. 1.

4.1   Pathways of Migration

In our work, the migration is modelled as the result of the animals finding a place for grazing and following existing pathways. The pathways are formed by their memorisation of the animals' previous movement and the initial pathways given from the beginning. The movement to the nearby area to locate grass is simply

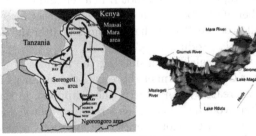

(a) Migration pattern   (b) Topography of the land

Fig. 1. Serengeti National Park

performed after the quantity of the grass in the current area is reduced by their consumption. When there is insufficient grass or if there is a strong pathway, the animals move to follow the pathway. To protect themselves from predators they tend to group and therefore, they avoid to be alone in a quiet location. On the other hand, they avoid crowded locations to maximise their chances to access the grass. On each movement they leave more marks (augmenting the pathway) which others will follow. Grass root will continue to produce blades of grass until the quantity reaches the maximum that can be produced in that area. The strength of a pathway will decay according to a decay factor in each interval of time due to being destroyed by natural events or being forgotten by the animals.

4.2 Life Cycle

Ideally, there should be at least three dimensions for their state space in animal life cycle: age, health, and physical periods. For this experiment, we simplified them to be one dimension with 10 stages of strength/wellness from $A0, A1, \ldots,$ $A9$. In every different stage animals will have its own behaviour parameters: death rates, feeding rates, birth rates. Pregnancy is limited only on stages $A6$ to $A9$. New born baby will be at $A0$. They will upgrade to one higher stage except at stage $A9$ when they gain food. Reversely, lacking the food will degrade to one lower stage except at the most left stage. The death rate will be higher to lower stages and the birth rate will be higher to higher stage. Their feeding rate will peak in $A6$ and $A7$. After giving birth they drop their condition 3 stages.

4.3 Objects

– Wildebeests: The animals of each stage will be represented as objects $A0$, $A1$, $\ldots$, and $A9$, movable animals, or $B0, B1, \ldots,$ and $B9$, in-digestion animals. As grass is being consumed, $A\langle S \rangle$ will immediately become $B\langle S \rangle$, then revert back to A with higher stage, $A\langle S + 1 \rangle$, after digestion is complete. This differentiation is intended to avoid other rule applicability being affected by the grass which is already being consumed.
– Grass: Grass will be represented as a root R in a cell and its quantity produced in a cell as a number of G. To create a delayed effect, that forces the animal to move, the root will produce H first then becomes G after the delay. Moreover, R can still continuously produce H.
– Counters: To ease some rules in considering the number of animals in some cells, object counter C whose number represents the number of animals in the same cell. One C is created when a birth rule is applied. In the death rule, A will become Ax first avoiding object C as a reactant followed by the rule that removes a pair of Ax and C. Moreover, the number of C changes due to the movement. Such a mechanism is performed by creating Ax in its origin and creating C in its destination.
– Pathways: A pathway is represented by object *path* which is a link. It will decay geometrically of a certain rate as the time passes. Links are refreshed

by the animal movements that create objects *path* in the cell. The number of objects *path* created by the movements varies depending on each movement's importance.

– Boundary objects: To limit the movement within an area, in each boundary cell a dummy object Z will be placed. Each movement rule will consider this object as the inhibitor in the destination cell.

4.4   Regions

A region is defined as a set of cells identifying an area. Associating a region with a rule implies associating its cells with the rule. Serengeti and its surrounding area are defined as a 50×50 grid of cells divided into *MovingSpace* region and *Boundary* region. *MovingSpace* is the grazing area. It is further divided into seven regions whose grass characteristics are different: *Ngoro2*, *West*, *Center*, *East*, *Mara*, *Northwest*, and *Centerwest*. They are characterized by the grass growth duration and the maximum grass quantity that can be produced by the land. *Initloc* is the region where the animals are initially placed. The regions are shown in Fig. 2.

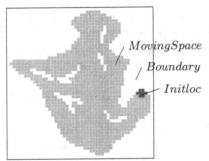

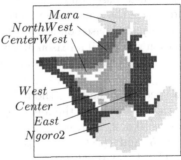

(a) *Boundary* and *MovingSpace* are complementary; *Initloc* is a subset of *Movingspace* where wildebeests were initially located in the simulation.

(b) The regions are defined as the subsets of *MovingSpace* whose different chararteristics of their vegetation (grass).

Fig. 2. Regions defined over the cells.

4.5   Reaction Rules

Firstly the rules were written and their parameters and initial objects were just roughly given. After running several combinations some adjustments were made. Insignificant rules were removed, whereas the ones representing important behaviours were modified by increasing their rates or lengthening/shortening their durations. Death/birth rates were also adjusted to approximate reasonable actual death/birth rates. The initial pathways were as little as possible to prevent animals from being trapped at the corners. Grass' growth parameters were

Table 1. Constants table for rules of life cycle

Stages	$\langle S \rangle$	0	1	2	3	4	5	6	7	8	9
Upstages	$ug\langle S \rangle$	A1	A2	A3	A4	A5	A6	A7	A8	A9	A9
Downstages	$dg\langle S \rangle$	A0	A0	A1	A2	A3	A4	A5	A6	A7	A8
Birthstages	$bs\langle S \rangle$	-	-	-	-	-	-	A3	A4	A6	A7
Birth rates	$br\langle S \rangle$	-	-	-	-	-	-	0.0017	0.0033	0.005	0.008
Death rates (nat.)	$dn\langle S \rangle$	0.05	0.035	0.021	0.015	0.011	0.008	0.006	0.004	0.003	0.002
Death rates (prey)	$dp\langle S \rangle$	0.5	0.35	0.21	0.15	0.11	0.07	0.005	0.003	0.03	0.015
Feeding rates	$fr\langle S \rangle$	1	2	4	6	8	10	15	20	16	0.1

Table 2. Constants table for grass growth

Region	$\langle R \rangle$	Ngorongoro	West	Center	East	Mara	Northwest	Centerwest
Max p. cell	$mg\langle R \rangle$	100	100	30	100	100	100	20
Duration est.	$gr\langle S \rangle$	1	1	15	1	1	1	15

set to assure right direction of migration. Ideally the time frame should be set up before defining parameters. However, the definition of "one year" was eventually justified based on the result instead. Then the migration cycle time length resulted from the simulation was taken as "one year" and finally the parameters were re-adjusted based on it. This method was repeatedly worked through many simulation runs until a reasonable behaviour was produced. The rules and parameters shown below illustrate one example that resulted in a stable migration cycles.

In specifying the rules the following constants are listed in Tables 1 and 2. Also, the rules refer to the following assignments.

$stages = \{0, 1, 2, .., 9\}$, $directions = \{1, 2, .., 8\}$, $declev = \{1, .., 10\}$, $Mnp = 5$, $Mng = 5$, and $\{(dr\langle x \rangle, dc\langle x \rangle) | x = 1..8\} = \{(-1, -1), (-1, 0), (-1, 1), (0, -1), (0, 1), (1, -1), (1, 0), (1, 1)\}$.

Consuming the grass, A becomes B,

$\forall \langle S \rangle \in stages.$ **Feeding**$\langle \mathbf{S} \rangle$: $G \; A\langle S \rangle \xrightarrow[1/4,M]{fr\langle S \rangle} B\langle S \rangle$

if $Feeding\langle S \rangle \in assoc(MovingSpace)$.

Food digesting is needed to create delay after the grass is removed and wellness level increases one level except at $A9$,

$\forall \langle S \rangle \in stages.$ **Digesting**$\langle \mathbf{S} \rangle$: $B\langle S \rangle \xrightarrow{1,M} ug\langle S \rangle$

if $Digesting\langle S \rangle \in assoc(MovingSpace)$.

Being unable to feed because of grass shortage, wellness level decreases one stage except at $A0$,

$\forall \langle S \rangle \in stages.$ **Starving**$\langle \mathbf{S} \rangle$: $A\langle S \rangle \xrightarrow{1/2,M} dg\langle S \rangle$ $[\; \lambda \;|\; G^{Mng/2} \;]$

if $Starving\langle S \rangle \in assoc(MovingSpace)$

Time needed to balance the death propensities,

$$\forall \langle S \rangle \in stages.\ \mathbf{Resting}\langle \mathbf{S} \rangle :\quad A\langle S \rangle \xrightarrow[1/2,M]{1} A\langle S \rangle$$

if $Resting\langle S \rangle \in assoc(MovingSpace)$.

Giving birth only at stages $A6, A7, A8, A9$ with different birth rates; after delivering a baby (at state $A0$) its wellness level decreases three levels,

$$\forall \langle S \rangle \in stages.\ \mathbf{Birth}\langle \mathbf{S} \rangle :\quad A\langle S \rangle \xrightarrow[5,M]{br\langle S \rangle} bs\langle S \rangle\ \ A0\ \ C$$

if $Birth\langle S \rangle \in assoc(MovingSpace)$.

Mortality because of natural factors; more healthy having lower death rate,

$$\forall \langle S \rangle \in stages.\ \mathbf{DeathNat}\langle \mathbf{S} \rangle :\quad A\langle S \rangle \xrightarrow[0.5,M]{dn\langle S \rangle} Ax\quad [\ C^{Mnp}\ \ |\ \lambda\ ]$$

if $DeathNat\langle S \rangle \in assoc(MovingSpace)$.

Mortality because of predators and natural causes due to grazing in a quiet place; the rate is higher than the normal,

$$\forall \langle S \rangle \in stages.\ \mathbf{DeathPred}\langle \mathbf{S} \rangle :\quad A\langle S \rangle \xrightarrow[0.1,M]{dp\langle S \rangle} Ax\quad [\ \lambda\ \ |\ C^{Mnp}\ ]$$

if $DeathPred\langle S \rangle \in assoc(MovingSpace)$.

Decreasing counter C after being mortality,

$$\mathbf{DecCount} :\ Ax\ C \xrightarrow{\infty} \lambda$$

if $DecCount \in assoc(MovingSpace)$.

Initial growth of grass; root R produces one unit of grass H until maximum capacity that the land can produce is reached,

$$\forall \langle R \rangle \in regions.\ \mathbf{Grass}\langle \mathbf{R} \rangle :\quad R \xrightarrow[gr\langle R \rangle,M]{1} R\ H\quad [\ \lambda\ \ |\ G^{mg\langle R \rangle}\ ]$$

if $Grass\langle R \rangle \in assoc(reg\langle R \rangle)$.

Grass growing to be available for future grazing,

$$\mathbf{GrassReady} :\ H \xrightarrow[25,M]{1} G\ \lambda$$

if $GrassReady \in assoc(MovingSpace)$.

Movement along the path unless there is enough grass for grazing,

$$\forall \langle S \rangle \in stages.\ \mathbf{MoveByPath}\langle \mathbf{S} \rangle :$$

$$A\langle S \rangle \xrightarrow{10,M} Ax\ A\langle S \rangle_{path}\ C_{path}\ path^{10} : path\quad [\ \lambda\ \ |\ Z_{path}\ G^{7Mng}\ ]$$

if $MoveByPath\langle S \rangle \in assoc(MovingSpace)$.

Random movement to a place having a plenty of grass (3, 6, and 9 times minimum quantity),

$$\forall \langle G \rangle \in \{3,6,9\}, \forall \langle X \rangle \in directions, \forall \langle S \rangle \in stages.\ \mathbf{MoveToGrass}\langle \mathbf{G} \rangle \langle \mathbf{X} \rangle \langle \mathbf{S} \rangle :$$

$$A\langle S \rangle \xrightarrow[1/2,M]{mr\langle G \rangle} Ax\ A\langle S \rangle_{(dr\langle X \rangle, dc\langle X \rangle)}\ C_{(dr\langle X \rangle, dc\langle X \rangle)}\ path^{pn\langle G \rangle} : (dr\langle X \rangle, dc\langle X \rangle)$$

$$[\ G^{Mng.\langle G \rangle}_{(dr\langle X \rangle, dc\langle X \rangle)}\ \ |\ G^{Mng}\ Z_{(dr\langle X \rangle, dc\langle X \rangle)}\ ]$$

if $MoveToGrass\langle G \rangle \langle X \rangle \langle S \rangle \in assoc(MovingSpace)$, and $\{mr\langle x \rangle | x = 3,6,9\} = \{20,25,35\}$, and $\{pn\langle x \rangle | x = 3,6,9\} = \{10,25,50\}$.

Table 3. Initial numbers of animals according to their levels

Level	A0	A1	A2	A3	A4	A5	A6	A7	A8	A9	Total
Number in a cell	10	10	15	25	30	50	60	75	50	25	350
Number in all cells	80	80	120	200	240	400	480	600	400	200	2800

Movement to a cell with a less dense grouping of animals due to overcrowding, $\forall\langle X\rangle \in directions, \forall\langle S\rangle \in stages.$ **MoveToLessDens$\langle$X$\rangle\langle$S$\rangle$:**

$$A\langle S\rangle \xrightarrow[1/2,M]{4} A\langle S\rangle_{(dr\langle X\rangle, dc\langle X\rangle)} \quad C_{(dr\langle X\rangle, dc\langle X\rangle)} \quad Ax \quad path^7 : (dr\langle X\rangle, dc\langle X\rangle)$$

$$[\ C^{10Mnp}\ C^{Mnp}_{(dr\langle X\rangle, dc\langle X\rangle)}\ |\ C^{5Mnp}_{(dr\langle X\rangle, dc\langle X\rangle)}\ Z_{(dr\langle X\rangle, dc\langle X\rangle)}\ path\ ]$$

if $MoveToLessDens\langle X\rangle\langle S\rangle \in assoc(MovingSpace)$.

Movement to a cell with a more dense grouping of animals due to quietness, $\forall\langle X\rangle \in directions, \forall\langle S\rangle \in stages.$ **MoveToMoreDense$\langle$X$\rangle\langle$S$\rangle$:**

$$A\langle S\rangle \xrightarrow[1/2,M]{8} A\langle S\rangle_{(dr\langle X\rangle, dc\langle X\rangle)} \quad C_{(dr\langle X\rangle, dc\langle X\rangle)} \quad Ax \quad path^7 : (dr\langle X\rangle, dc\langle X\rangle)$$

$$[\ C^{2Mnp}_{(dr\langle X\rangle, dc\langle X\rangle)}\ |\ C^{Mnp}\ Z_{(dr\langle X\rangle, dc\langle X\rangle)}\ C^{10Mnp}_{(dr\langle X\rangle, dc\langle X\rangle)}\ path\ ]$$

if $MoveToMoreDense\langle X\rangle\langle S\rangle \in assoc(MovingSpace)$.

Decaying of 10 % per an interval of time (7 time units),
$\forall\langle P\rangle \in declev.$ **Decay$\langle$P$\rangle$:**

$$path^{\langle P\rangle} \xrightarrow[7,M]{1} path^{\langle P\rangle - 1} \quad [\ \lambda\ |\ path^{ip\langle P\rangle}\ ]$$

if $Decay\langle P\rangle \in assoc(MovingSpace)$, and $\{ip\langle x\rangle | x = 1, .., 10\} = \{2, .., 9, 10, 0\}$.

4.6 Initial Configuration

4.6.1 Initial Population Size and Location
A total population of 2800 wildebeests is initially placed evenly in the cells of *Initloc* region. They were distributed in proportion to their wellness/strength stage, is shown in Table 3.

4.6.2 Grass and Grass Root
The numbers were set according to the figures from previous migration. Each region has a different duration in producing grass available from grazing. Grass growth is bounded to a maximum quantity per cell which is assumed as being caused by the different condition of the soil and water in each region. The following are the initial quantities of grass G per region: *Ngorongoro* 50 (50 %), *West* 40 (40 %), *Northwest* 20 (20 %), *Mara* 20 (20 %), *East* 2 (20 %), *Center* 12 (40 %) and *Centerwest* 2 (10 %).

4.6.3 Initial Pathways
Initially some pathways were placed in some regions especially at the corners (*West*, *Mara* and *East*, to avoid being isolated at the corners), at turning

positions (*East* to the tail of *Ngoro2*), and in *Center* (to force them going downward). Visually the initial pathways are shown in Fig. 4(a).

4.7 Results: Migration Movement

A simulation was run producing several stable cycles of migration. Figure 3 shows each "month" in the second cycle. In the fourth cycle a small group of animals was trapped in the tail part of Ngorongoro. They were mislead since the initial pathways were already overwritten by the new pathways created later. As more groups were being trapped, the size of the overall population was declined. By increasing the decay interval from 7 time units to 20 (to sustain the paths) there were no longer trapped groups until 7 cycles later.

The movement of frontiers were affected by the grass and movement of the followers were affected by the pathways. As the followers moved forward they become the next frontiers. Figure 4 shows the pathways in the beginning ($t = 0$) and at about the end of second cycle ($t = 17$).

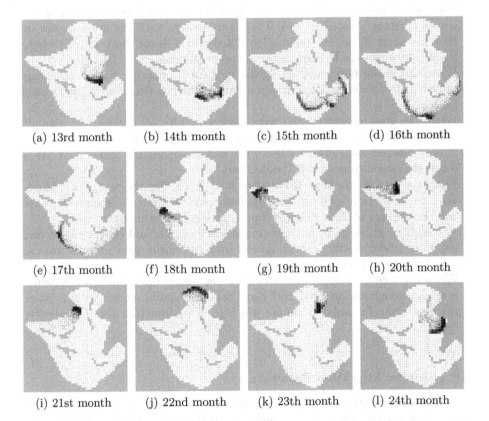

(a) 13rd month   (b) 14th month   (c) 15th month   (d) 16th month

(e) 17th month   (f) 18th month   (g) 19th month   (h) 20th month

(i) 21st month   (j) 22nd month   (k) 23th month   (l) 24th month

Fig. 3. "Monthly" sequence of migration at the second cycle since being started.

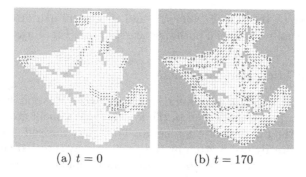

(a) $t = 0$ (b) $t = 170$

Fig. 4. Initial Pathways (at $t = 0$) and pathways at $t = 17$ (about the end of second cycle).

There are some interesting observations from the experiments by changing the rule parameters or adding/removing some other rules.

– When there was no initial pathway, animals were blocked by each other at the corner creating isolated groups. They stayed there until the grass regrew or they just died. Then, the population size declined faster. since in cells where isolated groups were located there was no more grass.

– When the initial pathways were given in a small quantity, similar isolations occurred after those initial pathways decayed. The population size also declined faster.

– When the grass characteristics were made equal for all regions, the animals divided into small groups moving without pattern in the area. Later some groups blocked each others when they met from opposite directions. As a result the overall population size declined.

– When the rate of rule MoveToPath was made exceeding the rate of rule Move-ToGrass, migration sped up, the population spread along the migration route and the average of their wellness dropped, thus increasing death rate.

– When initial grass quantities were made much smaller and the migration had not been realized, the animals spread over the entire grid and the overall population size quickly declined.

– When the rate of random movement was set higher the animals were evenly spread throughout an area and there was no significant migration. Since the death rate for isolated animal was high the population size immediately declined.

4.8 Results: Migration Pathways

The pathways created during the migration (at the end of second cycle) are shown in Fig. 4(b). They can be compared to the initial paths in Fig. 4(a). In each cell the animals passed through pathways were created in almost every direction. However, Fig. 4 shows only the pathway whose weight is greater than

0.30. Figure 4(b) shows that most initial paths were still there. After the fourth cycle most original pathways were overwritten by the new pathways.

5   Discussion

As described previously the model was simplified in some aspects compared to the real situation. The state space for life-cycle could be more complex than our ten-stage life cycle. The topology of the area was not fully represented. The parameters were not based on real-world measurements. The external events (rainfalls, temperature) and water availability which may affect the animal movements were not included. The resulting migration pattern has not been compared with actual migration patterns. However, this modelling effort was carried out with an experimental purpose rather than as a theoretical work of its biological domain. All parameters and behaviours expressed as the rules need to be further validated by the biologists. The main motivation of working on this case was to explore a new feature of the Grid Systems. As seen in the case its modelling required only expressing the behaviours in terms of rules and parameters. A working prototype simulator has been developed and used in our work. It was developed based on the semantics of the Grid Systems.

6   Conclusion and Future Work

A new feature of the Grid Systems is introduced. The new feature is the 'link' which is a special object that can carry pointers. The pointers carried by the links enable modelling the pathways for population movement in a more dynamic way. To illustrate the use of links a case was modelled and the model run using a simulator. The case study refers to a wildebeest population in Serengeti National Park, which performs seasonal migrations around the park area. The simulation of the model imitated the migration.

In our future work we aim at using real data for the same case or for others having similar problem characteristics.

Acknowledgments. This work has been supported by Macao Science and Technology Development Fund, File No. 07/2009/A3, in the context of the EAE project. Suryana Setiawan is supported by a PhD scholarship under I-MHERE Project of the Faculty of Computer Science, University of Indonesia (IBRD Loan No. 4789-IND & IDA Credit No. 4077-IND, Ministry of Education and Culture, Republic of Indonesia).

References

1. Adamatzky, A.: Identification of Cellular Automata. Taylor and Francis, London (1994)
2. Barbuti, R., Maggiolo-Schettini, A., Milazzo, P., Cerone, A., Setiawan, S.: Modelling population dynamics using grid systems. In: MoKMaSD 2012. LNCS, vol. 7991, pp. 172–189. Springer, Heidelberg (2014)

3. Barbuti, R., Maggiolo-Schettini, A., Milazzo, P., Pardini, G., Rama, A.: A process calculus for molecular interaction maps. In: Membrane Computing and Biologically Inspired Process Calculi (MeCBIC), pp. 35–49 (2009)

4. Barbuti, R., Maggiolo-Schettini, A., Milazzo, P., Tini, S.: Compositional semantics and behavioral equivalences for p systems. Theor. Comput. Sci. **395**(1), 77–100 (2008)

5. Barbuti, R., Maggiolo-Schettini, A., Milazzo, P., Tini, S.: A p systems flat form preserving step-by-step behaviour. Fundam. Inform. **87**(1), 1–34 (2008)

6. Barbuti, R., Maggiolo-Schettini, A., Milazzo, P., Tini, S.: An overview on operational semantics in membrane computing. Int. J. Found. Comput. Sci. **22**(1), 119–131 (2011)

7. Boone, R.B., Thirgood, S.J., Hopcraft, J.G.C.: Serengeti wildebeest migratory patterns modeled from rainfall and new vegetation growth. Ecology **87**(8), 1987–1994 (2006)

8. Durier, V., Graham, P., Collett, T.S.: Snapshot memories and landmark guidance in wood ants. Curr. Biol., Elsevier Science Ltd. **13**, 1614–1618 (2003)

9. Gillespie, D.T.: A general method for numerically simulating the stochastic time evolution of coupled chemical reactions. J. Comput. Phys. **22**, 403–434 (1976)

10. Goss, P.J., Peccoud, J.: Quantitative modeling of stochastic system in molecular biology by using Petri Nets. J. Bioinform. Comput. Biol. **95**, 6750–6755 (1990)

11. Holdo, R.M., Holt, R.D., Fryxell, J.M.: Opposing rainfall and plant nutritional gradients best explain the wildebeest migration in the Serengeti. Am. Nat. **173**, 431–445 (2009)

12. Kaupp, U.B., Kashikar, N.D., Weyand, I.: Mechanism of sperm chemotaxis. Ann. Rev. Physiol. **70**, 93–117 (2008)

13. Kohn, K.W., Aladjem, M.I., Weinstein, J.N., Pommier, Y.: Molecule interaction maps of bioregularity networks: a general rubric for systems biology. Mol. Biol. Cell **17**, 1–13 (2005)

14. Lohmann, K.J., Putman, N.F., Lohmann, C.M.F.: Geomagnetic imprinting: a unifying hypothesis of long-distance natal homing in salmon and sea turtles. Proc. Nat. Acad. Sci. **105**(49), 19096–19101 (2008)

15. Milazzo, P.: Qualitative and quantitative formal modeling of biological systems. Ph.D thesis, Università di Pisa (2007)

16. Pardini, G.: Formal modelling and simulation of biological systems with spatiality. Ph.D thesis, Università di Pisa (2011)

17. Priami, C., Regev, A., Silverman, W., Shapiro, E.Y.: Application of a stochastic name-passing calculus to representation and simulation a molecular processes. Inf. Process. Lett. **80**, 25–31 (2001)

18. Păun, G.: Computing with membranes. J. Comput. Syst. Sci. **61**, 108–143 (2000)

19. Regev, A., Silverman, W., Shapiro, E.Y.: Representation and simulation of biochemical processes using the π-calculus process algebra. In: Proceeding of the Pacific Symposium on Biocomputing, pp. 459–470 (2001)

20. Reynolds, C.W.: Flocks, herds, and schools: a distributed behavioral model. Comput. Graph. **21**(4), 25–34 (1987)

21. Rojas, R.: Neural Networks - A Systematic Introduction. Springer, Berlin (1996)

22. Rozenberg, G., Bck, T., Kok, J.: Handbook of Natural Computing. Springer, Heidelberg (2012)

A Computational Formal Model
of the Invasiveness of Eastern Species
in European Water Frog Populations

Roberto Barbuti, Pasquale Bove, Andrea Maggiolo Schettini,
Paolo Milazzo$^{(\boxtimes)}$, and Giovanni Pardini

Dipartimento di Informatica, Università di Pisa,
Largo B. Pontecorvo 3, 56127 Pisa, Italy
{barbuti,bovepas,maggiolo,milazzo,pardinig}@di.unipi.it

Abstract. European water frog populations are mainly composed by
two species: *Pelophylax lessonae* (pool frog) and *Pelophylax esculentus*
(edible frog). These populations are called L-E complexes. Edible frogs
are a hybrid form between *P. lessonae* and *Pelophylax ridibundus* (eastern lake frog) and they reproduce in a particular way, called hybridogenesis. These frog populations have been studied in the contexts of
evolution and speciation. In order to have stability of L-E complexes
(namely self-maintainance of the population structure) some conditions
are necessary. We present a computational formal model of European
water frog population based on a variant of P systems in which evolution rules are applied in a probabilistic maximally parallel manner.
Probabilities of application of rules will be computed on the basis of
parameters to be associated with each rule. By means of our model we
show how the stabilization of L-E complexes can be obtained. In particular, we show how the introduction of translocated eastern lake frogs in
such complexes can lead to the collapse of the populations. The study of
conditions for population stability and of possible threats to endangered
species is of particular importance for the maintenance of biodiversity,
which is an aspect of sustainable development.

1 Introduction

Lake frog (*Pelophylax ridibundus* Pallas, 1771) and pool frog (*Pelophylax
lessonae* Camerano, 1882) can mate producing the hybrid edible frog (*Pelophylax esculentus* Linneus, 1758). The edible frog can coexist with one or both of
the parental species giving rise to mixed populations. Usually the genotypes of
P. ridibundus, *P. lessonae* and *P. esculentus* are indicated by RR, LL, and
LR, respectively. In Europe there are mainly mixed populations containing
P. lessonae and *P. esculentus*, called L-E systems. Hybrids in these populations reproduce in a particular way, called *hybridogenesis* [6]. Hybridogenesis
consists in a particular gametogenetic process in which the hybrids exclude one
of their parental genomes premeiotically, and transmit the other one, clonally,
to eggs and sperm. This particular way of reproduction requires that hybrids

S. Counsell and M. Núñez (Eds.): SEFM 2013 Collocated Workshops, LNCS 8368, pp. 329–344, 2014.
DOI: 10.1007/978-3-319-05032-4_24, © Springer International Publishing Switzerland 2014

Table 1. Reproductive pattern of water frogs

	LL	LR
L_yL	L_yL LL	L_yR LR
L_yR	LR	RR not viable

live sympatrically with the parental species the genome of which is eliminated. In this way hybrids in a L-E system eliminate the L genome thus producing *P. esculentus* when mating with *P. lessonae*, and generating *P. ridibundus* when mating with other hybrids. Usually *P. ridibundus* generated in L-E complexes are inviable due to deleterious mutations accumulated in the clonally transmitted R genome [10,21,24]. Because of inviability of *P. esculentus* × *P. esculentus* offspring, edible frog populations cannot survive alone, but they must act as a sexual parasite of one of the parental species. In L-E complexes the reproductive pattern is the one in Table 1 where the subscribed Y indicates the male sexual chromosome.

Note that the Y chromosome, determining the sex of frog males, can occur only in the L genome, due to primary hybridization which involved, for size constraints, *P. lessonae* males and *P. ridibundus* females. Table 1 shows that only one of the three possible matings resulting in viable offspring produce *LL* genotypes. This would give an advantage to edible frogs which could outnumber *P. lessonae* and eventually eliminate them. This situation would result in an extinction also of *P. esculentus* which cannot survive without the parental species. In addition to their relative abundance which can be promoted by the above reproductive pattern, edible frogs show, by heterosis, a greater fitness than the parental species [2,12,23]. The sum of relative abundance and heterosis should out-compete *P. lessonae* in L-E complexes. The widespread distribution of L-E complexes reveals the existence of mechanisms which contribute to the stability of such complexes, namely to the ability of such populations to self-maintain their structure. Among such mechanisms sexual selection seems to be one of the most important: *P. esculentus* females prefer *P. lessonae* males with respect to males of their own species [1,5,9,19,20]. Many mathematical and computational models were devoted to the study of the influence of sexual selection in the evolution of populations, the models in [11,22] show how female preference is able to stabilize L-E complexes by counterbalancing both heterosis and reproductive advantage of edible frogs.

In this paper we are interested in modelling and simulating the dynamics of L-E complexes. The study of conditions for population stability and of possible threats to endangered species is of particular importance for the maintainace of biodiversity, which is an aspect of sustainable development.

P systems are a model of computation that has recently found new applications as a notation for the modelling of biological systems. We define a minimal variant of P systems that allows the dynamics of such L-E complexes to be formally described. Although defined with a specific example in mind, our variant of P systems will include features that allow it to be used to describe many other kinds of populations. We choose to adopt a formal notation based on P systems for the modelling of L-E complexes rather than directly implementing a computational model by using a general purpose programming language. This allows us to unambiguously define and describe the model. Moreover, in general the use of formal modelling notations for the construction of population models can enable the application of formal analysis tools (such as model checkers and static analysis tools) for the verification of properties of the populations of interest.

We analyze, by means of a P systems model, two aspects of L-E complexes. The first one is why L-E complexes generate almost all inviable *P. ridibundus* offspring. The second one is how female preference can contribute to stabilize the complexes. Finally, we show that the introduction of *P. ridibundus* can destabilize L-E populations. This is a real problem, as pointed out by Vorburger and Reyer in [25]. Their hypothesis is confirmed by our model.

2   A Variant of P Systems for Population Modelling

P systems (also known as *membrane systems*) are a bio-inspired model of computation proposed by G. Păun in [15] in the context of Natural Computing. P systems were originally aimed at investigating the computing capabilities of cells as new unconventional computing architectures. The motivation for such studies was that the extremely high (virtually unbounded) degree of parallelism in biochemical phenomena occurring within cells could have allowed the solution of computationally hard problems in short times. Many theoretical results have been achieved on P systems by considering many different variants of such a formalism (see [14, 16] for an overview).

The formalism of P systems falls in the category of rewriting systems, in which a structure with given characteristics evolves by means of application of some rewriting rules. In the case of P systems, the structure is inspired by the internal structure of cells, namely it consists of a hierarchy of *membranes*. Each membrane is identified by a unique label and in each membrane there can be a multiset of *objects* (representing molecules) that change over time by the application of rewriting rules (called *evolution rules* and representing chemical reactions). Each evolution rule consists of two multisets of objects (representing reactants and products of the described chemical reaction). A rule in a membrane can be applied only to objects in the same membrane. Some objects produced by the rule remain in the same membrane, others are sent *out* of the membrane, others are sent *into* the inner membranes (assumed to exist) which are identified by their labels.

Evolution rules in P systems are (usually) applied with *maximal parallelism*, namely at each step of evolution different rules can be applied at the same time

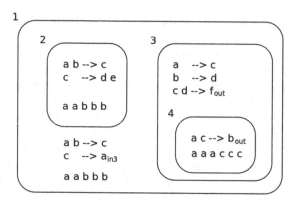

Fig. 1. An example of P system

(on different objects), the same rule can be applied more than once, and it cannot happen that a rule is not applied when the objects needed for its triggering are available (i.e. not used by any other rule). An example of P system is shown in Fig. 1, where membranes are depicted as boxes, objects as letters and evolution rules have the form $u \rightarrow v$, where u is a multiset of objects (reactants) and v is a multiset of object with target indication (products). Note that the target indication of products that remain in the same membrane is omitted.

In the last few years P systems found new applications as notations for the modelling of biological systems. In particular, quantitative extensions of P systems have been proposed that allow biochemical pathways to be suitably described and simulated [3,13,17,18]. In addition, variants of P systems have been applied to the modelling and simulation of populations and ecosystems [7,8].

The variant of P systems we define in this paper includes a minimal set of features necessary to model populations. We consider *flat P systems* [4], namely P systems consisting of a single membrane, since a membrane structure is not useful for our purposes. On the other hand, the key ingredients that we consider are (i) evolution rules with functional rates, (ii) probabilistic maximal parallelism and (iii) rule promoters. The aim of this new variant of P systems is to make modelling of populations easier, by avoiding in the modelling formalism unnecessary functionalities that are present in other similar variants of P systems.

In population models, evolution rules are used to describe events such as reproduction, death, growth, and so on. In general there may be several rules describing one of these events and involving the same individual. For instance, the same female individual may be involved in one of different reproduction rules, one rule for each possible kind of male it can mate with. Some of these rules may be more likely to be applied than others since the events they describe are more likely than others. (For instance, some females may have a sexual preference for some specific kinds of males.) Associating rates with rules allows the latters to be chosen in a probabilistic way, where probabilities are proportional to the rates. Moreover, by allowing rates to be functions, rather than constant values, we have that the probability of applying a rule can depend on the current state of the system (for instance on the size of the population, or on the number of individuals of a specific kind).

Although a form of probabilistic choice for evolution rules has to be considered, maximal parallelism is still useful since it avoids starvation of individuals. Indeed, populations often evolve by stages (e.g. reproduction, selection, etc...) in which (almost) all of the individuals are involved. By combining maximal parallelism with probabilistic choice of reactions we allow the whole population to evolve in a coherent way and, at the same time, each individual to follow its own fate.

Finally, since in each stage of evolution of a population different kinds of event may happen, we need a way to enable different sets of rules depending on the current stage. For instance, during a reproduction stage only reproduction rules should be enabled, whereas during a selection stage only death/survival rules should be enabled. In order to obtain this result we exploit rule promoters, that can be used to enable/disable a set of rules by simply including/removing an object from the state of the system.

We are now ready to define the variant of P systems we use for population modelling. We call it *Minimal Probabilistic P systems (MPP systems)*.

Definition 1 (MPP system). *A* Minimal Probabilistic P system *is a tuple* $\langle V, w_0, R \rangle$ *where:*

- *V is a possibily infinite alphabet of objects, with V^* denoting the universe of all multisets having V as support.*
- *$w_0 \in V^*$ is a multiset describing the initial state of the system*
- *R is a finite set of evolution rules having the form*

$$u \xrightarrow{f} v \mid_p$$

where $u, v, p \in V^*$ are multisets (often denoted without brackets) of reactants, products *and* promoters, *respectively, and $f : V^* \mapsto \mathbb{R}^{\geq 0}$ is a rate function.*

A state (or configuration) of a MPP system is a multiset of objects in V^*. By definition, the initial state is w_0. We denote a generic state of the system as w. Moreover, we denote with $|w|$ the size (number of objects) of the multiset w, and with $|w|_a$ the number of instances of object a contained in multiset w.

The evolution of a MPP system is given by a sequence of probabilistic maximally parallel steps. In each step a maximal multiset of evolution rule instances is selected and applied as described by Algorithm 1. Given w the current system state, the algorithm copies w into x, and then iteratively selects and applies applicable rules. At each iteration, one of the applicable rules (the set of which is denoted R') is probabilistically chosen. The probability of each rule to be chosen is proportional to the rate value obtained by applying its rate function to the current state w. Once a rule is selected, its application consists in removing its reactants from x and adding its products into y. The latter multiset will collect

---

Algorithm 1. Probabilistic maximally parallel evolution step

---

function STEP(w)

    $x = w$

    $y = \emptyset$

    while there exists $u \xrightarrow{f} v \mid_p$ in R s.t. $u \subseteq x$ and $p \subseteq w$ **do**

        $R' = \{u \xrightarrow{f} v \mid_p \in R \mid u \subseteq x \text{ and } p \subseteq w\}$

        choose $u' \xrightarrow{f'} v' \mid_{p'}$ from R' with a probability proportional to $f'(w)$

        $x = x \setminus u'$

        $y = y \cup v'$

    end while

    return $x \cup y$

end function

---

all products of all applied rules. Such products are not immediately added to x to avoid the application of a rule at the i-th iteration to consume objects produced by a rule applied in a previous iteration. Indeed, this iterative procedure simulates a parallel application of rules in which the reactions are applied all at the same time (their products are available only at the next parallel step). Once objects in x are such that no further rule in R can be applied to them, the algorithm stops iterating and returns the new state of the system $x \cup y$ (where x are the unused objects and y are the new products). Note that in order to determine (in the guard of the loop and in the definition of R') whether a rule is applicable reactants are checked to be contained in x (the remaining objects) while promoters are checked to be present in w (the system state at the beginning of the iteration).

Example 1. We consider a MPP system representing a reproductive event in a sexual population with XY sex-determination system. In the initial population there are females (f) and two types of males (m_1, m_2). Suppose that females prefer m_1 males with a preference value of 0.7, while they mate with m_2 males with a preference value of 0.3. We consider that the different traits of m_1 and m_2 are coded on the Y sexual chromosome. Thus the males in the offspring produced by m_1 and m_2 males are of kind m_1 and m_2, respectively. We consider also that each mating generates a single juvenile. The actual matings, in addition to female preferences depend on the availability of the two kinds of males.

    The MPP system representing the described reproductive event is the triple $\langle V_{fm}, w_{0fm}, R_{fm} \rangle$. The alphabet V_{fm} is defined as follows:

$$V_{fm} = \{f, m_1, m_2, f^j, m_1^j, m_2^j\}$$

where the j superscript indicates juveniles.

    The set of reproduction rules R_{fm} contains the following rules:

$$f\ m_1 \xrightarrow{f_{m_1}} f\ m_1\ f^j \qquad f\ m_1 \xrightarrow{f_{m_1}} f\ m_1\ m_1^j$$

$$f\ m_2 \xrightarrow{f_{m_2}} f\ m_1\ f^j \qquad f\ m_2 \xrightarrow{f_{m_2}} f\ m_1\ m_2^j$$

where $f_{m_1}(w) = 0.7 \cdot |w|_{m_1} \cdot 0.5$ and $f_{m_2}(w) = 0.3 \cdot |w|_{m_2} \cdot 0.5$. Note that the result of $f_{m_1}(w)$ is given by the preference of females for m_1 males multiplied by the number of m_1 males in the population and the probabilty of producing a male or a female (0.5). $f_{m_2}(w)$ is analogous.

Given the following initial population:

$$w_{0fm} = m_1, m_1, m_1, m_2, m_2, m_2, f, f, f, f, f, f, f, f$$

we obtain the following rates: $f_{m_1}(w_{0fm}) = 1.05$ and $f_{m_2}(w_{0fm}) = 0.45$. Note that two females cannot find a partner for reproduction in this event because there are not enough males.

3 Population Dynamics of L-E Complexes

In this section we study the dynamics of European water frog populations. In particular, we show that female preferences and the inviabilty of *P. ridibundus* offspring can stabilize L-E complexes. Moreover, we show how the introduction of translocated *P. ridibundus* in stable L-E complexes can lead to the collapse of the systems.

3.1 Deleterious Mutations and Female Preferences are Necessary for the Stability of L-E Complexes

The MPP systems model. We model a L-E complex by means of a MPP system $\langle V_{LE}, w_{0LE}, R_{LE} \rangle$ in which each individual of the population is represented by an object in the state of the system. Hence, the alphabet V_{LE} contains one object for each possible genotype of an individual. We use different objects for juveniles (immature individuals) and adults. Moreover, the alphabet includes some control objects used to realize alternation of reproduction and selection stages. As a consequence, we define $V_{LE} = V_{LEa} \cup V_{LEj} \cup V_{ctrl}$, where V_{LEa} represents adults, V_{LEj} represents juveniles and V_{ctrl} are control objects.

Since the R genome may contain a deleterious mutation or not, we use different objects for representing *P. esculentus* and *P. ridibundus* individuals carrying or not a mutation in their genotype. Thus, the alphabet representing adults is

$$V_{LEa} = \{\, LL\,,\, L_yL\,,\, LR_*\,,\, L_yR_*\,,\, LR_\circ\,,\, L_yR_\circ\,,\, R_*R_\circ\,,\, R_\circ R_\circ \,\}$$

where y represents the Y chromosome, and $*$ and $\circ$ represent the presence and the absence of a deleterious mutation, respectively. Note that according to the reproductive pattern of L-E complexes in Table 1 males with RR genotypes cannot be produced in a L-E complex. Moreover, note that object $R_\circ R_*$ is not present in V_{LEa} since the individual it represents is indistinguishable from the one represented by $R_*R_\circ$, and hence we use only one object to represent it.

The alphabet representing juveniles is

$$V_{LEj} = \{\, LL^j\,,\, L_yL^j\,,\, LR_*^j\,,\, L_yR_*^j\,,\, LR_\circ^j\,,\, L_yR_\circ^j\,,\, R_*R_*^j\,,\, R_*R_\circ^j\,,\, R_\circ R_\circ^j \,\}$$

where j denotes that the individual is a juvenile, and the other notations are as before. Note that $R_*R_*^j$ is allowed although it represents non viable genotype since in our model individuals with such a genotype will be allowed to be born, but they will not be allowed to become adults.

Finally, the alphabet of control objects is

$$V_{ctrl} = \mathbb{N} \cup \{REPR, SEL\}$$

where $REPR$ and SEL represent reproduction and selection stages, respectively, and natural numbers will be used as objects regulating the alternance of the two considered stages.

The set of evolution rules R_{LE} contains reproduction, selection and control rules. Hence, we have $R_{LE} = R_{LEr} \cup R_{LEs} \cup R_{ctrl}$.

Reproduction rules R_{LEr} are of the following form:

$$x\ y\ \xrightarrow{f_{xy}}\ x\ y\ z\ |_{REPR}$$

where $x \in V_{LEa}$ is any object representing a female and $y \in V_{LEa}$ is any object representing a male. Function f_{xy} gives the rate of mating of females of type x with males of type y by taking into account the sexual preferences of x females and the quantities of individuals of types x and y. In particular, given a multiset of object w (a system state), we have

$$f_{xy}(w) = k_{mate}(x, y) \cdot |w|_x \cdot |w|_y \cdot 1/k_{o\_kind}(x, y)$$

where $k_{mate}(x, y)$ is the preference of a female x for a male y, and $k_{o\_kind}(x, y)$ is the number of possible offspring kinds that can be generated by the mating of x with y. Remark that $1/k_{o\_kind}(x, y)$ distributes the rate of the mating event of x and y over the rules for this mating.

Finally, $z \in V_{LEj}$ is an object representing the newborn, and it is related with x and y as described in Table 1. For example, for $x = LL$ and $y = L_yL$ there are two rules, one with $z = L_yL^j$ and the other with $z = LL^j$. On the other hand, for $x = LR_*$ and $y = L_yR_o$ there is one single rule with $z = R_*R_o^j$. As a consequence, $k_{o\_kind}(LL, L_yL) = 2$ whereas $k_{o\_kind}(LR_*, L_yR_o) = 1$. The other combinations of x and y are analogous. The full list of reproduction rules is in the pre-proceedings version of this paper.

As regards selection rules R_{LEs}, they contain two rules for each individual of the population describing its survival and its death during the selection stage, respectively. The presence of these two rules for each type of individual together with maximal parallelism ensure that during a selection stage each individual will be faced with the two fates.

Survival and death rules are of the forms that follow. For each object $x \in V_{LEa}$ representing an adult individual we have:

$$x\ \xrightarrow{g_x}\ x\ |_{SEL} \qquad x\ \xrightarrow{g_x'}\ \epsilon\ |_{SEL}$$

where ϵ represent the empty multiset and g_x and g_x' give the probability of survival and death, respectively, of an individual of type x. Function g_x takes into account the size of the population, the carrying capacity of the environment and the fitness of the individual. More precisely, given $w \in V^*$ representing a system state, parameter cc representing the carrying capacity of the environment and parameter $k_{fit}(x)$ representing the fitness of individuals of type x, we have:

$$g_x(w) = \frac{1}{1 + \frac{|w|}{k_{fit}(x) \cdot cc}}$$

Function g'_x is such that for all $w \in V^*$ it holds $g'_x(w) = 1 - g_x(w)$.

For each object $x^j \in (V_{LEj} \setminus \{R_* R^j_*\})$ representing a juvenile (but not $R_* R^j_*$) we have:

$$x^j \xrightarrow{g_{x^j}} x \mid_{SEL} \qquad x^j \xrightarrow{g'_{x^j}} \epsilon \mid_{SEL}$$

where $x \in V_{LE}$ is the object representing the adult of the same type of x^j, and ϵ, g_{x^j} and g'_{x^j} are as before. In the case of $R_* R^j_*$ we consider only the death rule, since such a kind of juvenile is considered too unfit to be able to grow up. Hence, we have only

$$R_* R^j_* \xrightarrow{f_1} \epsilon \mid_{SEL}$$

where for all $w \in V^*$ it holds $f_1(w) = 1$.

Finally, as regards control rules R_{ctrl}, they are responsible for the appearance and disappearance of objects $REPR$ and SEL in order to activate alternatively reproduction and selection rules. For the sake of simplicity, we assume that the offspring of each female in each reproduction stage are exactly n. We also assume that each of the offspring is the result of a different mating (this is a very rough simplification that however should not change significantly the global population dynamics). Hence, the object $REPR$ has to be present for n subsequent steps, then it has to be replaced by SEL for one step, and these $n+1$ steps should be iterated forever. This result is obtained by ensuring that $REPR$ is in the initial state of the system and by using the following control rules:

$$1 \xrightarrow{f_1} 2 \qquad 2 \xrightarrow{f_1} 3 \qquad \cdots \qquad (n-1) \xrightarrow{f_1} n$$

$$n\, REPR \xrightarrow{f_1} SEL \qquad SEL \xrightarrow{f_1} 1\, REPR$$

where, as before, for all $w \in V^*$ it holds $f_1(w) = 1$.

The initial state w_{0LE} of the MPP system will change in different simulations. In general, it will contain the control objects 1 and $REPR$, and one object for each individual present in the considered initial population.

Parameters. In order to perform simulations we consider the following initial parameters (some of them will be changed later on).

- No sexual preference: for every female x and male y we have $k_{mate}(x, y) = 1$.
- 10 % higher fitness for hybrids (heterosis effect), namely

$$k_{fit}(x) = \begin{cases} 0.55 & \text{if } x \in \{ LyR_* \; LyR_\circ \; LyR^j_* \; LyR^j_\circ \} \\ 0.5 & \text{if } x \in V_{LEa} \setminus \{ LyR^j_* \; LyR^j_\circ \}. \end{cases}$$

– The carrying capacity cc is set to 400.
– The number of reproduction stages n is set to 3.

Results. We study the stability of L-E complexes by considering populations without deleterious mutations in the R genome of *P. esculentus*. We performed 1000 simulations with initial populations composed by *P. lessonae* frogs and a percentages of 10% of mutation-free edible frogs. The initial state of the system is hence described by the multiset w_{0LE} consisting of 90 instances of LL, 90 of L_yL, 10 of $LR_\circ$, 10 of $L_yR_\circ$ and of the control objects 1 and $REPR$.

We observe that, in all the simulations, the population evolves towards a mono-specific population of viable all-females *P. ridibundus* which eventually collapses for the absence of males (recall that the Y chromosome can occur only on the L genome). Figure 2 shows the outcome of a typical simulation. If viable *P. ridibundus* females are produced, the reproductive pattern becomes the

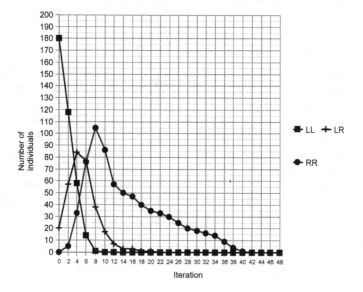

Fig. 2. Result of a simulation of a L-E complex without deleterious mutations.

Table 2. Reproductive pattern of water frogs without deleterious mutations.

	LL		LR		RR	
L_yL	L_yL	LL	L_yR	L_R	L_yR	L_R
L_yR	LR		RR		RR	

one depicted in Table 2. Edible frogs are numerically advantaged from possible mating between *P. ridibundus* females and *P. lessonae* males. It is clear from the table that this reproductive pattern generates a numerical disadvantage for pool frogs, the population of which decreases. The decrease in the *P. lessonae* population has, as a consequence, a decrease of produced L gametes, which, in turn, results in a bigger production of lake frogs. Thus the population of *P. ridibundus* females grows and eventually they out-compete the other species.

Let us now consider an initial population with the same percentages of edible frogs (10 %), but in which all the *P. esculentus* individuals carry the deleterious mutations on the R genome, that is *P. ridibundus* females are not viable and they do not appear in the population. The initial state of the system is hence described by the multiset w_{0LE} consisting of 90 instances of LL, 90 of L_yL, 10 of $LR_\circ$, 10 of L_yR_* and of the control objects 1 and $REPR$.

We performed 1000 simulations. We observe that also in this case the population collapses in all simulations. The cause of the collapse is due to the fact that both the reproductive pattern of Table 1 and the greater fitness of edible frogs give an advantage to *P. esculentus* frogs forcing the complex towards a mono-specific population. A population with *P. esculentus* alone cannot survive. Figure 3 shows the outcome of a typical simulation in this case.

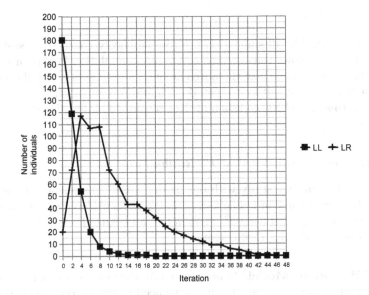

Fig. 3. Result of a simulation of a L-E complex with deleterious mutations.

Finally we introduce in the population a female preference towards L_yL males (observed experimentally in [1,9,20]). In particular, we set $k_{mate}(LL, L_yL) = 6$ and $k_{mate}(LR, L_yL) = 2$. Also in this case we performed 1000 simulations with the same initial state as before.

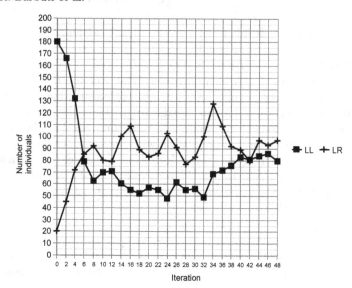

Fig. 4. Result of a simulation of a L-E complex with deleterious mutations and sexual selection.

We observe that in all simulation the complex evolves towards a stable L-E complex. Figure 4 shows the outcome of a typical simulation in this case.

Note that we do not show the outcome of simulations in a population with female preferences but without deleterious mutations in the R genome. Actually, also in this case the population evolves towards a all-females *P. ridibundus* population.

3.2 Invasion of Translocated *P. Ridibundus*

The main point that we study with our model is the consequence of the introduction of *P. ridibundus* in stable L-E complexes. *P. ridibundus* can mate both with *P. esculentus*, producing *P. ridibundus*, and with *P. lessonae* (primary hybridization), producing *P. esculentus*.

The MPP Systems Model. In order to study the dynamics of a L-E complex in which *P.ridibundus* can be introduced we need to extend our previous model (defined in Sect. 3.1). Indeed, we need to include in the model objects and rules describing the behaviour of *P.ridibundus* males.

Consequently, we define a MPP system $\langle V_{LER}, w_{0LER}, R_{LER} \rangle$ where $V_{LER} = V_{LERa} \cup V_{LERj} \cup V_{ctrl}$ and $R_{LER} = R_{LERr} \cup R_{LERs} \cup R_{ctrl}$, where, in turn, we have:

$- V_{LERa} = \{LL, L_y L, LR_*, L_y R_*, LR_\circ, L_y R_\circ, R_* R_\circ, R_{y*} R_\circ, R_{y\circ} R_*,$
$R_\circ R_\circ, R_{y\circ} R_\circ\}$

- $V_{LERj} = \{LL^j, L_yL^j, LR_*^j, L_yR_*^j, LR_o^j, L_yR_o^j, R_*R_*^j, R_{y*}R_*^j, R_*R_o^j,$
  $R_{y*}R_o^j, R_{yo}R_*^j, R_oR_o^j, R_{yo}R_o^j\}$
- R_{LERr} and R_{LERs} extend R_{LEr} and R_{LEs}, respectively, with analogous rules
  for *P.ridibundus* males
- V_{ctrl} and R_{ctrl} are as before

Note that, given the impossibility of mating between *P. ridibundus* male with *P. lessonae* females (for size reasons), L_*R_{yo} individuals cannot be produced. Note also that in reproduction rules involving *P.ridibundus* males with one mutation, namely R_*R_{yo} we have to consider more possibilities for the genotype of the offspring than in the previous cases. Indeed, by means of recombination a male of this type can produce four kinds of gametes: R_*, R_o, R_{y*} and R_{yo}.

The full list of reproduction rules is in the pre-proceedings version of this paper.

Parameters. In order to perform simulations we consider the following initial parameters (some of them will be changed later on) that we know, for the previous model, could lead to a stable L-E complex if deleterious mutations are present.

- Sexual preference:

$$k_{mate}(x,y) = \begin{cases} 6 & \text{if } x = LL \text{ and } y = L_yL \\ 2 & \text{if } x \in \{LR_*, LR_o\} \text{ and } y = L_yL \\ 0 & \text{if } x = LL \text{ and } y \in \{R_{y*}R_o, R_{yo}R_*, R_{yo}R_o\} \\ 1 & \text{otherwise} \end{cases}$$

- 10 % higher fitness for hybrids (heterosis effect), namely

$$k_{fit}(x) = \begin{cases} 0.55 & \text{if } x \in \{LyR_* \, LyR_o \, LyR_*^j \, LyR_o^j\} \\ 0.5 & \text{if } x \in V_{LEa} \setminus \{LyR_*^j \, LyR_o^j\}. \end{cases}$$

- The carrying capacity cc is set to 400.
- The number of reproduction stages n is set to 3.

Results. We performed 1000 simulations with initial populations composed by 80 % of *P. lessonae* frogs, 15 % of mutation-free edible frogs and 5 % of *P. ridibundus* frogs. The initial state of the system is hence described by the multiset w_{0LER} consisting of 80 instances of LL, 80 of L_yL, 15 of LR_*, 15 of L_yR_*, 5 of R_oR_o, 5 of $R_{yo}R_o$, and of the control objects 1 and $REPR$.

The results in this case are of two kinds: 73 % of simulations result in a monospecific *P. ridibundus* population while 27 % of simulations result in a collapse of the whole population. Figure 5 and 6 show typical population dynamics. Because the introduce lake frogs are mutation-free and because they can mate with *P.*

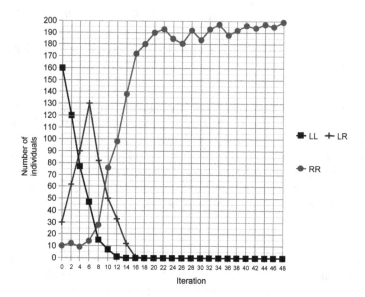

Fig. 5. Simulation of invasion leading to replacement of the population by lake *P. ridibundus* frogs.

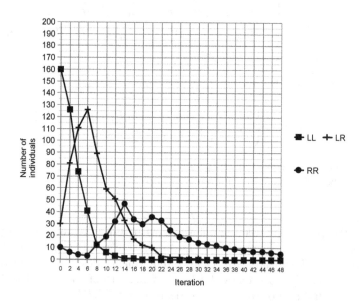

Fig. 6. Simulation of invasion leading to replacement of the population by lake *P. ridibundus* frogs.

esculentus frogs, deleterious mutations are gradually purged. Thus, the population evolves towards a mono-specific *P. ridibundus* system. In this situation, if males are present, the *P. ridibundus* population can survive, otherwise it will collapse. The survival of *P. ridibundus* males is threatened by female preferences towards *LL* males and the advantage of *P. esculentus* for their heterosis. In all cases, the initial L-E complex is destroyed, as predicted in [25].

4 Conclusions

In this paper we have faced the ecological problem of stability European water frog populations. We have shown how female preferences and deleterious mutations stabilize L-E complexes and also how the introduction of translocated *P. ridibundus* frogs can destroy such complexes. For modelling this phenomena we have used a variant of P systems and we have shown their suitability for describing real macroscopic ecological systems.

References

1. Abt, G., Reyer, H.U.: Mate choice and fitness in a hybrid frog: rana esculenta females prefer Rana lessonae males over their own. Behav. Ecol. Sociobiol. **32**(4), 221–228 (1993)
2. Anholt, B.R., Hotz, H., Guex, G.D., Semlitsch, R.D.: Overwinter survival of Rana lessonae and its hemiclonal associate Rana esculenta. Ecology **84**(2), 391–397 (2003)
3. Barbuti, R., Maggiolo-Schettini, A., Milazzo, P., Pardini, G., Tesei, L.: Spatial p systems. Nat. Comput. **10**(1), 3–16 (2011)
4. Barbuti, R., Maggiolo-Schettini, A., Milazzo, P., Tini, S.: A p systems flat form preserving step-by-step behaviour. Fundamenta Informaticae **87**(1), 1–34 (2008)
5. Bergen, K., Semlitsch, R.D., Reyer, H.U.: Hybrid female matings are directly related to the availability of rana lessonae and rana esculenta males in experimental populations. Copeia **1997**(2), 275–283 (1997)
6. Berger, L.: Systematics and hybridization in European green frogs of Rana esculenta complex. J. Herpetol. **7**(1), 1–10 (1973)
7. Besozzi, D., Cazzaniga, P., Pescini, D., Mauri, G.: Modelling metapopulations with stochastic membrane systems. Biosystems **91**(3), 499–514 (2008)
8. Cardona, M., Colomer, M.A., Margalida, A., Palau, A., Pérez-Hurtado, I., Pérez-Jiménez, M.J., Sanuy, D.: A computational modeling for real ecosystems based on p systems. Nat. Comput. **10**(1), 39–53 (2011)
9. Engeler, B., Reyer, H.U.: Choosy females and indiscriminate males: mate choice in mixed populations of sexual and hybridogenetic water frogs (Rana lessonae, Rana esculenta). Behav. Ecol. **12**(5), 600–606 (2001)
10. Guex, G.D., Hotz, H., Semlitsch, R.D.: Deleterious alleles and differential viability in progeny of natural hemiclonal frogs. Evolution **56**(5), 1036–1044 (2002)
11. Hellriegel, B., Reyer, H.U.: Factors influencing the composition of mixed populations of a hemiclonal hybrid and its sexual host. J. Evol. Biol. **13**(6), 906–918 (2000)

12. Hotz, H., Semlitsch, R.D., Gutmann, E., Guex, G.D., Beerli, P.: Spontaneous heterosis in larval life-history traits of hemiclonal frog hybrids. Proc. Nat. Acad. Sci. **96**(5), 2171–2176 (1999)
13. Manca, V., Bianco, L.: Biological networks in metabolic p systems. BioSystems **91**(3), 489–498 (2008)
14. Păun, G.: Membrane Computing: An Introduction. Natural Computing Series Natural Computing. Springer, Heidelberg (2002)
15. Păun, G.: Computing with membranes. J. Comput. Syst. Sci. **61**(1), 108–143 (2000)
16. Paun, G., Rozenberg, G., Salomaa, A.: The Oxford Handbook of Membrane Computing. Oxford University Press Inc., Oxford (2010)
17. Pérez-Jiménez, M.J., Romero-Campero, F.J.: P systems, a new computational modelling tool for systems biology. Trans. on Comput. Syst. Biol. VI. LNBI, vol. 4220, pp. 176–197. Springer, Heidelberg (2006)
18. Pescini, D., Besozzi, D., Mauri, G., Zandron, C.: Dynamical probabilistic p systems. Int. J. Found. Comput. Sci. **17**(01), 183–204 (2006)
19. Reyer, H., Frei, G., Som, C.: Cryptic female choice: frogs reduce clutch size when amplexed by undesired males. Proc. R. Soc. Lond. B Biol. Sci. **266**(1433), 2101–2107 (1999)
20. Roesli, M., Reyer, H.U.: Male vocalization and female choice in the hybridogenetic Rana lessonae/ Rana esculenta complex. Anim. Behav. **60**(6), 745–755 (2000)
21. Semlitsch, R.D., Schmiedehausen, S., Hotz, H., Beerli, P.: Genetic compatibility between sexual and clonal genomes in local populations of the hybridogenetic Rana esculenta complex. Evol. Ecol. **10**(5), 531–543 (1996)
22. Som, C., Anholt, B.R., Reyer, H.U.: The effect of assortative mating on the coexistence of a hybridogenetic waterfrog and its sexual host. Am. Nat. **156**(1), 34–46 (2000)
23. Tejedo, M., Semlitsch, R.D., Hotz, H.: Differential morphology and jumping performance of newly metamorphosed frogs of the hybridogenetic Rana esculenta complex. J. Herpetol. **34**(2), 201–210 (2000)
24. Vorburger, C.: Fixation of deleterious mutations in clonal lineages: evidence from hybridogenetic frogs. Evolution **55**(11), 2319–2332 (2001)
25. Vorburger, C., Reyer, H.U.: A genetic mechanism of species replacement in european waterfrogs? Conserv. Genet. **4**(2), 141–155 (2003)

Process Ordering in a Process Calculus for Spatially-Explicit Ecological Models

Anna Philippou and Mauricio Toro[✉]

Department of Computer Science, University of Cyprus, Nicosia, Cyprus
{annap,mtoro}@cs.ucy.ac.cy

Abstract. In this paper we extend PALPS, a process calculus proposed for the spatially-explicit individual-based modeling of ecological systems, with the notion of a *policy*. A policy is an entity for specifying orderings between the different activities within a system. It is defined externally to a PALPS model as a partial order which prescribes the precedence order between the activities of the individuals of which the model is comprised. The motivation for introducing policies is twofold: one the one hand, policies can help to reduce the state-space of a model; on the other hand, they are useful for exploring the behavior of an ecosystem under different assumptions on the ordering of events within the system. To take account of policies, we refine the semantics of PALPS via a transition relation which prunes away executions that do not respect the defined policy. Furthermore, we propose a translation of PALPS into the probabilistic model checker PRISM. We illustrate our framework by applying PRISM on PALPS models with policies for conducting simulation and reachability analysis.

1 Introduction

Population ecology is a sub-field of ecology that deals with the dynamics of species populations and their interactions with the environment. Its main aim is to understand how the population sizes of species change over time and space. It has been of special interest to conservation scientists and practitioners who are interested in predicting how species will respond to specific management schemes and in guiding the selection of reservation sites and reintroduction efforts, e.g. [12,21].

One of the main streams of today's theoretical ecology is the *individual-based* approach to modeling population dynamics. In this approach, the modeling unit is that of a *discrete individual* and a system is considered as the composition of individuals and their environment. Since individuals usually move from one location to another, it is common in individual-based modeling to represent

This work was carried out during the tenure by the second author of an ERCIM "Alain Bensoussan" Fellowship Programme. The research leading to these results has received funding from the European Union Seventh Framework Programme (FP7/2007-2013) under grant agreement no 246016.

S. Counsell and M. Núñez (Eds.): SEFM 2013 Collocated Workshops, LNCS 8368, pp. 345–361, 2014.
DOI: 10.1007/978-3-319-05032-4_25, © Springer International Publishing Switzerland 2014

space explicitly. There are four distinct frameworks in which *spatially-explicit individual-based models* can be defined [4] which differ on whether space and time are treated discretely or continuously. The four resulting frameworks have been widely studied in Population ecology and they are considered to complement as opposed to compete with each other.

In this paper, we extend our previous work on a process-calculus framework for the spatially-explicit modeling of ecological systems. Our process calculus, PALPS, follows the individual-based modeling and, in particular, it falls in the discrete-time, discrete-space class of Berec's taxonomy [4]. The extension presented in this paper is related to the issue of *process ordering*. In particular, simulations carried out by ecologists often impose an order on the events that may take place within a model. For instance, if we consider mortality and reproduction within a single-species model, three cases exist: concurrent ordering, reproduction preceding mortality and reproduction following mortality. In *concurrent ordering*, different individuals may reproduce and die simultaneously. For *reproduction preceding mortality*, the population first reproduces, then all individuals, including new offspring, are exposed to death. For *reproduction following mortality*, individuals are first exposed to death and, subsequently, surviving individuals are able to reproduce. Ordering can have significant implications on the simulation. Thus, alternatives must be carefully studied so that the ordering that best matches the observed behavior of the actual ecosystem can be concluded (see e.g. [27]).

In order to capture process ordering in PALPS, we define the notion of a *policy*, an entity that imposes an order on the various events that may take place within a system. Formally, a policy σ is defined as a partial order on the set of events in the system where, by writing $(\alpha, \beta) \in \sigma$, we specify that whenever there is a choice between executing the activities α and β, β is chosen. As a result, a policy is defined externally to a process description. This implies that one may investigate the behavior of a system under different event orderings simply by redefining the desired policy without redeveloping the system's description. To capture policies in the semantics of PALPS we extend its transition relation into a *prioritized* transition relation which prunes away all transitions that do not respect the defined policy.

Furthermore, we present a methodology for analyzing models of PALPS *with policies* via the probabilistic model checker PRISM [1]. To achieve this, we define a translation of PALPS *with policies* into the PRISM language and we prove its correctness. We then apply our methodology on simple examples and we demonstrate the types of analysis that can be performed on PALPS models via the PRISM tool. By contrasting our results with our previous work of [24], we observe that policies may achieve a significant reduction in the size of models and may thus enable the analysis of larger systems.

Various formal frameworks have been proposed in the literature for modeling biological and ecological systems. One strand is based, like PALPS, on process calculi, and constitute extensions of calculi such as CCS [17], the π-calculus [18] and CSP [13]. Examples include [6,9,15,26,29]. A different approach is that of

P systems [25], conceived as a class of distributed and parallel computing inspired by the compartmental structure and the functioning of living cells. P-systems have been extended in various directions and they have been applied to a wide range of applications including the field of ecology [5, 7, 20, 22]. Finally, we mention the calculus of looping sequences [3], and its spatial extension [2], *synchronous automata* [11] and *cellular automata* [8]. Similarly to ecosystem modeling carried out by Ecologists, these approaches differ in their treatment of time and space and can be considered as supplements as opposed to rivals as each offers a distinct view and different techniques for analyzing systems. In particular, the discrete-time approach, also adopted in PALPS, has proved useful and appropriate for studying predator-prey systems, epidemiology systems, and for studying population dynamics in other types of ecological systems in frameworks such as WSCCS [14] and P-Systems [5, 7].

Regarding the notion of policies employed in PALPS *with policies*, we point out that they are essentially a type of priorities usually referred to in the process-algebra literature as *static priority relations* (see e.g. [10]) and are similar to the priorities defined for P-Systems. In comparison to related works, as far as we know, PALPS *with policies* is the first spatially-explicit formalism for ecological systems that includes the notion of priority and employs this notion to experiment with different process orderings within process descriptions. Furthermore, via the translation to the PRISM language our framework enables to carry out more advanced analysis of ecological models than just simulation, which is the main approach adopted in the related literature. Possible analysis techniques are those supported by the PRISM tool and include model-checking, reachability analysis as well as computing expected behavior.

Structure of the paper. The structure of the remainder of the paper is as follows. In Sect. 2 we present the syntax and the semantics of PALPS *with policies* and we illustrate the expressiveness of the calculus via a number of examples. In Sect. 3 we sketch a translation of PALPS into the Markov-decision-process component of the PRISM language. We then apply our methodology on simple examples and we explore the potential of the approach in Sect. 4. Section 5 concludes the paper. For the full exposition of the PRISM translation and its correctness proof the reader is referred to [23].

2   The Process Calculus

In this section, we extend our previous work on the process calculus PALPS with the notion of a *policy*. A policy is an entity that accompanies the process description of a system and specifies precedence orders between the various activities that may take place within the system. In this section we review the syntax and semantics of PALPS, and we describe how policies are defined and how they affect the semantics of the framework. We illustrate the calculus via simple examples. For a more thorough presentation of PALPS and further examples the reader is referred to [23, 24].

2.1   The Syntax

In PALPS, we consider a system as a set of individuals operating in space, each belonging to a certain species and inhabiting a location. This location may be associated with attributes which describe characteristics of the location and can be used to define location-dependent behavior of individuals. Furthermore, individuals who reside at the same location may communicate with each other upon channels, e.g. for preying, or they may migrate to a new location. PALPS models probabilistic events with the aid of a probabilistic operator and uses a discrete treatment of time.

The syntax of PALPS is based on the following basic entities: (1) **S** is a set of species ranged over by $\mathbf{s}$, $\mathbf{s}'$. (2) **Loc** is a set of locations ranged over by ℓ, ℓ'. The habitat of a system is then implemented via a relation **Nb**, where $(\ell, \ell') \in \mathbf{Nb}$ exactly when locations ℓ and ℓ' are neighbors. For convenience, we use **Nb** as a function and write $\mathbf{Nb}(\ell)$ for the set of all neighbors of ℓ. (3) **Ch** is a set of channels ranged over by lower-case strings. (4) Ψ is a set of attributes, ranged over by ψ, ψ'. We write ψ_ℓ for the value of attribute ψ at location ℓ. Attributes may capture characteristics of a location e.g. its capacity or its temperature.

PALPS employs two sets of expressions: *logical expressions*, ranged over by e, and *arithmetic expressions*, ranged over by w. They are constructed as follows

$$e ::= true | \neg e | e_1 \wedge e_2 | w \bowtie c$$
$$w ::= c | \psi @ \ell^\star | \mathbf{s} @ \ell^\star | \mathbf{op}_1(w) | \mathbf{op}_2(w_1, w_2)$$

where c is a real number, $\bowtie \in \{=, \leq, \geq\}$, $\ell^\star \in \mathbf{Loc} \cup \{\mathsf{myloc}\}$ and $\mathbf{op}_1$ and $\mathbf{op}_2$ are the usual unary and binary arithmetic operations on real numbers. Expression $\psi @ \ell^\star$ denotes the value of attribute ψ at location $\ell^\star$ and expression $\mathbf{s} @ \ell^\star$ denotes the number of individuals of species $\mathbf{s}$ at location $\ell^\star$. In the case that $\ell^\star = \mathsf{myloc}$, then the expression refers to the value of ℓ at the actual location of the individual in which the expression appears and it is instantiated to this location when the condition needs to be evaluated.

The syntax of PALPS is given at three levels: (1) the individual level ranged over by P, (2) the species level ranged over by R, and (3) the system level ranged over by S. Their syntax is defined via the following BNFs:

$$P ::= \mathbf{0} \mid \sum_{i \in I} \eta_i.P_i \mid \sum_{i \in I} p_i{:}P_i \mid \mathsf{cond}\,(e_1 \rhd P_1, \ldots, e_n \rhd P_n) \mid C$$
$$R ::= !rep.P$$
$$S ::= \mathbf{0} \mid P{:}\langle \mathbf{s}, \ell \rangle \mid R{:}\langle \mathbf{s} \rangle \mid S_1 | S_2 \mid S \backslash L$$

where $L \subseteq \mathbf{Ch}$, I is an index set, $p_i \in (0, 1]$ with $\sum_{i \in I} p_i = 1$, C ranges over a set of process constants $\mathcal{C}$, each with an associated definition of the form $C \overset{\mathrm{def}}{=} P$, and

$$\eta ::= a \mid \bar{a} \mid go\,\ell \mid \sqrt{.}$$

Beginning with the individual level, P can be one of the following: Process **0** represents the inactive individual, that is, an individual who has ceased to exist. Process $\sum_{i \in I} \eta_i . P_i$ describes the non-deterministic choice between a set of action-prefixed processes. We write $\eta_1 . P_1 + \eta_2 . P_2$ to denote the binary form of this operator. In turn, an activity η can be an input action on a channel a, written simply as a, a complementary output action on a channel a, written as $\bar{a}$, a movement action with destination ℓ, $go \, \ell$, or the time-passing action, $\sqrt{}$. Actions of the form a, and $\bar{a}$, $a \in \mathbf{Ch}$, are used to model arbitrary activities performed by an individual; for instance, eating, preying and reproduction. The tick action $\sqrt{}$ measures a tick on a global clock. These time steps are abstract in the sense that they have no defined length and, in practice, $\sqrt{}$ is used to separate the rounds of an individual's behavior. Process $\sum_{i \in I} p_i : P_i$ represents the probabilistic choice between processes P_i, $i \in I$. The process randomly selects an index $i \in I$ with probability p_i, and then evolves to P_i. We write $p_1 : P_1 \oplus p_2 : P_2$ for the binary form of this operator. The conditional process $\mathsf{cond} \, (e_1 \rhd P_1, \ldots, e_n \rhd P_n)$ presents the conditional choice between a set of processes: it behaves as P_i, where i is the smallest integer for which e_i evaluates to true. Note that this choice is deterministic. Finally, process constants provide a mechanism for including recursion in the calculus.

Moving on to the species level, we employ the special *species process* R defined as $!rep.P$. This is a replicated process which may always receive input through channel rep and create new instances of process P, where P is a new individual of species R.

Finally, population systems are built by composing in parallel located individuals and species. An individual is defined as $P : \langle \mathbf{s}, \ell \rangle$, where $\mathbf{s}$ and ℓ are the species and the location of the individual, respectively. A species is given by $R : \langle \mathbf{s} \rangle$, where $\mathbf{s}$ is the name of the species. In a composition $S_1 \mid S_2$ the components may proceed independently on their channel-based actions or synchronize with one another while executing complementary actions, in the CCS style, and they must synchronize on their $\sqrt{}$ actions. Essentially, the intention is that, in any given round of the lifetime of the individuals, all individuals perform their available actions possibly synchronizing as necessary until they synchronize on their next $\sqrt{}$ action and proceed to their next round. Finally, $S \backslash L$ models the restriction of the channels in set L within S. As a syntactic shortcut, we will write $P : \langle \mathbf{s}, \ell, n \rangle$ for the parallel composition of n copies of process $P : \langle \mathbf{s}, \ell \rangle$.

2.2   The Unprioritized Semantics

The semantics of PALPS is defined in terms of a *structural operational semantics* given at the level of configurations of the form (E, S), where E is an *environment* and S is a population system. The environment E is an entity of the form $E \subset \mathbf{Loc} \times \mathbf{S} \times \mathbb{N}$, where each pair ℓ and $\mathbf{s}$ is represented in E at most once and where $(\ell, s, m) \in E$ denotes the existence of m individuals of species s at location ℓ. The environment E plays a central role in evaluating expressions.

Initially, we define the *unprioritized* semantics of PALPS. This semantics is then refined into the *prioritized semantics* which takes into account the notion of policies in Sect. 2.3. The unprioritized semantics is given in terms of two transition relations: the non-deterministic relation $\longrightarrow_n$ and the probabilistic relation

$\longrightarrow_p$. A transition of the form $(E, S) \xrightarrow{\alpha}_n (E', S')$ means that a configuration (E, S) may execute action α and become (E', S'). A transition of the form $(E, S) \xrightarrow{w}_p (E', S')$ means that a configuration (E, S) may evolve into configuration (E', S') with probability w. Action α appearing in the non-deterministic relation may have one of the following forms:

- $a_{\ell,s}$ and $\bar{a}_{\ell,s}$ denote the execution of actions a and $\bar{a}$ respectively at location ℓ by an individual of species s.
- $\tau_{a,\ell,s}$ denotes an internal action that has taken place on channel a, at location ℓ, and where the output on a was carried out by an individual of species s. This action may arise when two complementary actions take place at the same location ℓ or when a move action take place from location ℓ.

Due to the space limitations, the rules of the PALPS semantics are omitted. The interested reader may refer to [23] for the details.

2.3   Policies and Prioritized Semantics

We are now ready to define the notion of a policy and refine the semantics of PALPS accordingly. A policy σ is a partial order on the set of PALPS non-probabilistic actions. By writing $(\alpha, \beta) \in \sigma$ we imply that action β has higher priority than α and whenever there is a choice between α and β, β should always be selected. For example, the policy $\sigma = \{(\text{reproduce}_{\ell,s}, \text{disperse}_{\ell,s}) | \ell \in \mathbf{Loc}\}$ specifies that, at each location, dispersal actions of species s should take place before reproduction actions. On the other hand $\sigma = \{(\text{reproduce}_{\ell_1,s}, \text{disperse}_{\ell_1,s}), (\text{disperse}_{\ell_2,s}, \text{reproduce}_{\ell_2,s})\}$ specifies that, while dispersal should proceed reproduction at location ℓ_1, the opposite should hold at location ℓ_2.

To achieve this effect the semantics of PALPS need to be refined with the use of a new non-deterministic transition system. This new transition relation prunes away all process executions that do not respect the priority ordering defined by the applied policy. Precisely, given a PALPS system S and a policy σ then, the semantics of the initial configuration (E, S) under the policy σ is given by $\longrightarrow_p \cup \longrightarrow_\sigma$ where the prioritized nondeterministic transition relation $\longrightarrow_\sigma$ is defined by the following rule:

$$\frac{(E, S) \xrightarrow{\alpha}_n (E', S') \text{ and } (E, S) \not\xrightarrow{\beta}_n, (\alpha, \beta) \in \sigma}{(E, S) \xrightarrow{\alpha}_\sigma (E', S')}$$

2.4   Examples

Example 1. We consider a simplification of the model presented in [28] which studies the reproduction of the parasitic *Varroa mite*. This mite usually attacks honey bees and it has a pronounced impact on the beekeeping industry. In this system, a set of individuals reside on an $n \times n$ lattice of resource sites and go through phases of reproduction and dispersal. Specifically, the studied model considers a population where individuals disperse in space while competing for a location site during their reproduction phase. They produce offspring only if they have exclusive use of a location. After reproduction the offspring disperse and continue indefinitely with the same behavior. In PALPS, we may model the described species **s** as $R \stackrel{\text{def}}{=} !rep.P_0$, where

$$P_0 \stackrel{\text{def}}{=} \sum_{\ell \in \mathbf{Nb}(\text{myloc})} \frac{1}{|\mathbf{Nb}(\text{myloc})|} : go\,\ell.\text{cond}\,(\mathbf{s}@\text{myloc} = 1 \rhd P_1;\ \text{true} \rhd \sqrt{}.P_0)$$

$$P_1 \stackrel{\text{def}}{=} \overline{rep}.(p{:}\sqrt{}.P_0 \oplus (1-p){:}\overline{rep}.\sqrt{}.P_0)$$

We point out that the conditional construct allows us to determine the exclusive use of a location by an individual. The special label myloc is used to denote the actual location of an individual within a system definition. Furthermore, note that P_1 models the probabilistic production of one or two children of the species. During the dispersal phase, an individual moves to a neighboring location which is chosen equiprobably among the neighbors of its current location. A system that contains two individuals at a location ℓ and one at location ℓ' can be modeled as

$$System \stackrel{\text{def}}{=} (P_0{:}\langle \ell, \mathbf{s}, 2\rangle | P_0{:}\langle \ell', \mathbf{s}\rangle | (!rep.P_0){:}\langle \mathbf{s}\rangle) \backslash \{rep\}.$$

In order to refine the system so that during each cycle of the individuals' lifetime all dispersals take place before the reproductions, we may employ the policy $\{(\tau_{rep,\ell,\mathbf{s}}, \tau_{go,\ell',\mathbf{s}}) | \ell, \ell' \in \mathbf{Loc}\}$. Then, according to the PALPS semantics, possible executions of $System$ have the form:

$$System \stackrel{w}{\longrightarrow}_p (go\,\ell_1.\ldots{:}\langle \ell, \mathbf{s}\rangle | go\,\ell_2.\ldots{:}\langle \ell, \mathbf{s}\rangle | go\,\ell_3.\ldots{:}\langle \ell', \mathbf{s}\rangle) \backslash \{rep\}$$
$$\stackrel{\tau_{go,\ell_1,\mathbf{s}}}{\longrightarrow}_\sigma (\text{cond}\,(\ldots){:}\langle \ell_1, \mathbf{s}\rangle | go\,\ell_2.\ldots{:}\langle \ell, \mathbf{s}\rangle | go\,\ell_3.\ldots{:}\langle \ell', \mathbf{s}\rangle) \backslash \{rep\}$$

for some probability w and locations ℓ_1, ℓ_2, ℓ_3, where no component will be able to execute the $\overline{rep}$ action before all components finish executing their movement actions.

Example 2. Let us now extend the previous example into a two-species system. In particular, consider a competing species $\mathbf{s}'$ of the Varroa mite, such as the pseudo-scorpion, which preys on **s**. To model this, we may define the process $R \stackrel{\text{def}}{=} !rep'.Q_0$, where

$$Q_0 \stackrel{\text{def}}{=} \text{cond}\,(s@\text{myloc} \geq 1 \rhd Q_1, s@\text{myloc} < 1 \rhd Q_2)$$

$$Q_1 \stackrel{\text{def}}{=} \overline{prey}.Q_3 + \overline{rep'}.Q_4$$

$$Q_2 \stackrel{\text{def}}{=} \overline{rep'}.\sqrt{}.Q_5$$

$$Q_3 \stackrel{\text{def}}{=} \overline{rep'}.\sqrt{}.Q_0$$

$$Q_4 \stackrel{\text{def}}{=} \text{cond}\,(s@\text{myloc} \geq 1 \rhd \overline{prey}.\sqrt{}.Q, s@\text{myloc} < 1 \rhd \sqrt{}.Q_5)$$

$$Q_5 \stackrel{\text{def}}{=} \text{cond}\,(s@\text{myloc} \geq 1 \rhd \overline{prey}.Q_3, s@\text{myloc} < 1 \rhd \mathbf{0})$$

An individual of species s' initially has a choice between preying or producing an offspring. If it succeeds in locating a prey then it preys on it. If it fails then it makes another attempt in the next cycle. If it fails again then it dies.

To implement the possibility of preying on the side of **s**, its definition must be extended with complementary input actions on channel *prey* at the appropriate places:

$$P_0 \stackrel{\text{def}}{=} \sum_{\ell \in \mathbf{Nb}(\text{myloc})} \frac{1}{|\mathbf{Nb}(\text{myloc})|} : (go\,\ell.\text{cond}\,(\text{s@myloc} = 1 \triangleright P_1;\ \text{true} \triangleright \sqrt{.P_0}) + prey.\mathbf{0})$$

$$P_1 \stackrel{\text{def}}{=} \overline{rep}.(p{:}\sqrt{.P_0} \oplus (1-p){:}\overline{rep}.\sqrt{.P_0}) + prey.\mathbf{0}$$

In this model it is possible to define an ordering between the actions of a single species, between the actions of two different species or even between actions on which individuals of the two different species synchronize. For instance, to specify that preying takes place in each round before individuals of species **s** disperse and before individuals of species s' reproduce we would employ the policy

$$\sigma = \{(\tau_{go,\ell,\mathbf{s}}, \tau_{prey,\ell,\mathbf{s}'}), (\tau_{rep',\ell,\mathbf{s}'}, \tau_{prey,\ell,\mathbf{s}'})| \ell \in \mathbf{Loc}\}.$$

Furthermore, to additionally require that reproduction of species **s** precedes reproduction of species s', we would write $\sigma \cup \{(\tau_{rep',\ell,\mathbf{s}'}, \tau_{rep,\ell,s})| \ell \in \mathbf{Loc}\}$.

3   Translating PALPS into PRISM

In this section we turn to the problem of model checking PALPS models extended with policies. As is the case of PALPS without policies, the operational semantics of PALPS *with policies* gives rise to transition systems that can be easily translated to Markov decision processes (MDPs). As such, model checking approaches that have been developed for MDPs can also be applied to PALPS models. PRISM is one such tool developed for the analysis of probabilistic systems. Specifically, it is a probabilistic model checker for Markov decision processes, discrete time Markov chains, and continuous time Markov chains. For our study we are interested in the MDP support of the tool which offers model checking and simulation capabilities of PRISM models.

In [24] we defined a translation of PALPS into the MDP subset of the PRISM language and we explored the possibility of employing the probabilistic model checker PRISM to perform analysis of the semantic models derived from PALPS processes. In this paper, we refine the translation of [24] for taking policies into account. In the remainder of this section, we will give a brief presentation of the PRISM language, sketch an encoding of (a subset of) PALPS *with policies* into PRISM and state its correctness.

3.1   The PRISM Language

The PRISM language is a simple, state-based language, based on guarded commands. A PRISM model consists of a set of *modules* which can interact with each other on shared actions following the CSP-style of communication [1]. Each module possesses a set of *local variables* which can be written by the module and read by all modules. In addition, there are *global variables* which can be read and written by all modules. The behavior of a module is described by a set of *guarded commands*. When modeling Markov decision processes, these commands take the form:

[act] guard p_1 : $u_1 +$ ... $+ p_m : u_m$;

where act is an optional action label, guard is a predicate over the set of variables, $p_i \in (0, 1]$ and u_i are updates of the form:

$(x'_1 = u_{i,1})$ & ... & $(x'_k = u_{i,k})$

where $u_{i,j}$ is a function over the variables. Intuitively, such an action is enabled in global state s if s satisfies guard. If a command is enabled then it may be executed in which case, with probability p_i, the update u_i is performed by setting the value of each variable x_j to $u_{i,j}(s)$ (where x'_j denotes the new value of variable x_j).

A model is constructed as the parallel composition of a set of modules. The semantics of a complete PRISM model is the parallel composition of all modules using the standard CSP parallel composition. This means that all the modules synchronize over all their common actions (i.e., labels). For a transition arising from synchronization between multiple processes, the associated probability is obtained by multiplying those of each component transition. Whenever, there is a choice of more than one commands, this choice is resolved non-deterministically. We refer the reader to [1] for the full description and the semantics of the PRISM language.

3.2 Encoding PALPS *with Policies* into the PRISM Language

As observed in [19], the main challenge of translating a CCS-like language (like PALPS) into PRISM is to map binary CCS-style communication over channels to PRISM's multi-way (CSP-style) communication. Our approach for dealing with this challenge in [24], similarly to [19], was to introduce a distinct action for each possible binary, channel-based communication which captures the channel as well as the sender/receiver pair.

In PALPS *with policies* the translation becomes more complex because, at any point, we need to select actions that are not preempted by other enabled actions. For, suppose that a policy σ specifies that $(\alpha, \beta) \in \sigma$. This implies that, at any point during computation, we must have information as to whether β is enabled. To implement this in PRISM, we employ a variable n_β which records the number of βs enabled. To begin with, this variable must be appropriately initialized. Subsequently, it is updated as computation proceeds: once a β is executed then n_β is decreased by 1 and when a new occurrence becomes enabled it is increased by 1. Thus, if $(\alpha, \beta) \in \sigma$, execution of action α in any module of a model should have as a precondition that $n_\beta = 0$.

To translate PALPS into the PRISM language, we translate each process into a module. The execution flow of a process is captured with the use of a local variable within the module whose value is updated in every command in such as way that computation is guided through the states of the process. Then, each possible construct of PALPS is modeled via a set of commands. For example, the probabilistic summation is represented by encoding the probabilistic choices into a PRISM guarded command. Non-deterministic choices are encoded by a set of simultaneously enabled guarded commands that capture all non-deterministic alternatives, whereas the conditional statement is modeled as a set of guarded commands, where the guard of each command is determined by the expressions of the conditional process.

Unfortunately, the replication operator cannot be directly encoded into PRISM since the PRISM language does not support the dynamic creation of modules. To overcome this problem, we consider a bounded-replication construct of the form $!^m P$ in which we specify the maximum number of P's, m, that can be created during computation.

In the remainder of this section we present the translation of a simple PALPS model into PRISM considering the main ideas of the encoding. This model is an instantiation of the model in Example 1. The full details of the translation can be found in [23].

Example 3. Consider a habitat consisting of four patches $\{1, 2, 3, 4\}$, where **Nb** is the symmetric closure of the set $\{(1, 2), (1, 3), (2, 4), (3, 4)\}$. Let **s** be a species residing on this habitat defined according to the bounded replication $R \stackrel{\text{def}}{=} !^m rep.P_0$ and where:

$$P_0 \stackrel{\text{def}}{=} \sum_{\ell \in \mathbf{Nb}(myloc)} \frac{1}{2} : go\,\ell.\text{cond}\ (\text{s@myloc} = 1 \rhd P_1;\ \text{true} \rhd \sqrt{.P_0})$$

$$P_1 \stackrel{\text{def}}{=} \overline{rep}.(0.7{:}\sqrt{.P_0} \oplus 0.3{:}\overline{rep}.\sqrt{.P_0})$$

Now, consider a system initially consisting of two individuals, at locations 1 and 2:

$$System \stackrel{\text{def}}{=} (P_0{:}\langle \mathbf{s}, 1\rangle \mid P_0{:}\langle \mathbf{s}, 2\rangle \mid R{:}\langle \mathbf{s}\rangle)\backslash\{rep\}$$

Further, suppose that we would like to analyze the system under the policy where dispersal precedes reproduction: $\{(\tau_{rep,\ell,\mathbf{s}}, \tau_{go,\ell',\mathbf{s}}) | \ell, \ell' \in \mathbf{Loc}\}$.

In order to translate *System* under policy σ in the PRISM language we first need to encode global information relating to the system. This consists of four global variables that record the initial populations of each of the locations and a variable that records the number of enabled occurrences the higher-priority actions referred to in the policy σ, that is, of $\tau_{go,\mathbf{s},\ell}$. We also include a global variable i that measures the inactivated individuals still available to be triggered. Initially $i = m$. Finally, we make use of a global variable *pact* which takes values from $\{0, 1\}$ and expresses whether there is a probabilistic action enabled. It is used to give precedence to probabilistic actions over nondeterministic actions as required by the PALPS semantics. Initially, $pact = 0$.

```
module P1

st1 : [1..12] init 1;
loc1: [1..4] init 1;

[prob] (st1=1) -> 0.5:(st1'=2)&(n_g'=n_g+1)&(pact'=0)
                + 0.5:(st1'=3)&(n_g'=n_g+1)&(pact'=0);
[] (pact=0)&(st1=2)&(loc=1) -> (loc'=2)&(s1'=s1-1)&(s2'=s2+1)
                             &(n_g'=n_g-1)&(st'=4);
[] (pact=0)&(st1=3)&(loc=1) -> (loc'=3)&(s1'=s1-1)&(s3'=s3+1)
                             &(n_g'=n_g-1)&(st'=4);
... // All possible locations are enumerated

[] (pact=0)&(st1=4)&(loc=1)&(s1=1) -> (st1=5);
[] (pact=0)&(st1=4)&(loc=1)&(s1!=1) -> (st1=10);
... // All possible locations are enumerated

[] (pact=0)&(st1=5)&(i>0)&(n_g=0) -> (s1'=s1+1)&(i'=i-1)&(st'=6);
[rep_1_3] (pact=0)&(st1=6) -> (st1'=7)&(pact'=1);
... // All activation possibilities are enumerated
[prob] (pact=0)&(st1=7) -> 0.7:(st1'=10)&(pact'=0)
                         + 0.3:(st1'=8)&(pact'=0);
[] (pact=0)&(st1=8)&(i>0)&(n_g=0) -> (s1'=s1+1)&(i'=i-1)&(st'=9);
[rep_1_3] (pact=0)&(st1=9) -> (st1'=10);
... // All activation possibilities are enumerated

[tick] (st1=10) -> (st1'=11);
[] (st1=11) -> (pact' = 1)&(st1'=12);
[tick'] (st1=12) -> (st'=11);

[prob] (pact=1)&(st!=1)&(st!=7) -> (pact'=0)
endmodule
```

Fig. 1. PRISM code for an active individual

```
global s1, s2: [0,m+2] init 1;    global n_g: [0,m+2] init 0;
global s3, s4: [0,m+2] init 0;    global pact: [0,1] init 0;
global i: int init m;
```

We continue to model the two individuals P_0:$\langle s, 1 \rangle$ and P_0:$\langle s, 2 \rangle$. Each individual will be described by a module. In Fig. 1, we may see the translation of individual P_0:$\langle s, 1 \rangle$. Individual $P_0 \langle s, 2 \rangle$ is defined similarly.

In the translation of P_0:$\langle s, 1 \rangle$, we observe that its location variable $loc1$ is set to 1 and variable $st1$, recording its state, is set to 1, the initial state of the module. Overall, the module has 12 different states. Furthermore, all non-probabilistic actions have $pact = 0$ as a precondition.

From state 1 the module may non-deterministically decide on the location to which the individual will disperse (horizontal or vertical dispersal) while variable

n_g is increased by one as the *go* action becomes enabled. This is implemented from states 2 and 3 respectively where the number of individuals of the source and destination locations are updated accordingly and the variable n_g is decreased by one as there is now one fewer movement action enabled. Then, in state 4 the module determines if there exist more than one individuals in its current location. If yes, then the state progresses to 10 where the individual will synchronize on the *tick*. Otherwise, in state 5, assuming that there is no dispersal action available for execution ($n_g = 0$) and there is still an inactive individual to be activated ($i > 0$), variables i and s_{loc} are updated and the flow of control is passed on to state 7 where a synchronization with an inactive module is performed. This process is repeated in states 7–9 where a second offspring may be produced probabilistically. Finally, we point out that the tick action is implemented via three actions in PRISM (states 10–12): initially all modules are required to synchronize on the *tick* action, then they all perform their necessary updates on variable *pact* since a probabilistic action has become enabled and, finally, the modules are required to synchronize again before they may start to execute their next time step.

Moving on to the encoding of R, as we have already discussed, we achieve this via bounded replication which makes an assumption on the maximum number of new individuals that can be created in a system. Given this assumption, our model must be extended by an appropriate number of inactive individuals awaiting for a trigger via a rep_i_j action. It then proceeds with the code of P_0 just like an active individual.

Regarding the correctness of the proposed translation, we have proved the existence of a weak bisimulation between a PALPS model and its PRISM translation by showing that a move of the PALPS model can be mimicked by its translation in a finite number of steps, and that this set of steps is performed atomically, in the sense that no other action within the PRISM model may interfere with the execution of the PALPS step. Similarly, any move of the PRISM translation can be mimicked by the original PALPS system. This proof of correctness is presented in [23].

4   A Case Study in PRISM

In this section, we apply our methodology for the simulation and model checking of PALPS systems using the PRISM tool. We begin by considering the system in Example 1, Sect. 2.4, which was also considered in [24] and can thus serve as a benchmark for studying the effect of applying policies on systems and, in particular, the degree by which policies reduce the state space of a PRISM model. In our model we will assume a lattice of locations of size $n \times n$ (for $n = 4, 9, 16$). Furthermore, we assume periodic boundaries conditions so that the opposite sides of the grid are connected together and we instantiate $p = 0.4$.

The PRISM encoding of the system follows the translation methods presented in Sect. 3. We performed some obvious optimizations in order to reduce the size of our model. All the tests were performed on a G46VW Asus laptop with an

Table 1. Performance of building probabilistic models in PRISM with and without policies.

Case study size	Number of states	Number of transitions	Construction time (s)	RAM (GB)
No policy [24]				
3 PALPS individuals	130397	404734	8	0.5
4 PALPS individuals	1830736	7312132	101	1.9
Policy σ				
3 PALPS individuals	27977	64282	3	0.3
4 PALPS individuals	148397	409342	10	0.7
Extended policy				
3 PALPS individuals	20201	41602	3	0.3
4 PALPS individuals	128938	310393	9	0.6

Intel i5 2.50 GHz processor and 8 GB of RAM. We ran the tests under Linux Ubuntu 13.04 (Kernel 3.8.0_17), using PRISM 4.0.3 with the MTBDD engine for model checking and CI method for simulation, and Java 7.

As a first experiment, we explored and compared the effect of applying policies on the state space of the system in question. Specifically, individuals in the system may engage in two activities: reproduction and dispersal. Let us assume an ordering of these two activities so that reproduction follows dispersal. This gives rise to the policy $\sigma = \{(\tau_{rep,\ell,\mathbf{s}}, \tau_{go,\ell,\mathbf{s}}) \mid \ell \in \mathbf{Loc}\}$. In Table 1, we summarize the results we obtained. We may observe that applying policy σ has resulted in a reduction in the size of the states spaces by a factor of 10 (see cases *No policy* and *Policy σ*). A further reduction was achieved by further extending our policy to enforce an order between the execution of actions among individuals. Specifically, for each action (e.g., reproduction), the individuals executed the action in an increasing order in terms of their module identifier. This extended policy resulted in a further reduction of the state space by about 20 %.

As a second experiment, we attempted to determine the limits for *simulating* PALPS models. We constructed PRISM models with various numbers of modules of active and inactive individuals and we run them on PRISM. In Table 2, we summarize the results. It turns out that for models with more than 5000 individuals simulation requires at least 12 h (which was the time limit we set for our simulations).

Consequently, we redeveloped our model of the *Varroa mite* according to the description presented in [28]. In contrast to Example 1, the new model features mortality. Specifically, the new model has two parameters: b the *offspring size* and p the *probability to survive before breeding*. Each mite begins its life by being exposed to death and it survives with a probability p. In case of survival, it disperses to a new location. If it has exclusive use of the location then it produces an offspring of size b and it dies. If the location is shared with other mites then all mites die without reproducing. As before, we model space as a lattice with periodic boundary conditions and the probability of dispersal from a location to any of its four neighbors equal to $1/4$. As in the previous example,

Table 2. Performance of simulating probabilistic systems in PRISM.

Individuals	File size (MB)	RAM (GB)	Simulation time (s)
10	0.1	0.18	1
100	0.4	0.3	8
500	2.0	0.5	45
1000	4.2	1.0	300
1500	6.2	0.7	454
2000	8.2	0.9	820
5000	20.1	2.0	$> 12\,h$
10000	44.1	3.4	$> 12\,h$

in our system we employed the policy specifying that the process of dispersal precedes reproduction. Formally, the behavior of a mite is defined as follows:

$$P \overset{def}{=} p{:}P_1 + (1-p){:}\sqrt{.0}$$

$$P_1 \overset{def}{=} \sum_{\ell \in \mathbf{Nb}(\mathsf{myloc})} \frac{1}{4} : go\,\ell.\mathsf{cond}\ (\mathsf{s@myloc} = 1 \triangleright P_2;\ \mathsf{true} \triangleright \sqrt{.0})$$

$$P_2 \overset{def}{=} \overline{rep}^b.\sqrt{.0} \qquad \text{where } \overline{rep}^b \overset{def}{=} \underbrace{\overline{rep}...\overline{rep}}_{b\ times}$$

For our experiments, we took advantage of the model checking capabilities of PRISM and we checked properties by using the *model-checking by simulation* option, referred to as *confidence interval* (CI) simulation method. The property we experimented with is $R =?[I = k]$. This property is a reward-based property that computes the average state instant reward at time k. We were interested to study the expected size of the population. For this, we associate to each state a reward representing this size. In our experiments, we varied the size of the initial population (i), while the probability of surviving (p) and the offspring size (b) were fixed to $p = 0.9$ and $b = 3$, and the lattice was of size 4×4. The number of idle processes was fixed to $n \times b - i$, which is sufficient to avoid deadlocks. The results of the experiments, shown in Fig. 2, demonstrate a tendency of convergence to a stable state and an independence of the initial population for $i > 8$.

We also analyzed, for this model, the effect of the parameters b and p on the evolution of the average total number of individuals through time, with an initial population of 1 individual, as shown in Figs. 3, 4. The chosen values for p and b were selected so that they are close to the estimates of the parameters of the Varroa mite, namely, $b = 3$ and $p = 0.9$. Finally, we note that the results may also be applicable to other species that follow the same, so-called scramble-contest, behavior such as the bean bruchid that attacks several kind of beans.

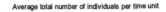

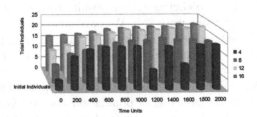

Fig. 2. Expected population size vs simulation time for different initial sizes of the population.

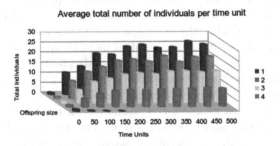

Fig. 3. Expected population size vs simulation time for different offspring sizes, for $p = 0.9$ and $i = 1$.

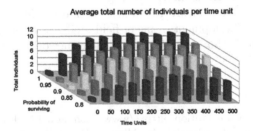

Fig. 4. Expected population size vs simulation time for different probabilities of survival, for $b = 3$ and $i = 1$.

5 Conclusions

In this paper we have extended the process calculus PALPS with the notion of a *policy*. A policy is an entity that is defined externally to the process-calculus description of an ecological system in order to impose an ordering between the activities taking place within a system as required for the purposes of the analysis. Furthermore, we have described a translation of PALPS *with policies* into the PRISM language. This encoding can be employed for simulating and model checking PALPS systems using the PRISM tool. We experimented with both of these capabilities and we have illustrated types of analysis that can be performed on PALPS models. We have also contrasted our results with those obtained for the same example in our previous work [24]. We have concluded that applying policies can significantly reduce the size of the model thus allowing to consider larger models. For instance, in the example we considered, the state space of the model was reduced by a factor of 10.

As future work, we intend to investigate further approaches for analysis of MDPs that arise from the modeling of population systems. One such approach involves the PRISM tool and concerns the production of PRISM input: we intend to explore alternatives of producing such input possibly via constructing and providing PRISM directly the Markov decision process associated with a PALPS system. We expect that this will result in smaller state spaces than those arising via our PALPS-to-PRISM translation. Furthermore, we would like to explore other directions for reducing the state-space of PALPS models e.g. by defining an enhanced semantics of PALPS to enable a more succinct presentation of systems especially in terms of the multiplicity of individuals, as well as defining a symbolic semantics which applies a symbolic treatment of environments.

Another direction that we are currently exploring is the application of our methodology to new and complex case studies from the local habitat and the exploration of properties such as extinction (e.g., the expected time until extinction), persistence (e.g., the long-term average of the number of sites occupied at a given time) and spatial indices (e.g., the correlation among nearby locations in space, patch shape analysis and the number of subpopulations in a spatially dispersed metapopulation) similarly to [27].

Finally, an interesting future research direction would be extend the work of [16] towards the development of mean-field analysis to represent the average behavior of systems within a spatially-explicit framework.

References

1. Online PRISM documentation. http://www.prismmodelchecker.org/doc/
2. Barbuti, R., Maggiolo-Schettini, A., Milazzo, P., Pardini, G.: Spatial calculus of looping sequences. Theoret. Comput. Sci. **412**(43), 5976–6001 (2011)
3. Barbuti, R., Maggiolo-Schettini, A., Milazzo, P., Troina, A.: A calculus of looping sequences for modelling microbiological systems. Fund. Inf. **72**(1–3), 21–35 (2006)
4. Berec, L.: Techniques of spatially-explicit individual-based models: construction, simulation, and mean-field analysis. Ecol. Model. **150**, 55–81 (2002)
5. Besozzi, D., Cazzaniga, P., Pescini, D., Mauri, G.: Modelling metapopulations with stochastic membrane systems. BioSystems **91**(3), 499–514 (2008)
6. Bioglio, L., Calcagno, C., Coppo, M., Damiani, F., Sciacca, E., Spinella, S., Troina, A.: A Spatial Calculus of Wrapped Compartments. CoRR, abs/1108.3426 (2011)
7. Cardona, M., Colomer, M.A., Margalida, A., Palau, A., Pérez-Hurtado, I., Pérez-Jiménez, M.J., Sanuy, D.: A computational modeling for real ecosystems based on P systems. Nat. Comput. **10**(1), 39–53 (2011)
8. Chen, Q., Ye, F., Li, W.: Cellular-automata-based ecological and ecohydraulics modelling. J. Hydroinf. **11**(3/4), 252–272 (2009)

9. Ciocchetta, F., Hillston, J.: Bio-PEPA: a framework for the modelling and analysis of biological systems. Theoret. Comput. Sci. **410**(33–34), 3065–3084 (2009)
10. Cleaveland, R., Lüttgen, G., Natarajan, V.: Priority in process algebras. Technical report, Langley Research Center, NASA, USA (1999)
11. Drábik, P., Maggiolo-Schettini, A., Milazzo, P.: Modular verification of interactive systems with an application to biology. Sci. Ann. Comp. Sci. **21**(1), 39–72 (2011)
12. Gerber, L.R., VanBlaricom, G.R.: Implications of three viability models for the conservation status of the western population of Steller sea lions (Eumetopias jubatus). Biol. Conserv. **102**, 261–269 (2001)
13. Hoare, C.A.R.: Communicating Sequential Processes. Prentice-Hall, Upper Saddle River (1985)
14. McCaig, C., Fenton, A., Graham, A., Shankland, C., Norman, R.: Using process algebra to develop predator–prey models of within-host parasite dynamics. J. Theor. Biol. **329**, 74–81 (2013)
15. McCaig, C., Norman, R., Shankland, C.: Process algebra models of population dynamics. In: Horimoto, K., Regensburger, G., Rosenkranz, M., Yoshida, H. (eds.) AB 2008. LNCS, vol. 5147, pp. 139–155. Springer, Heidelberg (2008)
16. McCaig, C., Norman, R., Shankland, C.: From individuals to populations: a mean field semantics for process algebra. Theoret. Comput. Sci. **412**(17), 1557–1580 (2011)
17. Milner, R.: A Calculus of Communicating Systems. Springer, Heidelberg (1980)
18. Milner, R., Parrow, J., Walker, D.: A calculus of mobile processes, parts 1 and 2. Inf. Comput. **100**, 1–77 (1992)
19. Norman, G., Palamidessi, C., Parker, D., Wu, P.: Model checking probabilistic and stochastic extensions of the π-calculus. IEEE Trans. Softw. Eng. **35**(2), 209–223 (2009)
20. Pardini, G.: Formal modelling and simulation of biological systems with spatiality. Ph.D thesis, University of Pisa (2011)
21. Pearson, R.G., Dawson, T.P.: Long-distance plant dispersal and habitat fragmentation: identifying conservation targets for spatial landscape planning under climate change. Biol. Conserv. **123**, 389–401 (2005)
22. Pescini, D., Besozzi, D., Mauri, G., Zandron, C.: Dynamical probabilistic P-systems. J. Found. Comput. Sci. **17**(1), 183–204 (2006)
23. Philippou, A., Toro, M.: Process ordering in a process calculus for spatially-explicit ecological models. Technical report, Department of Computer Science, University of Cyprus, 2013. http://www.cs.ucy.ac.cy/~annap/pt-tr.pdf
24. Philippou, A., Toro, M., Antonaki, M.: Simulation and verification for a process calculus for spatially-explicit ecological models. Sci. Ann. Comput. Sci. **23**(1), 119–167 (2013)
25. Păun, G.: Computing with membranes (P systems): an introduction. In: Rozenberg, G., Salomaa, A. (eds.) Current Trends in Theoretical Computer Science, pp. 845–866. World Scientific, Singapore (2001)
26. Regev, A., Panina, E.M., Silverman, W., Cardelli, L., Shapiro, E.: BioAmbients: an abstraction for biological compartments. Theoret. Comput. Sci. **325**(1), 141–167 (2004)
27. Ruxton, G.D., Saravia, L.A.: The need for biological realism in the updating of cellular automata models. Ecol. Model. **107**, 105–112 (1998)
28. Sumpter, D.J.T., Broomhead, D.S.: Relating individual behaviour to population dynamics. Proc. Roy. Soc. B: Biol. Sci. **268**(1470), 925–932 (2001)
29. Tofts, C.: Processes with probabilities, priority and time. Formal Aspects Comput. **6**, 536–564 (1994)

DISPAS: An Agent-Based Tool
for the Management of Fishing Effort

Pierluigi Penna[1,2]([✉]), Nicola Paoletti[1], Giuseppe Scarcella[2], Luca Tesei[1],
Mauro Marini[2], and Emanuela Merelli[1]

[1] School of Science and Technology, University of Camerino, Via del Bastione 1,
62032 Camerino, Italy
p.penna@an.ismar.cnr.it
[2] Institute of Marine Sciences, National Research Council of Italy,
Largo Fiera della Pesca, 60125 Ancona, Italy

Abstract. We introduce DISPAS, Demersal fIsh Stock Probabilistic
Agent-based Simulator, with the aim of helping to investigate and understand sustainability in the exploitation of fishery resources. The simulator has capabilities for exploring different fishing scenarios, focusing on
the case study of the common sole (Solea solea) stock in the Northern
Adriatic Sea (Mediterranean Sea). In order to assess and predict the
availability of the fish stock under different fishing efforts, the simulator
allows the user to specify fishing mortality rates (F) on a monthly basis.
We present some preliminary results simulating different scenarios.

Keywords: Ecosystem science · Simulation of biological systems ·
Agent-based methodologies · Fish stock assessment · Common sole ·
Adriatic Sea

1 Introduction

The World Summit on Sustainable Development (WSSD) [1], held in August
2002, laid the foundation for a radical shift about how marine ecosystems and
fisheries are to be managed in the future. In particular WSSD agreed to restore
the worlds depleted fish stocks to levels that can produce the maximum sustainable yield (MSY) on an urgent basis where possible no later than 2015.
After 10 years from the adoption of WSSD, Europe is still far from achieving
these objectives [2] especially in the Mediterranean area [3]. Most of the fish
stocks in European waters, 88 %, are estimated as being overfished and 30 % of
them are outside safe biological limits, which means they may not be able to
replenish [4]. To reach an healthy state of the resources it is important to know
their population dynamics, which is often difficult to estimate [5]. Thus, a big
effort of the scientific community has been directed towards the development
of modelling approaches and techniques (e.g. maximum likelihood methods and
Bayesian analysis) as new kinds of toolkit for understanding the dynamic of fishery exploited marine resources [6]. Within this framework, the use of agent-based

S. Counsell and M. Núñez (Eds.): SEFM 2013 Collocated Workshops, LNCS 8368, pp. 362–367, 2014.
DOI: 10.1007/978-3-319-05032-4_26, © Springer International Publishing Switzerland 2014

techniques represents - as in the present study - a new powerful tool in order to use the little pieces of information coming from scientific survey at sea in order to assure faithful modelling, towards sustainable exploitation of the stocks.

In this work, the simulator is used for the assessment of the common sole stock of the northern Adriatic Sea (Mediterranean sea). Only fishery-independent data, coming from a specific scientific survey (SoleMon survey) [7], were used. The case of Solea solea in the Northern Adriatic Sea is exemplary because the management of fishery resources, despite the results of the studies, has been defective. This is especially true for the young portion of the stock that continues to be exploited at unsustainably high levels [8], particularly in juveniles aggregation areas and periods [9]. Using the simulator it will be possible to understand the correct exploitation pressure on the stock. This can provide long-term high yields and low risk of stock/fishery collapse and can ensure that the sole stock is restored at least at levels that could produce the maximum sustainable yield.

2   Model of a Sole Behaviour

In [10] an automata-based formalism, extended probabilistic discrete timed automata (EPDTA), was introduced with the aim of modelling the essential behaviour of an individual of a fish population. An EPDTA is able to express time passing in a discrete domain - using special clock variables - and to specify constraints on the transitions from a state to another state of the individual. Such constraints depend on the values of clock variables or of other variables. Transitions can reset clocks and/or update the values of non-clock variables. The target state of any transition is determined probabilistically using a discrete probability distribution on the state space. We refer to [10] for the full definition of the EPDTA model. In Fig. 1 the simplified model (without breeding) of the sole behaviour is shown. The clock t measures absolute time, in months, since the starting of the system. The clock x is used for updating the sole on a monthly base. As common in their biological study, the sole population is partitioned in six classes, characterised by ranges of length. From state "class i", the invariant $x \leq 1$ combined with the transition guard $x = 1$ forces to go (with probability 1) to state "chkM i" while the age (in months) of the sole is increased by 1 and the new length is calculated using the function fVB. This function uses the The von Bertalanffy growth function [11] to estimate the length of the sole at its age and at the particular time t. This permits to model a different growth rate at different absolute times due to, for instance, abundance or scarcity of food. In state "chkM i" ("chkF i") the sole can die for natural causes with a certain probability PrM(i, t) (can be fished with probability PrF(i, t), respectively). The probabilities are inferred from real survey data and are distributed along the year with different weights, in such a way that, for instance, a temporary protection period of fishing can be modelled. If the sole does not die and is not fished, then it enjoys another month of life in the same class (returns in state "class i") or in the next class (goes to state "class $i + 1$") if, in the meantime, its length has been increased to the next class range. In both cases the clock x is reset to zero in order to let another month pass in state "class i" (or "class $i + 1$").

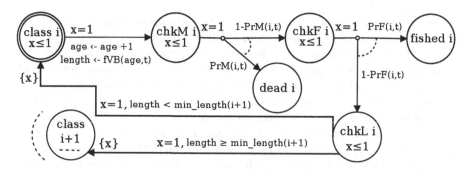

Fig. 1. Part of an EPDTA representing the behaviour of a sole in class i. The double circled state is the initial one when $i = 0$. From state chkL i the automaton goes to the next class $i+1$ if the length of the sole is sufficient to be considered in the new class.

3   From Model to Simulator

A population of virtual soles has been instructed, each with its individual behaviour, and they have been monitored along a (simulated) period of time of 10 years. Following the MAS (Multi-Agent System) paradigm, an environment has been created in which sole agents (about 500 in a simulated square kilometre) behave accordingly to the EPDTA model in Sect. 2.

We employed Repast Simphony, Recursive Porous Agent Simulation Toolkit [12], an agent-based modelling and simulation toolkit used in various application fields like biological systems, ecology, animal population, food chains, economy and financial markets. The initial configuration is stored in a file containing initial population, growth index, length-weight relationship, death index, and so on. Hence, the user can change the simulation parameters according to the target fish survey-based real data. In Repast Simphony one can change the properties of the scheduler. We used this feature for forcing all the agents to be updated simultaneously at discrete time points corresponding to months.

Accordingly to the species real habit, every year in June (i.e. months 6, 18, 30 and so on, in the simulation) the new born are added. For the first 7 years (2005–2011), which correspond to the period of the SoleMon survey, the number of the new born to add come from survey data. After 2011 they are added by randomly choosing a number taken from a normal distribution whose mean and standard deviation are calculated form the new born of the last 3 years.

Table 1 shows the probability of natural death and of being fished, related to fish length classes (0-5+). At each step (1 month) the probabilities $\mathrm{PrM}(i,t)$ and $\mathrm{PrF}(i,t)$ are read from the configuration file. $\mathrm{PrM}(i,t)$ remains fixed for the whole duration of the simulation while $\mathrm{PrF}(i,t)$ varies for each year.

In the first 7 years we derived $\mathrm{PrM}(i,t)$ and $\mathrm{PrF}(i,t)$ from surveys made by marine biologists. Afterwards, we used the values of $\mathrm{PrF}(i,t)$ of the last year available. Future scenarios can be created by modifying $\mathrm{PrF}(i,t)$ or other parameters. At each step the total biomass is calculated as the total weight of live agents. During the run it is possible to visualise, in real time, the charts about

Table 1. PrM(i, t) and PrF(i, t), related to sole length classes (0-5+) derived by the SoleMon scientific survey data.

Class	PrM				PrF			
		2005	2006	2007	2008	2009	2010	2011
0	0.041	0	0	0	0	0	0	0
1	0.024	0.122	0.121	0.131	0.100	0.171	0.084	0.115
2	0.020	0.115	0.114	0.155	0.087	0.093	0.144	0.117
3	0.017	0.152	0.153	0.178	0.080	0.195	0.280	0.182
4	0.017	0.129	0.129	0.158	0.080	0.159	0.177	0.139
5+	0.027	0.129	0.129	0.158	0.080	0.159	0.177	0.139

the evolution of the population (divided by age class) and of total biomass, as well as the 2D and 3D scenarios of the population. Furthermore, data are saved into external files in order to be processed with external tools. In the following, some results obtained using DISPAS are shown and commented.

Biomass trend. In Fig. 2, the red solid line shows the mean of total biomass computed by 50 runs. Dotted lines represent maximum and minimum values, while vertical bars show the confidence interval of 5 %. PrM(i, t), PrF(i, t) and other parameters come from the SoleMon survey data. Note that the total biomass tends to a mean level of almost 15,000 g over square kilometre.

Varying F. We fixed PrM(i, t) and other parameters according to the SoleMon data. PrF(i, t) is set differently to create different scenarios: virgin stock (PrF=0); PrF taken form SoleMon data; half of SoleMon PrF; and twice SoleMon PrF. Results are shown again in Fig. 2. The blue line (scale is on right axis) represents the biomass trend of the virgin stock, i.e. a sort of null model that indicates the ideal population dynamics. Other trends clearly denote the impact fishing on the total biomass (Fig. 3).

Varying F after the survey period (2005–2011). In this scenario we used the same PrF(i, t) as before, but we applied them after the period of the SoleMon scientific survey (2011).

4 Future Work

In order to validate our model, we plan to use SURBA (SURvey-Based Assessments) [13], a well-established model in the context of marine biology. In particular, SURBA will be fed with the simulation outputs from DISPAS and we will compare the results with the ones obtained feeding SURBA with real data from SoleMon. Moreover, we plan to devise a technique for calculating the optimal protection period of fishery in order to maximise the replenishing of the stock. Finally, we plan also to define a scenario for calculating the recovery time after overfishing, i.e. the time that the fish stock takes to reach again a sustainable level after simulating a period of strong fishing effort.

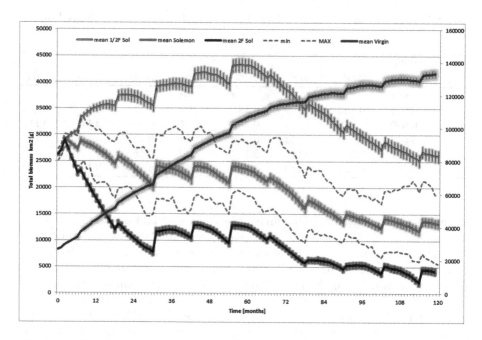

Fig. 2. Results of 50 simulations using SoleMon data (red), virgin stock (blue) and different fishing scenarios (green and black) (Colour figure online).

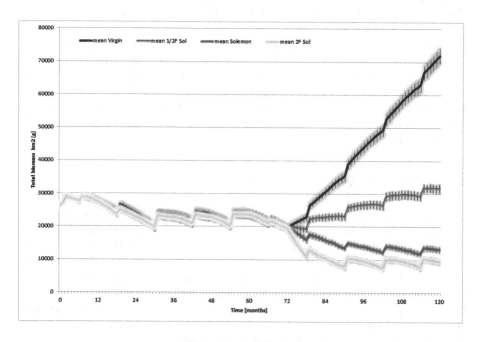

Fig. 3. Prediction in different fishing scenarios after 2011 (84 step/month).

References

1. United Nations: Plan of Implementation of the World Summit on Sustainable Development (2002)
2. Froese, R., Proel, A.: Rebuilding fish stocks no later than 2015: will Europe meet the deadline? Fish Fish. **11**, 194–202 (2010)
3. Colloca, F., Cardinale, M., Maynou, F., Giannoulaki, M., Scarcella, G., Jenko, K., Bellido, J., Fiorentino, F.: Rebuilding Mediterranean fisheries: a new paradigm for ecological sustainability. Fish Fish. **14**, 84–109 (2013)
4. European Commission: Green Paper Reform of the Common Fisheries Policy (2009)
5. Schnute, J.: Data uncertainty, model ambiguity, and model identification. Nat. Resourc. Model. **2**, 159–212 (1987)
6. Hilborn, R., Mangel, M.: The ecological detective: confronting models with data. J. Marine Biol. Assoc. U.K. **77**, 918–918 (1997)
7. Grati, F., Scarcella, G., Polidori, P., Domenichetti, F., Bolognini, L., Gramolini, R., Vasapollo, C., Giovanardi, O., Raicevich, S., Celi, I., Vrgo, N., Isajlovic, I., Jeni, A., Mareta, B., Fabi, G.: Multi-annual investigation of the spatial distributions of juvenile and adult sole (Solea solea, L.) in the Adriatic Sea (Northern Mediterranean). J. Sea Res. **84**, 122–132 (2013)
8. Scarcella, G., Fabi, G., Grati, F., Polidori, P., Domenichetti, F., Bolognini, L., Punzo, E., Santelli, A., Strafella, P., Brunetti, B., Giovanardi, O., Raicevich, S., Celic, I., Bullo, M., Sabatini, L., Franceschini, G., Mion, M., Piras, C., Fortibuoni, T., Vrgoc, N., Despalatovic, M., Cvitkovi, N., Pengal, P., Marceta, B.: Stock Assessment form of Common Sole in GSA 17. Technical report, ICES Working Group on Methods of Fish Stock Assessment (2012)
9. Scarcella, G., Grati, F., Raicevich, S., Russo, T., Gramolini, R., Scott, R., Polidori, P., Domenichetti, F., Bolognini, L., Giovanardi, O., Celic, I., Sabatini, L., Vrgoc, N., Isajlovic, I., Marceta, B., Fabi, G.: Common sole in the Northern Adriatic Sea: possible spatial management scenarios to rebuild the stock. J. Sea Res. (submitted)
10. Buti, F., Corradini, F., Merelli, E., Paschini, E., Penna, P., Tesei, L.: An Individual-based probabilistic model for fish stock simulation. Electron. Proc. Theor. Comp. Sci. **33**, 37–55 (2010). (Proceedings of AMCA-POP 2010)
11. von Bertalanffy, L.: A quantitative theory of organic growth (inquiries on growth laws II). Hum. biol. **10**(2), 181–213 (1938)
12. North, M., Collier, N., Ozik, J., Tatara, E., Altaweel, M., Macal, C., Bragen, M., Sydelko, P.: Complex adaptive systems modeling with repast simphony. Complex Adapt. Syst. Model. **1**(3), 1–26 (2013)
13. Needle, C.: Survey-Based Assessments with SURBA. Technical report, ICES Working Group on Methods of Fish Stock Assessment (2003)

OpenCert 2013

Certifying Machine Code Safe from Hardware Aliasing: RISC is Not Necessarily Risky

Peter T. Breuer[1]([⊠]) and Jonathan P. Bowen[2]

[1] Department of Computer Science, University of Birmingham, Birmingham, UK
ptb@cs.bham.ac.uk
[2] School of Computing, Telecommunications and Networks,
Birmingham City University, Birmingham, UK
jonathan.bowen@bcu.ac.uk

Abstract. Sometimes machine code turns out to be a better target for verification than source code. RISC machine code is especially advantaged with respect to source code in this regard because it has only two instructions that access memory. That architecture forms the basis here for an inference system that can prove machine code safe against 'hardware aliasing', an effect that occurs in embedded systems. There are programming memes that ensure code is safe from hardware aliasing, but we want to certify that a given machine code is provably safe.

1 Introduction

In a computer system, 'software' aliasing occurs when different logical addresses simultaneously or sporadically reference the same physical location in memory. We are all familiar with it and think nothing of it, because the same physical memory is nowadays reused millisecond by millisecond for different user-space processes with different addressing maps, and we expect the operating system kernel to weave the necessary illusion of separation. The kernel programmer has to be aware that different logical addresses from different or even the same user-space process may alias the same physical location, but the application programmer may proceed unawares.

We are interested in a converse situation, called 'hardware' aliasing, where different physical locations in memory are sporadically bound to the same logical address. If software aliasing is likened to one slave at the beck of two masters, hardware aliasing is like identical twins slaved to one master who cannot tell which is which. In this paper we will investigate the safety of machine code in the light of hardware aliasing issues.

Aliasing has been studied before [10] and is the subject of some patents [8,11]. There appears to be no theoretical treatment published, although the subject is broadly treated in most texts on computer architecture (see, for example, Chap. 6 of [1]) and is common lore in operating systems kernel programming. The 'hardware' kind of aliasing arises particularly in embedded systems where the arithmetic components of the processor are insufficient to fill all the address lines.

S. Counsell and M. Núñez (Eds.): SEFM 2013 Collocated Workshops, LNCS 8368, pp. 371–388, 2014.
DOI: 10.1007/978-3-319-05032-4_27, © Springer International Publishing Switzerland 2014

Suppose, for example, that the memory has 64-bit addressing but the processor only has 40-bit arithmetic. The extra lines might be grounded, or sent high, and this varies from platform to platform. They may be connected to 64-bit address registers in the processor, so their values change from moment to moment as the register is filled. In that case, it is up to the software to set the 'extra' bits reliably to zero, or one, or some consistent value, in order that computing an address may yield a consistent result.

We first encountered the phenomenon in the context of the KPU [6,7], a 'general purpose crypto-processor', a processor that performs its computations in encrypted form to provide security against observation and protection from malware. Because real encryptions are one-many, the calculation for the address 1+1 will mean '2' when decrypted, but may be different in value from another encryption of 2. If the two are both used as addresses, then two different memory cell contents are accessed and the result is chaotic. Data addresses are also encrypted differently from program addresses [5].

The same effect occurs in the embedded system that has processor arithmetic with fewer bits than there are address lines; add 1+1 in the processor and instead of 2, 0xff01000000000002 may be returned. If those two aliases of the arithmetic '2' are used as addresses, they access different memory cells. What is meant both times to be '2' accesses different locations according to criteria beyond the programmer's control.

There are programming memes that are successful in an aliasing environment: if a pointer is needed again in a routine, it must be copied exactly and saved for the next use; when an array or string element is accessed, the address must always be calculated in exactly the same way. But whatever the programmer says, the compiler may implement as it prefers and ultimately it is the machine code that has to be checked in order to be sure that aliasing is not a risk at run-time. Indeed, in an embedded environment it is usual to find the programmer writing in assembler precisely in order to control the machine code emitted. The Linux kernel consists of about 5 % hand-written assembly code, for example (but rarely in segments of more than 10–15 lines each). One of our long term objectives is to be able to boot a Linux kernel on an embedded platform with aliasing, the KPU in particular. That requires both modifying a compiler and checking the hand-written machine-level code in the open source archive.

An inference system will be set out here that can guarantee a (RISC [2,9]) machine code program safe against hardware aliasing as described. The idea is to map a stack machine onto the machine code. We will reason about what assembly language instructions for the stack machine do computationally. Choosing an inference rule to apply to a machine code instruction is equivalent to choosing a stack machine assembly language [5] instruction to which it disassembles [3,4]. The choice must be such that a resulting proof tree is well-formed, and that acts as a guide. The stack machine is aliasing-proof when operated within its intended parameters so verifying alias-safety means verifying that the stack machine assembly language code obtained by disassembly of the RISC machine code does not cause the stack machine to overstep certain bounds at run-time.

The RISC machine code we can check in this way is ipso facto restricted to that which we can disassemble. At the moment, that means code that uses string or string-like data structures and arrays which do not contain further pointers, and which uses machine code 'jump and link' and 'jump register' instructions only for subroutine call and return respectively, and in which subroutines make their own local frame and do not access the caller's frame (arguments are passed to subroutines in registers). These restrictions are not fundamental, but in any case there are no functional limitations implied by them; one call convention is functionally as good as another and data structures may always be laid out flat, as they are in a relational DB.

Mistakes in disassembly are possible: if a 'jump register' instruction, for example, were in fact used to implement a computed goto and not a subroutine return, it could still be treated as a subroutine return by the verification, which would end prematurely, possibly missing an error further along and returning a false negative. A mistaken return as just described would always fail verification in our system, but other such situations are conceivable in principle. So a human needs to check and certify that the proposed disassembly is not wrongheaded. The practice is not difficult because, as noted above, hand-written machine code at a professional standard consists of short, concise, commented segments. The difficulty is that there is often a great deal of it to be checked and humans tire easily. But our system reduces the burden to checking the disassembly proposed by the system against the comments in the code.

This paper is structured as follows: after an illustration of programming against aliasing in Sect. 2 and a discussion of disassembly in Sect. 3, code annotation is introduced in Sects. 4, 5 and 6, with a worked example in Sect. 7. Section 8 argues that code annotation gives rise to the formal assurance that aliasing cannot occur.

2 Programming Memes

We model aliasing as being introduced when memory addresses are calculated in different ways. That model says that a memory address may be *copied* exactly and used again without hazard, but if even 0 is added to it, then a different alias of the address may result, and reads from the new alias do not return data deposited at the old alias of the address. Arithmetically the aliases are equivalent in the processor; they will test as equal but they are not identical, and using them as addresses shows that up.

Table 1. Aliasing in function *foo*.

☠	✓
foo:	foo:
	gp = sp
sp -= 32	sp -= 32
... code ...	... code ...
sp += 32	sp = gp
return	return

That is particularly a problem for the way in which a compiler – or an assembly language programmer – renders machine code for the stack pointer movement around a function call. Classically, a subroutine starts by decrementing the stack pointer to make room on the stack for its local frame. Just before return, it increments the stack pointer back to its original value. The pseudo-code is shown on the left in Table 1. In an aliasing context, the attempt at arithmetically restoring the pointer puts an alias of the intended address in the **sp** register, and the caller may receive back a stack pointer that no longer points to the data. The code on the right in Table 1 works correctly; it takes an extra register (**gp**) and instruction, but the register content may be moved to the stack and restored before return, avoiding the loss of the slot.

Table 2. Aliasing while accessing a string or array.

string	☠	☠	✓
array	✓	☠	☠
	x = s[2]	s+= 2 x = *s	s++; s++ x = *s

Strings and arrays are also problematic in an aliasing environment because different calculations for the address of the same element cause aliasing. To avoid it, the strategy we will follow is that elements of 'string-like' structures will be accessed by incrementing the base address in constant steps (see the pseudo-code at right in Table 2) and array elements will be accessed via a unique offset from the array base address (see the pseudo-code at left in Table 2). This technique ensures that there is only one calculation possible for the address of each string element (it is $((s+1)+1)+0$ in Table 2) or array element ($s+2$ in Table 2), so aliasing cannot occur. The middle code in Table 2 gives address $(s+2)+0$ which matches exactly neither string nor array calculations. The decision over whether to treat a memory area like a string or an array depends on the mode of access to be used.

A RISC machine code processor consists of 32 (32-bit) integer registers R, a vector of 2^{32} (32-bit) integer memory locations M, and the program counter p. The latter gives the address of the current instruction. The **ra** register is used to hold a subroutine call return address. Only two instructions, **sw** and **lw**, access memory.

instruction	mnemonic	semantics
sw r_1 $k(r_2)$	store word	$M' = M \oplus \{R\,r_2 + k \mapsto R\,r_1\}$; $R' = R$; $p' = p+4$
lw r_1 $k(r_2)$	load word	$M' = M$; $R' = R \oplus \{r_1 \mapsto M(R\,r_2 + k)\}$; $p' = p+4$
move r_1 r_2	move/copy	$M' = M$; $R' = R \oplus \{r_1 \mapsto R\,r_2\}$; $p' = p+4$
li r_1 k	load immediate	$M' = M$; $R' = R \oplus \{r_1 \mapsto k\}$; $p' = p+4$
addiu r_1 r_2 k	add immediate	$M' = M$; $R' = R \oplus \{r_1 \mapsto R\,r_2 + k\}$; $p' = p+4$
addu r_1 r_2 r_3	add variable	$M' = M$; $R' = R \oplus \{r_1 \mapsto R\,r_2 + R\,r_3\}$; $p' = p+4$
nand r_1 r_2 r_3	bitwise not-and	$M' = M$; $R' = R \oplus \{r_1 \mapsto R\,r_2 \,\overline{\&}\, R\,r_3\}$; $p' = p+4$
beq r_1 r_2 k	branch-if-equal	$M' = M$; $R' = R$; if $(R\,r_1 = R\,r_2)$ $p' = k$ else $p' = p+4$
jal k	jump-and-link	$M' = M$; $R' = R \oplus \{\mathbf{ra} \mapsto p+4\}$; $p' = k$
jr r	jump-register	$M' = M$; $R' = R$; $p' = R\,r$

Notation. $M \oplus \{a \mapsto v\}$ means the vector M overwritten at index a with the value v; the processor arithmetic (bold font '**+**') is distinguished from the instruction addressing arithmetic (light font '+'); r_1, r_2 are register names or indices; k is a signed 16-bit integer; x and x' are respectively initial and final value after the instruction has acted.

Box 1. RISC machine code instructions and their underlying semantics.

3   Disassembly

Say that the stack pointer s is in the stack pointer register sp in the machine code processor. A corresponding abstract stack machine state is a 4-tuple $(\mathcal{R}, \mathcal{K}, \mathcal{H}, p)$, where $\mathcal{R}$ consists of the 31 registers excluding the stack pointer register, the stack $\mathcal{K}$ consists of the top part of memory above the stack pointer value s, the heap $\mathcal{H}$ consists of the bottom part of memory below the stack pointer, and the address p is that of the current instruction.

$$\mathcal{K}\,k = M(s+k) \qquad s = R\,\mathbf{sp}, \; k \geq 0$$
$$\mathcal{R}\,r = R\,r \qquad r \neq \mathbf{sp}, \; r \in \{0, \dots 31\}$$
$$\mathcal{H}\,a = M\,a \qquad a < s$$

The (hidden) stack pointer value s is needed to recreate the machine code processor state (R, M, p) from the stack machine state $(\mathcal{R}, \mathcal{K}, \mathcal{H}, p)$, so the latter is more abstract.

Box 2. Relation of processor to stack machine.

Nothing in the machine code indicates which register holds a subroutine return address, and that affects which machine code instructions may be interpreted as a return from a subroutine call. To deal with this and similar issues in an organised manner, we describe rules of reasoning about programs both in terms of the machine code instruction to which they apply and an assembly language instruction for a more abstract *stack machine* that the machine code instruction may be disassembled to and which we imagine the programmer is targeting.

The core RISC machine code instructions are listed in Box 1, where their semantics are given as state-to-state transformations on the three components of a RISC processor: 32 32-bit registers R, memory M and a 32-bit program counter p. The corresponding abstract stack machine is described in Box 2. The stack pointer address s in the machine code processor notionally divides memory M into two components: stack $\mathcal{K}$ above and heap $\mathcal{H}$ below. The stack machine manipulates the stack directly via instructions that operate at the level of stack operations, and they are implemented in the machine code processor via instructions that act explicitly on the stack pointer. No stack pointer is available in the abstract machine. Its registers $\mathcal{R}$ consist of the set R in the machine code processor *minus* the register that contains the stack pointer, usually the **sp** register. The program counter p is the same in the abstract stack machine as in the machine code processor, because instructions correspond one-to-one between programs for each machine. However, there is usually a choice of more than one abstract stack machine instruction that each machine code instruction could have been disassembled to, even though only one is chosen.

Table 3. Stack machine instructions: the n are small integers, the r are register names or indices, and the a are relative or absolute addresses.

```
s ::= cspt r | cspf r | rspf r | push n                        // stack pointer movement
    | get r n | put r n | ...                                  // stack access
    | newx r a n | stepx r n | getx r n(r) | putx r n(r) | ... // string operations
    | newh r a n | lwfh r n(r) | swfh r n(r) | ...             // array operations
    | gosub a | return | goto a | ifnz r a | ...              // control operations
    | mov r r | addaiu r r n | ...                            // arithmetic operations
```

Table 4. Machine code may be disassembled to one of several alternate assembly language instructions for a stack machine.

machine code	assembly language		machine code	assembly language
move r_1 r_2	**cspt** r_1		**lb** r_1 $n(r_2)$	**getb** r_1 n
	cspf r_2			**lbfh** r_1 $n(r_2)$
	rspf r_2			**getbx** r_1 $n(r_2)$
	mov r_1 r_2		**sb** r_1 $n(r_2)$	**putb** r_1 n
addiu r r n	**push** -n			**sbth** r_1 $n(r_2)$
	stepx r n			**putbx** r_1 $n(r_2)$
	addaiu r r n		**jal** a	**gosub** a
lw r_1 $n(r_2)$	**get** r_1 n		**jr** r	**return**
	lwfh r_1 $n(r_2)$		**j** a	**goto** a
	getx r_1 $n(r_2)$		**li** r a	**newx** r a n
sw r_1 $n(r_2)$	**put** r_1 n			**newh** r a n
	swfh r_1 $n(r_2)$		**bnez** r a	**ifnz** r a
	putx r_1 $n(r_2)$			

For example, several different stack machine instructions may all be thought of as manipulating the hidden stack pointer, register **sp** in the machine code processor, and they all are implemented as a **move** ('copy') machine code instruction. Thus the **move** instruction disassembles to one of several stack machine instructions as follows:

1. The **cspt** r_1 ('copy stack pointer to') instruction saves a copy of the stack pointer in register r_1. It corresponds to the **move** r_1 **sp** machine code processor instruction.
2. The **cspf** r_1 ('copy stack pointer from') instruction *refreshes* the stack pointer from a copy in r_1 that has the same value and was saved earlier (we will not explore here the reasons why a compiler might issue such a 'refresh' instruction). It corresponds to the **move sp** r_1 machine code instruction.
3. The **rspf** r_1 ('restore stack pointer from') instruction returns the stack pointer to a value that it held previously by copying an old saved value from r_1. It also corresponds to **move sp** r_1.

A fourth disassembly of the machine code **move** instruction, to the stack machine **mov** instruction, encompasses the case when the stack pointer is not involved at all; it does a straight copy of a word from one register to another at the stack machine level. The full set of stack machine instructions is listed in Table 3, and their correspondence with RISC machine code instructions is shown in Table 4.

We will not work through all the instructions and disassembly options in detail here, but note the important **push** n instruction in the stack machine, which can be thought of as decrementing the hidden stack pointer by n, extending the stack downwards. It corresponds to the **addiu sp sp** m machine code instruction, with $m = -n$. Also, the stack machine instructions **put** r_1 n and **get** r_1 n access the stack for a word at offset n bytes, and they correspond to the machine code **sw** r_1 n(**sp**) and **lw** r_1 n(**sp**) instructions, respectively.

The very same machine code instructions may also be interpreted as stack machine instructions that manipulate not the stack but either a 'string-like' object or an array. Strings/arrays are read with **getx/lwfh** and written with **putx/swth**. Table 4 shows that these are implemented by **lw/sw** in the machine code processor, applied to a base register $r_2 \neq$ **sp**. Stepping through a string is done with the **stepx** instruction in the stack machine, which is implemented by **addiu** in the machine code processor. Introducing the address of a string/array in the stack machine needs **newx/newh** and those are both implemented by the **li** ('load immediate') instruction in the machine code processor.

There are also 'b' ('byte-sized') versions of the **get**, **lwfh**, **getx** stack machine instructions named **getb**, **lbfh**, **getbx** respectively. These are implemented by **lb** in the machine code processor. For **put**, **swth**, **putx** we have byte versions **putb**, **sbth**, **putbx**.

4   Introducing Annotations and Annotation Types

Table 5. Non-aliasing subroutine machine code.

```
foo:
  move gp sp
  addiu sp sp -32
  ... code ...
  move sp gp
  jr ra
```

Consider the 'good' pseudo-code of Table 1 implemented as machine code and shown in Table 5. How do we show it is aliasing-safe? Our technique is to *annotate* the code in a style akin to verification using Hoare logic, but the annotation logic is based on the stack machine abstraction of what the machine code does. We begin with an annotation that says the **sp** register is bound to a particular *annotation type* on entry:

$$\{\, \mathbf{sp} = \mathrm{c}!0!4!8 \,\}$$

The 'c' as base signifies a variable pointer value is in register **sp**. It is the stack pointer value. The '!0!4!8' means that that particular value has been used as the base address for writes to memory at offsets 0, 4 and 8 bytes from it, respectively.

The first instruction in subroutine *foo* copies the stack pointer to register **gp** and we infer that register **gp** also gets the 'c' annotation, using a Hoare-triple-like notation:

$$\{\, \mathbf{sp}^* = \mathrm{c}!0!4!8 \,\} \; \mathtt{move} \quad \mathbf{gp} \quad \mathbf{sp} \; \{\, \mathbf{sp}^*, \mathbf{gp} = \mathrm{c}!0!4!8 \,\}$$

The stack pointer location (in the **sp** register) should always be indicated by an asterisk.

The arithmetic done by the next instruction destroys the offset information. It cannot yet be said that anything has been written at some offset from the new address, which is 32 distant from the old only up to an arithmetic equivalence in the processor:

$$\{\,\mathbf{sp}^*, \mathbf{gp} = \mathbf{c}!0!4!8\,\}\ \mathtt{addiu}\quad \mathtt{sp}\quad \mathtt{sp}\ \text{-}32\ \{\,\mathbf{gp} = \mathbf{c}!0!4!8;\ \mathbf{sp}^* = \mathbf{c}\,\}$$

Suppose the annotation on the **gp** register is still valid at the end of subroutine *foo*, so the stack pointer register is finally refreshed by the **move** instruction with the same annotation as at the start:

$$\{\,\mathbf{sp}^* = \mathbf{c};\ \mathbf{gp} = \mathbf{c}!0!4!8;\,\}\ \mathtt{move}\quad \mathtt{sp}\quad \mathtt{gp}\ \{\,\mathbf{sp}^*, \mathbf{gp} = \mathbf{c}!0!4!8\,\}$$

The return (**jr ra**) instruction does not change these annotations. So the calling code has returned as stack pointer a value that is annotated as having had values saved at offsets 0, 4, 8 from it, and the caller can rely on accessing data stored at those offsets. That does not guarantee that the *same* value of the stack pointer is returned to the caller, however. It will be shown below how this system of annotations may be coaxed into providing stronger guarantees.

5   Types for Stack, String and Array Pointers

The annotation discussed above is not complete. The *size* in bytes of the local stack frame needs to be recorded by following the 'c' with the frame size as a superscript. Suppose that on entry there is a local stack frame of size 12 words, or 48 bytes. Then here is the same annotation with superscripts on, written as a derivation in which the appropriate disassembly of each machine code instruction is written to the right of the machine code as the 'justification' for the derivation:

$$\frac{\dfrac{\{\mathbf{sp}^* = \mathbf{c}^{48}!0!4!8\}}{\{\mathbf{sp}^*, \mathbf{gp} = \mathbf{c}^{48}!0!4!8\}}\ \mathbf{move}\ \mathrm{gp\ sp}\quad /\ \mathbf{cspt}\ \mathrm{gp}}{\{\mathbf{sp}^* = \mathbf{c}^{32^{48}};\ \mathbf{gp} = \mathbf{c}^{48}!0!4!8\}}\ \mathbf{addiu}\ \mathrm{sp\ sp\ }\text{-}32/\ \mathbf{push}\ 32$$

$$\vdots$$

$$\frac{\{\mathbf{sp}^* = \mathbf{c}^{32^{48}};\ \mathbf{gp} = \mathbf{c}^{48}!0!4!8\}}{\{\mathbf{sp}^*, \mathbf{gp} = \mathbf{c}^{48}!0!4!8\}}\ \mathbf{move}\ \mathrm{sp\ gp}\quad /\ \mathbf{rspf}\ \mathrm{gp}$$

The **push** 32 abstract stack machine instruction makes a *new* local stack frame of 8 words or 32 bytes. It does not increase the size of the current frame. Accordingly, the 32 'pushes up' the 48 in the annotation so that 32^{48} is shown. This makes the size of the previous stack frame available to the annotation logic.

A different disassembly of **addaiu** r r n is required when r contains a string pointer, not the stack pointer, which means that register r lacks the asterisk in the annotation. The disassembly as a step along a string is written **stepx** r n, and requires n to be positive. In this case, the string pointer in r will be annotated with the type

$$\mathbf{c}^{\ddot{1}}$$

meaning that it is a 'calculatable' value that may be altered by adding 1 to it repeatedly. The form $\mathbf{c}^{\ddot{1}}$ hints that a string is regarded as a stack $\mathbf{c}^{1^{\cdot\cdot}}$ that starts 'pre-charged' with an indefinite number of frames of 1 byte each, which one may step up through by 'popping the stack' one frame, and one byte, at a time. So annotation types may be either like $\mathbf{c}^{32^{48}}$ or $\mathbf{c}^{\ddot{1}}$ and these may be followed by offsets !0!4!8! . . . . There is just one more base form, described below, completing the list in Box 3.

> Annotations a assert a binding of registers r or stack slots (n) to an *annotated type* t. One of the register names may be starred to indicate the stack pointer position. A type is either 'uncalculated', **u**, or 'calculated', **c**. Either may be decorated with '!n' annotations indicating historical writes at that offset from the typed value when used as an address. A **c** base type may also be superscripted by a 'tower' of natural numbers n denoting 'frame sizes' (see text), while a **u** base type may have a single superscript (also denoting size). We also use $\ddot{1}$ for a tower $1^{1^{\cdot\cdot}}$ of undetermined extent and a single repeated size. Also, formal type variables x, y, etc are valid stand-ins for annotated types, and formal 'set of offsets variables' X, Y, etc are valid stand-ins for sets of offsets.
>
> $$a ::= r^{[*]}, \ldots, (n), \ldots = t; \ldots$$
> $$t ::= \mathbf{c}^{[n^{\cdot\cdot}]}!n! \ldots \mid \mathbf{u}^{[n]}!n! \ldots$$

Box 3. Syntax of annotations and types.

The RISC instruction **lw** r_1 $n(r_2)$ is also disassembled differently according to the annotated type in r_2. As **get** r_1 n it retrieves a value previously stored at offset n in the stack, when $n \geq 0$ and r_2 is the stack pointer register. As **lwfh** r_1 $n(r_2)$ it retrieves an element in an array from the *heap* area. In that case, r_2 will be annotated

$$\mathbf{u}^m$$

meaning an 'unmodifiable' pointer to an array of size m bytes, and $m-4 \geq n \geq 0$. A third possibility is disassembly as retrieval from a string-like object in the heap, when, as **getx** r_1 $n(r_2)$, register r_2 will have a 'string-like' annotation of the form $\mathbf{c}^{\ddot{m}}$, meaning that it must be stepped through in increments of m bytes.

Similarly the RISC **sw** r_1 $n(r_2)$ instruction can be disassembled as **put** r_1 n of a value at offset n to the stack, or **swth** r_1 $n(r_2)$ to an array or **putx** r_1 $n(r_2)$ to a string, depending on the type bound to register r_2. These register types drive the disassembly.

6   Formal Logic

We can now write down formal rules for the logic of annotations introduced informally in the 'derivation' laid out in the previous section. Readers who would prefer to see a worked example first should jump directly to Sect. 7.

Table 6. Possible disassemblies of machine code instructions as constrained by the stack pointer register location changes (SP←SP) or absence (×), and changes to the stack content ('delta').

move r_1 r_2	r_1	r_2	stack delta
rspf r_2	SP ↻	×	yes
cspf r_2	SP ↻	×	no
cspt r_1	×	SP ↻	no
mspt r_1	SP←SP		no
mov r_1 r_2	×	×	no

addiu r_1 r_2 m	r_1	r_2	stack delta
step r m		×	no
stepto r_1 r_2 m	×	×	no
push $-m$	SP ↻		yes
pushto r_1 $-m$	SP←SP		yes
addaiu r_1 r_2 m	×	×	no

lw r_1 $m(r_2)$	r_1	r_2	stack delta
get r_1 m	×	SP ↻	no
lwfh r_1 $m(r_2)$	×	×	no
getx r_1 $m(r_2)$	×	×	no

sw r_1 $m(r_2)$	r_1	r_2	stack delta
put r_1 m	×	SP ↻	no
swth r_1 $m(r_2)$	×	×	no
putx r_1 $m(r_2)$	×	×	no

We start with a list of so-called 'small-step' program annotations justified by individual stack machine instructions, each the disassembly of a machine code instruction. The small-step rules relate the annotation before each machine code instruction to the annotation after. Table 6 helps to reduce a priori the number of possible disassemblies for each machine code instruction, but in principle disassembly to stack machine code does not have to be done first, but can be left till the last possible moment during the annotation process, as each disassembly choice corresponds to the application of a different rule of inference about which annotation comes next. If the corresponding inference rule may not be applied, then that disassembly choice is impossible.

Here is how to read Table 7. Firstly, 'offsets variables' X, Y, etc., stand in for sets of offset annotations '!k'. For example, the **put gp** 4 instruction is expected to start with a prior annotation pattern $\mathbf{sp}^* = \mathbf{c}^f!X$ for the stack pointer register. Secondly, the stack pointer register is indicated by an asterisk. Thirdly, f in the table stands for some particular stack frame tower of integers; it is not a variable, being always some constant in any particular instance. In the case of the **put gp** 4 instruction, f must start with some particular number at least 8 in size, in order to accommodate the 4-byte word written at offset 4 bytes within the local stack frame. Just '8' on its own would do for f here. Lastly, 'type variables' x, y, etc, where they appear, stand in for full types.

The table relates annotations before and after each instruction. So, in the case of the **put gp** 4 instruction, if the prior annotation for the stack pointer register is $\mathbf{sp}^* = \mathbf{c}^f!X$, then the post annotation is $\mathbf{sp}^* = \mathbf{c}^f!4!X$, meaning that 4 is one of the offsets at which a write has been made. It may be that 4 is also a member of the set denoted by X (which may contain other offsets too), or it may be not in X. That is not decided by the formula, which merely says that whatever other offsets there are in the annotation, '4' is put there by this instruction. At any rate, the annotation pattern for the **put gp** 4 instruction is:

$$\{\ldots; \mathbf{sp}^* = \mathbf{c}^f!X; \ldots\} \text{ put gp } 4 \ \{\ldots; \mathbf{sp}^* = \mathbf{c}^f!4!X; \ldots\}$$

Table 7. 'Small-step' annotations on assembly instructions.

$\{\ \}$	**newx** $r\ m$	$\{r=\mathbf{c}^{\tilde{m}}!X\}$	// Set reg. r content
$\{r_1=\mathbf{c}^f!Y; r_2=\mathbf{c}^{\tilde{m}}!X\}$	**putx** $r_1\ n(r_2)$	$\{0r_1=\mathbf{c}^f!Y; r_2=\mathbf{c}^{\tilde{m}}!n!X\}$	// Store word to string
$\{r_2=\mathbf{c}^{\tilde{m}}!n!X\}$	**getx** $r_1\ n(r_2)$	$\{r_1=\mathbf{c}^0; r_2=\mathbf{c}^{\tilde{m}}!n!X\}$	// Load word from string
$\{r=\mathbf{c}^{\tilde{m}}!X\}$	**stepx** $r\ m$	$\{r=\mathbf{c}^{\tilde{m}}!Y\}$	// Step along string
$\{\ \}$	**newh** $r\ m$	$\{r=\mathbf{u}^m!X\}$	// Set reg. r content
$\{r_1=\mathbf{c}^f!Y; r_2=\mathbf{u}^m!X\}$	**swth** $r_1\ n(r_2)$	$\{r_1=\mathbf{c}^f!Y; r_2=\mathbf{u}^m!n!X\}$	// Store word to array
$\{r_2=\mathbf{u}^m!n!X\}$	**lwfh** $r_1\ n(r_2)$	$\{r_1=\mathbf{c}^0; r_2=\mathbf{u}^m!n!X\}$	// Load word from array
$\{r_1=x; r_2^*=\mathbf{c}^f!X\ \}$	**put** $r_1\ n$	$\{r_1,(n)=x; r_2^*=\mathbf{c}^f!n!X\}$	// Store word to stack
$\{r_2^*=\mathbf{c}^f!n!X; (n)=x\}$	**get** $r_1\ n$	$\{r_1,(n)=x; r_2^*=\mathbf{c}^f!n!X\}$	// Load word from stack
$\{r^*=\mathbf{c}^f!X\}$	**push** n	$\{r^*=\mathbf{c}^{n^f}\}$	// New frame
$\{r_2^*=\mathbf{c}^f!X\}$	**cspt** r_1	$\{r_1,r_2^*=\mathbf{c}^f!X\}$	// Copy SP to reg. r_1
$\{r_1^*=\mathbf{c}^f!Y; r_2=\mathbf{c}^f!X\}$	**cspf** r_2	$\{r_1^*,r_2=\mathbf{c}^f!X\}$	// Copy SP from reg. r_2
$\{r_1^*=\mathbf{c}^{n^f}!Y; r_2=\mathbf{c}^f!X\}$	**rspf** r_2	$\{r_1^*,r_2=\mathbf{c}^f!X\}$	// Restore SP from reg. r_2
$\{\ \}$	**nop**	$\{\ \}$	// No-op, do nothing
$\{r_2=x\}$	**mov** $r_1\ r_2$	$\{r_1,r_2=x\}$	// Copy from reg. r_2
$\{r_2=\mathbf{c}^f!X\}$	**addaiu** $r_1\ r_2\ n$	$\{r_1=\mathbf{c}^0; r_2=\mathbf{c}^f!X\}$	// Arithmetic add

Notation. The X, Y, etc stand for a set of offsets $!n_1!n_2!\ldots$, for literal natural numbers n. The stack frame size (or 'tower of stack frame sizes') f is a literal natural number (or finite sequence of natural numbers). The x, y, etc stand for any type (something that can appear on the right of an equals sign)

and considering the effect on the **gp** register (which may be supposed to have the type denoted by the formal type variable x initially) and the stack slot denoted by '(4)' gives

$$\{\mathbf{gp}=x; \mathbf{sp}^*=\mathbf{c}^f!X\}\ \mathbf{put\ gp}\ 4\ \{\mathbf{sp}^*=\mathbf{c}^f!4!X; \mathbf{gp},(4)=x\}$$

because whatever the description x of the data in register **gp** before the instruction runs, since the data is transferred to stack slot '(4)', the latter gains the same description. Generalising the stack offset '4' back to n, and generalising registers **gp** and **sp** to r_1 and r_2 respectively, one obtains exactly the small-step signature listed for instruction **put** $r_1\ n$. Registers whose annotations are not mentioned in this signature have bindings that are unaffected by the instruction.

Small-step annotations $\{\Theta\}\ \kappa\ \{\Psi\}$ for an instruction ι at address a with a disassembly κ generate a so-called 'big step' rule

$$\frac{T \triangleright \{\Psi\}\ a+4\ \{\Phi\}}{T \triangleright \{\Theta\}\ a\ \{\Phi\}}[a \mid \iota / \kappa]$$

in which Φ is the final annotation at program end and T denotes a list of big-step annotations $\{\Psi\}\ a\ \{\Phi\}$, one for each instruction address a in the program (note that, in consequence, branches within the program must get the same annotation at convergence as there is only one annotation there). Thus the big-step rule is an inference about what *theory* T contains. The rule above says that if $\{\Psi\}\ a+4\ \{\Phi\}$ is in theory T, then so is $\{\Theta\}\ a\ \{\Phi\}$. The label justifies the inference by the fact that instruction ι is at address a, and disassembly κ has been chosen for it.

The big-step rules aim to generate a 'covering' theory T for each program. That is, an annotation before every (reachable) instruction, and thus an annotation *between* every instruction. The rule above tells one how to extend by one further instruction a theory that is growing from the back of the program towards the front.

Where does theory construction start? It is with the big-step rule for the final **jr ra** instruction that classically ends a subroutine. The action of this instruction is to jump back to the 'return address' stored in the **ra** register (or another designated register). The annotation for it says that there was a program address (an 'uncalculatable value', $\mathbf{u}^0$) in the **ra** register before it ran (and it is still there after), and requires no hypotheses:

$$\frac{}{T \,\triangleright\, \{r{=}\mathbf{u}^0\}\ a\ \{r{=}\mathbf{u}^0\}}[a \mid \mathbf{jr}\ r\ /\ \mathbf{return}]$$

The '0' superscript indicates that the address may not be used as a base for offset memory accesses; that would access program instructions if it were allowed. Calling code conventionally places the return address in the **ra** register prior to each subroutine call.

There are just three more big-step rules, corresponding to each of the instructions that cause changes in the flow of control in a program. Jumps (unconditional branches) are handled by a rule that refers back to the target of the jump:

$$\frac{T \,\triangleright\, \{\Theta\}\ b\ \{\Phi\}}{T \,\triangleright\, \{\Theta\}\ a\ \{\Phi\}}[a \mid \mathbf{j}\ b\ /\ \mathbf{goto}\ b]$$

This rule propagates the annotation at the target b of the jump back to the source a. At worst a guess at the fixpoint is needed.

The logic of branch instructions (conditional jumps) at a says that the outcome of going down a branch to b or continuing at $a + 4$ must be the same. But the instruction **bnez** r b ('branch to address b if register r is nonzero, else continue') and variants first require the value in the register r to be tested, so it is pre-marked with **c** ('calculatable'):

$$\frac{T \,\triangleright\, \{r{=}\mathbf{c}^f!\boldsymbol{X};\Theta\}\ b\ \{\Phi\} \quad T \,\triangleright\, \{r{=}\mathbf{c}^f!\boldsymbol{X};\Theta\}\ a+4\ \{\Phi\}}{T \,\triangleright\, \{r{=}\mathbf{c}^f!\boldsymbol{X};\Theta\}\ a\ \{\Phi\}}[a \mid \mathbf{bnez}\ r\ b\ /\ \mathbf{ifnz}\ r\ b]$$

The case $b < a$ (backward branch) requires a guess at a fixpoint as it does for jump. The annotated incremental history f, likely none, of the value in the tested register is irrelevant here, but it is maintained through the rule. The set of offsets $\boldsymbol{X}$ already written to is also irrelevant here, but it is maintained through the rule.

The RISC **jal** b machine code instruction implements standard imperative programming language subroutine calls. It puts the address of the next instruction in the **ra** register (the 'return address') and jumps to the subroutine at address b. The calling code will have saved the current return address on the stack before the call. The callee code will return to the caller by jumping to the address in the **ra** register with **jr ra**, and the calling code will then restore its own return address from the stack.

Because of **jal**'s action in filling register **ra** with a program address, **ra** on entry to the subroutine at b must already have a u^0 annotation, indicating an unmodifiable value that cannot even be used for memory access. And because the same subroutine can be called from many different contexts, we need to distinguish the annotations per call site and so we use a throwaway lettering T' to denote those annotations that derive from the call of b from site a. The general rule is:

$$\frac{T' \triangleright \{\mathbf{ra}=\mathbf{u}^0; \Psi\} \, b \, \{\Theta\} \qquad T \triangleright \{\Theta\} \, a + 4 \, \{\Phi\}}{T \triangleright \{\Psi\} \, a \, \{\Phi\}}[a \mid \mathbf{jal} \, b \, / \, \mathbf{gosub} \, b]$$

The '0' superscript means that memory accesses via the return address as base address for **lw/sw** are not allowed; that would access the program instructions. The stack pointer register has not been named, but it must be distinct from the **ra** register.

We have found it useful to apply extra constraints at subroutine calls. We require (i) that each subroutine return the stack to the same state it acquired it in (this is not a universal convention), and (ii) that a subroutine make and unmake all of its own local stack frame (again, not a universal convention). That helps a Prolog implementation of the verification logic start from a definitely known state at the end of each subroutine independent of the call context – namely, that the local stack frame at subroutine end (and beginning) is size zero. These constraints may be built into the **jal** rule as follows:

$$\frac{T' \triangleright \{\mathbf{ra}=\mathbf{u}^0; r^*=\mathbf{c}^0!\boldsymbol{X}, \Psi\} \, b \, \{r^*=\mathbf{c}^0!\boldsymbol{Y}; \Theta\} \qquad T \triangleright \{r^*=\mathbf{c}^f!\boldsymbol{Y}; \Theta\} \, a+4 \, \{\Phi\}}{T \triangleright \{r^*=\mathbf{c}^f!\boldsymbol{X}; \Psi\} \, a \, \{\Phi\}}$$

The requirement (i) is implemented by returning the stack pointer in the same register (r^* with the same r on entry and return) and with no stack cells visible in the local stack frame handed to the subroutine and handed back by the subroutine (the two 0s). The requirement (ii) is implemented by setting the local stack frame on entry to contain no stack, just the general purpose registers, which forces the subroutine to make its own stack frame to work in. Other calling conventions require other rule refinements.

As noted, the small-step and big-step rules can be read as a Prolog program with variables the bold-faced offsets variables $\boldsymbol{X}$, $\boldsymbol{Y}$, etc, and type variables x, y, etc.

7   Example Annotation

Below is the annotation of the simple main routine of a Hello World program that calls 'printstr' with the Hello World string address as argument, then calls 'halt'. The code was emitted by a standard compiler (*gcc*) and modified by hand to be safe against aliasing, so some compiler 'quirks' are still visible. The compiler likes to preserve the **fp** register content across subroutine calls, for example, even though it is not used here.

The functionality is not at issue here, but, certainly, knowing what each instruction does allows the annotation to be inferred by an annotator without reference to rules and axioms. The **li a0** instruction sets the **a0** ('0th argument') register, for example, so the only change in the annotation after the instruction is to the **a0** column. The annotator introduces the string type, c^1, into the annotation there, since the instruction sets **a0** to the address of the Hello World string. The annotator assumes that the stack pointer starts in the **sp** register and that 'main' is called (likely from a set-up routine) with a return address in the **ra** register. Changes are marked in grey:

$\{\,\}$	**newx** r m	$\{r = c^{\tilde{m}}!X\}$	// Set reg. r content
$\{r_1=c^f!Y; r_2=c^{\tilde{m}}!X\}$	**putx** r_1 $n(r_2)$	$\{r_1=c^f!Y; r_2=c^{\tilde{m}}!n!X\}$	// Store word to string
$\{r_2=c^{\tilde{m}}!n!X\}$	**getx** r_1 $n(r_2)$	$\{r_1=c^0; r_2=c^{\tilde{m}}!n!X\}$	// Load word from string
$\{r=c^{\tilde{m}}!X\}$	**stepx** r m	$\{r=c^{\tilde{m}}!Y\}$	// Step along string
$\{\,\}$	**newh** r m	$\{r = u^m!X\}$	// Set reg. r content
$\{r_1=c^f!Y; r_2=u^m!X\}$	**swth** r_1 $n(r_2)$	$\{r_1=c^f!Y; r_2=u^m!n!X\}$	// Store word to array
$\{r_2=u^m!n!X\}$	**lwfh** r_1 $n(r_2)$	$\{r_1=c^0; r_2=u^m!n!X\}$	// Load word from array
$\{r_1=x; r_2^*=c^f!X\}$	**put** r_1 n	$\{r_1,(n)=x; r_2^*=c^f!n!X\}$	// Store word to stack
$\{r_2^*=c^f!n!X; (n)=x\}$	**get** r_1 n	$\{r_1,(n)=x; r_2^*=c^f!n!X\}$	// Load word from stack
$\{r^*=c^f!X\}$	**push** n	$\{r^*=c^{nf}\}$	// New frame
$\{r_2^*=c^f!X\}$	**cspt** r_1	$\{r_1,r_2^*=c^f!X\}$	// Copy SP to reg. r_1
$\{r_1^*=c^f!Y; r_2=c^f!X\}$	**cspf** r_2	$\{r_1^*,r_2=c^f!X\}$	// Copy SP from reg. r_2
$\{r_1^*=c^{nf}!Y; r_2=c^f!X\}$	**rspf** r_2	$\{r_1^*,r_2=c^f!X\}$	// Restore SP from reg. r_2
$\{\,\}$	**nop**	$\{\,\}$	// No-op, do nothing
$\{r_2=x\}$	**mov** r_1 r_2	$\{r_1,r_2=x\}$	// Copy from reg. r_2
$\{r_2=c^f!X\}$	**addaiu** r_1 r_2 n	$\{r_1=c^0; r_2=c^f!X\}$	// Arithmetic add

That the '!' annotations are always less than the bottom element of the tower on the stack pointer annotation means that no aliasing occurs. Reads are at an offset already marked with a '!', hence within the same range that writes are constrained to.

The 'halt' subroutine does not use the stack pointer; its function is to write a single byte to the hard-coded I/O-mapped address of a system peripheral. The annotation for register **v1** on output is the taint left by that write.

```
halt:                                 # zero = c^0; ra = u^0
li v1 0xb0000x10 newh v1 ... 1 # v1 = u^1; zero = c^0; ra = u^0
sb zero 0(v1)    sbth v1 0(v1)  # v1 = u^1!0; zero = c^0; ra = u^0
jr ra            return         # v1 = u^1!0; zero = c^0; ra = u^0
```

The **zero** register is conventionally kept filled with the zero word in RISC architectures.

The *printstr* routine takes a string pointer as argument in register **a0**. A requirement that registers **v0**, **v1** have certain types on entry is an artifact of annotation. Since '$B' comes after writes to **v0**, **v1**, those two registers are bound to types at that point. The forward jump (**j**) to '$B' forces the same annotations at the jump instruction as at the target. But, at the jump, no write to **v0**, **v1** has yet taken place, so we are obliged to provide the types of **v0**, **v1** at entry. The table below is constructed using the same display convention as the table for *main*.

		sp*	ra	a0	fp	gp	v0	v1	(16)	(24)	(28)
main:		c^0	u^0		x		$c^i!0$	c^0			
move gp sp	cspt gp	c^0	u^0		x	c^0	$c^i!0$	c^0			
addiu sp sp -32	push 32	c^{32^0}	u^0		x	c^0	$c^i!0$	c^0			
sw ra 28(sp)	put ra 28	$c^{32^0}!28$	u^0		x	c^0	$c^i!0$	c^0			u^0
sw fp 24(sp)	put fp 24	$c^{32^0}!24!28$	u^0		x	c^0	$c^i!0$	c^0		x	u^0
move fp sp	cspt fp	$c^{32^0}!24!28$	u^0		$c^{32^0}!24!28$	c^0	$c^i!0$	c^0		x	u^0
sw gp 16(sp)	put gp 16	$c^{32^0}!16!24!28$	u^0		$c^{32^0}!24!28$	c^0	$c^i!0$	c^0	c^0	x	u^0
li a0 <helloworld>	newx a0 ... 1	$c^{32^0}!16!24!28$	u^0	c^i	$c^{32^0}!24!28$	c^0	$c^i!0$	c^0	c^0	x	u^0
jal <printstr>	gosub ...	$c^{32^0}!16!24!28$	u^0	c^0	$c^{32^0}!24!28$	c^0	c^0	$u^1!0$	c^0	x	u^0
lw gp 16(sp)	get gp 16	$c^{32^0}!16!24!28$	u^0	c^0	$c^{32^0}!24!28$	c^0	c^0	$u^1!0$	c^0	x	u^0
jal <halt>	gosub ...	$c^{32^0}!16!24!28$	u^0	c^0	$c^{32^0}!24!28$	c^0	c^0	$u^1!0$	c^0	x	u^0
nop											
lw gp 16(sp)	get gp 16	$c^{32^0}!16!24!28$	u^0	c^0	$c^{32^0}!24!28$	c^0	c^0	$u^1!0$	c^0	x	u^0
nop											
lw ra 28(sp)	get ra 28	$c^{32^0}!16!24!28$	u^0	c^0	$c^{32^0}!24!28$	c^0	c^0	$u^1!0$	c^0	x	u^0
lw fp 24(sp)	get fp 24	$c^{32^0}!16!24!28$	u^0	c^0	x	c^0	c^0	$u^1!0$	c^0	x	u^0
move sp gp	rspf gp	c^0	u^0	c^0	x	c^0	c^0	$u^1!0$	c^0	x	u^0
jr ra	return	c^0	u^0	c^0	x	c^0	c^0	$u^1!0$	c^0	x	u^0
helloworld:	⟨string data⟩										

The 'printchar' subroutine writes a character received in register **a0** to the hard-coded address of a printer device:

```
printchar:                  # a0 = c⁰; ra = u⁰
li v1 0xb0000000  newh v1 ... 1  # v1 = u¹; a0 = c⁰; ra = u⁰
sb a0 0(v1)       sbth a0 0(v1)  # v1 = u¹!0; a0 = c⁰; ra = u⁰
jr ra             return         # v1 = u¹!0; a0 = c⁰; ra = u⁰
```

Like *halt*, it does not use the stack pointer.

8   How Does Annotation Ensure Aliasing Does not Happen?

How to ensure memory aliasing does not happen is intuitively simple: make sure that each address used can have been calculated in only one way. There are in principle two constraints that can be enforced directly via annotation and which will have this effect:

(i) Both stack reads and writes with **get** and **put** may be restricted to offsets n that lie in the range permitted by the local stack frame size (look for a stack pointer tower $m^{\cdot}$ on the annotation before the instruction, with $0 \leq n \leq m - 4$);

(ii) stack reads with **get** may be restricted to offsets n at which writes with **put** have already taken place (look for a $!n$ mark on the annotation before the instruction).

Similarly for strings and arrays. It is (i) that makes memory aliasing impossible, but (ii) is also useful because it (a) reduces (i) to be required on writes alone, and (b) prevents 'read before write' faults. Without (i), code could validly try to access an element of the caller's frame, and that would fail because of aliasing via two distinct calculations for the same address, from caller's and callee's frames respectively.

If these constraints are satisfied, we argue as follows that memory-aliasing cannot occur. The base address used for access via the RISC **lw** or **sw** instructions is either:

1. The stack pointer (disassembly of the access instruction is to **put**, **get**, **putb**, **getb**);
2. the base address of a string, incremented several times by the string increment (the disassembly is to **putx**, **getx**, **putbx**, **getbx**);
3. the base address of an array (the disassembly is to **swth**, **sbth**, **lwfh**, **lbfh**).

and the offset in the instruction is in the first case less than the stack frame size, in the second case less than the string increment, and in the third case less than the array size.

Why are these and no other case possible? Firstly, if the program is annotated, then every use of a base address for the underlying machine code **lw** and **sw** instructions matches exactly one of these cases, because the annotation rules have no other option.

Next we claim that the annotations on a program are *sound*. This is a technical claim that we cannot formally substantiate in the space here that says that in an annotated program the annotations around each instruction reflect what the instruction does computationally. The full statement requires a model of each instruction's semantics as a state-to-state transformation and a proof that the big-step rules of Sect. 6 express those semantics. Given that, the three cases above for the base address used in a **lw** and **sw** instruction may be characterized thus:

1. It is the stack pointer, which is marked with an asterisk in the annotation and typed with $\mathbf{c}^f$ where the tower f consists of the sizes of current and calling stack frames;
2. it is a string pointer, which is typed with $\mathbf{c}^{\ddot{m}}$ in the annotation and is equal to the base address of the string plus a finite number of increments m;

3. it is an array pointer, which is typed with $\mathbf{u}^m$ in the annotation and is equal to the base address of the array, which is of size m.

In each of those three cases, the offset used in the **lw** or **sw** instruction is only permitted by the annotation to lie in the range 0 to $m-4$, where m is respectively the current frame size, the string step size, and the array size. The first of these cases implements condition (i), and the second and third implement the equivalent condition for strings and arrays respectively. I.e., there is only one calculation possible for each address used.

Similar arguments hold for byte-wise access via **lb** and **sb**. In addition, however, one must require that memory areas accessed via these instructions are not also accessed via **lw** and **sw**, in order to avoid different calculations for the addresses of the individual bytes in a word. The simplest way to ensure that is to forbid use of **lb** and **sb** entirely, relying instead on **lw** and **sw** plus arithmetic operations to extract the byte. The next simplest alternative is to allow **lb** and **sb** only on strings with step size less than 4 and arrays of size less than 4, which word-wise instructions are forbidden from accessing by the annotation rules.

9   Conclusion and Future Work

We have set out a method of annotation that can ensure that a RISC machine-code program is safe against 'hardware' aliasing. We model aliasing as introduced by the use of different arithmetic calculations for the same memory address, and successful annotation guarantees that a unique calculation will be used at runtime for the address of each execution stack, string or array element accessed by the program. Annotation also means disassembling the machine code to a slightly higher level assembly language, for a stack machine, and a human being is required to certify that the disassembly matches the programmer's intentions.

Note that one may add disassembly rules to the system that are (deliberately) semantically wrong, with the aim of correcting the code. For example, one may choose to (incorrectly) disassemble the RISC **addiu sp sp 32** instruction to a stack machine **pop** instruction. The RISC instruction is not a correct implementation of the higher level instruction in an aliasing context, although it was likely intended to be. But one may then replace the original RISC code with a correct implementation.

Also note that the equational annotations here may be generalised to quite arbitrary first-order predicates. It also appears that our system of types may be generalised to arrays of arrays and strings of strings, etc, which offers the prospect of a static analysis technology that can follow pointers.

References

1. Barr, M.: Programming Embedded Systems in C and C++, 1st edn. O'Reilly & Associates Inc, Sebastopol (1998)
2. Bowen, J.P.: Formal specification of the ProCoS/Safemos instruction set. Micoproc. Microsys. **14**(10), 637–643 (1990)

3. Bowen, J.P., Breuer, P.T.: Decompilation. In: van Zuylen, H. (ed.) The REDO Compendium Reverse Engineering for Software Maintenance, Chap. 10, pp. 131–138. Wiley, New York (1993)
4. Breuer, P.T., Bowen, J.P.: Decompilation: the enumeration of types and grammars. ACM Trans. Program. Lang. Syst. **16**(5), 1613–1647 (1994)
5. Breuer, P.T., Bowen, J.P.: Typed assembler for a RISC crypto-processor. In: Barthe, G., Livshits, B., Scandariato, R. (eds.) ESSoS 2012. LNCS, vol. 7159, pp. 22–29. Springer, Heidelberg (2012)
6. Breuer, P.T., Bowen, J.P.: A fully homomorphic crypto-processor design: correctness of a secret computer. In: Jürjens, J., Livshits, B., Scandariato, R. (eds.) ESSoS 2013. LNCS, vol. 7781, pp. 123–138. Springer, Heidelberg (2013)
7. Breuer, P.T., Bowen, J.P.: Idea: towards a working fully homomorphic crypto-processor: practice and the secret computer. In: Jörjens, J., Pressens, F., Bielova, N. (eds.) ESSoS 2014. LNCS, vol. 8364, pp. 131–140. Springer, Switzerland (2014)
8. Fischer, F.H., Sindalovsky, V., Segan, S.A.: Memory aliasing method and apparatus, 20 August 2002. US Patent 6,438,672
9. Patterson, D.A.: Reduced instruction set computers. Commun. ACM **28**(1), 8–21 (1985)
10. Sato, T.: Speculative resolution of ambiguous memory aliasing. In: Innovative Architecture for Future Generation High-Performance Processors and Systems, pp. 17–26. IEEE (1997)
11. Wing, M.J., Kelly, E.J.: Method and apparatus for aliasing memory data in an advanced microprocessor, 20 July 1999. US Patent 5,926,832

Soundness and Completeness
of the NRB Verification Logic

Peter T. Breuer[1]($\boxtimes$) and Simon J. Pickin[2]

[1] Department of Computer Science, University of Birmingham, Birmingham, UK
Peter.T.Breuer@gmail.com
[2] Facultad de Informática, Universidad Complutense de Madrid, Madrid, Spain
spickin@ucm.es

Abstract. A simple semantic model for the NRB logic of program verification is provided here, and the logic is shown to be sound and complete with respect to it. That provides guarantees in support of the logic's use in the automated verification of large imperative code bases, such as the Linux kernel source. 'Soundness' implies that no breaches of safety conditions are missed, and 'completeness' implies that symbolic reasoning is as powerful as model-checking here.

1 Introduction

NRB ('normal, return, break') program logic was first introduced in 2004 [5] as the theory supporting an automated semantic analysis suite [4] targeting the C code of the Linux kernel. The analyses performed with this kind of program logic and automatic tools are typically much more approximate than that provided by more interactive or heavyweight techniques such as theorem-proving and model-checking [10], respectively, but NRB-based solutions have proved capable of rapidly scanning millions of lines of C code and detecting deadlocks scattered as rarely as one per million lines of code [9]. A rough synopsis of the logic is that it is precise in terms of accurately following the often complex flow of control and sequence of events in an imperative language, but not very accurate at following data values. That is fine in the context of a target like C [1,12], where static analysis cannot reasonably hope to follow all data values accurately because of the profligate use of pointers in a typical program (a pointer may access any part of memory, in principle, hence writing through a pointer might 'magically' change any value) and the NRB logic was designed to work around that problem by focussing instead on information derived from sequences of events.

Modal operators in NRB designate the kind of exit from a code fragment, as **return, break,** etc. The logic may be configured in detail to support different abstractions in different analyses; detecting the freeing of a record in memory while it may still be referenced requires an abstraction that counts the possible reference holders, for example, not the value currently in the second field from the right. The technique became known as 'symbolic approximation' [6,7] because of the foundation in symbolic logic and because the analysis is guaranteed to be

S. Counsell and M. Núñez (Eds.): SEFM 2013 Collocated Workshops, LNCS 8368, pp. 389–404, 2014.
DOI: 10.1007/978-3-319-05032-4_28, © Springer International Publishing Switzerland 2014

inaccurate but on the alarmist side ('approximate from above'). In other words, the analysis does not miss bugs, but does report false positives. In spite of a few years' pedigree behind it now, a foundational semantics for the logic has only just been published [8] (as an Appendix to the main text, in which it is shown that the verification computation can be distributed over a network of volunteer solvers and how such a procedure may be used as the basis of an open certification process). This article aims to provide a yet simpler semantics for the logic and also a completeness result, with the aim of consolidating the technique's bona fides. It fulfils the moral obligation to provide theoretical guarantees for a method that verifies code.

Interestingly, the main formal guarantee ('never miss, always over-report') provided by NRB and symbolic approximation is said not to be desirable in the commercial context by the very practical authors of the Coverity analysis tool [3,11], which also has been used for static analysis of the Linux kernel and many very large C code projects. Allegedly, in the commercial arena, understandability of reports is crucial, not the guarantee that no bugs will be missed. The Coverity authors say that commercial clients tend to dismiss any reports from Coverity staff that they do not understand, turning a deaf ear to all explanations. The reports produced by our tools have been filtered as part of the process [4] before presentation to the client community, so that only the alarms that cannot be dismissed by us as false positives are seen by them. When our process has been organised as a distributed certification task, as reported in [8], then filtering away false positives can be seen as one more 'eyes-on' task for the human part of the anonymous network of volunteer certifiers.

The layout of this paper is as follows. In Sect. 2 a model of programs as sets of 'coloured' transitions between states is set out, and the constructs of a generic imperative language are expressed in those terms. It is shown that the constructs obey certain algebraic laws, which soundly implement the established deduction rules of NRB logic. Section 3 shows that the logic is complete, in that anything that is true in the model introduced in Sect. 2 can be proved using the formal rules of the NRB logic.

Since the model contains at least as many transitions as occur in reality, 'soundness' of the NRB logic means that it may construct *false* alarms for a safety condition possibly being breached at some particular point in a program, but it may not miss any real alarms. 'Completeness' means that the logic flags no more false alarms than are already to be predicted from the model, so if the model says that there ought to be no alarms at all, which implies there really are no alarms, then the logic can prove that. Thus, it is not necessary to construct and examine the complete graph of modelled state transitions ('model checking') in order to be able to give a program a clean bill of health, because the logic does that job, checking 'symbolically'.

2   Semantic Model

This section sets out a semantic model for the full NRBG(E) logic ('NRB' for short) shown in Table 1. The 'NRBG' part stands for 'normal, return, break,

Table 1. NRB deduction rules for triples of assertions and programs. Unless explicitly noted, assumptions $G_l p_l$ at left are passed down unaltered from top to bottom of each rule. We let $\mathcal{E}_1$ stand for any of $\mathbf{R}, \mathbf{B}, \mathbf{G}_l, \mathbf{E}_k$; $\mathcal{E}_2$ any of $\mathbf{R}, \mathbf{G}_l, \mathbf{E}_k$; $\mathcal{E}_3$ any of $\mathbf{R}. \mathbf{G}_{l'}$ for $l' \neq l$, $\mathbf{E}_k$; $\mathcal{E}_4$ any of $\mathbf{R}. \mathbf{G}_l, \mathbf{E}_{k'}$ for $k' \neq k$; $[h]$ the body of the subroutine named h.

$$\frac{\triangleright\{p\}\,P\,\{Nq\vee\mathcal{E}_1 x\} \quad \triangleright\{q\}\,Q\,\{Nr\vee\mathcal{E}_1 x\}}{\triangleright\{p\}\,P\,;Q\,\{Nr\vee\mathcal{E}_1 x\}}[\text{seq}] \qquad \frac{\triangleright\{p\}\,P\,\{Bq\vee Np\vee\mathcal{E}_2 x\}}{\triangleright\{p\}\,\mathbf{do}\,P\,\{Nq\vee\mathcal{E}_2 x\}}[\text{do}]$$

$$\frac{}{\triangleright\{p\}\,\mathbf{skip}\,\{N\,p\}}[\text{skp}] \qquad \frac{}{\triangleright\{p\}\,\mathbf{return}\,\{R\,p\}}[\text{ret}]$$

$$\frac{}{\triangleright\{p\}\,\mathbf{break}\,\{B\,p\}}[\text{brk}] \qquad [p{\to}p_l]\frac{}{G_l\,p_l\triangleright\{p\}\,\mathbf{goto}\,l\,\{G_l\,p\}}[\text{go}]$$

$$\frac{}{\triangleright\{p\}\,\mathbf{throw}\,k\,\{E_k\,p\}}[\text{throw}] \qquad \frac{}{\triangleright\{q[e/x]\}\,x{=}e\,\{Nq\}}[\text{let}]$$

$$\frac{\triangleright\{q\wedge p\}\,P\,\{r\}}{\triangleright\{p\}\,q\to P\,\{r\}}[\text{grd}] \qquad \frac{\triangleright\{p\}\,P\,\{q\}\quad\triangleright\{p\}\,Q\,\{q\}}{\triangleright\{p\}\,P\,|\,Q\,\{q\}}[\text{dsj}]$$

$$[Np_l{\to}q]\frac{G_l\,p_l\triangleright\{p\}\,P\,\{q\}}{G_l\,p_l\triangleright\{p\}\,P{:}l\,\{q\}}[\text{frm}] \qquad \frac{G_l\,p_l\triangleright\{p\}\,P\,\{G_l p_l\vee Nq\vee\mathcal{E}_3 x\}}{\triangleright\{p\}\,\mathbf{label}\,l.P\,\{Nq\vee\mathcal{E}_3 x\}}[\text{lbl}]$$

$$\frac{\triangleright\{p\}\,[h]\,\{Rr\vee E_k x_k\}}{G_l p_l\triangleright\{p\}\,\mathbf{call}\,h\,\{Nr\vee E_k x_k\}}[\text{sub}] \qquad \frac{\triangleright\{p\}\,P\,\{Nr\vee E_k q\vee\mathcal{E}_4 x\}\quad\triangleright\{q\}\,Q\,\{Nr\vee E_k x_k\vee\mathcal{E}_4 x\}}{\triangleright\{p\}\,\mathbf{try}\,P\,\mathbf{catch}(k)\,Q\,\{Nr\vee E_k x_k\vee\mathcal{E}_4 x\}}[\text{try}]$$

$$\frac{\triangleright\{p_i\}\,P\,\{q\}}{\triangleright\{Wp_i\}\,P\,\{q\}} \qquad \frac{\triangleright\{p\}\,P\,\{q_i\}}{\triangleright\{p\}\,P\,\{\bigwedge q_i\}} \qquad \frac{G_l\,p_{li}\triangleright\{p\}\,P\,\{q\}}{WG_l\,p_{li}\triangleright\{p\}\,P\,\{q\}}$$

$$[p'{\to}p, q{\to}q', p'_l{\to}p_l\,|\,G_l q'{\to}G_l p'_l]\frac{G_l\,p_l\triangleright\{p\}\,P\,\{q\}}{G_l\,p'_l\triangleright\{p'\}\,P\,\{q'\}}$$

goto', and the 'E' part treats exceptions (catch/throw in Java, setjmp/longjmp in C), aiming at a complete treatment of classical imperative languages. This semantics simplifies a *trace model* presented in the Appendix to [8], substituting traces there for state transitions here. The objective in laying out the model is to allow the user of NRB logic to agree that it is talking about what he/she understands a program does, computationally. So the model aims at simplicity and comprehensibility. Agree with it, and one has confidence in what the logic says a program may do.

A standard model of a program is as a relation of type $\mathbb{P}(S \times S)$, expressing possible changes in the program state as a 'set of pairs', consisting of initial and final states of type S. We add a *colour* to this picture. The colour shows if the program has run *normally* through to the end (colour 'N') or has terminated early via a **return** (colour 'R'), **break** (colour 'B'), **goto** (colour 'G_l' for some label l) or an exception (colour 'E_k' for some exception kind k). This documents the control flow precisely. In our modified picture, a program is a set of 'coloured transitions' of type

$$\mathbb{P}(S \times \star \times S)$$

where the colours $\star$ are a disjoint union

$$\star = \{\mathbf{N}\} \sqcup \{\mathbf{R}\} \sqcup \{\mathbf{B}\} \sqcup \{\mathbf{G}_l \,|\, l \in L\} \sqcup \{\mathbf{E}_k \,|\, k \in K\}$$

and L is the set of possible **goto** labels and K the set of possible exception kinds. We write the transition from state s_1 to state s_2 of colour ι as $s_1 \overset{\iota}{\mapsto} s_2$.

Table 2. Models of simple statements.

A **skip** statement is modelled as $$[\![\textbf{skip}]\!]_g = \{s \overset{N}{\mapsto} s \mid s \in S\}$$ It makes the transition from a state to the same state again, and ends 'normally'.	A **return** statement has the model $$[\![\textbf{return}]\!]_g = \{s \overset{R}{\mapsto} s \mid s \in S\}$$ It exits at once 'via a return flow' after a single, trivial transition.
The model of **skip; return** is $$[\![\textbf{skip; return}]\!]_g = \{s \overset{R}{\mapsto} s \mid s \in S\}$$ which is the same as that of **return**. It is made up of the compound of two trivial state transitions, $s \overset{N}{\mapsto} s$ from **skip** and $s \overset{R}{\mapsto} s$ from **return**, the latter ending in a 'return flow'.	The **return; skip** compound is modelled as: $$[\![\textbf{return; skip}]\!]_g = \{s \overset{R}{\mapsto} s \mid s \in S\}$$ It is made up of of just the $s \overset{R}{\mapsto} s$ transitions from **return**. There is no transition that can be formed as the composition of a transition from **return** followed by a transition from **skip**, because none of the first end 'normally'.

The programs we usually consider are deterministic, in that only at most one transition from each initial state s appears in the modelling relation, but they are embedded in a more general context where an arbitrary number of transitions may appear. Where the relation is not defined at all on some initial state s, we understand that that initial state leads inevitably to the program getting hung in an infinite loop, instead of terminating. The relations representing deterministic programs have a set of transitions from a given initial state s that is either of size zero ('hangs') or one ('terminates'). Only paths through the program that do not hang are of interest to us, and what the NRB logic will say about a program at some point is true only supposing control reaches that point, which it may never do.

Programs are put together in sequence with the second program accepting as inputs only the states that the first program ends 'normally' with. Otherwise the state with which the first program exited abnormally is the final outcome. That is,

$$[\![P; Q]\!] = \{s_0 \overset{\iota}{\mapsto} s_1 \in [\![P]\!] \mid \iota \neq \mathbf{N}\}$$
$$\cup \; \{s_0 \overset{\iota}{\mapsto} s_2 \mid s_1 \overset{\iota}{\mapsto} s_2 \in [\![Q]\!], \; s_0 \overset{\mathbf{N}}{\mapsto} s_1 \in [\![P]\!]\}$$

This statement is not complete, however, because abnormal exits with a **goto** from P may still re-enter in Q if the **goto** target is in Q, and proceed. We postpone consideration of this eventuality by predicating the model with the sets of states g_l *hypothesised* as being fed in at the point l in the code. The model with these sets g_l as parameters takes account of the putative extra inputs at the point labeled l:

$$[\![P;Q]\!]_g = \{s_0 \overset{\iota}{\mapsto} s_1 \in [\![P]\!]_g \mid \iota \neq \mathbf{N}\}$$
$$\cup \{s_0 \overset{\iota}{\mapsto} s_2 \mid s_1 \overset{\iota}{\mapsto} s_2 \in [\![Q]\!]_g, \ s_0 \overset{\mathbf{N}}{\mapsto} s_1 \in [\![P]\!]_g\}$$

Later, we will tie things up by ensuring that the set of states bound to early exits via a **goto** l in P are exactly the sets g_l hypothesised here as entries at label l in Q. The type of the *interpretation* expressed by the fancy square brackets is

$$[\![-_1]\!]_{-_2} : \mathscr{C} \to (L \twoheadrightarrow \mathbb{P}S) \to \mathbb{P}(S \times \star \times S)$$

where g, the second argument/suffix, has the partial function type $L \twoheadrightarrow \mathbb{P}S$ and the first argument/bracket interior has type $\mathscr{C}$, denoting a simple language of imperative statements whose grammar is set out in Table 3. The models of some of its very basic statements as members of $\mathbb{P}(S \times \star \times S)$ are shown in Table 2. We briefly discuss these and other constructs of the language.

A real imperative programming language such as C can be mapped onto $\mathscr{C}$ – in principle exactly, but in practice rather approximately with respect to data values. A conventional **if**(b) P **else** Q statement in C is written as the choice between two guarded statements $b \to P \mid \neg b \to Q$ in the abstract language $\mathscr{C}$; the conventional **while**(b) P loop in C is expressed as **do**$\{\neg b \to$ **break** $\mid b \to P\}$, using the forever-loop of $\mathscr{C}$. A sequence $P; l : Q$ in C with a label l in the middle should strictly be expressed as $P : l; Q$ in $\mathscr{C}$, but we regard $P; l : Q$ as syntactic sugar for that, so it is still permissible to write $P; l : Q$ in $\mathscr{C}$. As a very special syntactic sweetener, we permit $l : Q$ too, even when there is no preceding statement P, regarding it as an abbreviation for **skip** $: l; Q$.

Curly brackets may be used to group code statements in $\mathscr{C}$, and parentheses may be used to group expressions. The variables are globals and are not formally declared. The terms of $\mathscr{C}$ are piecewise linear integer forms in integer variables, so the boolean expressions are piecewise comparisons between linear forms.

Table 3. Grammar of the abstract imperative language $\mathscr{C}$, where integer variables $x \in X$, term expressions $e \in \mathscr{E}$, boolean expressions $b \in \mathscr{B}$, labels $l \in L$, exceptions $k \in K$, statements $c \in \mathscr{C}$, integer constants $n \in \mathbb{Z}$, infix binary relations $r \in R$, subroutine names $h \in H$. Note that labels (the targets of **goto**s) are declared with 'label' and a label cannot be the first thing in a code sequence; it must follow some statement. Instead of **if**, $\mathscr{C}$ has guarded statements $b \to P$ and explicit choice $P \mid Q$, for code fragments P, Q. The choice construct is only used in practice in the expansion of **if** and **while** statements, so all its real uses are deterministic (have at most one transition from each initial state), although it itself is not.

$\mathscr{C} ::= \mathbf{skip} \mid \mathbf{return} \mid \mathbf{break} \mid \mathbf{goto}\ l \mid c;c \mid x{=}e \mid b{\to}c \mid c \mid c \mid \mathbf{do}\ c \mid c{:}l \mid \mathbf{label}\ l.c \mid \mathbf{call}\ h$
$\qquad \mid \mathbf{try}\ c\ \mathbf{catch}(k)\ c \mid \mathbf{throw}\ k$
$\mathscr{E} ::= n \mid x \mid n * e \mid e + e \mid b\,?\,e : e$
$\mathscr{B} ::= \top \mid \bot \mid e\,r\,e \mid b \vee b \mid b \wedge b \mid \neg b \mid \exists x.b$
$R ::= < \mid > \mid \leq \mid \geq \mid = \mid \neq$

Table 4. The conventional evaluation of integer and boolean terms of $\mathscr{C}$, for variables $x \in X$, integer constants $\kappa \in \mathbb{Z}$, using $s\,x$ for the (integer) value of the variable named x in a state s. The form $b[n/x]$ means 'expression b with integer n substituted for all unbound occurrences of x'.

$$[\![-]\!] : \mathscr{E} \to S \to \mathbb{Z}$$
$$[\![x]\!]s = s\,x$$
$$[\![\kappa]\!]s = \kappa$$
$$[\![\kappa * e]\!]s = \kappa * [\![e]\!]s$$
$$[\![e_1 + e_2]\!]s = [\![e_1]\!]s + [\![e_2]\!]s$$
$$[\![b\,?\,e_1 : e_2]\!]s = \text{if } [\![b]\!]s \text{ then } [\![e_1]\!]s \text{ else } [\![e_2]\!]s$$

$$[\![-]\!] : \mathscr{B} \to S \to \textbf{bool}$$
$$[\![\top]\!]s = \top \qquad [\![\bot]\!]s = \bot$$
$$[\![e_1 < e_2]\!]s = [\![e_1]\!]s < [\![e_2]\!]s$$
$$[\![b_1 \vee b_2]\!]s = [\![b_1]\!]s \vee [\![b_2]\!]s$$
$$[\![b_1 \wedge b_2]\!]s = [\![b_1]\!]s \wedge [\![b_2]\!]s$$
$$[\![\neg b]\!]s = \neg([\![b]\!]s)$$
$$[\![\exists x.b]\!]s = \exists n \in \mathbb{Z}.[\![b[n/x]]\!]s$$

Example 1. A valid integer term is '$5x + 4y + 3$', and a boolean expression is '$5x + 4y + 3 < z - 4 \wedge y \leq x$'.

In consequence another valid integer term, taking the value of the first on the range defined by the second, and 0 otherwise, is '$(5x + 4y + 3 < z - 4 \wedge y \leq x)\,?\,5x + 4y + 3{:}0$'.

The limited set of terms in $\mathscr{C}$ makes it practically impossible to map standard imperative language assignments as simple as '$x = x * y$' or '$x = x \mid y$' (the bitwise or) succinctly. In principle, those could be expressed exactly point by point using conditional expressions (with at most 2^{32} disjuncts), but it is usual to model all those cases by means of an abstraction away from the values taken to attributes that can be represented more elegantly using piecewise linear terms The abstraction may be to how many times the variable has been read since last written, for example, which maps '$x = x * y$' to '$x = x + 1; y = y + 1; x = 0$'.

Formally, terms have a conventional evaluation as integers and booleans that is shown (for completeness!) in Table 4. The reader may note the notation $s\,x$ for the evaluation of the variable named x in state s, giving its integer value as result. We say that state s *satisfies* boolean term $b \in \mathscr{B}$, written $s \models b$, whenever $[\![b]\!]s$ holds.

The **label** construct of $\mathscr{C}$ declares a label $l \in L$ that may subsequently be used as the target in **goto**s. The component P of the construct is the body of code in which the label is *in scope*. A label may not be mentioned except in the scope of its declaration. The same label may not be declared again in the scope of the first declaration. The semantics of labels and **goto**s will be further explained below.

The only way of exiting the $\mathscr{C}$ **do** loop construct normally is via **break** in the body P of the loop. An abnormal exit other than **break** from the body P terminates the whole loop abnormally. Terminating the body P normally evokes one more turn round the loop. So conventional **while** and **for** loops in C are mapped in $\mathscr{C}$ to a **do** loop with a guarded **break** statement inside, at the head of the body. The precise models for this and every construct of $\mathscr{C}$ as a set of coloured transitions are enumerated in Table 5.

Table 5. Model of programs of language $\mathscr{C}$, given as hypothesis the sets of states g_l for $l \in L$ observable at **goto** l statements. A recursive reference means 'the least set satisfying the condition'. For $h \in H$, the subroutine named h has code $[h]$. The state s altered by the assignment of n to variable x is written $s[x \mapsto n]$.

$$[\![-]\!]_g : \mathscr{C} \to \mathbb{P}(S \times \star \times S)$$

$$[\![\mathbf{skip}]\!]_g = \{s_0 \xrightarrow{\mathbf{N}} s_0 \mid s_0 \in S\}$$

$$[\![\mathbf{return}]\!]_g s_0 = \{s_0 \xrightarrow{\mathbf{R}} s_0 \mid s_0 \in S\}$$

$$[\![\mathbf{break}]\!]_g = \{s_0 \xrightarrow{\mathbf{B}} s_0 \mid s_0 \in S\}$$

$$[\![\mathbf{goto}\ l]\!]_g = \{s_0 \xrightarrow{\mathbf{G}_l} s_0 \mid s_0 \in S\}$$

$$[\![\mathbf{throw}\ k]\!]_g = \{s_0 \xrightarrow{\mathbf{E}_k} s_0 \mid s_0 \in S\}$$

$$[\![P; Q]\!]_g = \{s_0 \xrightarrow{\iota} s_1 \in [\![P]\!]_g \mid \iota \neq \mathbf{N}\}$$
$$\cup \{s_0 \xrightarrow{\iota} s_2 \mid s_1 \xrightarrow{\iota} s_2 \in [\![Q]\!]_g,\ s_0 \xrightarrow{\mathbf{N}} s_1 \in [\![P]\!]_g\}$$

$$[\![x = e]\!]_g s_0 = \{s_0 \xrightarrow{\mathbf{N}} s_0[x \mapsto [\![e]\!]s_0]\} \mid s_0 \in S\}$$

$$[\![p \to P]\!]_g = \{s_0 \xrightarrow{\iota} s_1 \in [\![P]\!]_g \mid [\![p]\!]s_0\}$$

$$[\![P \mid Q]\!]_g = [\![P]\!]_g \cup [\![Q]\!]_g$$

$$[\![\mathbf{do}\ P]\!]_g = \{s_0 \xrightarrow{\mathbf{N}} s_1 \mid s_0 \xrightarrow{\mathbf{B}} s_1 \in [\![P]\!]_g\}$$
$$\cup \{s_0 \xrightarrow{\iota} s_1 \in [\![P]\!]_g \mid \iota \neq \mathbf{N}, \mathbf{B}\}$$
$$\cup \{s_0 \xrightarrow{\iota} s_2 \mid s_1 \xrightarrow{\iota} s_2 \in [\![\mathbf{do}\ P]\!]_g,\ s_0 \xrightarrow{\iota} s_1 \in [\![P]\!]_g\}$$

$$[\![P : l]\!]_g = [\![P]\!]_g$$
$$\cup \{s_0 \xrightarrow{\mathbf{N}} s_1 \mid s_0 \in S,\ s_1 \in g_l\}$$

$$[\![\mathbf{label}\ l\ P]\!]_g = [\![P]\!]_{g \cup \{l \mapsto g_l^*\}} - g_l^*$$
$$\text{where } g_l^* = \{s_1 \mid s_0 \xrightarrow{\mathbf{G}_l} s_1 \in [\![P]\!]_{g \cup \{l \mapsto g_l^*\}}\}$$

$$[\![\mathbf{call}\ h]\!]_g = \{s_0 \xrightarrow{\mathbf{N}} s_1 \mid s_0 \xrightarrow{\mathbf{R}} s_1 \in [\![[h]]\!]_{\{\}}\}$$
$$\cup \{s_0 \xrightarrow{\mathbf{E}_k} s_1 \in [\![[h]]\!]_{\{\}} \mid k \in K\}$$

$$[\![\mathbf{try}\ P\ \mathbf{catch}(k)\ Q]\!]_g = \{s_0 \xrightarrow{\iota} s_1 \in [\![P]\!]_g \mid \iota \neq \mathbf{E}_k\}$$
$$\cup \{s_0 \xrightarrow{\iota} s_2 \mid s_1 \xrightarrow{\iota} s_2 \in [\![Q]\!]_g,\ s_0 \xrightarrow{\mathbf{E}_k} s_1 \in [\![P]\!]_g\}$$

Among the list in Table 5, the semantics of **label** declarations in particular requires explanation because labels are more explicitly controlled in $\mathscr{C}$ than in standard imperative languages. Declaring a label l makes it invisible from the outside of the block (while enabling it to be used inside), working just the same way as a local variable declaration does in a standard imperative programming language. A declaration removes from the model of a labelled statement the dependence on the hypothetical set g_l of the states attained at **goto** l statements. All the instances of **goto** l statements are inside the block with the declaration at its head, so we can take a look to see what totality of states really do accrue at **goto** l statements; they are recognisable in the model because they are the outcomes of the transitions that are marked with $\mathbf{G}_l$. Equating the set of such states with the hypothesis g_l gives the (least) fixpoint g_l^* required in the **label** l model.

The hypothetical sets g_l of states that obtain at **goto** l statements are used at the point where the label l appears within the scope of the declaration. We say that any of the states in g_l may be an outcome of passing through the label l, because it may have been brought in by a **goto** l statement. That is an overestimate; in reality, if the state just before the label is s_1, then at most those states s_2 in g_l that are reachable at a **goto** l from an initial program state s_0 that also leads to s_1 (either s_1 first or s_2 first) may obtain after the label l, and that may be considerably fewer s_2 than we calculate in g_l^*. Here is a visualisation of such a situation; the curly arrows denote a trace:

$$\{s_0\} \quad {}^{\nearrow} \begin{array}{l} \{s_1\} \quad l: \quad \{s1, s_2\} \\ \quad \wr \\ \{s_2\} \quad \textbf{goto } l \end{array}$$

If the initial precondition on the code admits more than one initial state s_0 then the model may admit more states s_2 after the label l than occur in reality when s_1 precedes l, because the model does not take into account the dependence of s_2 on s_1 through s_0. It is enough for the model that s_2 proceeds from some s_0 and s_1 proceeds from some (possibly different) s_0 satisfying the same initial condition. In mitigation, **gotos** are sparsely distributed in real codes and we have not found the effect pejorative.

Example 2. Consider the code R and suppose the input is restricted to a unique state s:

$$\overbrace{\underbrace{\text{label } A, B.\ \textbf{skip};\ \textbf{goto } A;\ B: \textbf{return};\ A: \textbf{goto } B}_{Q}}^{P}$$

with labels A, B in scope in body P, and the marked fragment Q. The single transitions made in the code P and the corresponding statement sequences are:

$$s \overset{\textbf{N}}{\mapsto} s \overset{\textbf{G}_A}{\mapsto} s \qquad\qquad \text{\# } \textbf{skip};\ \textbf{goto } A;$$
$$s \overset{\textbf{N}}{\mapsto} s \overset{\textbf{N}}{\mapsto} s \overset{\textbf{G}_B}{\mapsto} s \qquad\qquad \text{\# } \textbf{skip};\ \textbf{goto } A; A: \textbf{goto } B$$
$$s \overset{\textbf{N}}{\mapsto} s \overset{\textbf{N}}{\mapsto} s \overset{\textbf{N}}{\mapsto} s \overset{\textbf{R}}{\mapsto} s \qquad \text{\# } \textbf{skip};\ \textbf{goto } A; A: \textbf{goto } B; B: \textbf{return}$$

with observed states $g_A = \{s\}$, $g_B = \{s\}$ at the labels A and B respectively.

The **goto** B statement is not in the fragment Q so there is no way of knowing about the set of states at **goto** B while examining Q. Without that input, the traces of Q are

$$s \overset{\textbf{N}}{\mapsto} s \overset{\textbf{G}_A}{\mapsto} s \qquad\qquad \text{\# } \textbf{skip};\ \textbf{goto } A$$
$$s \overset{\textbf{N}}{\mapsto} s \overset{\textbf{N}}{\mapsto} s \qquad\qquad \text{\# } \textbf{skip};\ \textbf{goto } A; A:$$

There are no possible entries at B originating from within Q itself. That is, the model $[\![Q]\!]_g$ of Q as a set of transitions assuming $g_B = \{\,\}$, meaning there are no entries from outside, is $[\![Q]\!]_g = \{s \overset{\textbf{N}}{\mapsto} s, s \overset{\textbf{G}_A}{\mapsto} s\}$.

When we hypothesise $g_B = \{s\}$ for Q, then Q has more traces:

$$s \overset{\textbf{N}}{\mapsto} s \overset{\textbf{N}}{\mapsto} s \overset{\textbf{N}}{\mapsto} s \overset{\textbf{R}}{\mapsto} s \qquad \text{\# } \textbf{skip};\ \textbf{goto } A; A: \textbf{goto } B; B: \textbf{return}$$

Table 6. Extending the language $\mathscr{B}$ of propositions to modal operators $\mathbf{N}, \mathbf{R}, \mathbf{B}, \mathbf{G}_l$, $\mathbf{E}_k$ for $l \in L$, $k \in K$. An evaluation on transitions is given for $b \in \mathscr{B}$, $b^* \in \mathscr{B}^*$.

$$\mathscr{B}^* ::- b \mid \mathbf{N}\,b^* \mid \mathbf{R}\,b^* \mid \mathbf{B}\,b^* \mid \mathbf{G}_l\,b^* \mid \mathbf{E}_k\,b^* \mid b^* \vee b^* \mid b^* \wedge b^* \mid \neg b^*$$

$$[\![b]\!](s_0 \overset{\iota}{\mapsto} s_1) = [\![b]\!]s_1$$
$$[\![\mathbf{N}\,b^*]\!](s_0 \overset{\iota}{\mapsto} s_1) = (\iota = \mathbf{N}) \wedge [\![b^*]\!](s_0 \overset{\iota}{\mapsto} s_1)$$
$$[\![\mathbf{R}\,b^*]\!](s_0 \overset{\iota}{\mapsto} s_1) = (\iota = \mathbf{R}) \wedge [\![b^*]\!](s_0 \overset{\iota}{\mapsto} s_1)$$
$$[\![\mathbf{B}\,b^*]\!](s_0 \overset{\iota}{\mapsto} s_1) = (\iota = \mathbf{B}) \wedge [\![b^*]\!](s_0 \overset{\iota}{\mapsto} s_1)$$
$$[\![\mathbf{G}_l\,b^*]\!](s_0 \overset{\iota}{\mapsto} s_1) = (\iota = \mathbf{G}_l) \wedge [\![b^*]\!](s_0 \overset{\iota}{\mapsto} s_1)$$
$$[\![\mathbf{E}_k\,b^*]\!](s_0 \overset{\iota}{\mapsto} s_1) = (\iota = \mathbf{E}_k) \wedge [\![b^*]\!](s_0 \overset{\iota}{\mapsto} s_1)$$

Table 7. Laws of the modal operators $\mathbf{N}, \mathbf{R}, \mathbf{B}, \mathbf{G}_l, \mathbf{E}_k$ with $M, M_1, M_2 \in \{\mathbf{N}, \mathbf{R}, \mathbf{B}, \mathbf{G}_l, \mathbf{E}_k \mid l \in L, k \in K\}$ and $M_1 \neq M_2$.

$$M(\bot) = \bot \qquad \text{(flatness)}$$
$$M(b_1 \vee b_2) = M(b_1) \vee M(b_2) \qquad \text{(disjunctivity)}$$
$$M(b_1 \wedge b_2) = M(b_1) \wedge M(b_2) \qquad \text{(conjunctivity)}$$
$$M(Mb) = Mb \qquad \text{(idempotence)}$$
$$M_2(M_1 b) = M_1(b) \wedge M_2(b) = \bot \qquad \text{(orthogonality)}$$

corresponding to these entries at B from the rest of the code proceeding to the **return** in Q, and $[\![Q]\!]_g = \{s \overset{\mathbf{N}}{\mapsto} s, \ s \overset{\mathbf{G}_A}{\mapsto} s, \ s \overset{\mathbf{R}}{\mapsto} s\}$. In the context of the whole code P, that is the model for Q as a set of initial to final state transitions.

Example 3. Staying with the code of Example 2, the set $\{s \overset{\mathbf{G}_A}{\mapsto} s, \ s \overset{\mathbf{G}_B}{\mapsto} s, \ s \overset{\mathbf{R}}{\mapsto} s\}$ is the model $[\![P]\!]_g$ of P starting at state s with assumptions g_A, g_B of Example 2, and the sets g_A, g_B are observed at the labels A, B in the code under these assumptions. Thus $\{A \mapsto g_A, B \mapsto g_B\}$ is the fixpoint g^* of the **label** declaration rule in Table 5.

That rule says to next remove transitions ending at **goto** As and Bs from visibility in the model of the declaration block, because they can go nowhere else, leaving only $[\![R]\!]_{\{\}} = \{s \overset{\mathbf{R}}{\mapsto} s\}$ as the set-of-transitions model of the whole block of code, which corresponds to the sequence **skip; goto** A; A : **goto** B; B : **return**.

We extend the propositional language to $\mathscr{B}^*$ which includes the modal operators $\mathbf{N}, \mathbf{R}, \mathbf{B}, \mathbf{G}_l, \mathbf{E}_k$ for $l \in L$, $k \in K$, as shown in Table 6, which defines a model of $\mathscr{B}^*$ on transitions. The predicate $\mathbf{N}p$ informally should be read as picking out from the set of all coloured state transitions 'those normal-coloured transitions that produce a state satisfying p', and similarly for the other operators. The modal operators satisfy the algebraic laws given in Table 7. Additionally, however, for non-modal $p \in \mathscr{B}$,

$$p = \mathbf{N}p \vee \mathbf{R}p \vee \mathbf{B}p \vee \bigvee \mathbf{G}_l p \bigvee \mathbf{E}_k p \qquad (1)$$

because each transition must be some colour, and those are all the colours. The decomposition works in the general case too:

Proposition 1. *Every* $p \in \mathscr{B}^*$ *can be (uniquely) expressed as*

$$p = \mathbf{N}p_{\mathbf{N}} \vee \mathbf{R}p_{\mathbf{R}} \vee \mathbf{B}p_{\mathbf{B}} \vee \mathbb{W} \, \mathbf{G}_l p_{\mathbf{G}_l} \, \mathbb{W} \mathbf{E}_k p_{\mathbf{E}_k}$$

for some $p_{\mathbf{N}}$, $p_{\mathbf{R}}$, *etc that are free of modal operators.*

Proof. Equation (1) *gives the result for* $p \in \mathscr{B}$. *The rest is by structural induction on* p, *using Table 7 and boolean algebra. Uniqueness follows because* $\mathbf{N}p_{\mathbf{N}} = \mathbf{N}p'_{\mathbf{N}}$, *for example, applying* $\mathbf{N}$ *to two possible decompositions, and applying the orthogonality and idempotence laws; apply the definition of* $\mathbf{N}$ *in the model in Table 6 to deduce* $p_{\mathbf{N}} = p'_{\mathbf{N}}$ *for non-modal predicates* $p_{\mathbf{N}}$, $p'_{\mathbf{N}}$. *Similarly for* $\mathbf{B}$, $\mathbf{R}$, $\mathbf{G}_l$, $\mathbf{E}_k$. $\qquad\square$

So modal formulae $p \in \mathscr{B}^*$ may be viewed as tuples $(p_{\mathbf{N}}, p_{\mathbf{R}}, p_{\mathbf{B}}, p_{\mathbf{G}_l}, p_{\mathbf{E}_k})$ of non-modal formulae from $\mathscr{B}$ for labels $l \in L$, exception kinds $k \in K$. That means that $\mathbf{N}p \vee \mathbf{R}q$, for example, is simply a convenient notation for writing down two assertions at once: one that asserts p of the final states of the transitions that end 'normally', and one that asserts q on the final states of the transitions that end in a 'return flow'. The meaning of $\mathbf{N}p \vee \mathbf{R}q$ is the union of the set of the normal transitions with final state that satisfy p plus the set of the transitions that end in a 'return flow' and whose final states satisfy q. We can now give meaning to a notation that looks like (and is intended to signify) a Hoare triple with an explicit context of certain '**goto** assumptions':

Definition 1. *Let* $g_l = [\![p_l]\!]$ *be the set of states satisfying* $p_l \in \mathscr{B}$, *labels* $l \in L$. *Then* '$\mathbf{G}_l \, p_l \triangleright \{p\} \, a \, \{q\}$', *for non-modal* $p, p_l \in \mathscr{B}$, $P \in \mathscr{C}$ *and* $q \in \mathscr{B}^*$, *means:*

$$[\![\mathbf{G}_l \, p_l \triangleright \{p\} \, P \, \{q\}]\!] = [\![\{p\} \, P \, \{q\}]\!]_g$$
$$= \forall s_0 \overset{l}{\mapsto} s_1 \in [\![P]\!]_g. \ [\![p]\!]s_0 \Rightarrow [\![q]\!](s_0 \overset{l}{\mapsto} s_1)$$

That is read as 'the triple $\{p\} \, P \, \{q\}$ holds under assumptions p_l at **goto** l when every transition of P that starts at a state satisfying p also satisfies q'. The explicit Gentzen-style assumptions p_l are free of modal operators. What is meant by the notation is that those states that may be attainable as the program traces pass through **goto** statements are assumed to be restricted to those that satisfy p_l.

The $\mathbf{G}_l \, p_l$ assumptions may be separated by commas, as $\mathbf{G}_{l_1} \, p_{l_1}, \mathbf{G}_{l_2} \, p_{l_2}, \ldots$, with $l_1 \neq l_2$, etc. Or they may be written as a disjunction $\mathbf{G}_{l_1} \, p_{l_1} \vee \mathbf{G}_{l_2} \, p_{l_2} \vee \ldots$ because the information in this modal formula is only the mapping $l_1 \mapsto p_{l_1}$, $l_2 \mapsto p_{l_2}$, etc. If the same l appears twice among the disjuncts $\mathbf{G}_l \, p_l$, then we understand that the union of the two p_l is intended.

Now we can prove the validity of laws about triples drawn from what Definition 1 says. The first laws are strengthening and weakening results on pre- and postconditions:

Proposition 2. *The following algebraic relations hold:*

$$[\![\{\bot\}\ P\ \{q\}]\!]_g \iff \top \tag{2}$$

$$[\![\{p\}\ P\ \{\top\}]\!]_g \iff \top \tag{3}$$

$$[\![\{p_1 \vee p_2\}\ P\ \{q\}]\!]_g \iff [\![\{p_1\}\ P\ \{q\}]\!]_g \wedge [\![\{p_2\}\ P\ \{q\}]\!]_g \tag{4}$$

$$[\![\{p\}\ P\ \{q_1 \wedge q_2\}]\!]_g \iff [\![\{p\}\ P\ \{q_1\}]\!]_g \wedge [\![\{p\}\ P\ \{q_2\}]\!]_g \tag{5}$$

$$(p_1 \rightarrow p_2) \wedge [\![\{p_2\}\ P\ \{q\}]\!]_g \implies [\![\{p_1\}\ P\ \{q\}]\!]_g \tag{6}$$

$$(q_1 \rightarrow q_2) \wedge [\![\{p\}\ P\ \{q_1\}]\!]_g \implies [\![\{p\}\ P\ \{q_2\}]\!]_g \tag{7}$$

$$[\![\{p\}\ P\ \{q\}]\!]_{g'} \implies [\![\{p\}\ P\ \{q\}]\!]_g \tag{8}$$

for $p, p_1, p_2 \in \mathscr{B}$, $q, q_1, q_2 \in \mathscr{B}^*$, $P \in \mathscr{C}$, and $g_l \subseteq g'_l \in \mathbb{P}S$.

Proof. (2–5) follow on applying Definition 1. (6–7) follow from (4–5) on considering the cases $p_1 \vee p_2 = p_2$ and $q_1 \wedge q_2 = q_1$. The reason for (8) is that g'_l is a bigger set than g_l, so $[\![P]\!]_{g'}$ is a bigger set of transitions than $[\![P]\!]_g$ and thus the universal quantifier in Definition 1 produces a smaller (less true) truth value. □

Theorem 1 (Soundness). *The following algebraic inequalities hold, for $\mathcal{E}_1$ any of $\mathbf{R}$, $\mathbf{B}$, $\mathbf{G}_l$, $\mathbf{E}_k$; $\mathcal{E}_2$ any of $\mathbf{R}$, $\mathbf{G}_l$, $\mathbf{E}_k$; $\mathcal{E}_3$ any of $\mathbf{R}$, $\mathbf{B}$, $\mathbf{G}_{l'}$ for $l' \neq l$, $\mathbf{E}_k$; $\mathcal{E}_4$ any of $\mathbf{R}$, $\mathbf{B}$, $\mathbf{G}_l$, $\mathbf{E}_{k'}$ for $k' \neq k$; $[h]$ the code of the subroutine called h:*

$$\left. \begin{array}{l} [\![\{p\}\ P\ \{\mathbf{N}q \vee \mathcal{E}_1 x\}]\!]_g \\ \wedge\ [\![\{q\}\ Q\ \{\mathbf{N}r \vee \mathcal{E}_1 x\}]\!]_g \end{array} \right\} \implies [\![\{p\}\ P\,;Q\ \{\mathbf{N}r \vee \mathcal{E}_1 x\}]\!]_g \tag{9}$$

$$[\![\{p\}\ P\ \{\mathbf{B}q \vee \mathbf{N}p \vee \mathcal{E}_2 x\}]\!]_g \implies [\![\{p\}\ \mathbf{do}\ P\ \{\mathbf{N}q \vee \mathcal{E}_2 x\}]\!]_g \tag{10}$$

$$\top \implies [\![\{p\}\ \mathbf{skip}\ \{\mathbf{N}p\}]\!]_g \tag{11}$$

$$\top \implies [\![\{p\}\ \mathbf{return}\ \{\mathbf{R}p\}]\!]_g \tag{12}$$

$$\top \implies [\![\{p\}\ \mathbf{break}\ \{\mathbf{B}p\}]\!]_g \tag{13}$$

$$\top \implies [\![\{p\}\ \mathbf{goto}\ l\ \{\mathbf{G}_l p\}]\!]_g \tag{14}$$

$$\top \implies [\![\{p\}\ \mathbf{throw}\ k\ \{\mathbf{E}_k p\}]\!]_g \tag{15}$$

$$[\![\{b \wedge p\}\ P\ \{q\}]\!]_g \implies [\![\{p\}\ b \rightarrow P\ \{q\}]\!]_g \tag{16}$$

$$[\![\{p\}\ P\ \{q\}]\!]_g \wedge [\![\{p\}\ Q\ \{q\}]\!]_g \implies [\![\{p\}\ P \,{}_|Q\ \{q\}]\!]_g \tag{17}$$

$$\top \implies [\![\{q[e/x]\}\ x{=}e\ \{\mathbf{N}q\}]\!]_g \tag{18}$$

$$[\![\{p\}\ P\ \{q\}]\!]_g \wedge g_l \subseteq \{s_1 \mid s_0 \xrightarrow{\mathbf{N}} s_1 \in [\![q]\!]\} \implies [\![\{p\}\ P : l\ \{q\}]\!]_g \tag{19}$$

$$[\![\{p\}\ P\ \{\mathbf{G}_l p_l \vee \mathbf{N}q \vee \mathcal{E}_3 x\}]\!]_{g \cup \{l \mapsto p_l\}} \implies [\![\{p\}\ \mathbf{label}\ l.P\ \{\mathbf{N}q \vee \mathcal{E}_3 x\}]\!]_g \tag{20}$$

$$[\![\{p\}\ [h]\ \{\mathbf{R}r \vee \mathbf{E}_k x_k\}]\!]_{\{\ \}} \implies [\![\{p\}\ \mathbf{call}\ h\ \{\mathbf{N}r \vee \mathbf{E}_k x_k\}]\!]_g \tag{21}$$

$$\left. \begin{array}{l} [\![\{p\}\ P\ \{\mathbf{N}r \vee \mathbf{E}_k q \vee \mathcal{E}_4 x\}]\!]_g \\ \wedge\ [\![\{q\}\ Q\ \{\mathbf{N}r \vee \mathbf{E}_k x_k \vee \mathcal{E}_4 x\}]\!]_g \end{array} \right\} \implies [\![\{p\}\ \mathbf{try}\ P\ \mathbf{catch}(k)\ Q\ \{\mathbf{N}r \vee \mathbf{E}_k x_k \vee \mathcal{E}_4 x\}]\!]_g \tag{22}$$

Proof By evaluation, given Definition 1 and the semantics from Table 5. □

The reason why the theorem is titled 'Soundness' is that its inequalities can be read as the NRB logic deduction rules set out in Table 1, via Definition 1. The fixpoint requirement of the model at the **label** construct is expressed in the 'arrival from a **goto** at a label' law (19), where it is stated that *if* the hypothesised states g_l at a **goto** l statement are covered by the states q immediately after code block P and preceding label l, *then* q holds after the label l too. However, there is no need for any such predication when the g_l are exactly the fixpoint of the map

$$g_l \mapsto \{s_1 \mid s_0 \overset{\mathbf{G}_l}{\mapsto} s_1 \in [\![P]\!]_g\}$$

because that is what the fixpoint condition says. Thus, while the model in Table 5 satisfies Eqs. (9–22), it satisfies more than they require – some of the hypotheses in the equations could be dropped and the model would still satisfy them. But the NRB logic rules in Table 1 are validated by the model and thus are sound.

3   Completeness

In proving completeness of the NRB logic, we will be guided by the proof of partial completeness for Hoare's logic in K. R. Apt's survey paper [2]. We will need, for every (possibly modal) postcondition $q \in \mathscr{B}^*$ and every construct R of $\mathscr{C}$, a non-modal formula $p \in \mathscr{B}$ that is weakest in $\mathscr{B}$ such that if p holds of a state s, and $s \overset{\iota}{\mapsto} s'$ is in the model of R given in Table 5, then q holds of $s \overset{\iota}{\mapsto} s'$. This p is written wp(R, q), the 'weakest precondition on R for q'. We construct it via structural induction on $\mathscr{C}$ at the same time as we deduce completeness, so there is an element of chicken versus egg about the proof, and we will not labour that point.

We will also suppose that we can prove any tautology of $\mathscr{B}$ and $\mathscr{B}^*$, so 'completeness of NRB' will be relative to that lower-level completeness.

Notice that there is always a set $p \in \mathbb{P}S$ satisfying the 'weakest precondition' characterisation above. It is $\{s \in S \mid s \overset{\iota}{\mapsto} s' \in [\![R]\!]_g \Rightarrow s \overset{\iota}{\mapsto} s' \in [\![q]\!]\}$, and it is called the weakest *semantic* precondition on R for q. So we sometimes refer to wp(R, q) as the 'weakest *syntactic* precondition' on R for q, when we wish to emphasise the distinction. The question is whether or not there is a formula in $\mathscr{B}$ that exactly expresses this set. If there is, then the system is said to be *expressive*, and that formula *is* the weakest (syntactic) precondition on R for q, wp(R, q). Notice also that a weakest (syntactic) precondition wp(R, q) must encompass the semantic weakest precondition; that is because if there were a state s in the latter and not in the former, then we could form the disjunction wp(R, q) $\lor$ ($x_1 = sx_1 \land \dots x_n = sx_n$) where the x_i are the variables of s, and this would also be a precondition on R for q, hence $x_1 = sx_1 \land \dots x_n = sx_n \to$ wp(R, q) must be true, as the latter is supposedly the weakest precondition, and so s satisfies wp(R, q) in contradiction to the assumption that s is not in wp(R, q). For orientation, then, the reader should note that 'there is a weakest (syntactic) precondition in $\mathscr{B}$' means there is a unique strongest formula in $\mathscr{B}$ covering the weakest semantic precondition.

We will lay out the proof of completeness inline here, in order to avoid excessively overbearing formality, and at the end we will draw the formal conclusion.

A completeness proof is always a proof by cases on each construct of interest. It has the form 'suppose that *foo* is true, then we can prove it like this', where *foo* runs through all the constructs we are interested in. We start with assertions about the sequence construction $P; Q$. We will look at this in particular detail, noting where and how the weakest precondition formula plays a role, and skip that detail for most other cases. Thus we start with *foo* equal to $\mathbf{G}_l\, g_l \rhd \{p\}\ P; Q\ \{q\}$ for some assumptions $g_l \in \mathcal{B}$, but we do not need to take the assumptions g_l into account in this case.

Case $P; Q$. *Consider a sequence of two statements $P; Q$ for which $\{p\}\ P; Q\ \{q\}$ holds in the model set out by Definition 1 and Table 5. That is, suppose that initially the state s satisfies predicate p and that there is a progression from s to some final state s' through $P; Q$. Then $s \overset{\iota}{\mapsto} s'$ is in $[\![P; Q]\!]_g$ and $s \overset{\iota}{\mapsto} s'$ satisfies q. We will consider two subcases, the first where P terminates normally from s, and the second where P terminates abnormally from s. A third possibility, that P does not terminate at all, is ruled out because a final state s' is reached.*

Consider the first subcase. According to Table 5, that means that P started in state $s_0 = s$ and finished normally in some state s_1 and Q ran on from state s_1 to finish normally in state $s_2 = s'$. Let r stand for the weakest precondition $wp(Q,q)$ that guarantees termination of Q with q holding. By definition, $\{r\}\ Q\ \{q\}$, is true and s_1 satisfies r (if not, then $r \vee (x_1 = sx_1 \wedge x_2 = sx_2 \wedge \dots)$ would be a weaker precondition for q than r, which is impossible). So $\{p\}\ P\ \{\mathbf{N}r\}$ is true in this case.

Now consider the second subcase, when the final state s_1 reached from $s = s_0$ through P obtains via an abnormal flow out of P. The transition $s_0 \overset{\iota}{\mapsto} s_1$ satisfies q, but necesarily an abnormal 'error' component of q as the flow out of p is abnormal, so $\{p\}\ P\ \{\mathbf{R}q \vee \mathbf{B}q \vee \dots\}$, as $\mathbf{R}q \vee \mathbf{B}q \vee \dots$ is the error component of q by Proposition 1.

Those are the only cases, so $\{p\}\ P\ \{\mathbf{N}r \vee \mathbf{R}q \vee \mathbf{B}q \vee \dots\}$ is true. By induction, it is the case that there are deductions $\vdash \{p\}\ P\ \{\mathbf{N}r \vee \mathbf{R}q \vee \mathbf{B}q \vee \dots\}$ and $\vdash \{r\}\ Q\ \{q\}$ in the NRB system. But the following rule

$$\frac{\{p\}\ P\ \{\mathbf{N}r \vee \mathbf{R}q \vee \mathbf{B}q \vee \dots\}\quad \{r\}\ Q\ \{q\}}{\{p\}\ P; Q\ \{q \vee \mathbf{R}q \vee \mathbf{B}q \vee \dots\}}$$

is a derived rule of NRB logic. It is a specialised form of the general NRB rule of sequence, availing of the 'mixed' error colour $\mathcal{E} = (\mathbf{R} \vee \mathbf{B} \vee \dots)$. Since $(q \vee \mathcal{E}q) \to q$, putting these deductions together, and using weakening, we have a deduction of the truth of the assertions $\{p\}\ P; Q\ \{q\}$.

That concludes the consideration of the case $P; Q$. The existence of a formula expressing a weakest precondition is what really drives the proof above along, and in lieu of pursuing the proof through all the other construct cases, we note the important weakest precondition formulae below:

- The weakest precondition for sequence is $wp(a; b, q) = wp(a, \mathcal{E}q \vee \mathbf{N}wp(b, q))$ above.

- The weakest precondition for assignment is $\mathrm{wp}(x = e, \mathbf{N}q) = q[e/x]$ for q without modal components. In general $\mathrm{wp}(x = e, q) = \mathbf{N}q[e/x]$.
- The weakest precondition for a **return** statement is $\mathrm{wp}(\mathbf{return}, q) = \mathbf{R}q$.
- The weakest precondition for a **break** statement is $\mathrm{wp}(\mathbf{break}, q) = \mathbf{B}q$. Etc.
- The weakest precondition $\mathrm{wp}(\mathbf{do}\ P, \mathbf{N}q)$ for a **do** loop that ends 'normally' is $\mathbf{wp}(P, \mathbf{B}q) \lor \mathbf{wp}(P, \mathbf{Nwp}(P, \mathbf{B}q)) \lor \mathbf{wp}(P, \mathbf{Nwp}(P, \mathbf{Nwp}(P, \mathbf{B}q))) \lor \ldots$. That is, we might break from P with q, or run through P normally to the precondition for breaking from P with q next, etc. Write $\mathbf{wp}(P, \mathbf{B}q)$ as p and write $\mathbf{wp}(P, \mathbf{N}r) \land \neg p$ as $\psi(r)$, Then $\mathrm{wp}(\mathbf{do}\ P, \mathbf{N}q)$ can be written $p \lor \psi(p) \lor \psi(p \lor \psi(p)) \lor \ldots$, which is the strongest solution to $\pi = \psi(\pi)$ no stronger than p. This is the weakest precondition for p after $\mathbf{while}(\neg p)\ P$ in classical Hoare logic. It is an existentially quantified statement, stating that an initial state s gives rise to exactly some n passes through P before the condition p becomes true for the first time. It can classically be expressed as a formula of first-order logic and it is the weakest precondition for $\mathbf{N}q$ after **do** P here.
  The preconditions for $\mathcal{E}q$ for each 'abnormal' coloured ending $\mathcal{E}$ of the loop **do** P are similarly expressible in $\mathcal{B}$, and the precondition for q is the disjunction of each of the preconditions for $\mathbf{N}q$, $\mathbf{R}q$, $\mathbf{B}q$, etc.
- The weakest precondition for a guarded statement $\mathrm{wp}(p \to P, q)$ is $p \to \mathrm{wp}(P, q)$, as in Hoare logic; and the weakest precondition for a disjunction $\mathrm{wp}(P \mid Q, q)$ is $\mathrm{wp}(P, q) \land \mathrm{wp}(Q, q)$, as in Hoare logic. However, in practice we only use the deterministic combination $p \to P \mid \neg p \to Q$ for which the weakest precondition is $(p \to \mathrm{wp}(P, q)) \land (\neg p \to \mathrm{wp}(Q, q))$, i.e. $p \land \mathrm{wp}(P, q) \lor \neg p \land \mathrm{wp}(Q, q)$.

To deal with labels properly, we have to extend some of these notions and notations to take account of the assumptions $\mathbf{G}_l g_l$ that an assertion $\mathbf{G}_l g_l \rhd \{p\}\ P\ \{q\}$ is made against. The weakest precondition p on P for q is then $p = \mathrm{wp}_g(P, q)$, with the g_l as extra parameters. The weakest precondition for a label use $\mathrm{wp}_g(P : l, q)$ is then $\mathrm{wp}_g(P, q)$, provided that $g_l \to q$, since the states g_l attained by **goto** l statements throughout the code are available after the label, as well as those obtained through P. The weakest precondition in the general situation where it is not necessarily the case that $g_l \to q$ holds is $\mathrm{wp}_g(P, q \land (g_l \to q))$, which is $\mathrm{wp}_g(P, q)$.

Now we can continue the completeness proof through the statements of the form $P : l$ (a labelled statement) and **label** $l.P$ (a label declaration).

Case Labelled Statement. *If $[\![\{p\}\ P : l\ \{q\}]\!]_g$ holds, then (a) every state $s = s_0$ satisfying p leads through P with $s_0 \overset{L}{\mapsto} s_1$ satisfying q, and also (b) q contains all the transitions $s_0 \overset{N}{\mapsto} s_1$ where s_1 satisfies g_l. By (a), s satisfies $\mathrm{wp}_g(P, q)$ and (b) $\mathbf{N}g_l \to q$ holds. Since s is arbitrary in p, so $p \to \mathrm{wp}_g(P, q)$ holds and by induction, $\vdash \mathbf{G}_l g_l \rhd \{p\}\ P\ \{q\}$. Then, by the 'frm' rule of NRB (Table 1), we may deduce $\vdash \mathbf{G}_l g_l \rhd \{p\}\ P : l\ \{q\}$.*

Case Label Declaration. *The weakest precondition for a declaration wp_g (**label** $l.P, q$) is simply $p = \mathrm{wp}_{g'}(P, q)$, where the assumptions after the* *declaration are* $g' = g \cup \{l \mapsto g_l\}$ *and* g_l *is such that* $\mathbf{G}_l g_l \vartriangleright \{p\}\ P\ \{q\}$. *In other words,* p *and* g_l *are simultaneously chosen to make the assertion hold,* p *maximal and* g_l *the least fixpoint describing the states at* **goto** l *statements in the code* P, *given that the initial state satisfies* p *and assumptions* $\mathbf{G}_l g_l$ *hold. The* $g_l y$ *are the statements that after exactly some* $n \in \mathbb{N}$ *more traversals through* P *via* **goto** l, *the trace from state* s *will avoid another* **goto** l *for the first time and exit* P *normally or via an abnormal exit that is not a* **goto** l.

If it is the case that $[\![\{p\}\ \textbf{label}\ l.P\ \{q\}]\!]_g$ *holds then every state* $s = s_0$ *satisfying* p *leads through* **label** $l.P$ *with* $s_0 \overset{l}{\mapsto} s_1$ *satisfying* q. *That means* $s_0 \overset{l}{\mapsto} s_1$ *leads through* P, *but it is not all that do; there are transitions with* $\iota = \mathbf{G}_l$ *that are not considered. The 'missing' transitions are precisely the* $\mathbf{G}_l g_l$ *where* g_l *is the appropriate least fixpoint for* $g_l = \{s_1 \mid s_0 \overset{\mathbf{G}_l}{\mapsto} s_1 \in [\![P]\!]_{g \cup \{l \mapsto g_l\}}\}$, *which is a predicate expressing the idea that* s_1 *at a* **goto** l *initiates some exactly* n *traversals back through* P *again before exiting* P *for a first time other than via a* **goto** l. *The predicate* q *cannot mention* $\mathbf{G}_l$ *since the label* l *is out of scope for it, but it may permit some, all or no* $\mathbf{G}_l$*-coloured transitions. The predicate* $q \vee \mathbf{G}_l g_l$, *on the other hand, permits all the* $\mathbf{G}_l$*-coloured transitions that exit* P. *transitions. Thus adding* $\mathbf{G}_l g_l$ *to the assumptions means* s_0 *traverses* P *via* $s_0 \overset{l}{\mapsto} s_1$ *satisfying* $q \vee \mathbf{G}_l g_l$ *even though more transitions are admitted. Since* $s = s_0$ *is arbitrary in* p, *so* $p \rightarrow \mathrm{wp}_{g \cup \{l \mapsto g_l\}}(P, q \vee \mathbf{G}_l g_l)$ *and by induction* $\vdash \mathbf{G}_l \vartriangleright \{p\}\ P\ \{q \vee \mathbf{G}_l g_l\}$, *and then one may deduce* $\vdash \{p\}\ \textbf{label}\ l.P\ \{q\}$ *by the 'lbl' rule.* $\qquad\square$

That concludes the text that would appear in a proof, but which we have abridged and presented as a discussion here! We have covered the typical case $(P; Q)$ and the unusual cases $(P : l, \textbf{label}\ l.P)$. The proof-theoretic content of the discussion is:

Theorem 2 (Completeness). *The system of NRB logic in Table 1 is complete, relative to the completeness of first-order logic.*

Theorem 3 (Expressiveness). *The weakest precondition* $wp(P, q)$ *for* $q \in \mathscr{B}^*$, $P \in \mathscr{C}$ *in the interpretation set out in Definition 1 and Table 5 is expressible in* $\mathscr{B}$.

The observation above is that there is a formula in $\mathscr{B}$ that expresses the semantic weakest precondition exactly.

4   Summary

In this article, we have complemented previous work, which guaranteed programs free of semantic defects, with guarantees directed at the symbolic logic used as guarantor. Soundness of the logic is proved with respect to a simple transition-based model of programs, and completeness of the logic with respect to the model is proved.

That shows the logic is equivalent to the model, and reduces the question of its fitness as a guarantor for a program to the fitness for that purpose of the model of programs. The model always overestimates the number of transitions that may occur, so when the logic is used to certify that there are no program transitions that may violate a given safety condition, it may be believed.

Acknowledgments. Simon Pickin's research has been partially supported by the Spanish MEC project ESTuDIo (TIN2012-36812-C02-01).

References

1. American National Standards Institute. American national standard for information systems - programming language C, ANSI X3.159-1989 (1989)
2. Apt, K.R.: Ten years of Hoare's logic: a survey: part I. ACM Trans. Program. Lang. Syst. **3**(4), 431–483 (1981)
3. Bessey, A., Block, K., Chelf, B., Chou, A., Fulton, B., Hallem, S., Henri-Gros, C., Kamsky, A., McPeak, S., Engler, D.: A few billion lines of code later: using static analysis to find bugs in the real world. Commun. ACM **53**(2), 66–75 (2010)
4. Breuer, P.T., Pickin, S.: Checking for deadlock, double-free and other abuses in the Linux kernel source code. In: Alexandrov, V.N., van Albada, G.D., Sloot, P.M.A., Dongarra, J. (eds.) ICCS 2006. LNCS, vol. 3994, pp. 765–772. Springer, Heidelberg (2006)
5. Breuer, P.T., Valls, M.: Static deadlock detection in the Linux kernel. In: Llamosí, A., Strohmeier, A. (eds.) Ada-Europe 2004. LNCS, vol. 3063, pp. 52–64. Springer, Heidelberg (2004)
6. Breuer, P.T., Pickin, S.: Symbolic approximation: an approach to verification in the large. Innovations Syst. Softw. Eng. **2**(3), 147–163 (2006)
7. Breuer, P.T., Pickin, S.: Verification in the large via symbolic approximation. In: Proceedings of the 2nd International Symposium on Leveraging Applications of Formal Methods, Verification and Validation, 2006 (ISoLA 2006), pp. 408–415. IEEE (2006)
8. Breuer, P.T., Pickin, S.: Open source verification in an anonymous volunteer network. Sci. Comput. Program. (2013). doi:10.1016/j.scico.2013.08.010
9. Breuer, P.T., Pickin, S., Petrie, M.L.: Detecting deadlock, double-free and other abuses in a million lines of Linux kernel source. In: Proceedings of the 30th Annual Software Engineering Workshop 2006 (SEW'06), pp. 223–233. IEEE/NASA (2006)
10. Clarke, E., Emerson, E., Sistla, A.: Automatic verification of finite-state concurrent systems using temporal logic specifications. ACM Trans. Prog. Lang. Syst. (TOPLAS) **8**(2), 244–253 (1986)
11. Engler, D., Chelf, B., Chou, A., Hallem, S.: Checking system rules using system-specific, programmer-written compiler extensions. In: Proceedings of the 4th Symposium on Operating System Design and Implementation (OSDI 2000), pp. 1–16, October 2000
12. International Standards Organisation. ISO/IEC 9899-1999, programming languages - C (1999)

Analysis of FLOSS Communities
as Learning Contexts

Sara Fernandes[1,2(✉)], Antonio Cerone[1], and Luis Soares Barbosa[2]

[1] United Nations University – International Institute for Software Technology,
Macao SAR, China
{sara.fernandes,antonio}@iist.unu.edu
[2] HASLab/INESC TEC, University of Minho, Braga, Portugal
lsb@di.uminho.pt

Abstract. It can be argued that participating in Free/Libre Open Source
Software (FLOSS) projects can have a positive effect in the contributor's
learning process. The need to collaborate with other contributors and to contribute to a project can motivate and implicitly foster learning. In order to
validate such statements, it is necessary to (1) study the interactions between
FLOSS projects' participants, and (2) explore the didactical value of participating in FLOSS projects, designing an appropriate questionnaire asking
FLOSS contributors about their experience in FLOSS projects. In this paper,
we illustrate how this questionnaire was designed and disseminated. We conclude the paper with results from 27 FLOSS projects contributors, determining
that, not only they contribute and collaborate to the project and its community,
but also that FLOSS contributors see that this type of activity can be regarded
as a complement to formal education.

Keywords: FLOSS · Communities of practice · Learning awareness

1 Introduction

Within 15 years the Web has grown from a group work tool for scientists at CERN[1]
into a global information space with more than a billion users [1]. Currently, it is both
maintaining its roots as a read/write tool and also entering a new, more social and
participatory phase. In particular, it is becoming a participatory tool for people to learn
and share knowledge. These trends lead to the feeling that the Web is entering a
"second phase" – a new and improved version, also defined as Web 2.0, which is
more than a set of new technologies and services. It is an enabler for participation and
interactions between users and used as an educative tool. However, there is a significant debate over the alleged advantages and disadvantages of incorporating new
technologies into mainstream education; particularly, to foster competence development of students [2]. To address such concerns, new pedagogical and information
design perspectives emerge and are closely coupled with Web 2.0 philosophy. Authors

---

[1] Conseil Européen pour la Recherche Nucléaire (European Council for Nuclear Research).

S. Counsell and M. Núñez (Eds.): SEFM 2013 Collocated Workshops, LNCS 8368, pp. 405–416, 2014.
DOI: 10.1007/978-3-319-05032-4_29, © Springer International Publishing Switzerland 2014

like Chatti, Jarke and Frosch-Wilke [3], present the concept of social software as a tool for augmenting human social and collaborative abilities; Downes [4], promotes the creation of an individual learning network using simple social tools; Happ [5], brings Web 2.0 into the mainstream advocating that is it more than technology and the human-element; Sclater [6], presents the pros and cons of using social networking systems such as Facebook in Learning Management Systems; or Wilson et al. [7] that explores a new design pattern for personal learning environments.

These perspectives help to rethink the purpose of technology-enhanced learning environments in education, to question the existing industry standards and to open the way towards competence development of learners.

According to Stephen Downes [6], knowledge informs learning; the learning outcomes inform community; and the community in turn creates knowledge. Looking from a reverse perspective, knowledge builds community, while community defines what is learned, and what is learned becomes knowledge. These three aspects − community, learning and knowledge, essentially model the same phenomenon, representations of communications and structures that are created by individuals interacting and exchanging experiences (knowledge) within communities [8].

As an example of the learning process explained above, Free/Libre Open Source Software (FLOSS) communities consist of heterogeneous groups of independent volunteers, who interact among them driven by different motivations [9]. Software developed by these communities is driven by collaborative, social modes of interaction and knowledge exchange, providing an example of peer-production [10].

Our research work focuses on studying how contributors to FLOSS projects learn and whether and how they recognize the learning process they experience through their contributions. Within such research frame, Fernandes, S. et al. [11] reported an initial experience using a stratified sampling, considering few FLOSS contributors playing different roles and with different demographics − i.e. gender and age. This paper extends such work by presenting results of a more extended sample with 27 respondents, committed to different activities, with diverse gender and age, but also representing different countries and possessing different backgrounds. In particular, the aim of this paper is to (1) study the interactions between FLOSS projects participants, and (2) assess the didactical value of their communities. The main contribution of the results presented here is bringing better understanding of how FLOSS contributors interact and the didactical value of such activity. The rest of this paper is structured as follows. Section 2 introduces some background and related work. Section 3 presents the methodology and the description of the instrument used for data collection. Section 4 presents results, while Sect. 5 the analysis of the results. Finally, Sect. 6 presents some conclusions pointing to envisaged future work.

2 Background and Related Work

At the end of 2006 Time magazine's Person of the Year was "You" [12]. On the cover of the magazine, and underneath the title of the award, is a picture of a Personal Computer (PC) with a mirror in the place of the screen, reflecting not only the face of the user, but also the general feeling that 2006 was the year of the Web − a new improved, user-generated web. This award and recent trends have led to a feeling that the Web is more and more a source of knowledge and that the activities performed there can be seen as a mean to develop skills.

As an example of collaborative and participatory trends, we focus on FLOSS projects. FLOSS projects are developed using the Web and it has been accepted that the participation in such projects represent a potential positive impact on the contributor's learning processes. The FLOSS community itself provides a valuable, though partial, source of information [10].

In fact, the use of FLOSS projects as learning tools have already gained significant supporters in higher education institutions, and implemented in regular courses. Brocco and Frapolli [13] report on the use of FLOSS projects in a computer science class at the University of Fribourg. Lundell et al. [16] report their experience from a practical assignment at the University of Skövde in Sweden. Papadopoulos et al. [14] reports on the use of an instructional method that utilizes FLOSS projects as tools for teaching software engineering at the Department of Informatics at the University of Thessaloniki in Greece.

In our previous work, we presented preliminary results obtained by conducting a stratified sampling for collecting data to study the learning process of contributors to a FLOSS project [11]. This paper extends such work, focusing on the FLOSS community and its contributors. In [11], and as a way to analyze whether FLOSS has a positive effect on contributors' learning, we decided to run an online questionnaire targeting few FLOSS contributors. The results, although with no statistical relevance, served to pave the way to further broader investigations. This paper extends the analysis mentioned above, after a re-design of the questionnaire and its dissemination to a broader audience.

Our hypothesis remains the same: long-term participation in FLOSS projects can have a positive effect in the contributor's learning process. And our main goal with the revised questionnaire continues to be to understand of how FLOSS projects contributors learn and whether and how contributors recognize the learning process them experience.

3   Methodology

This section provides details about the data collection process; in particular, the questionnaire construction and design, as well as the dissemination process.

3.1   Questionnaire Design

The questionnaire was structured into three main sections: Section A aims at collecting respondents' demographics; Section B aims at collecting data about the respondent's interaction with the project community, the motivations to start and continue contributing to FLOSS project; and Section C surveys where the respondents exploit the potential of FLOSS projects as learning environments. Each section comprises different types of questions. The questionnaire was formulated using open-ended and closed-ended questions. In the open-ended questions the possible responses were not given, allowing the respondent to write down the answers in his/ her own words. In the closed-ended questions, possible answers were provided for the respondent to tick the category that best describes his or her choice. In such questions, the clause "Other/please explain" was included to accommodate any response not listed. The use of these two forms of questions revert to the fact that close-ended questions are extremely useful for eliciting factual information and open-ended questions for seeking opinions, attitudes and perceptions.

In the closed-ended questions, we not only allowed multi-selection answers but also provided three types of Likert Scale answers: (1) to analyze the respondent's perception, including values like Strongly disagree, Disagree, Not sure/Not applicable, Agree, and Strongly agree; and (2) to analyze the frequency of certain respondent's behavior, including values like Ever, Once every year, Once a month, At least 3 times per month, and More than 3 times per month; and (3) to assess the relevance that the respondent assigns to a specific issue, including values like Not at all important, Not too important, Not sure /Not applicable, Somewhat important, and Very important.

In particular, Section A refers to the respondent age, country, language, background and the different FLOSS projects he/she have been enrolled in.

Section B explores the respondent's participation in a specific FLOSS project. In this section the respondent presents a specific project, to which he/she has (or is) contributing. The respondent is requested to describe how the participation started, the drivers what drove him to starting such activity, his/her role in the project, and how many hours he/she devotes to the project. The respondent has the opportunity to describe the type of relationships he has with community members, how they share information, or if they promote and have community meetings or events.

Section C aims at exploiting the potential of FLOSS projects as learning environments. In this section, the respondent analyzes whether the fact of being in a FLOSS community provides him with a learning opportunity, and if his background (professional or academic) facilitates the learning process while participating in a FLOSS project. We also explore who and what were the most important agents in his learning process, if FLOSS projects can be regarded as learning communities, if FLOSS can be seen as a possible alternative to formal education, and if FLOSS could be seen as an interesting complement to formal education.

3.2 Questionnaire Construction and Dissemination Process

The aim of the questionnaire was to (1) study the interactions between FLOSS projects participants, and (2) assess the didactical value of their communities. By interactions we mean the interactions between community members and the project, but also what drives an individual to start participating in FLOSS projects.

The questionnaire was carried out online using Google Docs Survey[2]. Following the same procedure as in [11], we tested the questionnaire, and performed a brief

---

[2] https://docs.google.com/a/iist.unu.edu/spreadsheet/ccc?key=0Akke8MV3ZtZidFpxdDRncTI3ekdj SlJzenFqNWVXNWc

analysis, representing the first phase of activities. For the second phase, and before launching the questionnaire to broader audience, we carried out a pilot test. First, the questionnaire was re-introduced to the same FLOSS projects contributors of the first phase. This pilot test lasted for two weeks in May 2013. With the received feedback, the questionnaire was revised and improved. As part of the dissemination process, we contacted several institutions from associations (Drupal Association, Associação Portuguesa de Programadores Perl), and foundations (Perl Foundation) to companies (Google, RedHat, Citrix, Linux, OpenSource.com) through their Websites, Facebook, or Twitter pages.

Finally, the questionnaire was officially launched on 1 June 2013 and preliminary results collected by 13 June 2013. After collecting this first data, the questionnaire will remain available, in order to increase the sample of responses.

4   Results

Two weeks after the questionnaire was released, we were able to collect data from 27 respondents, from 16 different countries, including Portugal, United Kingdom, Germany, India, France, Serbia, Finland, Netherlands, Belgium, Slovenia, USA, Macau SAR China, Canada, Argentina, Israel, and Brazil. From the respondents, 24 are men and 3 are women. Respondents have different academic levels. The majority has postgraduate studies (41 %), followed by undergraduate studies (33 %). As far as their professional activities are concerned, 29.6 % of the respondents are software developers, 18.5 % students – PhD and undergraduate, and 3.7 % are researchers. Concerning the list of projects, all respondents except one indicated only one project. The list of projects to which they contributed include: Perl, Perl Dancer, NetBSD, Gentoo Linux, Ubuntu Studio, Drupal, Kalkun, The Xen Project, and Joogie. A respondent who did not write any project name stated that he is involved in too many projects.

Results obtained in Section B are explained as follows. In Section A the respondents provided a list of projects. When asked to select a specific FLOSS project, 85 % of the respondents presented different projects, although within a similar field of activity. 48 % of the respondents work (or worked) on a project in the application software area, whereas 37 % at the level of operating systems. Although 70 % of the respondents participate in the correspondent project for more than 1 year, 19 % indicate their participation in the project lasts for less than 6 months, as shown in Fig. 1.

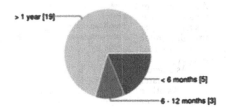

Fig. 1. Active participation in FLOSS projects

Although for 56 % of the respondents the challenge was what made them start participating in FLOSS projects, 52 % answered that it was the idea that triggered their participation, as depicted in Fig. 2.

The activities that one can perform in a FLOSS project are several and may go from observer to developer, from user supporter to tester. Although 41 % of the respondents stated that they started their participation as developers, it is important to notice that 44 % of the respondents declared they started in other ways (a way not included among the available responses), as depicted in Fig. 3.

Among others, the respondents said that they started in the selected project as owner, or translator. Also, we determined that respondents started their participation by having more than one role, such as, tester and developer, or as developer and observer. Although respondents said they started with a certain role, it is interesting to analyze that 70 % became active developers.

As far as the relationships are concerned, 33 % of the respondents state that they are friends with other group members, 33 % do not know any community members personally, 22 % declared that the relationship is professional, and 11 % have other types of relationships with community members. Concerning how often they collaborate with other group members, 56 % said that more than 3 times per month, and 15 % say they collaborate at least 3 times per month.

The channels used to share information and allowing collaboration in the community are diverse. They span from Wikis to Forums, from Mailing Lists to Chats. As far as the Wikis are concerned, 22 % said they use them more than 3 times per month, whereas 22 % said they never used them. As far as the Forums are concerned, 48 %

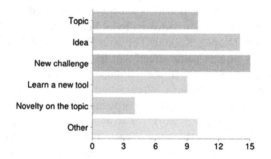

Fig. 2. Motivation to start contributing

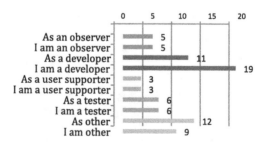

Fig. 3. Role at the beginning - As an...; and later - I am...

said they never use this type of channel whereas 22 % said they use them more than 3 times per month. As far as the Mailing lists are concerned, 44 % of the respondents use it whereas 22 % never use it. The channel with more usage is actually Chats where 63 % of the respondents said they use it more than 3 times per month. Overall, 96 % of the respondents use some sort of communication channel, whereas 4 % don't communicate more than 3 times per month.

As far as meetings are concerned, 74 % of the respondents have online meetings and 41 % have face-to-face meetings. Concerning the type of events each community organize, 37 % said conferences, 26 % workshops, and 37 % do not organize any types of events. Finally, 37 % of the respondents believe that their participation in the projects can be improved, 26 % strongly believes in that fact, whereas only 3 % disagree, as depicted in Fig. 4.

The results obtained in Section C include the following. Several areas where FLOSS can provide expertise were included, such as testing, programming, code reviewing, code analysis, writing documentation, or reading and writing documentation.

As depicted in Fig. 5 respondents assessed their perception on the learning opportunities provided by selected activities as follows: (1) testing - 59 % agree, (2) programming - 70 % strongly agree, (3) code reviewing - 70 % strongly agree, (4) writing documentation - 70 % strongly agree, (5) reading and understanding documentation - 41 % strongly agree. In addition, 89 % strongly disagree that participating in a FLOSS project does not provide a learning opportunity, 7 % only disagrees and 4 % does not have an opinion about if participating in a FLOSS project can or not provide a learning opportunity.

If, as seen before, participating in a FLOSS project can be considered as a learning opportunity. It is also important to determine whether the background of the respondent – academic or professional – is a factor to the success of such learning experience. To this questions, 56 % of the respondents agreed that their background is relevant for the success of their own learning process while participating in a FLOSS project, whereas 22 % is not sure if it has an impact.

As far as the agents involved in their personal learning experience, 59 % of the respondents agreed that themselves are very important in the learning process. 67 % recognize that group members such as manager, senior members of the community or others, are important agents. 56 % said that they are not sure if the end users are important agents, where 26 % agrees that the end users are important agents in the learning experience.

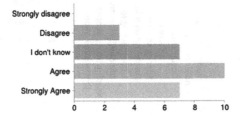

Fig. 4. Improvement through participation

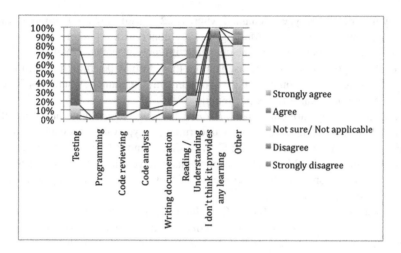

Fig. 5. FLOSS projects activities as learning opportunities

FLOSS projects can be regarded as an opportunity to perform several activities such as, attempting to understand shared code, programming, browsing and reading notes, documenting code, sharing concerns, contributing to the community forums, or reading formal publications such books, the answers. We have requested the respondents to evaluate such activities; responses are depicted in Fig. 6.

Respondents assess their perception on the relevance of conducting selected activities as follows: (1) attempting to understand shared code - 33 % as very important and 19 % as important, (2) programming - 44 % as very important, (3) browsing and reading documentation - only 37 % as somehow important, (4) documenting code - 30 % as very important and 22 % as somehow important, (5) sharing concerns, problems or solutions (using email, wikis, etc.) - 37 % as very important,

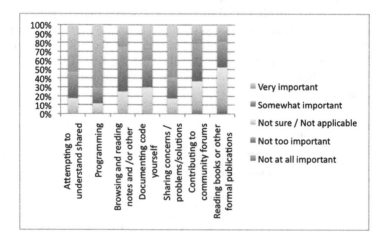

Fig. 6. Evaluation of different activities in FLOSS projects

(6) contributing to community forums - 30 % as somehow important, and (7) reading books or other formal publications - 33 % are not sure.

When asked who were the most important agents in the respondents' learning experience, 59 % of the respondents agree that themselves, and 41 % strongly agrees with such fact. Also, 67 % agrees that other group members are the most important agents in the respondents' learning experience, while only 26 % strongly believe in this fact. However, and although the software developed in FLOSS communities are for general use, 56 % do not see the End Users as agents of learning.

To the question, "has your involvement as a contributor in a FLOSS project changed the way you assess your own previous formal education", 37 % agree that it changed whereas 26 % are not sure.

In a more generic perspective, 48 % of respondents agree that FLOSS projects communities can be regarded as learning communities, 41 % strongly agree whereas only 4 % disagree.

When questioned if FLOSS projects can be regarded as a possible alternative to formal education, 33 % of the respondents do not agree. However, 59 % strongly agree that it can be regarded as a complement to formal education. Results to this question are depicted in Fig. 7.

5 Analysis

For analyzing the results, we focus on 5 main dimensions:

(1) *What* – determining the type of interactions present (internal and external);
(2) *How* – determining how the respondents start their interactions, the modality they use to promote interactions, the impact of documentation available and the tools they use to interact;

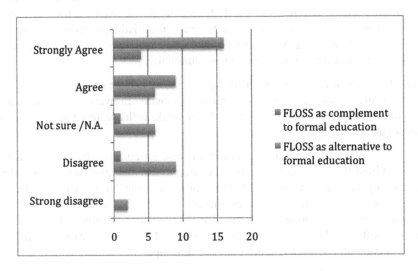

Fig. 7. Use of FLOSS projects in formal education

(3) *When* – focusing on the frequency of interactions and contributions;
(4) *Why* – assessing their motivation to start the contribution on a FLOSS project, the impact of their background, the learning opportunities while participating in a FLOSS projects and the benefits of such participation; and
(5) *Who* – evaluating what roles the respondent play in the community and its learning agents.

The analysis for the above dimensions follows.

What - To determine the interactions within a FLOSS community, we first analyze what type of interactions exist: either they are internal interactions - where the respondent focuses on his personal experience with the community and the project – or external, where the respondent presents how he promotes interaction with the community and to end-users of the product developed, such as events and meetings.

We have seen that nearly half of the respondents are friends with other community members. Nearly the remaining half simply does not know anybody in the community. Also, we have seen that nearly half of the respondents organize some sort of events. We believe that the high percentage of contributors that have a relationship, in this case, a friendly relationship, may have an impact on external interactions. The events organized, such as conferences and workshops, by default, promoting a direct contact among them.

How - In the questionnaire we presented many of the possible roles available in a FLOSS project. Interestingly, but not surprisingly, most of the respondents started their participation as developers and they continue being developers. They have online meetings and they use tools such as Wikis, Forums and Mailing lists to share information. Despite the intense use of such tools the majority of the respondents prefer chats to communicate. One of the main activities of the respondents is to develop software. As we know this is a type of work that is performed by single individuals. Such fact may indicate why contributors prefer chats to communicate. Besides chats, also mailing lists are very important to FLOSS contributors. Mailing lists are used as repositories by the community, as a way to share information, express concerns and achievements. Mailing lists, Wikis and Forums act as available documentation and are considered an asset for the project and the community.

When - From the results we determined that the majority of the respondents have been working in the selected project for more than 6 months. In average the respondents contribute to the project with more than 5 h per week, collaborating with other group members more than 3 times per month.

Why - The respondent background and initial motivations may have an impact on how committed he is to a project. It is interesting to see that most of the respondents said that they start participating in FLOSS projects as a challenge. Interestingly, 2 of the 3 women that replied to the questionnaire pointed that what made them start participation in FLOSS projects was the idea. As we know, the outcome of a FLOSS project is software. Not surprisingly the majority of the respondents have a background in computer science and are software developers.

Who - The respondents' background, academic or professional, may explain why they started their participation as developers and they continue doing so. However, having the same role does not mean they don't acquire knew knowledge. When asked who are the most important agents of their learning experience, the respondents indicate themselves and the community. To them, not only the community can be regarded as a way to improve the learning process but also participation in FLOSS projects can be seen as a complement to formal education, where students can learn by doing, representing a positive impact on the learner.

Summary – Addressing the two research questions formulated in the Introduction: (1) study the interactions between FLOSS projects participants, and (2) assess the didactical value of their communities, our analysis shows the following conclusions.

6   Conclusion and Future Work

The aim of this paper was to (1) study the interactions of FLOSS community members, and (2) to assess the didactical value of such participation. As we were able to analyze by our small sample of respondents, FLOSS projects participants collaborate and cooperate between them. This let us with the certainty that there are interactions in FLOSS community members, and they are driven by the same goal: to develop a software project. It is important to verify that FLOSS community members, do not believe that the participation in FLOSS projects can be an alternative to formal education, for example, to replace formal courses in software engineering in higher education institutions. However, they see that the "learning by doing" concept can be applied in FLOSS projects and therefore is an attractive complement to formal education, mainly in software engineering courses. As future work, we aim comparing the data collected with a pilot project that uses FLOSS projects as assignments in Software Engineering courses.

Acknowledgments. This work is funded partly by UNU-IIST and Macau Foundation in the context of the PPAeL project. This work is funded by ERDF - European Regional Development Fund through the COMPETE Programme (operational programme for competitiveness) and by National Funds through the FCT - the Portuguese Foundation for Science and Technology, within project FCOMP-01-0124-FEDER-010049.

References

1. Anderson, P.: What is Web 2.0? Ideas, technologies and implications for education. http://www.jisc.ac.uk/media/documents/techwatch/tsw0701b.pdf (2007). Accessed 11 Nov 2012
2. Fountain, R.: Wiki pedagogy. Dossiers Pratiques. Profetic. http://www.profetic.org:16080/dossiers/dossier_imprimer.php3?id_rubrique=110 (2005). Accessed 11 Nov 2012
3. Chatti, M.A., Jarke, M., Frosch-Wilke, D.: The future of e-learning: a shift to knowledge networking and social software. Int. J. Knowl. Learn. **3**(4/5), 404–420 (2007)
4. Downes, S.: Web 2.0 and your own learning and development. http://www.elearnspace.org/blog/2007/06/19/web-20-and-your-own-learning-and-development/ (2007). Accessed 10 May 2013

5. Happ, S.: The changing world of e-learning. http://besser20.de/the-changing-world-of-e-learning/44/ (2008). Accessed Dec 2012
6. Sclater, N.: Web 2.0, personal learning environments and the future of learning management systems. Educause Res. Bull. (13 Boulder, CO: Educause Center for Applied Research) (2008)
7. Wilson, S., Liber, P.O., Johnson, M., Beauvoir, P., Sharples, P.: Personal learning environments: challenging the dominant design of educational systems. J. e-Learn. Knowl. Soc. 3(2), 27–38 (2007)
8. Downes, S.: Knowledge, learning and community. http://www.downes.ca/post/57737 (2012). Accessed 10 Nov 2012
9. Fernandes, S., Cerone, A., Barbosa, L.S.: FLOSS communities as learning networks. Int. J. Inf. Educ. Technol. 3(2), 278–281 (2013)
10. Cerone, A., Sowe, S.K.: Using free/libre open source software projects as learning tools. In: OpenCert 2010, vol. 33 of ECEASST (2010)
11. Fernandes, S., Cerone, A., Barbosa, L.S.: A preliminary analysis of learning awareness in FLOSS projects. In: International Symposium on Innovation and Sustainability in Education (INSUEDU 2012). Springer, Thessaloniki (2012, in Press)
12. Times Magazine: http://www.time.com/time/covers/0,16641,20061225,00.html (2013). Accessed 5 May 2013
13. Brocco, A., Frapolli, F.: Open Source in Higher Education: Case Study Computer Science at the University of Fribourg (2011)
14. Papadopoulos, P.M., Stamelos, I.G., Meiszner, A.: Students' perspectives on learning software engineering with open source projects: lessons learnt after three years of program operation. In: Proceedings of the Fourth International Conference on Computer Supported Education (CSEDU 2012), pp. 313–322 (2012)
15. Magrassi, P.: Free and open-source software is not an emerging property but rather the result of studied design. In: ICICKM10 (2010)
16. Lundell, B., Persson, A., Lings, B.: Learning through practical involvement in the FLOSS ecosystem: experiences from a master assignment. In: Proceedings of the Third International Conference on Open Source Systems 2007, pp. 289–294 (2007)

Small World Characteristics of FLOSS Distributions

Jaap Boender[1]([✉]) and Sara Fernandes[2]

[1] Foundations of Computing Group, Department of Computer Science School of Science and Technology, Middlesex University, London, UK
J.Boender@mdx.ac.uk
[2] UNU-IIST, Macao SAR, China
sara.fernandes@iist.uni.edu

Abstract. Over the years, Free/Libre Open Source Software (FLOSS) distributions have become more and more complex and recent versions contain tens of thousands of packages. This has made it impossible to do quality control by hand. Instead, distribution editors must look to automated methods to ensure the quality of their distributions.

In the present paper, we present some insights into the general structure of FLOSS distributions. We notably show that such distributions have the characteristics of a small world network: there are only a few important packages, and many less important packages. Identifying the important packages can help editors focus their efforts on parts of the distribution where errors will have important consequences.

1 Introduction

It has long been a standard method in computing science to divide complex systems into components [10]. System processes are placed into separate components so that all of the data and functions inside each component are semantically related. Because of this principle, it is often said that components are modular and cohesive.

The modularity of components allows for easy debugging and maintenance, since components are small and generally focus on only one task. Cohesiveness allows components to work together towards a greater goal.

Free/Libre Open Source Software (FLOSS) software distributions are very good examples of component-based systems. They are very large (over 35 000 packages in the latest Debian release), heterogenous (they contain packages written by different teams, in different languages, with different release schedules, etc.).

Since FLOSS distributions are becoming more and more popular and complex, the fact is that to assure quality by hand becomes an impossible task. This forces the editors to search for automated methods in order to ensure the quality of their distributions.

The aim of this paper is to present some insights into the general structure and characteristics of FLOSS distributions. Identifying these can help distribution editors in concentrating their resources. For example, well-connected

S. Counsell and M. Núñez (Eds.): SEFM 2013 Collocated Workshops, LNCS 8368, pp. 417–429, 2014.
DOI: 10.1007/978-3-319-05032-4_30, © Springer International Publishing Switzerland 2014

packages with errors will have a greater impact than packages that have few connections. As another example, if there is a cluster of strongly connected packages, it might be useful to assign maintenance of these packages to the same person or team.

We have used the Debian and Mandriva distributions for our experiments. Debian was chosen because it is a very large distribution (in number of packages). Also, the semantics of its packaging system are well-defined, which makes it easier to interpret results. Mandriva was chosen because it is one of the distributions using the RPM system. The semantics of RPM are different from those of the Debian packaging system, so it is possible to assess whether characteristics are general for all FLOSS distributions or artefacts of a specific packaging system.

The rest of the paper is structured as follows. Section 2 introduces some background and related work. Section 3 presents the methodology. Section 4 presents the results and its analysis. Finally, Sect. 5 presents some conclusions pointing to envisaged future work.

2   Background and Definitions

FLOSS applications are often distributed in the form of packages, which are bundles of related components necessary to compile or run an application. For many FLOSS packages, the source code is freely available and reuse of the code for derivative works is encouraged.

Because of this, resource reuse is considered to be a natural pillar: a package is often dependent on resources in some other packages to function properly. Package dependencies often span between project development teams, and since there is no central control over which resources from other packages are needed or in what way, the software system self-organizes in to a collection of discrete, interconnected components.

The relationships between packages can be used to compute relevant quality measures, for example in order to identify particularly fragile components [1,4].

In a distribution, there are two main types of relationships, with totally different significance: dependencies (where one package needs another to function properly) and conflicts (where packages cannot function together). Also, syntactically, dependencies are directional, while conflicts are not. And finally, there are two different types of dependencies, conjunctive (the 'normal' kind, which can only be satisfied in one way) and disjunctive (where a dependency may be satisfied by one out of a list of packages). For formal definitions of these concepts, please refer to [7].

An example can be found in Fig. 1. If we want to install the package alpha, we will need to install bravo (a conjunctive dependency) and charlie or delta (a disjunctive dependency). Furthermore, delta is in conflict with foxtrot, so it is not possible to install them both together. In this case, the disjunctive dependency of echo on delta or foxtrot can be satisfied with either of these packages, but not both. This is because of the conflict: there is no problem in installing charlie and delta together.

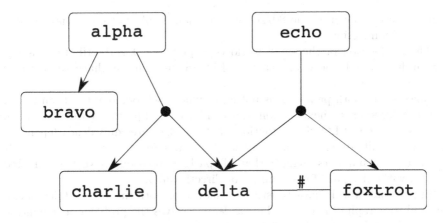

Fig. 1. Simple repository

If we look at a FLOSS distribution (which, after all, is nothing more than a set of packages with their relationships) as a whole, we can also identify quality measures. For this purpose, we will look at distributions as *networks*.

A network is an unweighted graph $G = (V, E)$ where V denotes a vertex set and E an edge set. Vertices represent discrete objects in a system, such as social actors, economic agents, computer programs, Internet sites, or biological producers and consumers. Edges represent interactions among these actors, such as Internet sites linking to each other.

Many of these networks exhibit a property known as the *small world* property, first described by Stanley Milgram in his famous paper about the 'six degrees of separation' concept [8]. A small world network is distinguished by the fact that the number of hops needed to reach one vertex from another is relatively small, at least compared to a random network.

This property has been observed in many products of human and biological activity, including the graph of the Internet [5], the graph of the World Wide Web [3] and other complex networks [2].

Formally, a network is deemed small-world if it satisfies two properties:

- The clustering coefficient, defined as the probability that two neighbours of the same vertex are connected, is significantly higher than that of random networks.
- On average, the shortest path length between two vertices is low (on the same order as that of random networks).

A small world graph has a high clustering coefficient (at least with respect to random networks), and also a low average shortest path length. Moreover, in a small world network, these two properties result in a network that consists of clusters, whose central vertices (or nodes) are highly connected, creating hubs. These have many connections, whereas the other nodes can have very few connections; thus, the degree distribution conforms to the well-known Pareto principle, also known as the 80/20 law—a small number of nodes have a high number of connections.

The application of the small world concept to FLOSS distributions is not new; it has already been proven that FLOSS distributions have small world characteristics [6,9].

However, in both papers, it is not clear which methodology has been used[1]. As we shall see in the next section, this can have an important effect on results, especially since in FLOSS distributions, not all edges are equivalent (dependencies are radically different from conflicts, for example).

In [6], the numbers suggest that all package relations have been treated equally, without regard for semantics or directionality.

In [9], small world characteristics are shown for both the graph of dependencies and the graph of conflicts. This at least resolves the problem of semantics, because dependencies and conflicts are treated separately.

The paper, though, contains a puzzling claim: it is stated that the small-world method does not hold for packages with very few or very many dependencies (the so-called 'saturation effect'). This claim is puzzling in that the entire basis of the small world phenomenon is the distinction between packages with few and packages with many dependencies. As we shall see, this is especially important in FLOSS distributions, as it gives us insights into the structure of the distribution.

In the next section, we present the methodology used in our measurements.

3 Methodology

In this section, we present the exact methods we have used to generate the distribution graphs and the measurements we have executed on them. We shall also discuss the different significance of these methods.

A distribution can be seen as a graph, where the packages are the vertices and relationships (dependencies and conflicts) are the edges. However, as we have seen before, not all edges are the same—the significance of a dependency is diametrically opposite to that of a conflict, and treating these edges the same can result in confusing results.

It thus becomes clear that, in order to draw any meaningful conclusions from a distribution graph, it is important to know *how* this graph is generated. We propose three methods, each with their own advantages and disadvantages.

Method 1 involves treating every edge equally, irrespective of their significance. We conflate conjunctive dependencies, disjunctive dependencies, conflicts, and any other relations between packages that are present. This gives us a distribution graph where two packages are connected if and only if they are possibly involved in some way in determining each other's installability.

In general, this is an overapproximation, since not every package that is mentioned as a dependency is actually used. The main advantage of this method is that it is easy to compute.

---

[1] Queries to the authors of these papers have gone unanswered.

In **method 2**, we connect two packages p and q if there is a path in the dependency graph from p to q. Another way of expressing the same concept is that q must appear in the transitive closure of the dependencies of p. In this way, a package p is connected to a package q if there is a possibility that q is installed to satisfy some dependency of p.

This method still is an overapproximation, though less so than the first method. It is not much more difficult to compute, though it no longer takes conflicts into account. The main advantage here is that now transitive dependencies are considered.

For **method 3** we make use of *strong dependencies* [1], a concept that subsumes both dependencies and conflicts. Informally, a package p strongly depends on another package q if and only if it is impossible to install p without also installing q.

Note that strong dependencies are a property of the entire distribution, not just of the packages involved: whether p strongly depends on q depends on the entire distribution, for *every* installation of p has to include q.

The advantage of using the strong dependency graph is that now we have a unified graph, where every edge has the same meaning, but which still takes both conflicts and dependencies into account. It is a slight underapproximation, since conjunctive dependencies where none of the alternatives is obligatory, but one will have to be installed nonetheless, do not end up as strong dependencies.

The main disadvantage is that the strong dependency graph is more difficult to compute, since it involves doing installability checks, e.g. with a SAT solver. However, it can still be done within reasonabletime (a few minutes for the latest distributions).

We have used all of these three methods to generate distribution graphs and measure their characteristics. In the next section we will present the results and discuss their significance.

4   Results and Discussion

In this section we present the results of measurements on the graphs obtained by the three different methods described above, for both the Debian and Mandriva distributions. We also discuss the significance of these measurements and the conclusions that can be drawn from them.

4.1   Debian

Let us start with the raw data for the latest Debian distribution (version 7) on the standard AMD64 architecture. Using the three different methods, we have generated distribution graphs and determined several key indices.

In this table, first we have the number of vertices (V) and edges (E) in the graph. At first glance, it might seem surprising that the method 1 graph has so few edges compared to the other two, especially since it uses every possible

Method	V	E	CC	APL	Comp	CpAvg	LComp
1	35 982	85 190	0.38	3.43	2 251	15.98	33 558
2	35 982	2 386 389	0.26	0.91	2 229	16.15	33 582
3	35 982	1 588 322	0.28	0.91	2 280	15.78	33 537

distribution used: debian/amd64 7 stable

package relation, but this can be explained by the fact that the method 2 and 3 graphs are transitive.

Then there are the main small world indices, the clustering coefficient (CC) and average shortest path length (APL). Both these characteristics show a small world effect in all three graphs, though we must note that the average shortest path length index is not indicative for graphs 2 and 3: these graphs being transitive, there is either no path between two vertices or a path of length 1. This results in the average shortest path length being less than 1.

Note that even though the number of edges is vastly higher in graphs 2 and 3, the clustering coefficient is actually lower. This might seem strange (more edges should result in more connection, hence a higher probability of vertices being neighbours) but it is caused by the fact that these graphs are transitive: the fact that vertices have a higher probability of being connected is balanced out by the fact that vertices have more neighbours to begin with.

We also show the component structure of the graph; in this case we use weakly connected components while ignoring direction. We show the number of components (Comp), average component size (CpAvg) and the size of the largest component (LComp). We can see from these measures that distributions consist of one huge connected component, encompassing over 90 % of the distribuition, with the rest of the distribution consisting of isolated or near-isolated packages.

In the rest of this section, we shall limit ourselves to a discussion of the strong dependency graph (method 3), as it is the most interesting one from a semantic perspective (every edge has an equal, well-defined meaning). All three graphs, however, exhibit small world characteristics.

Another characteristic of small world networks, demonstrated in Fig. 2, is that the distribution of degrees of their vertices follows a power law—as mentioned before, the Pareto principle. There should be few vertices with many edges and many vertices with few edges.

We can see this in the figure: the degree distribution forms a straight line in a double logarithmic plot.

In Fig. 3, we show the same plot, but now with in degrees and out degrees separated. We can see from this that the distribution consists of three main types of packages:

- Many packages with a small in degree and a small out degree;
- A few packages with a small in degree, but a large out degree;
- A few packages with a large in degree, but a small out degree.

Notably, there are no packages that have both a large in degree and a large out degree.

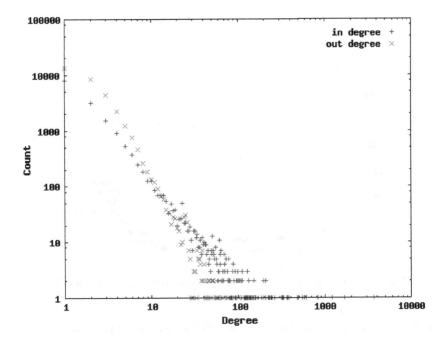

Fig. 2. Distribution of degrees in Debian `stable` (strong dependencies)

Examining these packages can shed some light on why this is the case. Here is a table with on the left the 10 packages in Debian with the highest in degree, and on the right the 10 packages with the highest out degree.

Highest in degrees			Highest out degrees		
Name	In degree	Out degree	Name	In degree	Out degree
gcc-4.7-base	31 708	0	gnome-desktop-environment	0	945
libc-bin	31 707	2	gnome	1	944
multiarch-support	31 706	4	task-gnome-desktop	0	746
libgcc1	31 706	4	gnome-core-devel	0	710
libc6	31 706	4	gnome-core	3	677
zlib1g	25 514	5	kde-full	0	643
libselinux1	21 695	5	task-kde-desktop	0	560
liblzma5	21 201	5	ontv	0	493
libbz2-1.0	21 108	6	kde-standard	1	473
tar	20 681	5	kde-telepathy	0	382

We see that the packages on the left are mostly libraries and base packages (`libc`, for example, or `tar`), and that on the right there are mostly high-level packages (*metapackages*) such as KDE or GNOME.

Figure 4 shows this in a schematic way.

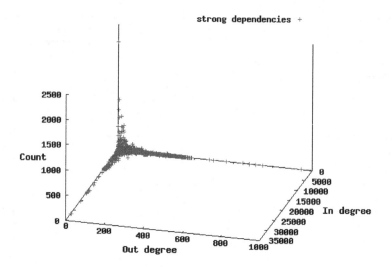

Fig. 3. In and out degrees in Debian `stable` (strong dependencies)

This data can be corroborated in a different way as well: in Debian, most packages carry *tags* that identify things like their role, whether they are part of a larger software suite, or the programming language they are implemented in. If we look at the tags that occur more than once in the packages in the top 10 shown above, we get the following table:

High in degrees		High out degrees	
Tag	Count	Tag	Count
`implemented-in::c`	7	`role::metapackage`	6
`role::shared-lib`	4	`interface:x11`	5
`devel::packaging`	2	`uitoolkit::gtk`	5
`interface::commandline`	2	`suite::gnome`	4
`role::program`	2	`suite::kde`	2
`scope::utility`	2		
`suite::gnu`	2		
`use::storing`	2		
`works-with::archive`	2		
`works-with::file`	2		

It seems that packages with a high in degrees are often shared libraries and implemented in C. Both of these characteristics point to system libraries.

Similarly, the packages with a high out degree are mostly metapackages, using the X window system and part of the GNOME or KDE suites. This also confirms the structure as shown in Fig. 4.

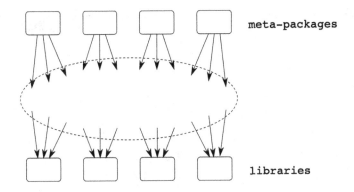

Fig. 4. Schematic repository structure

4.2   Mandriva

Debian, of course, is not the only distribution available. We have also analysed another distribution, Mandriva, which is based on RPM, a different but comparable packaging system. Let us see if the conclusions drawn for Debian also hold for Mandriva. First the raw data:

Method	V	E	CC	APL	Comp	CpAvg	LComp
1	7 566	84 855	0.47	7.49	289	26.18	7 273
2	7 566	1 170 721	0.25	0.94	333	22.72	7 230
3	7 566	721 162	0.25	0.94	339	22.32	7 223

distribution used: mandriva/x86_64 2010.1 main

Allowing for the smaller size of the distribution, the values are roughly similar. However, if we look at the first graph, we see that it has almost the same number of edges as its Debian equivalent, for roughly a fifth of the packages. This can be explained by a difference in semantics between the Debian package format and RPM: RPM packages and dependencies are more fine-grained, which makes for more edges in the graph[2]. We can also see this from the higher average shortest path length: there are on average more intermediate dependencies between two packages than in Debian.

We also see that the clustering coefficient of Mandriva is higher than that of Debian in the first graph, but slightly lower in the second and third. The higher clustering coefficent in the first graph can be explained by the difference in semantics mentioned above—there are simply much more dependencies, and the balancing effect of transitive graphs is not present here. For the difference in the second and third graphs, we will have to look at the actual degree distribution.

---

[2] This might seem at odds with the fact that there are many less packages in Mandriva than in Debian. The Debian distribution is, hoewever, very extensive and contains many packages not present in Mandriva.

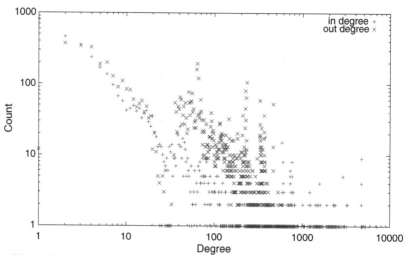

Fig. 5. Distribution of degrees in Mandriva 2010.1, strong dependencies

This degree distribution is shown in Fig. 5. We see that there is still a power law distribution, but it is not as clear as for Debian.

In Fig. 6, we have the degree distribution with in and out degrees broken down. This figure explains best why the clustering coefficient is lower: the figure looks comparable with its Debian equivalent (Fig. 3), but there are several outlying packages with a high out degree.

This is due to a specificity in Mandriva packaging: there are several packages that do not install files themselves, but are only there to fulfill a certain task, such as installing the X window system. These are similar to the meta-packages mentioned above, but they can have dependencies that are not at all related to each other. This explains both the lower clustering coefficient (dependencies of these meta-packages may not depend on each other) and the outlying packages (these will be like meta-packages in that they have a high out degree, but a low in degree).

Looking at the top 10 of high degree packages in Mandriva corroborates this:

Highest in degrees			Highest out degrees		
Name	In degree	Out degree	Name	In degree	Out degree
dash-static	7 106	0	task-kde4-devel	0	824
glibc	7 105	1	kimono-devel	0	683
lib64termcap2	5 862	2	ruby-kde4-devel	0	682
bash	5 861	3	qyoto-devel	1	681
perl-base	5 274	2	ruby-qt4-devel	1	680
libgcc1	5 206	2	smoke4-devel	4	675
libstdcc++6	5 201	3	kdenetwork4-devel	0	655
lib64pcre0	4 946	4	kipi-plugins-devel	0	651
lib64lzma2	4 836	2	kdepim4-devel	0	645
xz	4 825	5	kdeplasma-addons-devel	0	630

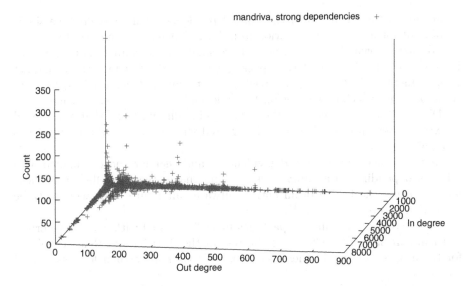

Fig. 6. In and out degrees in Mandriva 2010.1, strong dependencies

We see the same distribution structure: library packages on the left, with high in degree andlow out degree, and metapackages (and tasks) on the right, with high out degree and low in degree.

If we look at the list of task packages in Mandriva, they all have a low in degree and a high out degree. `task-kde4-devel` is simply the most glaring example; there are about 30 task packages in the entire Mandriva distribution, but they all have an out degree of over 100, and an in degree of under 10.

All in all, Mandriva shows much the same structure as Debian, and if we consider the task packages to be metapackages as well (which, in a sense, they are), the structure of Mandriva conforms to Fig. 4 as well.

4.3   General

We can conclude that there are two kinds of vulnerable packages in a distribution: the meta-packages that are vulnerable because they pull in a great amount of other packages, each with its own possible bugs, and libraries that are vulnerable because if they contain bugs, a large number of other packages will be influenced.

Identifying these packages in a distribution can help distribution editors focus their efforts.

5   Conclusion and Future Work

In the previous sections, we have presented a clear and precise method for creating graphs of FLOSS distributions, using three different methods. The most interesting of these three involves strong dependencies, where we create a single graph that incorporates information from both dependencies and conflicts.

We have shown that these graphs have small world characteristics for both Debian and Mandriva, and that packages can be divided into three distinct groups: meta-packages (top-level packages with many dependencies), libraries (base packages that many other packages depend on), and other packages.

Distribution editors can use these data to identify packages that are in need of extra surveillance, or that must be treated with extra care during upgrades or repairs.

Meta-packages have many dependencies, and therefore have a high probability of depending on a faulty package. This makes them excellent yardsticks for measuring the health of an entire software suite, since they will easily be influenced by errors in their dependencies.

On the other hand, library packages must be treated with care, since errors in them can have huge effects on the rest of the distribution. Release policies for these packages should therefore be more conservative than for less crucial packages.

The fact that FLOSS distributions have small world characteristics, provided that the methodology is clear, allows us interesting insights into the structure of these distributions that, we hope, will be used to make distribution editors' lives easier.

5.1 Future Work

We have so far used Debian and Mandriva for our tests. We do not expect huge differences in the results for other distributions such as Ubuntu and OpenSUSE, but it would be good to test these nonetheless—as we have seen from the discussion of the results for Mandriva, even small differences can be of interest.

It would also be interesting to have these tests run on a daily basis over a distribution to see how the data changes. This could not only be interesting for scientists who want to track changes to the structure of a distribution, but also for distribution editors, who could then identify vulnerable packages daily. They could also identify the effect of changes in dependencies on the distribution structure.

Acknowledgments. This work is partially supported by the European Community's 7th Framework Programme (FP7/2007-2013), grant agreement n°214898, "Mancoosi" project. Work developed at IRILL. This work is also supported by Macao Science and Technology Development Fund (MSTDF), File No. 019/2011/A1.

References

1. Abate, P., Di Cosmo, R., Boender, J., Zacchiroli, S.: Strong dependencies between software components. In: ESEM '09: Proceedings of the 2009 3rd International Symposium on Empirical Software Engineering and Measurement, pp. 89–99. IEEE Computer Society, Washington, DC (2009)

2. Albert, R., Barabási, A.L.: Statistical mechanics of complex networks. Rev. Mod. Phys. **74**(1), 47–97 (2002)
3. Barabási, A.L., Albert, R.: Emergence of scaling in random networks. Science **286**(5439), 509–512 (1999). http://www.sciencemag.org/cgi/content/abstract/286/5439/509
4. Boender, J.: Efficient computation of dominance in component systems (short paper). In: Barthe, G., Pardo, A., Schneider, G. (eds.) SEFM 2011. LNCS, vol. 7041, pp. 399–406. Springer, Heidelberg (2011)
5. Caldarelli, G., Marchetti, R., Pietronero, L.: The fractal properties of internet. EPL (Europhysics Letters) **52**(4), 386 (2000). http://stacks.iop.org/0295-5075/52/i=4/a=386
6. LaBelle, N., Wallingford, E.: Inter-package dependency networks in open-source software. CoRR cs.SE/0411096 (2004)
7. Mancinelli, F., Boender, J., Di Cosmo, R., Vouillon, J., Durak, B., Leroy, X., Treinen, R.: Managing the complexity of large free and open source package-based software distributions. In: ASE, pp. 199–208 (2006)
8. Milgram, S.: The small world problem. Psychol. Today **1**(1), 60–67 (1967)
9. Nair, R., Nagarjuna, G., Ray, A.K.: Semantic structure and finite-size saturation in scale-free dependency networks of free software. ArXiv e-prints (January 2009)
10. Szyperski, C.: Component Software: Beyond Object-Oriented Programming, 2nd edn. Addison Wesley Professional, Boston (2002)

Author Index